Julian Cope is a visiona ... ologist. His work with The Teardrop Expl... rks him as one of British music's great innovators. I ... dern *Antiquarian* and *The Megalithic European* have established hi... authority on ancient history. And his joyful surveys *Krautrocksampler* and *Japrocksampler* have become required musical reading. He has also penned two successful volumes of autobiography, *Head On* and *Repossessed*, and continues to perform, solo and with his band, the Black Sheep.

Further praise for *Copendium*:

'A lyrical map of sonic treasures.' Andrew Weatherall

'I think Julian is the best writer on rock and roll in the world today. No contest. Lester Bangs would love him if he were still alive. They'd be blood brothers. He's got the spirit alright. True faith.' Bobby Gillespie

'A combination of fastidiousness and freakout fervour means *Copendium* achieves its own aim of being an alternative head's guide to all and every music. It also documents a history just passed. Cope will always make us want to listen to this music again. He has also captured why the process of discovering it has changed forever.' *Wire*

'*Copendium* is a collection of album reviews, exactly ten years' worth, which Cope wrote for his own Head Heritage website. He homes in on the unsung, music that is unknown, unloved, even unreleased . . . If, like me, you thought you knew your musical onions, if you pride yourself on knowing or just owning the work of musicians whose mothers don't even know they exist, then reading *Copendium* is a humbling exercise . . . Every essay in *Copendium* is an adventure.' Roddy Doyle, *Irish Times*

'Phrase by phrase, Cope is the best music writer going. He has taste, anger, wit and a resplendent supracosmic vision. His decade's writings have now been compiled as *Copendium* . . . One hell of a book.' Toby Litt, *Herald* Books of the Year

'Each entry reads like a mission statement to convert you to the Arch-Drude's latest space-cake obsession. Whether raving about mid-'60s proto-metallers Blue Cheer or contemporary psych troop Sunburned Hand of the Man, Cope makes most other rock writing seem lifeless.' Andrew Perry, *Q Magazine* Books of the Year

'Julian Cope's *Copendium* provides an alternative history of popular music from the Fifties to the present. Cope is the well-read jester of English pop, a real one-off, and we're lucky to have him.' Ian Thomson, *Evening Standard* Books of the Year

'Downright irresistible.' Ben Thomson, *Independent on Sunday* Books of the Year

'Cult singer and songwriter Julian Cope's *Copendium* is a wonderful tribute to the misfits, outsiders and head-cases who have marked music's most magnificent margins. While heavyweights such as Miles Davis and Black Sabbath are loudly hymned, so are "underpraised" artists such as the Mops and Jex Thoth.' Rob Fitzpatrick, *Sunday Times* Music Books of the Year

---

by the same author

Autobiography
HEAD ON
REPOSSESSED

Musicology
KRAUTROCKSAMPLER
JAPROCKSAMPLER

Archaeology
THE MODERN ANTIQUARIAN
THE MEGALITHIC EUROPEAN

Copendium

Julian Cope

ff
faber and faber

First published in 2012
by Faber and Faber Ltd
The Bindery, 51 Hatton Garden,
London EC1N 8HN

This paperback edition published in 2013

Typeset by Ian Bahrami
Printed and bound by CPI Group (UK) Ltd, Croydon CR0 4YY

A CIP record for this book
is available from the British Library

TECHNICAL CREW OF THIS SONIC ANTIQUARIAN

Lee Brackstone
COMMISSIONING EDITOR

Dave Watkins
HEAD OF EDITORIAL TEXT MANAGEMENT

Ruth Atkins
EDITORIAL ADMINISTRATOR

Dave Sheppard
COPY-EDITOR

Ian Bahrami
PROOFREADER
PROJECT MANAGER

Eleanor Crow
JACKET DESIGN

Alison Worthington
THE INDEX

Jack Murphy
PRODUCTION CONTROLLER

Silvia Novak & Sarah Christie
PROPAGANDA

ISBN 978-0-571-27034-7

Printed and bound in the UK on FSC® certified paper in line with our continuing commitment to ethical business practices, sustainability and the environment.
For further information see faber.co.uk/environmental-policy

Contents

The Introduction

When I got kicked off Def American Records in 1995 CE for refusing to promote my new pradduct by flying to National Socialist Amerikkka, my erstwhile A&R man Marc Geiger informed me quite kindly that there was a thing coming called the Internet that would save me ever leaving Europe again. Ho-ho-ho-ho-ho-ho-ho-ho-ho-ho-ho . . . yessssss. But it was not until half a decade later – and only after the uphill '90s foot-slog of researching *Krautrocksampler* and *The Modern Antiquarian* – that I found myself in a position to take advantage of this fabulous Inner World Resource. And what a resource! Only then, through nightly direct experience with this serpentine, labyrinthine cybertaur of indescribable newness, did I grasp how a tenacious Luddite feistmeister motherfucker such as myself could rodeo-ride this magnificent World Ungraspable.

They'ze still making up their rules?

Yup.

Then nope.

'Cause now *I'm* making up their rules!

Motherfucker.

Yowzah, shrieked the mid-'90s me at the seemingly limitless educational and inspirational possibilities thrown up by this sinewy writher. And as a Gnostic and hero-worshipper who'd regularly praised Thomas Edison for facilitating my Invader-loud barbarian yawp, so now did I get down once again on my fucking hands and knees and grovel before him in my Household of His Many Appliances. And soon I remembered Robert Graves' inspirational five-year magazine stint as a poetry columnist and decided that, as my career was in a similarly fortunate position, surely now I could put into rock'n'roll literature what Graves had put back into poetic literature.

Head Heritage Album of the Month was born in May 2000 CE with my review of The Groundhogs' legendary 1971 LP *Split*, and would continue unceasingly for the next ten years no matter where my field research had temporarily taken me. Inevitably, certain reviews were scribed in fantastic locations – Pompeii for Randy Holden's *Population II*, the foothills of Mount Ararat for the Taj Mahal Travellers' *Live Stockholm* recordings – and just as inevitably did that foreign travel lead me to such lost gems as Italy's Le Stelle di Mario Schifano, British Columbia's Sacrificial Totem, Denmark's Alrune Rod, hell, that entire *Danskrocksampler*. And while further Scandinavian travels revealed a whole slew of unique and contemporary folk artists doing their barely announced strung-out thing in their singularly chilly Scando manner, feisty and more hot-blooded cultural equivalents revealed themselves through travels across the Iberian peninsula and obscure corners of the Mediterranean. And while those Sardinian one-on-every-hilltop proto-barbershop quartets known as the 'Tenores' could be experienced deep in the island's interior, vocally free-forming their local populations into the myths, even careful burrowing far closer to home in nearby Brittany yielded braying, tinnitus-inducing marching bands delivering twenty-minute-plus drone extravaganzas of no little meditative appeal. One thing is clear from my clandestine raids on other cultures: when Bonio and Bob Geldof arrive in African villages replete with TV crew, fanfares and four-week warnings, these lordly Dublin Vikings always receive the same doctored and distorted truth as Queen Victoria progressing through nineteenth-century Dorset. Clean up, clean up, Queen Bone-O's on the Phone-O! But when I arrive unannounced (occasionally even disguised) in some precipitous hamlet teetering on the very edge of culture, I get a genuine insight because the band plays on unaware and unimpressed by this Hairy Russky (or whatever the locals have currently mistaken me for). Odin always travelled in disguise, and it has certainly worked for me.

However, my Culture Hero mission – and please never doubt the gravity and Truth of that Lofty Intent – was never just to plumb the unsung depths of the lost Music Underground. Rather, I was always here to raise up and bring to the attention of the Heads all and every type of underpraised music, be the artist obscure or even already of World Importance. For the latter example, just check out Funkadelic's 1981 LP

The Electric Spanking of War Babies for Sly Stone's stellar vocal'n'drums performance 'Funk Gets Stronger' and ask yourself why knowledge of such errant genius is not commonplace among all soul and funk fans? For shit damn sure that epic piece carpet-bombs Sly's later lame-o comeback discs. Kicks their dicks into the dust, brothers'n'sisters. Similarly, why was *Tonight's the Night* – CSNY megastar Neil Young's drunken 1976 tribute to two dead compadrés – first released only in Germany? On account of Warner Brothers Records' fear of its lack of World Commercial Potential? Moreover, Young's heroically struggling and poetically flailing LPs *On the Beach* and *Time Fades Away* were similarly ignored for decades and even refused a CD release by Warners in case the Joni Mitchell/Carole King/James Taylor AOR folkies took offence to his seemingly demented mewling, clueless to the fact that the genu-whine nature of Neil's mewling had long ago eclipsed the lisping preciousness of those aforemenched silly, self-righteous old sods-in-stasis. From my angle, therefore, it's only through persistently mining the peripheral seams of forgotten rock culture that these obscure gems of Krautrock, Japrock, hard-rock, glam-rock and their ilk can be restored to a righteous and appropriate place.

Now just whom should you blame for this 17,000-page *Copendium*? Not me, not me, says I. Nope, I'm just John Belushi in *The Blues Brothers* cowering and robo-repeating, 'It's NOT my fault!' For only a canny visionary of epic proportions AND with their powerful trigger finger on the cash register could dare have implemented such a T O M E as *Copendium*. So both the blame and the heaped praise should be in this case snow-shovelled at the door of one Lee Brackstone, commissioning editor and Lord Bollocks of Faber's Upper World. This is yer man, kiddies – what a genius, what a rogue! But then, it's a slow-burning truth that *Copendium* peddles not a single Roman blow to the bonce, but instead seemingly endless Keltic pummels to the body . . . until the reader – worn down by evidence and exhaustion – screams, 'Enough already, Cope! I get it, now just leave me [the fuck] alone!'

The 1950s

Righteous it is that the two ur-ancestors on which this entire work stands – Tom Lehrer and Lord Buckley – have gained special early access to this tome due to their being a full decade before the rest. Futuristic over-achievers! But did anyone ever sound so modern, so confrontational or so marginal as Tom Lehrer did back in 1953? Undoubtedly, Lehrer's songs about sado-masochism, drug dealing, incest, STDs, prostitution and sex-with-the-dead sneaked past US censors only because his self-published debut LP was mainly aimed at fellow students and academics and, moreover, was cannily delivered to listeners' earholes with all the wide-eyed, bucolic charm of Winnie the Pooh and Piglet engaged in a game of Poohsticks. Lord Buckley's seasoned and worldly nightclub audiences, on the other hand, mainly inhabited Chicago's murderous gangster underworld, facilitating the Lord's Utopian anti-religious message of mind expansion, self-betterment and anti-Kapitalism, and all delivered in an obsessively proto-L. Bruce patois so far ahead of its time that '60s icons Frank Zappa and Sly Stone were still worshipping, nay, copying Buckley's methods a full decade later.

And so, with these two World Apostates installed as the Twin Towers of *Copendium*'s fundament, I can sleep sounder, knowing that time is still on my side and that the obscene fudge of Western culture's hobbling, guilt-obsessed Political Correctness can never be more than a 'semblance of the truth', as Thomas Carlyle would have it; nobbut a temporary blip in that great and ever-advancing scheme of All Things.

Lord Buckley in Concert

(Fontana, 1958)

SIDE ONE

1 Supermarket (3.36)
2 Horse's Mouth (1.00)
3 Black Cross (4.05)
4 The Naz (10.10)

SIDE TWO

1 My Own Railroad (4.48)
2 Willie the Shake (2.56)
3 God's Own Drunk (6.34)

I once saw a Sly Stone documentary in which the Family Stone's trumpeter Cynthia Robinson did Sly's mid-'60s DJ patter for the camera. It was entirely copped (word for word) from the opening lines of 'The Naz' sketch from this Lord Buckley LP. Years later, I put this LP on and was shocked at the sheer enormity of its lucid-dreaming, psychobabbling, ampheto-minging influence on me, too. Dammit, it was like listening to myself speak. This was fundamental shit on the same level as the MC5's John Sinclair, the 13th Floor Elevators and The Stooges . . . at least. I'd always presumed I'd copped the whole 'greedheads' schtick from Sinclair's scene; but, hey, Sinclair and Rob Tyner were all jazzers before they were Beats, and I'd known this Lord Buckley LP at least eight years afore I knew Sinclair's texts. Richard Bock, a.k.a. Lord Buckley, had been spouting this stuff in the jazz clubs of Chicago since before WWII! Hail yeah, this was the shit and the heads had to know! I'd even sampled Lord Buckley for my *Radio Sit-In* release and know sucker nude it . . . Know? No! And if mebbee some o'them did already knew'd, then they had to be re-knew'd! Yup, it's payback time! We gots to honour the ancestors!

'We Gotta Knock Out the Greedheads!'

There are only two things I've ever stolen at a truly revolutionary level, that is, on a mystical, higher-consciousness level in which I knew (on a specifically Gnostic level) that my ownership of said colossal artefact/great spiritually endowed document would, in the long term, turn the world off its kilter, however imperceptibly at first. One was John Sinclair's dementedly essential revolutionary text *Guitar Army*, and the other was this record.

It was 1981 and I was a drug-addled pop star, stalking London's underground record stores. I hit one shop just as some Beefheartian voice came screaming out over their sound system: 'But first, we gotta knock out the greed-heads!' For the next forty minutes, this howling priest, this blathering, stuttering Loki, this African shaman, this Cheyenne medicine man, this stentorian, bicameral British Raj colonel-cum-Vachel Lindsay in full flight proceeded to mewl and sing, rail and wail, coo and sigh, pelt and belt out helter-skelter rant after tumultuous, damning tirade about rotten politicians, city planners and the first supermarkets with their low, low prices, and how – by loading up your stuff on a shopping trolley and schlepping it around the place – you were working for *them*, 'the greed-heads'. This was 1958 and the prices of groceries were going up and up; by pushing the 'mother cart', yooz working for them. You'll even take shopping carts and push 'em into other carts, noted M'Lud Buckley.

Man, I laughed and I cried, and sat goggle-eyed in the corner of this tiny record store and wondered, 'What the fuck?' (I never pushed another shopping cart back to the entrance again, I can tell y'all.) What had we lost? If this druid was telling us it's bad in the late '50s, what was the real deal in early '81? And what, then, is the deal three decades later?

And all this immaculate conception that Lord Buckley was trotting out, here in the record store, veered wildly from pedantic, Disneyesque, *Toad of Toad Hall* stuff to delta-blues-wailer-on-the-edge-of-time: a 'John Lee Hooker isn't a Looper', which up-ended my love of Captain Beefheart in one fell swoop from this one-time airing. *Fast and Bulbous*? Got me? Not any more, Cap'n. For Beefheart had entirely copped, note for note, every bit of Lord Buckley's very own speshul hip-patwah! I was now foaming and drooling in some Soho diskery, giving Noddy and Big Ears to a 1950s LP laid down over seven years before Don Van Vliet's first record. Indeed, I never listened to the Beef after 1981 for this very reason. You think I was without compassion? Will you check this sucker out before you judge me? Lend your ears to the rolling, as-it's-a-happening 'God's Own Drunk' and tell me it ain't 'Orange Claw Hammer' without the bogus field-recording interference hiding the edits.

Fer shoor, I believe you can cop somebody's riff over and over, but note for note just don't make it with me. Take 'Satisfaction' and sing other words over it, great; it's generic rock'n'roll and it should be public domain. But, however much I loved the MC5, I hated them nicking The Troggs' 'I Want You' and crediting it to themselves. Rip it off, babies, cop the lick in its entirety, but declare its provenance when the press come a-knocking! That undeclared shit is for the Led Zeps of this world.

So, you think I was happy to hear some voice unknown declaring in Beefheartian tones how 'God's lantern was a-hangin' in the sky'? Here I am sitting on the Soho sofa and my being a fucking pop star is clearly winding up the proprietor of this shop no end. He was doing all he could to ignore me, but being on drugs, I was dancing around like I'd found the Grail (which I had). I needed this LP like no other, but being managed by Bill Drummond I had no money, natch. Finally, the counter guy starts eye-balling me and in an instant he knew I was some remarkably hip aristocrat with one long-term eye on the world. 'Take it, brother,' says he: he was telling me to take the motherlode and spread its gospel. I could pay him back when next I hit the Soho swamps. 'Don't hold your breath,' mutters this punk into me booties and Lord Lucan'd it down the street.

U Dug Him Before . . . Re-Dig Him Now!

So, why am I telling you all this? The fact is, you can't review this Lord Buckley LP without describing his patter. And seeing his patter on paper is unlovely because the jungle fires of his rhythm and the cut of his jib and the slip of his tongue as the air leaves the lung remains unreachable outside the hearing of it. Of course, I may just be a sack-o-cack writer, but that's my alibi and I'm shielded behind it.

How do you review a '50s guy who defines cool as having 'the sweet fragrance of serenity', or who refers to Jesus as 'The Naz' and calls him a 'carpenter kiddie' who heals 'a little cat with a bent frame'? How d'you tell your potential audience that on the first run through of this LP they're gonna miss half the jokes in a furious flurry, an onslaughter of slanguage? But hang in there whatever, brothers and sisters, because it's a priceless commodity forged in the heads of the backwards-facing 'goodbye' witch doctors of the American (astral) Plains; a Zoroastrian anti-chariot rant by a pedestrianised priest of the pastoralists; a barking Odin versus Loki, I-know-you-are-but-what-am-I? tell-athon in the mead halls of Valhalla, reconstituted in the Chicago jazz club hinterlands in a wooden-structured, Odinesque temporary watering hole . . . How d'you paraphrase a piece like 'Willie the Shake' that takes Shakespeare and reshapes famous quotes to such as: 'The bad jazz that a cat blows wails long after he's cut out.' When it comes to Brother Bock,[1] all I can do is be the dude who brings the doodoo.

This record is even more superb because of the strange jazz instrumentation that supports his derailed stream-of-consciousness muse, as piano, trumpets, drums and even a female gospel singer orchestrate the proceedings. Buckley had been a child in the '20s; he was a comedian born of the Chicago ganglands.

As the sleeve-notes to his Frank Zappa-released *A Most Immaculately Hip Aristocrat* album stated, Buckley was described by friends as 'a combination of Salvador Dalí, a madman, a dandy and a real lord'. Part Indian, born in Stockton, California, in 1906, Buckley had an enormous ability to take all of his influences, wide ranging as they were, and subsume them into a multiple, *You're Never Alone with a Schizophrenic* character who leapt from class to class (hell, from race to race) mid-sentence, and would probably have been pretty adroit at changing species if the point could thus be better made. Historically, Buckley was at the end of his career with this LP and would live only two years after its release, dying in 1960 at the age of fifty-four. When he croaked, his obituary, as reproduced in the aforementioned sleeve-notes, read:

1 Having consulted the Goddess Sophia on the etymosophy of Richard Bock/Lord Buckley, his aberrant muse seems clearly to have been motivated by his ur-provenance as the ancient buca, or brownie; that sparrying spirit that gleefully undermines authority. We see it also in the character of Shakespeare's Puck and in the crazy West Country spirit of Bugley of Cley Hill, both of whom derive from the same root as the bogeyman, the 'boggart', the Scottish 'buckie' or the Welsh 'bwci'; all interfering, underworld supernaturals with a naughty little bugger's mission to undermine. This is Lord Buckley inner nutshell. Note should also be made of the Bock, the Germanic buck, or horned stag – the demonising of the horned god being the reason that figure has come to have two entirely polarised meanings: one as the aforementioned naughty little bugger, and the other as horny, anal rapist fuck-up.

Sir Richard Buckley – Lord of Flip Manor, Royal Holiness of the Far Out, and Prophet of the Hip – has gone to his reward. It probably won't be as swinging as his life, but Valhalla will have a hard time keeping him down. It is terribly difficult for anyone who really knew Richard Buckley to think of him as dead. It is more like he has been on an extended engagement in Reno and can't get back to town.

Amen. And, when you listen to this LP and look for a context in which to see him, remember that one early-'60s magazine wrote of Lord Buckley that his

. . . presence is felt strongly in the Mort Sahls and Lenny Bruces of today. The 'blast 'em and insult 'em' school of comedians popular today was actually started by Buckley when, back in the twenties, he became the pet of one of the big Chicago gangsters, who set him up in a nightclub because he liked the way [Lord Buckley] put on the suckers. Of course, [Buckley] had the protection of this gangland element during that period, and possibly he never got over it. He carried a bit of it with him always. He never really expected retribution to come or be paid. [Lord Buckley] always figured he would get away with it, and he usually did. It seemed predestined that Dick could never really become successful during his lifetime. He used up all his luck just staying alive.

There's unsung and there's *unsung*, babies. I really feel we got one of the latter here.

Discography

Lord Buckley in Concert (World Pacific, 1964. Originally released as *Way Out Humor*, World Pacific, 1959)

The Best of Lord Buckley (Elektra, 1969. Much of the same material previously released by Vaya Records, 1953)

Songs by Tom Lehrer

(Decca, 1959)

1 Oedipus Rex (1.42)
2 The Old Dope Peddler (1.29)
3 I Wanna Go Back to Dixie (1.55)
4 The Wild West Is Where I Wanna Be (2.05)
5 The Irish Ballad (3.03)
6 She's My Girl (1.51)
7 My Home Town (2.41)
8 The Masochism Tango (3.05)
9 In Old Mexico (4.10)
10 Be Prepared (1.34)
11 I Hold Your Hand in Mine (1.30)
12 When You Are Old and Grey (1.54)
13 Lobachevsky (3.13)
14 We Will All Go Together When We Go (3.29)

'Be It Ever So Decadent, There's No Place Like Home'

Born poor, in 1890, and raised the thirteenth child of older parents, my Grandma Cope's cultural sensibilities remained so locked into the pre-WWI mind-set that her son, my father, would regularly lullaby me to sleep with Victorian ballads – often incurring the wrath of my terribly modern mother: 'Good God, Alan, sing him something from this century, can't you?' But no, he really couldn't. For it was late 1959, and we were lodgers at Grandma Cope's house in Two Gates; worse still, surrounded by ancient Cope elders, most of whom reckoned WWI to have been merely the midpoint of their extremely long lives. Indeed, my Uncle Sam Knight, Grandma's eighty-two-year-old brother who still lived next door, had fought in the Boer War of 1899–1902, and once – when I was old enough to talk – described to me his terror while viewing a Zeppelin raid over Birmingham in the winter of 1916. Meanwhile, here in good ole '59, my dad rocked me to sleep by candlelight upstairs at Grandma Cope's, crooning the Boer War anthem 'Goodbye Dolly Gray', while downstairs my mother planned her appointment with the twentieth century.

By spring 1960, however, my parents and I had finally moved into a brand new house at 588 Main Road, Glascote Heath, four miles distant, and all of Grandma Cope's Victoriana was purged by my mother, swept away in a tidal wave of nowness. Unlike Grandma Cope's, the house in Glascote Heath had an indoor toilet, a bathroom, electricity and plumbing upstairs, as well as car parking space and – supplied by a pushy ex-suitor of my mother's – a heavy, walnut radiogram, with a single eight-inch speaker, which played records at thirty-three, forty-five or seventy-eight rpm.

Cannily, the ex-suitor also provided my parents with their first LP, a ten-inch record called *Songs by Tom Lehrer,* to go with the radiogram and, thus, we were all introduced to the dulcet tones of this cheerful Harvard mathematician. I say 'we' because I was always included in social gatherings at Glascote Heath, wielded as a one-metre mascot and magical totem by my mother, who loved showing off my memory and voice by parading me in front of her friends to sing note-perfect renditions of Tom Lehrer songs. That Lehrer's lyrics were somewhat 'off colour' (to use the vernacular of the day) only added further grist to my mother's Modernist mill, and she claimed throughout my teenage and early adult years, to anyone who would listen, that I had known all of Lehrer's best songs by heart by the time I was three and a half years old. And, dammit, from the trouble Lehrer's lyrics got me into throughout my childhood, I believe she may have been right.

Tom Lehrer was the ultimate wolf-in-sheep's-clothing; a bespectacled and über-mild-mannered academic within whose 'tra-la-la' catchy-bastard songs were contained endless tales of incest ('Oedipus Rex'), drug use ('The Old Dope Peddler', 'Bright College Days', 'Be Prepared'), xenophobia ('In Old Mexico'), violent institutionalised racism ('I Wanna Go Back to Dixie'), violent homicide ('The Irish Ballad', 'I Hold Your Hand in Mine, Dear') and violence to animals ('In Old Mexico' again, as well as 'Poisoning Pigeons in the Park'). All these songs sat quite happily alongside more acceptable targets of the day such as communist spy paranoia and the atom bomb ('The Wild West Is Where I Wanna Be') and the end of the world, courtesy of the Cold War policy of Mutually Assured Destruction ('We Will All Go Together When We Go'). Even a raunchy-sounding love song like 'She's My Girl' in actuality celebrated the poor personal hygiene of the singer's girlfriend. And, thus, material that would have got a feistmeister such as Lenny Bruce sacked immediately was, in the hands of this congenial Harvard academic, easy enough to sneak past the unsuspecting authorities, as unnoticed as Sidney Vish warbling 'You cunt, I'm not a queer' at the beginning of 'My Way'. I mean, no one but Tom Lehrer would have dared, back in 1959, to introduce a number like so: 'This is a song about a young necrophiliac who achieves his childhood ambition by becoming coroner.'

Unbeknown to me until very recently, Lehrer's debut LP had first been released as a private pressing way back in 1953, but his legend had been growing inexorably and to such an extent that, in 1959, Decca Records released British versions of his first two LPs. So, when my parents finally fled Grandma Cope's for their own home, that raunchy gift from the ex-suitor was blasted often and loudly in celebration of finally having their own space.

According to my mother, everybody who visited them was at first so embarrassed by Lehrer's lyrics that they insisted on listening with the lights turned off like giggling schoolkids. That's quite possible, I suppose, although my own later memories are of my father singing every song as though it were no more offensive than selections from Joan Littlewood's 1963 WWI spoof, 'Oh, What a Lovely War'. He was one of nature's innocents, my father, bursting into Lehrer's 'The Masochism Tango' at the drop of a hat – and sod the consequences:

I ache for the touch of your lips, dear,
But much more for the touch of your whips,
dear,
You can raise welts like nobody else,
As we dance to the masochism tango.

On car journeys, my father actually led the family in Lehrer singalongs, goggling my mother in a constant series of glassy-eyed epiphanies, even harmonising (for fuck's sake) on his favourite bit of 'The Old Dope Peddler':

He gives the kids free samples,
Because he knows full well,
That today's young innocent faces will be
tomorrow's clientele.

And as liberal, go-ahead, postwar, post-British Empire free-thinkers (and quite poor, to boot), both my parents relished Tom Lehrer's love of putting his great USA down; relished it as only pass-the-guilt children of the previous World Enslavement Regime could. So you can imagine with what gusto they uttered 'I

Wanna Go Back to Dixie', Tommy's impassioned paean to Confederate racism down in 'The land of the bo-weevil/Where the laws are medieval':

I wanna talk with Southern gentlemen,
And put my white sheet on again,
I ain't seen one good lynching in years.

In the post-everything twenty-first century, it's utterly impossible to conjure up the kind of antipathy generally displayed to Tom Lehrer's songs back in the day. But the establishment was right to have feared his influence on the next generations, for Lehrer was most certainly, for me, the marijuana that led to heavier drugs like Lenny Bruce. Lehrer ducked and dived, bluffing and swerving by interspersing his heavy comments with simplistic, sick songs like 'Poisoning Pigeons in the Park', work which was merely gauche, albeit highly enjoyable. Gradually, over time, my parents utterly forgot how shocking such words were to those hearing them for the first time, and they'd long forgotten that other people took offence at raunchy songs such as Lehrer's 'Oedipus', and fretted over incest-alluding rhymes like:

On one thing you can depend is,
He sure knew who a boy's best friend is.
So be sweet and kind to mother,
Now and then have a chat,
Buy her candy and some flowers or a brand new hat,
But maybe you had better let it go at that.

For my parents, Lehrer's 'evil' had become subsumed into an all-purpose popular-entertainment stew along with the aforemenched 'Oh, What a Lovely War'. So, when Lehrer's Australian tour was cancelled halfway through thanks to the local media's outraged response to his lyrics, my parents blamed it all on the slightness of Australian culture. When my primary school music teacher hit me over the head for singing Lehrer's version of 'No Place Like Home' ('Be it ever so decadent/There's no place like home'), my mother simply phoned the school and raged at them until they apologised unconvincingly.

Even I eventually awoke from my parentally induced Lehrer stupor one day, aged eleven, while listening alone to the singer's concert recording, *An Evening Wasted with Tom Lehrer*. I'd heard the record umpteen times before, spent whole weekends with it throughout my childhood; I loved it to death, I did. But, this time, alarm bells screeched as one word of that aforementioned spoken introduction made sense at last; holy shit! Let's take another look at that: 'The next song is about a young necrophiliac who achieves his childhood ambition by becoming coroner.'

Now, I heard it! I knew, at last, what that sentence meant, but I could barely believe it was true. So I summoned the mighty *Oxford Dictionary* and discovered, to my horror, that my parents – not me, note – yes, my own parents listened to songs about having sex with the dead! I was so disgusted, in my pre-sexually aware state, that I immediately sneaked all the Tom Lehrer records out of the house and fucked them up royally.[1] But I was still distraught. No wonder I'd received a clout from the music teacher; my folks were mentally ill and they needed help. It was all down to that ex-suitor of my mother; what an effing bee . . .

The period between 1969 and 1974, of course, was one during which I discovered and played only the Rock,[2] and almost all childhood fetishes were cast to one side. Indeed, next time I encountered Tom Lehrer was deep into my teenage years, when I earned Brownie points with my refusenik History teacher for singing 'Poisoning Pigeons in the Park' word perfectly. It was the sixth form. Teenage girls were less hung up about stuff then, and my teacher's endorsement of Lehrer suddenly made my friends pay attention to him. In truth, Lehrer's words and his infuriatingly catchy melodies have never left me for very long. Even nowadays, if someone rips me off I still leap around the room waving the offending object, quoting Lehrer's song 'Lobachevsky': 'Plagiarise, let no one else's work evade your eyes/ So, plagiarise, plagiarise!'

Do give this Album of the Month a chance; it's old and archaic and a real curiosity, I know, but Lehrer is one of the real Ancestors and deserves to be honoured within the portals of the pantheon.

Discography

'Poisoning Pigeons in the Park' b/w 'The Masochism Tango' (single, Decca, 1961)
Songs by Tom Lehrer (Decca, 1953)
An Evening Wasted with Tom Lehrer (Decca, 1959)

1 I still have those trashed records, although only as totems as they're unplayable now. Long after punk happened, I came to claim them, and bought my parents new copies.

2 Speaking of the Rock, Tom's opening lyric in 'She's My Girl' is worthy of *Raw Power*-era Iggy Stooge ('Sharks gotta swim and bats gotta fly/I gotta love one woman till I die').

The 1960s

The legendary Skip Spence gained his nickname on account of his being a Skip Allen lookalike, and as anyone who has viewed that late-'65 footage of The Pretty Things at Paris Olympia will know, the Look and the Way of this drummer/freakshow from every aspect beats The Who's Keith Moon by several miles. Indeed, it was only Moon's teenage gorgeousness and the sustaining genius of The Who that prevented him from being at least temporarily eclipsed by the monumental I'm-just-being-myself-ness of Skip Allen. As if having a male singer with hair so long he shoulda been called Susan wasn't enough in 1965, The Pretty Things also deployed this MoD Mod LSD-gobbling manimal percussionist Gunner S. Allen, whose forays into the audience and press enclosures caused genuine panic and occasional but futile attempts of authoritarian clampdown. 'Reincarnation, who needs reincarnation?' pouts Susan over a drumless two-chord organ–guitar–bass riff so shabby that Les Rallizes Dénudés could play it correctly, the singer all the time guffawing at the antics of his Tasmanian Devil drummer out in the audience. Even before the arrival of Skip, however, a lack of professionalism had pervaded every Pretty Things incarnation, and it's said that early drummer Viv Prince was the primary muppet inspiration for our boggle-eyed Skip. Yup, brothers'n'sisters, these Pretty Things wuz Born Never Arsed a full decade too early. Performing their 1966 single 'LSD' for the TV, not only does Skip Allen walk into view kicking and drumming upon a beer barrel, but their Susan singer Phil May even starts miming four bars early, looks around like a smirking cunt and starts again. It's a Nutter Classic performance.

Intuitive non-career movers always, The Pretty Things soon substituted madman Skip for another madman, Twink, who immediately accepted that upstaging Phil May was an unwritten given throughout his drumming assignment. Watch Twink miming 'Private Sorrow' on French TV, in that performance more beautiful even than Marc Bolan, Kevin Ayers or Nico herself. Of course, Twink was too freaky even for The Pretty Things, and soon headed off to rejoin the Pink Fairies Marching Band, or was it the reformed Deviants? Anyhow, back came the impossible Skip Allen again. For a while anyway . . .

The 1960s as told through this section of *Copendium* contain several lofty, sociopathic tales similar to my *prettythingsbabble* above. This section tells of unsung heroes and heroines whose sole crime was their refusal to be driven by Kapitalism as their prime motive. And while Nico, Soft Machine, Kim Fowley and Blue Cheer miraculously found major-label patrons of a kind, ensembles such as Italy's Le Stelle di Mario Schifano found only private art-house LP pressings available to them. Worse still, New York's Henry Flynt and the Insurrections and Sweden's Pärson Sound released nothing at all during their existence, while Blue Cheer's Randy Holden had his gear repossessed, lost his home and waited twenty years to see a worthy pressing of his classic *Population II* hit the racks. So please devour these '60s tales of compressed, distilled, hi-youthful achievement, and – having drizzled the events gently into your thoughts – do allow yourself to subsume them all into your melting polytheistic minds, along with all the other Rock'n'Roll Heroes'n'Heroines. For all of these lonely druids, each and every one of them, deserve that cherished place in the Gallery of Eternal Rock.

The Godlike Genius of Blue Cheer

(The above title was invented for the purposes of this eulogy and actually refers to tracks culled from the first two Blue Cheer albums, *Vincebus Eruptum* and *Outsideinside*, both released in 1968)

SIDE ONE (JULY 1968)

1 Doctor Please (7.53)
2 Out of Focus (4.08)
3 Second Time Around (6.17)

SIDE TWO (OCTOBER 1968)

1 Feathers from Your Tree (3.34)
2 Sun Cycle (4.18)
3 Just a Little Bit (3.30)
4 Gypsy Ball (3.01)
5 Come and Get It (3.18)

Although the twenty-first-century myth of Blue Cheer as *the* ur-power trio is nowadays so suffused with incandescent, post-everything, twenty-twenty hindsight that Messrs Peterson, Whaley and Stephens sit quite snugly alongside the other great Ancestors (the MC5, The Stooges and Pentagram) on most stoner rock.commer's record shelves, it's still particularly important, after Mein Hairy Dickie Peterson's untimely October 2009 demise, to remember that Blue Cheer's story only even began to resurface during the grungy, Sabbath-informed-in-a-Melvins-stylee, St. Vitus-propelled early '90s, as a whole new generation of orphan rockers suddenly asked: 'Whence sprung our current mung-worship?' And, 'Who were these pre-Sabbathians who bequeathed us these snottiest of lick scraps and riffic mishaps?'

Had the more literate among them trawled the then-current selection of blues-rock treatises available on the high-street bookshelf, they'd have been alarmed to discover that Blue Cheer had been entirely passed over by the bluesologists – those prim, Robert Cray'n'Elick Crapton authenticists relegating Dickie'n'co. to that sub-category just below Hendrix and Cream copyists known as 'garage'.

Yup, alongside the MC5 is where

Blue Cheer dwelled throughout the '70s and '80s: it was *they* who were the world's forgotten boys (not Nincompoop and The Stooges). Ahem, anyway, even Charles Shaar Murray's big, 1982 blues tome *Crosstown Traffic* didn't give 'em a mench, Murray not even dignifying the Cheer with a snidey one-line putdown. Their absence in the index says it all. Squish.

So, what is the real truth of it? Well, let's take a look at the sonic evidence, that is, the music contained within this particular Album of the Month. All of it was released between July and October 1968, when the original version of Blue Cheer was at its Mekong Delta-strafing height. Yup, the Cheer unleashed two hugely dynamic and killer albums barely fourteen weeks apart, each one being chock-full of great, bludgeoning soul, berserk, off-kilter (so-called) blues-rock and hefty, free-form bass'n'drum excursions of sheer cranium-pummelling intensity, over which white-noise ramalama was inappropriately daubed as often as was possible.

Was this actually blues at all? Search me; I hate the blues and love Blue Cheer, so what does that say? Besides, being managed by Hell's Angels and named after a brand of LSD, Blue Cheer was the absolute antithesis of the Zeitgeist, singer Dickie Peterson later commenting, infamously: 'We were the ugly stepchildren. Everybody of the San Franciscan scene was all "kiss babies" and "eat flowers". We were sort of "kiss flowers" and "eat babies"; we weren't peace and love.' No shit, Sherlock!

Blue Cheer's debut album *Vincebus Eruptum* was an absurdly unbalanced adventure playground of screeching white-noise guitar drool and Exxon-levels of axe spillage from Leigh Stephens, clumsy shed-building drum assaults from Paul Whaley and Mae Westian, corner-of-the-mouth vocal asides from bass player Dickie Peterson; each band member showing next to no regard for the standard soul or blues chord patterns that struggled to be heard far, far below. Buoyed up by their freak occurrence US Top Twenty hit versh of Eddie Cochrane's 'Summertime Blues', the rest of this first LP wedded the Cheer's brutally tough soul and blues rhythm section to Leigh Stephens' inordinately disconnected take on the role of the modern lead guitarist, almost every solo commencing as though the guitarist had been caught on tape actually in the act of giving up guitar playing. Chaos ensues every time his turn comes as Stephens' inner demons force him through the solo ('Come on, Leigh, you daft, tripping cunt; you can give up guitar after this one final assault').

Three months later, in October '68, the gentlemen of the ensemble returned with album number two, entitled *Outsideinside* – another catalogue of drunken, midnight dodgem shunts, amphetamine, stop–start buzzsaw sprawls and even the occasional moment of delightful pin-drop silence, this time occasionally overladen with mucho stacked soul harmonies (MC5-style, but a year ahead) and some exquisitely heavy keyboard contributions from a divinely ordained guest pianist/organist, Ralph Burns Kellogg.

So, What's It Sound Like?

The July portion of this *Vincebus Eruptum/Outsideinside* meld commences with the near-eight-minute-long free-rock bonanza 'Doctor Please', throughout which the three band members assault us with all of their choicest manoeuvres, again and again and a-fucking-gain. Blue Cheer sound like forgotten technicians jamming with long-obsolete weaponry aboard some abandoned space freighter; Paul Whaley's incredible and relentless drumming providing a clattery backdrop of 'busy canteen'-style mid-range as a vehicle for Stephens' solipsistic and arhythmical guitar flailing. In comparison, the soulful strut of 'Out of Focus' is a catchy slab o'tambourine-driven loveliness; that is, until Leigh Stephens interrupts proceedings with a solo so inappropriate that it could be a whole other song – hell, a whole other ensemble!

The July side concludes with the Cheer's ultimate avant-garde garage epic, the six-minute-long 'Second Time Around', on which these gentlemen prove once and for all that their sense of dynamics was both intenser and immenser than the other boys'. Repeatedly, the Cheer do their utmost to false-end us to death, each time returning to that same, barely restrained pulsing silence. There is one massive final shoot-out and all is silence. Albeit briefly, however.

The October 1968 side opens like some tsunami at sunrise, as the massive and resounding piano chords of Ralph Burns Kellogg herald *Outsideinside's* epic opener, 'Feathers from Your Tree', and the multi-voiced, searching, searching choir anticipates the harmony vocals of the MC5's *Kick Out the Jams*, then still over a year away.

'Sun Cycle' sounds like Jimi Hendrix's Experience attempting something from the third Velvets LP; that is, until Paul Whaley kicks in the hardest, most stentorian drum beat available, and the three Cheers cycle over and over, inserting just plain weird in-joke stop/starts, until the whole thing collapses and peters out beautifully.

Continuing Whaley's over-drumming motifs, 'Just a Little Bit' is another simple, cycling, riff song, entirely based around his phased amphetamine percussion lunacy; even Leigh Stephens' contribution is reduced to hurling in the occasional sonic hand-grenade. But there's no let-up from Whaley, and the final seconds of this raging song sound as colossal as any hundred-piece orchestra and as elemental as Niagara Falls.

Then we're off into the stumbling grunge of 'Gypsy Ball', a jaunty snorkel across the shallow end of the swimming pool; a sub-sub-Hendrix, sub-Troggs gadabout of the kind *Madcap*-period Syd Barrett could have served up while backed by Soft Machine's arch overachiever Robert Wyatt on drums.

This compilation concludes with the archetypal rummage-sale ramalama of 'Come and Get It', in which Dickie P lets fly a spirited series of fatuous lyrical declarations declaimed with such intensity that they sound positively life enhancing – the Cheer, for this final statement, now cast as Norse trailblazers, galloping off into the sunset as Leigh Stephens, sitting bareback astride Odin's eight-legged horse, Sleipnir, hurls down thunderbolts and epic stereo squalls of molten axe-murder into both speakers simultaneously.

In Conclusion

And then they were gone; that is, as the flame-thrower-wielding, bolt-throwing artillery division, ur-power trio. With truly poetic correctness, Leigh Stephens quit Blue Cheer when he went deaf, being replaced by Oxford Circle guitar genius Randy Holden, who lasted barely long enough to contribute a side of material to the third Blue Cheer LP, *New! Improved!*, before quitting to record his own legendary *Population II* opus.

Next, drummer Paul Whaley left to deal with his heroin addiction and new members came and went as Dickie Peterson refashioned the band, first as a blue-eyed, hippie-soul squad, thereafter as a really fucking fine band of songwriters, as captured on 1970's *The Original Human Being* and 1971's *Oh! Pleasant Hope*: great songs, great sound, but no fucker was expecting Badfinger from such badasses.

Dribbling on into the mid-'70s, even miscreant Svengali Kim Fowley attempted to prop up Blue Cheer's stinking carcass with a fairly excellent and abrasive four-song demo recorded in Hollywood. But, by then, the band had become a period piece à la the MC5, an anachronism too early and too punky for the real metal heads – only journalist Lester Bangs daring (with mucho hindsight, mind you) to comment positively about the 'bracing atonality' of Leigh Stephens' playing.

The mid-'70s saw them forced to compete in a Jon 'I Produced MC5 into the toilet bowl' Landau-informed, post-Cream, pro-virtuoso corporate-rock world that made The Stooges pay for their sonic ineptitude with alcoholic death and heroin addiction, and even dared question the transcendental, godlike genius of the MC5's rhythm section of Michael Davis and Dennis 'Machine Gun' Thompson. Sheesh!

In those dark, mid-'70s days of soft-rock, overseen by a bunch of Hollywood soft-arses, Blue Cheer could only sit and wait it out until the time again arrived when being a thunderous Viking poet with a canon of proto-metal anthems counted for something . . . anything.

And so, with Dickie Peterson no longer among us, it seems appropriate to celebrate the fact that he at least lived long enough to experience the pleasure of being accepted as one of rock'n'roll's important originators. For myself, I'd just like to let out a corvine screech of thanks to ye Bass Lord of Blue Cheer: Dickie, may ye drink Valhalla dry!

Henry Flynt and the Insurrections

I Don't Wanna

(Recorded in 1966, first released by Locust Music, 2004)

SIDE ONE	SIDE TWO
1 Uncle Sam Do (2.42)	1 Jumping (2.57)
2 Goodbye Wall Street (2.54)	2 Sky Turned Red (2.27)
3 Go Down (2.49)	3 I Don't Wanna (3.12)
4 Corona Del Max (2.54)	4 Dreams Away (7.14)
5 Missionary Stew (4.25)	Plus: Blue Sky, Highway and Tyme (15.53)

(The inconsequential organ instrumental 'Corona Del Max' has been omitted here in favour of 'Blue Sky, Highway and Tyme', a fifteen-minute-long guitar meditation from Henry Flynt's solo record *Back Porch Hillbilly Blues Volume 1*.)

The Image of the Untrained 'Folk Creature' as Avant-Gardist

When I first heard the New York guitar music on this album, I was gobsmacked and derailed by the agitated attack of Henry Flynt's bluegrass-meets-hillbilly-meets-rock'n'roll guitar sound, and the manner in which he took Troggs-simple riffs and upended them into dustbowl dances for tigers on Vaseline. Where had this horseless rodeo been all my life? Contained within these Flyntian grooves was a dehydrated atmosphere of such simultaneously biblical ancientness and futurist heathenism that it appeared as though some petty sub-Jehovah had chosen to install our man Flynt unfairly and squarely into the darkest episodes ever torn from the pages of J.F.K.'s tome *A Nation of Immigrants*. If this guy owned a car, it was a kaput Model T drawn by mules, for shit damn sure; if this guy owned a chicken coop, it was most likely that same Model T. Furthermore, the manner in which Flynt commandeered his own riffs, or even whole tracks, for crooning new songs over at a later time ('Missionary Stew' is also 'Uncle Sam Do', for example) really blew my mind – especially as the artist himself (hardly yet out of adolescence) looked like a cross between Stork from *Animal House* and Napoleon Dynamite.

Moreover, brothers and sisters, this guy was a true Zelig of the underground – an everywhere and nowhere baby whose name cropped up time and time again in articles about the American Civil Rights Movement, the modern New York art world and the new socialist philosophies being thrown up at the cusp of the '50s/'60s. And although no real articles appeared to have been written about Henry Flynt, from the various snatches of information that I could discover from biographies of his more celebrated contemporaries I gleaned that Flynt had always been considered a heavy conceptual artist, nay, for some people *the* original conceptual artist. But even for the few souls who knew Henry Flynt's work, he never was a guitarist but a violinist, and a musical theorist to boot. Indeed, in an essay written for Yoko Ono's 1992 boxed CD set *Onobox*, *New York Times* rock critic Robert Palmer referred to Henry Flynt as a 'composer, violinist, and the theorist who coined the term "concept art"'. Palmer went on to include Flynt in his list of the very earliest of the Fluxus artists – John Cage, Yoko Ono, La Monte Young, Richard Maxfield – whose art was so named by the gallery owner George Macunius for having been permanently in a state of flux; that is, forever at the moment of becoming.

And yet the difference between Henry Flynt and most other conceptual artists of his time is that the more you play *I Don't Wanna*, the more you need to hear it. I know Flynt initially conceived this album in a flurry of post-Exploding Plastic Inevitable excitement, probably as nothing more than an adjunct to his more serious violin drone music, but for listeners who get the picture, repeated plays soon become an emotional and cardiovascular necessity. You want to steep yourself in his hip, spiky yokel-drones and his catch-all, pop-art lyrical take on the protest movement, and you want to blast the fucking world to rights.

Flynt's formulaic approach is the difference between the obnoxious and obsessively listenable genius of Takeshisa Kosugi's majestic 1975, proto-Martin Rev ur-drone, *Catch Wave*, and the excessively intellectual, violin-tapping non-muse of that same artist on his *Live in New York* album, five years later. Or the difference between Bill Nelson's barely contained and primal '70s guitar tantrums with Be-Bop Deluxe and his pale, David Byrne-worshipping world music-isms of the following decade. And, in terms of being a truly intuitive, non-career mover, Henry Flynt really did take the fucking cake, limiting his releases to a few private cassettes from time to time; indeed, refusing proper releases for any of his works until the beginning of the twenty-first century.

But, while I rant and rave about the epic quality of this music, lay back awhile and let The Insurrections burn a few holes on your inner carpet while I relate to y'all how Mr Flynt reached this magically (and timelessly) funky place. Hell, motherfuckers, as George Clinton noted on Funkadelic's *The Electric Spanking of War Babies*: 'Funk can sit and sit and never go sour.' Well, beloveds, this Insurrections stuff is well over forty years old and (like Captain Scott's bully beef) it's still as fresh as the day they laid it down.

Avant-Bumpkin Hillbilly Joyriders of the Coming Revolution

In the early months of 1966, during Andy Warhol's Exploding Plastic Inevitable performances at The Dom, and just before The Velvet Underground recorded their first LP, the band's bassist and viola player, John Cale, became so sick, courtesy of the VU's unhealthy lifestyles, that he was forced to take some time away from their performances. Determined to replace himself with a valid substitute capable of understanding the ur-drones necessary for fulfilling The Velvets' highly specific metaphor, Cale asked his friend and fellow La Monte Young acolyte Henry Flynt to fill in for him. Unfortunately, this young experimental violinist and early Fluxus member was himself currently obsessed with reawakening his North Carolina roots. And so, Flynt brought to the Velvets not the removed and numbing sophistication of Cale's wind-tunnel viola, but a brutally hickish and highly volatile hoedown that had the young Southerner coming to physical blows with VU leader Lou Reed. Henry Flynt says of the experience:

> *Reed taught me their repertoire in about five minutes, because basically he just wanted me to be in the right key. At one point I got in a fight with him on stage because I was playing a very hillybilly-influenced style on the violin and that upset him very much. He wanted a very sophisticated sound; he didn't*

want rural references in what was supposed to be this very decadent S&M image that they were projecting.[1]

However disastrous the experience was, Flynt struggled through several further performances with the band, and, in lieu of payment, received six hour-long lessons of guitar tuition from Lou Reed himself. Taking this apprenticeship extremely seriously, and stimulated by Bob Dylan's recent adoption of rock'n'roll in the face of huge criticism, Henry Flynt decided immediately to process and utilise this new sonic information as a vehicle for his other main obsession – political activism. Or, as he wrote later:

Given my political engagement, I had been waiting for an impetus to try songs with 'revolution' lyrics.[2]

Initially comprised of Flynt, on vocals and electric guitar, accompanied only by his sculptor friend Walter De Maria on drums, the duo was nevertheless a superb and highly volatile agit-punk outfit that soon went by the name of Henry Flynt and the Insurrections. Rehearsals initially took place at De Maria's downtown loft, where the duo swung rhythms around and against each other and battered smart 13/8 and 5/4 time signatures so hard that they sounded like old vinyl caught in a locked groove.

Released temporarily from his La Monte Young-fixated violin drones, but still determined 'to reject the claim of cultural superiority which musicology made for European classical music',[3] Flynt's spangly and disorientating guitar licks and tumultuous Reedian rhythm-playing came on like Armand Schaubroeck's Churchmice playing frenetic Bulgarian wedding music; or John Fahey as fed through the Boards of Canada filter. Moreover, this neo-New Yorker's refusenik, motor-mouthed verbal onslaughts were delivered in an ultra-southern preacher twang said to have been far stronger than when he'd first stepped off the train from North Carolina several years previously. Behind Flynt, Walter De Maria's drumming was a swirling and bruising snare-led Dervish dance, inspired by a desire to jettison

1 Victor Bockris, *Transformer: The Lou Reed Story* (Simon & Schuster 1994). Search out the ten-minute-long violin drone entitled 'Jamboree' from *Back Porch Hillbilly Blues,* and you will belly-laugh at the sheer preposterousness of such a violent violin style having been foisted upon the unfortunate Velvets.

2 Henry Flynt, *The Meaning of My Avant-Garde Hillbilly and Blues Music* (essay, 1980).

3 Ibid., point 2.

the indolent thuggery of his previous band, The Primitives, whose now-legendary forty-five 'The Ostrich' had almost been an accidental hit in 1965 for its writers, Lou Reed and John Cale.[4]

Such was the musical effect of Henry Flynt and the Insurrections on its protagonists that they soon attempted to validate their group in the eyes of the New York art community by adding a bass player and organist. However, both Flynt and De Maria were overtly paranoid about the possible unbalances that could be wrought by unsympathetic playing from new members. And so, it was with some trepidation that they asked their friends, organist Art Murphy and upright bassist Paul Breslin, to extend The Insurrections into a quartet. We shall never know, however, quite how this four-piece incarnation would have fared in a live situation, for, due to Flynt's wariness of the commercial music business, they were disbanded after recording just one LP's worth of material, in 1966. Flynt would later claim that it was the music-hall approach of The Beatles that was to rid pop music of the essential ethnic qualities that had attracted him to it in the first place; while the assassination of Martin Luther King would – for Flynt – be the final nail in the coffin of the civil rights movement, driving this delicate soul underground forever.

Flynt's assumption that his playing 'would entail commercial success as a by-product' was severely battered by the absolute chart failure of The Velvet Underground, so recently championed as the New York avant-gardists' answer to The Rolling Stones. It all seemed evidence enough to Flynt that popular rock'n'roll had become 'Uniformly loud in a way which was vulgar, mechanical, and bloated.'[5]

Here was a perfect excuse for Henry Flynt to bow out of mainstream culture entirely and disappear for good, rather than 'competing with musicians for whom the last step in composing a piece is the sale – musicians for whom a bad piece that sells is a good piece'. Thereafter, this marginalised (and highly shell-shocked)

4 Incredibly, such was the incestuous nature of New York's early-'60s art and music scene that Walter De Maria's first attempt at making music had taken place in his New York loft back in 1963 with Andy Warhol and La Monte Young. It was during this same period and in this same loft space that Flynt was working on his 'new American ethnic music' project snappily entitled *From Culture to Veramusement*.

5 Ibid., point 2.

artist chose a strictly non-combative path, still quietly exploring his theory of a new American ethnic music in the face of what he called the 'Youth Disintegration Industry', but damning all post-'69 rock'n'roll as a 'one-way march towards grotesquerie and defilement'.

By 1984, Henry Flynt had given up playing music of any kind and had retired inwards into his art theories. He appears to have gained some kind of solace in the notion that all Western art movements were equally pervasive, equally brutal and equally unjust.

The Timelessness of I Don't Wanna

But where does this leave Flynt's sole recorded statement made with The Insurrections? At times, this guy is as much of a Zoroaster, staring down the Iranian charioteers, as is Van der Graaf Generator's Peter Hammill, and – after eighteen months of repeated listening – I personally consider the record to be a truly dislocated and barbarian classic. Moreover, although I've attempted several times to make *I Don't Wanna* into Album of the Month, I have previously always backed down at the last minute in case it was just my ultra-compassionate or overly romantic side talking. But still I'd come back for one more spin and fall in love all over again.

The recorded evidence contained within the grooves of this album reveals such an astonishing quicksilver energy of interplay between the guitar and drums that it all sounds completely contemporary. While De Maria's drumming ricochets around the heavens and, at times, makes no more attempt to keep down the beat than did Mickey 'Circle Sky' Dolenz at Monkees' concerts, Henry Flynt's guitar melds Sterling Morrison's cyclical mantras to Lou Reed's free-rock abandon with effortless ease, all the while his vocalising conjuring up a bucolic and biblical imagery utterly at odds with the downtown New Yorkscape in which the recordings were made.

Except for the seven minutes of 'Dream Away', each of the songs is concise, most being less than three minutes in length, and each inevitably sounding somewhat reminiscent of Reed's playing in his pre-Velvets groups (which I could never get enough of). Does *I Don't Wanna* truly qualify as having been made by a group? Perhaps not, for 'Jumping' is a duel between Guitar Henry and an overdubbed Violin Henry, with ne'er a thought for the other three guys in the band; while 'Dreams Away' is virtually solo Henry throughout its entire seven minutes. It seems that, in choosing a double-bass jazzer such as Paul Breslin over an electric bassist, Flynt was clearly intending his sideman to be seen (for credibility's sake) and not heard (as Leo Fender commented in 1951, the double bass was always 'the doghouse' – inaudible to all but the front rows of the audience and *never* in tune).

Perhaps the highly respected Breslin was put in place to make The Insurrections *feel* more like a 'proper' group to outsiders. But you can strain your ears all you wish and barely hear a pulse from that double bass, other than the occasional boogie down on 'Sky Turned Red'. Furthermore, that Art Murphy's organ playing was equally secondary to the powerhouse of Flynt and De Maria is also clearly evidenced on *I Don't Wanna*, being audible only during the unnecessary and slight instrumental 'Corona del Max' (which sounds more like the work of a typical organ-led, garage-rock band such as The E-Types than hefty musical dudes from a NY seminary). However, as Murphy went on to play with both Steve Reich and Philip Glass in the 1970s, perhaps he too was added to the line-up to infuse psychic heftiness in this otherwise guitar'n'drums-only 'quartet'.

Whatever his reasons, Henry made his single most magical statement with this self-styled 'protest band', The Insurrections, and mighty thankful should we be for the release of this hitherto unknown gem. Indeed, so should our man Flynt. For, with such a substantial statement now in place, much of Henry Flynt's other performance work (from the 'Dreamweapon' appearances with La Monte Young to a slew of more recent releases on the Locust Music label) will be much easier to access by utilising this record as the gateway to his skewed and elliptical underworld.

My compassion for this anguished theorist grows with everything new I learn about the man, especially as his own writings reveal no anger at his lack of commercial success but instead betray all the compassion for modern humanity of a prophetic voice truly crying out in the desert. As Mr Flynt so percipiently commented, back in 1980: 'I have to believe that the audiences which support the deluge of crass, gross music experience a far greater misfortune than I . . . Under the circumstances, the horrible symbiosis represented by mass culture cannot be upstaged by one iconoclast.'

Discography

Back Porch Hillbilly Blues Volumes 1&2 (Recorded throughout the 1960s, released by BoWeavil, 2004)

Raga Electric (Recorded 1963–71, released by Locust, 2002)

I Don't Wanna (Recorded 1966, released by Locust, 2004)

Hillbilly Tape Music (Recorded 1971–78, released by Locust, 2003)

C Tune (Recorded 1980, released by Locust, 2002)

Graduation (Recorded 1981, released by Ampersand, 2001)

Purified by the Fire (Recorded 1981, released by Locust, 2005)

Kim Fowley

Outrageous

(Imperial, 1968. Reissued by Ascension Records, 2000)

1 Animal Man (2.42)
2 Wildfire (4.08)
3 Hide and Seek (2.09)
4 Chinese Water Torture (0.43)
5 Nightrider (2.22)
6 Bubble Gum (2.27)
7 Inner Space Discovery (4.01)
8 Barefoot Country Boy (2.01)
9 Up (14.28)
 i Up
 ii Caught in the Middle
 iii Down
10 California Hayride (1.17)

The Shaman as Doorway

The problem with someone like Kim Fowley is that the intellectuals know that, on a long-term, sensible career level, he doesn't mean any of what he says. So they dismiss him because they've fallen for the idea that you gotta mean what you say in the first place in order for it to have value. Baloney! The innate truth of rock'n'roll shamanism is such that it can still ooze out and inform the world, even from the works of those who claim to be engaged in nothing more than some form of parody.

So, while The Doors took you to the underworld in a manner that was deadly earnest, The Fugs did it by employing mock incantations and magical chants which had superficially ridiculous lyrical content but which were still ultimately mysterious enough to entrance the listener in the same way that Latin intoned during a church service can still unexpectedly transport the most secular and un-spiritual of visitors. In other words, act like a shaman and you may become a shaman. Affect a ritual in your living room, with all the mock solemnity that it entails, but don't be surprised when half the people involved become moved and emotional. Hell, if we could persuade Britney to lend us her name for a coupla massive, meditational groove albums, we'd see such an emotional and electric response from Western teendom that it would feel like Woodstock all over again – it wouldn't matter a damn that she didn't mean it; her name on the record would be enough seal of approval.

Eat and Run

The shaman has always been the doorway between worlds. The shaman acts as some bizarre, bozo-interface mixing the serious and the ridiculous, the sacred and the profane, the super-dangerous and the embarrassingly twee; which is where Kim Fowley comes in. Or, more specifically, this is where *Outrageous* comes in, because with this album Fowley became the ultimate examplar of that bozo-interface. And, like a petrified rubber figure of Bart Simpson excavated from under one of Stonehenge's trilithons, *Outrageous* is probably the most unprovenanced piece in the whole history of rock'n'roll. It sounds like nothing else. It came out of nowhere. There wasn't even an attempt at a follow-up. Fowley just did it and then walked away.

Outrageous contains song after song, and great ones at that. But, far more than all of these, it was a shamanic rock'n'roll album made by the ultimate chancer/huckster/gleeman. And its lack of commercial success in no way undermines its genius as an album of transformation. Indeed, this album could probably be used as a blueprint for those seeking to create a Pied Piper effect on our contemporary teenage wasteland.

How could this be? When I make the claim for *Outrageous* lacking provenance, I'm talking about this urine-stained, street-hustler Fowley guy who, back in 1966, was having a novelty hit as Napoleon 14th, with 'They're Coming to Take Me Away', after failing one year before with his bandwagonning forty-five 'The Trip'. Four long years before that, he'd been the doo-wop producer of naff Leiber and Stoller rewrites such as the Hollywood Argyles' chart-topper 'Alley Oop'. Hell, back in 1960, this guy was writer, producer and performer of that hoary forty-five 'Nut Rocker' – yup, this man *was* B. Bumble and the Stingers (in fact, overseeing Rendezvous label session musicians, notably Al Hazan playing the signature, Tchaikovsky-derived piano melody).

I guess the greed of late-'60s expectations must have taken over. An opportunist schmoozer-loser such as Fowley must have known he had to act quickly as soon as he clocked other contemporaries from the early '60s transforming themselves *and* being taken seriously, as did his mate Little Ritchie Marsh, who had become the proto-flower child Sky Saxon.

Do It and Then Move On

Like Vachel Lindsay, who heroically walked across America at the turn of the twentieth century, writing poems for bakers and Chinese laundry-owners in return for a loaf of bread and clean undies, Kim Fowley was always the gleeman rather than the true poet – the conjuror of words, the raiser of psychic hackles on the backs of the great and the gifted, and the self-styled 'Lord of Garbage', as he called himself on *Outrageous*.

Of course, aside from their hugely ostentatious and frantic styles of vocal delivery, the only other artistic elements which Vachel Lindsay and Kim Fowley could be said to have shared was an insatiable desire to encapsulate in their art everything which pertained to be America *right now*. To capture your own culture in its state of flux is to comprehend that culture is always in that state of flux – that culture is always in the act of 'becoming'.

And what better medium through which to capture the moment than rock'n'roll? Even in these cynical days of *Q* magazine's Nick Drake Award for Melancholic Unshavenness, most journalists prefer to write about a rock'n'roll which at least attempts to sound as though it captured the moment. Murky or bright, bass-heavy or drum-less, stupid or smart, rock'n'roll just *is*. You book your studio on a rainy Tuesday morning and you make your classic right then and there. Fuck Memphis and 'the vibe'; the vibe's where *you* are, motherfucker. Would countless neo-Krautrock bands now be asking engineers to replicate Neu!'s drum sound if guitarist Klaus Dinger hadn't given up searching for a drummer to make the rhythms he kept hearing in his head and, out of sheer exasperation, played the fucking drums himself? After adoring Can's legendary *Ege Bamyasi* and having it inform huge chunks of my whole musical aesthetic for twenty years, did I really need Jaki Leibezeit to let on that, all along, he'd thought his drums were too loud on that record? No fucking way! Did any of us need to hear Johnny Thunders complain that Todd Rundgren's mix of the first New York Dolls LP was too murky? Hail no! Besides, it just reinforces the image of Thunders as the puppet of his more powerful producer.

All of which brings us to Kim Fowley and his spirit of ultra-ultra-ultra-ultra-ultra-ultra immediacy. Hey, and in these neo-Tears for Fears days of Coldplay, and so-called artists like Richard Ashcroft employing Paul Young 'fugees such as bass player Pino Packadildo, we need as much now, now, now as we can grasp a hold of; which (again) is where Kim Fowley comes in – or, more specifically, where *Outrageous* comes in.

Although its rent-a-wreck homage to The Doors, the Mothers and Jimi Hendrix is immensely satisfying, in a Teddy and His Patches sort of way, it isn't the music on *Outrageous* which continues to leave twenty-first-century listeners gasping. No, no, no; the genius of this 1968 album is all contained in the dizzyingly portentous and truly whacked-out vocal delivery which Fowley chooses to foist upon us. And it's a delivery which, I might add, entirely pre-empted '70s Iggy Pop and must have (at least temporarily) kicked Jim Morrison's dick into the dust. And hearing the various members of Steppenwolf trying to keep up with Fowley's heart-attack vocalese is mesmerising in itself – and all this at a time when iconoclastic recording acts were commonplace enough to be almost expected.

Let's Go Out of Our Minds to Get Back In

Outrageous opens with the brief Gatling-gun drumming and lightweight Hendrix-ish psychedelia of 'Animal Man'. Like The Standells playing The Music Machine's hit 'Talk Talk', the music exists entirely on its own, working well as an instrumental and merely laying down a foundation on which Fowley sets out his stall: 'I'm ugly/Uh-huh/Dirty, filthy, sneaky, horrible/I'm gonna kill you/Are you straight?/Well, I'm Animal Man.'

Right now, he's still courting us. This is pathetic, right? The music here is way too bubblegummy to be anything more than a cute diversion. The second verse is just as lame and the music is great, generic, psychedelic garage-rock, at least one year out of date. Cue verse three: 'I'm a love addict/Public enemy number one/I'm gonna butcher all the girls on my loving-room floor.' A Suzy Creamcheese-type voice then announces: 'Oh Animal Man, you're so rough and so . . . big.' Seven seconds of grunting (count 'em) and Fowley comes like a sixteen year old. 'It's too dirty, it'll be banned,' he chuckles, and that's where you start liking the guy.

'Wildfire' really kicks *Outrageous* in.

Meaning and meaninglessness shag each other senseless, as a Gothic minor-key blues guitar riffs over a slouching, lurching drum beat, and the voice of a singing cadaver croaks: 'Oh yayer, yayer, someone's been setting fire in my neighbourhood . . ./ An old car has been . . ./Somebody tell me . . ./And who's been setting the fire?' Fowley doesn't finish any sentence, just leaves a space for us to fill in and moves on. 'Wildfire . . ./It's wild figh-figh-figh-figh-figh-fire/The fire inspector came up to me and he said to me, "How do you know? How do you know? How do you know?"/ And I asked him, "How do you know? How do you know? How do you know?"'

Genius. I'd love to have watched *that* conversation.

Then Kimmy continues: 'And I said to the fire inspector, "What bothers you about everything?"' Out of the ether, shuffling and shoe-gazing, trucks a reluctant nerd chorus which, at the behest of a cajoling Fowley, reluctantly moos out a truly bovine 'Reality!' This is done with about the same achingly embarrassing non-conviction that Steve Hanley exhibited when singing 'Popstock' on the second Fall LP. It's fabulous. 'What bothers you about everything?' asks Kim. 'Reality,' they chunter, slowly warming to his cause. 'So what bothers you about reality?' he counters, before answering on their behalf: *'Everything!'*

Yes, it's deadly obvious, but it's a beautiful pay-off. Too beautiful for Kimmy, who gets bored easily and switches off immediately. 'I'm not crazy/I'm going to sleep,' states Kim. 'I wanna go to sleep/I wanna go to sleep,' he repeats over and over at Mach 1, motormouth speed. 'Help me go to sleep/Help me go to sleep.'

Next up is the let-down. 'Hide and Seek' is an excellent, funky, early Sly-type instrumental and a so-what forgettable waste of your time in the context of this album. You could see its inclusion as a clue to why Kim Fowley remains utterly unsung.

'Chinese Water Torture', however, is the most abject form of genius; a forty-three-second 'Horse Latitudes' for paranoid teen masturbators. Hilariously, contemptibly rubbish, fake-oriental intoning excites the drummer into a stomping frenzy until a super-paranoid Fowley insists that the police have just walked in and made them stop playing – and by the way, we're all dead. Excellent.

'Nightrider' commences as a gigantic circular instrumental with an amazing guitar riff and only later does a tripping vocalist appear, coming to terms with the fact that contact lenses really must be cleaned every couple of months or they'll dry up like husks right there in your eyes: 'Aaaaaaaaaargh! Whoaoaoaoaoaoa! Wowowow-waughghghghghgh!' Here, Fowley takes the archetypal garage-rock scream and punishes until his throat is razor raw and his haemorrhoids are inflated to the size of grapes from the Hanging Gardens of Babylon. There's only one lyric in the entire thing:

You say you want me every night,
Running around with the angels of light,
You say you want a natural man, girlchild.
Whoaoaoaoaoaoaoaoaoaoaoaoaoaoaoaoa oaoaoaoa!

This is a man with Pete Burns up his ass . . . Unlucky.

'Bubblegum' opens with a truly euphoric, Robbie Krieger-like, ever-ascending guitar line and an atmosphere straight out of The Doors' *Strange Days*. 'Your name is Bubblegum/Live for moon and sun,' coos Fowley. Oh, 'Bubblegum' is brief, beautiful, deeply sexy and groovy-groovy-groovehhhh!

'Inner Space Discovery' is that bozo-interface I was mentioning earlier, where The Fugs meet The Doors (indeed, where The Godz meet the Patti Smith Group, and where the Nihilist Spasm Band meets the MC5). One of the session engineers, David Brand, flatly states: 'Take four, *insane version*,' to which the other engineer, Bruce Ellison, blandly insists that this must be delivered in the 'Mark Lindsay voice, Kim'. And so this glorious 'Inner Space Discovery' takes off, although utterly devoid of any Mark Lindsay voice whatsoever.

This song – its tone of voice, its solipsistic asides, the whole schmeer – must have been the blueprint for the Iggy Pop of the '70s, and almost a decade before Iggy got there. That's not to put down the Ig – you've got to admire his genius for even recognising that a career could be forged out of this kind of vocal delivery. And Iggy was also smart enough to smokescreen any direct Fowley comparisons with his famous, damn-with-faint-praise comment: 'Kim Fowley is bullshit, but it's a better class of bullshit!'

Next follows the flatulence of 'Barefoot Country Boy'. What, here, is basically bog-standard, proto-retro-rock'n'roll in the style of 'Star' from Bowie's *Ziggy Stardust* or the Plastic Ono Band's 'New York City' becomes possessed and ultra-weird when used as musical support for someone snorting, belching, straining and sneezing their way to a heart attack. As Fowley asserts on the record sleeve, the answer to the city dweller's neuroses must include acts of 'animalism, vulgarity, and pure madness', but the most charming aspect of this method of song delivery is the way in which Fowley occasionally surprises even himself. 'Whoa . . . rock'n'roll!' he shouts in alarm as one particularly ripe greeny whizzes past the mic.

I'll Sleep When I'm Dead

Finally we're into the biggie – the transformation freak-out which sets *Outrageous* apart from all but the best. 'Up' is the definitive audience-led, stream-of-unconsciousness descent into madness; fourteen and a half minutes of soul-review-from-hell ritual abuse by a tripping and paranoid maniac who may even not be on drugs. When I say audience-led, I simply mean that Kimmy, here, is totally affected by every look, grimace, whisper and nip-to-the-bog which his hippie studio cortege makes. As always, this is Kim the observer, and everything he sees, even in the safety of his own recording studio, is out to get him. The fat, smoking girl who brought in the whip comes in for some particularly strong criticism. A couple of minutes further into this death trip and he screams in apparent surprise, and apparently to no one/everyone: 'You're not dead'. What a give-away – he's tripping his socks off. 'I just woke up next to Ay-dolf Hitler's body/Is this hell?/Is there a drummer somewhere in hell?' The questions are coming too thick and fast, now. 'Do you wanna bury the straight people?/"Straight People's Funeral Song", please,' he continues. Cue cheesy-cheesy organ theme. 'Well, the straight people are going nowhere/And we're gonna get you/We're coming after you.' He goes on. 'I am the Lord of Garbage/I sit in a dirty room next to a gas station/On weekends I wait for local straight chicks to walk up the hill/I have one thing on my mind/You know what I'm gonna do to those straight chicks?/What am I gonna do?/Yeah, yeah, yeah/Yeah, heah, heah, yeah, yurgh, yurgh, yurgh . . .'

Then he does a tasteless rap about how white guys have to get used to finding black women beautiful because 'black negroes' are taking all the white chicks. And still it won't let up. We get some shit about the Chinese invading the USA in 1987, and what will we say to those invading troops? According to Kim, American couples will walk up to them and scream: 'Yeah, yeah, yeahhhhhhhhhhhh!'

'Up' dies in echo only to be followed by the insane, vocal-only coda 'California Hayride'. This brief, final track is a whole pre-Altamont, pre-Manson dialogue between the screaming, incoherent, belching Fowley and the compassionate, frankly unbelievable, world-changing charlatan Fowley. Everything that the latter character asserts is instantly undermined by belches and stun-grunts from the other speaker. It's fantastic.

In conclusion, Fowley chants 'We're rough,/We're tough/We've had enough!' over and over and fucking over again, before the engineers pull the plug and a strangely delightful silence pervades the room. Transformation, transformation, transformation!

From Y to Z and Never Again

Listeners shaking their heads in wonder at the sheer cantankerous perfection which Kim Fowley achieved on *Outrageous* may well wish to leg it to the nearest record store and attempt to stock up on some more of these gems. However, there are none; zero; zilch. Our intuitive non-career-mover chose to populate his next album with all kinds of Sunset Strip detritus, dignifying them with cameo roles right there on his own vinyl grooves, and calling the debacle *Good Clean Fun*. That in itself is a pretty major statement of intent. Right now, somewhere in the ultraworld, Kimmy is at work formulating the next 'moment'. He is another of the world's truly forgotten boys, but he's smart enough to know that a genius like his will always have its Dante Gabriel Rosetti waiting in the wings of some future theatre, preparing to champion his skinny ass; as Fowley once wrote: 'I never wanted to be a mainstream rock star! I did succeed.'

Randy Holden

Population II

(Hobbit GRT Records, 1970)

SIDE ONE	SIDE TWO
1 Guitar Song (5.42)	1 Blue My Mind (5.34)
2 Fruit and Iceburgs (8.05)	2 Keeper of My Flame (9.23)

In the wake of the cryptic allusions to this record on my own *Rome Wasn't Burned in a Day* album cover, and its being blasted over the speakers throughout those *Rome* shows (plus Ethan Miller from Comets on Fire heckling me to give it an Album of the Month slot), it seemed like a good time to tell this sad, sad tale. That the artist himself believed *Population II* to have never been commercially released is weird enough, but the betrayal of this supreme guitar hero by his management when they impounded and sold all his equipment on the eve of the album's release is a tragedy of titanic proportions, especially when both Randy's guitar *and* his beloved Sunn amplifiers could, in his unique case, be considered to have been his muse above any female in his life.

Randy Holden deserves to go down in history not for what he achieved but for what he *wished* to achieve. Reading some of the comments he's made about rock'n'roll music and the effect of the electric guitar puts me in mind of Faust – the group *and* the literary character. Those comments certainly define Randy Holden as having a truly shamanistic nature; probably somewhat akin to the more resilient Mizutani from Les Rallizes Dénudés. That *Population II* is as good as it is, is almost a bonus. That Randy was as forward-thinking a motherfucker set him way back and probably cost him his entire career.

'Scuse Me While I Kiss This Guy

Population II is a legendary album for several reasons, but none more than it being the most strung-out, wrung-out, ambient hulk of metalwork to rise from the mystic portals that crossed the 1960s over into 1970. When Andrew Marvell wrote about 'desarts of vast eternitie' in the seventeenth century, he was surely anticipating Randy Holden's *Population II.* It's definitely the most aptly titled record ever, for it sounds like the musical equivalent of two loners in the Belfast shipyard, working after hours, heads down and walleyed, to create a solo aircraft-carrier of Howard Hughesian proportions. Yes, it's that big, that lonely, that singular: a friendless, featureless musicscape that rivals Skip Spence's *Oar* and Klaus Schulze's *Cyborg* for sheer doing-my-thing-till-I'm-damned proportions.

Maybe that's why so few have even heard this sucker. Like punks who name-dropped The Stooges during '77 when they'd only ever heard *Lust for Life*, even metallers and guitar freaks who've never heard *Population II* allude to it in conversation. For it so irrigates the souls of those in the know that their descriptions waft into the collective consciousness of outsiders who quickly beg, steal or borrow a burn from any friend-of-a-friend-of-a-friend-of-a-friend . . . However, unlike most of the supposed 'lost gems' that fetch big money in collectors' circles, *Population II* is a genuinely life-changing experience.

Recorded in an opera house, using twenty Sunn amps wired in parallel ('It was the only place we could rehearse that would carry all the amplification,' Holden told *Trouser Press*), by this ex-member of instrumental surf loons The Fender IV, this Sons of Adam lead guitarist (whose cover of Arthur Lee's 'Feathered Fish' is a lost classic), this co-writer with the slow, slow, semi-achieving The Other Half (whose solitary LP Randy rightly dismisses, despite their wonderful 'Mr Pharmacist' forty-five), *Population II* sounds absolutely unlike any other LP (even the similarly epic-styled Side Two of Blue Cheer's *New! Improved!*, which Randy wrote alone, before disappearing).

When this surf-punk's career began, in 1964, instrumental music was at its height and he always maintained that he 'wanted to do nothing but the instrumental thing . . . because the instrumentation was where I really got my joy'. Well, it seems to me that he was still just as resistant to vocals five years later, when *Population II* was cut. You might think Jimi Hendrix's vocals were just throwaways, there to provide punctuation to a bunch of jams, but Randy Holden's vocal style makes them sound essential by comparison. And just as Kiss's Gene Simmons must have written his bass lines around his punches in the air, Randy Holden probably wrote down every yelp, howl and grimace on paper; which is why I love this Randy LP so fucking much.

The album approaches genuine sonic meltdown in the manner in which it smears layer upon layer of sludge-trudge guano riffery until you get the impression that the brick walls of that empty opera house will be forever imbued with the sonic ur-klang of this Yankee Reaper. And if the forced march of Black Sabbath's first three LPs' slowies was partly informed by the lumpen metal of Side Two of Grand Funk Railroad's red-sleeved *Grand Funk* (especially 'Winter and My Soul', 'Paranoid' and 'Outside Looking In'), then they were equally caught in the thrall of the post-Leigh Stephens Blue Cheer beast that Randy coaxed back into life for one last swansong before seeing them consigned to the good-time soul of Delaney & Bonnie (ho-est of hums). That Randy managed only one side with Blue Cheer is a damn near perfect metaphor for the whole careering showbusiness of this guitar druid. 'Once you get started, ooh it's hard to stop,' sang Chaka Khan. Tell that to Randy Holden, baby; his career was more stop–start than a rush-hour hitch-hike through Tijuana contraflow ('Watch out for that dead German Shepherd with the distended belly! Oops, too late!').

Population II doesn't start, it just fades in like it's been going around and around since the beginning of time . . . as though 'Hey Joe' was walking through Hungerford, killing the same thirteen people over and over, and we could still go there and witness it if we were to board a plane right this minute.[1] As if calling the opening track 'Guitar Song' was not enough, Randy then seeks to re-emphasise this obsession by singing: 'I love the sound of a guitar playing/I love the way it makes me feel inside.'

The main riff is a Troggsian 'Purple Haze', shot so full of largactyl that it keeps slowing down, while Randy is commander-in-the-field, howling out instructions in a sub-Mae West style to his sole underling. That's right, babies, we ain't talking about a three-man army here – this

1 I wrote this review in room forty-six of the Hotel Forum, Pompeii, kids. Now, just how fucking Rawk is that? Mount Vesuvius was just five kilometres away but it's Randy who's smokin'!

is a power duo! And, from the Kwalo Klobinskyian outer limits future-warrior sound emanating from this couple of annointed bozos, Randy must have chosen Chris Lockheed as his drummer mainly because Lockheed was the aviation company which made the Starfighter – the USAAF's ultimate plane-crash disaster that got sold on to West Germany's post-war Luftwaffe. Randy once said of guitar-manufacturing pioneer Leo Fender: 'He was a brilliant man. He took military technology and turned it over . . . Pretty amazing when you think about it.' A beautifully poetic thought, Herr Holden. You could, however, turn that right around and suggest that with *Population II*, Randy took rock'n'roll and turned it over to the military, although I guess if they'd played this sucker outside General Noriega's house instead of Barry Manilow's 'Mandy' on endless repeat, Noriega would have held out longer, thinking heroically that the entire Yank army was at his door. Meanwhile, amidst this chaos, Mae West Hendrix is still issuing more incomprehensible orders and declaring: 'And I'm in love/I'm in love/I'm in love.'

This is one darkly erotic muse that Randy Holden has caught by the short'n'curlies. She shrieks and howls in gorges and on hilltops; she fakes death in her own mound then rises like a phoenix; she manipulates and she engorges; she is penetrated as she consumes, and all the time Breakneck Holden is a-holdin' on for dear life – a paraglider towed behind a careering 1934 Chrysler Airflow, with Cruella DeVille at the wheel.

Fading in next comes the re-recorded, proto-Sabbathian 'Fruit and Iceburgs', the Dantean doom descent that Randy originally sung on Side Two of Blue Cheer's *New! Improved!* (one of only two new songs that Blue Cheer learned in the entire time he was in that group). But whereas Dickie Peterson and Paul Whaley merely played their leaden parts as though learned by rote, here the now pumping rhythm track is consumed by a Jeff Beckian scythe guitar (the kind perfected on 'Under Over Sideways Down') melded into a twin-harmony doom-raga that, according to Randy, made Blue Cheer sound 'quiet, placid and peaceful; what you listen to when you're eighty years old, in your rocking chair'. Randy sings the vocal line along with the guitar, creating an *Emerge*-period The Litter-at-sixteen rpm feel, crumbling to a halt every so often as wildly unrestrained and excessive Glenn Ross Campbell-style atonal, arhythmical, sun-bleached slide guitar broncos across the stereo panning with a numbing slowness that must have been truly out-to-lunch in those late-'60s days of speed and dexterity.

Then, out of nowhere, comes the brief intermission of 'Between Time' – a backwards 'You Really Got Me' version of 'Jumping Jack Flash'. 'I been loving this guitar for a long, long time,' sings Randy. No shit, Sherlock Holden. 'Well, the rhythm of the music will a-thrill your soul/Till you got no time to get old/And it's all right now,' opines Randy. Then it's cut back into the second, purely instrumental half of 'Fruit and Iceburgs', this time treading a line between the barren-ness of 'Ladytron' from the *Roxy Music* LP and some of the more ominous of Van der Graaf Generator's stuff. Randy's guitar is truly transcendental, as though becoming both Andy Mackay's oboe and David Jackson's saxophone simultaneously.

Intermission – or the Present Day Power Duo Refuses to Die

Thus endeth Side One, in which you really do get the impression that Randy Holden was moved by some greater ur-force. For myself, when considering even some of my most full-on peers, I've noticed that life for them has just recently started to 'wear off' in the past half decade. But even in 1995, Randy still spoke of his guitar muse as though she was some succubus who devoured him every night, calling his relationship with his instrument 'a total, full-blast, full-on love affair. The louder and clearer that baby was, the more beautiful it was. Hitting that guitar string on a voluminous [*sic*] amp was just heaven, and people felt it.'

In that same year, Randy recorded an album called *Guitar God* for Japan's Captain Trip label, and it was damned good. Not quite such singular, earth-shaking savagery as *Population II* but still a motherfucker (almost) all the way through. Who played drums? Paul Whaley from Blue Cheer! Twenty-five years on and these druids were still at the mound invoking the reluctant, sleeping goddess like the Odinesque Svipdag in the Norse myths!

Population II *(Slight Return)*

Side Two opens with the truly cinematic roar of 'Blue My Mind', in which Randy finds himself at a porn show where he's watching his new girlfriend, the star of a blue movie that's truly blown his tiny mind. 'Is it really you that I'm watching?/That I'm seeing . . .' he croaks, still in his bestest, most defiant Mae Westian, 'come-up'n'see-me' style. 'I hope this ain't true/Don't you think I don't know what you're doing?'

Now, ordinarily, I'd be on Randy's side and feeling bad for the dude. But, if her misdemeanours can conjure up such errant guitar savagery, then I'm all for her taking her exhibitionism to new heights just to piss him off. Just as the Five could take a song as simple as the Troggs' 'I Want You' and melt it down into something akin to Beethoven's *Fifth*, so Holden and Lockheed here create as thunderous an orchestration as ever helped shore up the walls of Asgard. That Randy Holden was aiming for something at least akin to the aforementioned description is somewhat supported by this comment he made in *Trouser Press* magazine, in 1973, about the force of the 'lecky guitar:

I once thought at some depth what a nuclear bomb would sound like in close proximity. I concluded it would be so overwhelming it wouldn't be heard, but simply be all-encompassing, beyond imaginable experience. I was so affected by the idea of what such sound would feel like that I wandered into the arena of attempting to produce a sound that would be so overwhelming, it would create a silence all its own.

A 'silence all its own', babies: it makes me cry just to think about this poetic soul adrift in a post-Mansonic world of Linda Ronstadt and Jann Wenner's *Rolling Stone* magazine, musing in his room about guitar music so loud it would 'create a silence all its own.' This multiple Sunn amp-marshalling, former surf-punk was on a proto-Glenn Branca trip a decade too soon. Randy should've been in Germany or Japan or Scandinavia or somewhere else crazy where they'd have had the intellectual capacity to realise his vision; anywhere but California in the early '70s.

OK, I'll get off my soapbox and tell you that *Population II* concludes with the nine-minutes-plus of 'Keeper of My Flame', the best song on the LP and anutha mutha that fades in and halts, as Randy Mae hiccups: 'Hey, baby.' Then we're off into the only mid-tempo track on the entire LP. Indeed, it sounds fast as a bastard compared to the rest, and only here does Randy's muse manifest as a real (although still unapproachably shadowy) lady. Chris Lockheed's tom toms are totally unsupported by bass, and the groove kicks and kicks and yooz soon dancing around the room, fist in the air, screaming 'Randair! Randair! Randair! Randair!' – as if each time you call his name will carve him deeper into the bedposts of history. Soon, out of nowhere, comes a glam descend to end all fucking glam descends; it's right in the pocket of that whole tradition of

'Maggot Brain', 'Safe Surfer', 'Pyjamarama', and the 'Moonage Daydream' tail-out, and it is one deadly beauty. But, just when you want it to last twenty minutes, in comes the sonic traffic accident: a stop–start breakdown somewhere between Sir Lord Baltimore's 'Pumped Up' and Zep's 'Whole Lotta Love'. Around six minutes and fifty seconds comes the halting slow-down to end all slow-downs, and we're off into another singular, signature tail-out, the only difference being that this was the one that signalled the end of Randy Holden's career. Call in the remixer! We needs an ambient metal version *right now*! Four songs across two sides ain't nothing to be unhappy about, but I would have appreciated them all being twice as long. The problem was that this record should've been the beginning of something huge, and ended up as the end of something not less than disastrous.

What Happened Next? Or How Several Abject Motherfuckers Fucked Up a True Motherfucker

With Randy waiting around for *Population II* to get any proper release, he went into 'a state of deep shock' when a Hobbit Records executive accused him of spending all his time having fun. 'I worked my butt off for twenty hours a day rehearsing, writing, just total devotion, seven days a week, and this clown is sitting there with some illusion that I'm going to the beach.' In a state of severe despair, Randy then learned that an equipment manager at his management company had sold all twenty of his Sunn amplifiers and his Gibson SG Deluxe guitar to a Hollywood music store. It proved to be the end for Randy Holden's poetic mind, and he was utterly destroyed ('I really wasn't sure if I was gonna be alive the next minute, it was so bad,' he told *Trouser Press*). By the end of that same year (1970), he'd abandoned all hopes of making music and moved to Hawaii, where he took up fishing and the buying and selling of boats. 'People in the business have this way of taking an emotionally vulnerable musician . . . and making them feel like they're garbage and worthless,' he concluded.

To say I understand how Randy Holden felt is something of an understatement; indeed, to write this now is to glimpse once again my own impotent rage of many years ago. However, whereas I rose out of it because my muse was real, female and strong, Randy Holden was consigned to the rubbish tip for the rest of his natural.

I'd been promising *Population*

II as an Album of the Month for some time and, finally, I've at least skimmed the surface of this truly spectacular LP. In decades to come, it will, for shit damn sure, become the subject of an entire book.

Randy, I love you and know yooz still out there. Your *Guitar God* album is also fucking superb – so just give us some more of that Mae Westian sludge and make it endless, ambient and brain damaging, like the twenty-first century so clearly *needs*! Until then, ladies'n'gentlemen, I present you with *Population II* by Randy Holden – probably the only guy to have talked it as poetically as he walked it.

Nico

The Marble Index

(Elektra, 1968)

SIDE ONE	SIDE TWO
1 Prelude (0.50)	1 Julius Caesar (Memento Hodié) (4.57)
2 Lawns of Dawns (3.12)	2 Frozen Warnings (4.00)
3 No One Is There (3.36)	3 Evening of Light (5.33)
4 Ari's Song (3.20)	
5 Facing the Wind (4.52)	

This review was written to celebrate the re-release of Nico's second and third LPs, *The Marble Index* and *Desertshore,* united on Rhino Records' double CD as *The Frozen Borderline,* with extra songs and new versions of already released material. While I'm mainly out of synch with current music trends, it was wonderful to be able to write about one of my all-time favourites at the same time as members of the press are celebrating her. However, I have chosen only to write about the original LP, rather than include the extra songs included on the new Rhino reissue, as three decades with this record has made me too subjective to comment on the extra stuff, beautiful though it may be. Finally, many thanks to my darling wife Dorian for allowing me free access to the notes of her book, *Miss X: The Muse in Rock'n'Roll.*

This review is dedicated to Nico in her many roles: as the Artist, as the Muse and as the Norn tending the well at the foot of Yggdrasil, while simultaneously playing the role of Groah the goddess informing Odin as the traveller Svibdag. Hail Nico, enduring, hail Nico, forever becoming . . .

Voyaging Through Strange Seas of Thought, Alone

In the freezing winter mornings

of late February 1978, my first wife would leave our one-room bed-sit in Liverpool's Prospect Vale at seven-fifteen in the morning for her teaching job ninety minutes away, and I would throw this record on to our hairdryer-sized portable record player and do the few dishes with a single kettle-full of boiled water, and contemplate my possible future life as a full-time artist over a cup of hot, sweet tea, clothed in t-shirt, pyjamas, two dressing-gowns, three pairs of socks and a night-cap. Layers, they're what keep you warm. Layers and a copy of Nico's *The Marble Index.*

I'd scored it earlier that month from Dave, at Liverpool's Backtrax store, for two pounds fifty, and had to avoid the shop thereafter once he'd found out how badly he'd under-priced it. I'd been a fan of Nico since the big hoo-ha that had surrounded the *June 1 1974* concert/album starring Kevin Ayers, John Cale, Nico and Eno, but (in those pre-reissue days) this particular LP was the Grail, talked of in hushed tones by Velvets fans and owned only by thirty, or less, overly hairy hippie-chicks who'd spent the free-sex days of the late '60s alone with their cats and Dion Fortune books.

Was there ever an album like *The Marble Index* released before or after? Why, what an absurd question . . . of course not. The moment I'd popped it on to the record player, any possibilities of a so-called real world had retreated so far away from our flat that even our ever-complaining landlady had not thought that the strange emanations coming yet again from the young punk couple's room could actually have been music-related. With no drums nor percussion, and precious little guitar, our pious landlady probably thought I'd been temporarily saved by some religious cult. Besides, on *The Marble Index*, however eloquent John Cale's orchestrations may be, mere exposure to Nico's voice guarantees that we are led out of the so-called real world, far out of the city, across uninhabited Scandinavian wastes.[1] Frame it within an environment informed entirely by Cale's damaged, La Monte Youngian viola drones, his stentorian piano hammering, his Edgar Froese/early Tangerine Dream-like looped guitar phrases and his *Lorca*-like, overly

1 Richard Witts, *Nico*, p. 174, Virgin Books, 1993. I'm sure Lou Reed dumped Nico not just because he wanted the glory of singing his own songs, but because The Velvet Underground was a determinedly urban sound, as evidenced by his dumping hillbilly drone violinist Henry Flynt as a temporary replacement when John Cale was out of town.

recorded low-end electric piano and you have a recipe for instant connection with the gates of Hel (one 'l' – the Norse myth variety). Furthermore, even without Cale's contributions, *The Marble Index*'s harmonium drones alone separated the record from every other LP released by a so-called rock'n'roll company – with the possible exception of Ivor Cutler's mid-'70s Virgin releases (which emitted a similarly disturbing religious-Gothick charm, despite their being marketed as being humorous).

More out of time even than The Stooges themselves, Nico chose to name her second LP after a quote from a poem, *The Prelude,* about the genius of Sir Isaac Newton, penned by northern England's then-unfashionable mystical bard, William Wordsworth:

Where the statue stood of Newton,
With his prism and silent face,
The marble index of a mind forever,
Voyaging through strange seas of thought alone.

As those who've lived in thrall to *The Marble Index*'s singular genius will happily attest, no one, not even Nico herself, again reached the unfathomable and Norn-like depths that this artist, formerly known as Christa Päffgen, dredged up on her most soul-searching and heart-rending of records. Why, its magnificent follow-up, *Desertshore,* sounds positively extrovert in comparison, coming over like the abandoned soundtrack to some lost D. W. Griffiths movie about the refusenik pharaoh Akhenaten. And, even three decades and more after scoring my own vinyl copy, even after having played it to death on an array of equally battered, hairdryer-sized buzz-boxes in homes throughout England, still this record retains precisely the same level of mystery as it did on that cold, nay freezing February day in 1978 when I first laid the needle upon it. Indeed, as I write this, I've insisted on listening to that original, red-labelled Elektra copy scored so long ago, and placed it upon the most portable and singular turntable affair located in our rock-gear-infested house.

Nico's harmonium playing on *The Marble Index* was the reason I bought my own such instrument three months later, for thirty pounds, paid over six months in instalments of five pounds, writing grave elegies like The Teardrop Explodes' 'The Great Dominions', 'The Culture Bunker', 'You Disappear from View', 'Window Shopping for a New Crown of Thorns', 'Screaming Secrets' and 'Passionate Friend', most of which would, in the studio, become superficially transformed into upbeat anthems, but whose underlying themes reeked of desperation, artistic doubt and loss.

So, why is this review so interwoven with my own personal experiences? With regard to my own relationship with *The Marble Index*, there's not a moment, an instant, a flicker of its bizarre, Gothic underworldly timelessness that does not/has not/will not continue to reduce me not only to tears, but to an amphibian wreck upon my own psychic ocean floor, because its drones, its dreams, its fantastic Germanic heroinism reveal Nico to have been far, far beyond any archetype we have before experienced. And, in as deeply patriarchal and homosocial an environment as rock criticism, it's essential for someone as free of that bullshit as myself to come out fighting and raging and say . . . Nope, Nico was not just the singer of three songs on the first Velvets LP, she was not just the lucky lover of Iggy Pop, Jackson Browne and Jim Morrison, she was way beyond all of that; a law unto herself, a goddess, a muse, yes, but also a lawmaker and a priestess.

Just as the Jews symbolise the adventure into monotheism, yet were in reality a pursued and persecuted tribe of itinerant ex-slaves barely equipped to deal with such a ridiculously portentous conceit as Moses' Akhenaten-informed concept of Jehovah, so Nico's *The Marble Index* was (despite being the *summum bonum*, the shit, the absolute zenith of all the artistic achievements made through the tryst between John Cage's post-war musical experiment with super Zen and Andy Warhol's obsession with The Jaynetts' 'Sally Go Round the Roses') still an unfathomably unlikely candidate for such a title considering that its composer, barely one year before, had been unfairly written off as no more than a pretty-faced figurehead or passenger aboard her beautiful although over-produced debut, *Chelsea Girl*, with its myriad contributions from superstar songwriters Bob Dylan, Lou Reed, Jackson Browne and Tim Hardin. The *Los Angeles Times* review best captured its glorious failure: 'It is a wanly beautiful collection of nice songs by great writers. It would be better if the songs were great and the writers nice.' For Nico, that debut LP had been a disaster ('I cried when I heard the album'[2]), impossible to perform in concert, even if she had wished to do so, which she didn't. Verve's staff

2 Perhaps this Nico rebirth will justify the reprint of my friend Richard Witts' aforementioned Nico biography.

producer, Tom Wilson, had over-orchestrated the simple guitar songs and daubed flute, willy-nilly, wherever he'd found a space ('I cried because of the flute,' lamented Nico. 'There should be a button on record players; a "No Flute" button'[3]). Ousted from the Velvets and considered a royal pain-in-the-ass, Nico decamped to California briefly and met Jim Morrison, who saw her for what she really was, and pretty soon Nico realised that she must demand of herself what she saw in Jim and what Jimbo saw in her, saying later: 'I thought of Jim Morrison as my brother . . . He is my soul brother. We exchanged blood. I carry his blood inside me . . . We had spiritual journeys together . . . We went into the desert and took drugs.'

And so, from her musical beginnings within the supposed superficiality of Andy Warhol's Factory,[4] the newly artistic Nico returned to New York from LA as a heavyweight artist replete with new harmonium chops whose drones were destined, nay, cosmically designed to drive every future roommate to the edge of distraction. To the New York scene she'd so recently left, she must have appeared to have re-emerged as complete and fully formed as Athena bursting forth from the head of Zeus; indeed, even her rejection of stylish clothes in favour of monkish coveralls appalled the effete Warholians.

That male rock'n'roll writers instantly looked to credit John Cale, Leonard Cohen or absolutely anybody but Nico herself for this outrageously accelerated learning curve is highly understandable, but it is to Nico herself that the real glory must go. For, even despite her soul brother J. Morrison's recognition of her mounting inner flame, there never was any great patriarch to watch over La Päffgen – already ten years into her modelling career and used to having things done for her – as she contemplated how on earth to ease egression into the troubling and easily capsized world of the itinerant, self-contained artist, carefully considering the correct instrument on which to write songs before finally buying that first harmonium from a San Francisco hippie in 1968. It was an instrument chosen for its portability, its religious-sounding drones and its acoustic nature, and, ultimately,

3 Ibid., p. 174.

4 Although Nico made her musical name while on the Warhol scene, Andy had picked her up after hearing her Immediate Records single 'I'm Not Saying', produced the previous year, 1965, by Jimmy Page and Rolling Stones' manager Andrew Loog Oldham.

because it meant: 'I do not have to rely on guitarists, who are unreliable people to work with.'[5]

I'm sure almost no one in the world would have considered Nico to have been a pragmatic artist, but so she was, pedalling her beloved harmonium on stages across Europe and America, self-reliant and proud of it, pedalling out songs in a warm, heroin-induced blanket in umpteen freezing, candle-lit squats throughout the '70s and '80s, ironically still pedalling when she died of a heart attack while taking exercise on her pushbike in 1988.

The Recording of The Marble Index

So it was that, for her second album release, Nico took just one song (the enormously long 'It Was a Pleasure Then') from her debut LP and built her future sound upon the interwoven drones of that sole track which had, somewhat righteously, burst into life from Lou Reed, John Cale and Sterling Morrison's sterling decision to jam over one of Nico's own melodies. After the poor sales of her debut got her dropped from Verve Records, Nico was picked up by Elektra at the behest of NYC scenester, Danny Fields, who persuaded Elektra boss Jac Holzman to put up the money for *The Marble Index*. However, although it's funny and seems nowadays vaguely criminal that John Cale was not credited as producer for this masterpiece, it's fair to accept that the Elektra boss was rightly wary of two such East Coast crazies putting together a record, and was determined to bring them into his own orbit out in California, at least to be able to bring some kind of psychological proximity to bear upon them. That Holzman insisted on a producer like Frazier Mohawk, who everyone involved with the LP has subsequently claimed had doodley squat to do with achieving its overall sound, may have been a clueless decision, but I sincerely doubt it. For the simple truth of rock'n'roll is that a producer often achieves great results just by knowing enough to keep out of the fucking way. To his credit, once Mohawk saw the empathy between Nico and Cale, he confidently chose to stand to one side and let them hammer through it all, later commenting that he and engineer John Haeny 'just stood back and tried to document this wonderful little event as best we could'.[6]

Moreover, we must also remember

5 Ibid., p. 194.

6 Sleeve-notes from *The Frozen Borderline* (Rhino Records, 2007).

that John Cale was, at this time, no more than an ousted member of a failed rock'n'roll band; troubled, lacking in self-confidence and desperate to have a career in record production. Indeed, Cale himself saw this record as an important apprenticeship, a chance to shine in front of the hip dollar-wielders of the day, and its recording was what won him the production of The Stooges' debut.

Combining Nico's new harmonium songs with Cale's huge experience in the avant-garde field of John Cage and La Monte Young proved to be the kind of high artistic one-off success that happens only every few decades. On paper, *The Marble Index* should have been arch and intolerable, with a former model singing songs in a foreign language to an ad-hoc backing of a one-man chamber orchestra. The truth, however, was nothing less than stunningly great. From the first moment of 'Prelude', with its bells, celeste and jazzy, bell-tone guitars, *The Marble Index* captures our hearts, its weird mix of the atonal, the traditional, the novel, the folksong, the hymnal and the classical colliding to create in the listener the kind of disorientating and visionary dream state barely hinted at by ninety-nine percent of so-called psychedelic records. Barely fifty seconds later, Nico is weaving her spell, as the bizarre back-and-forth of 'Lawns of Dawns' edges into view, singing over harmonium and guitars:

Can you follow me?
Can you follow my distresses?
My caresses, fiery guesses?
Swim and sink into early morning messes.

With the music gently, inexorably sawing through our melted plastic brains, Nico's words appear at first to be vehicles for her voice and its sheer joy at being allowed to play with sounds and simple melody, no more than that. Yet, as we see with her phrase 'early morning messes', she dared to use idiosyncratic words and lines which only the most confident of artists would deploy ('Janitor of Lunacy' surely being her ultimate example). In truth, those words set up such a host of powerful dream images that the intoxicated listener clues into them as though they were part of some religious text. Perhaps they are. 'Lawns of Dawns' is as lyrically unreachable but as poetically truthful as ? and The Mysterians' '96 Tears', and musically comparable only to the most out-there moments of Tim Buckley's *Lorca*. Can you follow me? Yes, I think we can, but we don't know why we are doing so.

He blesses you, he blesses me,
The day the night caresses,
Caresses you, caresses me,
Can you follow me?

The second verse commences with the incredible words 'Dawn, your guise has filled my nights with fear,' and the listener begins to see each lyric as the closing of one door and the opening of another; like death and life, night and day are constantly startling each other awake as this foreign, nay alien, priestess brings us closer and closer to the meaning of our own language by using it as pure sound.

By the time 'No One Is There' begins, we are captivated, slaves to this new world that Nico and Cale have created for us – a string section heralding Nico's description of yet another bizarre half-world happening:

I crossed from behind my window screen,
Nina's is dancing down the scene in a crucial parody,
Nina's is dancing down the scene,
He is calling and throwing his arms up in the air,
And no one is there.

This is the world of dreams that Westerners have, for too long, been taught to ignore. Indeed, the early-twentieth-century mystic and psychologist George Gurdjieff fought against sleep as though it were the greatest evil ever. And yet, as Nico's powerful dream imagery reveals, the dream state is often as real as any waking world could possibly be. Indeed, if we are created to spend around a quarter of our lives asleep, is it not churlish of us to resent those hours spent in the land of Nod?

Next, 'Ari's Song' begins with the reedy pipes of Nico's harmonium, as she once again embarks on as timeless a melody and refrain as even the hoariest folkie could summon up:

Sail away, sail away my little boy,
Let the wind fill your heart with light and joy,
Sail away my little boy.
Let the rain wash away your cloudy days,
Sail away into a dream,
Let the wind send you a fantasy,
Of the ancient silver sea.

Now, she breaks the theme and makes her case for the dream state in the extraordinary middle eight: 'Now you see that only dreams can send you where you want to be,' and we can begin to reflect on this sad seeress whose last decades were spent scoring heroin in a cosmically daft cycle of narcotic dreams and physical pain. And yet the desperate truth is that no transcendental art can be made without those willing to walk at the edges on our behalf. As the great Hunter S. Thompson commented: 'The edge? The only ones who know where it is are those who've gone over it.'

Side One closes with the kind of insane, reckless piano that John Cale applied to his Terry Riley collaboration *Church of Anthrax*, and not much else. Indeed, there's not much in the whole of rock'n'roll's canon of work that transcends 'Facing the Wind' for pure, raw, ritual sacrifice. Over a recurring harmonium drone, Cale's mythical piano beast climbs out of its nest, baring its eighty-eight black-and-white ivory teeth, and slowly, slitheringly descends the Tree of Life as Nico, apparently chained to some unknown sacrificial altar, calls out:

It's holding me against my will and doesn't leave me still,
Amazons are riding out to find a meaning for the name,
My name in the rain – my spinning on my name in the rain, in the rain
When did it begin?
When did it begin?
Why am I not facing the wind?
My mother and my brother
Are facing the wind.
Why are they facing the wind?
Why are they facing the wind?

Side Two begins with the pastoral sounds of 'Julius Caesar (Memento Hodié)', in which Cale's violas spiral and weave in and out of one of Nico's most traditional, almost barrel-organ-styled drones, over which she tells two tales simultaneously: Adam and Eve's apple conjoined with the betrayal of Julius Caesar:

Amidst water lily fields white and green grows a tree,
And from the tree hang apples . . . not for you to eat.

With its melancholy refrain of 'mirth, birth, reverie', in this song, subtitled 'Memento Hodié' (In the Present Time), Nico brings to the present the power of ancient times with her wonderful lines: 'Beneath the heaving sea?/Where statues and pillars and stone altars rest/For all these aching bones to guide us far from energy.'

Then we are confronted with the most beautiful song that Nico ever recorded, 'Frozen Warnings', on which John Cale's years of John Cagean meditations were finally compressed into five, perfect minutes of pure Henry Flynt rural drone, as Nico tells her exquisite autobiographical tale of the friar hermit.

Friar hermit stumbles over the cloudy borderline,
Frozen warnings close to mine,
Close to the frozen borderline,
Frozen warnings close to mine,
Close to the frozen borderline.

When she sings of the 'railroad station tracks', the listener is immediately transported to some freezing frontier town in the Yukon, the parallel iron rails creating an apparently arbitrary territorial break across the previously untamed land mass, as Cale's tumultuous and cyclical guitar spits out like some over-caffeinated back-porch mandolinist aping Henry Flynt's transcendental hillbilly utterings.

The album then concludes with the cataclysms of 'Evening of Light', a song about a song; a song about *her* song, describing in detail what is going on in this particular song. 'Midnight winds are landing at the edge of time,' she intones, and could any lyric be more all-encompassing than that simple statement? As Cale's cosmic shower of mandolins throw out shards of light to which he responds with angular, overdubbed viola, Nico repeats the phrase: 'Mandolins are ringing to his viol singing.'

Gradually, over Nico's child-like, repeated melodies, Cale's orchestration builds into a shed-constructing competition as he saws through a succession of violas with cartoon intensity, their gut strings transformed into an indignant and bucking pack-mule which finally submits to the cruel load of blankets that the mischievous Cale expects him to carry. The album grinds to its shattering conclusion in a Blakean sky of cosmic reverb and shuddering, juddering, seismic plate-shifting.

'My Life Follows Me Around' (Nico)

For most of her old friends from the Warhol scene, *Chelsea Girl* was Nico's only real solo record because it saw her successfully playing the role in which they'd always known her. The beautiful '50s model that La Päffgen had once been had easily adjusted to the superstar ideal. But on *The Marble Index* Nico became herself for the first time, declaring to her former manager (and manager of The Factory) Paul Morrissey: 'I don't want to be beautiful any more.' However, just as her obsession with dawn, doorways, borders and shorelines shows, Nico was the true female shaman of her time, a priestess of the threshold, no less than mythic Ireland's Brigid herself. She was the troubled gatekeeper whose art straddled language barriers through sheer willpower, straddled wide cultural barriers from the shallowness of fashion to the highest, most redemptive art, and a woman whose life wires were so uninsulated that she turned to heroin because it 'made my good thoughts run slower and my bad thoughts go away'.

John Cale has commented about how her lack of regular timekeeping made her tambourine impossible to follow during Velvets shows, and how her lack of respect for musical rhythm was so important to the artistic success of *The Marble Index*. Once, during the album's recording, after she'd showed up hours late on three consecutive days, Cale asked her what her problem with time was. She replied: 'When I was working in The Actors' Studio, Elia Kazan told me to do things in my own time. I took him at his word.' In this corporate world, with its increasingly Romanized scheduling, we can only be thankful for Nico's singular attitude to time-keeping. Throw away your timepieces and embrace *The Marble Index*.

The Godlike Genius of Pärson Sound (1966–1968)

(This compilation was constructed by Julian Cope for the purposes of this review)

1 India (13.06)
2 Skrubba (28.57)
3 Tio Minuter (10.30)
4 From Tunis to India in Fullmoon (20.57)

A Time of Great Ambitions

Issuing from that same great La Monte Youngian musical glacier from whose colossal base oozed the Velvets' perpetual motion 'Venus in Furs', Stockholm's six-piece Pärson Sound brought forth – between 1967–68 – a raging musical stream, nay, a torrent of huge, drawn-out, adventuresome pieces, mostly so caffeinated and belligerent, so pugilistic and so feisty that, even to we Moderns, this electric cello'n'bass-driven ensemble still has the sound of Midgardsorm – the Ouroboros, the Serpent of the World – writhing for its freedom in the great mitt of Thor. It's the sound of confident motherfuckers, it's the sound of a live installation, not a studio: its perpetual motion rampage could've maybe been replicated in the USA only if an avant-garde-ised Kim Fowley had found the time to bully The Vejtables into uniting with Friendsound in order to re-record their epic single 'Shadows' as a side-long piece. Nothing else is really like it. Furthermore, the music of Pärson Sound occupies a musical topography so fucking enormous and eternal that it would be easy to believe that there was – on some lonely Zoroastrian hill-top – a black-robed, sonic imam right now mixing up vats of this heathen-sounding stuff.

Like the mantric music of the Dream Syndicate, these mental-men sound as though they wuz sucked clean out of Mother Earth by some county council gulley clearer, extracted in one swift movement, then manipulated'n'sold directly to the general public in sonic pessary form. Down our way, we call it 'The Crude'. Like raw Krautrock, you can buy this multi-purpose, Scando-Germanic stuff in large, sealed jars from Lidl, spooning out just a few tablespoonfuls every time you wanna exercise, seek enlightenment or simply knob your tart. It's eternal, like *Schwingungen*-period Ash Ra Tempel or the eerie canals of Beefheart's endless *Strictly Confidential*; it's eternal like every early Amon Düül II extended piece, as seemingly infinite as the Arabian caravan underlying Can's 'You Doo Right'; it even approaches the twenty-two-minute totality of Agitation Free's perfectly La Montean 'Looping'.

Their music rendered only and always in Cinemascope, these edgy Mu-Sicians were saving their own lives when they played together. Somewhat incredibly, however, Pärson Sound's singular genius remained unknown to the rock listener until 2001, when their first *ever* release – a huge, self-titled, pop-art-clad, double-CD masterpiece – knocked everyone at Head Heritage for six and had our Unsung forums buzzing for months with eulogies and where-have-they-been-all-our-lives questionings.

That a Sound as great as the Pärson had never been committed to vinyl seemed downright impossible, yet it was true. These druids had never once glimpsed the inside of a record company, nor even made the attempt during their entire 'career', inhabiting instead the world of galleries and art museums; a Revox, thirty-ips, hi-fi world in which reel-to-reel tapes of the band swapped hands, as patrons commissioned yet another twenty-minute-plus piece to illustrate yet another art exhibition.

Like Tokyo's conservatory-based Taj Mahal Travellers, and the sheltered-by-Andy early days of The Velvet Underground, Pärson Sound operated so far outside the orbit of da music biz that they were ever free to expand musically *and* spiritually way beyond any bands with even remote commercial expectations, simply because they never interfaced with greed-head kapitalist cunts at any level. Hammond organist Torbjörn Abelli even jettisoned his own instrument on joining forces with Bo Anders Persson, instead choosing to play the latter's Hofner bass in this strange 'continuous seminar', as he would later describe the band.

Moreover, observe how forcefully Abelli emphasises the Utopian attitudes of *all* the band members with this comment:

And so came a time of great ambitions. More and more, people came to realise that the new world order had to come. There were several opinions on what it would look like, from militant Marxist to more blackredgreen anarchist . . . And how could one find a music with potential to transform the sense, a music that could make way for the new world order? Pärson Sound were born out of these crossings and tensions.

Scandinavia's Cultural Revolution was, throughout the 1960s, rising at a steep trajectory that plateau'd in summer '67 with the highly controversial release of Swedish film director Vilgot Sjöman's movie *Jag Är Nyfiken – Gul* (*I Am Curious – Yellow*). However, while the 'crossings and tensions' that Abelli describes above may arguably be named as the elemental swamp that 'Pärson Sound were born out of', the band's formation actually occurred for a far more prosaic, although still highly artistic, reason. For it was the arrival in Stockholm, in February 1967, of American avant-garde minimalist composer Terry Riley that caused Pärson Sound to be formed.

Working on a small budget, desperate to save money and searching for a European ensemble capable of playing his newly famous piece, *In C*, Riley commissioned his Stockholm-based former student Bo Anders Persson to put together a quintet ready for his arrival. A series of truly inspired musicians were then hired by Persson to create an ensemble that delighted both Riley *and* the musicians themselves, each of whom immediately recognised the possibilities that this line-up could achieve.

All in their early twenties – and each between five to ten years younger than their guitarist band-leader – the new members added a raging rock'n'roll youth spirit that turbo-charged the tumbling mantric monotony envisaged by Terry Riley for *In C* and presented huge possibilities to the rhythm-obsessed Bo Anders Persson. Indeed, rhythm was entirely the key to Persson's dreams and plans for this heady ensemble. With the aforementioned Torbjörn Abelli now playing bass, Persson further reinforced those rhythmical lower reaches with the addition of electric cellist Arne Ericsson, a fellow student at the Royal College of Music, whose churning and sawing rhythms blunted the attack of the lower register into an almost proto-Sabbath monotony; a seminary Troggs. On drums, Thomas Mera Gartz was a wildman, displaying in his free-rock blitz both a relentlessness *and* a jazzy lightness of touch similar to that provided by Danny 'D. Secundus' Fichelscher in his work with Popol Vuh and Amon Düül II, while – on the heaviest of jams – an equally Amon Düül II-style twin drummer set-up was adopted with guests Bengt Berger or Björn Fredholm. The band's upper registers were taken care of by the organ, guitar, effects and flute of Persson himself and by poet/vocalist Thomas Tidholm, whose mid-'60s travels up and down the American West Coast would lend a psychedelic 'authenticity' to these Scandos-at-the-edge-of-Western-Culture.

Aping Charlie Parker and Ornette Coleman, Tidholm also took up plastic soprano sax on joining the ensemble, but it was Tidholm's nomadic spirit and 'anarchistic personage' that would make him the band's totem; their Bruce Palmer, if you will. Struggling to find a catchy pop-art moniker for this kinetic band, Persson then racked his brains until he . . . gave up! In the end, Persson just anglicised his own surname in an effort to appear more Western, and Pärson Sound was born. Yup, that's what passed for a pop-art moniker in crazy old '60s Sverige!

Anyway, while I'll admit that the four songs I'm presenting y'all in this Album of the Month reveal Pärson Sound at their most distilled, this is only because I felt a duty to sweeten their pill by consciously excluding all the rehearsal tapes and solo Bo Anders Persson tracks from the original double CD. That's because I'm on a mission to raise the profile of this criminally undervalued band in a manner that befits their genius (so the false starts and Persson's solo, wah-mouth vocal gymnastics will have to wait until you're all aboard their trip).

These four epic tracks – 'India', 'Skrubba', 'Tio Minuter' and 'From Tunis to India in Fullmoon' – will widen your horizons considerably, and have you all wondering why on earth this incredible ensemble failed during their own lifespan to make even one genuinely contemporary Pärson Sound vinyl document. And, afore I quit y'all, a word to all you young kiddies who missed out first time around: please do keep remembering that this music was mostly recorded two full years ahead of the Krautrock bands' experiments, Pärson Sound having been kick-started by the arrival of Terry Riley – one of the True Masters.

Playing this extraordinary music recently for my Krautrock-obsessed daughter, Albany, I was both shocked and distressed to remember that I'd never yet got around to writing about these gentlemen. Still, love is more than words . . . or better late than never, as Arthurly would have said. So if ya dug Pärson Sound then, re-dig them now; and if this is all new to ya, then – dammit – I'm jealous!

Le Stelle di Mario Schifano

Dedicato a . . .

(BDS Records, 1967)

SIDE ONE

1 Le Ultime Parole di Brandimante, dall'Orlando Furioso, ospite Peter Hartman e Fine (da ascoltarsi con tv accesa, senza volume) (17.20)

SIDE TWO

1 Molto Alto (3.12)
2 Susan Song (3.36)
3 E Dopo (2.09)
4 Intervallo (2.30)
5 Molto Lontano (a Colori) (2.45)

The sole album release of Le Stelle di Mario Schifano (The Stars of Mario Schifano) was a Warholian contrivance of the Italian pop-art painter/sculptor guru who gave his name to this 1967 project. This is the story of the album's astonishing, seventeen-minute-long freak-out which filled all of Side One, with an attempt to contextualise the record with the pop-art, multi-media events of its day.

EPI with Twenty-Twenty Hindsight

Although *The Velvet Underground & Nico* LP was considered by its creators and their record company to have been lost in the psychedelic flood which deluged America and Britain throughout late 1966 and early 1967, its super-confident air of 'total package' was, in actuality, an immediate counter-cultural hit. Especially in the fashion capitals of London, Paris, New York, Rome and Berlin, Andy Warhol's Exploding Plastic Inevitable (EPI) was received as a holistic pop-art vehicle with such a thoroughness of design that it successfully created an instant and revolutionary archetype of the ultimate kind. That most European underground scenesters could never have hoped to attend an EPI performance was in no way a distraction once the Velvets' long-delayed first album had been released. And blurry photographs of Lilithian Mary Woronov and the whip-wielding Gerard Malanga, caught mid-ritual, prostrated before the statue menhirs of John Cale, Lou Reed, Sterling Morrison and Maureen Tucker, only served to overdrive the already heightened imaginations of Western artists, poets, pop stars and entrepreneurs.

But wishing for a European equivalent of the EPI and achieving it were hardly the same thing, as other hip artists out to ape Warhol soon found out. The Factory's amphetamine infrastructure supported a surprisingly Bronze Age hierarchy, and if one superstar croaked, the next one waiting in the wings was doing so word perfect and in full costume. And so it is that, over four decades down the line and operating with twenty-twenty hindsight, I would suggest that the closest Europeans ever came to achieving that total Warholian package were, in reverse order of success: London's Hapshash and the Coloured Coat (twenty percent); Stockholm's Pärson Sound (thirty percent); and Rome's Le Stelle di Mario Schifano, in at the top with a groundbreaking fifty-percent pass mark. I have chosen to cite these three as examples because all of them centred around established underground 'stars' who, similarly to Andy Warhol, held genuine artistic credentials with a sound provenance.

Guy Stevens' London Happenings

Hapshash and the Coloured Coat were a design team led by designers Nigel Weymouth and Michael English. This pair had already designed many famous psychedelic concert posters (Jimi Hendrix at the Filmore, Pink Floyd at UFO), album and single sleeves and pop artefacts (The Who's 'I Can See for Miles' artwork, for example) before they teamed up with the insane producer-genius that was Guy Stevens. As conceptual artists, Hapshash were happy to take Stevens' Island Records band, the variously named VIPs/Art/Spooky Tooth, as their sonic springboard to multi-media heaven. Stevens, Weymouth and English invited all their friends to the album's recording, naming them the Heavy Metal Kids especially for the occasion, while the omnipresent Guy Stevens here adopted the magnificent name The Human Host.

Describing the whole package artefactually as well as sonically, the Hasphash LP was a red-vinyl, proto-Amon Düül percussion-athon of considerable charm which came in a silver inner sleeve, but whose outer package, although displaying a beautiful ufology'n'occulture'n'folklore centrepiece, ultimately failed because of its un-epic, un-sumptuousness.

Neither was it any musically barbarian classic. Indeed, it was a pale shadow of the subsequent Krautrock which, ironically, it would soon inspire. But at least the sixteen minutes of Side Two's 'Empires of the Sun' showed Guy Stevens' fundamentalist hooligan attitude to slaking the shamanic thirst, coming on as a skeleton, bass-driven soul mantra closest in sound to Amon Düül's double LP *Disaster*, still two long years away. But, as no other fucker was coming close to this sound in 1967, it was generally dismissed at the time as amateur garbage of the highest order. Thirty years down the line, this wholly sympathetic writer suggests that, while the album was enough to help get cosmic freak-out music started, we shouldn't exactly hold our breath for the next Hapshash revival.

Andy Warhol and Terry Riley in Stockholm

However, the seemingly unlikely location of Stockholm's Moderna Museet (Museum of Modern Art) had, in late 1966, become the home of a genuine multi-media bunch led by experimental artist Bo Anders Persson, as discussed in the entry for Pärson Sound. The experimental electronic music which Persson had made prior to the formation of Pärson Sound had helped his introductions to the world of high modern art. But, in any case, Sweden was already a society looking to its young artists for navigation, and the formation of a so-called 'rock band' by a credible experimental artist such as Persson was bound to catch the attention of both underground and mainstream Swedish media. Indeed, so successful were Pärson Sound on stage that they would later provide the live performance soundtrack for Andy Warhol's 1968 Moderna Museet exhibition, *Screens, Films, Boxes, Clouds and a Book.*

More than tragically, as we have learned, Pärson Sound's heraldic, post-Terry Riley, proto-Velvets urdrone became totally lost to culture, and their mid-'60s live performances resulted in no contemporary album releases. The ensemble remained together into the '70s, but later changed their moniker with every subsequent album release; names such as International Harvester, Trad, Gras os Stenar (Trees, Grass and Stones) and the comically unhip The Hot Boys. More unfortunately, each increasingly difficult-to-pronounce name took them a stage further from the pop art which had spawned them.

Spend Bubble Hour in your Dream-Machine

So it was that only Rome's Mario Schifano came to even temporarily challenge Andy Warhol's mid-'60s multi-media supremacy. Nowadays, Schifano is probably most famous to British rock'n'rollers for having temporarily stolen Marianne Faithfull from Mick Jagger. Certainly, every '60s freak knows the famous press shot of Marianne and her young son, Nicholas, bundled up in Schifano's car as they prepared a hasty exit from Jagger and Faithfull's Cheyne Walk home. But that was in 1969, and in order to understand how the Italian could have wielded enough power to have even temporarily relieved Jagger of his muse, we must backtrack to mid-1966, when Mario Schifano and his then-girlfriend, Anita Pallenberg, were hanging out with London's young, hip aristocracy.

Throughout that summer, Schifano and Pallenberg had stayed at the Chelsea home of Lord Harlech, whose children, Jane, Julian and Victoria Ormsby-Gore, were all obsessed with The Beatles and The Rolling Stones. In the same circle were the art dealer Robert Fraser, the antique dealer Christopher Gibbs and the Guinness heir Tara Browne, who later 'blew his mind out in a car'.

It was in this environment that Mario Schifano began to understand that, however cool he could be as a painter and sculptor, no artist in the '60s could ever hope to approach the level of adulation and respect that could be brought by being a member of a pop group. This must have been particularly galling for an incredible painter such as Schifano. Born in Libya in 1934, his exhibitions of pop art had been wild successes since the late '50s.[1]

Understanding the level of intrigue which Andy Warhol had created with his multi-media packages in New York, Mario Schifano set out to emulate this success. But, feeling that such a thing could be easily lost in the Swinging London of late 1966, Mario Schifano percipiently chose to set up his project back home, in Rome. And, rather than aim for a merely achieving replica

1 Schifano continued to be a successful fine artist, presenting many of his favourite paintings at New York's Guggenheim Museum in 1994, during their exhibition *The Italian Metamorphosis 1943–68*.

of Warhol's idea, Schifano decided that the music created by his protégés could only gain ground if it was perceived by the hip intelligentsia as being part of the genuinely radical avant-garde.

Schifano adored the way the front sleeve of *The Velvet Underground & Nico* bore no other legend than the words 'Andy Warhol' – which is how he hit upon the self-aggrandising group name Le Stelle di Mario Schifano, or 'The Stars of Mario Schifano'. Now, how fucking *Me Generation* is that?

In Rome, Schifano collected together four unknown musicians and schooled them in the kind of sounds which he was expecting from them. Urbano Orlandi was a skinny guitarist with a Sterling Morrison haircut and a scything, simplistic, fuzz-tone sound. Organist Nello Marini was an Afro-headed and moustachioed avant-gardist, whose dedication to the cause of atonal jazz clusters hid his considerable classical schooling. Sergio Cerra's drumming was excellent but less important than his dazzling looks and excruciatingly Milanese fashion obsessions. Of cumbersomely named bass player Giandomenico Crescentini, nothing is known, from either before or after his tenure with the group.[2]

In live performance, screens, lights, even clothes aped The Velvet Underground. Schifano hired massive amounts of amplification, lights and projectors, and booked his new group into Rome's Piper Club, where they played and prepared under their guru's paranoid direction. To help them at the Piper Club, Schifano brought in his friend, the film producer and pianist Ettore Rosboch, who had agreed to co-produce the project. Rosboch dug what he was hearing, but felt that any album produced by this ensemble was gonna be way too lightweight and standard-sounding without considerable outside help. Rosboch suggested that Schifano should uproot the project and shift it to Turin, where the experienced and radical engineers of the Fono Folk Stereostudio would help them turn this thing into the heavyweight trip worthy of the name Schifano.

In Turin, the group began the recording of their album and soon had five stage favourites finished. Schifano adored the results – but

2 Ironically, early bootleg reissues of this album were signed exclusively by bass player Giandomenico Crescentini. Stranger still, the most recent reissue, on Italy's Akarma Records, is also licensed by him.

for Ettore Rosboch it was not nearly enough. It was now that Rosboch suggested the whole of the album's first side should feature one incredible cosmic jam – something which would pitch the record way outside the mainstream and be perceived as something worthy of a scene-maker such as Mario Schifano. The previous year – 1966 – had already seen Love's *Da Capo* give premature birth to the twenty-minute jam phenomenon with the appalling 'Revelation'. Later that year, Frank Zappa had utilised 'auxiliary' musicians for the side-long 'Return of the Son of Monster Magnet', which had closed The Mothers of Invention's debut double album, *Freak Out.* Even The Rolling Stones had closed *Aftermath* with the eleven minutes of 'Mother Sky'-period proto-Can they called 'Goin' Home'. Ettore Rosboch and Mario Schifano brazenly decided that, in order that they should be perceived as having gone further than everyone else, they could not afford to hide away their masterpiece on Side Two. No, this motherfucker was gonna be the opening statement.

TV On, but the Sound Off

At the Fono Folk studio, the three engineers set up microphones throughout the building and added individual delays to the two grand pianos in the principal live room. For this main event, Ettore Rosboch invited the German experimental pianist Peter Hartman to play one of the pianos, whilst Rosboch himself chose to play the other. A percussionist and a flautist were brought in to add to the sonic soup, and the ballad singer Franscesca Camerana pre-recorded a brief 'Greensleeves'-type haunting ballad, which was to be inserted into the recording during the final mix. And so it was that the freak-out with the most unwieldy title ever came to grace the whole of the album's first side.

'Le Ultime Parole di Brandimante, dall'Orlando Furioso, ospite Peter Hartman e Fine (da ascoltarsi con tv accesa, senza volume)' is the only track I've ever known which actually includes listening instructions and special guest star right there in the song title, for it translates as something like: 'The Last Words of Brandimante, as taken from Orlando Furioso, with guest Peter Hartman; which should be listened to with the TV On, but the Sound Off'.

The record begins with hip Italians in a recording studio speaking rock'n'roll English and Italian simultaneously, and demanding this and that from their engineers. 'Piano! Piano!' screams one at the overly loud drum sounds blasting his ears. 'It's fucking red!' As each musician toys with his individual instrument, it is clear that there ain't gonna be much normality here to pin down the general sound. Touch the organ keys and the sound zooms off into outer space; tinkle the ivories and the music of the spheres cascades across the firmament; beat the drum and an army of percussive orcs disappears over the sonic horizon. Then Francesca Camerana sings her Spanish-guitar madrigal with tuning up and cosmic percussion-tinkering alienating her – a front-line nurse singing 'Greensleeves' to her dying soldier/lover, with clueless first-time musicians in the hallway undermining her melodies. Get this mawkish chick out of here!

Peter Hartman and co-producer Ettore Rosboch punish pianos as Nello Marini assumes the position and begins to 'Irmin Schmidt' the organ with karate chops. Out of the murk, remedial pre-schooler rhythms arise amidst screams, and the pianos weave around the dual drummer and percussionist soloist. Horrible, horrible organ plinks and maracas *s-s-s-shake*, while graveyard vocals holler under the multiple piano rolls. The shitty bass playing is about as malformed as that three-string affair the Canadian Nihilist Spasm Band used to feature, looming and booming around the walls of the studio. Then, around six minutes into the track, the chaotic rhythms drop down into a monolithic epic of ass-clenched and clichéd fuzz guitar, as a whole mystical other takes over. From here, we enter the genius of true turds on a bum ride! For it is at this moment that they locate *the path*. The navigation is over and the doorway leads to dissonant sonic magnificence, in Aladdin's chambers of enlightenment.

All the Hapshash and Parson Sound (and Amon Düül and Velvets) comparisons dissolve as a raging intoxication of otherworldly anti-rhythm globalises your senses and mobilises your troops. You attempt to tear off your headphones but you ain't wearing any. Ace Ventura, Pet Detective is driving your white van and no amount of Red Bull is gonna sort you out now, as the record moves out of all accepted musical forms into the truly avant-garde. Wind from Uranus tears this fart apart, and spreads it thin and streaky along the underside of your kitchen ceiling. You kangaroo-hop across Vauxhall Bridge in shrieking first gear, smooth as taking a suburban cul-de-sac full of sleeping policemen at seventy mph. The percussionist has all the feel of a fat alderman shaking his heavy mayoral chain. And sack that fucking bass player – Prometheus is bound upside down but he ain't the hanging man tonight. Odin, Loki and Graham Simpson off the first Roxy Music album attempt some Bavarian skank, as coyote vocals howl and yelp. Exhausting to describe and exhausting to listen to, you grab the oldest, coldest, stickiest can of fizz from the back of the refrigerator and pour it over your belly. The whole thing finishes on a long looming note of guitar resonance, it merges into an excerpt from some classical trumpet piece, a beautiful series of end-chords and you're off the fucking hook, finally! Get thee behind me, Santa!

In total contrast to the first side, Side Two is wholly at odds with freak-out chic and is, instead, chock-full of extremely catchy stuff. 'Molto Alto' opens the side, coming on almost like a '70s take on psychedelia, but so full of stock '60s devices that it's like something off Faust's *Last* LP. If you know the amazingly claustrophobic production of The Seeds' most full-on album, *Future*, then imagine that with crunching snare and a sort of Circus Maximus-type raga meeting head-on with The Deep's awesome forty-five 'Color Dreams'. Maybe the psychedelic guitar is actually background, but with the whole track fading in and out totally, it gives off a haunting, Blue Things-plays-The Yardbirds flavour.

'Susan Song' follows with its string section and mournful Ruby Tuesday-ness, like some aural netherlander midway *Between the Buttons* on the horns of *Aftermath*. Mournful and yearning for some long-lost moment, an exquisite, rippling piano hooks you in like the tragic 'Atridsvisan' of Sweden's Sammla Mammas Manna.

'E Dopo' is one more truly catchy mother, and sounds just like a single. Imagine 'Granny Takes a Trip' by The Purple Gang meets *Aftermath*-period Stones, but played by *Da Capo*-period Love; then into 6/8 scythe lead guitar over a backing track which reminds me of John's Children's 'Smashed! Blocked!' And it doesn't hang around to bore you, either. A coupla minutes in and they're already hitting the American radio fade button . . . bang, zoom, outta here.

OK, so then 'Intervallo' brings us back to Faust again. It's cliché upon cliché, and it's wonderful. Cylindrical lead guitar duels with itself over Sounds Incorporated organ, and it's the party that everyone thought the '60s was. We're listening to The Monkees' 'Goin' Down' as played by The Chocolate Watchband on the set of the movie *Psyche Out*. The guitar is pure garage-blues 'Psychotic

Reaction'. There's plenty of laughing, screaming and groovy, shattered times. And, thus, the album closes with the tragedy-laden 'Molto Lontano (a Colori)', as flute, by the extraorchestrally named Anton Mario Semolini, dances around peculiar and mournful vocal declarations and a lilting guitar/organ thing.

As I told you, Side One is the real reason for this making Album of the Month, but it's all pretty great. And the glorious artwork and sleeve inners do tend to get stared at as you listen to Side Two. Also, there are more dedications than any Chocolate Watchband LP (or even the Mothers' *Freak Out*), which is a strange sort of success in itself.

Finally, for those of you unsure of freak-out LPs in general and this one specifically, I've gotta tell you that I did not lightly choose to review this record. Indeed, I've had it in my collection since the end of the last millennium, and it still gets played all the time. For me, its ur-klang sits right up there with Amon Düül II's *Phallus Dei*, Aphrodite's Child's nineteen-minute 'All the Seats Were Taken' from *666*, and 'Why Don't You Eat Carrots?' from the Faust clear vinyl/sleeve album. Sadly, Mario Schifano died in 1998, but I'm sure he'd have been made up to see his long-lost 'pop' project up there with such bad company.

Early Soft Machine (1966–1968)

PHASE ONE: 1967

1 I Should Have Known (7.29)
2 Feelin', Reelin', Squealin' (2.51)
3 Memories (2.58)
4 Love Makes Sweet Music (2.31)
5 She's Gone (2.27)
6 We Know What You Mean (3.09)

PHASE TWO: 1968

1 A Certain Kind (4.14)
2 Why Am I So Short?/So Boot If at All (9.02)
3 Lullabye Letter (4.42)
4 We Did It Again (3.46)
5 Plus Belle Qu'un Poubelle (1.01)
6 Why Are We Sleeping? (5.32)

As a big fan of *The Soft Machine* debut LP, I was initially tempted to proffer that whole record as Album of the Month. Instead, however, I've picked only my very fave raves from the debut, inserting them all into 'Phase Two: 1968'. I've dedicated 'Phase One: 1967' to the band's debut forty-five ('Love Makes Sweet Music' b/w 'Feelin', Reelin', Squealin''), interspersed with the quartet's two most successful Giorgio Gomelsky demos ('I Should Have Known' and 'Memories'), plus an unreleased B-side from '67 ('She's Gone') and one BBC *Top Gear* session from September '67 ('We Know What You Mean').

Repping the Intuitive Non-Career Mover

Recorded in the seventeen short months between December '66 and April '68, the intensely psychedelic music contained within this Album of the Month displays such a rush and roar of Mithraic fire, such a manic intensity of youthful ardour and such a burning desire to capture the spirit of Right Now that, despite having been recorded in umpteen different studios and with four very different, highly successful producers (Giorgio Gomelsky, who produced The Yardbirds' hits; Chas Chandler, producer of Jimi

Hendrix's *Are You Experienced*; Tom Wilson, who produced The Velvet Underground and The Mothers of Invention; and Kim Fowley, who produced everyone), nevertheless on these early recordings it is still only the extraordinary sound of Soft Machine that ever shines through . . . that and the excellence of their self-written songs, of course.

Back then, in the heaving and heady days of 1967, Soft Machine's forever bare-chested singing drummer Robert Wyatt was a brazen and burning warrior-elf with a dulcet tone like Dionne Warwick and a splatter-clatter drum style unlike any outside the jazz scene; while the band's leather-coated organist, the six-plus-footer Mike Ratledge, evinced a keyboard sound close to that of The Animals' Alan Price . . . but with wings. On guitar and several years older than the rest of them was the band's mentor, the Australian beatnik poet (and future Gong founder) Daevid Allen, whose days in Paris had led him to novelist William S. Burroughs, from whose 1961 novel The Soft Machine took their name.

But the band's two high aces were undoubtedly their songwriters: singer/bassist Kevin Ayers and roadie Hugh Hopper, who had played bass in Robert Wyatt's earlier band The Wildeflowers. His hair receding by his early twenties, with buck-teeth and ugly as sin, Hugh Hopper nevertheless wrote poetic and desperately aching, lonely songs that the R&B-obsessed Wyatt could deliver with heart-rending sincerity. In stark comparison to Hopper, the occasionally face-painted Kevin Ayers was a beautiful and beguiling, psychedelicised Hans Christian Andersen figure, a Pie-eyed Piper with a flair for writing archetypally great Sandozian pop songs (check out 'We Know What You Mean' and 'She's Gone', included herein), or intoning, nay, doxologising, lead vocals in a register deeper than Lee Marvin, and deploying – from his archaic-looking Gibson EB2 – a molto-munting, semi-acoustic bass sound even more radical than that of Jefferson Airplane's Jack Cassady's always-overloading (and equally archaic-looking) Epiphone hollow-body.

Love Makes Sweet Music

In September '66, having followed Daevid Allen's international beat connections from cloistered Canterbury up to London, The Soft Machine found themselves performing at one of the Marquee Club's earliest Spontaneous Underground performances, soon afterwards being invited to share the stage of Tottenham Court Road's UFO Club with Syd Barrett's Pink Floyd. It was in this fertile and lysergic atmosphere of experimentation that Soft Machine rose to the challenge of rearranging and deconstructing all the best songs that Hugh Hopper and Kevin Ayers could heave at them. Producers flocked to oversee the band's debut single, but it was sleazoid LA scumbag Kim Fowley who dragged them through the portals of CBS Studios and successfully transformed Kevin Ayers' darkly monstrous and highly experimental 'Feelin', Reelin', Squealin'' – a real Ayers vocal and bass tour de force – into a veritable Boris-the-Spiderthon. Displaying typical Fowleyan overkill, the producer emphasised the doomy discord of Ayers' lyrical bombinations by layering the supersweet choruses with extra-saccharine harmony vocals from Daevid Allen and Robert Wyatt, then undermined the entire song with an almost *musique concrète* approach to its bizarre instrumental section of piano and flute cut-ups, all achieved in a manner guaranteed totally to blow the band's collective mind. Daevid Allen later commented:

> *The thing about Kim Fowley was, he was a complete codeine freak. So he never stopped talking. But, secondly, he astonished everybody by taking the 8-track master tape and cutting; splicing the eight-track master tape, which nobody had ever seen done (laughs). It was really wild to make 'Feelin', Reelin', Squealin''. So [Fowley] made these huge massive splices right across all of the 8-track . . . if you fuck it up, that's it, that's the end of the master.*[1]

Believing Fowley's recording of 'Feelin', Reelin', Squealin'' to be an excellent B-side but just too uncommercial for the single, a mere one month later the band entered London's Advision Studios with Jimi Hendrix's producer Chas Chandler, who'd chosen for the prospective A-side another highly catchy Kevin Ayers song, 'Love Makes Sweet Music', with Robert Wyatt as lead singer. This time the delightful results were picked up for a one-off record deal by Polydor Records, who released both tracks in February '67, a full month before Pink Floyd's own debut single, 'Arnold Layne'.

Unfortunately, despite mucho airplay from John Peel and Radio Caroline, 'Love Makes Sweet Music' totally failed to chart. The band was

1 Daevid Allen interview with Richie Unterberger.

nonplussed. To the fascinated media, The Soft Machine were considered, alongside Pink Floyd, to be heralds of the so-called psychedelic underground. And yet, with no long-term record deal forthcoming, no money could be made available to them for recording a debut LP. Refusing to appear discouraged, the band now entered London's De Lane Lea Studios with Yardbirds producer Giorgio Gomelsky, with the sole intention of creating a demo with which to sell themselves to a record company. Unfortunately, the sessions were haphazardly prepared and the results extremely patchy: the incredible clatter of Wyatt's drums being lost in the colossal reverb of the studio; the sinewy, Stylophonic Ratledge organ oft reduced to nowt but a distant chordal pad; Daevid Allen's guitar, too, often merely perfunctory; and the molto-hefty Ayers bass merely dancing around the head of the listener, rarely landing a truly sonic K.O.

Inappropriately, time that should have been better spent on new songs by Kevin Ayers and Hugh Hopper was instead forfeited on a couple of Robert Wyatt's oldest, most jazzy mid-'60s songs ('You Don't Remember' and 'That's How Much I Need You Now'), which, here in spring '67, sounded merely anachronistic. Despite all of this, a wonderful version of Hopper's magnificent 'Memories' was committed to tape, replete with Allen's moody signature blues lines, as was a stupendous seven-minute burn-up of Hopper's 'I Should Have Known', today perhaps the only true recorded evidence of Daevid Allen's guitar genius during his entire time in the band.

In late April, The Soft Machine joined The Move, The Crazy World of Arthur Brown, The Flies, The Deviants and the Floyd at Alexandra Palace for the now-legendary all nighter, The 14 Hour Technicolor Dream,[2] but their recordings with Gomelsky had clearly come to nothing. In June, two new recordings of Hugh Hopper's songs 'She's Gone' and 'I Should Have Known' were made for a possible second Polydor single, but no offer was to be forthcoming. Without a record deal, the summer was spent jamming almost unpaid at various happenings

2 Former anarchist and Deviants singer Mick Farren, commenting on the backstage arrangements at the legendary psychedelic event, The 14 Hour Technicolor Dream, said that many of the members of even the most supposedly illuminated and experimental of bands exhibited a disturbing 'brown ale consciousness'.

throughout France. However, disaster struck on August 24 when, on returning to the UK, Daevid Allen was refused re-entry for having previously overstayed his visa stipulation. Continuing as a trio, Ayers, Ratledge and Wyatt made several European TV appearances throughout the autumn, also making their first trio studio recordings for the BBC's *Top Gear*, before joining The Who, Eric Burdon, Tomorrow, Pink Floyd and Jimi Hendrix at London's Olympia for December '67's Christmas On Earth Revisited.

It was here that Jimi Hendrix's managers, Chas Chandler and Mike Jeffrey, offered the flagging band a management contract plus the support slot on Hendrix's forthcoming US tour. Touring with Hendrix throughout February and March '68, the trio honed their songs into such immaculately performed jewels of turbo-charged performance that they at last secured a deal with ABC Records, who booked the band recording time at New York's Record Plant Studios, to be overseen by Velvets/Mothers of Invention producer Tom Wilson.

At long last, The Soft Machine received their belated opportunity to create a worthy LP statement, and the results were spectacular. Gone was the lumpen chord work which had pervaded the weaker performances of the original quartet, replaced instead by a sound of extraordinary economy. Where once both Daevid Allen and Mike Ratledge had been content to punctuate the sound with stabs and sweating chords, now Ratledge entirely backed off, forfeiting his chordal organ washes for the sweet harmony vocals of Ayers and Wyatt. Where the quartet's guitars and organ had previously drizzled sound across the entire rhythm section, now vast sonic spaces appeared that teased out every drum roll, every atonal freak-out, every overdriven, proto-Lemmy bass chord that Kevin Ayers thrummed out of his big semi-acoustic bass.

More importantly, despite its rewrite, this self-titled trio album was a masterful exercise in jagged, futuristic song experiments; numbers such as the expansive and exhilarating 'Lullabye Letter' and 'Why Are We Sleeping?' radically confident garage-soul songs quite unlike the cocktail jazz-tinged psychedelic R&B/soul hybrid of just one year earlier.

Despite its excellence, however, *The Soft Machine* was also far too little and far too late. Further held up until November '68 for its US release, the album would not even gain its own UK release until the 1970s.

Exhausted by their seemingly

endless US tour, and unable to control his naturally hedonistic ways,[3] Kevin Ayers quit the band to pursue a solo career. Their psychedelic beginnings clearly over, roadie Hugh Hopper now laid to rest his years of superb songwriting and replaced Ayers on bass, joining Mike Ratledge on his curious quest to turn Soft Machine into a pure jazz-rock ensemble.

In Conclusion

So, listen now to this Album of the Month and think of what might have been. With the plethora of hip producers already involved in creating the early Soft Machine canon, I've often fantasised how great the band's debut LP could have been had strung-out soul visionary Guy Stevens been hired as their producer in late 1966. With their R&B and soul fixations, perhaps Messrs Ayers, Allen, Ratledge and Wyatt would have followed the Hapshash and the Coloured Coat trajectory and delivered us a stylish and free-form psychedelic-soul debut LP on the Minit Records label. I know it's daydreaming, but let me daydream. Music this adventurous should make its listeners daydream. Furthermore, just take one final look at the sheer visionary breadth of musical and songwriting talent (barely) contained within the ranks of the early Soft Machine and try *not* to gasp at the possibilities and potential of what could have been.

3 In the same interview with Richie Unterberger, Daevid Allen remarked of Kevin Ayers: 'I've never seen anybody take so much alcohol, so much damage. It would kill anybody else. I've never seen anyone drink like him. He's got an extraordinary ability to drink, and an extraordinary ability to rejuvenate himself. He goes right to the edge, and then he goes swimming and runs around for a week and then comes out and starts again. I've never seen such an extraordinary level of ability to drink so much, and get away with it. He's gotten away with amazing amounts of stimuli. He really put it away.'

Various Artists

High Vikings

(Cider Kellar Records, 1987)

SIDE 1

1 Steppeulvene: Du Skal Ug Hvor (2.31)
2 The Moondogs: Trying to Make You See (2.16)
3 The Crowd: Junk (2.29)
4 The Stomps: My Parents (2.32)
5 Young Flowers: City of Friends (3.08)
6 The Drys: My Flash on You (2.46)
7 The Coins: My Sadness (3.57)
8 Young Flowers: Like Birds (3.21)
9 The Moondogs: I'm Gonna Step on You (2.34)

SIDE 2

1 The Noblemen: I'm Mad Again (3.25)
2 The Beefheaters: Lad Mig Bilve Noget (4.23)
3 The Drys: I'm So Glad (8.09)
4 The Beefeaters: LSD-25 (3.13)
5 Dandy Swingers: Stay with Me Baby (3.13)
6 Master Joseph: All Your Love (5.52)
7 The Beefeaters: Night Flight (3.18)

Although I'd known various Danish garage forty-fives and random album tracks since the '70s, when John Peel would foist them on us from time to time on his nightly BBC radio show, my real interest in Danish rock only truly kicked in when, in November 1995, I received in the post a copy of the monstrous eight-hundred-and-ninety-four-page Danish-language rock encyclopaedia *Politikens Rock Leksikon*, by the author Jan Sneum. The hardback had been sent to me as a gift by rock writer Jan Paulsen, a researcher on the project and long-time Cope fan who'd interviewed me on umpteen occasions. Slumping on the sofa under the weight of this glossy motherlode, I dutifully checked the index for Denmark's all-time biggest, coolest, psychedelic band, The Savage Rose, in the hope of getting myself directed to whatever Jan

Sneum called the 'Danskrock' section. I scanned the index again and again but Savage Rose was not there. How could this be? The Savage Rose was seminal stuff. I checked out the only other Danish bands I could remember, but neither Burnin' Red Ivanhoe nor Young Flowers graced the index, either: eight hundred and ninety-four pages of international rock music in Danish, but not a Danskrocker amongst the throng.

How could this be? I mean, Burnin' Red Ivanhoe had even had an LP out on John Peel's Dandelion label. This bunch was hip. Upon inspection of my own index entry, I was, therefore, somewhat shocked to discover my own brother's name indexed twice just above mine. Checking the first 'Joss Cope' entry, I deduced from the Danish text that it was commenting on his being signed to Creation Records with his then-current band. The other 'Joss Cope' entry was just a reference in an article about me, declaring that I had a brother of that name. Again, how could this be? On their own home turf, the eight-album Savage Rose had been sacrificed at the altar of Rock, dissed in favour of my own brother's two-single Creation Records deal. I winced. How could Jan Sneum have produced so vast an undertaking and yet missed/dissed all and every Danish band?

Over the next decade, I travelled many times to Denmark and gradually built up a good collection of 'Danskrock' stuff from the '60s, something which accelerated after picking up a later Savage Rose LP, *Dodens Triumf*, for twenty pence in a Melksham charity shop.

I recently received in the post a large compilation of Danish rock, as a gift from my publisher friend, Ole Knudsen of Copenhagen. The double CD contained several classics that I'd heard before during my garage-rock fixation, and so I duly fished out this garage compilation, *High Vikings*, as Album of the Month. I figured that as no one knew how those early '70s bands (as described in *Danskrocksampler*, later in these pages) got their sounds, this compilation was a good place to start.

This review is dedicated to Ole Knudsen, for keeping me up-to-date with the reissue goings-on concerning his extraordinary scene.

Fear the Norsemen!

Like all of my favourite garage-rock compilations, *High Vikings* is a barbarian charge through the late '60s, spearing randomly selected victims (herein The Noblemen, The Drys, Young Flowers, etc.) at high speed, then binding them up, one after the other, and fusing them on to twelve-inch vinyl, forever after bonded together at thirty-three rpm. When Bruce Planty and his cohorts were at the peak of their garage compilation frenzy, around 1985, little could they have guessed that a whole future generation of trash-rock obsessives would thereafter come to associate the fade-out of Larry and the Bluenotes' 'Night of the Phantom' with the impending introduction of The (Swamp) Rats' incredible and iconic 'Rats' Revenge (Parts 1 & 2)', just because of a (random yet momentous) decision made in some anonymous Queens basement on a stoned, too-beery Tuesday evening because a particular disc happened to be closest to hand. Believe me, for certain sociopaths the aforementioned occurrence (Larry and the Bluenotes *then* The Rats) is as much a fact of life as night following day, as death following life, as 'Rock'n'Roll' following 'Black Dog' on *Led Zeppelin IV*.

Being Danish, and just a little behind the British and US scenes, the bands on *High Vikings* not only tend to have been doing their thing around a year later than London, New York, LA, etc., but – like Krautrockers and Japanese Group Sounds outfits – managed simultaneously to embrace the then all-pervading US and Brit trends without *entirely* dissing the stuff from two years previously. With hindsight, this trick has enabled the so-called 'rock provinces' such as Denmark, Japan, Germany, Italy, etc. (once rediscovered by rock's seekers) to sustain the interest of international rock nutters, because those so-called 'provincials' never felt the need to dump such things as early-'60s, Sonics-styled frat-rock sax for the next incoming trend – wah-wah guitar, say – in the manner that the too-cool Brits and Yanks felt compelled to do. Instead, the provincials just mixed it all up, keeping phasing long after '67, deploying 'Apache'-style 1960 Hank B. Marvin spangly solos over early-'70s analogue synth and gruff Hammond solos ('Didn't Zappa do it on *Lumpy Gravy*, Peder? Then so can we do it, even if it is sunny old 1972').

Many of the bands on *High Vikings* had emerged from the mid-'60s beat era. In Britain, by '67, beat groups were, of course, stodgy and uncool, but Denmark still rang to the clamour of outfits with such prosaic monikers as The Stoke Sect, Ola and the Janglers, Pils and His Pilsners, Little Freddie and His Rockboys, The Stamping Bricks, Ranthe-Birch's Smashband, Melvis Rockband (who later became The Medley Swingers because they'd spent so much money on having each of their shirts embroidered with a large capital 'M'), The Clidows, The Five Danes, The Teenmakers, The Hitmakers, Sir Henry and His Butlers, and my all-time favourite name for a Danish beat group, Roy and Decent People. Come on! Imagine the conversation that went down before they came up with that winner! In a spectacularly international mixing of the metaphors, Denmark's Cliff Richard-inspired surf band The Cliffters scored their biggest success far away in Japan, where their jazzy-styled surf song 'Django' was a massive hit. Neither were these Scando-Germanic surfers on their own in their Japanese/Euro-surf success. Sure, the term 'Euro-surf' sounds like an oxymoron, but there were several such bands worthy of Japanese obsessions, not least Belgium's red-velvet-suited The Jokers, who struck gold with unlikely singles such as 'Football Boogie' and 'Spanish Hully Gully', before topping the charts with their surf LP *Beat on Christmas*.[1]

Because of the wide range of music contained in the grooves of *High Vikings*, it's probably best that we address what is known (or even unknown) about each band in the order in which they appear before us on the compilation. The album's running order is certainly not chronological, but the styles of its sixteen songs never venture any wider than those '60s sounds on Lenny Kaye's original *Nuggets* double LP. Moreover, many of the performers on *High Vikings* went on to greater things by playing major roles in the bands described in *Danskrocksampler*, including The Dandy Swingers' Annisette, who became the voice of The Savage Rose, and Povl Dissing, Denmark's answer to Van Morrison, here showcased in his R&B group The Beefeaters. The Stomps' sinus-toned vocalist was Leif Roden, future leader of psychedelic progressive giants Alrune Rod, while Steppeulvene ('Steppenwolf')

1 But, then again, the Japanese were entirely on their own in celebrating Finland's unlikely surf combos The Quiets and the soberly-dressed quartet The Sounds, whose matching honey-maple Fender guitars and royal-blue suits gave them a ghoulish glow somewhat akin to The Shadows lost in the Nordic underworld. A surfing version of Rimsky-Korsakov's 'Troika Chase' anyone? Japan's Philips label certainly felt that it was worth a shot! Ironically, The Sounds' big Japanese hit, 'Mandschurian Beat', would, three years later, be covered by their heroes, The Ventures, who would, ironically, only get to hear it for the first time on their own Japanese tour in 1965.

– through the otherworldly utterances of their poet/leader Eik Skaloe – inhabited a Brechtian half-life, midway between the privileged and educated yet wasted and low-life styles evoked through the Cale/Nico/Edie Sedgwick tendency of The Velvet Underground, and Jim Morrison's Eurodrunk guise on The Doors' 'Moon of Alabama (Whisky Bar)'.

It's fitting, therefore, that Steppeulvene should have opened *High Vikings* with their hugely catchy 1967 single 'Du Skal Ug Hvor', originally released by Hamburg's Metronome Records. For it was singer Skaloe who first dared to sing rock'n'roll in his native language (thereby consigning himself to a Denmark-only career), and whose disappearance in the Indian city of Ferozepore in 1968 fixed Steppeulvene's legend forever in the Danish collective psyche as those islands' only truly authentic answer to Britain's Brian Jones and the American axis of Jimi, Jimbo and Janis. The two and a half minutes of heavy bar-room piano and bizarre vocal delivery suggestive of a male hybrid of Marlene Dietrich and Mouse and the Traps tells us that this could only be Steppeulvene. Around fifty seconds into the song, a bracing, branging guitar solo and grating key change accelerate the song one hundred percent, tumbling'n'cascading into a delightful vocal middle eight. The song collapses to a conclusion in precisely the same manner as Bump's magnificent 1968 single 'Winston Built the Bridge'.

Next up, The Moondogs' 'Trying to Make You See' is a superb cross-pollination of The Who's 'Pictures of Lily' and The Rolling Stones' 'Jumping Jack Flash', similar to Massachusetts band The What Fours' classic 'Basement Walls' – especially so with the vocals being delivered by a hairy choirboy somewhat reminiscent of Peter 'Herman' Noone if he'd been petrol-injected with a more Keith Relfian cultiness. The Crowd's extremely peculiar 1969 single 'Junk' kicks off next, and is more out of time than anything else herein.

Apart from the yearning, Rob Tyner vocals, this song's minimalist, post-'Whole Lotta Love' riffery is spectacularly subdued considering it emerged from rock'n'roll's most Plant, Farner'n'Gillanised, chest-beating period. Instead, The Crowd dare to take the hoary Zep riff into a kind of Subway Sectian territory, replete with weird time signatures (nope, those ain't skips, brothers'n'sisters), before opening up into chords at the very final pass through. Nicely restrained, chaps.

We slip back three years, now, to The Stomps' frustrated, mid-1966 complain-athon 'My Parents', originally released on Indspillet Records. Over a generic, Stonesy stomp, future Alrune Rod-er Leif Roden declares his disbelief that these two ur-stooges sitting before him hunched in front of the TV had something to do with bringing his triumphant ass into the world. Featuring the great refrain 'This we have in common/Not a word not a sound,' the music heaves with suppressed fuzz guitars that finally break free of their bondage, heralding an enormous middle eight which shudders with early-Who drum chaos and amplifier overload . . . Magnificent.

Coming right after the archaic Stomps, it's difficult to imagine that the barely suppressed, squealing axe-worship of Young Flowers' 1967 single 'City of Friends' was recorded just one year later, for the Sonet label. But, as I explain further in *Danskrock-sampler*, the impact in 1966 of the power trios Cream and The Jimi Hendrix Experience was particularly potent on these Danes, all of whom had previously played in well-known beat groups.

Cast in the role of the first Danish supergroup, Young Flowers were an often blues-based but otherwise highly original bunch. Too damn right, although Young Flowers exhibited an early Barrett/Floydian approach to their trio playing, often stretching their album tracks into ten-minute excursions through free-rock territory, their beat-group roots allowing the band members to retain at all times their original three-minute-single sensibility – conveniently, for it enabled them to score big hits with classy, concise statements like the song included herein.

I'd guess that almost every classic garage compilation includes either a version of 'Hey Joe' (The Leaves/Byrds/Love arrangement) or Arthur Lee's take on said song via his own 'Feathered Fish' (Zachary Thaks' was the definitive versh) and 'My Flash on You' (also covered brilliantly by Thee Sixpence). It's the latter song that upholds the tradition on *High Vikings*, delivered with undue, Thor-like gusto by an unknown band called The Drys. In possession of a manic bass-drummer and a swooping bassist in the tradition of Golden Cups/Speed, Glue & Shinki's Masayoshi Kabe, and powered by a monolithic garage organist on a par with the ultra-long-haired Masao Tonari, of Japanese early Soft Machine addicts Datetenryu, The Drys' manic version of this Arthur Lee song may swirl with *Da Capo*-style flute, à la Tjey Cantrelli, but even its recording engineers were hell bent on stirring up Woden's Wild Hunt on this utterly berserk version.

Next, the whole album emotionally tumbles with 'My Sadness', The Coins' ham-fisted tale of love, which comes on like some garage take on Bobby Goldsboro's mawkish 'Summer the First Time'. Personally, I find its mistranslated lyrical botch fascinating and strangely moving, especially this bit: 'And she received me lying there on the beach/She was my instrument and we played a lovely tune.'

Better still is this four-minute song's wah-wah overhill guitar solo, which kicks in at about one minute thrity-nine seconds and just keeps in there for almost a minute and a half. Including a weird and super-lumpen middle-eight key change, 'My Sadness' is a highly inventive psychedelic ballad despite the glorious failure of its lyrics.

Young Flowers return next with the huge guitar tour de force that is 'Like Birds', another of their 1967 singles released on Sonet Records. What was it about these massively long guitar solos? Again, less than one minute into the song demonic axe-wielding kicks in and proceeds to tear the place apart for over a minute of overt manglism.

Side One concludes in fine traditional style with The Moondogs' pubescent 'I'm Gonna Step on You', the kind of generic adolescent beat song that appeared on the more melancholic Moulty Records compilation *The New England Teen Scene* (especially The What Fours' 'Eight Shades of Brown' and The Rouges' 'The Next Guy'). Again, the poorly translated lyrics provide major entertainment when the singer declares to his girl: 'You put me down, and tread on me like I'm a piece of ground.'

Side Two opens with The Noblemen's 'I'm Mad Again', a dry, dry, staggering 'I'm a Man' one-chord blues. Like the best Cuby and the Blizzards material, this arid complain-athon is up there with some of the finest *Pebbles* stuff.

Then we're off into the strange soul world of The Beefeaters, whose 'Lad Mig Bilve Noget' would probably be nothing more than a basic Memphis/Detroit R&B instrumental if not for vocalist Povl Dissing's old-man-of-the-mountains, abject, pleading vocal delivery. However, this in itself sets The Beefeaters far apart from *everyone*, Dissing being in possession of a crackle mouth right up there with Captain Beefheart, Feargal Sharkey and 'You Ain't Seen Nothing Yet' by BTO. Dissing's yammer raises the stakes no end, and immediately explains how this gravel-breather was able to ride through the '70s on a high-powered solo career.

The wah organ-dominated Drys return next with their eight-minutes-plus take on Cream's 'I'm So Glad', a song I wouldn't give a thank-you for in the hands of Clapton and co., but which shakes itself alive here like a dormant sea monster from the ocean floor. The subterranean flute and growling rhythm guitar mung this version no end, allowing more Masayoshi Kabe-style bass to hubbub in and out of the mix the same way he does on The Golden Cups' epic B-side version of 'Hey Joe'. Using 'I'm So Glad' as their vehicle for a sonic onslaught, The Drys manage effortlessly to enter the same garage legend as Oxford Circle's massive 'Mind Destruction' or 'Psychedelic Journey Parts 1 & 2' by Long Island's guitar mercenaries The Mystic Tide.

Next, we're back with Povl Dissing's street-corner-drunk for The Beefeaters' magnificent take on The Pretty Things' 'LSD'. Here accompanied by wailing blues harp, this was the B-side of The Beefeaters' 1966 debut single 'Big City', released on Ecco Records.

Dandy Swingers' horn-driven 1966 version of Percy Sledge's 'Stay with Me Baby' is an incredible, Spectorised soul revue, anticipating The Savage Rose's higher revelations as their future singer, Annisette Hansen, takes the Janis Joplin route but transcends it effortlessly, her higher register shriek-outs clearly preparing the way for Björk's future volvic wailing.

Master Joseph's near-six-minute-long 'All Your Love' is a shimmering, late-night, organ'n'guitar-thunder original, heavily influenced by The Allman Brothers as delivered in the style of the American West Coast sound. Two minutes into the slow groove, the beat picks up into a superb, Booker T-meets-Ray Manzarek organ solo and whoever Master Joseph is cops some sober falsetto, before the whole thing implodes and re-enters its glorious soul soup.

High Vikings concludes with 'Night Flight', a 1967 soul instrumental by The Beefeaters that could have been by The Chocolate Watchband or one of those Mike Curb studio creations. The generic guitar solos of 'Dark Side of the Mushroom' are overwashed with the sound of jetliners passing across the stereo, as Povl and co. pretend to be checking in at Copenhagen Airport (yeah, it coulda been at Jutland's provincial Aarhus Airport over to the west, but there are never enough passengers to create that kind of five-people-plus crowd action).

And so we conclude *High Vikings*, an almost comprehensive overview of the post-beat-era Danish scene at the height of its psychedelic garage assault, delivered on a single vinyl record. Nice. Although this record has been unavailable for over two decades, you'll be happy to learn that several of these essential tracks are now reissued on Sonet's massive triple CD, *Derfra Hvor Vi Stod – Sange Med Mervaerdi* (Sonet UMD 987 411 4). Completed with copious notes (in Danish, natch), this snappily titled compilation contains tracks from the beat era right up to the mid-'70s. Check it!

The 1970s

I hated the 1970s until the punk thing happened. I lived through them. Boring? Fucking hell, what a travesty those first few years were. It felt like the carnival floats carrying the '60s had all driven by and we were there to pick up the discarded dog-ends and roaches. Many '70s rockers – feeling utterly eclipsed by the technology-wielding Moonwalkers of NASA – did battle not by shagging more groupies nor by Blue Cheering their Deep Purple riffs, but instead by totally abandoning their Afro-American roots in favour of an Olympian musicianship of a near classical kind. Hell, prog-rock bands added entire orchestras to their stage sets! Didn't get away with it . . . but still did it. Worse still, many former classical musicians grew their hair and formed bands like Curved Air and The Flock, combining hyper versions of classics along with their own songs. Worser still, most of those clueless axe heroes chose to do battle with these classical nitwits, diminishing rock'n'roll's raw fury in a tragic attempt to validate it as an authentic art form. Authentic? Kiddies, those guys was taking the piss. Concentrating like grannies in a knitting contest, prog-rockers took their performances Inside, shutting out their 1970s audiences until the Rock . . . died, brothers'n'sisters.

I knows it. I was there and I suffered, too. Denied access to the Rock until 1970 by a teacher mother who believed the *Daily Mail*'s every Rolling Stones exposé, aged thirteen I lived at first on a diet of *Who's Next*, Creedence's *Cosmo's Factory* and . . . ahem, The Moody Blues' *A Question of Balance*. Yeah, yeah, I know. Moreover, my enduring and very real hatred of The Beatles' *Sergeant Pepper* LP – highly useful credentials during punk, brothers'n'sisters – emanated not from a simple backlash against my parents' love of John,

Paul, George and Gringo, but from their vicarious 'appreciation' of the Moptops' finer points, as 'revealed' through the prissy filter of the *Sunday Times*' music critic Derek Jewell. Thereafter, my entire '70s anti-rock methodology involved (1) rejecting any song that I suspected could have been singalong'd to quite happily by my Boer War Uncle Sam; (2) accessing the Inner Moron through Krautrock, Fripp and Eno, and the *Clockwork Orange* soundtrack; and (3) celebrating prog-rock only through heathen reprobates such as Amon Düül II, Van Der Graaf Generator, Magma, Todd Rundgren, The Velvet Underground, The Doors and The Edgar Broughton Band.

But even these last mentioned enlightened beings were history when, in late summer '76, I espied in *Melody Maker* a pathetic polio youth wearing a t-shirt emblazoned with the legend 'I HATE PINK FLOYD'. J. Rotten's Two-Minute-Hate movement Pol Potted everything right back to the Stone Age. True, it didn't kill all the fuckers dead, but it surely created a more righteous new order, as those genuine non-sellout counterculture heroes of that now-outlawed '60s generation gradually crossed over into the new wave through post-punk's Rock Against Racism movement, Kevin Millins' militant and beguiling Final Solution shows and, of course, Rough Trade Records. Thereafter, such was the generational integration achieved that even The Fall's Mark Smith could admit to me in 1978 that he'd failed an audition to join Cambridge commies Henry Cow the previous year.

My rock'n'roll writing about '70s music is, therefore, entirely informed by those blazing '70s Incorruptibles, those beautiful Visionaries, rock'n'rollers and avant-gardists who never bowed down to corporate wishes and for whom every recording was a kick in the smug mug of the '70s Rock Establishment: Bobby Liebling's Pentagram, Todd Clark's New Gods, Billy Miller's Dark Shadows/Cold Sun, John Garner's Sir Lord Baltimore, Cleveland's too-soon-for-punk triumvirate Electric Eels, Mirrors and Rocket from the Tombs – all were forced to exist at a level so far below '70s record-company standards that most of their recordings still sound breathtakingly new and inspirational to this day. Ignored and left to rot by contemporary companies, their studio songs have suffered no contamination by commercial expectations, so they pick up new and genuine rock'n'roll fans every day. Read their stories in *Copendium* and weep that they were ignored back in the day.

Alice Cooper

Don't Blow Your Mind

(Recorded live in Toronto, 1970)

1 Don't Blow Your Mind (12.30)

Alice Cooper: A Group of the Future

You may be thinking, 'What a sneaky way to try and get us into Alice,' and you'd be right. For a start, this isn't even an LP; it's just a live bootleg of twelve-and-a-half-minutes duration, but it's my Album of the Month even if it is really only an EP's worth. And it's totally merited in any case because this 1970, live-in-Toronto version of 'Don't Blow Your Mind' (a single for the band when they were still known as The Spiders) was recorded when Alice Cooper was still a group of ascendant longhairs led by two dudes called Vince Furnier and Dennis Dunaway.

This bad-ass, wise-ass, dumb-ass recording of a cumbersomely raging garage ritual was made long before Bob Ezrin added his whole cash'n'carry-size can o'Canuck AOR'n'B, proto-Seeger colliery brass band to the proceedings. No, babies, this prehistoric sucker was ooh-flung-dung on the cusp of the '70s – indeed, outta the very beginnings of that Straight Records period when Frank Zappa was trying to sell them as just five more bogies from his ever-growing Snot Colony. You've heard the GTO's, Wild Man Fischer and Captain Beefheart – now here's Alice Cooper: the singer's a reincarnation of a seventeenth-century witch and sings like Lennon *and* McCartney over an inept space-jam backing of wannabe Magic Band meets early Floyd, stuck in an M25 contraflow. Sounds too contrived to sustain a career? U-betcha!

As a rock'n'roll group, Alice Cooper were always so much more than those first two horrible/brilliant

LPs – and even they were genuine experimental rock of the Frankenstein kind. That is, they fell on their face at least seventy percent of the time, but struggled ever upward towards some Doorsian light at the end of the tunnel. Tell me the furry freakiness of 'Swing Low Sweet Cheerio' couldn't have a place in your twilight heart, you brutes. Tell me 'Mr and Miss Demeanor' ain't the lost, sacred twin of 'Moonlight Drive' and I'll weep for ya! Surely 'Living' is really 'Paperback Writer' as played by lost African bush men who've been taught about Western culture by anthropologists armed only with second-generation, reel-to-reel copies of the film *Help!*. Surely the *Paradise Lost* space-rock of 'Levity Ball' is the truest kissing cousin of 'Astronomy Domine' to ever grace your turntable. Hear me, babies, even the cargo cults of the south-western Pacific couldn'ta played good old rock'n'roll weirder than these guys. Face it, if they'd split in 1971, we'd all be shelling out mini-fortunes for these records. As it is, I've been scoffing up original Straight copies around Britain for the price of new Manic Street Porter releases. If it had a Brain label, we'd have intuitively subsumed it intravenously into our cultural consciousness light years ago.

Although 1969's *Pretties for You* and 1970's *Easy Action* may have always been perceived as mere psychic noogies that you really have to work hard at just to get all the way through a single side, they ain't a helluva way removed from their label-mate, good old Captain Beefheart's *Lick My Decals Off, Baby* – only far more chock-full o'licks and hooks and sing-alongs from the (perceived) dog-end of psyche. Indude, the last time I put that particular Beefheart old-timer on the turntable, its sheer arrant, self-conscious twerpiness had me returning it to the Unplayed Classic section of my collection in no time flat. And at least the Coop's first two LPs sounded like The Beatles in a liquidiser – *Lick My Decals Off* sounded like fucking Henry Cow jamming late-period Pere Ubu. Mercy!

It's just that Alice Cooper became a Hollywood golfing no-mark while Captain Beefheart became a holier-than-thou sepia print by Anton Corbijn. Alice may have become arena dross, but Beefheart opted out of music altogether. And, in my book, choosing the art-gallery scene over the arena-rock scene is a far bigger crime against humanity. But then, my love of music is such that, for me, even T'Pau, Living in a Box and the Jools Holland Big Band together doing reggae versions of

'The Macarena' comes closer to approaching the divine than the passive, dry-wank snore-athons of meaninglessness spewed up by the I've-got-my-personal-neuroses-and-I'm-not-afraid-to-use-them brigade of Tate Modern masters.

So, why have I been humming and hawing for so long before writing about Alice Cooper? I really dunno. I suppose it's because he coulda been great but he never shoulda kicked the cute longhairs into touch. Alice wasn't even the greatest thing about Alice Cooper, the band, in the beginning. Because the cute longhairs *were* Alice Cooper. Because Michael Bruce wrote all the best songs and then got unceremoniously kicked out without so much as a champagne handshake. Because when I was a teenager, Dennis Dunaway was my favourite bass player, *and* he was the most experimental, *and* he did it on a silver-glitter Gibson SG bass, dressed as a skinny, pre-teen zombie.[1] Because Neal Smith was a six-foot-six-inch drumming freak-show who took the rhythms into African places that scared me – *and* he wrote 'Black Ju Ju' on his own! The best slice of recorded, post-Doors schlock/shock rock-theatre since The Guess Who's 'Friends of Mine' and the fucking drummer wrote it! Because *Love It to Death* is the best MC5/Detroit rock'n'roll LP of all time not made by a Detroit band. Because *Killer* is the too-brutal-to-be-prog, art-rock LP of life experience, which they sensationally topped with the 'School's Out' forty-five, then lamely followed up with the *School's Out* LP – a bare half-hour-long cash-in unworthy of Mike Curb. Because they saved the day with *Billion Dollar Babies*, even if the rot was setting in by then (and *only* then, all you motherfucking non-believers). Because nostalgia is about yearning for a time that you didn't even realise was that cool while it was happening. And, while Alice Cooper the group got it completely right all too rarely, Alice Cooper the guy got it completely right *never*. Damn you, son of a preacher man.

What am I moaning about? What am I raging about? I'm howling for the hicks from the provinces, can't you see? I'm weeping for The Troggs in Andover and I'm blarting for Simply Saucer in Hamilton, Ontario. I'm blubbering for Les Rallizes Dénudés in Japan, and I'm moping for the Electric Eels in Cleveland. Man, I'm kicking my legs and throwing a

1 The Gibson SG bass is known as the EB0 or EB3, depending whether it has one or two pick-ups, respectively.

tantrum at the sheer tragedy of all the genius geek-rock still laying there in the vaults, unheard, unreleased, unsung and unknown. And Alice is worse because Alice is famous and *still* he's unheard and unknown!

Like the best Alex Harvey stuff, primo-period Alice Cooper was too casually heard to be considered worthy of re-evaluation. Well, we must re-evaluate *now*! Shit, I saw a fucking rock rag call Tears for Fears' albums 'classic' the other day. What am I reading, a car magazine? The Mark II Cortina is thirty years old – it must be a classic; an Austin Allegro and that wedge-shaped Austin Westminster? They *must* be classics – they're dead old . . . Fuck 'em all and the horse they rode in on. Rock'n'roll is life affirming. Rock'n'roll is life, full stop. Without it we'd all be Christians. Christianity equals death: bye-bye.

So, listen to this here piece of free-rock heathenstompf they called 'Don't Blow Your Mind' and dig it as their 'Black to Comm'[2] – as their group mantra and the setting out of their stall. And sure, you can dig the way they slow down into the choruses like Ash do on 'Goldfinger', and smile as you dig the way the chords echo 'Hey Joe'. But dig even more the other bits, which sound like guys standing rampantly long-haired in front of huge Marshall speaker cabs, with the drummer playing a solo, wearing welding goggles so big that he can't see the kit and keeps falling off his stool. And dig that all this is going on soon after the release of Stanley Kubrick's *2001: A Space Odyssey*, so the ape scene with the monolith has to be included so they can all worship the monolithic speaker cabinets and *oo-oo-ah-ah* at each other across the big, rock-festival-sized stage. And dig that the group are all Anglophiles and, therefore, fans of Patrick McGoohan in *The Prisoner*. So they

2 Unlike, for example, the great hardrock-cum-meditational Krautrock pieces such as Ash Ra Tempel's 'Amboss', any of Guru Guru's *UFO* LP or GAM's 'Gam Jam', both the MC5's 'Black to Comm' and Alice Cooper's 'Don't Blow Your Mind' are successful for their disrupture of rhythm and the role of their lead singers – both of whom provide a virtual dyslexicon of shamanic stutter'n'holler on these two tracks. It is the stop–start which may be most annoying to the general listener, but it is precisely this stop–start which enables the tracks to develop their drawing down of the Muse. Much of the free-jazz which attempts this is a stone-cold bore to me because I hate the acousticness of the chosen instrumentation. But gimme the feedback and the arhythmic wail-athon can go on all night.

greedily try to incorporate all this into one big human orgy of rock ritual which can't possibly succeed, but still does in any case because of their sheer exuberance. And, while you're listening, dig that the whole thing was being filmed by D. A. Pennebaker – the guy who filmed that *Don't Look Back* film of Bob Dylan slagging everyone off. So this whole thing is a moment captured forever.

And remember that when the guy at the end of the song screams 'Ladies and gentlemen, Alice Cooper – a group of the future!' he really meant what he was saying. Alice Cooper *was* a group. The MC really meant those words, so listen like he meant them. Really *hear* the whole thing: the future, the future . . . Because we all belong to the future, babies. We're all constantly in the process of becoming . . . we know not what.

It used to be that, when a man wanted to say a woman was beautiful, he would say she was 'becoming'. And that, ladies'n'gentlemen, is what I love so much about this recording. It's becoming. It's twelve and a half minutes of evolution. It's a sonic celebration of all that's human: the physical, the cerebral and the pan-shamanic flip-out amidst total control. It's the sound of young people . . . *becoming.*[3]

3 In the Norse myths, the Triple Goddess manifests as the Norns: three women who tend to the roots of Yggdrasil, the Tree of Life. The meaning of their names, Urd, Verdandi and Skuld, has, in the past, been generally translated as meaning Fate, Being and Necessity, but some scholars have translated Verdandi as meaning 'Becoming'.

ALRUNE ROD

Hej Du

(Sonet Records, 1970)

SIDE ONE

1 Du Taler Og Si'r (7.51)
2 Hej Du (15.11)

SIDE TWO

1 Perlesøen (21.51)
i Prelude
ii Nu
iii Prov
iv ?
v Invitation
vi Neden/Under
vii Ny Dag
viii Finale

As shown in my book *Krautrocksampler*, and in several articles on the Head Heritage website, not bringing much by way of artistic merit to the swinging '60s party until the tail-end of '69 ultimately worked in favour of the West German and Japanese rock'n'rollers, because their sheer physical distance from the party allowed time for them to subsume into both their own music and lyrics the later ghastliness of Altamont and the Manson Family *and* the earlier, well-meaning idealism of the 'All You Need Is Love' ethos of 1967. And so, that calamitous mix of simultaneous rampant expectation and utter devastation that so depressed British and American youth after the multiple collective '60s high ultimately made far more poetic sense to German and Japanese youth, still picking their way through their own shattered (and so recently Americanised) homelands. However, as I illustrate in the *Danskrocksampler* entry, other peripheral yet slightly less damaged youth cultures (ignored or dismissed at the time as Johnny-come-lately art statements) nowadays yield a high level of excellent rock'n'roll, with much still awaiting serious excavation. That this is the case no longer surprises me; hell, motherfuckers, if twenty-first-century underground rock'n'roll is virtually impossible to keep track of, what chance have we of keeping up with the remote past?

Neverending Compositions

It's the spring of 1970 (cue feedback guitars and doomy riff organ), and two longhairs are walking down Stroget, Copenhagen's King's Road, talking it like they're walking it and wondering how long it's all gonna last. Both are musicians but one is the poet too, and he says to his mate (as translated from the Danish by my publisher friend, Ole Knudsen):

Brother, today you have that same manic gleam in your eyes that I saw first time I met you. Here we are, lucky to be striding down Stroget, but you still spend half the time neurotic that all this is an illusion. How much more free can you get? Get on with being it now! You crow about not being tied to your missus, but where would you live without her flat? You say you're not scared of the police, but you'd never have the guts to go to a country where losing your freedom would be a real possibility.

And so, this classic *Hej Du* album begins amidst hippie idealism, the new Danish youth realism and a joyously abandoned musical soundtrack that vibrates like the sum total of all of the West's best underground psychedelic soul music. Themes, man, this band has a fucking plethora of them. Most especially über-catchy is the song playing out as they stride down Stroget, entitled 'Du Taler Og Si'r' (You Talk and Say). The aforementioned poet is Leif Roden, a tall, ultra-skinny longhair with a Holger Czukay moustache and a sunburst Fender Precision bass that propels what the Danish press have dubbed Alrune Rod's 'Neverending Compositions': long, psychedelicised TCB soul revues of ever-building epiphanies and cascading, angelic vocal refrains, occasionally regrouping into ambulant drifts of rhythmless, formless, still-waterscapes.

The joy of *Hej Du* is that it sounds like all late-'60s heavy music simultaneously *and* like none of it specifically. Organ, guitar, bass and drums were rarely used more sparingly than on Alrune Rod's records, with no real lead instruments at all and lots of 'ooh' angelic vocals and plane, train, automobile sound-effects thrown in.

This is predominantly a band of groovers informed equally by the Chambers Brothers' epic 'Time Has

Come Today' work-out and British organ-dominated art-rock such as Pink Floyd, The Nice and The Crazy World of Arthur Brown. So, despite it being 1970, these are guys who still wanna look ultra-cool and score with the dollies. Which means the so-called lead guitar is in reality more of an FX extravaganza-cum-shrine to the tasty lick – Davy O'List from The Nice springs to mind, or Peter Banks-period Yes, or maybe what Steve Winwood did on the first couple of Traffic LPs.

In Alrune Rod's music, fuzz riffs and noises proliferate and throw off-kilter the overdriven curtains of dirge and stewing Hammond organ, which is itself a cross between the drones of Floyd's Rick Wright on 'A Saucerful of Secrets' and the R&B-based, driving riffs of Yes's Tony Kaye, with Jon Lord of Deep Purple and Van der Graaf Generator's Hugh Banton also thrown in.

But the main reason that Leif Roden has such a spring in his step as he navigates the Stroget pavements is that he's full of hope for the Rod's future. The group's first LP had done well on the Danish scene and now Roden's working on copping some more hip Anglo-Americanisms to Danskify for instalment number two – indeed, even the album title *Hej Du* (literally 'Hey You') was the popular Danish hippie greeting of the time, reflecting Roden's drive to give it all a local context.

I have to admit that the main reason *Hej Du* has been so heavily rotated these past months (I even listened to almost all twenty-one minutes of 'Perlesøen' in the carwash the other day, around two in the afternoon, when no one was behind me, waiting) is because it takes me back sonically without merely being something I listened to as a kid. Sometimes, when I feel the need to play punk-rock without all the attendant associations of the past, I put on *Minutes to Go* by The Sods, and right at that moment their late-arrival swoop of breathless stupidity sums up punk better in one twenty-minute side of vinyl than all the originators could. Similarly, playing the title track from The Sweet's *Sweet Fanny Adams* does glam-rock better for me in five minutes than umpteen repeated listenings to 'The Jean (yawn) Genie' ever could. And, for Alrune Rod, being Danish allowed them to retain in their sonic mash certain ingredients that had, by 1970, become shut out and shunned as 'old gimmickry' in the lands of the originators. Guitar phasing, organ phasing, 'Astronomy Domine'-style howling-at-the-moon; all these add-ons might hide shortcomings in the musicians themselves, but their presence also allowed the overall musical effect to be one of psychedelia rather than progressive-rock. Hell, *Hej Du* even gets a long, rambling and very mid-'60s set of poetic sleeve-notes for stoners to giggle at as they listen.

All three epic tunes on this record remind me of the title track from Amon Düül II's *Yeti*, insofar as they shift from beacon to terrific beacon of raging sun-worship via valley pathways of intriguing, low-key mystery. Did you ever wish that the four-piece Soft Machine of the 'Love Make Sweet Music' forty-five had made an entire LP of that exquisite psychedelic soul, rather than just padding out the sublime 'Why Are We Sleeping?' with thirty minutes of so jazz/so what free-form dry-wank? Or wished that organ-grinding behemoths such as Mountain and Vanilla Sludge – rather than indulging in some typically undignified and seemingly endless, twelve-minute 'Heavy Rigby' *en suite* cover version *du jour* – had instead dared to knee popular music in the nuts by slinging out such semi-coagulated spittoon fodder as the ultra-monolithic Iron Butterfly's seventeen-minute 'In-A-Gadda-Da-Vida'? Yeah, me too; which is why this particular Alrune Rod LP deserves its place as an Album of the Month . . . not because of the many musical barriers it broke at the time of its release, but because of the confident manner in which its Danish creators accepted all the various ingredients in the menu being served up to them by the various chefs of British and American rock'n'roll.

Just as William Burroughs suggested that an author in a dry spell is best engaged in creative reading, so Leif Roden took on the job of creative hoarding. Riffage, rhythms, intros, tail-outs, you name it, they were all grist to Roden's Alrune Rod mill. But, like the cultural kleptomania of T. S. Eliot's *The Hollow Men*, the songs of Alrune Rod that annexed so shamelessly sections of other people's work did it so seamlessly and with such witty craftsmanship that the listener quickly gives up yelling 'Oi, I know that bit' and just gets on with enjoyment of the overall piece.

There's little point in my telling you precisely where I reckon Leif Roden got all his source material from, because I'm not enough of a know-it-all to be up for the job, nor is Leif Roden merely the smart sonic cut'n'paster I'm in danger of accusing him of being. The strength of this record is the manner in which it all hangs together, building, dipping, dropping down, swaying, regrouping then building again and again.

Moreover, Alrune Rod had the luxury of being able to stretch out their material over two, twenty-minute-long LP sides only after Sonet Records had, in mid-1969, sought to kick-start the band's career with a nice, safe piece of institutional psychedelia as their first single, a five-minute-long equivalent to Keith West's 'Excerpt from a Teenage Opera' hit, to show they meant business. Typically of the time, this first forty-five, 'Pigen Pa Stranden', was a bit of a curveball and quite unlike their real direction. Just as Van der Graaf Generator hiccupped their way into existence via a doom single especially penned for them by George 'The Beatles' Martin, so Alrune Rod's earliest commercial venture was a Danish Tin Pan Alley rewrite of Cat Stevens' hoary doom-vehicle 'The First Cut Is the Deepest'. Written by Danish singer-songwriter Bent Birkholm, its huge, stop–start organ cross-pollinated the aforementioned with Procol Harum's 'Whiter Shade of Pale', without laying to rest the spectre of either. Much better was the Rod's own gleeful B-side, 'Tæl Aldrig Imorgen Med', which conjures up the same Daft Vader atmosphere of Hammill's later 'Imperial Zeppelin'. Fucking beautiful, man!

However, I'll conclude this by telling y'all that *Hej Du* is damned listenable, refreshing and stonkingly groovy. Alrune Rod's self-titled debut LP (their name means 'mandrake root') was also quite killer, but this second LP is definitely the real shit. The later LPs have their moments (especially *Alrune Rock*) but are in most ways too generic. Focus now on the largeness of *Hej Du* and allow its riffs to cascade over your melted plastic brain and tell me these gentlemen achieved one delightful motherfucker of a long-playing record. And, while I try hard not to become ensnared in cosiness in my rock'n'roll, something about the pulse, the heartbeat of *Hej Du*, for me, really captures how marvellously soul music and psychedelically styled music could occasionally unite. As Leif says in the title track: 'Your ears are used to lies/But your body can find its way towards yourself.'

A.R. & Machines

Echo

(Polydor, 1972)

SIDE A

1 Invitation (20.32)

SIDE B

1 The Echo of the Present (10.08)

2 The Echo of Time (13.05)

SIDE C

1 The Echo of the Future (18.13)

SIDE D

1 The Echo of the Past (19.38)

Over a decade and a half since the first publication of *Krautrocksampler*, I'd presumed there was hardly anything left in the genre to champion. My job was done, and, anyway, there was a whole new generation of maniacs who, by now, probably knew even more about the Krautrock scene than I'd ever known. So I was a bit freaked out to discover from a couple of good friends and major heads that poor old Achim Reichel's big psychedelic space-outs had never received the treatment they deserved.

It was Steve Freeman, from specialist record emporium Ultima Thule, who clued me into this particular sprawling, eighty-three-minute monster back in 1995. Soon after the publication of *Krautrocksampler*, Steve sent me a cassette tape which, in turn, got copied on to DAT and whizzed around other head-scratching innerspacers, each of whom waited with baited breath for a proper re-release which never came.

Then the physical writing of *The Modern Antiquarian* took over, and Krautrock in the Cope household got temporarily sidelined by my return to the gonzo, proto-metal of The Stooges, Funkadelic, Black Sabbath and the MC5, all fleshed out by new loves such as Sir Lord Baltimore, Blue Cheer and even early Grand Funk.

But, of course, there were still those happy accidents, nay designs, which straddled both camps so successfully that I was soon back on track. And so it was inevitable that I should eventually return to this huge and sprawling inner world which Achim Reichel, a.k.a. A.R., decided to call *Echo*.

And what an inner world this album is. Over four sides of vinyl, Reichel created a vast parallel otherworld which allowed listeners to sink so deep within themselves that the return to the real world at the end of Side Four always came as a genuine shock. Even more so than Walter Wegmuller's *Tarot*, which allows the listener to rove from emotion to emotion, *Echo* operates on such a singular level that listeners actually start to feel inhabited by this record. It is such a long recording that Thighpaulsandra and I had difficulties transferring it to CD because we both became taken over by the sound. We'd worry about the length of time between each track, we'd try and add more treble to it when it was unnecessary purely because Achim Reichel's super-echoed guitar was just too watery to listen to over and over without entirely losing perspective. Man, it just took hours.

But it was surely worth every moment. For this 1972 recording is a giant of an album, and any move that will help to push Polydor into its late re-release is nothing less than essential. Indeed, it was only when I called Steve Freeman at Ultima Thule, to get a CD copy of *Echo*, that I discovered the album's unavailability. I'd just presumed that the job had been done long ago. Of course, with hindsight it's possible to explain the oversight thus: Achim Reichel is nowadays a very successful German actor with seemingly no interest in his Krautrock output. He had begun as leader of The Rattles, Germany's mid-'60s answer to The Beatles, before jumping on to the 'heavy' scene introduced into Germany at the turn of the decade. From The Rattles, Reichel took Frank Dorstal and Dicky Tarrach with him to form Wonderland, after which a brief period of experimentation with the echoed electric guitar saw the recording of 1970's *Die Grüne Reise*. This stupendously weird and outrageous vocal, guitar and whatever-happens-to-be-around piece of post-psychedelia was then released on Polydor as *A.R. & Machines* first official LP. Five further albums of varying quality and experiment escaped during the 1970s, but Reichel himself had abandoned the project by the end of the decade and returned to making pop music. The jump from music to acting had obviously only alienated him still further from this idealistic work of the early '70s.

But, if artists themselves are uninspired by a particular period of their earlier work, as Achim Reichel has been shown to be, it is up to others more motivated to make that work available. And, when that work could be utilised by major heads for some serious shamanic endeavour, instead of lying unloved in a freezing and damp corporate catacomb, then it is time for the forward-thinking motherfuckers to shine a light in the darkness and scream out: 'Navigation! Navigation! Navigation!'

So, please excuse the nature of this long and unwieldy introduction, and do please understand that, in these heady, long-post-Krautrock days, it was first necessary to hip you to the Achim Reichel scene before I could, with any real sense of conviction, punch my fists MC5-like in the air and scream: 'Bring it on!'

Echo opens with the massive, low-key, twenty-minute rumbles of 'Invitation', in which hugely echoed, watery electric guitars minor-chord their way across a vast sky of long tape-phasing, as rhythms of subterranean dripping punctuate the caverns of your unlit mind and send listeners back into a proto-Gollum state. The tape-phasing spirals ever up and up as the cavern route takes you ever more down and down: like your head is travelling to Jupiter and your arse fell into the sub-sonic wells of eternity. Your newly dead body is being rouged with face paint, to prepare you for the next world, by chattering unseen spirit forms who minister to the bodily needs of your former corporeal self. Around seven minutes into the music, strange orchestras lining the route to your future home set up another massively tape-phased heraldic theme as Thor, or even some Armenian proto-Thor (Tarhunda/Tork), hammer-wielding and mounted on the first of eight, black flying warhorses, burns across the sky. He's an arc-welding forward-thinker with both eyes on the future, and his cohorts are elegant saxophone gods and a sure-footed, mercurial drummer with a seven-league bounce in his stride who kicks in a big 6/8 rhythm as the sky gods' practise aerobatics overhead. It's as though the Red Arrows were passing through some cosmically sized ring modulator with hundreds of yards of one-inch recording tape trailing off the back of their tail-planes. Intense co-ordination of musicianship is counted as a big plus in this Pantheon of gods and goddesses, and they've clearly been playing a higher form of Krautrock since the early Bronze Age. Indeed, these were probably the ur-deities who brought the first news of wire guitar strings to Ash Ra

Tempel. For this is the territory in which we find ourselves – a mounting *Schwingungen* landscape lit by flares of pitch and torches of burning tar, each carried by some unknown horse-mounted earth spirit.

It's an ever intensifying, ever-speeding-up, multi-guitar-led rock'n'roll rampage across the ancient starlit skies without so much as one hoary cliché passing across any of the guitar strings. Theme after theme opens out upon yet further themes, as drums build then break down to accommodate, then build up again only to fail like waves breaking on some ancient musical shore. When the drums break down for the last time, Mellotron-like, real-voiced cyber-choirs have taken over to orchestrate our descent into the end of the track with perfect spiritual aplomb. 'Invitation' is a big, beautiful, pagan darkness with the bright-eyed, soon-come Zoroastrian promise of a wide-mouthed and smiling, beaming enlightenment.

Four musical massifs straddle the next three sides of vinyl, each song dedicated to illustrating, respectively, 'The Echo of the Present', 'The Echo of Time', 'The Echo of the Future' and 'The Echo of the Past'. It's so important (and so easy) to accept the artist's metaphor when his vision is as clear and strong as it is on this record. Although Reichel's music here never sounds like it, *Echo*'s mystery approximates similar emotions in Klaus Schulze's later masterwork, *Dune*, in which muttering voices (in Schulze's case, including that of Arthur Brown) are used so effectively to conjure up the sounds of lost ancestors.

Side B's 'The Echo of the Present' begins almost as 'Invitation' had done; that same watery, minor guitar preparing us for a sweet, howling vocal, which, in turn, propels drums and multiple percussion off into another horse-mounted march through Middle Europe. Once more there are gods on the landscape, bringing themes to the peasant population, all interwoven with an undulating and indefinable poetical gabbling. A.R. and his posse are here and they're spreading mystery and enlightenment with sound and rhythm. Catch a few words and they say something about the mountains, something about coming from far away, and something about urging the populace to 'come on'. Then the whole ensemble arrives at some musical ford, whereupon Achim declares: 'When I was a little boy/Six thousand years . . .' As he declaims grandly about his 'fathers' and his 'mothers', his lieutenants are searching the river bank to the north and south, determined to cross this wide stream in order to get to the other side, where a magical music is generating as if from some enormous Mother Machine. With resolve and care, they eventually find a route, as if on stepping stones hidden just below the surface of the water. Achingly slowly, they begin to cross to the other side, whereupon the musical Mother Machine opens her mouth and sucks them up in a flash. Blink and they are gone – through a cosmic portal of immense proportion.

Within micro-seconds, we are on the other side of that parallel world, with children playing in some forever playground. It's a place where ancient life-forms dance around the maypole of some half-life medieval fair. This is 'The Echo of Time'. Reichel and his horsemen briefly investigate this other world before continuing on their epic journey. Reichel is the seer of forever, the intoner of magic, inventor of words, poet of existence, and we are just there to be dragged onwards into his musical vision. Leaving the ensemble but still declaiming wildly, he climbs to the very top of a sacred mountain, which rears up before us. At the summit, he calls out: 'There's a man on the moon/There's a woman in the sun!'

Remember, right now, that 'real time' for Achim is 1972; the astronauts are up there on the moon's surface and cosmic humanity is truly at hand. Remember also that Achim is a German, for whom the sun is a goddess (*noun* Sonne *f.*) and the moon is a god (*noun* Mond *m.*). Being of both Keltic and Scando-Germanic stock, our British psyche conveniently allows us to see sun and moon as being of both sexes. But that also allows us to often regard them as being of neither sex, so there *are* disadvantages. Instead, we must here open our minds to a female sun of constancy, and to a hunting moon which dances across the sky in a manner which is seemingly impossible to anticipate. *This* is the shamanic moon; the moon of chaos and Lugh-nacy. The moon which draws the menstrual blood-flow from women is the same moon which causes the tidal flows of Mother Earth's oceans to gravitate upwards, and whose energy pulls our shamanic other out through our third eyes and guides us up towards it. For the shaman belongs to Lugh; as shamanic Iggy was wont to announce: ''Cause I'm Lugh's.' We are lupine or, as shamanic Ozzy was wont to announce, 'barking at the moon'.

Down and down and down and down goes the music, until roaring rock'n'roll chords possess us and send huge legions of Amon Düül Dervish drummers upon us. We are then sent through another portal into yet another driving, simmering and seething horse-borne riff. And on and on and on and on and on and on and on and on, until all mystery implodes on itself and the sounds of forever subside into a deep and relieving silence at the end of Side B, leaving only the static crackle of the needle in the groove. Indeed, five minutes of silence right now woulda been very enjoyable. But we're here, stuck in a digital land where the CD determines when and where we should listen. Be brave, because we're moving on.

Side C takes us deep into the ur-heart of this double LP. For it is here that we get beyond Achim Reichel's stylings and into a pure, pure form of music. This side-long piece known as 'The Echo of the Future' commences with electro-zither and strummed piano strings, as Turkish percussion and Eastern European tunings herald yet more massed ranks of fast-strummed, vivacious electro-acoustic guitars. It could be the middle of Walter Wegmuller's *Tarot* right now, or even the massive side-long 'Hoch-Zeit' from *Lord Krishna von Goloka.* We've entered a multi-layered sonic world of confusion and inspiration, where the higher spirit unites with other higher spirits to create a vast and cerebrally abandoned beauty. Endless layers of echoed vocals 'aaaaaaaaaaaah!' and 'ooooooooh', as Reichel declaims ludicrous and enthralling lyrics about the universe. It's like Rainer Bauer's delightful pseudo-English on Amon Düül II's 'Sandoz in the Rain', and makes you realise just how perfectly English works as the language of rock'n'roll. No wonder Germans, Italians, French and Japanese are happy to scream such things as 'Right On', 'Motherfuckers', 'All Right!', and all those other hoary rock clichés, never feeling the need to translate it into their own respective languages. These time-honoured underground words register all higher forms and feelings of rebellion, release, obstinacy and youthful cerebration/celebration.

Meanwhile, back at the track, we're still travelling deep into a musical landscape of vast horizons and endless flattened plains. Ancestor spirits lurk in every corner of this piece, muttering to themselves in some transcendental post-language that approximates Japanese here, delta blues there, Burroughsian, Pig Latin desert-song elsewhere . . .

And so we come, at long last, to the final track, known as 'The Echo of the Past'. This side-long weird-out is close to twenty minutes long and is the wildest and most eclectic track of all. Beginning like a real song with real lyrics, 'The Echo of the Past' kicks off like a more accommodating version of something from Peter Hammill's *The Silent Corner and the Empty Stage*. But too soon, and most bizarrely, it degenerates into a cosmic chimp-out. Remember those apemen at the end of Tangerine Dream's *Atem*? Well, they're here with a vengeance – indeed, these babies arrived a full year earlier than Edgar and co. But then, these babbling droolers are only giving the listener more of what A.R. & Machines had delivered one year earlier on their first album, 1970's *Die Grüne Reise*. Ever wondered what possessed Marc Bolan to finish certain early Tyrannosaurus Rex LP tracks by letting them just degenerate into a psychobabble, something akin to an acid-fuelled bar mitzvah led by a Jewish Donovan? I surely have. But I sure wouldn't change those moments of inspired, deformed madness for a fucking T. Rex LP, no way. And so it is with the bizarre ending which Reichel chose for *Echo*. It even gets weirder – a full-sounding and beautiful orchestra starts up out of the blue and we're soon digging the same trench as John Cale did on his legendary *The Academy in Peril*. Remember 'Legs Larry at Television Centre'? Well, he's here again. And this time he's accompanied by David Ackles, ready to perform his magnificent 'Montana Song'. See what I mean? What kind of wide references are these? From three sides of minor-chord, electric horse-riding to orchestras and the ur-men's tea party, this wild double LP is one greedy motherfucker.

And, just as you're at your most confused and beginning to think in a kind of Stanley Unwin-ese, an incredible *musique concrète* of bells, pipes and woodwind tends to your poor outraged (and outreached) mind, and soothes, soothes, oh how it soothes. On and on and on go the bells until they inevitably begin to fade and a sense of termination-any-minute-now descends upon the reluctant listener. Too soon the record is finished and the needle is glitching heartlessly. Why, if Thighpaulsandra were in charge, we'd all be guaranteed at least ten additional minutes. But greed is an ugly trait, and Achim Reichel must only be praised for his incredible and wide-reaching musical vision. Indeed, without a negative thing to say about the actual content of this album, I'd prefer to end this review by urging you to petition your local record shop, your local Polygram office, your neighbours, everyone that you *need* this record! The mental health of the West can only be uplifted by its re-release!

Battiato

Fetus

(Bla Bla, 1972)

SIDE ONE

1 Energia (Energy) (3.01)

2 Fetus (Foetus) (2.30)

3 Una Cellula (A Cell) (2.50)

4 Cariocinesi (Karyokinesis) (2.00)

5 Fenomenologia (Phenomenology) (4.56)

SIDE TWO

1 Meccanica (Mechanics) (6.13)

2 Anafase (Anaphase) (5.32)

3 Mutazione (Mutation) (2.48)

This record was originally released back in the '70s, on the influential Italian label Bla Bla. While most of Franco Battiato's output was released under his own name, the albums *Fetus* and *Pollution* were released by just 'Battiato', in the heavy-rock style of that period. If you enjoy *Fetus*, you really should make an effort to get a hold of *Pollution*, too. This second album of 1972 has a far more spaced-out quality and is another record which, in places, sounds like Walter Wegmuller's epic double LP, *Tarot.*

Throughout my early-'90s reappraisal of Krautrock, umpteen records were pushed my way, accompanied by the comment: 'If you like so-and-so, you'll love this lot.' It was in this manner that I discovered the ambient genius of Russia's Mikhail Chekalin, the rush and roar of Günter Schickert's GAM, the Italian, Warholian freak-outs of Le Stelle di Mario Schifano, the monochrome psychedelia of the lost Czech refusenik 'ensemble' M.C.H. and a whole other raft of strange European bands. I even rediscovered the middle-period genius of Magma's *Mekanik Destruktiw Kommandoh* and *Köntakösz*, both of which I had loved during my pre-punk teens but never thought to revisit. But my dedication to defining the lost art of Krautrock meant that many of these other non-German pioneers got lost in the shuffle as their albums slipped out of pole position and back into the racks marked 'undefinable'.

It was only when this amazing 1972 record by Franco Battiato was recently issued in its English-language version that I dusted off my copy of the original and realised how much I'd once played it. Bloody hell, I knew every note on the album; and I knew its near neighbour, 1972's sister album *Pollution*, almost as well.

With the added excitement of this new English version, I decided to turn *Fetus* into an Album of the Month. It is a stunningly catchy but impossibly strange record which inhabits that netherworld of pop music, electronics, politics and experimental rock; a '70s demi-monde which I grew up with, yet one which takes so many chances that it makes the whole work sound quite timeless.

Fetus is an album beyond all definition. It's a masterpiece of daring and almost stupid risks that work every single time. Some of my forthcoming descriptions of these songs will appal you – you'll think there's no way it can sound good with all the ingredients I'm describing. But it doesn't sound good; it sounds *great*. In little more than half an hour, Battiato takes us through eight uniquely super-detailed songs that tug at the heart strings as no other experimental record ever could.

Fetus is an entirely studio album, audaciously psychedelic and sonically estranged in the manner of Kalacakra's mysterious *Voyage to Llasa* LP, Witthüser & Westrupp's *Trips und Träume*, and the first album by Dalek I Love You. Out of nowhere, acoustic-guitar songs reduce themselves to unaccompanied solo-piano licks, horde nations of backing vocals rush to agree with the lead vocalist and even the hoariest classical tunes will be commandeered to accompany famous events. Its mystery is in its unashamed use of clichés, juxtaposed with the most un-obvious elements. The best example is surely the Stéphane Grappelli-style 'Georgia Brown' violin which is used to orchestrate a drum-machine-driven psychological song.

With such a wide range of musical influences, Franco Battiato is a real mystery, too. Indeed, from the sheer volume and scope of his output from the late 1960s onwards into the 1990s, Battiato most reminds me of myself. Beginning as an Italian pop singer, Franco Battiato moved into the '70s on the crest of the progressive-rock wave, which is where we find him for the recording of both *Fetus* and *Pollution.* Battiato was briefly signed to Island Records, and it was during this period that the English-language version of *Fetus* was made. Franco Battiato had plans to make it big in Britain, and played two fairly high-profile shows at London's Roundhouse, supporting first Magma and later Ash Ra Tempel. And it was at this time that Frank Zappa, on hearing *Pollution*, famously called Battiato's work 'Genius'.

Unfortunately for us all, the British period of his trip was brief and unsuccessful, probably because of the car crash which forced Battiato to return to Italy for hospital care. Further British shows with the Japanese artist Stomu Yamashta had to be cancelled, as did a proposed tour with John Cage. Indeed, the car crash so affected Battiato's career that the English-language *Fetus* was shelved indefinitely and he was forced to return to Italy permanently.

In the light of Battiato's subsequent change of musical direction, whether this temporary relocation to Britain could ever have worked, given a little more success, is a moot point. In the long run, Battiato was far too excited by the musical possibilities thrown up by Stockhausen and the Krautrock scene to stay in song mode for very long, and he soon submerged himself in electronic works such as the more experimental sound of the instrumental LP *Clic.* Several other such releases saw him in this guise, until he appears to have rejected this method entirely and returned to his first love – the role of pop singer.

Taking a look at his website recently, I was impressed to see that Franco Battiato has sustained a huge output, which has latterly extended into classical releases and even an opera. But the Franco Battiato whom I know and love occupies a narrow seam of early-'70s experimental rock, and it is to this period which we must now return.

Fetus begins super-dramatically with 'Energia', in which multiple recordings of babies crying and goo-goo speaking fade up, in stereo, through the murk, as backwards play-room music fades in, reminiscent of *Sparky's Magic Piano* meets Samla Mammas Manna's classic 'Astrid's Vision'. Then a synthesised and pulsating electric piano announces Franco, who sings to us about all the women he's bedded and all the babies who have been lost down the drains of Europe in his quest for a good life. That may sound desperate, but it's melancholy only in a tragic and uplifting way. Like 'Wilhelmina', Peter Hammill's embarrassingly frank and frankly absurd-to-the-point-of-being-laughable lullaby to his growing daughter, 'Energia' employs a chord sequence so obvious that it's like the first thing you would play as a sixteen-year-old, then probably dismiss immediately. Tom toms and electric rhythm guitars are accompanied by brassy, out-of-tune polyphonic synthesizers in a mawkishly emotional blitz. Indeed, being out of tune elevates the whole fucking thing.

The short title track arrives next. An unaccompanied and heavily reverbed heartbeat introduces 'Fetus', as Battiato's lonely, melancholy voice sings, in a single verse, a heart-rending story from the point of view of an unwanted, unborn child:

I wasn't yet born, and I felt the heartbeat,
And that my life was born in hate,
I drag myself slowly through the human body,
Down through the veins, going to my faith.

As the verse unfolds, understated wah-wah guitar chords and plucked piano strings shudder in the stereo distance. A brutal edit into incredibly beautiful music cuts us short; it's another lost child's play-room, this time with a mind-manifesting sound akin to that of The Residents' 'Edwina', from their definitive LP, *Not Available*. The music builds quicker and quicker until it is frightening and overpowering, as wailing and howling monophonic synthesizers annex the mix and kidnap it screaming and blindfolded into the mystic night. In two and a half minutes, Battiato takes us from silence to slack-jawed incomprehension. It's incredible.

Next comes the cliché of clichés. 'Una Cellula' is a Mediterranean sob-fest of mawkish, sub-chicken-in-a-basket chords unfit to be outtakes on a Demis Roussos LP. This time, in less than three minutes, Battiato, rapes our sensibilities with his unholy combinations. He takes a chord sequence reminiscent of true drivel and lends it dignity by playing it in the manner of the truly experimental. It's here that Battiato enters that shameless Dalek I Love You territory located in outlands so far beyond twee that only the most confident truth-seeker may go there. By now, he's the Igneous Fatuus, the Foolish Fire, a Morris dancer who cares not one jot that he appears to the outside world to be line dancing in a stone circle.

'Cariocinesi' is the crazy, Stéphane Grappelli-styled violin and drum-box-propelled song I mentioned earlier. What could be more incongruous than a two-minute gypsy-jazz song with staccato, Beatles piano about a nucleus splitting itself, delivered by a singer who sounds as though he's saluting the sunrise? Nuff said. In either English or Italian, this song is unlikely. That it works probably has more to do with its novelty than its being great art, but I ain't never got bored with it yet because it says its piece then sods off – and pronto, Tonto.

Side One then concludes with the longest song so far, and even this is less than five minutes in duration. 'Fenomenologia' is a dramatic epic in multiple parts, beginning with portentous minor-chord acoustic and Spanish guitars over which Battiato hums wordless 'da-da-das'. His voice tells us that he's living lost and in a fog, until the guitars drop away to reveal a tragic, reverbed, lonely mountain-top solo piano and fuzz bass accompanying Battiato's admission: 'I've already forgotten my dimension/And I have no power standing away from myself.'

But Battiato's fog is clearer than most people's sunny day. He's on Carn Ingli living with the angels of the Preseli Mountains, and a squall of Enochean synthesizers comes down from the heavens to meet him. Then more acoustic guitars and plainsong vocals mourn some dreadful recent event, and the angels of Carn Ingli wordlessly lament him in a harmony of rhythmless and touchingly formless beauty. Like the deeply felt themes of Acid Mothers Temple's *La Novia*, the stereo mix is awash with different voices squeezing deep meanings from 'da-da-da-da-das' until the mystery of the mix consumes the human sounds and wrings them out through a sonic mangle, like your old grandma used to have in the kitchen.

In common with the rest of this mystical LP, time has no place in this song. In less than five minutes, Battiato has sent us on to the moors where the triple goddesses weave and spell, and created a timelessness that lesser artists would claim requires a double LP to achieve. In the fifteen minutes of Side One, *Fetus* has greedily gorged itself on more emotions than many modern guitar bands approach in a career. Fuck 'em all, I say. Fuck their self-pitying, inexperienced asses. But then compassion kicks in and I can only wish that every musician could glimpse the moments that Franco Battiato captures here.

Side Two opens with the hugely stereo FX pianos of 'Meccanica', in which a ludicrous instrumental keyboard theme is hammered out with fuzz guitars, screaming synthesizers and high-pitched, wordless voices all essaying the same moronic tune. Until, that is, fast-strummed twelve-string guitars, more gypsy violin and obvious/dumb bass, propelled by a pitter-patter drum-box, shoot out over the horizon. This new theme continues at a substantial pace until dropping right down to five miles per hour in order to allow a dryly recorded and claustrophobic Franco to have his say:

My eyes are mechanical – my heart is made of plastic,
My brain is mechanical – the taste is synthetic,
My fingers are mechanical – made of moon dust
In a laboratory – the genes of love.

Perhaps I'm simply more affected than most by translated lyrics, but I do find the extreme brevity of these one-verse Battiato songs truly moving. His economy of sound and words is stunning, and the way he juxtaposes moods is breathtaking.

In a move reminiscent of The Moody Blues, this whole shebang fades into a banshee choir of female voices which give way to the voices of *Apollo 11*'s Neil Armstrong and Buzz Aldrin at their most child-like and excited. As they delightedly scoot around the moon's surface, they speak aloud whatever comes into their minds, through telephone-quality microphones. Over this moving exchange, Battiato audaciously fades in J. S. Bach's 'Air on a G-String', here put through delays and given an otherworldly quality possibly thanks to being passed through (I would guess) a VCS3 synthesizer, or something very similar. I know what you're all thinking, punks. Sounds like clichéd doggy-do on paper, don't it? Well, babies, believe me, it's a truly moving thang!

'Anafase' begins as a Latin-Bowie-by-numbers exercise, again with the now typical Battiato one-verse'll-do-me approach to lyrics. Over lonely acoustic guitars, he sings a tune reminiscent of the Bach piece which has so recently faded:

I will go far away beyond the limits of the air,
Towards the immensity,
Above the astronauts,
Towards the interstellar stations.

It's 'Space Oddity' meets 'Starman' for a few moments; it fades out, and then fades back in, accompanied by military clatter-drums which bring us to a huge piano explosion. Then we're catapulted into that low-hum, *musique concrète*, ambient world which Battiato is clearly so fond of. Juddernaut synthesizers stereo-trip across the speakers looking for The Clangers, who are staying in their holes, thank you very much. A spaceship captained by Pac-Man lands and brings us the master tapes of Florian Fricke's briefest church-organ piece ever! Battiato kicks him clean into touch with further ponderous 'da-da-das' over pensive acoustic guitars, and then he's going, going, gone.

Fetus finishes with all the hope of a Utopian priest, as the three-minute-long, four-chord 'Mutazione' builds gently around deadly obvious strummed acoustic guitars. Again, he's a Latin Ziggy Stardust hovering above Planet Earth waiting for his moment. It's a post-Christian and Erich von Dänikenised, still-Christian worldview. But, just because that's ultimately the same as viewing a Picasso from behind a garden fence with a peephole drilled in it, this doesn't stop a truly visionary artist such as Franco Battiato from striking chest-beatingly uplifting possibilities in all but the most cynical of us. I rarely print lyrics in album reviews because they rarely have anything to say when removed from the music. But, once again, the translated words of 'Mutazione' are indisputably poetic and true:

Thousands of years of sleep have blocked me
in my cradle,
And now I return.
Something changed, I'm not aware of signals
of life,
And yet I'm aware of vibrations.
What will my eyes see next?
There will be stone bodies,
I hear them coming,
I hear them coming,
I hear them coming,
I hear them coming . . .

It's the classic lost daddy of the universe story which has permeated our patriarchal consciousness for so long. Of course, it would be nice to discover that all the world's problems were just caused by dad fucking off, and, naturally, it's highly romantic and unbelievable. But just 'cause it ain't true don't mean Battiato hasn't given it the kind of poetic truth which allows even this heathen to, at least temporarily, accept his metaphor and sigh along with everyone else.

Be-Bop Deluxe

Axe Victim

(Harvest, 1974)

SIDE ONE

1 Axe Victim (5.01)
2 Love Is Swift Arrows (4.05)
3 Jet Silver and the Dolls of Venus (3.57)
4 Third Floor Heaven (2.19)
5 Night Creatures (3.26)

SIDE TWO

1 Rocket Cathedrals (2.54)
2 Adventures in a Yorkshire Landscape (3.19)
3 Jets at Dawn (7.02)
4 No Trains to Heaven (6.24)
5 Darkness (L'Immoraliste) (3.10)

Although oft dismissed (even by its composer) as no more than a Johnny-come-lately at the burn-out, tail-end of the glam-rock scene, *Axe Victim* has edged towards rock'n'roll respectability in recent times. Indeed, Dylan Carlson's proto-doom band Earth even (mis)named their album, *Sunn Amps and Smashed Guitars*, in homage to a misheard lyric on the title track of this record, which eventually led to the rise of Greg Anderson and Stephen O'Malley's mighty Sunn O))) in the mid-1990s. That there was no lyric sheet included within the non-gatefold sleeve of most US editions of *Axe Victim* was probably down to Harvest Records not applying enough heft to their EMI distributors, for the lyrics were surely written large enough across the gatefold of the original British versh. However, rock'n'roll has always benefited from misunderstandings, and Bill Nelson's lyrics certainly increased in vibe when refracted through Herr Carlson's cracked, faulty, gunked-up ear trumpet. *Axe Victim* certainly ain't a faultless album by any stretch of the imagination, but whenever a combo lags so far behind its visionary frontman as did the rest of Be-Bop Deluxe (Mark I), be in no doubt, yooz gonna get some seriously be-jewelled barbarian crappola going down!

'We Hit the Road to Hull . . . Sad Amps and Smashed Guitars'

This Album of the Month was the mighty opening statement of virtuoso guitar execution by a young and poetic young man called Bill Nelson. For me, it was an example of the shamanic artist displaying his powers to the wider public, here given the role as gatekeepers of the first cosmic portal. However, on *Axe Victim* the moment had a particular poignancy because Bill Nelson was demonstrating his blazing magic to a demanding music business which would soon decide that, no, his cohorts with whom he had made his earliest moves were not about to make the trip with him. Indeed, despite Bill Nelson's propensity for overplaying, overachieving, being massively moved to every point of the compass and informed by the previous couple of years' Bowiefied 'rock'n'roll supermen' antics, *Axe Victim*'s deeply rock overtones were to become obscured – initially by the make-up, then perceived as a false start or hiccup by its own author – before being cacked out into the sewers (seemingly) forever along with the merely-achieving pub-rock and other assorted eclectic musical junk that so inspired the impending punk pogrom.

But, as the truth eventually flickers through, *Axe Victim*'s remarkably cohesive, post-post-*Ziggy* statement is now at the stage when its delightfully contiguous construction has begun to sound more like a Ray Davies/Pete Townshend-informed paean to the English 1960s than any 'fag-end of glam-rock', as the *Melody Maker* summarily dismissed all such music at that time. Furthermore, listening to June 1974's *Axe Victim* butt-to-butt with Television's Eno-produced Island Records demos, from December of that same year, it seems pertinent to suggest that two such fey, yet axe-wielding songwriters as Bill Nelson and Tom Verlaine were always gonna be more dependent than most, firstly, on the charming manner in which the musical ineptitude of their cohorts was captured on record and, secondly, on the devious manner in which their management/record companies would choose to make their precious muses available to the public. Moreover, as David Bowie's metaphor was so transparently informed by Lou Reed's Warholian period, to the point of scrawling VU eulogies on his LP sleeves, it seems unfair that all such subsequent offerings were to be dismissed as ersatz when Gentle Giant and their ilk were making a living from far more musical untruths. And even more especially when someone like Bill Nelson seemed perfectly aware of the tightrope between the portentous and the pretentious that he was treading.

That he was smooching a Hoyer Les Paul copy guitar on the back of the LP sleeve seems to sum up perfectly Nelson's grasp of the metaphor. What was ersatz and what was real? If he'd been playing the Hoyer all along the north-eastern seaboard, then got a Gibson in for the Mick Rock photo-sesh, wouldn't that have been pretentious? But he was honest enough to look inside and recognise that embracing the Hoyer was his strange and convoluted truth. Besides, 'pretentious' is a horribly over-used word, and one that doesn't stand up to much excavation when you talk about a barbarian concept such as the Rock. Half of the rock-est stars were nerds whose pretences were what launched them into a situation in which others could start to believe in them.[1]

Ziggy himself had showed us that glam could be as revelatory and Gnostic as Krautrock if we did but look below the poorly applied panstick.[2]

1 When Bonnie Prince Charlie was known as The Young Pretender, it did not mean that his claim to the English throne was in any way phoney; it meant instead that his case was genuine as 'a person who mounts a claim, as to a throne or title'. However, when The Platters' Tony Williams sang 'Yes, I'm the Great Pretender,' you can see from the context that the poor geek ain't gotta throne to go to and is deluding himself entirely.

2 It all comes down to how we interpret the Glam, I suppose. Wasn't it all best summed up when that shitty *Velvet Goldmine* flick came out a few years back? Me, I chortled with embarrassment at the pitifully shallow take on glam-rock revealed by whosoever was in charge of the soundtrack. Hail, babies, these non-heads were operating on twenty-twenty hindsight and still couldn't hack what had counted for real and what was just glow-in-the-dark, mince-alonga-Bolan. These revisionists had done their best to refit glam as a strictly gay phenomenon, when it had most evidently been nothing more than a Kelto-Viking brickies-in-lipstick kneez-up supreme with a coupla real fags in tow (Jobriath Running In – Please Pass). On the road to gay salvation, *Velvet Goldmine* had, therefore, missed such crucial excavations as the two Mick Ronson LPs (where the fuck was 'Billy Porter' and the excruciating phased-guitar mayhem of 'Angel Number 9'?); *Slade Alive* ('sequinned top hats and post-Plastic Ono Band hollering don't fit our revisionist straitjacket at all, dear'); Alex Harvey's entire teenage *Vambo* Utopian rock theatre ('yes, I know he sings Brel and has a harlequin guitarist but he's old and Glaswegian, darling'); the first six Kiss studio LPs (c'mon guys, where was Fowley's 'I Mean Like . . . Do Ya?' not to mention Gene Simmons' 'Great Expectations' being the greatest Mott the Hoople song never recorded by Ian Hunter); and watt abaht the later, Hunterless Mott LPs (*Drive On* being an almost perfectly executed late glam record); or Neil Merryweather's Space Rangers LPs

But thereby hangs a tale: you still can't be considered serious *and* clothe your rock unseriously, because the ugly interleck-chew-alls will have a tantrum and ignore you or deplore you, as the holier-than-thou, so-jazz members of Traffic did when they slagged off their 'too-flash' Island Records label-mates, Mott the Hoople, on the album *The Low Spark of High Heeled Boys*. Yup, if yooz pretty, glamorous or like dressing up, there's nothing down for you. Unless yooz Richey Manic, and then you have to carve '4 Real' in your arm and disappear at the mystical portals (Aust Services) between heaven and hell (England and Wales, in whichever order you so choose). Even the self-styled Dionysian Jim Morrison was forced to ugly out later on in his career in an effort to fit in somewhere; and if Patti Smith hadn't had the muzzy, she'd have been shat on, fer sure.

(when it comes to mawkish but poetically truthful Hunteresque songs about writing songs, can Merryweather's 'The Groove' ever be topped?); or even Sweet's magnificent greed in wishing simultaneously to straddle Chinnichap and chinning the audience (surely their lyric on 'Sweet FA' is the summit of all glam – who could possibly better: 'If she don't spread/I'm gonna bust her head'?).[3] All the aforementioned are contemporary ball-busters that woulda blazed on that *Velvet Goldmine* soundtrack and lifted it considerably, had any genuine motherfucker found time to trawl their record collections beyond the easy-find CD re-ishes. And it ain't just me – every sucker I know had the same complaints.

3 Excuse the footnote-within-a-footnote, but what about Sweet's 1974 *Sweet Fanny Adams* LP finishing with a boogie-woogie track called 'AC/DC' about a bisexual girlfriend? Malcolm and Angus Young have always been coy about the roots of their band's name, and are known to have been glam-rockers in the group's earliest inception. As Malcolm's first band had been called The Velvet Underground (sic) and fifteen-year-old Angus had worked as a printer at the porn magazine *Ribald*, isn't it coherent to suggest that they – dwelling as they did as Aussie teens fixated with the sleazy underbelly of British and American culture – chose to take their name from this Sweet track, rather than (as they ingenuously asserted in their biography *AC/DC: The Definitive History*) Angus' dubious and deeply boring alternative claim: 'My sister Margaret suggested something she'd seen on the back of a vacuum cleaner: AC/DC. It had something to do with electricity . . .'. Evidence is strong, just from my collection of American *Cream* magazines, that glam-rock bands such as The Sweet were perceived abroad as being no less credible than any other. It's for precisely this reason that The Stooges were happy to support Slade on their 1974 US tour, and why Kiss' Ace Frehley had no problem having a solo hit with a cover of Hello's 'Back in the New York Groove'. Glam was always so deeply rooted in heavy rock that it never coulda got away with being truly queer, play-queer being quite close enough for most of these proto-Cro-Magnauts.

'Paintings and Songs That I'd Done in a Day'

All of which brings us to why Bill Nelson's *Axe Victim* was such a conundrum at the time and still, today, mystifies almost everyone. Here was a guitar-hero guy from up north on his first LP, presumptuous/naïve enough to be quoting Cocteau in untranslated French and confident enough to be writing about his beloved Yorkshire hills ('Adventures in a Yorkshire Landscape') rather than imagining losing his cherished six-string razor on the way to Memphis. Like the Zig, Bill was happy dressing like a total nance and crediting himself as 'William Nelson', all the time his whole trip being backed up by lead-booted troglodytes with clothes grants off the local council. And, like Ian Hunter, David Bowie and Kiss, the Bill Nelson of *Axe Victim* was fascinated by the process of the song and the show, and that mysterious area in-between.

Sure, Nelson's muse was mightily 'affected' by David Bowie, but this angular harlequin was more the Ziggy Stardust character than Bowie himself. For a start, boy, could he play guitar! Much as I worship Mickey the Ronce's tween-time, wah-wah Les Paul, there's so much truly heart-rending (and often inappropriate) Nelsonic guitar soloing going down on *Axe Victim* that he must only be described herein as a Gonzoid Virtuoso. If you are hearing this album for the first time, don't speak to anyone as it goes down; let it all cascade over your shoulders. Granted, his lyrics lag far behind his musical dexterity, but unless William Nelson had reduced his vocals merely to moaning, screeching and belching, there weren't no words the equal of this boy's laughably over-reaching muse. Indeed, the first time I heard this offering, I did just that – laughed and laughed, outraged at Nelson's shamelessness and inspired by his will to power. And, all throughout the period in which he was jamming good with Weird and Gilly, they were probably to be found legless in the back of the Transit, without even 'a beer-light to guide them'.

The evidence of all this is, of course, that Nelson split this band just one year later in the middle of a Cockney Rebel tour-support and appropriated half of Steve Harley's band from under the Psychomodo's very inward-looking gaze. When that didn't work out, Nelson regrouped with two monster session guys and blasted out the manic euphoria of *Futurama*, a second LP which is patchy but (unsurprisingly) over-reaching and contains probably

Nelson's finest ever number, 'Swansong' – a glam slam that still makes me cry every time I hear it. In true Nelson form, he glam/hams it up on the back sleeve of *Futurama*, too, dedicating the whole oeuvre to 'The Muse in the Moon' and appearing as a monochrome harlequin, so very, very madly *into it* that his two new cohorts are having to physically restrain him!

But, I state, with great dollops of hindsight, that it is on *Axe Victim* that Nelson really nailed what he was trying to say, even if he would most likely disagree. Faust referred to it as 'the time between concept and reality', and Lou Reed nailed it more poetically with the words: 'Between thought and expression lies a lifetime.' Well, that gulf is never so beautiful as on the kind of rock'n'roll which yearns to be far more than it can ever really reach. Which is why *Axe Victim* is, in its partly bungled, partly punk, partly overly zealous get-outta-Yorkshire earnestness, far more real and coherent and still more sustainingly pertinent to the twenty-first century than all of the eloquent Be-Bop Deluxe LPs that Bill would subsequently record with technically greater musicians.

Axe Victim's striving, *ernie-ernie-ernie*, dying-seagull guitar overkill and more-than-occasional overly twee, self-obsessed lyrical preciousness are its inner strengths because, although it *was* informed by *Ziggy Stardust*, it was just too excited to give a damn about hiding the fact. And what would we really prefer? Sure, at the time Blue Cheer must have sounded like Jimi Hendrix had just sneezed a big greenie across the California faultline. But Leigh Stephens' artless and uncontrollable Technicolor yawns are certainly far more pertinent to the twenty-first century than anything Hendrix laid upon us. And who wants Cream's oh-so-delicate 'Sunshine of Your Love' when you can hear it refracted through Iron Butterfly's foggy lens on 'In-A-Gadda-Da-Vida' and then again (and even more sludge-trudged) for Sabbath's 'Lord of This World'? *Axe Victim* makes me wanna hear the original pre-EMI demos complete with (inevitably) toe-curlingly inept bass mistakes, *and* rip the suckers off wholesale for my new record.

Making Love in Strange Autos

Axe Victim kicks off with the title track, armed with the kind of 'Snowblind', stop–start tempo changes and super-indulgent guitar gratuities that immediately sort out the men from the supermen. The scene is set up perfectly when Bill sings to us:

You came to watch the band,
To see us play our parts,
We hoped you'd lend an ear,
You hoped we'd dress like tarts.

Fairy nuff, Mr Nelson; I think we all know precisely where we stand from that pair of couplets. Especially as Bill's guitar frenziedly (and polyrhythmically) punctuates every dramatic lyrical assertion with the kind of teenage girl, 'hearts drawn above every "I"' (and sideways-on email smileys) effusiveness that set him up as an amphetamine Richard Clayderman of the guitar. Indeed, each of *Axe Victim*'s songs is at least ninety seconds longer than necessary thanks to the sheer heart-attack obsessiveness of the guitar soloing, and this is precisely what makes the album so special – that is, once you've allowed the artist his peculiarly solipsistic metaphor.

'Love Is Swift Arrows' follows on at a reckless, acoustic-driven pace, catchy as a motherfucker and strewn with more of the same garrulous, call-and-answer from Nelson's guitar and gob. It's like the blues just got sucked into Toni Visconti's mind and got belched out, be-sequinned, as Edgar Winter's unlikely *They Only Come Out at Night* LP cover, Nelson's words answered by his guitar volleys thus:

Room in the east invested with meaning (ernie-ernie-diddler-diddler),
Open to none but the strange and the wild (stupidly explosive overachieving guitar crash),
Sunset encounters with destiny's chances (guitar impersonating a 737),
Envelopes marked for the personal life (guitar impersonating a 747).

As I declared earlier, *Axe Victim*'s greatest strength is in Side One's contiguous construction, in which each song seamlessly segues into the next, like some Moody Blues cross-faded eternal flow, and gives a tremendous eloquence to the otherwise charmingly bozo assertions coming out of Sweet William's mush.

'Jet Silver and the Dolls of Venus' has a delightfully expansive, harmonically appealing, descending chorus, but it's ultimately the Peter Pan lyrics that most capture the listener, especially the bit where we can 'See the town, in midnight eiderdown/ Wrapped in your dressing gown.'

'Third Floor Heaven' is the only song on the record in which Nelson steps outside what he knows and tries to walk on the wild side. Luckily, he's smart enough to make no bones about its being a rip, and just cops 'Sweet Jane' and 'Queen Bitch' in much the same way that Michael Bruce did for Alice Cooper's 'Be My Lover' on the *Killer* LP. Even stranger is the fact that this was still a time when a homosexual could be referred to in a rock'n'roll song as 'one of those'!

Side One closes with the Ziggy-in-Wakefield, proto-goth of 'Night Creatures', in which Billy Boy lists a whole string of Soho wannabes stuck under the arches of the Leeds–London mainline and desperate to hitch out of there, down the A1 to London.

Side Two opens with a real tell-tale glitch – the only Be-Bop Deluxe song not written by the Nelse. And what a noise 'Rocket Cathedrals' turns out to be! Written and sung by soon-to-be-given-the-push bass player Rob Bryan, it's a space-boogie that successfully crosses 'Silver Machine' with the imagery of the then-recent 'Rocket Man'. The crash, bang, wallop lyrics may be highly at odds with Nelson's iron butterfly approach, but they make for a superb bit of stomp-athon relief, and the bit about 'sinking a bottle of gin' as an antidote to 'thinking about the state I'm in' is really funny after the previous side's overly precious allusions.

But, with the blunderbuss having shot its wad, it's back to form for the rest of Side Two, which is entirely the property of Herr Nelson. Coming, as he did, from Wakefield, a place 'where wakes or festivals take place', it was probably Bill Nelson's destiny to eulogise his area in an overly sentimental manner. So it well befits 'Adventures in a Yorkshire Landscape' to begin as a precious, acoustic, 6/8, Spiders-from-Mars-y take on Rodgers and Hammerstein's 'My Favourite Things', here transplanted to the 'Buildings pulled down' and the 'Pylons that crack/With singing sad wires to council-house mystics.' Like Krautrock in the mid-'70s, only very provincial musicians would have dared lay a phased guitar solo on their public. But, here, Nelson veers from erudite stratospherical euphoria to youth-club Les Paul copy cliché and back without missing a beat, in much the same way that The Guess Who's mainman, Burton Cummings, could do with his keyboard playing, and get away with it (probably only because he was both Canadian and a bozo Dionysus in the Morrison tradition). But, then again, you can get twenty minutes into some truly far-out Les Rallizes Dénudés burn-up and Mizutani will do exactly the same thing, pulling out a cliché *and* pulling it off purely because no other sucker ever dared commit such a travesty on record.

Starting in an English country garden, complete with birdsong, the seven-minute-long 'Jets at Dawn' is truly lovely and simultaneously annoying (almost as precious as

Jon Anderson) and conjures up the ubiquitous TV theme from 'White Horses'. But once you allow the 'young thing' his metaphor, 'Jets at Dawn' becomes a uniquely open-eyed, open-mouthed delight, until – hail, English motherfuckers – you wanna salute the Union Flag like those damned shameless Yankees do, without stint or moderation.

'No Trains to Heaven' is gonzoid to the extreme, with a kind of off-kilter Bang/Edgar Broughton riff that is pure 1970. Six minutes of dubious harmonic guitar riffs and spindly, dual-boogie sputter and spit as a clichéd lyric kicks in about 'burning the prisons in which your children live'. Uncomfortable call-and-answer vocals follow the dumb-ass riff, and the shameless William vocally scats, *Made in Japan*-style, along to his own guitar solo.

But it's the final song, 'Darkness', with its subtitle, 'L'Immoraliste', that really nails the gonzo medal to the gatepost. I can't blame the raggedy-ass backing band for this winner as the performance is Bill's and Bill's alone – well, along with a norkestra or three. Cringe you may for the first coupla listens to words such as 'Darkness, you are my true love,' especially as the tune is deffo ripped off from Neil Sedaka's 'Solitaire'. And when Bill proclaims, 'Darkness, you're with me most every night,' you gots to wonder what the nights are like when he manages to banish her. I wanna be there! I wanna be there! And yet, even here, at his closest moment to taking a massive Brechtian Brel-y flop off the nearest bridge, it still fucking works! Am I the most compassionate dupe alive or is this a really beautiful song? I think the latter. This little jewel sums up goth in a nutshell and five years before the phenomenon was named. The Hollywood choirs of angels, the Gallic subtitle, the detectable northern accent, the portentous key changes, the French horn, the stops and starts, it all works and shows that it is (as Nelson shamelessly proclaims) 'no fashionable disguise'. Gimme William Nelson on this record, because he approaches humanity in a disarming and delightedly unnerving manner; add to all of this the classic Mick Rock photography, the Gibson 335-done-up-as-a-skull artwork, the French quotes from Cocteau and the subtitle 'Some rock'n'roll madness from Be-Bop Deluxe', and yooz got a timeless classic just waiting to be sung back to life, children. To William Nelson and his slow riders of the Wake Field, please raise your overflowing cup . . . and sup!

Black Sabbath

Behind the Wall of Spock

(Seidr, 2003)

DISC 1

1 Killing Yourself to Live (6.41)
2 Hole in the Sky (4.31)
3 Snowblind (6.40)
4 Symptom of the Universe (4.40)
5 War Pigs (8.26)
6 Megalomania (11.00)
7 Sabbra Caddabra (5.19)
8 Jam/Guitar Solo (7.52)
9 Drum Solo/Jam (6.07)
10 Supernaut (2.11)
11 Iron Man (6.16)

DISC 2

1 Orchid/Rock'n'roll Doctor/Don't Start (Too Late) (8.45)
2 Black Sabbath (6.45)
3 Spiral Architect (5.14)
4 Embryo/Children of the Grave (6.01)
5 Paranoid (3.03)

For those of you who always felt that *Live at Last* was too little too late, here's a chance to dig Sabbath at their very best on this unofficial release. It boasts the best album title ever and should be scoffed up by anyone with a CD player.

Blabbath

He loves to talk inanely, does Ozzy Osbourne, but I wouldn't have it any other way. As it's always been my assertion that June 1975's *Sabotage* is the most rounded, finished, complete statement made by Black Sabbath, this double live CD couldn't really come from a better period, and Ozzy gassing just makes for a better show. Recorded at New Jersey's Asbury Park Convention Hall just before the release of that album, we get the best of every world. Yes, the preceding *Sabbath Bloody Sabbath* was their worst album of the main sequence of six, but it was still a stupendous statement from everybody's favourite Wodenists, marred only by one too many cack-handed Ionni-isms (yes, 'Fluff' yer bastard!). That apart, 'Supertzar' predicted Kiss' mighty (and mightily ignored) *The Elder* by over half a decade and entirely reshaped the sound of those other ham-fisted cosmicians, Hawkwind, who would swoop on the *Sabbath Bloody Sabbath* sound and assault-and-batter it in *Warrior on the Edge of Time* (via false starts during *Hall of the Mountain Grill*) to create a Goths/Vandals/Huns-at-the-gates-of-Rome signature that really ain't even been approached since. Furthermore, these live versions manage to sod off all the arrangement detritus without losing the essential Mellotronia, which probably comes care of some unsung crew member, retaining all the make-you-cry-isms and defiantly in-your-face, too-uncool-to-be-uncoolisms that only The Troggs and The Seeds coulda got away with, had they ever had the technical back-up of '70s technology, and which The Moody Blues shoulda done more with (being equally Midlands but possibly too genuinely enlightened – and too democratic – to make real).

There's no real point in giving you the whole double CD to wade through, as it's a given you're right now on the way to score this sucker. Besides, whoever needed 'Orchid' or 'Embryo' besides Iommi's grandma?

'I've Watched the Dogs of War Enjoying Their Feast/I've Seen the Western World Go Down in the East'

So, 'Supertzar' provides the fanfare intro tape, and comes on very *A Clockwork Orange* when played in a massive concert hall. Man, it's inspiring me: straight after this review, I gots to listen to Edgar Froese's 'Metropolis' from the *Ages* double LP. Then I shall follow it up with Kiss' majestic 'Under the Rose'! Man, it really musta been great to get rid of Peter Criss for a couple of albums! Even Eric Carr's make-up was better! Anyway, talking of better drumming, it should also be noted that Bill Ward's throwing-Bibles-at-the-sofa drum fills sound fuck-off on this recording. We love you!

'Killing Yourself to Live' is monstrous and the subterranean bass is so much better without any support whatsoever, so the descending chord solo actually becomes the song 'N.I.B'. I guess the best bands all descend into a kind of Odinist, ur-version of themselves right in the middle of their trip. The Five did it, as did The Doors, the Pistols, The Clash and The Stooges, so it's righteous that Sabbath do, too. We love you! It even brings the weirder bits out, like: 'I'm telling you believe in me/Nobody else will tell you.' And that Zappa-esque vocal-following-guitar riff is always a Juicy Luicyan shock (same Vertigo spiral label, all you vinyl nerds) and the laugh is up there with Ian Hunter and the Gillan cackle at the end of 'Speed King'. Oh, then there's that brilliant, mysterious 'I don't know but I've been told' melody with the lyric about how 'The colours of my life are all different somehow/Little boy blue's a big girl now.'

'Little boy blue' now being a big girl still shocks in the context of Sabbath's canon of the law. Indeed, it's like finding out your Viking sons have been practising seidr so you gots to kill them, like really happened in the eleventh century. Spookeh!

'We love you!' shouts the Oz. It's the first of thirteen thousand such proclamations on this record. 'This is off our new album, sorry it's been delayed; you probably don't know it. Listen, you might like it.' OK, you passed the audition, guy, we paid already. He might have recorded it already, but Ozzy surely ain't got the lyrics to 'Hole in the Sky' in his head for this show. In typical Gillan manner, we get repeated first verses and even flat-as-flat-fluffs but it's done with such braying, Roger Chapman heathen-grace that it just doesn't matter. In fact, you get the impression he repeats 'I'm living free because the rent's never due' just because he's riffing on it and thinking how very Oz it is. Moreover, the lyric from 'Hole in the Sky' hits you even harder today than it did in the '70s: 'I'm looking through a hole in the sky/I'm seeing nowhere through the eyes of a lie.'

Man, doesn't that just about sum it all up? I know if I see any more BBC news shots of RAF Brize Norton with nothing going on in the background, I'll scream the place down. (We love you!) However, if there's one thing this album does, it is to reinforce how great most of the Sabbath lyrics are, and how pertinent they have been throughout my lifetime. Most of them were written by Geezer Butler, whom Tony Iommi had always referred to as 'the Keltic Poet'. Forget the Tap context, babies, it's my theory that said with a Brummie accent (which is after all just an industrialised Danish accent[1]), he become Gazer Butler – as in star-gazer, got me?

1 This point is further enforced by the Midland pronunciation of the 'street' as 'straight', which is what it was to the Saxons and Vikings anyway (or should that be 'any road'?).

I've seen the stars disappear in the sun,
The shooting's easy if you've got the right gun,
And even though I'm sitting waiting for Mars,
I don't believe there's any future in cars.

C'mon, babs, a statement like that last line is realistic genius (We love you!) and poetic genius wrapped up in one, while the bit about it being easy shooting when you've got the right gun just about sums up the smug arrogance of Rumsfeld and co. (We love you!) without even attempting to make sense.

Smoke It

'Snowblind' is almost as beautiful and death's-bed as it is on *Volume 4*, but the Oz is too happy and even sneaks an 'I love you!' in the aside before Iommi's guitar is consumed by Hel's fleshy upper half. Shit, Oz sneaks another 'We love you!' in and starts a lower skeletal half-boogie-ing (can you do that?). We love you! This guy means it, however throwaway it is; it's oozing out of his every pore. He finishes with a climactic 'Yeah!', as if death is life (which of course it is).

Ozzy introduces the album like he's at Tamworth Youth Club and it's the make or break of the group. 'Go!' says Ozzy, like a dead ringer for Reg Presley. 'Symptom of the Universe' is perfection, complete with flat 'yeahs'. Dammit, this is a great album. Straight into 'War Pigs', and Ozzy has them clapping. Same Ozzy every night and it's heavy as they can sound, so you don't even miss the air-raid siren (which Amon Düül II woulda got together on tape, as would Hawkwind, which only serves to remind us of the 'that'll-do' power-trio, ur-nature of Sabbath: you-need-no-more is what they show us here). After the instrumental section, more inappropriate clapping at the behest of John Osbourne – he's a clapping, We-love-you-ing, behemoth from Hel. 'We're gonna do another off our new album . . . Plug . . .', he announces. Yup, he's a smooth bastard is our John. Even at pre-arena stage, he's a shameless market trader.

Watching Eyes of Celluloid Tell You How to Live

Stripped of its Renaissance/Gentle Giant acousto-chintz, the live version of 'Spiral Architect' really starts to move me. I'd always had a soft spot for it, but secretly suspected (We love you!) that it was me just being a soft-arse. Of course, Sabbath fans at school and college were always way too insular and emotionally autistic to admit that their fave band could stick their hooves the wrong side of sentimental – not batting a give-away eyelid even when Ozzy struggled through '(I'm going through) Changes' on *Volume 4*, now how dutiful is that? Oz even shamelessly substitutes 'audience' for 'memories' in the second verse:

Of all the things I value most in life,
I see my audience and feel their warmth,
And know that they are good,
You know that I should.

U know watt? I never watched *The Osbournes*, so there might be a whole crowd of you reading this going, 'What's Cope on this week?' All I can say is, yes (We love you!), the Oz is a clueless knobshiner with killdozer kids, but this Skellig Michael hermit/Viking ain't complaining one bit. Ozness ain't tarnished his inverted cross in this household because that programme never got watched. Sorry to offer that cop-out aside, but fuck you (We love you!) if you don't believe me. Besides, 'Symptom of the Universe' is next, so the riff will drown out whatever you yell at me.

Take me through the centuries to supersonic years,
Electrifying enemy is drowning in his tears,
All I have to give you is a love that never dies,
The symptom of the universe is written in your eyes.

Even the Saxon cavalry rhythms at the end sound better than the studio album, dammit. Is this more of the Scando-Germanic Midlander thing? I know the Vikings were a sea people, but their poems always alluded to hooved animals, with their ships being 'horses of the breakers' and 'ocean-striding bisons' and 'horse of the lobsters' heath' and 'fjord elks'. Even a flotilla of ships was poetically named 'a fleet of the otter's world'. And so, just as we're brought up to believe that the Vikings merely blundered upon the monastery at Lindisfarne, rather than sitting in mighty Trelleborg for months seething at those shaven, ingrown cop-outs with all their cloistered wealth, then consciously blasting across the Baltic with tonsured death on their minds, we tend to believe that Sabbath, too, just kinda shambled upon their trip by reading a coupla Dennis Wheatleys after getting some late-night Hammer Horror down them as they're drunkenly necking Wednesbury curry take-aways of a Friday night. But somehow I think we need a bitovva rethink. I'm talking intuitive genius, of course, 'cause these weren't no educated types – but does it matter when you got Wednesbury primary schools with names like Noose Lane Juniors?

I think a fairly hefty *not*!

Next up is 'War Pigs', with its legendary clap-along-a-Sabs: 'Generals gathered in their masses (We love you!)/Just like witches at black masses.' The tragedy of this lyric is just how on the case it is. And all those evil minds that plot destruction really are sorcerers of death's construction. And, in the oilfields, where the bodies are burning, the war machine keeps turning. Britain is contributing to the death and hatred of mankind by further poisoning their already brainwashed minds (We love you!) . . . Oh Lord, yeah! I have seen the many faces of the gods, and I call them all rock'n'roll!

'Megalomania' is just behemothian on this record, like Joy Division meets Hawkwind, and consumes both of those bands, despite Gazer's accidentally reading a psychology magazine article while he was in the doctor's waiting room renewing his Junior Aspirin prescription. How long is this thing? It must be two hours at least. And then 'Sabbra Caddabra' is as lyrically bereft as a Sabbath love song should really be: gleeful and life-affirming and huge. If this was one of those southern boogie-woogie bands, we'd be gagging, but they got the Anglo-Scando-Germanic so running, nay coursing through their veins they're about as American as a Ford Consul Capri. This song could be on *Volume IV*, played like this. It only takes one listen to this version to remind me what I hate about so much of *Sabbath Ruddy Sabbath*, and it's the gods' damn production. Sabbath ain't doing anything different; it's that sumptuous swamp they've hosed over everything. Dry the fucker up and I guarantee we'd play it as much as the other five.

Then we come to the big climb, Max (We love you!). Keep the drum solo on, by the way. Give it some *hommer*. It's brief, too, before a 'Children of the Grave'-style Saxon cavalry jam starts up. Again, it's an Iommi everysolo from bagpipe theme tune to obliterati seethe-werk via fairly believable Keltiberian Beltane Awakening. U know me and I don't give a dry-wank about authenticity, so this soup doggy dog must be the pig's business or it'd be off the turntable next to *Argus* (great sleeve though, eh?).

Babies, I finished this review. I can't just crash through descriptions of Sabbath songs like this. What's the evidence that it's a great album? Well, I've played it shit-loads and it even kept me buoyant in those dark days of Rumsfeld and co. Have a listen and tell me that finishing with 'Children of the Grave' and 'Paranoid' ain't the best finish to a (Nunnofishal) live double LP evvah!

We love you!

Blue Öyster Cult

In Your Dreams or In My Hole

(*In Your Dreams or In My Hole*, or *Ten Cuts from the Golden Age of Leather*, was culled from the first three Blue Öyster Cult LPs in the late summer of 2005. It has never been released)

1 Patti Smith Invocation
2 Transmaniacon MC (3.21) (from *Blue Öyster Cult*)
3 Before the Kiss, a Redcap (4.59) (from *Blue Öyster Cult*)
4 Screams (3.10) (from *Blue Öyster Cult*)
5 Subhuman (4.39) (from *Secret Treaties*)
6 Hot Rails to Hell (5.12) (from *Tyranny and Mutation*)
7 ME 262 (4.48) (from *Secret Treaties*)
8 O.D.'d on Life Itself (4.47) (from *Tyranny and Mutation*)
9 The Red and The Black (4.24) (from *Tyranny and Mutation*)
10 Workshop of the Telescopes (4.01) (from *Blue Öyster Cult*)
11 Flaming Telepaths (5.20) (from *Secret Treaties*)

This forty-four-minute compilation was created in order to ease egression into BÖC's obscure and now shadowy trip. Unfortunately, the 1976 international hit '(Don't Fear) The Reaper', and the subsequent release of far too many catch-all, bland-out albums on into the 1980s, has left the prospective BÖC fan mouth agape and listless at the record-store checkout. So forget the multiple compilations, the 'best ofs', the rip-offs, etc., and please give this short compilation just three-quarters of an hour of your time.

The Patti Smith invocation which opens the album was snipped from the beginning of the Cult's 'The Revenge of Vera Gemini', which was itself based on Smith's poem 'Vera Gemini' and was released on the band's *Agents of Fortune* album.

That Hideous Strength

Would you be intrigued by five

contrary motherfuckers spewing out a hi-amped, post-Elevators conspiracist blues whose unrestrained debut LP opened with a 'Born to Be Wild'-alike biker-rock anthem ('Transmaniacon MC') with Roky Erickson's Bleib Alien-gone-to-hell lyrics that imagined the movements of the Hell's Angels in those final hours just prior to their brutal, jackboot policing of The Rolling Stones' Altamont fiasco? Yeah, me too . . . And how about if the second track of that same debut LP was a fetishist's anthem named 'I'm on the Lamb But I Ain't No Sheep', whose lyrics celebrated the dubious antics of the Canadian Mounties and what they did with their whips in their spare time? Yup, me three. And just suppose that same rock'n'roll band had all opted for the Jimbo Morrison-fronting-Steppenwolf regulation look (black leather'n'shades, each one), except for a Jerry Garcia-styled, all white-clad guru who opted for the enlightened name of Buck Dharma? Sounds amazing, don't it, motherfuckers? Even more amazing when you notice that the singer had shamelessly appropriated Jagger's '69 dog-collar look twelve months *after* Iggy. And what if all the song titles were just as intriguing as the aforementioned? In other words, all so fucking obvious or so damned cryptic that merely reading them altogether on an LP sleeve caused them to occupy in your head the larger place and further psychedelicised your already melted plastic brain? And wouldn't all this be somehow even more intriguing if the major lyric writer was perceptive enough to have flexed his inner moron with catchy-bastard press quotes such as: 'I like to use naïve, densely stupid terms' (Sandy Pearlman)?

Moreover, if that same band of outlaws had had Patti Smith as their muse and co-songwriter, along with a whole slew of other intellectual rock'n'roll and sci-fi scribes (Michael Moorcock, Richard Meltzer, Jim Carroll, Helen Wheels . . .) waiting at their beck and call, could these itinerant motherfuckers have really failed? Add to all this the fact that their super-astute producer/sometime lyricist Sandy Pearlman (again) was canny enough to admit that with BÖC he was attempting to meld Alice Cooper's *Killer* with Black Sabbath's *Master of Reality*, and you have a pre-punk rock'n'roll band hip enough to have had The Clash's Mick Jones successfully petition the rest of his band to have Pearlman produce *Give 'Em Enough Rope*. And yet BÖC's current place in the rock'n'roll pantheon is right down the rock'n'roll pan.

Why? Because, brothers and

sisters, Blue Öyster Cult started something they couldn't finish. You start out as hot as this bunch claimed to be, and yooz destined either to explode by the third album amidst drug problems and suicides, hit the Number One spot with every release – bang, bang, bang – or you, with your 'crypto-intellectual lyrics', as some contemporary rock critics deemed them, ain't the real deal, ain't really hard, West Coast bikers at all, ain't really occultists, just fairly heavy readers. So you persist for a further twenty-odd years with ever-increasing amounts of record company tinkering, gradually substituting Nuremberg Rally-sized shows at aircraft hangars for local clubs as your rock'n'roll temple. Unfortunately for both we the audience and the Cult themselves, the latter course was the path they chose, or rather that which fate chose for them.

It ain't that there wasn't mighty music contained somewhere within the grooves of most early BÖC records, it's just that they had no frontman of note, and far too little charisma and stage presence between them (my wife saw them three times and said they were faceless), too many contributing songwriters to maintain the focus of their metaphor (which the musicians themselves didn't have a clear enough grasp of) and not enough genuine weight within their own ranks to tell said contributors to fuck off occasionally. Oh yeah, and at a time (1972–76) when the double live LP was god, the Cult's *On Your Feet or On Your Knees* was rotten to the core. I know, because I bought it for the title and sleeve alone, and then howled in protest any time anyone sang their praises. 'Those guys are the pits,' I'd shriek, and never listened again until my memory banks had been well and truly erased.[1]

And another fucking thing: speaking from personal experience, when you dress your sleeve with such mysterious symbols and sing songs of the kind that the Cult were laying on their audience, you betcha sorry ass you gots to know what the fuck it's all about, or all those Richard Meltzer and Patti Smith lyric contributions are gonna get short shrift from the journalists who ain't in on the deal. Lester Bangs especially had it in for the Cult. 'It was only inevitable that

1 In order to re-acquaint myself with *On Your Feet or On Your Knees* for the writing of this article, I was determined to cop a double-vinyl example like my first copy. Sure enough, I put the thing on and it all happened again. Except for flashes of genuine brilliance, there's still nothing down for this thirty/seventy heap of crap.

groups like Blue Öyster Cult would come along, singing in jive chic about dehumanization while unconsciously fulfilling their own prophecy albeit muddled by performing as nothing more than robots whose buttons were pushed by their producers,'[2] he wrote. Bangs was wrong about the musicians being true puppets because the Cult's inner circle consisted of such old friends that all were well used to Sandy's in-jokes and lyrical wordplay. Besides, who could never have failed to make the connection that they were all Pearlman's oyster boys? Especially when Pearlman's lyric for 'Subhuman' includes the line: 'Oyster boys are swimming for me.'

However, the band members themselves didn't make the accusations of puppetry any easier with such 'search me' comments as drummer Albert Bouchard's disingenuous: 'Sandy might have believed in some of our image . . . the rest of us didn't know enough to believe in all that voodoo and whatnot.'[3] You could've asked him then, mate, rather than just hoping it was all kosher and above board. But ain't that always the way with musos? I mean, if Slash didn't say nothing to Axl about the racist lyrics to 'One in a Million' bothering his own Afro-American sensibilities, maybe Albert the drummer was genuinely too intimidated to ask Mr High Falutin' Pearlman for fear of sounding like a dummy. Besides, such was the hype and wall of secrecy around the Cult that it's personally taken me twenty-five years to komprennay where they was a-coming from.

It's for all these reasons mentioned above that I should now ask heavy Cultists to (please) accept that I've felt duty-bound to appropriate any scrap of evidence from anywhere in the band's early career in order to further the greater BÖC cause (which will, in the long run, be a great result for rock'n'roll). That Blue Öyster Cult never achieved a wholly great LP should hardly preclude our investigating, excavating and unlocking the greatness from within the grooves of that main sequence of patchy bastard LPs (offsprings all of post-Altamont hard-rock), namely the ten-inch mini-album *In My Mouth or On the Ground*, plus *Blue Öyster Cult*; *Tyranny and Mutation*; *Secret Treaties*; and *On Your Feet or On Your Knees*. Besides, I've never personally had a problem with artistic inconsistency, being prone to it myself at times. Unfortunately, while Blue Öyster Cult certainly sustained

2 Lester Bangs, 'Kraftwerkfeature', *Creem* magazine, September 1975.

3 Wayne Jancik and Tad Lathrop, *Cult Rockers* (Simon & Schuster, 1995).

their trip for several years, they ultimately snatched defeat from the jaws of victory simply because the blood-letting possibilities of the band's massive canine overbite were overwhelmed by the psychic plaque and icky residue of their ever-increasing eclecticism.

'I'm After Rebellion . . . I'll Settle for Lies'

But who were these be-leathered men, and their strangely monikered, white-clad guitar guru? Perhaps this *In Your Dreams or In My Hole* compilation will work best as an introduction if y'all just listen in, while I lay upon ya some hefty historical/chronological fax. Indeed, a quick perusal of their convoluted pre-history soon reveals that Blue Öyster Cult began in crisis, endured in crisis and celebrated crisis, with a side order of . . . crisis.

In 1970, after the unexpected success of Black Sabbath's first two LPs had given the incredulous American music industry apoplexy, Columbia Records' A&R man and all-purpose folk-music expert Murray Krugman let it be known to his *Crawdaddy* magazine rock writer/lyricist friend Samuel 'Sandy' Pearlman that Columbia was on the look-out for a home-grown Sabbath equivalent. Claiming to have the very band they required, Pearlman convinced Krugman to give him demo time at Columbia's own studios. What Pearlman didn't tell Murray Krugman was that his band, known as the Stalk-Forrest Group, was on the verge of splitting up after three fruitless years of courting Elektra Records, where they had made an unreleased LP and a single ('What Is Quicksand?' b/w 'Arthur Comics') that had never got beyond its initial two hundred radio promo copies. Neither did Pearlman tell Krugman that the Stalk-Forrest Group had only reluctantly changed their name from their preferred original title, Soft White Underbelly, after a gig so disastrous that carrying on in that guise would have left them without promoters. Furthermore, Pearlman was careful to make no mention of the fact that Elektra's executives had signed the otherwise imageless band only thanks to singer Les Braunstein's striking visual similarity to Jim Morrison. Indeed, Elektra had dumped the band when Braunstein had unexpectedly quit, leaving everyone concerned rudderless and unable to promote their album without the vocalist who had sung its songs.

However, with Murray Krugman's insider information resounding in his head, Sandy Pearlman convinced his lyricist/cohort Richard Meltzer and the other members of Stalk-Forrest

Group/Soft White Underbelly to pull together to give it one last try and bring Columbia Records what the label required. OK, you know what's gonna happen, but this is the Blue Öyster Cult story, and with these guys it ain't gonna have any kind of ending until we hit several seams of crisis. So, first, we gots to excavate even further into the murky depths of the late 1960s.

Rue d'Awakening

Soft White Underbelly had originally been formed on Long Island, in 1967, as a free-form psychedelic band, after two Stoney Brook College students, Richard Meltzer and Samuel 'Sandy' Pearlman, hooked up with a group of rock'n'roll musicians who lived in a large house near the college campus. Pearlman it was who'd suggested they call themselves Soft White Underbelly, and Pearlman again who'd introduced Richard Meltzer as lead vocalist and main songwriter. After years of playing seemingly endless cover versions of Beatles, Temptations, Beach Boys and Rolling Stones songs that were the expected repertoire in bars around Long Island, drummer Albert Bouchard and his guitarist friends Donald Roeser and Allen Lanier saw the band as a healthy respite from crowd-pleasing, even more so because Pearlman, their strategist from the off, had insisted on giving them each a wild, Captain Beefheart/Frank Zappa-styled nickname to go with their band's ultra-weird moniker. Lanier was renamed 'La Verne', Albert became 'Prince Omega', Roeser became 'Buck Dharma', with Pearlman himself taking the name 'Memphis Sam'. When the band recruited bass player Andy Winters, who worked at Pearlman's father's drugstore, 'Memphis Sam' took over as lead vocalist, but soon realised that he himself was no better than Meltzer had been. Albert Bouchard suggested they invite their poetess friend and sometime lyricist Patti Smith to join, but no one else wanted a female in the band. And so, while the lead-singer problem remained, Albert, as 'Prince Omega', and Donald, as 'Buck Dharma', took over temporarily, during which time Soft White Underbelly successfully supported Jefferson Airplane, The Grateful Dead, The Band and Muddy Waters.

However, the band's fortunes rose considerably when singer Les Braunstein jammed with them one night. With his sense of extreme drama, everyone except Meltzer considered Braunstein an ideal frontman, his Lizard King style and baritone voice lending authority to the sound, and his stage presence being a welcome change from the others' anonymity. But when Braunstein demurred from taking a Pearlmanising nickname, everyone but Buck Dharma decided to ditch theirs, too.

The new, Les Braunstein-fronted version of Soft White Underbelly soon gained the attention of Elektra Records president Jac Holzman, who – seeing in Braunstein a possible East Coast version of Morrison – signed Soft White Underbelly in the autumn of 1968. This was typical of Elektra's methods at the time; indeed, you only gotta listen and look at the packaging of the label's earlier Clear Light LP to see that they had already attempted precisely the same move with that band's singer, Cliff DeYoung. Anyway, when the newly wedged-up Underbelly crossed the bridge to Manhattan with their Elektra dollars to score some new gear at Sam Ash Music, on 52nd St., Les Braunstein bumped into Eric Bloom, an old friend from his Hobart College days. Braunstein raved to the others about Bloom's singing in Manhattan band Lost and Found, who had recently split up, leaving Bloom at a loose end. Being himself a Long Islander but three years older than the members of the Underbelly, Bloom accepted the band's invitation to become their sound engineer and brought with him his own massive PA system, transported in his own van.

Recording their debut LP turned into a traumatic and protracted disaster for the Underbelly, who saw their relationship with Braunstein crumble into dust as song after song caused the singer problems. Shortly after the sessions were concluded, a calamitous gig supporting The Jeff Beck Group and Jethro Tull at the Fillmore East drove Braunstein to quit the band, closely followed by Andy Winters. Elektra flipped out. First they cancelled the band's contract, then, reluctantly, agreed with Pearlman's pleas to give the group time to find a new singer and bass player. Albert's kid brother Joe Bouchard now took over on bass, while soundman Eric Bloom was given the singer's gig. But this new configuration of the band would still have to audition for Elektra in order to satisfy the label. Grudgingly, Elektra agreed to keep the Underbelly, but it was to be only temporarily.

The first recordings of the Eric Bloom-fronted band, newly renamed Stalk-Forrest Group, were deemed adequate enough for an Elektra single release, but a kind of lethargy now hung over the project. Although Pearlman's manoeuvring enabled them to cling on to their contract until early 1970, at this time Elektra kicked them off the roster, which is where we came in at the start of the story, with Columbia Records still searching for a Yank Sabbalike.

From the Pearlman to His Oyster Boys, a Sign . . .

Whereas Sandy Pearlman had, during the first two incarnations of the band, mainly concentrated on such managerial tasks as booking shows and song production, the crisis at Elektra made him no longer happy to be leaving the band's songwriting to Richard Meltzer and drummer Albert Bouchard. As a writer for *Crawdaddy*, Pearlman had watched the heavy music of 1968–69 transform into the so-called 'heavy metal' of 1970, the term being first used by Metal Mike Saunders in his *Creem* review of Sir Lord Baltimore's debut LP *Kingdom Come.*

Post-Woodstock hippies generally opted for the overly self-reflective singer-songwriter soft balladry of Joni Mitchell and Crosby, Tween and Nash, while America's industrial heartlands riposted with such monolithic broadside outcasts as Dust, Bang, Dragonfly and Bloodrock. Ironically, that music-industry chasm had destroyed many of the 'heavy' originals, first causing ur-pioneers Blue Cheer (amidst heroin and hearing problems) to jump the fence to become a Delaney & Bonnie-styled soul quartet. The other early behemoths, Vanilla Fudge, soon after exploded into two rival stupor-factions (although the moronic rock of Cactus was no match for the frankly charming ball-bluster of Mark Stein's short-lived Boomerang). Most mysterious of all was the high-velocity upward ascent of Grand Funk Railroad, whose overly earnest, brothers'n'sisters fodderstomp take on the MC5's Detroit grudge-grunge soul had catapulted three former backing musicians from Michigan six-time losers The Pack[4] past The Beatles, selling out Shea Stadium's fifty thousand seats even faster than John, Paul, George and Gringo.

Studying all of these goings-on while seeing his welcome at Elektra Records rapidly diminishing, Sandy Pearlman decided to take the reins of the band and began to write darker songs specifically aimed at fulfilling Murray Krugman's insider brief. Pearlman harangued the band members for losing focus and playing

4 With only one US Top Fifty placing to show for their seven single releases between 1965 and July '67, singer Terry Knight finally got the message and left his own band! Choosing to manage his former backing musicians, The Pack, it must have been with a strange melancholy that he watched them spring to international fame within fourteen months of the first LP.

shows under such random names as The Santos Sisters and Oaxaca. What was the point? Three years of psychedelia and heavy rock had got them nowhere, and the musicians seemed no closer to understanding what they were trying to achieve. As writer Colin Murray noted in a career overview of BÖC: 'Whereas Sabbath had no idea why they were popular, Pearlman wanted the Cult to be popular and understand why they were.'[5]

Having just completed a song named 'The Blue Oyster Cult', Pearlman suggested it as a possible band name, but initially the musicians unanimously rejected the idea. However, as the Elektra days became a distant dream, and all concerned gradually became interested in becoming a part of Murray Krugman's 'dark' project at Columbia, so the name Blue Oyster Cult was resurrected. Guitarist/organist Allen Lanier suggested adding an umlaut over the 'O', as it was in keeping with Sandy Pearlman's new, über-Teutonic lyrics. At Columbia, Murray Krugman thought the new Blue Öyster Cult project ideally suited for the company, and decided to produce the band with the help of Pearlman himself.

And so, arduous though the thirty-six months of navigation had been, Sandy Pearlman now knew that the path to the Cult's first LP statement had finally been cleared of obstacles. Next, he set about devastating the role of Richard Meltzer in this upcoming adventure by writing a series of rock lyrics that would kick the words of Pearlman's lyrical foil into the dust. Uh, look out!

The Making of Blue Öyster Cult

Blue Öyster Cult's self-titled debut LP was an intriguing package of cryptic song titles, Steppenwolf-meets-Electric Prunes biker-rock and geometric, John Michellian-styled imagery. Clothed in a hand-finished cover of mysterious, monochrome, sacred geometry, *Blue Öyster Cult* opens with a whooping, on-the-hoof battle cry which, from bar one, sets out the band's vindictive vagabond stall most eloquently. 'Transmaniacon MC' is an itinerant and un-righteously inverted 13th Floor Elevators hot-rod howl, as though the commentary of lyricist Tommy Hall had been achieved while still in his pre-psychedelicised, white-supremacist state. Indeed, the Pearlman lyric technique is veritably the anti-Tommy, being executed with

5 'Sandy Pearlman and The Blue Öyster Cult' by Colin Murray, taken from *White Stuff*, issue 7, February 1978.

the same violent lashings of pedantry and excessive elocution that Malcolm McDowell would dish out a coupla years later in the movie version of *A Clockwork Orange*. Herein, they really nailed Sandy Pearlman's vision of mystery, myth and darkness. Take a gander at these malevolent openers:

With Satan's hog no pig at all, and the weather getting dry,
We're heading south from Altamont in a cold-blooded travelled trance,
So clear the road my bully boys and let some thunder pass,
We're pain, we're steel, a plot of knives,
We're Transmaniacon MC.

The exquisite interplay between each of the guitarists creates a kind of high-amped road poetry, in which each bike takes it in turn to set the pace, gears shifting and rhythms increasing, some falling back as others engage the throttle.[6]

And surely we did offer up behind that stage at dawn,
Beers and barracuda, reds and monocaine,
Pure nectar of antipathy behind that stage at dawn,
To those who would resign their souls,
To Transmaniacon MC.

Cry the cable, cry the word, unknown terror's here,
And won't you try this tasty snack, behind the scenes or but the back,
Which was the stage at Altamont, my humble boys of listless power,
We're pain, we're steel, a plot of knives,
We're Transmaniacon MC.

If anyone ever found a better description for an errant motorcycle club than that penultimate line ('We're pain, we're steel, a plot of knives'), then clue me, druids, 'cause for me, they nailed that fucker shut.[7]

6 In the summer of 1972, just two months after this LP was released, I was one of two fifteen-year-old longhairs running the main café on the coast road between Torquay and Teignmouth. One day, twenty-five members of The Wessex Chapter motorcycle club, the meanest Hell's Angels in the west of England, descended and demanded free food and water. We'd been to see The Edgar Broughton Band the night before, and still wore our Nick Turner mascara thickly the next day to weird-out the local tourists. I never took make-up off so quickly as the day the Wessex Chapter arrived without a reservation.

7 Verse three's inventory of drinks and drugs consumed from off the tailgate of an artic trailer is so strikingly vivid that each listen takes me back to several occasions between 1981–88, when crossing the Windsor Bridge from the US into Canada, where crews and band members would lovingly and tragically dispose of all illegal drugs before delivering ourselves – by now squirming, grimming, bug-eyed and hyperventilating – exhausted, into the rubber-gloved hands of those bastard Canadian customs men.

At this point, another Pearlman epic careens across our bows, going by the stunning name 'I'm on the Lamb But I Ain't No Sheep'. Herein, the Canadian Mounties ('a police force that works') are eulogised for their red and black uniforms and extreme leather whippery. Gay, in the modern sense, this song is delivered at an even more breakneck pace; an all Nuge-d out Amboy Dukes, balls-to-the-wall guitar trek, somewhere in the realms of The Yardbirds' 'Train Kept a-Rolling' and AC/DC's version of 'Baby, Please Don't Go'. However, the first side of this debut was then rendered patchy, firstly by Buck Dharma's dreary, off-metaphor tale 'The Last Days of May', in which college boys get murdered in a drug deal and the singer cares. Wrong, rule-breaking motherfuckers! Better, through its sheer pace, was Richard Meltzer's 'Stairway to the Stars', with its facile and uncool wordplay unable to drag the song right down due to the utter exuberance of the music of Albert Bouchard and Buck Dharma.

However, Side One closes with the crypto-nightmare scenario of Pearlman's epic, 'Before the Kiss, a Redcap', among whose eleven verses bikers and sexy women down at Conry's bar get into an all-night 'shroom and wine and coke and speed-informed gang-bang with definite ('why did we ever start?') sinister overtones. The rhythm change mid-way takes these bikers into hoedown territory, as Pearlman tells the tale of Suzy and her cohorts and the 'Awful things [that] are happening':

Their lips apart like a swollen rose,
Their tongues extend, and then retract,
A redcap, a redcap, before the kiss, before the kiss.

As future Cult LPs were often wont to do, Side Two falls to pieces conceptually. Opening with the excellent, Electric Prunes-oid dark psychedelia of Joe Bouchard's 'Screams', the late-'60s roots of the Cult show through most effectively, whereas the following song, Richard Meltzer's ingloriously titled 'She's as Beautiful as a Foot', despite its pulverisingly shit imagery and arduously sustained metaphor, is a raga of positively royal proportions. However, Side Two again belongs to Pearlman, here with two epics: the Fritz Lang totalitarianism of the self-explanatory 'Cities on Flame with Rock'n'Roll', and the outrageously worded 'Workshop of the Telescopes', with its Tycho Brahe worldview seemingly refracted through a camera obscura. In order to sing such obtuse lyrics, Eric Bloom adopts the voice and one-eyed, scowling personality of an idiot savant-cum-blues mage somewhere between Lord Buckley, Dr John Creaux's 'Danse Kalinda Ba Doom' and W. C. Fields:

By silverfish imperetrix [sic], whose incorrupted eye,
Sees through the charms of doctors and their wives,
By salamander, drake, and the power that was undine,
Rise to claim Saturn, ring and sky,
By those who see with their eyes close,
They know me by my black telescope.

Kinda makes the idea of a Merlin in black leather seem like a fairly hefty proposition, don't it? And although this fairly focused debut album thereafter petered out with the comparatively light, Pearlman-worded 'Redeemed', nevertheless *Blue Öyster Cult* remains a hefty rock event – even the obvious failures being worthy of more than a couple of rotations. However, Sandy Pearlman's assertion that they eclipsed Alice's *Killer* with this record is way off the mark. *Killer* was a hard, otherworldly boogie that appropriated the trappings of British prog – then zapped those chatchkas with stinging garage-guitar riffs and genuinely psychedelic moments; the sonic landscape created therein by the Coop's original team of Dennis Dunaway, Neal Smith, Glen Buxton and Michael Bruce revealing a viciously talented bunch of glamorous super-longhairs. And – hey – the primo talents of 'Toronto' Bob Ezrin were barely yet kicking in.

Tyranny and Mutation

When *Tyranny and Mutation* hit the shops in April 1973, your average rocker could have been forgiven for thinking this was just a repackage of the debut. Contained within another cover depicted in the same, mysterious, hand-drawn style, the album even commenced with yet another (although far superior) Yardbirds-paced, turbo-driven version of 'I'm on the Lamb . . .', here renamed 'The Red and The Black'. However, like Little Feat's penchant for re-recording earlier songs ('Willin'', 'Cold, Cold, Cold'), the Cult's slight return appears to have been more a desire to nail the song than any real shortage of material.

Next up comes the immaculately named 'O.D.'d on Life Itself', whose sub-Grand Funk boogie, hooting analogue synthesizer and *Raw Power*-styled vocal cackle really puts me in mind of early Pere Ubu. Man, I love this band when they get down and dirty. Soon, however, we're off into Joe Bouchard's euphoric Cult classic, 'Hot Rails to Hell'. Joe's music and lyrics have a real obvious, melodic charm to them, one that is always informed by the clanging drones of The Who or The Electric Prunes or some such *Nuggets*-style garage music. 'Hot Rails to Hell' clatters along as the best example of his work, describing nothing more than a sweaty summer subway ride through Manhattan on the 1277 express. But, boy, does this song burn. Time and time again, it all breaks down to zilch, whereupon some Cult member or other yelps out one more chorus and kick starts the whole tune back to life once again.

Side One closes with the Cult's classic '7 Screaming Diz-busters', whose soundtrack I've omitted here because it straddles that weird jazz that both Zappa and Todd Rundgren had a habit of shoe-horning into their songs, and which The Tubes and their ilk later appropriated, however inappropriately. Despite its absence here, the song is indeed a real wonder, a seven-minute-long leviathan and full-on rumbustuous tale of seven itinerant, horse-borne paladins and their relationship with Lucifer, or Lugh, in his pre-Christian role as the Horned God of the Hunt.

Patti Smith's 'Baby Ice Dog' opens Side Two with the wonderful lyrics: 'I had this bitch, you see/She made lies to me.' Strangely, the song itself is a piano-based ballad like something we could find on *Easter* or *Wave*, and it's easy to imagine La Smith doing her own versh. Nevertheless, the power of Side Two dwindles from here on in, particularly the Bouchard brothers' own 'Wings Wetted Down', with its clichéd, prog-rock vision of black horses, like something off Wishbone Ash's *Argus*. Again, the Cult is trying to break open its own tightly drawn metaphor with a nutcracker so big that it can only shatter the entire trip.

Richard Meltzer's sole contribution to this LP was the throwaway 'Teen Archer', a song whose repeated lyrics and lack of moment certainly justify its position in the boneyard.[8] Even Pearlman shows a lack of stamina with the album closer 'Mistress of the Salmon Salt'. This long, Todd Rundgrenian-styled tale just never takes off and leaves the album inconclusive and unsatisfying after the first side's highly orchestrated and technologically superb series of rock moves. Still, this is why the Cult ain't where they wanted to be, and why we gots to excavate through the cack.

8 The boneyard is the term used to describe the penultimate track on the second side of a vinyl album – the place you put a filler track when it ain't quite good enough but you don't gotta better offering to take its place. Of course, I never experienced such a problem and have left a trail of boneyard-free records. Hmm . . .

Secret Treaties

It was one year later, in April 1974, that the Cult released what is arguably their best LP of all. On *Secret Treaties*, BÖC abandoned the sacred geometry of their previous sleeves in favour of a line drawing of the band standing next to a Messerschmitt 262; the turbo-jet that Adolf Hitler hoped would be Germany's ultimate secret weapon. Ironically, despite the menacing presence of the aircraft (and Eric Bloom's cape!), the sound of this record was never quite up to the power of the first two LPs, although *Secret Treaties* did at least capture the glorious mix of influences that had so long (and so clearly) inspired the musicians and their producers. Herein, Doors riffs collided with Alice Cooper melodies, and by now David Bowie's *Ziggy Stardust* had begun to inculcate its glamorous self into the American hard-rock psyche.

This time, Patti Smith got to write the album opener, 'Career of Evil'. Coming on like the Coop's own 'Eighteen' or maybe something off *Billion Dollar Babies*, 'Career of Evil' was a rearrangement of her own 'Poem of Isidore Ducasse'. Unfortunately, despite having been written about the nineteenth-century French author of the same name, whose book *Les Chants de Maldoror* was published under the pseudonym Comte de Lautréamont, 'Career of Evil' was a fairly pedestrian song, with an even more boring arrangement. Indeed, I've even chosen to leave it off this compilation. However, as this is, after all, a little-known Patti Smith piece, I've reproduced the lyrics below:

I plot your rubric scarab,
I steal your satellite,
I want your wife to be my baby tonight,
I choose to steal what you chose to show,

And you know I will not apologise,
You're mine for the taking,
I'm making a career of evil.

Pay me, I'll be your surgeon,
I'd like to pick your brains,
Capture you,
Inject you,
Leave you kneeling in the rain,
I choose to steal what you chose to show,

And you know I will not apologise,
You're mine for the taking,
I'm making a career of evil.

I'd like your blue-eyed horseshoe,
I'd like your emerald horny toad,
I'd like to do it to your daughter on a dirt road.
And then I'd spend your ransom money, but still I'd keep your sheep,
I'd peel the mask you're wearing, and then rob you of your sleep,
I choose to steal what you chose to show,

And you know I will not apologise,
You're mine for the taking,
I'm making a career of evil.

'Career of Evil' splices directly into 'Subhuman', which has to be one of the Cult's greatest and most evocative tunes, and a showcase for the versatility of Eric Bloom's voice. Over a generic West Coast riff, Bloom adopts a female, almost Helen Reddy-like vocal style for Pearlman's ultra-mysterious libretto:

I am becalmed, lost to nothing,
Warm weather and a holocaust,
Left to die by two good friends,
Abandoned me, and put to sleep,
Left to die by two good friends,
Tears of God flow as I bleed.

Yet another Cult classic follows in the form of 'Dominance and Submission' (again omitted here). Drawing accusations of his having an obsession with Teutonic and overly patriarchal imagery, Sandy Pearlman here flexed his lyrical genius by employing S&M imagery to describe the Beatles-led British Invasion of 1964, and the manner in which the American media knelt down before the Anglo tidal wave. Reminiscent of Lou Reed's 'Rock and Roll', Pearlman's lyric describes 'Suzy' and her kid brother 'Charles' riding around listening to Little Eva's 'The Loco-Motion' in 1963, then hearing the Anglo-led cultural shift on the radio, the band chanting 'Dominance' to Eric Bloom's ever-increasingly stuttered: 'Sub-mission . . . sub . . . mission . . . sub . . . mission . . . sub . . . mission.'

Side One closes with the power-boogie of 'ME 262', whose subject matter is that aforementioned twin-engined Messerschmitt turbo-jet featured on the LP sleeve. It's late 1944 and the Germans are losing the war; Hermann Göring's freaking out because for close to two years the Luftwaffe's had this new machine that could bring the RAF to its knees, if only the Führer hadn't been so hung up about employing the plane as a 'revenge weapon'.[9] Here's this ME 262 monster waiting to annihilate RAF Bomber Command, yet poor old Herman G's still running for cover like every other sucker because his obstinate leader remains unconvinced of what a spectacular job Dr Willie Messerschmitt has done:

Göring's on the phone to Freiburg,
He says: 'Willie's done quite a job,'
Hitler's on the phone from Berlin,
He says: 'I'm gonna make you a star.'

9 William Green, *Fighters, Volume I* (Hanover House, 1960).

Göring looks up at these massive, four-engined Allied planes and muses poetically, not believing his bad luck:

They hang there dependant from the sky
Like some heavy metal fruit,
These bombers, ripened, ready to tilt,
Must these Englishmen live that I might die?
Must they live that I might die?

Although the song's antecedents are clearly Bowie's 'Suffragette City' and Alice's 'Under My Wheels', 'ME 262' is a huge roar of a song with hysterically funny lyrics and a chorus that revolves around chanting the name of the aeroplane's engine, the Junkers Jumo 004. And so, Side One closes with the band alternately chanting either the engine serial number or 'Must these Englishmen live that I might die?', as Eric Bloom wails dispassionately: 'It was dark over Westphalia, in April 1945.'

Now c'mon, motherfuckers, who couldn't boogie to that lyric? No wonder Richard Meltzer thought his erstwhile cohort was consciously bumming him out of the equation.

After the megadeth of 'ME 262', Meltzer's 'Cagey Cretins' is ultra-throwaway, an admittedly cute, proto-Ramones drivel-on that (mercifully) sods off before it really has a chance to leave an aftertaste. On a higher plain of existence, however, is the superbly titled 'Harvester of Eyes', Meltzer's massive ode to the Grim Reaper as a hopeless drug addict. Suffused with imagery that appears to be an Odinist take on Alice's epic 'Halo of Flies', this tight-assed caffeine blues straddles that bizarre, mid-'70s hinterland between Joe Walsh's delightfully clodhopping 'Rocky Mountain Way' and the post-Todd meltdown of The Tubes' 'White Punks on Dope'. It's one of Eric Bloom's finest vocal performances and one which he obviously relished, recounting how the Reaper – so 'high on eyes' – needs 'all the peepers' he can harvest not only as evidence that the donor of those eyes is truly dead, but also to satisfy his hopeless drug-lust, or 'Ocular TB', as Meltzer terms it. Nailed it this time, motherfucker!

Another real Cult classic follows in the form of 'Flaming Telepaths', over whose soaring guitar theme and portentous boogie Bloom sings Pearlman's words of genuine transformation and alchemy, before summing up the world both of the teenager and the mystic in the brilliant line: 'I'm after rebellion . . . I'll settle for lies.' I must also note the extreme Be-Bop Deluxe qualities of this song. It's as though Bill Nelson had focused on this one aspect of the Cult's muse, taking it up several notches one year later on Be-Bop Deluxe's *Futurama* album.

Secret Treaties closes with the delightful, piano-based epic 'Astronomy', its Spectoresque orchestra-scapes and self-mythologising wordplay even more powerful thanks to the Helen Reddy vocal style that Eric Bloom once more adopts. Like 'Before the Kiss, a Redcap' and 'Dominance and Submission', we are again accompanying Pearlman's Suzy character into some cosmic dreamscape, awash with shamanic portals, accessed via a strange cocktail bar when 'The clock strikes twelve':

Two doors locked and windows barred,
One door set to take you in,
The other one just mirrors it.

For those critics who accused the Cult of 'crypto-intellectual lyrics', I gotta say they could be mighty specific when they chose to be, and the above lyric sounds like an instruction manual to enlightenment. Unfortunately, no one in the world could get away with such shit as 'it's the nexus of a crisis', so consider my argument totally null'n'voided just a few lines later.

But hell, y'all, who really cares if the Cult broke their own rules occasionally? We must always remember that, despite their rock'n'roll being propelled by a savage and occultist Pearlmania, *Blue Öyster Cult*, *Tyranny and Mutation* and *Secret Treaties* were gassed up and driven by sanguine motherfuckers with one eye on the ticking clock and a long career in mind. Yeah, but think how cool they'd have been if Sandy Pearlman's dad had owned a chain of Long Island drugstores instead of just the one. Mr Pearlman Senior coulda provided his son with enough of a financial safety net to let Memphis Sam really explore the occult properly, and the wider world woulda benefited royally.

All the Voodoo and Whatnot

After the relative failure of those first three LPs, and with the taxman nipping at his itinerant ass, Pearlman chose to lead BÖC down the already time-honoured path of other non-sellers such as Kiss, Ted Nugent and Peter Frampton – that trackway that leads to the double live LP, in which the best of the studio stuff was distilled and offered up as a mid-price, gatefolded ticket to the truth. Yet whereas *Kiss Alive* had kicked Gene and co.'s overly tinny studio LPs into the dust, the Cult double, *On Your Feet or On Your Knees*, was ultimately nothing more than a fake blood feast of dropped notes and ill-conceived 'take-it-down' cul-de-sacs full of nothing to say. When Eric Bloom comes on like the Lizard King, he fumbles his raps like Ian Gillan on a bad night; yup, that bad. Whenever he sings a particularly poignant passage, Bloom jettisons all melody in an effort to be jazz. Mean mistreater. Even a delicate classic such as 'Subhuman' gets the same torture. Similarly, Buck Dharma in concert certainly ain't no Iommi nor a Ritchie Blackmore, neither, being more of a late-'60s anachronism in the Alvin Lee tradition. His solo blitz-out, 'Buck's Boogie', contains far too many uncool quotes from inappropriate sources – old-timer shit like 'Aint' She Sweet, even some lame Beatles' Merseybeat from my primary-school days called 'You Can't Do That'. Yeuwck! Even BÖC's version of The Yardbirds' 'I Ain't Got You' features Buck quoting from the opening bars of The Doors' 'LA Woman'. And, for shit damn sure, you gotta be able to improve on the guitar solo when yooz playing twice as fast as that studio disc version which the audience is all holding as the mythological blueprint in their collective mind.

Ironically, however, it was Buck Dharma's '60s fetish that finally propelled the Cult to stardom the year after the live LP, with his Byrds-alike song '(Don't Fear) The Reaper'. Although this song would have benefited considerably from a *Raw Power*-style vocal, it was still a beautiful, out-of-time piece somewhat in the tradition of The Flaming Groovies' 'Shake Some Action' of that same year. But the song's phenomenal success truly battered BÖC's mission and commenced a series of moves that would eventually sideline Sandy Pearlman as successfully as he had once done to Richard Meltzer.

By the time of 1977's *Spectres*, dressing up as mages and pretending to be zapping extra-terrestrial cosmic forces was the only way the Cult could maintain even a nominal hold on their original dark metaphor. They just didn't know enough about what they were claiming to be writing about, and, frankly, sounded laughable at times. Even throwing in the occasional Patti Smith lyric couldn't drown out the disco and Springsteen beats and achingly trite love songs that spewed out of the Cult's stable. Indeed, the more occult the LP sleeves became, the less occult was the content.

In Conclusion

From this reassessment of Blue Öyster Cult's early work, it seems now that there were just too many cooks in the band's kitchen. You look at the song credits and everybody's a fucking writer. Nine people take credits on the debut, with seven writers on the following pair of LPs. Shit, even their A&R man was writing for them by the 1980s! Perhaps the Cult's biggest flaw was being overly open-minded about which songwriters should be allowed to represent them. Personally, I believe that when conceptual groups such as BÖC, Kiss, Faust, Neu!, Grand Funk Railroad, etc., can only be enjoyed by their audience's total acceptance of each group's tightly drawn, self-imposed metaphor, then that group has an extra-tough duty to stay within those guidelines, even if it means less people can reach where they're coming from. Besides, I ain't no fucking evangelist – just a Gnostic rock'n'roll dementoid with a demon's zeal for turning on the few with ears pointy enough to listen. And I most certainly do have a bee in my bonnet about Blue Öyster Cult and how faintly they have been praised, compared to just how useful they've been down the years. Indeed, some conservative (or just plain hung up) modern rock crits still impede our way into BÖC for the most minor of reasons. America's Chuck Eddy surely scanned the writing credits of Cult LPs before lazily offering up such facile criticisms as: 'How come Eric Bloom sings like he's reading cue cards?' 'Hey, motherfucker,' says I, 'how come you perceive that as bad?' I mean, Eric is singing Patti Smith, fer Chrissakes, and even Patti delivers her own words like they're on cue cards. For shit damn sure, half the charm of the Cult's wordplay was their Tom Lehrer-like struggle to fit the words in. Moreover, surely half the charm of the 13th Floor Elevators was Roky Erickson's lack of authority as he struggled in vain through their *Easter Everywhere* and *Bull of the Woods* albums, attempting to turn Tommy Hall's Gurdjieffian wordplay into bite-size, Buddy Holly-isk chunks. Hey, Chuck, don't listen to Andy McCoy's Hanoi Rocks lyrics or any Krautrock whatsoever, motherfucker, or yooz gonna belly-laugh all the way to cardiac arrest.

So where does this leave Blue Öyster Cult, in twenty-first-century rock'n'roll terms? Personally, I think Patti Smith's silence on the subject says it all. She's ignored her role and clearly wants us to do the same. Or is it that simple? Somehow, I suspect Patti Smith's reasons for silence are twofold. Her contributions are slight in terms of the overall Cult oeuvre, but her more majestic, piano-based *Wave* and *Easter* music certainly bears more than traces of those first three BÖC LPs. What is regularly attributed to Smith's Springsteen links may well have been more to do with the Cult.

It was for this reason that I kept the compilation short – ten tracks only. I want you to get into this shit slowly . . . ooze into it. With care, the Cult's music can almost get your heathen ass into the afterlife, but not quite. However, you may find it's still well worth further trawling, nay navigating through all the other cack I've not discussed, because BÖC's brand of intellectual bludgeon riffola and wilful obscurity did deffo help not actually to spawn, but certainly majorly inform such errant genius as The Tubes, Rocket from the Tombs, Radio Birdman, Television, early Pere Ubu and even (as evidenced by the version of 'Black Blade' on the new Southern Lord compilation) Joe Preston's exceptional Thrones project.

Humankind is so magically metaphorical that if the moon is hidden behind clouds, you can meditate just as successfully with a glow-in-the-dark moon. Similarly, if the Christian Church has caned your pagan rituals by burning all the books and the practitioners thereof, you can always substitute it with a degraded form and still get there, albeit in a degraded form. Know what I mean? Rock'n'roll is such a barbarian art form that merely alluding to the underworld can get you to that underworld. So, for want of the genuine article, a substitute will always do nicely if yooz a magical motherfucker. It's for that very reason that I never had a yen to be authentic – stick your Les Paul copy through the same fuzz and distortion pedals as a real Gibson and, chances are, no sucker'll win the Pepsi Challenge, 'cause they'll sound just the same.

All of which suggests that the darkest corners of Blue Öyster Cult are portals to the same underworld as the darkest Sabbath, darkest Alice and darkest Jimbo. And so, although they were a very erratic and somewhat Guess Who-like hit'n'miss ensemble, Blue Öyster Cult will, with a little tweaking and *a lot* of editing, send your visionary ass precisely where your visionary ass needs to go. Yowzah!

Select Discography

In My Mouth or On the Ground (Reichsdag, 1972)
Blue Öyster Cult (Columbia, May 1972)
Tyranny and Mutation (Columbia, April 1973)
Secret Treaties (Columbia, April 1974)

James Brown

The Payback

(Polydor, 1974)

SIDE 1

1 The Payback (7.35)

2 Doing the Best I Can (7.50)

SIDE 2

1 Take Some . . . Leave Some (8.22)

2 Shoot Your Shot (8.08)

SIDE 3

1 Forever Suffering (5.42)

2 Time Is Running Out Fast (12.37)

SIDE 4

1 Stone to the Bone (10.05)

2 Mind Power (10.35)

We Got a Right to the Tree of Life

When James Brown released *The Payback*, in April 1974, it was the leanest, wisest, most self-assured record of his outstanding career. Here, within the grooves of four long sides of twelve-inch vinyl, was a distillation of his most streamlined late-'60s and early-'70s meditational funk. Although it was neither his first double LP, nor even his first studio double, *The Payback* was so spectacularly laid out that it transcended time itself. Indeed, I once had a five-and-a-half-hour wait in Malaga airport, which I passed by playing *The Payback* on endless heavy rotation. Sure, there are still two (extremely long and portentous) slowies fighting away in the grooves of this album, but even these so-called 'ballads' are themselves pretty damned groovy; so groovy that they are almost lost among those other six massive meditational assaults, each of which ranges from between seven and a half and twelve and a half minutes in length.

Something else was very different about this record. *The Payback* was housed in a wonderfuelled gatefold sleeve depicting the self-styled Godfather of Soul omnipotent and looking down benignly over black culture, his hat ablaze with the remarkable statement: 'We got a right to the tree of life.' Whereas the record sleeves of Brown's previous albums had always opted for either the showbiz or the bland, the artwork for *The Payback* was a Black Power statement of considerable depth. And it was a statement that could only have been instigated by the lyrical themes that James Brown had worked up for the album.[1]

Sleeve-notes by Alan M. Leeds inside the gatefold commenced: 'It all began with forty acres and a mule . . . a simple desire for one whose personal branch on the tree of life struggled to protect itself from the dangerous branches of lust and greed.' Black Americans' removal from ownership of the land was countered on the inner gatefold by sleeve art which depicted an idealised black farmer. And on the back sleeve was step two of the Godfather of Soul's Utopian grand design. Here was the stylised profile of a black man, his cranium fizzing and illuminated with mathematical equations, while overhead hovered large yellow buzz-words: 'Mind Power'.

As though all these statements were not proof enough of James Brown's incredibly high intentions, so further evidence could be seen in the form of *Damn Right, I Am Somebody*, a companion album packaged in similarly weighty style. Repeated banner quotes across the album sleeve screamed the headlines: 'Positive Thinking, Positive Thinking, Positive Thinking'; and all this interspersed with 'Think That You Are Somebody and You'll Be Somebody.'

This LP was released on James' People label and credited to Fred Wesley and the J.B.'s, the former being the Godfather's long-time musical producer. In its totality, James Brown was now providing a whole cultural package with which to educate, empower and shamanise his audience. For those who still wished only to dance, hey, these grooves were from down below. But for those who also wanted to be in the know, James Brown's decades of searching *within* were finally being enlisted to look after those *without*.

But before we address the enormous weight of the music on *The*

1 I write 'worked up' because of the immediacy of many of the grooves on *The Payback*. Often James' technique of giving the ensemble a limited palette of song parts and responses enabled him to come upon far more than was ever actually written. Elsewhere, I have written of James Brown's own obvious delight when a riff, lyric and groove all switch on simultaneously.

Payback, I'll take you on a brief 'non-soulboy' trip back through Brown's early career. This is necessary in order to at least show that there was downright will at work in the experimental ways of James Brown which led him inexorably towards that incredibly spaced-out funk which was so dangerously distilled to perfection on *The Payback*.

The Birth of 'On the One'

Nobody in music, no one, nowhere, never, *so* validated my argument for the rock'n'roller as shaman like Mr James Brown. From his apprentice days in the 1950s as a Little Richard copyist, through the multiple single release-after-release-after-endless-release showbiz days of the 1960s, via his sustained cultural heights as teacher and bringer of wisdom to his beleaguered black American audience, which he attained throughout the 1970s, even to his fabled two-state police chase and subsequent jail sentence in 1988, James Brown has always epitomised what the shaman spirit could be and could achieve. On his records he's a godlike figure ('the hardest working man in show-business') summoning up songs right here and right now, often as charmed, intrigued and mystified by his own abilities as are the members of his ensemble and his audience. Indeed, listen to 'Funky Drummer' and we can almost hear him thinking to himself, 'Did I just come up with that? *Awl-righttt!*'

Even more shamanic has been James Brown's ability to not only influence such greats as Sly Stone, Miles Davis and George Clinton, but to be, in turn, influenced by them. That is the confidence of the truly great. As T. S. Eliot pointed out, talent imitates, genius steals; and James Brown, at his height, was a master musician and singer so sure of himself he often didn't even need to play or sing on his own records, confident in the knowledge that the musicians laying down the music were all of his own choosing. Sure, he was an organist supreme and added hugely to the sound made by his backing band, The Famous Flames, but only when *he* chose to do so. Even as early as 1961, instrumentals had been staples of James Brown's singles release schedule.

Of course, such massive LPs as 1962's *James Brown Live at the Apollo* sustained the career of James the Showman. But all the time, a parallel figure existed in the form of James the Shaman. What I mean is that James the Orchestrator, James the Fixer and James the Figurehead were all slowly merging into James the Forerunner of every future rock'n'roll shaman, from Jim Morrison to Iggy Pop; from Malcolm Mooney to Damo Suzuki; from Shaun Ryder to Keith Flint.

Probably most influential of all was James Brown's dedication to putting all his songs 'on the one'. Whereas music of the day chose to emphasise the 2/4 or the 4/4 time signature, the Godfather stupefied his early producers by insisting that the first beat of each bar be where the accent lay, giving his music a tumbling, endless groove which would influence all future music. Indeed, later soul giants, from Parliament in the late '60s to Trouble Funk in the mid-'80s, sacrificed and submerged their songs and arrangements in order to achieve the continuous performance which the Godfather himself had instigated.

James Brown changed the focus of the song until it shifted dramatically from the original two minutes of verse/chorus/verse to anything-goes, umpteen-minutes-with-maybe-a-coupla-hollers-if-yooz-lucky. And when you think about it, most casual fans of James Brown would be unaware that the signature exhortations to 'Get up', 'Get on up', 'Get into it' and 'Get involved' were actually sung by his cohort and long-time MC Bobby Byrd. This was a shaman's confidence in his apprentice; and it was a confidence which Miles Davis would later emulate during his own mid-'70s funk period. Unfortunately, coming outta jazz and lacking James Brown's incredible dancing, Miles Davis churlishly chose to turn his back on his (admittedly mainly white intellectual) audience, standing, eyes closed and trumpet lowered, taking in the scorching wah-funk of his much younger musicians. This was to become an acceptably aloof stance for the later rock'n'roll shaman – PiL-period John Lydon, for example – but it was only accepted by Miles' audience because they were, in the main, white and middle-class. And whereas Miles was the son of wealthy black parents, and a Juilliard-schooled jazzer playing to an intellectual crowd, James Brown was raised in his aunt's brothel and initially aspired only to entertain audiences at Harlem's legendary Apollo Theatre. James Brown may have later called himself a greedy man, but, really, he's always just been a very hungry man; someone who pulled himself out of poverty but never truly left it behind. And had he ever done a Miles Davis and turned his back on his audience, they would have kicked his underachieving ass and bundled him right off the stage.

Which brings us, conveniently, to James Brown the dancer. For in

James' need to become the consummate entertainer, his dancing turned him into a showman so fine that, as a slo-mo replay of his steps confirms, he was moving in another dimension. As I commented earlier, true shamans constantly reappraise themselves and constantly serve new apprenticeships. Like the incredible Dervish dances which George Gurdjieff taught his ensemble in the early 1900s, James Brown repeated his dance steps so often and invested so much time in perfecting them that his dancing became, to all intents and purposes, superhuman. Indeed, I truly believe that, in the late '60s and the '70s, James Brown glimpsed the divine so many times that he even temporarily dwelled in it. Not in some removed, Christ-like way; not separated from his everyday but *right down in it*, like George Gurdjieff himself but even greater. For James Brown was not only picking up the money at each show himself, schooling the musicians and sacking the underachievers, running his own production company and doing the deals himself; he was also putting food on the tables of all those who worked for him, and nourishing the lives of all those who listened to his songs on a completely different level to any white artist. He was getting down in it and becoming the eye of the hurricane.

The personnel in James Brown's band would change so often during this period that it would be impossible to explain any such protracted goings-on. Suffice to say that when Bootsy Collins famously but temporarily swelled the ranks, then left due to in-concert, LSD-influenced ineptitude, it made sod all difference. Now, how funky is that? James was the Godfather of Soul, and never was a nickname so magnificently placed nor so accurate.

By the late 1960s, James Brown was so funky it defies description. James Brown singles had become quicksilver things which altered the very smell and touch of your surroundings. And if a single was not doing the business, it could be withdrawn and replaced with another version of the same song.

But the push towards the new decade was a time of massive progression for soul music, and the sound of James Brown slimmed down and down until it streamlined into the pure rush of grooves such as 1968's 'I Got the Feelin'', 1969's 'The Popcorn' and 'Funky Drummer', and 1970's amazing 'Brother Rapp'. Armed only with words, explaining to the ignorant, what was the effect on those listening to such mysteriously syncopated singles? 'Mother Popcorn (You Got to Have a Mother for Me)' is as abstract as describing the spiritual merits of a Methodist church service to a Born Again Christian. But James continued to up the stakes and pushed his sound ever tighter, becoming ever more mercurial.

Then, in March 1970, the mind-blowing austerity of 'Ain't It Funky' made all his recent singles seem as leaden as contemporary hard-rock, and anything of his, even just a coupla years old, such as 'Cold Sweat', suddenly seemed as antiquated and ostentatious as 'MacArthur Park'. It was as if only James and the drummer were left in this band. How could such a large musical ensemble make such massively subtle contributions to music?

Open Up the Door: I'll Get It Myself

Of course, this is just a review of what I consider to have been James Brown's shamanic height, so please excuse some of the seemingly random musicology. But any jump from showman to shaman needs explaining because so few really do it. Little Richard was so far ahead of the pack that he actually joined the clergy that he was supposed to have been subverting/replacing. Frank Zappa could have achieved it if he'd just had a little more faith in the musicians he'd hired. But, like many genii, Zappa didn't understand himself well enough to admit his own ignorance, even to himself. Jim Morrison did it so easily (but so briefly) that only the coolest people in the world recognise it. Off the top of my head, I can think of no one else.

James Brown, on the other hand, sustained and ordered the chaos around him for almost two decades. In the 1970s, his hard-work policy grew and grew until it was out of all proportion. And although the fundamental funk album *Hot Pants*, with its eight-minute title track and almost ten-minute-long opener 'Blues and Pants' was born out of that policy, so was a lot of the regular soul ballad-type material which is of no use to us here. *There It Is* featured the genius of 'Talking Loud and Saying Nothing' and 'Greedy Man', but was still full of soul schmaltz. Similarly, so was too much of the huge double LP *Get on the Good Foot.* And, unfortunately, there were also a couple of patchy live albums: *Super Bad* and the double, *Sex Machine.* A couple of film-soundtrack albums, *Slaughter's Big Rip Off* and *Black Caesar*, contained some incredible grooves, but (in terms of usable shamanic tools) the sheer weight of James' output was undermining the groove itself.

But I don't want to say negative

things about a genius like James Brown just because his music is not always the tool that I require. If the critical listener's expectations are outside the parameters of the artist's intentions, our judgement ain't worth shee-it! Accept the artist's metaphor or butt out, I say.

'I Don't Know Karate but I Know Ker-Ayyzee'

Opening with the massive, seven-and-a-half-minute-long title track, *The Payback* immediately locks into a hugely compulsive space-groove. Grinding guitar is punctuated with seven-league bass, as a reverbed and mysterious call-and-answer unisex choir responds emotionally to the Godfather's tales of cuckolding, hoodwinking, sell-outs and lowlife morality. James wants revenge for it all and now is the time to collect. 'Revenge, I'm mad,' he shrieks. The opening moments of the album are all spent in this confusion of angry claims. When James, out to get any low-life mother, threatens: 'I don't know karate but I know ker-ayyzee,' the choir reverentially but uncomprehendingly respond in unison: 'Yes, we do.'

This fucking groove is too much – it sounds as though James is walking down the street threatening everyone. The choir appears out of doorways and alleys just in time to answer his defiant stance, before ducking back inside. The brass is hanging on every street corner, waiting for Mr Brown's poetically timed arrival. Ba-ba . . . Ba-ba . . . *Bap!*

Then a strange and abrupt climax segues into the lush Mancini-rations of 'Doing the Best I Can'. Here, we're deep in unjudgeable areas for the kind of review I'm intending. It's an 'I'm-for-real-man-questioning-his-woman's-leaving' song which I have to culturally almost sidestep. The call-and-response of 'I'm for Real' is a beautiful and hauntingly mournful cycle which continues for three long minutes until it becomes a proto-meditation in the same vein as The Jaynetts' 'Sally, Go Round the Roses'. James is vamping on 'Me and Mrs. Jones', and Fred Wesley is playing the trombone of a starving man. It's a chillingly slow, stoned groove which closes Side One of this album.

Side Two consists of a pair of massive grooves. 'Take Some . . . Leave Some' is eight and a half minutes of ever-circling skeletal bass, cycling round a brass and drum theme from an imaginary TV cop series, with James explaining the nature of a life thinking about food. And this life, thinking about food, is being inevitably worked into the fabric of *The*

Payback. Getting out of second-hand-me-downs is the next priority, but it's way behind the food. We're now listening to the first of several allusions to the practicality of Mind Power, not as an aid to the higher spirit, but as a way of transcending hunger. When James tells us that his friends all 'need it', the report is about good food, new shoes and a suit of clothes. But, says James, you can't be greedy. And, all the time, this cycling groove is arcing clockwise around the room like an ever-upwardly spiralling elevator.

Then, *ver-rooom*, we're into the 'Shaft'-like 'Shoot Your Shot'; eight minutes-plus of fast ricochet funk that spunks us to the wall like an outta-control firehose. James is in one helluva mood as he declares: 'Shoot your shot or get the shit shot out of you.' Now, there's the 'Poet' that Sly was talking about in *There's a Riot Goin' On*.[2] Mesmerised and cross-eyed, the structural interior of the listener wearing headphones begins to shake and flutter at the syncopation of this mighty rhythm.

Side Three opens with the 6/8 blues of 'Forever Suffering', with its endless choruses of 'Suffering.' Then we're blown to pieces by the twelve minutes of 'Time Is Running Out Fast'. The beginning is a strange mix of moods from the sampled orchestra, plucked from the front of the earlier 'Doing the Best I Can', directly into an African groove which anticipated and must have inspired Funkadelic's amazing 'Brettino's Bounce' from their *The Electric Spanking of War Babies* album. 'Time Is Running Out Fast' is a strident monster with a quasi-Cuban shaman, of the Alan Vega variety, ya-ya-ya-ya-ing pre-verbal, proto-Hispanic over Fred Wesley's hungry-man trombone. It's an epic groove through backstreets and alleys in the middle of a scorching sunny day, and it kicks my dick into the dust.

And so to the final and most major side of *The Payback*, which kicks off with the startling brass of 'Stone to the Bone': ten minutes of the most shuffling 'on-the-one' so far. We're deep in the heart of the album by now and it's this side which pushes *The Payback* into transcendental territory; on and on and deeper and deeper in we go, riding a deadly meditational groove. James tells us how he has got a good

2 James Brown's companion albums are a real source of nourishment. My other favourites include The J.B.'s monumental groove album *Hustle with Speed* and the Cope family's primo party album, *Breakin' Bread*, credited to Fred Wesley and The J.B.'s.

thing that he ain't gonna give up. He wants permission to holler from the ensemble. 'Sure, James,' say the band, holler and howl all you want. But still James pleads for permission. Then he's off to the organ to add the kind of spaced, bell-toned precision Hammond that takes away this white punk's hope. Soon he's back at the mic to tell the arriving brass that they 'must turn me loose!' He ain't gonna give it up, and the sheer joy and the wrath of James inspires the ensemble, to a man, to say they ain't gonna give it up, either. Can James holler again? Sure, then off into a claustrophobic and more subdued version of the song's primary riff. The cleanness of the studio is an advantage with this music, so perfect and clear is the sound. You sort of wanna be informed that the cleaning lady kept it spruce and litter-free, too.

And so we find ourselves in the final and superlative space-grooves of 'Mind Power', the ultimate track both artistically and chronologically. What is this groove? Space is everything, and 'Mind Power' features the most economical bass line ever. It's a single boom every four beats for the whole of the opening groove, a ploy which anchors the track in a way that still allows the boat to move forwards. James explains that we're living in the most crucial time he's ever known, and the sense of urgency so evident in his vocal delivery lends real portent to even the supposedly light asides. And James Brown on this record is a very funny man, talking to the ensemble, egging them on, suggesting riffs, even throwing around biblical allusions. Here, James is telling his audience that what they have had to survive upon is 'Mind Power'; what people in Britain call 'vibe'. Others know it as ESP, but James likes to call it what it is. He's giving it all a cultural context and in so doing he's dignifying the whole process. Perhaps there's no point in even explaining this monumental groove and the presence of James Brown upon this track. Suffice to say that his presence is warming, uplifting, invigorating and totally liberating. And I guess what's most surprising is just how much of what James was saying in 1974 is still pertinent today. And again, over that empty, taut tightrope groove, in which space between instruments makes the sound actually austere, his band sing 'What-it-is-and-what-it-is' as the song tails out into a long, slow fade.

And so, as we close *The Payback* down and wonder where all the time went, we consider had we not better just put it back on again and stare at the moon for another hour.[3] Obviously, I have a belief that real deep exploration of this period of James' groove could bring finely tuned shamanic results. Of course, the huge use of James Brown samples in modern music is evidence enough of our current need for this timeless rhythm. But, like the motorik Neu! grooves which propelled much of the Krautrock-inspired, mid-to-late-'90s music, the groove of *The Payback*, once discovered or relocated, is there for us all to use not in a dance setting but as one of the accepted propellants of the modern urban meditation music.

3 If you get the chance to listen to *Damn Right, I Am Somebody*, a whole other world of sub-plots and undergrooves soon emerges. James Brown continued in this direction for quite some time afterwards, delivering further expansive double LPs, my favourite being *Hell*, with its long, slimmed-down Side Four, which featured the single track 'Papa Don't Take No Mess'.

Chrome

Chromeology

(2005)

(The music on *Chromeology* was recorded between 1976–79, and was put together for streaming purposes only. It has never been released)

1. TV as Eyes (2.16) (from *Half Machine Lip Moves*)
2. The Monitors (2.23) (from *Alien Soundtracks*)
3. March of the Chrome Police (3.36) (from *Half Machine Lip Moves*)
4. Slip It to the Android (4.01) (from *Alien Soundtracks*)
5. Return to Zanzibar (3.51) (from *The Visitation*)
6. Chromosome Damage (3.42) (from *Alien Soundtracks*)
7. Kinky Lover (3.31) (from *The Visitation*)
8. ST-37 (3.12) (from *Alien Soundtracks*)
9. You've Been Duplicated (2.38) (from *Half Machine Lip Moves*)
10. Nova Feedback (5.58) (from *Alien Soundtracks*)
11. Pharaoh Chromium (3.27) (from *Alien Soundtracks*)
12. All Data Lost (3.22) (from *Alien Soundtracks*)
13. My Time to Live (4.20) (from *The Visitation*)

Chromeology is my attempt to conflate the first three Chrome LPs in one lavishly streamlined package in order to sweeten their noise enough to lure a few of you unsuspecting motherfuckers into the wider trip of this late-'70s San Francisco band. I still exercise regularly to Side One of *Alien Soundtracks* and Side Two of their fourth LP, *Red Exposure*, and find that Chrome's pulse helps me take on a superman/automaton guise during the process. However, pretty much all of the early Chrome records are important and generally useful to those on the heathenising programme; moreover, all of the first four LPs still work as a holistic canon with which to blow yer brains out.

Modern Equipment Can't Take the Abuse

Damon Edge! Helios Creed! John L. Cyborg! Gary Spain! Now those are motherfucking names to conjure with . . . maybe there were indeed giants walking the earth back in the late '70s. Unfortunately, the catchy, proto-industrial bastard that was Chrome has not easily asserted its place in rock'n'roll history, for its seventy percent massively stylised and unrighteously holy mix of Jagger-mouthed robot soul, sweating, lo-fi 'Bogus Man' dubby-skank ('drums'n'tea tray', Swell Maps stylee), *Neu! 2*-styled, art-house cut-ups, and berserkely feral, fuzz-saw Detroit-ness (all projected to the public via record sleeves depicting a monolithically clichéd, postwar view of the future) does not sit well with the band's other thirty percent – a perverse underbelly comprised of cumbersomely arhythmic, UFO-crash-landed-behind-the-gasworks, alien-engineers-trying-to-blowtorch-the-door-open soundtrack. Nor was it ever meant to, of that I'm quite sure. But, damn me, if it ain't still (once yooz evicted certain obversely perverse miscreants) a fucking glorious rush of sound with which to clear the twenty-first-century custard. A row, a racket, a bull in a china shop – Chrome certainly was all these things. But, no, no, no, Chrome were nobody's dry wank and that's a fact, just fabulous future cretins with a silver-foil fixation – one that lasted far longer than their allotted fifteen minutes, merely because their leader, Damon Edge, proved he had shit to say, and wasn't about to fuck off until he'd said it *all*.

Yup, Chrome's alien alliance of garage Krautfunk and Jaggeresque electro-dub was the obtuse collision and singular vision of singing drummer and vengeful lyricist Damon Edge, a hard-to-photograph, occasionally be-lipsticked, oft leather-gloved vision – like Frank Zappa's Afterbirth of the Underworld. Although, vocally, Damon Edge was an older and braver kissing cousin of Electric Eels' über-sniveller David E, the lyrical twists of his many snide-boy broadsides were often submerged under their Don Buchla-informed[1] electronic bray of

1 Don Buchla created some of the most intriguingly experimental synthesizers of the early period, building keyboardless analogue instruments which operated on a key system that seemed to mirror the workings of his own mind. Looking at them now, it's easy to see why they failed commercially. Unlike the ever pragmatic Bob Moog, who began as an instrument salesman working out of the back of his car (and therefore grasped what the market 'required'), Don Buchla stayed in his laboratory, digging deeper and deeper. Like Chrome, Ed Wilcox's Temple of Bon Matin has also used Buchla synthesizers with dramatic success.

hideous radioactive mid-range that Edge insisted on fly-tipping over every Chrome recording. And while R2D2 getting into punk would have chosen Chrome over the Pistols every time, because you could dance to them, regular humans, like me, always wore oven gloves when handling their discs for fear of death via some hitherto unknown space disease.

Chrome were '80s before the '80s ever happened, and boy did they have the funk – a funk so degraded and so abrasive and so alienating that its single reference point was, from the inception of their career, the arid cocaine mix of Sly's *There's a Riot Goin' On*. Indeed, 1976's 'Kinky Lover' should be considered a more naturally automaton sequel to Sly's lights-are-on-but-no-one's-home performances on *There's a Riot Goin' On* than the fake effusiveness of *Fresh* ever coulda been. At our punk club, Eric's, in Liverpool, 'Slip It to the Android' was a big dance-floor smash because it ran James Brown's 'Cold Sweat' through engineer John L. Cyborg's alien filter to create a Faust clear album/early-Mothers horn arrangement that had you body-poppin' before any sucker had even come up with the term.

And yet Chrome do not seem to have filtered happily or naturally into the official 'I Was a Punk Before You Were a Punk'[2] list of bands, as did their West Coast contemporaries The Residents, or Cleveland's Rocket from the Tombs, Electric Eels and Mirrors, or even Canada's Simply Saucer. Why's that, I hear you cry? Well, it's probably because Damon Edge continued recording under the Chrome moniker for so long after they passed their sell-by date that potential new fans – badly burned by their first and inappropriate Chrome purchase – thereafter give up (or wait for a mate more monied than they to do the shelling out). Chrome are now in a similar situation to other once-greats who soldiered on with a few original members making music unworthy of the name. How many teenagers who, on a whim, bought Can's late-period *Saw Delight* LP or Blue Cheer's *Oh! Pleasant Hope* glimpsed even vestiges of the beasts that once inhabited the world under that name? Chrome, too, now suffer from too many releases that look the

2 Ironically, Chrome's 'Electric Chair' (from *Red Exposure*) was covered by Mikey Wild on his twenty-five-years-too-late album *I Was Punk Before You Were a Punk*. However, this Johnny Rotten-come-lately chose not to credit Chrome for the song and re-named it 'The Crucifier'. Despite that failure, it's an excellent drunken sprawl, well worth searching out.

part but just don't pass muster.

And yet time was when the appearance of a new Chrome record in the racks was guaranteed to send seismic shockwaves of expectation through the underground. Throughout the ominous daylight of '77 and '78, imported and too-expensive Chrome LPs used to leer at me conceitedly from behind their elite, US-only shrink-wrappings in the import section of Liverpool's Probe Records. Unlike the soon-to-be-dog-eared copies of Throbbing Gristle's *Second Annual Report* and other British handmades of their ilk, Chrome's cut-up, paste-board, art-statement sleeves always rested far more dignified and more overly validated than their UK counterparts simply because record manufacturers in the US felt the need to protect their product with that ultimate enhancer, the aforementioned shrink-wrapping – still a two-years-away concept here in Merrie Olde England. And so, like those LPs of The Residents, Suicide, Pere Ubu, Afrika Corps, etc., Chrome's *Neu!*-like graffitoid canvases were sacred documents whose contents had to be learned at all costs. However, these suckers had been factory-sealed behind an impregnable clear plastic wall that was penetrable only by those with massive amounts of dosh, indeed *import* amounts of dosh . . . Gosh!

The owner of Probe Records, Geoff Davis, was far too hardened a businessman to fall for us listening without buying – hell, I'd tried it on too many times and got it in the ear from him concerning The Residents and Armand Schaubroeck. So we had to wait for some other poor sod to shell out, and cop an earful of their copy. In the meantime, with only hardened (and monied) punks and experimentalists buying Chrome LPs, Damon Edge and co. were hunting around for that elusive UK record deal, which was not gonna be forthcoming until the early 1980s, courtesy of Beggars Banquet. Unfortunately, by the time those records would be released, both the real fire and the most focused musicians had quit Chrome, leaving Edge and his ever-increasing slew of side-men to tour until there was nowt but a husk to be had.

Right, with that little history out of the way, weez now gonna go back and focus on those first three LPs that make up this so-called *Chromeology* . . .

The Visitation

Being on the cusp of just about every rock'n'roll crossroads you'd care to mention, Chrome's debut, *The Visitation*, is a particularly strange hybrid, having been conceived and executed during that unforgiving hinterland between 'The Death of Prog' and 'The Birth of Punk'. Recorded in San Francisco throughout 1976, and replete with poorly photocopied lyric sheets and generally arty detritus, this self-released first LP's home-made sleeve implied far more vicious contents than the opening tracks delivered. Like the MC5's *Kick Out the Jams*, the opening song (no, two songs) of Chrome's debut LP bore nothing more than a passing resemblance to the general canon of work that Edge and co. would put out in the coming years – the debut even employing the services of a soon-to-be-jettisoned lead-singer geezer who went by the unconvincingly normal name of Mike Low, plus the chameleon-like lead guitarist John Lambdin, who seemed able to deliver whatever Damon Edge asked of him. On neither opening song ('How Many Years Too Soon?' and 'Raider') was there much evidence of the unprovenanced ur-scrawl that the insane record cover implied, Low's euphoric pleading and whining set over the kind of well-recorded, Hendrix-inspired heavy-rock (Uli Roth's *Earthquake* LP meets Flower Travellin' Band) that would, elsewhere, have us all creaming in our jeans. However, hard-rock and psychedelia is never what Chrome should be thought to have represented. And only on the third track, 'Return to Zanzibar', did the Chrome beast of legend finally shake itself from its dormant repose, as Damon Edge's now familiarly scrawny complain-athon vocal style – here particularly reminiscent of Fred 'Sonic' Smith – and Klaus Dinger-on-an-exercise-mat-drum kick into the kind of white trash, junkie-funk that New York's no-wave bands would appropriate two years hence.

After that tune, Mike Low's vocals finally get with the Chrome programme for the steaming, hot-house funk of Side One's closer, 'Caroline' – vocally approximating Edge, although without the bark or the rabid bite.

Side Two's 'Riding You' opens with all the Chrome elements in place, as disorientating tapes of laughter and effects, in the manner of Pere Ubu's Allen Ravenstine, set the scene, but Lambdin's frenetically strangled lead guitar is still way too straight for its musical setting. The Chrome classic, 'Kinky Lover', which follows is an outrageous piece of clattering industrial funk which uses for its main riff John Cale's brooding minor-key take on Elvis' 'Heartbreak Hotel'.[3]

3 Recorded on Cale's LP, *Slow Dazzle* (Island Records, 1974).

'Sun Control' is a euphoric piece of drum'n'tea-tray insanity, and Mike Low's vocals are by now a positive gift to the overall sound, as further overly flanged funk riffs baste the listener, until a beautiful, Be-Bop Deluxe-style coda ushers the song out.

The Visitation finishes disappointingly with the bland and overly long, percussion-driven, West Coast psychedelia of 'Memory Cords Over the Bay', which concludes the LP with Chrome still retaining one foot in the old world.

Alien Soundtracks

However, as the late-'76 punk explosion changed the sonic temples of the rock'n'roll landscape out of all recognition between the release of Chrome's debut and their follow-up, the trashing of the old ways brought many musicians not only in line with Chrome, but also actually into a position to surpass them. Chrome, however, rose to the occasion, as vocalist Mike Low disappeared over the horizon forever, leaving guitarist John Lambdin at the mercy of Damon Edge, now free to work on his lupine howl, unobstructed. And with the release of Chrome's second sacrificial offering, *Alien Soundtracks*, the band absolutely nailed their muse to the floor. For herein was contained all of the yawp and thunder, all the bark and bitter rage of removal, all the homunculus ennui and editing-room-floor psychedelia that best represented Damon Edge's unvented brainium. And while the forms, cut-ups, splices, segues and collages of the record are never more extreme or lustfully executed than within the grooves of this LP, *Alien Soundtracks* still successfully walked that tightrope between horribly more-ish direct hits and the sheerly perverse barf-athons which so obviously delighted Edge himself.

The change in sound and honing down of direction appears to have been due specifically to the appearance of a new member: the legendary, mythically named guitarist Helios Creed, whose arrival tipped the scales so far in Damon Edge's direction that every song on *Alien Soundtracks* would be a compositional collaboration between the drummer and the newcomer, leaving previous songwriter John Lambdin orphaned in his own band.

Alien Soundtracks commences with the three-part mini-epic, 'Chromosome Damage', which kicks off with about forty seconds of frenetic drumming and lo-fi fuzz guitar, over which Edge announces 'I wanna fly away,' before the whole freight-train groove collides with the buffers of an industrial terminal. Sonic effects reminiscent of Pere Ubu-meets-Grand Funk's 'Winter and My Soul' (all TV and shortwave radio) breaks in until, fading out of the ether, comes a foul, gloopy, dual-guitar solo announcing the death of the previous LP in final style.

Incoming, then, is the careering, distorto-monomaniacal riffery of 'The Monitors', replete with a killer punk-along chorus. Then, sucked out of the ether, come the almost Residents-like harmonised vocals of 'All Data Lost', which anticipates Monoshock's 'Leesa' by about a decade and a half, as analogue synthesizer drones and distant, Joy Division-like theme guitars herald the fade. The ensuing 'SS Cygni' is nothing more than a highly catchy but typical Chrome lo-fi funk groove, with intertwining fuzz guitars that hit a plateau and then just motor to a fade.

Side One concludes with one of my all-time favourite Chrome pieces, the six-minute-long, 6/8 time, flanged, stellar waltz of 'Nova Feedback', in which John Lambdin and Helios Creed create layer upon layer of fuzzy, crunching melody over an Edge skank rhythm reminiscent of Moebius and Plank's *Rastakrautpasta*.

The six minutes of 'Pygmies in Zee Park' opens Side Two, like some weird hybrid of Yello, Tuxedo Moon and *Duck Stab*-period Residents, as wild, dislocated voices howl and hoedown over frenetic, distracted sambas, before the whole schmeer breaks down into a Hawkwind/Neu! motorik groove over which Damon Edge croons, shamelessly aping Roy Orbison. Soon this gives way to an infuriating electronic Prince Buster skank, albeit weighted down under heaped mattresses of distorted and ring-modulated electronic brass stabs.

Track Two is the aforementioned 'Slip It to the Android', a James Brown-catchy, 'on-the-one' soul piece, complete with George Duke/Herbie Hancock funky ARP 2600 synth soloing, John Lambdin's slinky electric violin and a robot MC crowing '*Sleep eet to thee ann-droid*' over and over and fucking over again – a braying cartoon Mexican mule sneerily, cheerily chewing your lobes like there's zero airspace between performer and audience.

'Pharoah Chromium' is Chrome's take on Sam the Sham and The Pharaohs, in which a bogus 'Casbah Rock' meets 'Rock the Casbah' meets The Modern Lovers' 'Egyptian Reggae', as filtered through Damon Edge's melted plastic brain. Kinda makes me think Adolphe Sax woulda had second thoughts had he known such noise addicts were gonna get their mitts on his beloved invention. On second thunks, you remember that Mothers of Invention track off *Freak Out* entitled 'The Chrome-Plated Megaphone of Destiny'? Well, I'm sure that's the instrument Edge and co. employed in order to achieve this braying ass of a sound.

The three minutes of 'ST 37' follows, a pachuco spider-on-roller-skates barn dance with spiky, picked electric guitar, clattering snare drums and lowest-common-denominator lyrics about getting in a Winnebago and going to San Diego. That this song gave its name to one of the '90s best American space-rock bands is certainly evidence that not everyone had forgotten Chrome, although, as with Bowie's 'TVC15', I've no idea what the title means.

Alien Soundtracks concludes with the 'Iron Man'-like instrumental riffery of 'Magnetic Dwarf People', as the sparks fly upward and the skank of nations drags us, with biblical intensity, westward across the night sky, forever chasing the sunset. Beautiful . . . fucking beautiful . . . If anyone asks you about Chrome, tell 'em *Alien Soundtracks* nailed it, end of story.

Half Machine Lip Moves

That said, when their third LP hit the streets, one year later, I gots to admit that – although patchy and shatteringly unlistenable in places as it was – nobody ever started an album with as much fire as Chrome did with the opening of *Half Machine Lip Moves.* Hell, the first time I heard the guitar riff in 'TV as Eyes', I thought I'd died and gone to rock'n'roll heaven. The second time, I knew it. This song remains my favourite beginning to any rock'n'roll record, surpassing even Iggy and The Stooges' *Raw Power*, Blue Cheer's *Outsideinside* and Pere Ubu's *The Modern Dance.* On it, flanged, fuck-everything, arhythmical guitars whoop like itinerant, eunuchised priests of Frey pushing their ox-carted god across a field, until the greatest, most monolithic punk guitar riff ever bursts forth, and Damon Edge parps:

I don't know why I should wait there,
I don't know why.

I gotta find a way there,
I don't know why.

Something you feel inside,
I don't know why.

Something I feel inside,
I don't know why,
Writing in the back of my poor mind.

Edge expels each syllable so radically, so sneeringly, so droolingly that his cud-chewing gob John Garner-ises beyond the words 'TV as Eyes' then collapses into the motorik Neu!-ness of 'Zombie Warfare' which proceeds to fall in on itself, becoming a faceless industrial skank permeating the perished air vents of some disused industrial estate. 'March of the Chrome Police' returns us to super-catchy chorus territory, as Damon serenades us over a typical (if bass-less) garage-rock riff, as usual, undermined by the sheer sibilance of the hi-hats and the immensely bad mic technique of the backing vocalist, who sneers and agrees with the lead vocals, although at a volume at least twice as loud. 'A cold, clammy bombing will ruin your town,' yammers Edge. 'We'll shit on your town.'

'You've Been Duplicated' is another Damon Edge 'hit', containing an irresistible chorus and twanging, Wild West guitar, although its bright, melodic light is sunk beneath layers of those exquisitely hissing drums that Chrome went out of their way to achieve. Unless these guys spent hours just building up supplies of readymade *musique concrète* with which to pour over otherwise sonically acceptable songs, it surely cannot have been easy to create a sound this degraded, this stinky, this contaminated.

Side One concludes with the vile anarchy of 'Mondo Anthem', whose interminable three minutes of cut-ups shoehorns together drum-machine freak-outs, buzzing, riffy guitar bludgeon and sped-up '50s vocal music, as though produced by Frank Zappa having dropped acid with Faust, thereafter disowning all his classical allusions in favour of home-made, Harry Partch-style percussion. Imagine The Residents' 'Six Things to a Cycle' through a ring modulator, and yooz somewhere close.

The album's title track, which commences Side Two, is, again, deep in Residents' territory and about as catchy as their 'Satisfaction'. It still presents me with shocks after three decades of playing it. The vocals are as arch as those of the Mothers on *Absolutely Free*, and each track segues mercilessly and seamlessly into the next, creating as psychedelic a trip as ever there was. However, I gots to admit Chrome lost even me on this side of the disc. It really is 'too, too, too to put a finger on'. Is this track 'Abstract Nympho', or was that last fade-out a part of 'Turned Around'? I dunno. Keep listening and keep navigating and maybe we'll find a signpost, a side street, a lay-by, anything to help us in this disorientating morass of sound-effects.

Sometimes, a moment of coherence – a punk reference – slips through, but each time things revert back to the tidal wave of chaos. Only with the less than two minutes of 'Turned Around' does anything like a catchy chorus surface out of the ether, but we're soon overtaken by Turkish robots playing Hawkwind's 'You Shouldn't Do That (Zero Time)', or two minutes of late Can as played by *Babyfingers*-period Residents ('Creature Eternal'). A whole LP of this stuff would be a settler for the listener, a storming chaos that could act as a psychic poultice to the tortured brain. Unfortunately, there's not enough of anything for it to act positively and 'Critical Mass' concludes the LP disappointingly, being no more than a tough but highly anonymous riff with which to fade back into the ether.

And Thereafter Did They Slowly Change and Dissolve

Much of Chrome's Buchla confusion and tinnitus-inducing, drumled groove receded into the middle distance after the salvo of the three opening LPs. Unfortunately, signing to Beggars Banquet in the UK coincided with the band's reducing to just the kernel of Edge and Helios Creed. *Red Exposure* contained many fine moments from the duo; indeed, Side Two of that record is as gloriously scripted and consistent a piece of Chrome work as any. But Chrome's fire-breathing dragon no longer had an amphetamine pessary up his psychic jacksie, and each subsequent release paled before the sounds of its predecessors. When Helios Creed left to record the first of many intriguing solo LPs, Chrome became a successful vehicle for Damon Edge – his subsequent European career facilitated by French musicians. But these late records bear none of the Chrome hallmark sound, as Edge now neither drummed nor applied that smear-mouth, radioactive, gum-chewing vocal to his songs.

Nevertheless, anyone who chooses to equip themselves with the records discussed above will soon discover that *Alien Soundtracks* especially, and *Half Machine Lip Moves* to a slightly lesser extent, are definitely as important a musical Year Zero as the albums of their more eulogised contemporaries. Moreover, uncovering more of the early Chrome trip can still be a fragmented and frustrating gas, as I discovered when I missed, by minutes, the opportunity to win on eBay a rare reel-to-reel tape of their *Ultra Soundtrack*, a real Holy Grail Chrome relic that was recorded in

San Francisco for a porn show but never used. So re-excavation of the Chrome canon can only irrigate the muse of those who choose to shine their own flashlight into that intriguing and mythical place, and I'm sure that much still awaits us down in Damon Edge's basement . . . if you'd care to go down there.

Essential Discography

The Visitation (Siren, 1976)
Alien Soundtracks (Siren, 1978)
Half Machine Lip Moves (Siren, 1979)
Red Exposure (Siren, 1980)

Culpeper's Orchard

(Polydor, 1971)

SIDE ONE	SIDE TWO
1 Mountain Music (Part One) (6.27)	1 Your Song and Mine (5.34)
2 Hey, You People (1.29)	2 Gideon's Trap (5.44)
3 Tea Party for an Orchard (6.10)	3 Blue Day's Morning (2.12)
4 Ode to Resistance (5.55)	4 Mountain Music (Part Two) (7.33)

Although I briefly mention this Anglo-Danish quartet in *Danskrocksampler*,[1] this, their self-titled debut LP, was such a consistent work that I figured it would make perfect listening during long, Midsummer days.

What Time Is It? The Seventeenth Century?

Replete with extremely catchy songs, fiery, Dervish-like guitar solos, confidently self-referential lyrics from poet/guitarist Scott 'Wino' Weinrich, all the while the entire ensemble spewing euphoric vocal harmonies over intricate and furiously hard-edged arrangements, this Album of the Month owes its artistic success not to any great dream of originality, but to the wild spirits of each of its performers and especially that of its primary writer – one Cy Nicklin

1 Back then, I wrote: '*Culpeper's Orchard* was a highly involved and heavily vocalled and rocked-out take on "No Time"-period Guess Who/late Buffalo Springfield as played by *The Yes Album*-period Yes, with lashings of Procol Harum's "Whiter Shade of Pale" and Thunderclap Newman's "Accidents" thrown in, and (ooh-er) Dieter Dierks at the soundboard. If that sounds horrendous, then it's my fault because it's compulsive and euphoric and wholly authentic. This lot was led by an ex-pat Yank by the name of Cy Nicklin, whose self-referential trip is occasionally too twee and cloying, but mainly it's authentic in a manner similar to that of Burton Cummings, and hefts their trip up considerably. Methinks readers of these Cope articles are gonna love or hate this band unreservedly, with no in-betweens. Me, I love this record because I already love and therefore accept its references; but then I loved *Axe Victim* by Be-Bop Deluxe *because*, not in spite of, its Ziggyphilia.'

– and his clear desire to contribute highly accessible, hippie-dream music that sat well alongside such million-selling contemporary heroes as The Moody Blues, Crosby, Tween, Nash and Young, Led Zeppelin, Traffic and The Who. *Ooh-er*, missus, get that lot wrong and it coulda been God's Own Abortion. Ah, but the über-thorough Nicklin and co. made damn sure they goddit entirely right.

So, the wonderful results are somewhat like that vigorous, enormous and ever-unfolding medley on Side Two of The Beatles' *Abbey Road* as executed by the overtly power-trio-muscular but acoustically driven *Four Sail*-period Love, featuring The Obsessed's Scott 'Wino' Weinrich on lead vocals. There, now we're approaching Ye Culpeper's Orchard pleasure centre. Add to that several dollops of Buffalo Springfield's elongated and countrified version of 'Bluebird', and a few of the more uproarious moments of Yes' 1970 album *Time and a Word* and 1971's *The Yes Album*, and you've probably hit the nail on the head . . . never forgetting (natch) the obvious influence of Mason Williams' ubiquitous 'Classical Gas', the infectious licks of which pervade the very veins and arteries that fuel this entire body of Anglo-danskwerk. Phew!

So, for sure, this is wannabe music from back in the day, but it's the kind of artfully constructed and heftily executed wannabe music that presses all the appropriate buttons at the right times and still sounds mighty fresh. So if yooz looking for something new from your nostalgia and you need a disc that rocks like Wishbone Ash's *Argus* but one that doesn't also immediately remind you of being dissed by some chick at the youth club, you've come to the right place. Or maybe you never dare mention The Moody Blues because work friends always just say 'Nights in White Satin', while you still secretly seek the euphoric rush of bliss that cascades over your entire outer mantle whenever Justin Hayward's Hank B. guitar solo kicks in over M. Pinder's stentorian piano on the tailout of 'The Story in Your Eyes'. Then, baby, you just arrived home and *Culpeper's Orchard* is the album for you.

Released on Polydor, Denmark, in 1971, to absolutely no international response whatsoever, this LP was entirely the work of two Danes (lead guitarist Niels Henriksen and bassist Michael Fries) and two Copenhagen-based ex-pats, English drummer Rodger Barker and American former Sandy Denny associate and songwriter Cy Nicklin. Following a brief Danish tour with Denny,

Nicklin had become ensconced at the Free Christiania Commune, just outside Copenhagen, where he briefly joined the band Day of Phoenix. But the arrival from the UK of drummer Barker prompted Nicklin to put together a band specifically to perform his newest songs. Providentially, Culpeper's Orchard's early signing to Polydor's Danish division allowed the band's songs to gestate, facilitated by the renting of a huge farmhouse in which to 'get it together in the country', in the style of The Band, Traffic and suchlike. There's certainly a genuine sense of rich artistic remove from the everyday urban bustle informing, nay, pervading this record; Nicklin even included a verse about rushing out to see a storm, only to discover that the noise was actually 'Rodger, practising the drums.'

Culpeper's Orchard opens with the euphoric, six and a half minutes of 'Mountain Music (Part One)', a masterful offering that commences with a Krauty, Amon Düül II/Curved Air-style riff, over which Cy Nicklin declaims in a husky voice somewhere between Steve Stills, Burton Cummings and Justin Hayward. An almost Who-ian madness ensues in the form of one hell of an elongated guitar power-drive from Niels Henriksen, until some semblance of order is restored in the last minutes, wherein reed organ and harmony vocals take over.

Then we move into the ultra-brief, rent-a-hippie, CSNY, catchy-catchy chorale of 'Hey, You People', which concludes violently with a terrific Pete Banks-informed, early-Yes steal, before melding seamlessly into the epic, six-minute prog ballad 'Tea Party for an Orchard'. This is the closest we get on the whole LP to a truly twee, sub-Dave Mason moment, but as this song is still one helluva catchy bastard, we forgive its trespasses moments later when the whole mix up-ends and sends us off into a spaced-out, 7UP world of ring modulators, Dieter Dierks-stylee.

Thereafter, the band performs a live edit which allows them to change horses and cop the most unashamed 'Yours Is No Disgrace' tailout you could imagine, just like Side One of *The Yes Album* as played by *Déjà Vu*-period Crosby, Stills, Nash and Young (not that the two are so far apart, anyway). The near-six-minute-long epic 'Ode to Resistance' closes Side One and is pure *Wheatfield Soul*-period Guess Who, as interpolated through the stereo effects in 'Yours Is No Disgrace'. Ooh ja, mein hairies!

As I note in the *Glamrocksampler* entry, I often experience a real yearning for that genre's massed clatter (the glitterstompf thump, the dive-bombing Les Paul guitars and the Mick Ronson and/or Tony Visconti post-*Imagine* string sections of archetypal glam-rock), without ever wishing to resort to one more spin of hoary faves such as 'The Jean Genie' or 'Metal Guru'. I admit also that I often seek, and *find*, solace in certain lost glam efforts, not because they are as artistically sound as those so-called greats, but because these lost tracks – in accepting the glam-rock metaphor as delivered to them by the masters – often contain all of the aforementioned glam ingredients, but carefully regurgitated in a manner that gives them the appearance of being new. It is in that same manner that *Culpeper's Orchard* works so well today. The album is thorough, consistent and horribly more-ish.

'Your Song and Mine' opens Side Two with huge acoustic guitars and the sensational opening lyric: 'Rainbow from your arse will fill the skies/ Blows your tears away.' Whoa! Go, Cy, go! Maybe he figured that to lay it out all Shakespearean-like would render the lyric more opaque and therefore less offensive to Danes, especially over a demented and catchy-as-a-bastard Moody Blues/ Buffalo Springfield hybrid.

Then follows the bizarre and vast ballad 'Gideon's Trap', a kind of funereal 'A Day in the Life'-meets-Thunderclap Newman's nine-minute-long behemoth 'Accidents', although in possession of a mighty and euphoric tail-out, somewhat akin to Mick Ronno 'Moonage Daydreaming' over 'A Whiter Shade of Pale'. It's effortlessly beautiful. Propelled shamelessly by Rodger Barker's play-in-a-day-like-Beatle-Ringo blip-blop-der-bop-der-bop bop bop, this song reaches a cosmic climax not because it is possessed of greatness, but because the recorded version just absolutely refuses to back off.

Next up, and stuck quite appropriately in the boneyard, the super-brief 'Blue Day's Morning' is just all right 'Through My Sails', common-or-garden, ho-hum, CSNY fodder.

Nevertheless, it's with Cy Nicklin belting his head off in his best, proto-'Wino' Weinrich dialect that this wild album concludes.

Even better, the mighty seven minutes-plus of 'Mountain Music (Part Two)' is an entirely different musical beast to its opener namesake on Side One. Sure, it's another intricately arranged hard-rock song, but this one has a strangely ornate production that kind of pre-empts *Sabbath Bloody Sabbath*, as the final two minutes of this album reach higher and higher, as though a fuzz-toned,

Paranoid-period Tony Iommi had become accidentally caught in the lush and overly elaborate rigging of 'Spiral Architect', only to discover that his volume and tone knobs had jammed. Luckily for us, or watt! It's an epic conclusion to a fabulous piece of work.

In Conclusion

Thus endeth another Album of the Month, our heroes forgotten temporarily but hardily in a situation that is unexcavable. Purely on the quality of its songs, arrangements and performances, *Culpeper's Orchard* is guaranteed a place in future rock'n'roll history. Since first mentioning this album in *Danskrocksampler*, I have discovered that its successor, *Second Sight*, was a disappointing and patchy record. On it, drummer Rodger Barker was replaced by Danish superstar Ken Gudmand, of Young Flowers, but the great songs were few. Still, *Culpeper's Orchard* remains one classic debut LP and an enduring testament to the healthy state of so-called progressive-rock back in 1971, a time when the music played by bands of that genre still owed more to the robust post-psychedelia of The Youngbloods, The Guess Who, The Moody Blues, etc., than to the tempo gymnastics of ELP, Gentle Giant and their unctuous, conservatory-bumming ilk.[2]

Indeed, 1971 was, in hindsight, a veritable doorway of decision-making for the prog-rockers: do we continue to mine the healthy song-based seams as excavated by fine, forward-thinking, late-'60s songwriters (Steve Stills, Neil Young, Syd Barrett and Arthur Lee come to mind)? Or do we admit to ourselves that we ain't got a single original tune in our bourgeois heads and, instead, hoodwink the audience by choosing the orchestral path of Vanilla Sludge, thus gaining valuable *Sunday Times* credibility by modifying barely known Eastern European classics by such highly regarded (and rarely heard) Russky composers as Son-of-a-Bitch and Suck-me-off? As evidenced by the geographically challenged band members who recorded *Culpeper's Orchard*, even for those without a brain, 'twas a no-brainer. The song mattered. And so, like the druids before them, Culpeper's Orchard

2 Although Curved Air was sold to us in 1971 by Warner Brothers' hype entirely based on the presence of a virtuoso classical violinist (Eddie Jobson), the gimmicky twelve-inch picture disc was of such poor quality that the murky results sounded enticingly Gothic and truly psychedelic in an Amon Düül II-meets-Jefferson Airplane/*Crown of Creation* manner.

said nothing new; but they said it with such poetic aplomb and respect for the traditions that this music resonates with almost the same truth as that of the Truly Greats. Yowzah or what?

Discography

Culpeper's Orchard (Polydor, 1971)
Second Sight (Polydor, 1972)
Going for a Song (compilation, Polydor, 1972)

Miles Davis: On the One

(1974–75)

In Praise of *Get Up with It*, *Dark Magus*, *Agharta* and *Pangaea*

In May 2001, a long, two-part documentary of Miles Davis' career was broadcast on British TV. As my wife and I sat down to watch, she looked at me and said sarcastically: 'Hey, I'll bet they spend *ages* on the period you like!' She was ragging on me because the only Miles Davis I listen to is his (to the high-minded jazz fan) 'sell-out' period from 1974–75. Of course, when the documentary came to this favourite period of mine, it was summarily dismissed not as a less-achieving, tail-end of Miles' most fertile era, but as the actual beginning of his artistic winter. Whoa! I felt so intensely un-served by the documentary that I was moved to write this long essay on what I see as a truly extraordinary and extra-perceptionary period of this great artist's life. In so doing, I would like to make clear the fact that I do not approach this from the angle of a jazz fan; indeed, quite the opposite. I here judge Miles Davis' most-dismissed musical era from the point of view of a rock'n'roll, Krautrock and cosmic-music devotee with a long-standing quest for the shamanic other. Rite On!

In choosing both *Dark Magus* and *Pangaea* for this Album of the Month, I felt that it was imperative to give these records a greater context, and, in so doing, it really needed an entire article to be written around them. I am not a jazz fan in any shape or form, but, as aficionados around the world have long been at pains to point out, Miles Davis' music in the mid-'70s was not strictly 'jazz' at all. Rather, it was a shamanic funk that reached for the same stars which had earlier shone for Ash Ra Tempel, Can and early Amon Düül

II. *Downbeat* magazine writer Greg Tate probably hit the nail on the head when he called Miles' combo of this era: 'The world's first fully-improvisational acid-funk band.'

Right Off: Towards a Meditational Funk

In 1974 and 1975, Miles Davis recorded and released a series of albums deemed by his legions of fans (both in and outside the music business) to be so far out that they were only worthy of release in Japan, or were otherwise consigned to total obscurity until rescued in the mid-'90s. Miles was burned out, maintained the critics. He was looking for a young, hip, black audience, they said. After those LPs, he stopped recording for five years – proof positive that he was nowhere; or so they said.

I beg to differ. Throughout my prolonged shamanic search for a sustained sonic obliteration, I have on occasion been led, open-minded and open-mouthed, down several blind alleys. But, far more often, I have found myself travelling down wide-open avenues leading to music which is tantamount to a blueprint for third-eye travel. The side-long freak-outs of Krautrock, sure, Japanese improvisation and free-rock, natch, indeed even proto-metal has caught me out with its wildly long work-outs on great rock'n'roll songs; yet my discovery of Miles Davis' astonishingly visionary and inspired, but nowadays critically detested, 1974–75 'sell-out to funk' period has made me understand more than ever that the necessary requirements for the soundtrack to shamanic flight may be found in the most unlikely quarters of all.

Miles Davis, sheesh! I never thought I'd be writing about him in a million years. I hate jazz as much for the instruments they use as for the rhythms themselves: saxophone, trumpet and flute? Get lost! I always loved the musicians themselves and their stories and their lives and their aims, too. But the result was always a total no-go area for me, or so I thunk. How wrong I was!

The music of Miles Davis during 1974 and 1975 was the epitome of sonic shamanism. In four double albums, he distilled all that he had learned in the previous decades into a sustained and punishing maelstrom of sound – truly that third-eye travel blueprint which I had been searching for. For this new music, Davis dumped whole accepted areas of jazz and, instead, adopted the wildly loud and distorted freak-out guitar of Jimi Hendrix and Funkadelic's Eddie Hazel, and the 'on-the-one' rhythms of turn-of-the-'70s James Brown. Then he extended James' ten-minute grooves into half-hour jams taking up whole LP sides, and took the role of a witch doctor/musical director, often standing motionless in his bizarre Sly Stone shades, his trumpet reduced to no more than a baton with which to command the troops. When Miles did contribute notes to this fury, it was frequently without the trumpet he had become so legendary for playing. Instead, he commandeered Sly Stone's organ sound and played it Irmin Schmidt-style – wearing an oven glove! Chord structures were entirely abandoned in favour of rhythm; often it was left to the underpinning Fender bass of Michael Henderson alone to give any hint of acceptably orthodox musical content.

Sax player Dave Liebman has even written of the, admittedly brief, relief he and the other musicians would feel at hearing an A-minor chord emanating from the Davis organ, before this oasis of sound would evaporate, returning them all to the desert of percussion and howling which Miles so obviously craved.[1] No bones for the dogs! There's even a famous story about how Miles came around to Sly's house and started playing his jazz 'clusters' on Sly's keyboard – fistfuls of notes at a time, with no semblance of chordal consonance. The gospel-choir-educated Sly Stone called Miles 'a motherfucker' and kicked him out for playing such unrighteous 'voodoo' in his house.

Who Says a Jazz Band Can't Play Funk Music?

Evidence shows that the story of Miles Davis and his funk trip has been obscured from history by a jazz crowd embarrassed by what they perceived as a series of slipshod Miles records, when, really, they just couldn't get to grips with the place he was so clearly headed towards. Listening to hugely acclaimed Miles 'classics' such as *On the Corner*, *In a Silent Way* and *Live Evil*, it became clear that, through their sonic fury yet musical overplaying, Miles' next step, into the period which I'm now praising, was mainly to do with his completely letting go of any remaining 'classical' jazz-musician aspirations, instead embracing the truly barbarian. Wonderfully schooled jazz musicians, such as Miles' sidemen John McLaughlin and Billy Cobham, were, in this 'meditational

1 Dave Liebman, *Dark Magus* sleeve-notes.

funk' period, replaced by guys from R&B and soul backgrounds. Reggie Lucas came in on exclusively wah-wah'd rhythm guitar, while the Afro'd, ex-Muddy Waters guitarist Pete Cosey took up the frenzied lead position on a Fender Telecaster put through multiple effects pedals and a small, monophonic synthesizer.

For this new, super-loud ensemble, the ungroovy double bass was replaced by a Fender Jazz wielded by Stevie Wonder's aforementioned bassist Michael Henderson, a musician who brought a whole new sense of punctuation to the house party. On drums was the amazing Al Foster, whom Miles had discovered playing in a New York club. Foster it was who took the 'on-the-one' route to its ultimate conclusion. As Miles Davis would later write in his autobiography: 'Al could set shit up for everyone to play off and then he could keep the groove going forever.'[2]

Completing the rhythm section was Miles' young friend James Mtume, who facilitated Davis' increasingly Afro-centric fixation with his use of log drums, African hand percussion, water drums and a rudimentary drum machine played with an intriguing and strangely arhythmic attitude.

But it would seem that the only way into this Miles Davis period is to be alerted by some head in the know. Miles fans hate it all and rag on people for liking it – even my friend, the American rock'n'roll writer Michael Krugman, says it's trash. He once took my wife aside and commented, of me, 'He only likes the weird Miles shit!' And he's generally a forward-thinking motherfucker . . .

But the more I heard of Miles' 1974–75 period, the clearer it became that he never sold out at all. Instead, what the critics have called burn-out' in the mid-'70s happened not because of what has been perceived as Miles' desire merely to attract a young and hip black audience, but as a result of his sheer determination to create what I call 'meditational funk'.

For what the jazz-loving Miles Davis fan would consider to have been an affronting (and even uncool) sell-out turns out, to this forward-thinking Krautrock and Funkadelic maniac, to have been nothing less than the great Cunt of the Mother opening in a manner in which she had rarely opened before. For Miles to have created the music of this period by accidental burn-out would have been impossible. Had he burned out, he would have given up the reins of arrangements to his producer,

2 Miles Davis, *Miles, The Autobiography* (Simon & Schuster, 1989).

Teo Macero, who would surely have employed far more stock, hip, Afro-American devices in the music. Had Miles really burned out and sold out, there would surely not now be such an enormous body of evidence of his apprenticeship-serving in the form of such LPs as *A Tribute to Jack Johnson*,[3] *On the Corner* and *Live Evil*. For me, it makes sense that this early-'70s music has long been regarded as visionary genius in both jazz and rock-music circles, for it is the most emulated, most acrobatic (or noodling), and it was chock-full of future jazz-rock stars like John McLaughlin, Billy Cobham and all those guys who crossed over to rock audiences.

But, at this earlier point, it was still jazz rising up out of the '60s maelstrom. And it is my assertion that it was only in 1974, when he had purged himself and his band of all those jazzers, that Davis was able to create music beyond ego, in which everyone, himself included, became subsumed into the raging sonic torrent. Only then could Miles Davis embark on these perfect meditational funk LPs, all of them doubles and all of them dedicated to picking up a groove and maintaining it at all costs.

Get Up with It

Released in January 1975, *Get Up with It* had far more soul-brother style in its LP jacket and James Brown-like title than in any of its actual musical content. Miles loomed huge yet mysterious across both outer faces of the gatefold sleeve; his hexagonal shades alluding to Sly Stone, and the sepia printing echoing James Brown's classic 1973 refusenik double LP *The Payback*. Yet the eight tracks within its, at first, seemingly impenetrable grooves are undermined by Miles' decision to open this monster work with the half-hour-long kosmische music known as 'He Loved Him Madly'.

If this was a guy seeking a young

3 Check out Miles' 1971 documentary soundtrack, *A Tribute to Jack Johnson*. Its two, side-long tracks are worth hearing just for the depths of slackness which Miles' goads such luminaries as John McLaughlin and Billy Cobham into de-achieving. The opening of 'Right Off' is truly such a eulogy to sloppiness that the first few listens can cause actual laughter in the listener. Miles' interest in the black champion-boxer Jack Johnson, and the problems of envy which his success caused the white population, sent Miles into the boxing gym four times a week during this period. He claimed that he understood how Johnson felt when he was fined a hundred dollars for driving an unlicensed Ferrari, something which, he maintained, would never have happened had he been white.

audience, he surely weren't looking very hard. For the incredible beauty of this opening piece is the manner in which it hangs in mid-air, almost motionless yet light as the breeze. Imagine suspending a huge child's mobile from the ceiling of Wookey Hole caves with a drawing-pin night-light and then measuring its movement. This is the motion of 'He Loved Him Madly' – it's a tethered and chloroformed flight of butterflies and dragonflies and fireflies, spacily and dazedly encircling the night-light, never completely leaving their tight orbit.

Miles' wah-wah trumpet and Dave Liebman's lyrical flute guide the way, as three extremely restrained, bluesy wah-guitars fuss and fidget in the near distance. Hollow congas barely punctuate the hugely reverbed sound for the first half of the track, until Al Foster finally picks up the beat, elevating into an insistent but bass-less 'on-the-one' reminiscent of James Brown's epic 'Mind Power', but even more ambiently groovy. It is difficult to say precisely what each instrument is doing here, but then, during this curious period, Miles Davis had openly expressed his wish 'to confound critics, so they couldn't tell what instrument was responsible for what sounds'.[4]

The same group of musicians open Side Two, but the twelve minutes of 'Maiysha' are something else; a hugely loose soul-bossa nova propelled by Miles' overdriven wah-organ and 'Superfly'-style guitar chords, which seem to have no idea just when Miles will make his change. This is a peculiar combination: using a fairly defined musical base on which to add experimental chordal elements which are totally out of place and at odds with the fundamental style of the piece. Out of nowhere, a distorted, FX'd lead guitar howls out of the right-hand speaker, while *Stand*-period Freddie Stone-type choppy guitar slashes a rhythmic path through the broad swathes of verdant chords which sing out of Miles' fertile keyboard.

For 'Honky Tonk', with its funky multi-keyboards and drumless beginning, Miles reached back to earlier days, from a time when the band was populated by more famous and more seasoned jazz musicians like John McLaughlin, Billy Cobham, Herbie Hancock and Keith Jarrett. Indeed, this recalls the early '70s, when Miles Davis recorded his excellent *A Tribute to Jack Johnson* LP. 'Honky Tonk''s loose, wah-wah beginning is reminiscent of the Family Stone's workout,

4 Kevin Whitehead, *Pangaea* sleeve-notes.

'Sex Machine', also on *Stand.* And, when the drums finally come in, the groove affects a huge sense of relief in the listener.

'Rated X' closes Side Two: it's a fierce and hugely ominous, organ-dominated, African-and-Indian-percussion-led piece, in which the wah-guitar of Reggie Lucas and the sitar of guest player Khalil Balakrishna conspire to harry the rest of the musicians, like snarling jackals worrying a much larger prairie animal. The piece slowly builds and builds to a deafening climax of organ chords; only then, as the sound collapses and subsides, revealing the bell-like piano chords of guest Cedric Lawson.

The whole of Side Three is given over to the brilliant half an hour-plus of 'Calypso Frelimo', in which Miles subsumes his personality further than ever into the music, contenting himself with themes on organ and piano, while guest sax player John Stobblefield takes his instrument into areas previously only inhabited by the trumpet flights of Miles himself. The whole thing sounds like a massive jam on Can's *Ege Bamyasi*-period mini-epic 'Pinch'. Michael Henderson's bass playing is all punctuated pop and groove, wholly reminiscent of Holger Czukay, while the furious wah-guitars of Reggie Lucas and Pete Cosey chatter and gas in the margins (panned far right and left in the speakers).

About a third of the way through this clatterstomp, the rhythm drops way, way down into its boots, and Michael Henderson puts out a pulsing, Larry Grahamesque riff as the wah-guitars howl their heavy metal into the night. Miles continues his theme intermittently, a theme to which he would return again and again throughout this period (sometimes in seemingly the most inappropriate places), and John Stobblefield's sax continues to ape his master's horn in the deep darkness of reverb. Then the track picks up again and continues in its deeply Can-ish manner.

'Red China Blues' is a real anomaly on *Get Up with It*, a big, brassy, 6/8 blues with wailing harmonica and Cornel Dupree's big-bodied rhythm-guitar chords slashing out a relentless melody. It's fine, I guess, but if it wasn't here, then I surely wouldn't miss it.

Wait, instead, for the curiously named and curious sounding 'Mtume', named after Miles' percussionist, James Mtume. This extravagant rhythmic piledriver of a sound is driven by the choppy wah-guitars of Pete Cosey and Reggie Lucas and the log drum of Mtume himself, while Miles' atonal, squally wah-organ chords do their best to undermine the entire sound. Again, although here it is far more thunderous and disorderly, we're close to approaching a sound similar to Can's *Ege Bamyasi*, released two or three years previously. If Miles Davis was serious about his awareness of Stockhausen, is it possible that he was unaware of Can at this time? It seems almost impossible to me.

At one point deep in the tune, he blasts the entire band with a cluster of shattering organ non-chords, akin to zapping them with a ray gun, but soon they're back on that jittery freak-beat and they ain't about to give any of it up. Miles has now taken James Brown's jungle groove and left it breathless and scorched on the outskirts of the desert.

Get Up with It finishes with the even more curiously titled 'Billy Preston', a steaming and insistent, James Brown-like African soul dance. Again, it's also extremely Krautrock-like, in a Can kind of way, and Michael Henderson's Holger Czukay-style bass is here syncopated to create a sort of bass-marimba effect. The regular gang is here, joined by guests Cedric Lawson on organ and Khalil Balakrishna on sitar, while the lead is taken by the sax of Carlos Garnett, who, like John Stobblefield before him, manages to ape the horn sound which is pure Miles.

While Miles Davis employed the same general pool of musicians throughout this period, it's worth noting that he also used the same stable of instruments, processed through the same configuration of effects pedals. So, whatever the personnel each night, the limits of their musical palette were always very clearly laid out.

Get Up with It is an extraordinary double LP, meticulously dedicated to locating a very specific groove. But however brain-frying this massive statement was, it was still only the beginning of a sequence of extraordinary albums. And, as we will see, Miles Davis was determined to further distil his sound until it was honed down and down and ever further down.

Dark Magus

Recorded in concert at Carnegie Hall, on March 30 1974, *Dark Magus* is located, therefore, both earlier and later than the *Get Up with It* sessions. But, while the latter album works hardest to define the new, shamanic Miles sound, *Dark Magus* is probably the most musically concise because it was captured on tape in one single evening of fury. Indeed, of all four double LPs under discussion here, *Dark Magus* is the most tightly drawn and the most mysterious and difficult to fathom.

Unyielding and as narrowly defined in its musical parameters as reggae or ska, the music of *Dark Magus* revealed that Miles was by now so dedicated to the 'on-the-one' rhythm which James Brown had instigated and George Clinton had championed that even his biggest admirers were having problems following him. Indeed, *Dark Magus* initially only saw release in Japan.

The wah-guitarists Messrs Cosey and Lucas were here joined by a third guitarist, Dominic Gaumont, and all three conspired with the rhythm trio of Al Foster, Michael Henderson and James Mtume to unleash a savagery which would not let up for the entire concert. Indeed, sax player Dave Liebman's sleeve-notes admit that none of them knew where one piece ended and another began, and Liebman himself believes that Miles only much later gave the music individual titles in order to bring some hint of order to the primordial soupiness of the proceedings.

I use the phrase 'some hint of order' because *a hint* is really all we get. When I explain that Disc One's tracks are 'Moja (Part 1)', 'Moja (Part 2)', 'Wili (Part 1)' and 'Wili (Part 2)', you could be forgiven for thinking that it was all a big wind-up intended to confuse us even further. But, when I explain that Disc Two's tracks are 'Tatu (Part 1)', 'Tatu (Part 2) (Calypso Frelimo)', 'Nne (Part 1) (Ife)' and 'Nne (Part 2)', then it becomes clear that Miles was surely intending to cloak the entire trip in some impenetrable mystery.

And so it is best to listen to *Dark Magus* as a whole, preferably on repeat for hours on end. Its fury rarely subsides, and, soon, the whole of the listening space becomes a shamanic environment where time is meaningless and the world outside is forgotten.

Agharta

So now we come to the monster that is *Agharta*, an album which even turns up in lists of people's favourite heavy-metal records. All right! Recorded in the afternoon of February 1 1975, at Osaka Festival Hall, Japan, *Agharta* opens with the soberly titled 'Prelude', a twenty-two-minute wah-wah-wah from the bowels of Mother Earth. Miles opens the ritual with a super-groovy, now-where-have-I-heard-that-before? organ, every riff of which sounds as though he's playing the tune of Dr John's 'I Walk on Guilded Splinters' in a Funkadelic, 'Music for My Mother' stylee. Then we're coupled to a long freight train with a cargo bound for the heart of the every-desert.

You wanna know the sound of this Mongol horde nation on the move? It's *wah-wah-wah-wah-wah-wah-wah-wah-wah-wah-wah-wah-wah-wah-wah-wah-wah-wah-wah-wah-wah-wah!* Stampeding elephants, running parallel to our train, trumpet and bray, but they just can't keep up. Compassionate Miles stops the train for a moment to let them catch up; then we're off again, through the brush and cactus, as Sonny Fortune stands astride the observation car and blows a small, straight, soprano saxophone as though the lives of this entire migrant nation depended on it.

If you love the sound of all seven CDs from The Stooges' *Funhouse* boxed set played simultaneously throughout the house on small, inferior ghetto-blasters, then you'll adore this fucking sound. If you ever wondered how Can's 'Mushroom' would sound if the band members were clones of each other and could all play exactly one beat ahead of the other, well, you've got it!

Jazz critics, set on blaming someone other than Miles for the music of this period, were quick to say that bassist Michael Henderson was out of his depth. Out of his fucking depth! This is the Very Reverend Michael Henderson, Lord of 'The One' and Crown Prince of Simplicity when all around him is a Montserratian volcano of chaos. And proof of this dedication is most clearly evidenced in the magnificence of the *Aghartan* storm known as 'Prelude'.

So, anyway, you fade out of 'Prelude' and stick Side Two on the turntable, and what do we got? More of the fucking same! Another ten minutes, already! 'Prelude Part Two'! By now, Sonny Fortune's soprano sax has joined forces with Miles' horn to create some of the most contrary a-sectional brass-playing this side of the Laughing Clowns' *Mr Uddich-Schmuddich Goes to Town*. Meanwhile, the guitars are buzzing around like locusts in a royal shit-storm. Reggie Lucas' rhythmic, *wokka-wokka-wokka-wokka-wokka-wokka-wokka* is, as ever, relentless and dedicated to the groove, while Pete Cosey's car-alarm guitar solos shudder and judder in the far-left corner. Then, without hesitation, we're suddenly propelled into the light-as-a-breeze super-cool of 'Maiysha', here rogered by Cosey's Ernie Isley-like, FX'd lead guitar. The beat drops completely, leaving Cosey exposed and raging. He sounds like his guitar is going through that synthesizer he's often credited with playing. Then back we drop into the light flute of Sonny Fortune, as Lucas provides a cool, cool, bluesy-toned, soul rhythm guitar.

Side Three is entirely taken up by the twenty-six minutes of 'Interlude', another soberly titled freak-out which kicks off at a typically furious, *Dark Magus*-like pace; an Al Foster-driven chariot race through ancient city streets. Sonny Fortune's alto saxophone wails like Miles' own trumpet and the track thunders through phase after phase of new groove. A strident sax blitz occupies the centre section, its walking bass placing the music deep-inner-heart-of-the-city. But the atonality soon returns in the shape of a strange and elliptical groove, in which Pete Cosey sets his monophonic synthesizer (it sounds like a Moog Rogue or something equally rudimentary), and lets it fizz and buzz around the hall like some motor-bike-engined V1 terror weapon.

By this time, we're getting into pure space-rock territory and the clusters of organ chords combine with Lucas' primal electric guitar to confound any eavesdropper, preventing them from ever guessing the provenance of this magical and timeless sound.

And so on to Side Four's reinterpretation of 1971's 'Theme from Jack Johnson'. Like Alan Vega's take on Hot Chocolate's 'Everyone's a Winner', this Miles Davis 'version' of his own song is a completely new piece. Gone is the choppy sloppiness of the catchy McLaughlin/Cobham-driven original, replaced by this ensemble's by-now notorious let's-strangle-Ernie-Isley lead guitar and heavily booming, percussive proto-funk. Towards the end of the piece, we're being steered into a looming and humming, howling and zinging ancient amphitheatre of percussionless electronic sound-effects, tone generators, feedback and noises of the universe. In truth, *Agharta*'s long Side Four fade-out sounds more like Dr Fiorella Terenzi's marvellous *Music from the Galaxies* LP than anything even slightly alluding to jazz.

I suppose we're getting back to Miles' desire to create one fourteen-armed musical beast out of seven individuals. Non-musicians could argue: 'But why does the music get credited entirely to Miles Davis rather than to the ensemble?' To which Miles would most likely have replied: 'Replace any one of them and you'll still get almost this sound. But replace me and they would be lost and directionless, for I am the shaman and their facilitator. There are no chords because I dictate that. The beat is on-the-one because I stipulate it. The musicians have untold freedom to play what they wish, *but* only within the exceedingly narrow boundaries which I have set.'

Like an Andy Warhol painting on which Andy himself chooses the subject matter, the canvas size, paint type and the four desired colours, but which he never actually touches, this music is governed by extreme pre-sets. It can only sound one way. Like Stockhausen's *musique concrète*, it is the purest form of music imaginable. Like Japan's Taj Mahal Travellers, who never even gave their tracks titles, it has returned us to a time so long before classical civilisation that even our hands and feet and lips and throats and asses become musical instruments. Sure, the jazz of the city will surface once in a while (and Miles himself is bound to try and sneak in an organ theme from 'Calypso Frelimo'). But, again and again, those same, stock primal percussions and electro-motifs will conspire to keep anything too learned from struggling to the surface for very long before being cut down, smitten, and subsumed back into the whole.

Agharta is an album of truly mystical significance, greater than both *Get Up with It* and *Dark Magus*, although I do listen to the latter most of all. Nonetheless, *Agharta*'s greatness is that it is the album which, more than any other, sets up the newest archetypes for the musicians to play off. A new rock'n'roll band could form around 'Prelude' alone and still have a three-album career. Another band could exist primarily to investigate the relationship between Pete Cosey's lead and Reggie Lucas' rhythm guitars. 'Interlude' could keep any ardent Krautrock fan happy for years with its sonic shiver'n'shake appeal. Even the reinterpretation of 'Jack Johnson' is eye-opening in its looseness and wide-awake, hunter-gatherer attitude to music.

Pangaea

Pangaea is a very different kettle of killer whales. Captured at Osaka's Festival Hall in February 1975, in the evening immediately following *Agharta*'s afternoon concert recording, *Pangaea* is a far more distilled take on this music, and it enters the ring with the same, Al Foster drum-driven fury as *Dark Magus*. Indeed, the opening beats of the forty-one-minute-long epic 'Zimbabwe' almost replicate the opening of *Dark Magus*' 'Moja'. Miles chose to dub this torrent of sound 'Zimbabwe' – a real Afro-centric, forward-thinking motherfucker of a name, as the country we now know as Zimbabwe was then still white-ruled Rhodesia, awaiting momentous changes not just in name.

The sameness of the rhythm secured the listener in the knowledge that here was an African equivalent to the strictly defined rhythmic parameters of reggae. I forget now which of Miles' sidemen it was who argued against biographer Roy Carr's use of the term 'anchor' to describe the bass and drums. It may have been Al Foster who claimed that the metaphor is weak as the anchor stops the ship from going anywhere at all.

Actually, I would counter-claim that anchors, in their ancient role, were often used in multiples known as drogue stones, which allowed the buffeted ship above to slow its journey to a navigable crawl without being sent around in dizzying circles by the mighty swell of the ocean.[5] As such, the bass and drums of Michael Henderson and Al Foster are indeed anchors, providing a stable platform on which Miles, Cosey, Lucas, Mtume and guests can perform their sonic oceanic rites.

Following the heavy weather of 'Zimbabwe' is the three-quarters-of-an-hour-long mystical ride known as 'Gondwana', named after the original ur-continent which, three hundred million years ago, split up into Africa, Australasia, Antarctica, South America and southern Asia. The music opens with an intense but far more subdued groove, led by Sonny Fortune's beautiful, dove-like flute, undermined by outrageously weird and dissonant wah-guitar chords. As someone who only enjoys the flute when it is set over a backdrop of extremeness, I am here reminded most of all of the soaring lotus flute which rises out of the sonic turbulence of Tangerine Dream's amazing 'Fly and the Collision of Comas Sola' from *Alpha Centauri*.

But 'Gondwana' retains its ocean-voyage-like mystery almost to the end, often dropping down into a becalmed ambience inhabited only by the popping of Mtume's hand percussion and water drums. And the lack of real jazz-chord content ensures that the music always appears to take place far from the cool of cityscapes, allowing it a feeling of true ancientness and bucolic timelessness. Until the thirty-third minute, that is, when Miles' ornery horn inspires Michael Henderson to pick up the groove with a walking bass which catches the band's imagination and has them mouthing off 'Yeah, that's right,' and several other time-honoured jazzisms.

At this point, their boat of a million years sails right up the flooded avenues of *No New York* and on into

5 Even as far back as the biblical tale of Noah's Ark and its Eastern equivalent, *The Epic of Gilgamesh*, there are many references to anchors, or drogue stones, being used for this purpose.

post-Atlantean Harlem, far uptown, where James Brown, George Clinton, Sly Stone and the ghost of Jimi Hendrix are all waiting to board from the upper windows of the legendary Apollo Theatre. As Miles wrote in his autobiography, 'I never end songs; they just keep going on and on.'

Bollocks to the Lot of Them

As I said, it's been argued by his detractors that Miles was burnt out and spiritually lost during this period. They say that his five-year absence from the recording studio is the evidence. But I personally believe that these four double LPs connote the end of the shamanic/druidic/Masonic/call-it-what-you-will apprenticeship of Miles Davis. They are the *summum bonum*, or distilled ur-essence, of Miles Davis as Shaman Warrior King. And, if he was nowhere in this period, then nowhere is where we shamans all should be.

As the opening poem of *The Modern Antiquarian* so flatly stated, I have been so brought to my knees by the Great Mother who is my muse and mentor that I can only be contemptuous of the cheap New-Age fix. But, in Miles' attitude, experience and practice of this period, there is evidence of a dedication to a Gurdjieffian-type physical and emotional exhaustion – the kind that can hardly have been hit upon by accident or through loss of the muse. Indeed, as I wrote earlier, had Miles lost the muse, he would surely have done everything possible to have maintained the illusion of one still in control. Instead, he chose to scream 'Fuck it!' as loudly and as often as possible.

Over all other arts, music is eternal and allows us to touch the divine. And I believe that because of its physical element, rhythmic music which inspires the dance brings us even closer to that point and more quickly. And it is because the end result of such intense and shamanic musical endeavours is the elevating of some of humanity (no matter how few) that the true musician will always say, 'Then so be it.'

Dogs live dogs' lives, but one discarded scrap of cake lets them glimpse humanity. Humans live human lives, but one brush with the eternal lets them glimpse Divinity – and, once touched, they will *never* forget it. In 1974–75, Miles Davis did so much more than merely glimpse eternity – he actually embraced it.

Electric Eels

God Says Fuck You

(Homestead, 1991)

1 Cyclotron (2.05)
2 Refrigerator (3.28)
3 Tidal Wave (2.20)
4 Agitated (2.10)
5 Anxiety (3.54)
6 Natural Situation (5.23)
7 Cold Meat (2.16)
8 Cyclotron (Giganto) (3.44)
9 Sewercide (3.59)
10 No Nonsense (1.45)
11 Jaguar Ride (1.48)
12 Accident (3.33)
13 Bunnies (4.21)
14 Cards and Fleurs (2.09)
15 As If I Cared (5.42)
16 Spin Age Blasters (3.47)
17 You're Full of Shit (2.32)

It has been generally established that it was the music and attitudes of The Velvet Underground which most completely prepared and predicted the way of all future rock'n'roll music from the '70s clear through to the millennium. But, writing in 1970, Lester Bangs claimed that the only Velvets-influenced band of the time was The Stooges. Now, neither The Stooges nor the Velvets really sound like 1977-vintage punk-rock, and neither should we expect them to. But does this mean that the British and US punk scene's fixation with The Velvet Underground sprang fully formed out of a general 1976 consensus to return rock'n'roll to its roots? Or were there any other unsung groups after 1970, but before 1977, which predicted punk by wrestling the Velvets' baton from The Stooges and carrying it further? Of course, I'm not gonna count anomalies such as the MC5 or early Roxy Music, or strange blips such as Peter Hammill's ultra-punky LP *Nadir's Big Chance*, from 1975; for these artists had all achieved some degree of success on their own and within their own context. No, this is a brief quest for rock'n'roll artists who, in the pro-muso, pro-progressive early '70s, forfeited any possibly successful contemporary career by being wantonly and boundlessly anarchic and out-of-step (we must include looking for similar apostate signs to Iggy's cantankerous short hair-do when everyone else was a longhair).

The first place to check out would have to be Boston in 1972, where Jonathan Richman was singing a love song entitled 'I'm Straight' to hippie audiences, a song in which he berates the girl of his dreams for going out '. . . with hippie Johnny/ He's never straight, he's always stoned.' If attitude and self-reliance score heavily in the anti-static kling-klang of the I-was-a-punk-before-you-were-a-punk boxing ring, then Jonathan Richman is Mr Golden Gloves and everybody else can fuck off. But I would have to exclude those first recordings by The Modern Lovers, which were made in 1971 and 1972 by Kim Fowley and John Cale. Although I love their sound, it is still too rooted in the soul and garage of the '60s, so they ultimately sound like Jonathan Richman working out his Lou Reed fixation over a backing track of The Mar-Keys playing ? and the Mysterians. Magnificent indeed, but not the Holy Grail we're searching for.

So where would that place Canada's Simply Saucer? By 1973, they were claiming to be younger brothers of The Stooges, early Roxy Music and Syd Barrett's Pink Floyd. Right fucking on! But what was the reality? Well, the truth is that they were fucking great and came on like all those bands were put through a blender. Conservative Canada wouldn't give 'em the time of day, so they were left to germinate/vegetate alone and unlistened to, a fate which had befallen The Monks a decade before in Germany. But, wonderful as Simply Saucer's music is, it's fairer to call it a post-psychedelic '60s afterflash (made in the same spirit as most Krautrock) than any proto-punk statement. Their songs were long, space-punk workouts and, from photos, they also look like their stage presence and dress sense, so essential to punk, was nil (v-necks and curly perms).

How about Debris, from Oklahoma, then? Starting out in 1974 as Victoria Vein and the Thunderpunks, they played in suburban shopping centres to no applause whatsoever and howled/stuttered songs of urban alienation over a skeletal backing of scratchy, trebly guitars, uncontrolled, cheap monophonic synths and proto-X Ray Spex shit-sax. Intriguing 1975 photographs of them in lab coats and aircraft goggles playing white-noise TV sets say they should have been brilliant. Unfortunately, their recordings nowadays sound way too clear to hide a total lack of catchy songs. Really short songs, which is dead punky, but all shit. Unlucky!

Full of great songs and looking twenty times better than Debris were Tom Verlaine and Richard Hell's Neon Boys. Their 1974 Velvets-indebted, all-night-workers stance was also buoyed up by Hell's pre-Rotten spiky hair, but everything else was unessential retro, from The Beatles-in-Hamburg photos to Verlaine's choice of stage name.

To Germany, then; by 1975, Neu! had embraced their proto-punk phase via the first Harmonia album, with Side Two of *Neu! 75* finding them effectively predicting punk rhythms, Sex Pistols' key-changes and even Johnny Rottenesque vocal asides. Hell, if you forgive his previous *Aladdin Sane* fixations, drummer Klaus Dinger even looked like a punk on the album sleeve. Here is the ten-out-of-ten, one-hundred-percent heart of proto-punk, and it's here where we shall also find Electric Eels.

Yeah, Electric Eels, from Cleveland – the same city that birthed Rocket from the Tombs, and from pretty much the same period, too. It's the industrialised heartland of North America again, and it's here that we find the Antichrist's Holy Grail. Legend has it that Electric Eels' guitarists John Morton and Brian McMahon were so grossed-out by their straight, blue-collar surroundings that they would enter working-men's clubs and start necking just to get a fight going. There was so little facility for the statement they wanted to make that the Eels only played six gigs in their entire career. John Morton was said to have duct-taped large wrenches to his clothes and have operated a gas-powered lawnmower on stage to lively things up, while their singer, David E, always had his school clarinet nearby for free-form freak-outs in case the audience's reaction was too muted. Those finding Captain Beefheart's *Mirror Man*-period, free-form 'first time musette' as the inspiration for David Thomas' Pere Ubu squawking are hereby directed to listen to David E on this here CD. It seems most likely that Thomas was directly inspired by David E when his former band, the aforementioned Rocket from the Tombs, supported Electric Eels in Cleveland in 1975.

The sound of the Electric Eels is one so snotty, so abrasively degraded, so militantly into its own thing that their first single was only released in 1979 (four years after its recording), and it still sounded advanced! Electric Eels songs were ultra-brief explosions of sticky antipathy condensed into a purely Orwellian, two-minute hate. In 1975, say-it-quickly-and-fuck-off was a whole new thing in itself. Ask the Ramones. Yet 1975-vintage Electric Eels songs contained all the stock elements that would come to characterise '77 punk. Traditional bubblegum call-and-answer verses and choruses butted right up against pure sonic-feedback experiment. Hook lines as catchy as chicken pox rise out of dreadfully recorded, Buzzcockian cissy-boy rants about who-the-fuck-knows-what, before being consumed by sheer ear-splitting wodges of furiously strummed twin rhythm guitars. And always at the expense of the rhythm section; hell, there ain't even any drums on some of the stuff, although they play it just as hard and rhythm-based as if there were.

Electric Eels never released an album during their lifetime, so *God Says Fuck You* offers twenty-twenty hindsight and still doesn't answer all the questions. There also seem to be several versions of this record, but as I've got two of the different versions myself, I've picked my favourite with which to lambaste you.

The album opens with the insanely catchy 'Cyclotron', which might be about some piece of '60s domestic Americana for all I know, but what the hell, rock'n'roll is meant to be mysterious. Lyrics about Daffy Duck, hating girls and war being fun are bawled out by Pee-Wee Herman's jammy-faced nipper brother, as an argument of I-know-you-are-but-what-am-I? intellect is acted out over staccato machine-gun guitar and snare drum. It's the sound of two guitarists playing loud through one amp captured on the condenser mic of borrowed recording equipment in a how-long-before-we-gotta-pack-up? rented rehearsal space.

'Refrigerator' has the same sound, this time clod-hopping round and round a monolithic 'Stand by Me' (they wish) chord sequence, while David E relates some suburban mystery story. The whole band 'ooh ooh' in agreement, before the riff breaks down into guitar-solo surrender, like the end of Buzzcocks' 'Friends of Mine' from *Spiral Scratch*, and you wonder how they managed to submerge the drums amidst the cacophony when they'd started out so loud.

Next up, 'Tidal Wave' is just fucking genius, coming on like it's the middle of a guitar solo; then it's stop–start, complain-complain, as David E tries in vain to keep up with the guitarists, recounting how sharks like to bite him, until he has to 'swim like a tuna fish' because '. . . help, help, help, here's a tidal wave'. Oh, fuck off and drown, you bastard! I never needed my rock'n'roll heroes to be likeable, which is good, because I wanna kill this guy. He's Jerry Lewis at a British Library dinner party, dosing the punch with cooking speed and threatening the hostess with amphetamine pessaries. Howling, piercing, emotional guitar car-crashes the song to its thank-fuck conclusion; and then they're off again, and on to the next song.

'Ohhhhhhhh, I'm so agitated/I'm so convoluted,' whines David E at the beginning of 'Agitated'. 'It's 5am and I'm crawling the walls/Waiting for imaginary telephone calls.' Now David's taken all the speed himself and he's run out of domestic appliances to clean, so he's started on the lightbulbs, while the band truck along on a Stonesy 'I'm a Man' drummerless, twin-guitar riff. Hey, this has musical references!

As does 'Anxiety', which takes the maddening, boogie drudge-sludge of David Bowie's magnificent 'Cracked Actor' and repeats it round and round and fucking round, until enough already! Oh, it's beautiful. Electric Eels just restore the riff to its netherworld roots in the most clamorous de-glamourising of a song ever. Replace Mick Ronson's Les Paul with an Asda equivalent, as played by Alvin, Simon and Theodore from The Chipmunks, and you've got this.

The side finishes with the one-minute cyclical hypochondria of 'No Nonsense', which is The Jaynetts' 'Sally Go Round the Roses' without any of its constituent parts whatsoever, with David E repeating the title as though 'twas the biggest hit since 'Hang on Sloopy'. Its riff, which is about as arty as a turd-filled ox cart pulled by giant slugs (eight feet high and with 'Mom' tattooed on their shoulders), maybe should never have seen the light of day, it's so repellent and underachieving. It's the first riff a sixteen-year-old plays at rehearsal to see if their amp's warmed up, and their mates jam along for a moment before saying, 'OK, let's do something real now.'

Side Two opens with their most obvious song of all. 'Jaguar Ride' is as catchy as The Rivieras' 'California Sun' or any of those surfing tunes. It's just that there are no drums, again, and so you get the eeriest feeling that not knowing what exactly happened on this particular Jaguar ride is a big plus.

'Accident' is just hilarious, and

is the ultimate example of the city-dweller's self-consciousness. A true Velvets-like driving riff has David E complaining to himself: 'Hope no one sees me in this accident/With my feet down through the floor-boards and my head up through the busted glass/My face smashed against the dash.' But he's too late, because the group happen to be passing and, sure enough, they've seen him in there amongst the wreckage: 'Let's go see who's in the accident/Nyah nyah nanna-nanna.' Howling, squealing, strangulated guitars penetrate the entire song, as observances by onlookers clog David E's embarrassed brain: 'Someone said it was a reckless u-turn,' and 'There's no attraction like a fatal crash.' You hate him for being bothered, but you love him so much for daring to register that he is.

What is 'Spin Age Blasters' about? A horrible, horrible twin-guitar riff cycles round and round, as the group tells us 'you know what this is' over and over. Like a shit-list of turn-offs made by a gang of bored teenagers, this song is written in some heightened ultra-slang which is comprehensible only to its creators. Then, just as you're sitting more clueless than Job, the guitar riff drops out and the backing vocalist picks up the story with all the confidence and technique of a drunk doing Telly Savalas' version of 'If': [aside] 'Now listen to this/The skin-diver dived off the bank/He disconnected his airtank (You know what this is)/His face went totally blank (You know what this is)/And down to the bottom he sank (You know what this is).' No, I don't have a fucking clue what this is about.

The album finishes with the ultra-catchy complain-complain of 'You're Full of Shit', a song of proto-barbarian, avant-garage intensity driven by yet more of David E's malcontent ramalama. He hits below the belt and stops at nothing to get another barbed comment in. He stoops to conquer, so low it makes even him look stupid. But he doesn't care. He'll I-know-you-are-but-what-am-I? you to death if needs be. For David E, even the most abject pyrrhic victory is worthwhile. Besides, he's got the coolest band in the world and no one's gonna know for twenty-five years. So fuck 'em all.

Yeah, fuck 'em all; this is an unconditionally brilliant album from a lost time. It's tragic to relate the fate, or non-fate, of Electric Eels. None of them made it, except for their magnificent and sometimes inaudible drummer, Nick Knox, who went on to fuel The Cramps throughout the late '70s and '80s. But Electric Eels will be one day recognised for their miraculously tuneful noise-against-all-odds. As Chuck Eddy wrote, in New York's *The Village Voice*, they were '. . . absolute antisocial provocation as a life force – whether you approve or not'.

Friction

'79 Live

(Pass, 2005)

1 Automatic-Fru (4.35)
2 Pistol (3.17)
3 Big-S (3.23)
4 Kagayaki (4.28)
5 A-Gas (2.43)
6 Cool Fool (3.15)
7 Cycle Dance (3.00)
8 I Can Tell (3.51)
9 Out (6.51)

Friction was a late-'70s Tokyo band that missed a place in *Japrocksampler* on account of their having commenced their career just over a year later than that book's self-imposed time limits. However, two of the band's members – Reck and Chico Hige – featured in earlier bands 3/3 and ○△□ (a.k.a. Maru, Sankaku, Shika – literally, 'Circle, Triangle, Square'), both of whom appear in the book's Top Fifty album reviews.

Whatever

When this excellent live album first surfaced a couple of years ago, I gots to admit it was a delightful revelation to me to experience Friction sounding as I imagine their leader, Reck, had originally intended. Indeed, with three decades and several oceans between us, and the dryness of their original studio sound herein replaced by the inevitable sonic spillage of a cheap concert recording, the catchiness of Friction's racket finally made perfect sense, as Reck's driving bass melded together with Chico Hige's drums and Tsunematsu Masatoshi's splashy-scratchy guitar to create a triple-headed, post-punk behemoth. Heck, even Reck's overly arch J. Rotten vocals now sounded less like Butler Rep's dental drool and more like a genuine lead-vocalist proposition, as really fucking catchy Japanglish choruses – admittedly often of barely more than a coupla duplicated words' duration – emerged from the dungeonous gloop.

But whereas the repeated vocals of songs such as 'A-Gas' ('Gas mask/Gas, gas, gas/Gas tank/ Gas, gas, gas/Anarchy') and 'Cycle Dance' ('Red light switch/Black light switch/White light switch/ Switch, switch, switch, switch') added little more than a glimpse of humanoid personality to Friction's dislocated, 'Cloud 149'-meets-*No New York* muse, elsewhere Reck's still highly minimalist vocals contained choruses catchily hefty enough to corral, momentarily, some of the wild atonal funk tableaux into which they had been released.[1] For example, however much the jarring skronk of 'Cool Fool' tried to alienate the listener with its bombardment of Japanese verse lyrics, Reck was smart enough to render the song unforgettable after just one listen with his ultra-sardonic, repeated English pay-off: 'Oh baby, you're so cool, fool.'

'Automatic-Fru' followed the same formula, Reck belly-aching on in Japanese for a coupla minutes before tying it all up again in English with the gloriously catchy so-called chorus: 'Style, style, Japanese style/Style, style, Japanese style.' Even better, 'Big-S' captured the on-and-on-and-fucking-on nihilism of the time in the most poppy (and weirdly translated) manner imaginable:

You wanna suicide in your room,
You wanna suicide in your city,
You wanna suicide in your country,
You wanna suicide on your TV set,
You wanna suicide on your planet,
You wanna suicide on your phone.

Man, if Richard Hell and the Voidoids' *Blank Generation* LP had managed even just one chorus as memorable as that sucker, we'd all still be spinning the disc.[2] Even the live versions of Friction's boringly derivative debut single ('I Can Tell' b/w 'Pistol') gain considerably from the graininess of this concert recording, 'Pistol' sounding especially fucking riotous here.

Nine songs in thirty-five minutes is very Van Halen or AC/DC, dontcha

1 OK, they still weren't exactly real pop choruses. But they did truly inject structure into the songs, somewhat on the lines of The Rolling Stones' über-linear and Germanic disco-song 'Shattered', which had appeared one year previously on *Some Girls*.

2 Better still, all those ancient TV punk pundits wouldn't have to keep mentioning Hell's brief role in Madonna's vile movie *Desperately Seeking Susan* just to remind us who he was.

thunk? But does the success of this live record mean the first studio LP is now worthy of a reappraisal? Back in 1980, as well as being busy with my own career and in light of that first Friction seven-inch having been such a big disappointment, I really hadn't paid much attention to the album. At the time, it sounded far too much like an admittedly ingenious but cynical case of cultural kleptomania: a too-simplistic ploy to conflate the crankiness of 1978's PiL/Banshees and New York no-wave noise with the punk ramalama of the previous year's Pistols and Voidoids. Fabulous if yooz the only purveyor of such a sound, but being at that time a Liverpool snotbag of epic proportions, I felt that Friction were peddling precisely the same formula as that which ninety percent of my then contemporaries were barfing out (yeah, I'll admit I was wrong, but I think you can forgive my mashed brain for misreading the overall situation as I'd spent most of late '78 and all of '79 on the same bills as scratchy guitarmeisters A Certain Ratio, Joy Division, Crispy Ambulance, Wire, Gang of Four, Scritti Politti and the Bunnymen[3]).

However, with twenty-twenty hindsight and my continuing fascination for the manner in which the Japanese send every occidental trend through a rigorous Nihonese filter, much of that Friction debut LP now sounds remarkably fresh and inventive. And although 'I Can Tell' and 'No Thrill' (a wholly pointless ESG copycat instrumental) still bore me stiff, the LP versions of 'Cool Fool' and 'Big-S' positively vibrate with an ectoplasmic energy all their own. Moreover, the studio versions of 'Cycle Dance' and 'Out' are a whole new thing, both being suffused with sub-sub-sub-Junior Walker sax, courtesy of drummer Chico Hige. Indeed, 'Out' concludes the album beautifully and artfully, like Van der Graaf Generator during their *Nadir's Big Chance* period playing Flipper's 'Sex Bomb (My Baby)' in a Berlin disco. Git down!

History

Let us now briefly discuss both Reck and Chico Hige's decade-long descent into the heart of punk darkness. Like the members of Crass in the UK, it was the richness of the late-'60s cultural route trodden by this rhythm-section duo which allowed

3 Fucking hell, just goggling at that list of Keith Levine-o-philes, it's no wonder I kicked Mick Finkler out of The Teardrop Explodes in June 1980!

them to navigate so successfully into the so-called 'no wave'. Of course, those of you who've already read my *Japrocksampler* may now wish to bleep this section out and proceed to the conclusion. But even those heads in the know will do well to remember that Friction's roots lay not in hard-rock, but in the free-music commune music of Tokyo's late-'60s Futen scene. For it was here that the teenagers Reck and Chico Hige began their musical careers as face-painted members of ○△□, a wild septet led by former Murahatchibu[4] drummer and communist street-activist, Kant Watanabe. Although ○△□ performed their shows only on the streets of Tokyo's Shinjuku district, they also released three sub-Amon Düül commune LPs[5] between 1971–73, each sounding as ramshackle and over-recorded as the other.

Thereafter, Reck and Chico Hige quit the ensemble to form the UFO/Stooges-influenced power trio 3/3 with Kohji 'Tôhchan' Miura, another former member of ○△□, playing sporadic gigs with such harsh-sounding festival bands as Yellow, Gedo, Too Much and The M; loose biker-rock aggregations made up of former commune members. Throughout 1975, 3/3 cut a whole album's worth of lo-fi demos before Reck and Chico Hige quit Japan for New York just as punk was being ushered in. However, as the high point of their New York stay was Reck's brief tenure as bass player in the final incarnation of Lydia Lunch's Teenage Jesus and the Jerks, the pair opted to return to Japan in 1979 as heralds of the new sound.

Seemingly not wishing to miss one single new-wave move, Reck and Chico Hige named their new Tokyo band after a classic song from Television's *Marquee Moon*, and Reck cast himself thereafter as your all-purpose Final Solution, none-more-black Nihonese nihilist.[6] And what an act of genius his decision turned out to be! By first divining, then covering all the most essential '77/'78 bases, Reck was able to demand that history be more than kind to himself and his cohorts. Dammit, (as I mentioned before) with three decades and several oceans between us,

4 The Murahatchibu story is protracted but essential to early-'70s Japanese music, and is told in detail in *Japrocksampler* (pages 117–27).

5 These three LPs were released in 2003 as a three-CD set by Tokyo's Captain Trip Records.

6 Even sartorially, this Reck druid was smart enough to keep away from the dreaded, and soon-to-represent-only-The-Knack'n'The Cars, skinny tie.

Reck's catch-all vision of the West's 1977–78-period Lutheran readjustment has revealed itself as one of the truest, nay, *the* truest that we could wish for.

Listen to these Friction albums and, for sure, you'll also hear snatches of early Subway Sect, early ATV, Television's 'Little Johnny Jewel', mucho Pere Ubu (their Hearthan-label period, natch), Mars, The Contortions, even Patti Smith's 'Gloria'. But unlike other similarly motivated but far less talented overseas ensembles (compare Friction's arsey gonadism with the always enjoyable but mostly *Sun*-reader punk pastiches of Denmark's The Sods), what proves Reck to have been a true motherfucker was that he was smart enough (and *old* enough) to know which musical elements to keep *out* of his mighty distillation process, forever displaying an uncanny ability to subsume all of those aforementioned artists into Friction's musical stew and still have the result sound like nothing other than themselves. Such an obsessive thoroughness towards his cultural research was bound to elevate Reck's work above that of his contemporaries. But it was the combination of his experience on the NY scene with his Crass-style grounding in a previous protest movement that set Friction head and shoulders above the rest. For, paradoxical as it may appear, the punk movement of 1977–78 was for most (J. Rotten included) not the death of hippiedom but rather hippiedom reawakened and retailored. And the power at the heart of Reck's nihilism was still entirely based on a fierce Utopianism, which is paradoxical for sure, but true nonetheless.

Select Discography

'I Can Tell' b/w 'Pistol' (single, Pass, 1979)
Friction (Pass, 1980)
'79 Live (Pass, 2005)

German Oak

(Witch and Warlock, 1972)

Like many of the more obscure choices in Head Heritage's Album of the Month, this German Oak LP is currently available in two different formats. An American twelve-inch vinyl LP, reissued in its original configuration, can be still sought out online, while Germany's Witch and Warlock Records are responsible for a CD version. The latter is endorsed by members of German Oak and contains three extra tracks. My review is of the original 1972 LP, followed by a detailed description of those extra songs on the CD.

In the strange, Olympic summer of 1972, Düsseldorf instrumental group German Oak entered the Luftschutzbunker (air-raid shelter) in order to record their eponymous first LP. Following in the footsteps of the percussive and organic Organisation and the remarkable Dom, German Oak had every reason to believe that this third in a triumvirate of early-'70s albums by Düsseldorf groups would be warmly received. Unfortunately, German Oak were not only wrong in assuming that locals would embrace their music, but even Düsseldorf record shops wouldn't stock the group's LPs. Such was their lack of success that 202 of the original 213 pressed copies were stored in the basement of the group's organist until the mid-'80s, when a thirst for undiscovered Krautrock finally brought German Oak back from the dead.

Just what is the sound of a group that was so rejected during its time of recording? Well, imagine a brutally recorded, brazen and ultra-skeletal industrial white funk played with all the claw-handed, crowbar technique of The Red Crayola recording their infamous 'Hurricane Fighter Plane', over which are superimposed the what-instrument-could-that-be? rumblings of Günter Schickert's GAM meeting the

Electronic Meditation incarnation of early Tangerine Dream – that is the sound of German Oak. Imagine Faust's reverb-y schoolroom in Wümme being party to a jam between *There's a Riot Goin' On*-period Sly Stone on itchy-scratchy bass and the pre-Kraftwerk ensemble Organisation playing 'Milk Rock', without their being formally introduced, and with all the hang-ups that this would entail. Again, this is the sound of German Oak.

Theirs is a strangely skin-of-the-teeth genius. It is a toe-curlingly heartfelt method-acting of the most in-your-face kind. In places, it's a sort of gormless Gong, even a moronic Magma – a Teutonic tribe standing in the ruins of some Roman temple, playing barbarian riffs on classical instruments two sizes too small. Aerosmith's Joe Perry once said: 'When all you've got is a hammer, everything looks like a nail.' He must have been listening to German Oak.

With this band, what seems after two minutes to be a simplistic and worryingly trite riff becomes, after eight minutes, the only really honest riff in town. Like the legendary death-blues of Josephus' (similarly sixteen minutes-plus) epic 'Dead Man', this is music which does not hit you instantly in the face; it is an accumulative groove, building and building on the endless repetition of some bog-standard, soul-type 'Please, Please, Please' bass line or rhythm-guitar sequence.[1]

There is a remarkable space within German Oak's music, which may have been caused by their ultra-rudimentary playing, or may have been because they just listened ultra-attentively to each other as each player struggled for the notes. Whatever the reason, German Oak conjured up a mythical sound in the grand Krautrock tradition. And, as a quintet without a lead singer, they were a rare five-piece who never got in each other's way. Throughout the music of German Oak, the bass and the lead guitar are frequently mistakable for each other, until the fuzzy lead slowly claws itself out of the sonic mire and drags itself arduously and inelegantly to the top of the heap. The drumming is often furious

1 Armand Schaubroeck's double LP *Live at the Hollywood Inn* has this same thuggish atmosphere, in which songs such as 'King of the Streets' and 'Streetwalker' are played with such fierce brutality that they sound like a hack house band playing perfunctory versions of classics. In many ways, this makes the songs sound great, and gives the illusion that, were they to be played subtly, they would perhaps be even better. A lie, but a smart move!

and even overplayed, yet it is often the single constant within the group's sound.

Perhaps German Oak hit the nail on the head when they credited group members as the 'crew' and refused to give full names. Such was their sense of space that they often sounded like a trio and hardly ever like a quintet. Perhaps, like Can, they worked in pairs and recorded in parallel as opposed to one live performance. Somehow I doubt it; the recording quality and attention to sound separation is far too slack and haphazard. No, I'm sure the reason that the characterless 'crew' credit sums up German Oak's attitude best is because it conspires to make them all sound like the dwarves whose job it was to hold up the four corners of the Viking worldview. Separately they were nothing; together they were everything.

Wolfgang Franz Czaika, here known only as Caesar, is credited with 'Lead-and-Rhythmguitar'; the busy flourishes of insistent drumming are by Ullrich Kallweit, here known only as Ulli 'Drums/Percussion'; his brother, Harry Kallweit, billed simply as 'Harry', contributes 'Electric bass/voice'. This leaves the tail-gunner's places to be filled by the wonderfully named Manfred Uhr, a.k.a. Warlock, on 'Organ/fuzz-organ/voice' and Norbert Luckas, a.k.a. Nobbi, on 'Guitar/A77/Noises'. And, like the simple Amon Düül I credits, the friendly nicknames somehow make the group appear even more mysterious and out of reach.

The German Oak LP consisted of two very long Kraut-grooves, one on either side of the vinyl, bookended by a short, organ-themed instrumental intro and outro. Side One begins like a crusty hunt led by hunt saboteurs, as the one minute and fifty seconds of 'Airalert' fades in from the mists of time with a hopeful if amateurly recorded organ. The remainder of the side is then given over to the enormous, eighteen-minute-long 'Down in the Bunker', where feedback whistles and screams and factory-interior-sized organ roars, while relentless hammering on metal suggests that the workers are in there, building something over the din. Portentous, manically bowed, cello-style film-theme bass guitar and scraping cymbals rise out of the maelstrom to prepare the listener for the onslaught to come. Sonically, it is pure sound, like the primal intro beauty of GAM's *1976* album, Guru Guru's *UFO*, or the opening section of Ash Ra Tempel's 'Amboss'.

As though recorded in a deep river gorge from beyond time, with dozens of old fridges and cookers strewn across its banks, this proto-industrial sound truly invokes the ancestors. And it is perfectly understandable that German Oak's sleeve-notes read: 'As we played down there in the old bunker, suddenly a strange atmosphere began to work. The ghosts of the past whispered.'

Far from being deluded, the German Oak crew are understating – for this track is alive with the dead, awash with a flood of ur-spirits from the recent past and the days of yore. Banshee-like glissando guitars and Mani Neumaieresque voices creep up the north side of the track, mount the battlements and howl at us and the members of the group.

Side Two begins with the reverbed, minor-key horseback charge of 'Raid Over Düsseldorf'. The bulk of the second side is taken up by this furious and rudimentary psychedelic ride, reminiscent of The Chocolate Watchband. Indeed, my friend and Brain Donor guitar cohort Doggen has suggested that it is the rhythm of the horse which heavy-rock most often emulates. I would tend to agree with this assertion, as this rhythm can be found everywhere in rock, from the central spine of The Doors' 'Roadhouse Blues' to the middle of David Bowie's 'Width of a Circle'. I would even cite Robert Browning's nineteenth-century poem 'How They Brought the Good News from Ghent to Aix' as an example of how pre-rock'n'roll this galloping rhythm really is.

The album's finale is the two-minutes-short '1945 – Out of the Ashes', which returns to the organ-led hunting sound of the opening 'Airalert' before cross-fading into the tolling of a lone bell.

Although I am rarely a fan of extra tracks being added to CD reissues, we must count ourselves lucky in this case to have been handed the three superb, pre-LP German Oak workouts located herein. The five-minute-long 'Swastika Rising' sounds like the Plastic Ono Band meeting both Faust and Organisation; all rudimentary organ, splatter drums and a barely coherent and wandering psychedelic fuzz guitar. Following this, the ten-minute 'The Third Reich' starts with a rallying Hitler speech, before slipping inside yet another hypnotic and insistently mesmerising, teen-Funkadelic groove, with scything and Scythian psychedelic guitar. A brazen, disabled lead guitar mindlessly scatters seedling riffs across an infertile field of unidirectional bass riffing and extremely formulaic drum fills, played relentlessly and robotically.

The final extra track, 'Shadows of War', is like an overladen Chinook helicopter struggling to lift off from its pad, the organ chords seemingly weighted down by the reverbed wodges of clawed bass. Then another Hitler rally cut-up sends us into a collage of over-hasty milk delivery as an obligatory Stuka raid finally cuts us down in a single, all-terminal bomb blast.[2]

I noted in *Krautrocksampler* that the German postwar youth scene was trying to work itself free of its recent Holocaust history, and German Oak in particular seem to have wrestled with these demons for longer than most. Their sleeve-note dedication seems all the more poignant and moving for its bathos and poor translation: 'We dedicate this record to our parents which had a bad time in World War 2.'

2 I must note that this album in its Witch and Warlock CD reissue guise chooses, strangely, to present the three extra tracks *before* the actual LP itself. If this is the version which you find, make sure that you begin your listen with 'Airalert'!

Grand Funk Railroad

Live Album

(Capitol, 1971)

SIDE ONE

1 Introduction (2.30)
2 Are You Ready? (3.34)
3 Paranoid (6.20)
4 In Need (9.50)

SIDE TWO

1 Heartbreaker (6.58)
2 Inside Looking Out (12.22)

SIDE THREE

1 Words of Wisdom (0.55)
2 Mean Mistreater (4.40)
3 Mark Say's Alright (5.10)
4 T.N.U.C. (11.45)

SIDE FOUR

1 Into the Sun (12.10)

All you compassionate, forward-thinking motherfuckers dig The Monkees, right? Yeah, me too! Most likely, you dig 'em for the TV series that premiered in September 1966, and for that superb refusenik movie *Head*, which closed their 'official' career three years later to the month; but probably, most of all, you dig 'em for the seven monster forty-fives they barfed out in-between. However, you know in your hearts that the seven accompanying (count 'em[1]) LPs they delivered between January '67 and September '69 are ultimately nothing more than a patchwork of underachievement (cynically created sessioneering cash-ins, comedy goof-offs and Hollywood-meets-Brill Building hack

1 How about this for an LP release schedule? Entitled simply *The Monkees*, their debut LP came out in January 1967, followed by: *More of the Monkees* (April 1967); *Headquarters* (July 1967); *Pisces, Aquarius, Capricorn and Jones Ltd* (January 1968); *The Birds, The Bees & The Monkees* (May 1968); *Instant Replay* (May 1969); *Head* (September 1969); and *The Monkees Present . . .* (October 1969).

jobs) constructed specifically to rip off 'The Kids', grand stylee.

Well, now that I've brung to your attention what you intuitively knew all along, but didn't wanna address because y'all had so much childhood nostalgia invested in them moptop-a-likes, what I'm asking is that you please extend a little of that Monkees grace to a hard-working band that never had the luck to be granted their own TV series, got it all together themselves (along with their particularly inspirational manager) and, in their first half-decade, pumped out umpteen patchy-but-listenable LPs that would have distilled into five very excellent albums had their Monkees release-schedule-style work-rate been taken at a more moderate and carefully edited pace.

So, ladies'n'gentlemen, I now present to you those worthy journeymen musicians Mark Farner, Don Brewer and Mel Schacher – collectively, Grand Funk Railroad. Moreover, this *Live Album* is the specific record which inspired me to form Brain Donor back in the summer of '99 – not the MC5 or Blue Cheer as everyone has presumed. But hey, it's so long ago even I'd forgotten about the monumental vibe on these discs until a coupla shows at Reading and Brighton playing with Dogntank, whose band members collectively still worship at the shrine of this double LP.

Come and Geddit While It's Hot!

Imagine an American band fixated on the raw, white soul-blues of The Animals and the sheer raging and seemingly endless tragedy and joy pumping out of their neighbouring Tamla Motown label. This was a band surrounded and inspired by the massive automobile works of Michigan's Detroit, Pontiac and (their home town) Flint, and all the attendant blue-collar, 'hard-working man' values that surround such a scene; a band that fused the vibe of The Spencer Davis Group's 'I'm a Man' with Count Five's 'Psychotic Reaction', then segued directly into riffola somewhat akin to Eddie Floyd's massive, descending 'Big Bird', via obvious-to-the-point-of-being-generic heavy-soul stomps along the lines of Aretha's 'Save Me', The Supremes' 'You Just Keep Me Hanging On' and Otis Redding's 'Respect' (Deep Purple/Vanilla Fudge-stylee), yet who also threw in raging and unaccompanied raga-rock solos in the style of Jimmy Page's 'White Summer', while the ultra-athletic singer/guitarist took every opportunity to run, bare-chested, around the arena, randomly flashing peace signs and arbitrarily screaming 'brothers and sisters' at the audience throughout. Imagine all of this description being about neither the equally collectively naked MC5[2] or Scott Morgan's wonderful Rationals, or even Funkadelic themselves, but about a band that were Top Ten regulars in the American album chart throughout the early '70s.

Musically, the album is a stew of ingredients so very obvious that the results are actually not that obvious at all.[3] Commencing with that same heightened sense of sonic moment located within the grooves of the two other best 'live' albums of the late-'60s/early-'70s cosmic portal, namely the MC5's *Kick Out the Jams* and The Who's *Live at Leeds*, Grand Funk Railroad's awesomely massive *Live Album* was a stone killer that distilled their first three studio LPs (the excellent debut, *On Time*, the schizophrenically lop-sided but essential for the proto-doom'n'dirge of its second side *Grand Funk*, and the charmingly self-righteous but deeply sexist protest-by-numbers of *Closer to Home*) into a one-hour-twenty-minute-long double album of the kind of demented, tight-assed heavy acid-soul that San Francisco's Flipper would distil even further, one decade later, into their legendary, eight-minute-long 'Sex Bomb'.

Live Album saw Grand Funk take umpteen traditional-to-the-point-of-clichéd musical vehicles and work them so damned relentlessly, so speed-freak-cleaning-the-lightbulbs thoroughly, and with such a Plymouth Rock, straight-edged puritan work-ethic attitude that the psychic hackles of even The Wire-readingest dude will rise eventually (albeit reluctantly) as your twenty-first-century self glimpses, just for one second, precisely what the 1970 world then believed it might still become. Because Grand Funk Railroad was the biggest and they wuz Utopian to a man (and in a deeply late-'60s, man's, man's, man's world, these motherfuckers wuz some seriously

2 Wrong! No one comes close to appearing naked on their LP sleeves as often as Grand Funk Railroad. They are entirely naked on *We're an American Band* and merely loin-clothed on both *Survival* and *Phoenix*, while elsewhere Farner is bare-chested always.

3 Indeed, this album's so fucking cosmically and hysterically great that the whole thing reminds me in places of that startlingly Sabbath-plays-Traffic, euphoric bludgeon riffola as served up on John McLaughlin's 1970 platter *Devotion*. Yup, I've lost my head and I ain't gonna find it listening to this record.

sexist Utopians![4]). And, of course, by conflating three canons of work into one fairly short double LP (plus, of course, enriching it all further with the addition of a highly potent audience, nay, crowd) you get the *Kiss Alive* effect, in which all the boneyard detritus and filler is scummed off the top and the deeper, more successful grooves which the band most loved to play live come rising to the surface like juicy worms in the furrows of a newly ploughed field (d'you dig my righteous and honest man o'the land metaphor, fellow Grand Funksters?).

Grand Funk

Furthermore, even a hardened Grand Funk Railroad fan like me is forced to admit that the only truly essential releases they ever made were this *Live Album* and the debut, *On Time* (OK, Side Two of the second album makes it essential, too). Mainly, Grand Funk studio LPs were, in comparison to this concert record, dry and boxy. Indeed, you only have to see a coupla moments' footage of Farner's bare-torso'd psychedelic gymnast persona going mental in front of a blue-collar, proto-Sabbath audience to understand that without the collective dead-end mentality of that audience (Homer Simpson is a fan of this lot – which sums it up perfectly), their LPs weren't gonna sustain beyond the 1970s. Musta been hard being Mark Farner. Hell, crossing the fittest dude in the football team with the greatest stoner in the basement is one thing, but adding to it perpetual priapism and cosmic earnestness without an 'off' switch is beyond the beyond.

My being English and not able quite to reach Grand Funk's place in rock'n'roll history, I always wondered if Pere Ubu had got Ken Hamann in to engineer their albums because they wuz Grand Funk fans; did Farner and co. aim for that dry-to-the-point-of-being-parched studio sound, or was it foisted on them by their manager/producer/mentor Terry Knight? Well, the evidence is here on these concert discs, where they lose the tappity boxiness and spread out into an enriched, healthy vegetal wildness almost approaching James Brown's *Live at the Apollo*; groove to the rhythms of your own

4 As a father of a teenage daughter, it's hard to accept that earnest Mark Farner had no problems writing the horribly unrighteous 'She Got to Move Me' from 1973's *Phoenix*, in which he's fucking a fourteen-year-old. Weirder still is that the song is one of their most beautiful grooves, coming on like a precursor to The Black Crowes' most soulfully syncopated *Amorica* period.

tinnitus, all you metal heads and soul brothers, and tell me it ain't so!

One listen to the energy of this double LP should have any male with a full sack in his shorts deludedly marching for 'Freedom' and 'The Truth', at least for the duration of these four twelve-inch discs. For the atmosphere and intensity of this record is a Woodstockian night rally and Mark is The Führer – hell, no one else would dare include track titles such as 'Words of Wisdom' and 'Mark Say's Alright' [*sic*, *sic*, *sic*].

Rising from the ashes of mid-'60s teen stompers Terry Knight and the Pack, Grand Funk was created by The Pack's rhythm section, bassist Mark Farner and drummer Don Brewer, in 1968 as a call-to-arms. Eight consecutive flop singles informed Terry Knight that his time as a Country Joe/Kim Fowley-a-like lead singer was up, so he threw in his lot as the manager of this 'heavy metal band'.

The previous year had seen John Sinclair, located a mere thirty miles south-east from Knight's Flint home town, in Detroit, so successfully politicise and mobilise his protégés, the MC5, that they had gone from being perceived as a garage-band-in-stasis to free-jazz explorers aligned with the Black Power struggle, outlawed in their own state and accompanied to gigs by fleets of motorcycle cops. Inspired by the so-called 'Struggle' going on down in Detroit against what Terry Knight called 'Violence, pollution and desperate dying elders,' the new manager hired a brick rehearsal hall in Flint, while his old bass player Mark Farner swapped over to guitar, and he and Brewer added Mel Schacher from ? and The Mysterians on bass.

In every way, Terry Knight and the Pack were to Grand Funk what Yuya Uchida and the Flowers were to The Flower Travellin' Band. The portentous sleeve-notes and wider 'world-views' [*sic*!] all seem to have been those of Terry Knight, but the cod-revolution all came from the pen of the bare-chested, quasi-Native American Mark Farner. And, if ever a band simultaneously straddled righteous, unrighteous and self-righteous more effortlessly than Grand Funk Railroad and their leader, Farner, well, I ain't yet found them.

Self-appointed champion and spokesman of just about everybody in the world: the indigenous native population; women (when it suited him); the godless (when it suited him); and most of all (like those other never-done-a-proper-day-job-in-their-lives-refusenik-blue-collar-hippies Neil Young and Bob Dylan), spokesman for all those hard-done-to, all-American working stiffs. Like Eric Burdon's similar appropriation of LSD, Black Power, heavy music and Native American rights throughout the 1960s and '70s, Grand Funk, too, took up whatever 'The Cause' currently was and hammered it until no fucker gave a damn any longer. Which is why, like longhairs during punk's heyday, Grand Funk have been virtually written out of the Detroit story for so long – essentially because they wuz just too gauche, too in-yer-face and, moreover, because they petered out in a welter of mild-and-boogie, *so what* releases. But it's time for me to shut the fuck up about all that and tell y'all exactly why *Live Album* is Album of the Month.

So, Watt's It Sound Like?

Live Album opens with your typically portentous 'there's too much chaos in this hall for the band to play' jobsworth-type announcement; arena crowd, drug'n'booze crazoids taking up the whole of the opening piece, which is the same length as a contemporary forty-five. 'Are You Ready?' then kicks in with some of the best MC5-ian soul a boy could wish for. Following in the great tradition of songs about how good the show's gonna be, 'Are You Ready?' is up there with 'Hello There' from Cheap Trick's *Live at Budokan* for sheer heart attack. Originally the first track from their *On Time* debut LP, the soul on this overheated versh shines hard enough to sear through your undies to your boogieing butt. Mel Schacher's bass at the end of the song is insanely compulsive (as it will remain for the entire duration of this disc) and the dual Don Brewer/Mark Farner vocal is just beautiful.

Herein, this live 'Paranoid' kicks in far harder than its Cleveland-esque punk studio version from Side Two of the band's red-jacketed second LP *Grand Funk*. That version has immense charm, it must be asserted, but this take has a grind that no studio could even hope to reach. Farner's wah-wah guitar sounds like a clavinet with ancient strings, occupying an underworld, dead-soul groove that leaves Mel Schacher's finger-played Fender Jazz to provide all the melody, although before long even the bass becomes subsumed into the grunge as a fuzz-pedal-from-hell kicks our collective dicks into the dust. 'Paranoid' is a great place for first-time Grand Funk listeners, as it provides the stop–start, over-and-over riff-building that smoked my pole from the very beginning, and surely provided Sabbath with so much of their Butler/Iommi, first-your-riff-then-my-riff attitude to songwriting.

As this type of performance is nowadays such a stand-up show, it's too weird – in these long-past-punk times – to hear Farner telling people to get off each other's shoulders and stop spoiling it, but that was the way they wanted it because, unlike the Grande Ballroom and the other places that the Five played, Grand Funk was out there in front of fifty thousand every night.

'In Need' pisses all over the too-spiky studio version from *Grand Funk*, kicking in at over ten minutes here, and being almost as heavy on crowd participation as music. Farner's harmonica-and-huffing'n'moaning over the bass and drums is just a joy and the excitement is a truly intense tidal wave – again, they move seamlessly from riff to riff, building endlessly. In this live situation, it's Farner's corralling of 'everyriffs' and generic, brotherly love lyrics that makes the songs so massively appealing. The band is an effortless freight train that totally delivers the goods. The aforementioned raga solo at the end of this 'soul catalogue' is a kind of take on Dave Arbus' amazing violin solo at the end of The Who's 'Baba O'Riley', via the tail-out of 'Egyptian Gardens' from Kaleidoscope's *Side Trips*. Farner's achievement is that he provides peak-experience-by-rote entertainment worthy of both *Kiss Alive I* and *II*, and leaves Deep Purple's *Made in Japan* standing on the landing.

Side Two hefts in with a massive version of the debut LP's 'Heartbreaker', with its multi-part 'rock ballad' structures and massive 6/8 introduction that creates a kind of barbarian Ottomans-at-the-walls-of-Vienna magnificence that is shockingly soulful for a so-called power trio. Even the cod-Spanish guitar solo is so undermined by the one-hundred-and-fifty percent coda that the sheer exhilaration defies the intellectual and allows the moron to break free from the shackles of Earth's gravity. Also, the end of 'Heartbreaker' is surely where Sabbath nabbed the 'Snowblind' riff from (and don't believe Geezer Butler when he disingenuously claims not to know what 'paranoid' meant at the time – it was a commonly used head's term).

Next up, comes Grand Funk's cover version of The Animals' 1966 classic 'doing-time' forty-five 'Inside-Looking Out', originally found on the *Grand Funk* LP. It's hard to beat that dry, oppressive, nigh-on-ten-minute-long studio version, but Farner and co. do it with comparative ease, pushing the track to a hefty fourteen minutes. Especially endearing herein are Farner's crowd-pleasing tactics, which include changing the studio lyrics: the prisoner now 'sewing nickel bags' instead of 'burlap bags'.

Although Grand Funk were real cunts when it came to a too-obvious cover version ('The Loco-Motion' and 'Gimme Shelter', for example), this fairly obscure Animals song (a Number Twelve on the UK chart but a failure in the US) follows their beloved Eric Burdon's lead and is one of the greatest, most storming results for rock'n'roll that ever there was. It careers along at varying stop–start speeds of ninety, twenty and fifty-five miles per hour, like a V8-powered cherry picker with the band playing at the highest point to which the hydraulics will lift it.

Side Three is the 'work-out' side, with its grooves and open-ended ramalama being underpinned only by the ballad 'Mean Mistreater'. The side's opener, 'Words of Wisdom', is preceded by Farner being his righteously, almost self-righteous, Rock Police self, which I happen to find endearing: 'Brothers and sister, there are people like you who look just like you, but they're not. And, when they hand you something, don't take it.'

Then it's off into their *Closer to Home*-period single, the piano-based, Number Forty-Seven hot hit 'Mean Mistreater', in which a proto-Todd Rundgren, blue-eyed soul ballad conjures up an overloaded fury that would be horribly undermined by future blandishments such as Hall & Oates (*Abandoned Luncheonette*? What the fuck?) but which is here just stupendous and insane and gimme more right now, ta very much. Then they're off into the non-album B-side of the previous single in the shape of the jungle-rhythm'd and burning geetar-mayhem of 'Mark Say's Alright' (love the spurious apostrophe, punctuation freaks!).

The artless female-putdown 'T.N.U.C.' is really just a vehicle for Don Brewer's merely-achieving drum solo, which ain't a patch on 'Moby Dick' or 'The Mule' for boring muso shit. Indeed, this sucker has excellent crowd participation and is even a bit good . . . although not good enough to bear listening to all the way through, even once!

The final side is taken up by the debut LP's massively brilliant (if cliché-ridden) soul-galleon 'Into the Sun', whose themes include the standard soul riff on which The Doors based their *LA Woman* opener 'The Changeling', played here as frigging speed-freak-fast and frantically as any punk band. In some kind of cosmic energy exchange, the great main line was 'interpreted' by Wishbone Ash one year later for 'Blowing Free', on their *Argus* album.

Weirdly, the song really does seem to be about Farner getting into being a sun-worshipper on a hippie level, and leaving behind, temporarily, the problems of getting paid on time.

In conclusion, this is one hell of a raucous achievement from a time when the double live LP was becoming almost essential to any rock'n'roll band that considered itself to have legs and a place in the future. The Grand Funk that played these shows was so big that the entire audience stormed the police cordon and broke on through to the other side, whereas memory relegates them to several leagues below contemporaries who were, at the time, only a fraction of their size. This recording is, however, timeless and raging and snot-nosed enough to redeem Grand Funk's situation, if enough people relate to the incandescent grooves *and* don't feel duty-bound to search through The Guess Who-like over-release schedule of ever-increasingly keyboard-led, good-time drivel with which they ultimately kicked their own golden asses into touch. Recorded way before that earnest pomp, and before added keyboard player Craig Frost turned Mel Schacher into just 'the bass player', listen herein and rage hard as you dig Messrs Farner, Brewer and Schacher. For, on this record especially, this American band got it totally right.

Select LP Discography

On Time (Capitol, September 1969)
Grand Funk (Capitol, January 1970)
Closer to Home (Capitol, July 1970)
Live Album (Capitol, January 1971)
Phoenix (Capitol, September 1972)

Hairy Chapter

Can't Get Through

(Bacillus, 1971)

SIDE ONE

1 There's a Kind of Nothing (5.50)
2 Can't Get Through (10.48)

SIDE TWO

1 It Must Be an Officer's Daughter (8.05)
2 As We Crossed Over (3.39)
3 You've Got to Follow This Masquerade (4.47)

'My education will never let me be free' (Harry Unte of Hairy Chapter)

In 1971, this Nordelic K.O. of an album saw the immaculately named German band Hairy Chapter briefly joining the warrior guitar gods of their ancestral dreams. They'd made albums before which were all-right-now, in a fuzzy, garagey way, but with the release of *Can't Get Through* Hairy Chapter finally recorded a righteous, royal shit-stirrer which should be in the collection of every twenty-first-century head. For *Can't Get Through* was a blood-lusty and maniacally lunar combination of the first Funkadelic LP, Alice Cooper's *Love It to Death*, *Led Zeppelin II* and Amon Düül II's *Yeti*. All of the aforementioned sum up the male aspects of this rave, but maybe Sir Lord Baltimore playing Fleetwood Mac's 'Green Manalishi' forty-five more accurately describes the spectral she-muse summoned up on this monstrous slab of Bonn sub-culture. For, like the hoary whore-shadow which inhabits the first Baltimore LP, the whole of *Can't Get Through* seems to be a mare's nest motivated by some hidden (or perhaps accidentally invoked) White Lady who is determined to punish both the guitarist and the singer unless they overachieve far beyond their hitherto wildest dreams.

The Laser's Edge magazine once referred to this LP's 'uninhibited guitar debauchery', and it would be churlish in the extreme not to award some sort of posthumous Golden Guitar medal to so unsung an axe hero as Hairy Chapter's Harry Titlbach. He coaxes, caresses and finally wrings out such heathen howls from his instrument that it is impossible not to visualise him as anything other than a cartoon. In my mind's eye, I see him wild-eyed and tormented, making endless prowls back and forth across the stage, from the foot-pedal of his ever-more distorted amplifier to the mic stand of his singer and cohort, the equally tortured longhair known as Harry Unte. Yes, this group was led by two guys called Harry and, on this album, they were both demented. Maybe they should have been called *Harry* Chapter! Perhaps it was some crazy in-joke, lost in the mists of time.

For this *Can't Get Through* LP, singer Harry Unte was inhabited by the same spectral muse as his guitar partner. Listen to the vocal delivery and you soon understand that, whatever mysterious force it was which had him by the balls, this singer may have needed the revolution right now, but, more than that, he needed to get cosmically laid, and pronto, Tonto! 'Gimme your body,' he howls. 'I wanna ball you all night long,' he wails. 'I wanna hold your luscious breasts in my hands,' he implores. Best of all, he pleads, 'I . . . I . . . I wanna see your twenty-seven fingers explode in my body.' Hell, Harry, doesn't everyone?

Hairy Chapter had been together since the late '60s, but by 1971 these longhair guys were Bonn punks with the bit between their teeth. They had a big new record label behind them and a big-time record producer helping them. And, from the Funkadelic-like start of *Can't Get Through* to its blazing, Amon Düül II, stun-guitar photo-finish, they were far out, flat out and putting the cat out. As though aware that their other albums didn't cut the mustard, and unaware that this was to be their goddess-fuelled swansong, everything on the record is weighted with a real sense of moment and dread.

In 1969, they had recorded the obscure *Electric Sounds for Dancing* LP, followed by the disappointing *Eyes* album for the tiny Opp record label.[1]

1 For an instant comparison between 1971's *Can't Get Through* and 1970's *Eyes*, get hold of both on one CD, released on the Second Battle record label, catalogue number 038.

But the passing of one whole year and the release of a slew of 'heavy' albums from other bands turned Hairy Chapter from slack, Yardbird-alikes into a proud warrior caste with a post-barbarian *Guitar Army* battle-plan. Gone were the late-'60s fuzz leads and the blues structures and the muted guitar-blasts of 1970's *Eyes*. Replacing them came long, intricately arranged barrages of compelling mood and mania; undulating hoodoo which pulled the carpet from under the feet of listeners and sent them down sonic tunnels into underground wells of pure mystery.

Of course, it may well be that the arrival of Dieter Dierks as their producer imbued the members of Hairy Chapter with a sense that this was finally their moment. *Can't Get Through* was recorded for the new and hip Bacillus record imprint, and this was only the second release for the company, which had been conceived as the German Polygram label's answer to the genuinely underground companies which had sprung up during the 1960s. Unlike labels such as Ohr and, much later, Brain Records, which concentrated on real Krautrock (being the most German-sounding music they could find), the strategy at Bacillus seems to have been based on marketing music which could compete with the output of British and American bands. So money and expectations abounded with the recording of *Can't Get Through*, and the genius of Dieter Dierks was there to channel and manipulate it. And he truly kept his part of the deal. Although Hairy Chapter were in no way a Krautrock band, being far too convinced of their status as genuine competition for the British and Americans, powerful elements of Krautrock are still contained within these grooves, and having Dieter Dierks at the sound desk is surely the reason. It was Dierks who confronted Hairy Chapter's hard-rock with outright psychedelic production, and he even co-wrote one of the songs.

Can't Get Through begins with the chiming Hendrix Funkadelia of 'There's a Kind of Nothing', which summons the ur-klang of the Krautreaper but all too soon breaks down into a low-key, weird acoustic thing. I say all too soon because their one mistake was not making this opening track ten minutes long; or, perhaps, even beginning the album with the epic, nine-minute title song which follows, for 'Can't Get Through' is epic in a heavy way, the way that early-'70s groups only got when they'd played this stuff live on stage before recording it. Coming on like something from The Groundhogs'

Split, all arranged and furious, it features Harry Unte's classy words 'Reality has got to die' and 'My education will never let me be free.' The vocals are confidently snotty and unselfconsciously whining, and the guitar and drum interplay is epic in the same way that Alice Cooper's *Killer* actually supersedes *Love It to Death* both musically and emotionally. Does Harry Unte really sing 'My parents tried to make a white person out of me'? It surely sounds that way, before Total Guitar Wars take over the song and huge psychedelic metal riffs obliterate the whole band. Finally, unaccompanied wild, rhythmless soloing reminds all of us that Dieter Dierks is, of course, the dread at the controls.

But my favourite song is definitely 'It Must Be an Officer's Daughter', the eight-minute behemoth which opens Side Two. For here it is that the White Lady really strikes hardest. Yes, this is the one in which Harry Unte wants to ball her all night long and feel her luscious breasts and feel her twenty-seven fingers explode inside his body. Anyone who has felt Peter Green's White Lady at his back when listening to 'Green Manalishi' will stiffen and blanch at the psychic hand-job that the singer receives on this song.

By the time Hairy Chapter get to 'As We Crossed Over', they've taken on elements of Amon Düül playing *The Man Who Sold the World*, as Gothic choral vocals and solo piccolo trumpet illustrate a tale of breaking through into the Underworld, or through the Berlin Wall, or both. Its acoustic mystery is pure Bowie Krautrock and it totally intrigues my psychic ass.

Can't Get Through finishes with the Amon Düül II-riffing of 'You've Got to Follow This Masquerade' – more of that White Lady-on-my-trail vocal, cut with the epic guitar wolf-howl of Harry Titlbach. The entire album comes in under forty minutes, and they're done and gone forever. The Hairy Chapter was a brief one, with few pictures but a definite way with words and vats of spare rock'n'roll riffs just looking for their moment. As Dag Erik Asbjornsen so accurately commented in his marvellous book *Cosmic Dreams at Play*, *Can't Get Through* is 'one of those screaming diz, dumbo IQ-reducing monsters that some people can never get enough of'.

Right ON!

HIGHWAY ROBBERY

For Love or Money

(RCA, 1972)

SIDE ONE	SIDE TWO
1 Mystery Rider (3.03)	1 Bells (3.24)
2 Fifteen (2.57)	2 Ain't Gonna Take No More (4.16)
3 All I Need (4.19)	3 I'll Do It All Again (4.16)
4 Lazy Woman (5.44)	4 Promotion Man (6.06)

This Album of the Month is for all you Detroit-obsessed believers in the electric-guitar powerdrive as the über-sacrament – the amphetamine pessary, the Jolt Cola-enema-to-the-motherfucking-stars! Yeah, I'm talking to all you dragster slide-guitar worshippers at the altar of Ronnie Montrose's 'Bad Motor Scooter', those whose priapic meditation is mostly upon Jimmy Pagan's 'When the Levee Breaks', the oozy, suicidal G-force descent of The Litter's 'Blue Ice', and the bucking-bronco axe-shudder of Sir Lord Baltimore's 'Pumped Up'. And – laid-eez and gentlemunters – so do I have to lay upon y'all ye saddest of tales in the tellbook, for this is the tragedy of Michael Stevens, songwriter, guitarist and sometime seer of rock'n'roll, a musician whose artistic life was too brief, too imperfect and too beholden to ye money men to make any headway at the time of his actual playing. But for those elite few heavy-music fanatix whose lives are en-fuelled by ye aforementioned Utopian, hard-driving, nose-diving, axe-wielding rock'n'roll . . . well, motherfuckers, ah thunk we gotta live one!

I've chosen to sequence the album in the same running order as the songs were laid down in the studio, as I felt this better introduced the band to the world than did RCA's early-'70s compromise. Two songs, the esspecially recorded, too-soft rock single 'All I Need' and the sugary power ballad 'Bells', are deemed not only inappropriate to the Highway Robbery trip, but were record-company devices designed to capture a wider audience. Ha bloody ha, as the release of the former as a single effectively killed the band stone dead in the water!

Professor Longhair, or 'Sonically Speaking'

It do rage, it do blast, it do spit-roast and baste us, ye outrageous stop–starts of this singular burnt offering do pummel then lambaste us. A cartoon-octopus wine waiter on roller skates, its shrieking, high-octane, unbeaten black-and-blues burns and blazes, razes us clean to the ground. Here in the grooves of *For Love or Money* greedily we experience the sky-high energy-guitar complete control of the MC5 ('Looking at You', 'Sonically Speaking'), the bludgeoningly idealistic, Stephen Stills-inspired gospel-metal of Grand Funk Railroad's *Survival*, and the doom death-march of *Vincebus Eruptum*-period Blue Cheer ('Doctor Please', 'Out of Focus' . . .). Furthermore, the songs on *For Love or Money* even, at times, attempt to include all of the above extremes in the same tune!

And so, brothers and sisters, this LP is one hell of a statement to have lain unexcavated for so long. Only slightly flawed by RCA's typical early-'70s record-company requirement for a 'radio-friendly ballad', *For Love or Money* is almost as intensely *out there* as Sir Lord Baltimore's *Kingdom Come* debut from two years before, and contains several performances so extreme that the songs appear at first to be no more than a vehicle for the raging talents of the three musicians: Mike Stevens (guitar/songwriter), Don Francisco (singer/drummer – yowzah!) and John Livingston Tunison IV (singer/bass player/most immaculately hip aristocat).

Led by Stevens, a crazy and psychedelicised Mark Farner wannabe, there were few still alive on the planet during that immediately post-'60s period for whom such an incredibly supercharged guitar vision as Highway Robbery could have made any sense at all. One moment faster than The Wig's 'Crackin' Up' or anything by Ted Nugent's Amboy Dukes, the next minute as slow and sludgy as Juan De La Cruz's version of 'Wanna Take You Home' or Bang's 'Future Shock', but burning with a slow-building intensity several octanes higher than both, Highway Robbery was a Viet vet's wet dream, the ultimate all-purpose, do-everything, ideal, off-road sonic vehicle. And dolloped – nay, ladled – across this bare-bones racket of Red Indian war drums'n'wires was a thawing chocolate sundae of sticky-sweet power-harmonies brung in to bill'n'coo and Spectorise these heathen proceedings.

And yet several listens in to *For Love or Money* it becomes clear that it's the tough internal structure of each of those songs that allows them to have been so rigorously disassembled during the performance, almost, at times, to the point of total dissolution. Ooh yeah, part Indian braves and part dandy highwaymen, with Stevens acting the war-painted outlaw nine years before Adam Ant, Highway Robbery may have been constructed as a safe-house for the loner who led the band – that is, Stevens, the 'real' songwriter. But, as a true power trio, Highway Robbery was also a canny unit of proto-metal artisans with a real eye for facilitating the release of the Beast.

Ain't Gonna Brown-Nose the Blues No More!

But stranger than all of this is the fact that this mother of all experimental power trios had to be constructed especially for the mainman himself by a high-powered Hollywood management team. Cobbled together from other bands and furnished with an RCA record contract and the services of a legendary engineer-producer named Bill Halverson, whose supreme experience had included work with Eric Clapton, Delaney & Bonnie and Crosby, Stills, Nash & Young (*Déjà Vu*, no less), the question for Highway Robbery was never 'if' but only ever 'how soon' it would all take off for them.

Just two years before, as the door of the '60s had closed shut forever, a similar experiment way over on the East Coast had ended in miserable failure when a group of New York record businessmen – led by impresario Dee Anthony – had brought songwriters Jim Cretecos and future Springsteen manager Mike Appel together with Jimi Hendrix's engineer-producer Eddie Kramer to do a number on that insane power trio by the name of Sir Lord Baltimore. That the artistic results were amazing but resulted in the total ejection from the music business of all the band members will be well-known to readers of Unsung's pages. But both hindsight and a historical overview were unavailable to these illuminated souls about to record *For Love or Money*. When yooz standing on the verge of getting it on, guess u gotta keep your mind open . . .

Besides, Stevens felt that he had nothing to lose, having spent his

1960s high-school years in a semi-nomadic existence, flitting between the gymnasium, the football field and the basements of his garage-band buddies. Consumed by the lost culture of the Plains Indians who had so recently been evicted from this Californian landscape on which he walked, Stevens – like so many other West Coast rockers – believed that he felt the still-burning embers of their camp fires beneath his bare feet. And so Stevens remained the loner, his combination of physical fitness and rock'n'roll seemingly mismatched and impossible to reconcile with any fixed teenage scene. That is, until the arrival of Grand Funk Railroad in late September 1969.

For Mike Stevens, the bare-chested and fist-waving Mark Farner and his power trio were a massive and magical distillation of everything he'd aspired to. Coming out of Flint, in the heart of the Michigan Motor City conurbation, Grand Funk's tight and brutally simple soul-revue arrangements espoused a Luddite, anti-robot revolution in a brazen and basic blue-collar manner – and all recorded at such a workaholic pace that their four LPs had, between September '69 and Christmas '70, yielded three Top Tens. More than Farner's songs about modern life, his lyrics about the plight of Native Americans, sung in beautiful harmonies over crude wardance rhythms, inspired the romantic Mike Stevens so intensely that he simplified his own songs accordingly to embrace similarly screeching, ninety-degree rhythm changes, multiple-voiced harmonies and the kind of woven structural arrangements that only the simplicity of a power trio can accommodate.

The trouble was that Stevens was hardly a great lead singer and the early incarnations of Highway Robbery lacked the craziness required to carry the primeval bombast he envisaged. However, when the band supported Maurice White's early incarnation of Earth, Wind & Fire, Stevens' own performance was exciting enough to convince White's hot-shot Hollywood managers to sign him immediately. Here was the break Stevens had awaited, for his new management team of Robert Cavallo and Joseph Rufallo were already looking after Little Feat, Weather Report and The Lovin' Spoonful's John Sebastian, as well as having produced several Hollywood films. And when Stevens declared his intention to unite lightning-strike guitar playing with the kind of awe-inspiring harmonies that Steve Stills had brought to his own two solo LPs and the majesty of CSNY's *Déjà Vu*, Cavallo and Rufallo went straight to the engineer of that sound – the aforementioned Bill Halverson – and booked him as producer. Out went the garage-band drummer and in came the immaculately named Don Francisco, whose previous leadership of the now faltering power trio Crowfoot immediately endeared him to Mike Stevens' Red Man sensibilities.

Born Donald John Francis, this acrobatic and hugely confident singing drummer had taken his stage name from the seventeenth-century religious poet Don Francisco Placido, whose ministry had taken place among the Aztecs. Blond, urbane and supremely confident, the manner in which Francisco sung Stevens' songs dumped all the blues melodies and replaced them with the kind of spaced-out, shrieking vocal acrobatics that John Garner had brought to Sir Lord Baltimore (and which that beautiful cosmic brother, the late Ron Goedert, would eventually bring to White Witch's *A Spiritual Gathering*). For both Francisco and Stevens, it was a hallucinatory union. Retaining original bass player Jan Tunison, now portentously renamed John Livingston Tunison IV for his Swedish antecedents, Highway Robbery began to record their debut album without so much as one show having been performed. But on the day that the trio entered the recording studio, Mike Stevens pinned up his great manifesto over the doorway. These were to be their sleeve-notes and their words to live by. They read:

Declaration
For love or money, Highway Robbery hereby dedicates itself to roar, to drive, to sensitive joy and, above all, the emission of the highest levels of energy rock. Let it be known that Michael Stevens – lead guitarist, vocalist, writer of all material contained herein, child of a gypsy commune – carries out this pledge in the true manner of his forebears. Further be it known that he is in allegiance with Don Francisco – drummer, lead singer and a New York native whose main influences have been traditional New Orleans-based bands such as Robert Parker & the Royals and Deacon John & the Ivories; and with John Livingston Tunison IV – bassman, vocalist and painter, whose first sound memories are of Muddy Waters and B. B. King. FOR LOVE OR MONEY: signed, sealed and created by the aforementioned Highway Robbery, in this age, on this day, in the name of storming, beautiful rock and roll.

For Love or Money was recorded at a furious pace, played as hard as bleeding hands could allow and always at insane volumes, often causing engineer Richie Schmitt to run screaming from the control room. Beginning the proceedings with the incendiary 'Ain't Gonna Take No More', Schmitt soon found himself unable to bring the soundboard under control as what began as a kind of Uncle Tom-ing Janis-meets-Garner slide blues erupted into a cacophonous jackhammer more akin to *Led Zeppelin II* as played by Sir Lord Baltimore. With Francisco's uncannily female banshee wailing off the Richter scale and Stevens' shameless appropriation of the middle eight from Jefferson Airplane's 'She Has Funny Cars', the song then veers off into a double-time, 'Psychotic Reaction'-style coda, long-fading with wailingly beautiful multi-tracked power chords; altogether, as uniquely disturbing a piece of sonic cut-and-paste as any young band has ever laid down.

Next up, 'Fifteen' is Stevens' lament at his discovery, at such a young age, that adults generally knew shit. And what a lament this was. Imagine Sabs' 'Children of the Grave' played by The Litter during their *Emerge* period, with the 'School's Out' riff thrown in every thirty-two bars. It speeds up, slows down, stops and starts; this motherfucking barrage of relentless yawp is a blow to the cosmic fundament, make no mistake. And it beats Alice's 'Eighteen' by three full years of incomprehension.

The next libretto to be stapled to the gates of hell is 'Mystery Rider', the soon-to-be opening track on which Halverson unleashed a 'River Deep, Mountain High' sensibility of multiple-layered vocals that elevated the song into a euphoric initiation into the underworld. As an opening track, its lyrics appeared to speak directly to the guardian gatekeeper of the album itself, endowing the work with an immediate mysticism. The song was a ride with the Red Man that would end all rides – a Spector soundalike *summum bonum* of Grand Funk's gospel-chorused *Survival* anthem 'I Want Freedom', created through a laborious and protracted process of harmony-vocal multi-tracking, but ultimately still a sonic cinch to achieve for Bill Halverson by comparison with his labours for Crosby, Stills, Nash & Young.

Schmitt's shattered hearing must've eased considerably when the quiet 6/8 blues of 'I'll Do It All Again' commenced its squawking. But even with its inward-looking 'Signed D.C.' self-reflection, the song held masterful surprises, as the superbly confident Don Francisco let forth lupine yelps of John Garner-esque vocal mannerisms guaranteed to tear to shreds the remaining sensibilities of his captive audience – i.e. their long-suffering engineer.

When Don Francisco refused to sing two of Mike Stevens' most powerful songs on account of their crass lyrical content, both 'Lazy Woman' and 'Promotion Man' were more than successfully bawled out by bassist John Livingston Tunison IV, whose hilarious and unforgettably balls-to-the-wall style gives us all an idea of how Steve Jones and Michael Anthony would have fared as lead singers. Both songs were chosen as side closers because who the fuck could follow that? Despite its Todd Rundgren-like, phased, descending-harmony vocals on the chorus, the furious adolescent rush and roar of 'Lazy Woman' is pure Detroit teen riffery; a Kiss-take on Hendrix that Mountain woulda died for. And the guitar coda is a motherfucker, a faster, more distilled version of Hendrix, Page or Beck than even Louis Dambra coulda conjured up; indeed, it's up there with Gary Rowles' solo on Love's 'Love Is More Than Words, or Better Late Than Never'.

Better still was the album's epic closer, 'Promotion Man', and funny as fuck, too. Played with a desperation and last-stand violence that only those on the edge of oblivion could muster up, 'Promotion Man' was Michael Stevens' plea to the record people to make him a motherfucking star at any cost: 'We need the dues/We need the exposure/Hell, we'll take anything you got,' barks the ornery Tunison. And in the final verse, after singing to an audience of fifty thousand people ('I really love this crowd'), the singer hears his postman downstairs and . . . realises it was all a fucking dream . . . ending the song exactly the way the English teachers always tell you not to: '*But then I woke up!*'

Perhaps it's too much to suggest that the band members knew this was to be their only chance. But, upon hearing the sessions, the executives at RCA first shelved the album, then asked Stevens for a couple of radio hits to sugar this bitter sonic pessary. Naturally, when the naïve Stevens obliged, it was to the sanctuary of the bland 'All I Need' that the marketing team ran, ensuring that Highway Robbery's first and only single bore no resemblance to the rest of their work. It makes you wonder what woulda happened had this piece of crap by some fluke given the band a Top Forty hit. Would those people have then returned the LP because it blew their fucking arms off?

As the obvious disaster unfolded, the management team of Cavallo and Rufallo realised that their all-or-nothing approach had hit a brick wall. Still, they had plenty of other projects to keep them busy if their golden Cherokee could not deliver for them, while the ever-professionally minded Don Francisco jumped ship and settled for the simpler role of drummer with Wha-Koo, led by original Steely Dan singer David Palmer. The marketing people had said all along there was no focal point in the group, that singing drummers had always failed, and that a coupla songs having been sung by the bass player was even more confusing when the super-talented Pete Townshend-type guy whose trip propelled it all was nowhere near enough in evidence.

And so, after one superb LP, Highway Robbery were dropped by both RCA and Cavallo–Rufallo Enterprises, and promptly forgotten. Unlike Deep Purple, who'd got to make four shockingly average LPs before they managed to muster up *In Rock*, and even Sir Lord Baltimore, who'd managed to squeeze out a hugely toned-down second helping, Highway Robbery were in truth shafted by the sheer high calibre of their representatives, whose Hollywood credentials ensured that the hype was just that: briefly full-on but momentary, with nothing left over for Michael Stevens to build upon.

It seems that a truthful description of this music by Highway Robbery should most accurately be described as 'over the top', for verily its leader did vault WWI-style into the music-business minefield and was reported missing in action just days into the war. For those of us who dig the mayhem unleashed by this lost trio, I'll wager we will all return to their performances again and again, and that *For Love or Money* will grow into a future barbarian classic, guaranteed to occupy in all of our heads The Larger Place.

Discography

'All I Need' b/w 'Mystery Rider' (single, RCA, 1972)
For Love or Money (RCA, 1972)

MAGMA

Köhntarkösz

(A&M, 1974)

SIDE ONE

1 Köhntarkösz (Part One) (15.24)

2 Ork Alarm (5.27)

SIDE TWO

1 Köhntarkösz (Part Two) (15.59)

2 Coltrane Sündïa (4.11)

'How impossible it is to deny the personal influence of individual great men on the history of the world.' (Sigmund Freud, *Moses and Monotheism*)

A Kelt in a Krautrock-style

On July 6 1978, I found a copy of Magma's then four-year-old LP *Köhntarkösz* in a junky second-hand shop on the corner of Belmont Road, Liverpool. My friends Paul Simpson and Smelly Elly green-eyed it greedily as I paid over the one-pound-thirty, while the singer in our 'band', a prude called Ian McCulloch, legged it out of the shop as quick as you like, saying he'd always suspected I was a 'fucking jazz-rock fan!'

I had had a difficult relationship with Magma since 1972, way back when my Mahavishnu Orchestra-loving mate Herb Leake had bought their insane, black, gatefold-sleeved debut double LP and tried to convince me that it wasn't just Blood, Sweat & Tears on an astral plane. Sure it was, I'd argued relentlessly; the singer's David Clayton-Thomas and they're on bloody Philips. How un-rock can ya get?

But I secretly held Herb Leake in high esteem for forking out such big dosh for such a big Euro-double. And, although he often admitted to me that the record wasn't nearly as far out as Faust or Amon Düül II, we both got a big kick out of this strange, super-gloss gatefold packaging with its ultra-annoying/intriguing end-flaps, which you wanted to cut off because they so easily ripped, yet couldn't because they held inordinate amounts of information.

However much I dismissed them for being a kind of Blood, Sweat & Tears, in the early '70s only Magma would have dared appear (all eight of them) in fitted, black, flared one-piece jumpsuits and matching occult medallions; three of them saluting the sun, while the other five just stared you out, as though thinking: 'Yeah? Whatchyew gonna do about it?'

Yup, even back then Magma weren't no ordinary, brassy, jazz-based octet. Whereas the impressionism of Faust and the German bands intrigued you with the sheer lack of information, Magma assaulted you with wave upon wave of *meaning*. And what meaning! While the bottom right-hand corner of their album waylaid ya with the mysterious words 'Univeria Zekt', the names of the tracks were 'something else again' (as we fifteen-year-old proto-heads loved to say). 'Nau Ektila', 'Stoah', 'Muh' and 'Thaud Zaia' were hardly French, although not German either. And how did you even attempt to pronounce 'Schxyss'? Hey, I'm gonna be hanging with these guys when I grow big enough balls.

As all the copious sleeve-notes were in French, it took all our powers of decoding to discover that the mysterious Attaturko-Rumanian grunting of the Clayton-Thomasian lead singer was actually in an invented language called Kobaian, which had been especially made up for Magma by their unbelievably talented and mysterious drummer, Christian Vander. Shit, it was all run by the bloody drummer! We all ran around using words like 'pretentious' for a coupla months. Well, not words *like* 'pretentious' – we actually just said 'pretentious' and let that do us. It was a time when 'pretentious' could even be used positively – a bit like 'paranoid', a word which I'm absolutely sure Black Sabbath themselves never really understood. Every stupid get in the school was 'paranoid' at some point, just as every no-mark doing metalwork or technical drawing yearned to be a temporary poet in order to be called 'pretentious'.

Theusz Hamtaahk

In my Tamworthian neck of the woods, nothing more was heard of Magma for a year or so. Apparently, they had released another LP, called *1001 Degrees Centigrade*, but no one got beyond ogling its imported sleeve in Birmingham's Virgin Records, except Herb Leake's reggae mate,

Puddle, who claimed that it sounded a lot like the first one, as though he'd have a clue. Anyway, what with it just having the single sleeve, it was hardly worth the bother, or so we all comforted ourselves.

Then something truly insane happened. In February 1973, Magma signed to A&M Records and released an album of true genius – a classic. It was a record so weird and catchy-at-the-same-time that you could sing it straight-faced and piss off all the soul boys at school to such an extent that they wanted to disarticulate you right there and then. And it was on A&M – the fucking Carpenters' label, run by Herb Alpert the trumpeter! It's 1973 and the world has gone insane. Fucking hell, it was weird enough seeing the late copies of Faust's first LP, no longer the clear-vinyl copies which had howled 'statement', but black vinyl ones with a standard red Polydor label. Trainspotter-y, great-coated fifteen-year-olds such as we were needed solid cultural contexts by which to live. There were traditions to uphold. Slade was red-label Polydor, not Faust! And A&M was certainly never gonna be Magma.

Except that it very definitely *was*. Magma's new album appeared in such a high-grade black and gold gatefold that we all felt empowered by this strangely magical act. Magma seemed to have made it, and the record was a new totem to keep on the outside of your weighty, underarm LP collection to be conspicuously paraded as you struggled, great-coated and unshaven, around Tamworth every Saturday afternoon.

And what was the name of this mighty new release? I'll tell ya, kiddies; it was *Mekanïk Destruktïw Kommandöh* . . . Catchy, huh? And what was it about? Well, y'know – mechanical destructive commandos and everything that they do. Bloody obvious, I woulda thought.

It turned out that *Mekanïk Destruktïw Kommandöh* was actually the third part of an unfolding, nine-LP series known as *Theusz Hamtaahk*. In Christian Vander's Utopian mind, rock'n'roll was now at a cultural place in the collective conscious of humanity where it could possibly be used to help us take giant, progressive leaps, via a few forward-thinking motherfuckers such as he; people with a true tale to tell. And so *Theusz Hamtaahk* was Vander's vehicle for healing the world.

Those first two releases, in which the singer Klaus Blasquiz had appeared to be gargling endless portentous phlegm, now made some kind of sense. Those two albums, *Magma* and *1001 Degrees Centigrade*, had been telling the tale of future humans leaving polluted Mother Earth, travelling to their new home on planet Kobaia, returning as evangelists to Earth, then being imprisoned as dangerous neo-aliens before being released by the authorities, who had been informed by Kobaian command that Earth would be disintegrated should they refuse. Cool.

So Why Was Mekanïk Destruktïw Kommandöh *Such Unfettered Genius?*

The real reason that *Mekanïk Destruktïw Kommandöh* was so good was that it appeared utterly complete and fully formed to most people. It had the backing of a big record company and, like Athena bursting from the head of Zeus, it had no apparent provenance. If you listened to just *Mekanïk Destruktïw Kommandöh*, it had no influences to grab hold of, no background of any kind, just a bunch of humanoids with the weirdest names who all hung out together and spoke their own language; a bit like Dexy's Midnight Runners during their Buddhist-boxers phase.

Three fundamental changes in Magma's line-up had sent their sound into hyperspace. Firstly, their new producer was Giorgio Gomelsky, the Swinging London impresario who had been former manager of the Yardbirds and producer of the very psychedelic early Soft Machine. Secondly, gone was the first bass player and gone with him was the jazz – replaced by the scariest and greatest, shaved-bald, middle-European ur-human of all time. And with the greatest name of all time, too: Jannik Top.

Jannik Top! I'm shaking in me booties just thinking 'bout him. Jannik Top was a Gene Simmons for people with their own IQ. He played the bass like a Tyrannosaurus Rex skinning a Stegosaurus. He was at least eight feet tall and had claws instead of hands. His bass sound made the night fall early and kept the moon from rising at all. He didn't have amplifiers, he just plugged straight into the National Grid and drained the neighbourhood. Upon the ogreish arrival of Jannik Top, the early brass section of two saxophones and trumpet had left, bloodied, sweating and teary – exit three cool-schoolers pursued by a bear.

The other change was the arrival of five Valkyries – a spectacular and oracular choir of women with wonder-fuel Teutono-Frankish names: Muriel Streisfeld, Evelyne Razymovski, Michele Saulnier, Doris Reinhardt and, last but not least, her just-as-Highness Stella Vander in her role as (to give her full Kobaian appellation) *Organik Kommandeuhr.* The first two records had featured poor Klaus Blasquiz on his lonesome vocal jacksee, howling up a lupine storm like the Alaskan shaman Igjugarjuk with the white authorities hot on his trail – a Michael Ryan figure, picking off innocent Hungerford bystanders and garnering zero compassion from the listener. *But* the magical effect of having five Tungerman death goddesses singing along with him suddenly made Klaus into a combination of Superman, Spiderman, Ultraman *and* all sixteen of his brothers simultaneously!

Whereas, on the first two LPs, lonely Klaus was often an irksome intrusion (often mixed down lower than the brass), on *Mekanïk Destruktïw Kommandöh* the whole vocal system became a visionary call-and-answer divine dialogue of epic proportions. Imagine this piece of libretto, a translation of that album's '*Ïma Süri Dondaï*', screamed out in Kobaian, and tell me it's not genius:

'I have seen the Angel of Light and he smiled at me.
He smiled at me; he smiled at me, the Angel of Light.'
And the others, surprised, question him:
'The Angel of Light smiled at you?'
He answers with growing conviction:
'He smiled at me, the Angel of Light.'
And the others again ask him:
'He smiled at you, the Angel of Light?'
And he answers:
'He smiled at me, he smiled at me.'

And so it goes on. If teenage mates of mine came to *Mekanïk Destruktïw Kommandöh* cold and loved it, I never blew it for them by telling them that the band had made two jazz-based semi-achievements beforehand. I could even have shown them the first two expensive imports in Virgin Records and they'd never have guessed – without hearing the music, the sleeves looked great and, in the early '70s, imports were a no-no to listen to on Virgin headphones unless you were a real grown-up with plenny o'dough. And so the mystery continued.[1]

Köhntarkösz

By June 1974, Magma had changed all over again, and the low-key opera known as *Köhntarkösz* was released. Emotionally, it's probably best

1 If you need to hear some of *Mekanïk Destruktïw Kommandöh,* check out WSYM's Thighpaulsandra programmes. One of them features the album's opening track, 'Hortz Fur Dehn Stekehn West'.

described as Amon Düül II's Renate Knaup and Lothar Meid meets the reformed Van der Graaf Generator on an unvisitable and otherworldly plateau.

'Köhntarkösz (Part One)' opens with furious beat-the-kit-into-submission and telegraph-wire bass lines over droning, hanging, one-chord organ, before Klaus Blasquiz leads the ensemble into a punctuated, angular, descending riff, kinda like The Doors' 'America'. This mutates into a slow, slow, portentous Do-Re-Mi of pianos and mob-handed bass, as waspish fuzz organ irritates the choir, buzzing around their collective asses, getting permanently shooed elsewhere. Klaus hisses and cajoles the music, as though he's trying to cop off with the many heads of Medusa simultaneously, but he's fighting a losing battle and he's in danger of them all sussing his two-facedness any minute. Bass oozes from every aural orifice as the fuzz organ becomes untethered and pushes forwards, overly loud and brazen. *Star Trek*-ian females 'ooh' and 'aah' soothingly, but we're in that same netherland which Van der Graaf Generator found themselves in throughout *Godbluff*, and no one feels soothed at all. According to the sleeve-notes, we're now entering the tomb of Emehnteht-Re and only the rhythm section and bass piano dare play, until . . . *aaaaah!* Horrible, horrible, zapping, loud, synthesized organ ker-monsters your senses out of the right-hand speaker, picked up by the female voices and rhythm which continues to rise and fight the fuzz organ. This then subsides and lets the ensemble continue on their way into the ancient tomb. Gentle oriental pianos cascade over brooding distorted Yamaha organ, until the whole track slowly fades.

Then we're off into the storm of 'Ork Alarm', Jannik Top's ever-ascending, cello-driven Blasquizian, proto-human mantra. Stereo clavinets echo across the speakers as pumping, driving cellos and waspish, Yoko Ono-like female vocals shiver and shake, inspiring a strangled lead guitar to wring out a hoodoo of notes. No drums at all. A Christian Vander album and *there are no drums*! So rhythmic, so charged . . . and all without drums! Until the final moments, that is, when the intense paranoia has become just too much and the super-stereo effects, like crunching Iron Man electro-footsteps, come raging up some Milky Way path of gravel stars and bring the whole claustrophobic thang to a conclusion of sweet relief.

In total contrast, 'Köhntarkösz (Part Two)' is a huge and epic mantra, a heathen movie score for an unfilmed religious epic. It's the closest Magma ever get to approaching that unchanging Krautrock-ian spiralling that Can and Popol Vuh loved so much, building slowly and gently around just three notes, getting progressively louder and louder and more and more furious until the whole track finishes with the low, rasping tongues of Buddhist monk-type chanting.

Köhntarkösz concludes with the delicate beauty of 'Coltrane Sündïa', a short eulogy to the late John Coltrane. This multiple-piano and guitar piece would be at home on Popol Vuh's *Einsjäger und Siebenjäger*, hanging in a kind of suspended animation as rippling waterfalls of piano notes tumble out over a gorge of rumbling bass throbs. Perhaps these are the last notes of the perfect Magma ensemble, or perhaps I'm being a romantic and claiming something which could never have been quite so simple.

It may be that Jannik Top just tried to take over. It may be that Christian Vander decided that *Theusz Hamtaahk* was no longer achievable. It may be that A&M came to their senses and heard Joan Armatrading. But, whatever it was, *Köhntarkösz* and *Mekanïk Destruktïw Kommandöh* were destined to remain the only A&M releases ever made by Magma. The detective work is all there waiting to be done by some journalist with a good ear for an occult tale. If you've read my book *Repossessed*, then you'll know the weirdness of Christian Vander's Spanish-castle magic battle with big Jannik, and how my/their tour manager Martin Cole was reduced to driving from one hilltop to another in an attempt to make both of them see some sense.

Beyond the Valley of Jannik Top

The albums after *Köhntarkösz* do have some insanely great moments, but as time moves on they get increasingly few and far between. Two particular albums, however, must be appraised for their hidden genius. On 1976's extremely patchy *Udu Wudu*, Christian Vander even attempted to trump the death of his mighty ensemble by letting Jannik Top entirely loose on the berserker magic of the side-long epic 'De Futura'. But a Magma in which Jannik held sway was a Magma in which Klaus Blasquiz was returned to his Igjugarjuk/Michael Ryan role. And I do believe even he himself recognised this – the vocal credit on *Udu Wudu*'s 'Zombies' merely reading 'Klaus Blasquiz – growl'. For me, *Udu Wudu* fails not because Magma has become a kind of augmented power trio – that's fine, and Blasquiz, Top and Vander make an almighty machine – but because it's really a return to jazz-rock. Clothe it any Teutonic or Utopian way you wish and I still can't stand the stuff.

Far better was the more ensemble-based *Attahk*, which saw Jannik Top totally ousted. Yet the opening track and long main themes again generally suffered from the same bugger-digger jazz bass lines and brittle percussive onslaught that I can't abide. However, the real 'songs' – the piano-based 'Spiritual', 'Rinde', 'Nono' and 'Dondai' – inhabited a kind of magical and impossibly beautiful Afro-Teutonic space that makes you desperate for an entire album with this sense of loss. Imagine Norman Whitfield at his Undisputed Truth-period experimental best putting out a German-only release on R. U. Kaiser's Pilz label, and you glimpse the moments that these later Magma tracks still generated. Or maybe Tim Buckley's 'Get on Top'/'Sweet Surrender' vocal gyrations over one of the longer tracks from the Cosmic Couriers' *Tarot*.

On 'Nono', Klaus Blasquiz gets more tearful than Clarence Carter on his soul-weepy 'Patches'. On 'Dondai', reunited at last with his new soul Valkyries, Klaus becomes the greatest and most abandoned operatic soul diva of all time – Sylvester meets Klaus Nomi meets Alan Vega meets *Don't Stand Me Down*-period Kevin Rowlands on a railway platform, waving goodbye to all hope, all possibilities, all family, all relationships; a squirming, writhing apostate soul brother stomping at the Pillar of Irminsul, desperately willing the newly converted King Charlemagne to 'Spare that tree!'[2]

But music of this yearning and intensity never came about from a good sensible strategy meeting; it was clearly born in the euphoric high heavens of the central European plain and dragged its migratory self by the knuckles, sacrificing itself to itself at every monolith and significant tree, in the true shamanic tradition. The closest that Christian

2 Like all visionaries and genuinely forward-thinking motherfuckers, as time moved on Christian Vander remained as true to the trail as ever. Speaking to Ed Vulliamy in the London *Evening Standard* on January 16 1988, Vander was still claiming that Magma's music was there to be used to confront strong and violent emotions and to dissolve them through 'a new consciousness in which we no longer have to take time to land from our moments of aggression, and we understand exactly the place where we are and what things are around us. We are telling always the same story, of the same *douleur* [pain/distress] and the same *souffrance* [suffering] in order to achieve the same goal.'

Vander and Jannik Top ever got to a compromise was in not killing each other.

Probably the ultimate reason I hate the Romans so much is because of their pragmatism – as every Roman animal sacrifice doubled as a barbecue, was it even a sacrifice at all? Surely it meant no more than Bill Nelson's guitar sacrifices during his Be-Bop Deluxe days, in which he would play a Gibson all evening, then substitute that Gibson for a cheap copy, before ceremoniously setting it afire. Like the Romans before him, Bill made it look great, but it didn't have to hurt his pocket. Was it, then, really any more of a sacrifice than the wishing well is nowadays, in which we throw in ten pence to make a wish while patting the tenner lodged firmly in our back pocket?

For Christian Vander and Jannik Top, this was a true soul sacrifice. And when Top awoke one Spanish morning to discover that his former partner/boss had caused him to rip open his own chest during the night, whatever despair he then lived through must have eventually been overtaken (perhaps much, much later) by the realisation that, together in temporary unity, a bass player and a drummer had not only glimpsed that Kobaian paradise which they had projected into the heavens, but, like Igjugarjuk himself, they had sustained long enough to visit that imagined planet and its Utopian culture and bring us all back a piece.

Buy and listen to *Köhntarkösz* and *Mekanïk Destruktïw Kommandöh*, then go to an oldies record shop and check out the sleeves of the other LPs. You don't need *all* these records, but you sure as hell gotta grab the two classics. Then the genius of Christian Vander will slowly become subsumed into your consciousness, and you'll want to own the others just because of what he symbolises. And then, little by little, bit by bit . . .

Montrose

(Warner Brothers, 1973)

1 Rock the Nation (2.57)
2 Bad Motor Scooter (3.41)
3 Space Station Number 5 (5.18)
4 I Don't Want It (2.58)
5 Good Rockin' Tonight (2.59)
6 Rock Candy (5.05)
7 One Thing on My Mind (3.41)
8 Make It Last (5.31)

The first time I played this LP to my American wife, she was furious. As a proto-rock teen-chick of the '70s, Dorian couldn't believe that this record had not been massive in the US. But no, this first Montrose release was ignored and went chartless in America, although it hit the Top Fifty in Britain in spring 1974 and caused a real stir amongst heads at my school when we saw Sammy Hagar und cohorts parping and hollering through the BBC's geriatrically sedated *Old Grey Whistle Test.* And it was a yawpy and incendiary, almost Detroit-type credibility which saw them through punk and later accepted enough to have Stiff Little Fingers nick the opening of their 'Space Station Number 5' for the latecomer punk anthem 'Suspect Device'.

I commented in *Head-On* about how revisionists had written the longhairs out of the beginnings of punk. Well, here's another missing link, and it's a primal example of how bad-asses were cutting the cheese in those early mid-'70s. This isn't righteous-music-in-the-face-of-Altamont like the MC5 and Funkadelic, nor is it unrighteous like The Stooges always were. No, this is far more unconscious than that; for a start, its political agenda was about as token as the vegetarian menu on a North Sea ferry. So I'm not judging it in that way; this album was, after all, just the soundtrack to every 1970s Saturday night nutjob's failed blowjob. Too drunk to fuck? U-betcha! But even during this legendary time when guitar masters of rock were the new alchemists, this Montrose album was the philosopher's stone. Yes, Montrose were never a wanna be – they wuz always a gonna be. So file away your Neu! albums and strap back, it's time to partayyy!

For years, Ronnie Montrose had been a your-time-is-gonna-come Jimmy Page-rising, until his part in the freakazoid success of Edgar Winter's glam-blooz *They Only Come Out at Night* LP (with its attendant 'Frankenstein' and 'Free Ride' hit singles) left him with a big Warner Bros. contract and lots of high expectations all around. So, like Jimmy Page did with Zeppelin, the hugely experienced Montrose picked two young unknowns and one session vet with whom he formed this brilliant quartet around his own surname.

Like Montrose himself, bass player Bill Church had played on Van Morrison's *Tupelo Honey*, and the jacket of this first LP features these two most prominently in the photographs. In contrast, drummer Denny Carmassi is given a secondary billing, while an extremely shy-looking and nervous young Sammy Hagar hangs even more in the background.

The album's songs are split evenly between Hagar and Montrose compositions, and even the cosmic, Beefheartian, big-eyed blues powerdrive which fuels the whole sound is still secondary to obvious and damn-catchy riff-athons. Warners house producer Ted Templeman co-piloted this album, but it is Ronnie Montrose's co-production and sense of space and thrill which made the record into a guitar dream from the beyond. Throughout the length of this too brief assault, fuzz guitars, phasers and all manner of stereo effects heave and sweat, while the bass climbs the walls and undercuts the massive drums. It is also the strut and yawp and '30s gangster, side-of-the-mouth, young-teen-being-a-fax-of-a-man which defines this whole sound.

The two minutes and fifty-seven seconds (great length!) of 'Rock the Nation' opens the album with all the ur-klang of The Who's *Live at Leeds*. Lean, spacious, metal chord riffs peal off a monstrous bootboy beat, as Sammy Hagar muses cool, cool mutterings about how he's going to give us the business. And he surely does. His asides and vocal inflections are those of a young man walking down the street saying hello to every local he meets, assured and adored in his own environment. Like the easy confidence of Ian Gillan on Purple's 'Highway Star', like the strut/saunter rhythm of Hendrix's 'Highway Chile' (hell, the song even quotes licks from Neil Young's 'The Loner') the song doesn't make any attempt to shoot its load then and there. Instead, it's a declaration of intent. It says we're-gonna-shoot-our-load-but-we-won't-tell-you-when-or-where. And for the next thirty-five minutes they do it again and again and fucking again. The second half of the song introduces a wildly catchy, Zeppelin'd-*Abbey Road* guitar arpeggio and then it's gone. Boom!

Next up is 'Bad Motor Scooter', which they did on the *Whistle Test.* Super stereo stun-guitar intro effects powerhouse into a Texan, Elevators-styled rave-up with lyrics to write home to your ma about: 'If you get lonely on your daddy's farm/ Just remember I don't live too far.' Rock! As the rarely proud owner, in 1974–76, of a 1964 Lambretta Li150 scooter with no mod/northern soul/post-suedehead affiliations whatsoever, it was only this song which made my lonely, late-evening, two-stroke refuellings behind Tamworth's only shopping precinct seem more acceptable.[1] And Sammy was a true punk in this song, leaving the bravado way behind with the killer admission: 'I'd come over to your place but I'm afraid of your dad.' Then it's time for Ronnie to 'zip up my guitar' in an overt 'Sun Zoom Spark'-stylee, before a bumping car-crash, dodgem-shunt guitar solo, like the whole track suddenly has taken the tea-cup ride. And, as the song finishes, he lets out a long, looming note . . . and lets it float.

'Space Station Number 5' starts

---

1 In 1974, my Lambretta Li150 was shit because:

(a) You couldn't bank without grinding the rubber footboard trim off the base of the barely-retractable stand;

(b) You couldn't rough-ride it without caking up the wheel-arches so much that the whole thing resembled a scrawny, long-necked adolescent mallard duck straining to escape from some polluted beach oil spill;

(c) I hated the knobhounds who covered their scooters with multiple mirrors, but became inexorably associated with them as some lesser cousin because I didn't play the game, preferring instead to spray-paint the whole thing matte black with gold side-panels;

(d) In the cold, those gold side-panels regularly fell off on the A5 between Atherstone and Wilnecote (late at night), because the spring contraptions which held them on were hard to click into place all the way without cutting yourself, when still covered in oily gunk from rough-riding around the Tamworth mound;

(e) The riding position was about as Rock as arriving in a sedan chair. The long, foamy sit-up-and-beg bench seat conspired with the ribbed footboard to make you feel you were no more out-of-doors than if you'd been waiting to jump down from the back of a double-decker bus.

with all the *Lonesome Crow* hammy mysticism of very early Scorpions, and it works. Indeed, it's great and it makes you want to reach out your hands to imaginary laser lights tracking across the ceiling. Then the bludgeoning of the soon-to-be 'Suspect Device' riff looms large and pumps out of the dirge, until we're trammelling along like *Sabotage*-period Black Sabbath playing 'Paranoid'. We even get a kind of sub-Granicus/Woody Leffel/*Led Zeppelin VII* (second side) bogus stream-of-consciousness spoken word. It's what Stephen Holden would have called 'Hi-amp speechsong', and it still sounds effective and real, even in these twenty-first-century days. The rise in the middle of the chorus has always reminded me of a cross between the Bunnymen's 'Crocodiles' and Cheap Trick's Nirvanaesque *Live at Budokan* version of 'Come On, Come On'. The primary riff then speeds up and up and up into a Whirling Dervish tape-effect conclusion in the same tradition as Sabbath's 'Wheels of Confusion'.

I suppose 'I Don't Want It' is an almost mundane and perfunctory way to end Side One after such all-out assault; as Sammy states so succinctly on this Black Sabbath boogie: 'Well, I gave it a chance and it shit back in my face.' But, oh ja, you got to allow Hagar the Horrible his Iron Age metaphor in order to allow him to truly creep into your heart. And even though Sammy's 'making toothpicks out of logs', and praying hurts his knees, he's working his thing out with such success that we can only benefit. And, seen in terms of a-truly-great-singer-can-sing-the-back-of-a-menu-and-get-away-with-it, Sammy Hagar is up there on the B+ list, alongside Sir Lord Baltimore's John Garner, Ash Ra Tempel's John L. and Granicus' Woody Leffel, and just below Iggy, Ozzy, Damo and the Lizard King.

Side Two jump-starts with the Utopian 'Good Rockin' Tonight', an ascending and bubbling frat-boogie 'All Right Now' sung in anticipatory David Lee Roth voice. It's a fresh and clean-sounding, Townshendian 'Long Live Rock' clarion-call to the pure, mod-youth shamanic act of getting Saturday-night fucked-up seven evenings a week. In contrast, 'Rock Candy' is a Rock of Gibraltar – it's 'When the Levee Breaks' played by a two-ton drummer in slo-mo; broad-based and tight/fat-assed as Kiss would get on their classic 'I Love It Loud' forty-five (and probably the inspiration for High Rise's ultra-monolithic 'Door'). I guess that 'Bonhamian' should be the term for this earthbound piece of Kashmir.

This song surely can't fly, so it won't bomb you. But it invades like a horde nation sweeping across your open plains.

Now, I'd argue that the Ted Templeman production and formatting of this album became the actual set-in-stone modus operandi for almost every Van Halen album. But not only that, even the lyric of the Utopian-sounding and Who-ian 'One Thing on My Mind' predates by half a decade David Lee Roth's method of writing seduction lyrics to some invisible female in a way which totally reduces the band to a back-up role. By 1980 and Van Halen's third album, *Women and Children First*, Diamond Dave had surpassed himself with the hysterical lyrics of 'Everybody Wants Some'. But the roots of his muse are right here, and it's interesting that Van Halen graduated to Sammy Hagar when Diamond Dave became just too, too fucking eclectic for even his biggest fans. (I say graduated because Sammy Hagar is much better at articulating his muse than Diamond Dave. And even though David Lee Roth's autobiography proves him to be in many ways a true mystic,[2] the proof of the trip in rock'n'roll is shown simply by listening to the fucking music.)

By the time the genius of 'Make It Last' kicks off, I'm a foamer. The rock-solid Bonhamian beat crosses the Polish border at the average speed of a 1939 Panzer tank. The slab guitar chords pave it in instant-drying sonic concrete which ossifies on the feet of huge Viking weather gods stomping across the landscape in their new, instant-fancy piston boots. It's an 'I Love Rock'n'Roll' Joan Jett-riding-a-real-lead-zeppelin way to finish the album.

Tragically, Montrose never maintained the heights of this debut. By the time of their second album, *Paper Money*, just six months later, Bill Church had gone, and Sammy Hagar quit soon after that. But, for that brief period in late '73/early '74, Montrose could surely rock any place.

2 Even in fifty-thousand-seater arenas, David Lee Roth would ignore the jibes of Edward and Alex Van Halen and, before the show, take a brush and pail and clean the stage on which he was to perform, in order to better communicate with his surroundings and audience. After shows, he would cycle the midnight streets of cities he had played, in further efforts to communicate with them. In his autobiography, his flip attitude is constantly undercut by genuinely mystical phrases such as: 'We are only at our best when we are ascending towards something.' Right on!

Billy Miller

Three Visionary Songs

(This album was created by Julian Cope for the purposes of this review)

1 Fall (7.12)
2 Ra-Ma (11.19)
3 Here in the Year (8.54)

How Billy Miller Invented Post-Punk in 1970

In 1970, visionary lyricist and electric autoharp wielder supreme Billy Miller recorded these three astonishing songs with his quartet Cold Sun – a.k.a. Dark Shadows – in Texas' legendary Sonobeat Studios,[1] creating a startlingly rich-but-ragged, heathen-as-fuck, post-psychedelic sound that many believe was way ahead of its time. Like Van der Graaf Generator, these gentlemen sounded punky, defiantly imperfect (although rhythmically masterful) and appeared to share most in common with groups of the post-punk late '70s: the euphonically atonal Blue Orchids; Vic Godard's raging weaklings Subway Sect; and the spiritedly 'off' chorales of ex-Saint Ed Kuepper's *Mr Uddich-Schmuddich Goes to Town*-period Laughing Clowns.

Miller's ensemble brought forth an erotically satanic sound, something like early Una Baines-period The Fall attempting The Savage Rose's take on The Doors, via *Easter Everywhere*-meets-Van der Graaf's proto-Johnny Rotten fist-shaking, Zoroastrian defiance. Phew! Furthermore, Billy Miller's barbarian lyrical yawp exuded a post-'hippie dream' knowingness similar to that of much later groups such as the Patti Smith Group and The Neon Boys/Television, while Miller's experimental, Terry Rileyan

1 Sonobeat Records was the home of Johnny Winter's early releases, and later of psychedelic band The Conqueroo.

electro-strumming was so wanton, so urgent, so pestering, so spiritedly untutored and rule-breaking that it's hard to imagine these poor dudes was plying their trade so long ago that they had to tolerate the opinions of Cream fans. Sheesh! You think Blue Cheer was slagged off as 'inauthentic'? Fergettaboutit! At least those druids came bearing electric guitars. With our man Billy Miller, it's get the Joe Meek freak with the plug-in angel's harp! Mercy!

Since his lizard'n'snake-collecting youth, Billy Miller had long been a follower of the nightmare antics of England's outrageous Screaming Lord Sutch, and a devotee of one-time Sutch producer Joe Meek and his stratospheric, Selmer clavioline-driven 'Telstar' sound,[2] along with Del Shannon's equally mysterious and equally clavioline-driven hit 'Runaway'.[3] The piercing oscillations of this bizarre 1955 monophonic miniature keyboard (replete with knee-operated chrome volume lever) plagued and obsessed the young autoharpist, who began searching for an 'electrifying' method with which to integrate his own 'too quiet' folk instrument into a rock'n'roll context. The answer was not easily forthcoming in those barren Texas surroundings, besides which many contemporary musicians regarded the autoharp as far too passive an instrument with which to accompany any singer of rock songs, the instrument being held hard against the chest with the left hand and 'thrummed' with the right hand, rendering the performer rigid and almost preacher-like – a far cry from every rock'n'roll archetype Billy Miller had thus far encountered. This was, however, a time for destroying archetypes. And when the first wave of rock'n'rollers bit the dust – Elvis into the army, Chuck Berry off to gaol, Little Richard to the ministry, Eddie and Buddy to the afterlife – the next truly interesting wave of artists that inspired this young songwriter was led by one of the greatest rock'n'roll iconoclasts in all of ye rawk history: ladies'n'gentlemen, please welcome

2 The unearthly sound of the clavioline was something of an all-purpose secret weapon in the sci-fi and horror-obsessed early '60s. Indeed, Joe Meek united the twin obsessions on the 1961 Parlophone single 'Night of the Vampire' by The Moontrekkers, forcing electronic epiphanies into the burning tail-out of each refrain before concluding the song in a barrage of screams and backwards effects.

3 Del Shannon's musical collaborator, Max Crook, so modified his own clavioline that he renamed it a Musitron, and tried unsuccessfully to patent his modification as a brand-new design.

that mythical and jug-wielding Gurdjieffian scholar Mr Tommy Hall and his 13th Floor Elevators! Yee-har!

Delighted by the psychedelic hootenanny conjured up by the jug-informed Elevators sound, and inspired by the strange manner in which Buddy Holly-obsessive Roky Erickson was obliged to get his caterwauling tonsils around Tommy Hall's extraordinarily instructive and esoteric lyrical observations, autoharpist Miller threw all caution to the wind and brought forth an inspired series of tumbling and ever-becoming, tempo-changing compositions, whose breathtaking musical flights, abrupt halts and sudden airlifts evoked nothing less than the switchback Peyote ride of some brave-but-clueless native Texas shaman astride the great Night Mare of the Norse myths (recently imported by Whitey) as she vainly attempts to dislodge him from her saddle-less back. And within these new and highly arranged compositions the extremely demanding and focused songwriter carefully itemised all the musical highpoints of his life thus far and, like some psychedelicised carnival barker luring unsuspecting kids to his midnight carousel, disgorged the entire contents of his Peyote'n'sci-fi mind into the music of his band.

Herein, the unearthly and electronic Joe Meek-isms stood shoulder-to-shoulder with *Easter Everywhere*-style lyrical poetry of great, protracted beauty, while elsewhere Miller's raging ensemble united other bizarre, early-'60s pop experiments such as The Jaynetts' creepy 'Sally Go Round the Roses' and The Shirelles' titanic 'Baby, It's You' with the darkest moments of such near contemporaries as The Music Machine, The Doors and Burton Cummings' The Guess Who at their most malevolent.[4]

4 There are three stages to The Guess Who's career. Led by Randy Bachman and bespectacled singer Chad Allen, this Canadian outfit began in the early '60s as a beat combo with some great singles. Next, a very young singer/pianist/flautist called Burton Cummings took them to international success, singing his own and Randy Bachman's hit songs while releasing bizarre Doors-wannabe LPs totally at odds with their housewife charm. Finally, Bachman left to form Bachman-Turner Overdrive, leaving Cummings to work out his Jimbo fantasies on the awe-inspiringly crass LP *Live at the Paramount* (with its seventeen-minute version of 'American Woman' and drug anthem 'Truckin' Off Across the Sky'), before succumbing to an innate Canadian conservatism that eventually nosedived into a swamp of moustachioed, merely-achieving-ness. It's fascinating, but do be wary!

Billy Miller was joined in these experiments by drummer Hugh Patton, bass player Mike Waugh and close friend and fellow Velvet Underground obsessive Tom McGarrigle, whose own guitar style was an unlikely mix of fuzzed-out, staccato, Seedsian, Jan Savage-ry, cyclical Sterling Morrison-isms and pure white-light feedback of the kind even the hoity-toity Lou Reed would have approved.

So when the Velvets fetched up in Austin for their now-legendary autumn 1969 Texas tour, both Miller *and* McGarrigle were equally absorbed by the manner in which Messrs Reed, Morrison, Tucker and Yule had subsumed the cacophony of their earlier LPs into a far more palatable (even occasionally 'alien MOR') listening experience; yet one that still remained just as clean, just as uncluttered and almost as meditative as those early Terry Riley/John Cage/La Monte Young-inspired, John Cale-led, minimalist drone experiments on top of which Lou's first Velvets songs had been superimposed. And so it was that Billy Miller's Cold Sun, a.k.a. Dark Shadows, worked up a whole set of highly original songs, alongside several others (some co-written with McGarrigle) that fitted in more successfully with the West Coast mores of the period.

Fortunately, or unfortunately, for us, no one was able to place the band's Sonobeat recordings with a major record company, and the project soon lay dormant, before being shelved as the four musicians became the backing band of the recently released king of the psychedelic jailbirds, Roky Erickson. Seemingly going nowhere and then being invited to become musical director of his fave singer's band, Billy Miller jumped at the chance.

Renamed Blieb Alien by their new boss, the band forgot their beginnings, and this current Album of the Month material lay forgotten for close to two decades until it was released by America's Rockadelic Records in 1989. I have only a passing interest in the general Cold Sun canon of shorter songs, as they were, to my mind, essentially no more than nice meditations on typical West Coast, 'Greasy Heart'-style workouts – all a little 'so what?' at this late stage in the game. So let us now take a look at these three visionary songs, songs which so set Billy Miller aside as a rare, Gnostic poet. For all three compositions are possessed of a clarity, a daring and a sense of adventure that makes them transcendental.

'Fall'

Commencing with a hugely compressed cross-kit drum roll, the seven-minute, ingrown majesty of 'Fall' casts off like some cartoon hoedown; a steam-powered and agricultural rave-up; an Okie Doors fronted by a straw-chewing, wide-eyed, teenage Keltic bard whose mind is so o'erflowing with imagery and life force that his mush-mouthed proclamations to his muse skip and trip from his errant gob at such a rate he can barely keep tabs on what's been did and what's been hid. Querulous as early Neil Young and earnestly spazmo as Crispin Clover as *Back to the Future*'s George McFly, Billy Miller's delivery herein is probably the most confidently unconfident this side of Jonathan Richman's on the first Modern Lovers LP. One day, young men will woo beautiful women successfully by invoking these very words:

This hour, your everlasting form,
Waves from the windowsill,
And I see your moonlight eyes,
Turning this way still.

Once I was a drunken mass of men,
At the garden wall,
Now I'm a dancing Prince of Light,
Who knows no fear at all.

I'll never go to war,
I've been there before,
Napoleon is standing fast,
On the battleground,
Bullets, cannons, roaring past . . .

Kiddies, how often am I drawn to type out the words, fer Chrissakes? This is the shit, brothers'n'sisters . . . declaimed like a youthful Vachel Lindsay ranting from atop a flatbed at a Springfield, Ohio, agricultural show. For two full minutes, Miller sustains this magical and wonder-fuelled gush, until the whole track halts abruptly; a biblical mist rises up and a brand-new declaration takes us over, this time performed according to the Frankie Laine system. Now we're experiencing deathly country and western, as morose as Scott Walker's *Scott 4*, as a spectral army treks across an Armenian spaghetti-western landscape, with Mount Ararat rising at their backs.

As vast and simple as Hawkwind's Mellotron 400-fuelled *Warrior on the Edge of Time* period and reminiscent of Creedence's meditative marathons 'Pagan Baby' and 'Ramble Tamble', this Billy Miller song was, back in 1970, undoubtedly music of the future. Hereafter, 'Fall' descends into a bludgeoning post-punkiness that comes over like The Badgeman playing Salem Mass' 1970 epic

'Witch Burning'; same use of so-called satanic chords to scare the elders and entice the young. The song finally concludes after some truly euphoric chordal autoharp/guitar interplay that reeks of the Velvets, but is *n* degrees more moving. Indeed, it's always put me in mind of Donald Ross Skinner's contribution to my 1990 version of Roky's 'I Have Always Been Here Before'. But then, we *were* attempting to sound like Billy Miller . . .

'Ra-Ma'

Next up, the lone drums that kick off the eleven epic minutes of 'Ra-Ma' invoke Creedence's proto-Krautrock version of 'Suzie Q', but the divine autoharp soon intercedes and Miller delivers us into very eerie and discordant territory. Then, what the fuck? Out of nowhere, the band launches into a bizarre hybrid of *The Soft Parade*'s title track and the Velvets' 'The Murder Mystery', as the whole band speak–sing across each other. Then, just as abruptly, a scything scuzz-fuzz riff kicks in, and in no time Billy's invoking ancestral Roky from atop some ancient Texan law-hill. Another change follows, into a rampant and deadly sleazy/stripper music, an Alice Cooper-like Jimbo rip (I shit you not!), and we're soon stratosphere-bound with an adolescent space-trek that opens out into the Simply Saucer variety of punk Floyd. Just as quickly, ye wide-eyed bard from the album's beginning returns to claim his tune:

All is calm, back to life again,
You are young,
Open your eyes, begin,
Take me off to the woods,
Beyond the wind,
Find a place to be grown – to fit in . . .
The tortoise before you saw da Gama as he landed,
We can make our life in a temple of stone,
It took an age or two to get home,
Now, see the tree and how it has grown,
It was a seed in my hand when the tortoise was born . . .
Here, down on to the falling land,
From your feeling hand I step on the wind,
Now I know they can never hurt you again,
Infant Vision lives at higher than pilot's airflow . . .

At this point, Billy Miller and the whole ensemble accelerate into the greatest dream music I've heard since Neu!; it's the music they'll play on the elevator that takes me down into hell, for shit damn sure. Bury me to this music. Drape your bodies over my coffin and wail for me to *this* music. Then, ye final tempo change, at eight minutes and forty-one seconds, delivers us into the divine brothel, a heavenly womb/tomb full of bosomy, loving, sacred whores/houris, carrying bongs'n'endless pints of beer and chanting sacred texts, with a tuxedoed Roky Erickson as the in-house chanteur. Some songwriters have long careers and never nail as many poetic truths as this one song.

'Here in the Year'

The nine-minute-long behemoth that is 'Here in the Year' is a true wolf in sheep's clothing, greeting us with all the seeming festive tradition of some Rabbie Burns ode set to music, toppled over a waterfall of guitar notes similar to that perplexing instrumental beginning tacked on to the start of the *Loaded* versh of 'Sweet Jane'. That the song is nothing of the sort becomes apparent only well after listeners' minds have been successfully hoodwinked by enough hoary Bach-ian fugues, cascading *Einsjäger und Siebenjäger*-period Popol Vuh/Daniel Secundus Fichelscher electric guitar and arcane lyrical allusions. Thereafter, we're lured further underground by the venerable and dignified 'Wishful Sinful'-ness of it all. There's no doubt that, lyrically, this gorgeous and extraordinary song is a true offspring of Tommy Hall, whose own highly wordy songs forced upon Roky Erickson such a tumbling and unsettled delivery that it made Arthur Lee and Bob Dylan look positively languid.

Then we're suddenly thrust, unprepared, into the Valley of Van der Graaf Generator and Alrune Rod (these entrenched fuckers have been at war for years), and we get shot by both sides before being zipped down, down, down a sonic corridor back into post-punk. Yup, it's 1979–83 all over again and The Chills are 'Pink Frosting' us to death. Whoa, we've shifted again, and now, over cascading Joe Meek-ian Bach fugues, the Miller's lamenting Jim Morrisonesque, as though through a Ray Collins/Mothers filter. Man, this send-up sure is moving. I mean, this poet is goofing maximum stylee and still I'm blarting big old puddles round the base of my pewter computer.

Clang, all change into a Van Dyke Parks-ian knees-up, and . . . whoosh, out we are sucked through the asshole of a goose into (yup, again) some clattersome post-punk of The Blue Orchids variety . . . ten years early. I would imagine it's highly likely that the extremely fundamentalist and hip Cleveland band Mirrors had heard this bunch, for there are major similarities in their twin obsessive takes on L. Reed and co.

Open Sesame

As my dear friend and 13th Floor Elevators biographer Psychedelic Paul Drummond commented at the dawn of the publication of *Krautrocksampler*, it is not in the interest of most rock writers to re-evaluate their chosen pantheon of great '60s/'70s artists, because they already have too much emotional and career baggage invested in their preferred muses; i.e. they have already devoted so much of their time to investigating the lives of J. Lennon, J. Morrison, S. Barrett, B. Dylan, R. Erickson, L. Reed, I. Stooge et al. that it would be debilitating to 'fess up and admit there may still remain some possibly even greater artists awaiting discovery. History tells us otherwise, however, as evidenced by the careers of Vincent van Gogh and William Blake. Neither was recognised until long after death, *and* Blake had to suffer the double indignity of being close friends with one of the most famous and esteemed artists of his day, one John Flaxman. Who he? Exactamundo! As Lenny 'Romeo Blue' Kravitz once sang: 'It ain't over till it's over.' In other words, the aforemenched list of '60/'70s luminaries doesn't even count historically until everybody's taken their rightful place in the line-up; and that includes underground heroes such as Todd Clark, Mizutani, Klaus Dinger and Alexander 'Skip' Spence, whose records were only released locally or with minimal advertising. Likewise, the songs of Billy Miller need first to be rehabilitated and sent out into the so-called 'real world' before we can see with what wider truth they resound for the listening public.

Back in the '80s, Skip Spence's legendary *Oar* LP was generally (under)classed as a spirited-but-sub-*The Madcap Laughs* work. Hell, kiddies, pre-*Krautrocksampler* most UK journos shared David Quantick's *NME* description of German '60s/'70s music and musicians as 'overlong sub-Mike Oldfield dirge made by humourless men with Bavarian landlord moustaches and exchange student haircuts'. Oops. Nowadays, this music is so accepted that German national TV even made a six-part documentary about Krautrock. Perceptions change with time. So please check out the excellent (and well-meaning) 'new' Cold Sun album on Germany's World in Sound Records, and please do make the effort to struggle through the more average Clear Light/sub-Doors/sub-Jefferson Airplane material, for the Miller's truly bejewelled and gold-encrusted nuggets still lie in the sheltered depths of the album's boneyard, awaiting your appreciative uncovering.

In the meantime, please give this Album of the Month another spin, and delight in the knowledge that, even if many unique and Herculean artistic events evade discovery for decades, some intrepid and forward-thinking motherfucker will eventually glimpse their obscured genius glinting down there in the gloaming and haul them blinking and coughing once more into the daylight. To Billy Miller: come on!

Mirrors

(Underground Records, 1982; recorded 1974–5)

SIDE ONE	SIDE TWO
1 How Could I? (2.44)	1 Shirley (4.37)
2 All My Life (3.50)	2 Cindy and Cathy (1.32)
3 She Smiled Wild (4.03)	3 I've Been Down (4.12)
4 Inside of Here (3.04)	4 Hands in My Pockets (2.14)
5 Fog-Shrouded Mist (4.41)	5 Violent Shadows (5.17)

Preparing an article on Monoshock several years ago, I was fascinated to learn that they'd done a version of the Mirrors song 'Everything Near Me' for the other side of their remake-remodel-in-a-sandstorm 'Model Citizen' forty-five. As a huge early Pere Ubu devotee, I'd dutifully obtained the other Hearthen Records releases and especially loved The Girls' Ubu-esque 'Jeffrey I Hear You'/'The Elephant Man' single. However, Mirrors' sole Hearthen forty-five didn't touch me one jot and I didn't even keep a hold of it; too much Velvets retro at a time when everything great seemed entirely new, perhaps . . . But hearing Monoshock's cover made me pull out this unofficial French LP I'd picked up back in 1982, and it shocked me how excellent the whole thing was. Since then, I've been playing it continuously and it's just got better and better.

What's Up with That?

Jamie Klimek had great long hair, strummed a deep-green Gretsch Tennessean guitar, wrote obvious melodic rock'n'roll songs in the style of Lou Reed, and had a surname like 'climax'. Now, how rock is that? Klimek once wrote that: '. . . when we saw the Velvets at [Cleveland venue] La Cave, I saw God . . . and, realizing that I needed only two-thirds of my vast musical knowledge to play "Heroin", we were off . . . I studied the V.U. Sub-Moronic Easy Guitar Book . . . From the start, we rehearsed originals along with Velvets covers . . . aside from loving them we did the Velvets because they were easy.'

Good start, innit? Sounds like the beginning of a classic rock autobiog. I know they did 'I Can't Stand It' and 'Some Kinda Love', as well as sub-Velvets stuff such as Eno's 'Baby's on Fire' and his 'Here Come the Warm Jets' instrumental. So how come Jamie Klimek isn't name-dropped alongside the rest of the '70s anti-prog clowns and refuseniks that wouldn't take Yes for an answer? Unfortunately, I *can* tell you why. It's because he emerged out of the mid-'70s Cleveland scene alongside Electric Eels and Rocket from the Tombs, and we all know what happened to them, don't we, kiddies? They were ignored. With no contemporary commercial releases, Mirrors were quickly forgotten, reassessed, then forgotten again until the Int'net comes along and finally allows the cybergeeks and megaraks to have their say. Unfortunately, since what they're saying ain't worthy of hawking into a spittoon, yooz stuck with little old eye[1] to seal the deal! So here goes.

She's Not There

In the post-Tin Pan Alley/pre-prog days of 1960s rock'n'roll, Jamie Klimek's singular use of Lou Reed songs as vehicular access to his own sweet muse was a fairly acceptable method. Hell, if you spend all day learning somebody else's chord sequence, it seems kinda commie to keep their words and give 'em full song credit when you could just change the lyrics (which probably didn't mean shit in any case) and bask in the reflected glory of the great man yooz ripping. I mean, who wants to be known for doing Dylan covers when you could just change the words and become legendary for writing songs that are 'Dylanesque'?

Besides, in those bad old days it used to be that certain of the more eclectic pop groups had such a wide range of styles that once in a while a song might be released that the

---

1 One piece of errant bollock-consciousness that riled me was this nugget (as printed in the sleeve-notes to the aforementioned compilation album *Those Were Different Times*): 'Debate amongst commentators is often around the subject of whether Mirrors were proto-punk or proto-no wave?' Bull-ownee! No wave? Like James Chance and DNA and Mars and all the other we-ain't-got-no-songs-but-how-the-smack-flows, numb-numbs? I think not.

public definitely needed more of. But the originators were just so totally *on one* it surely weren't gonna be them who provided it; wasn't 'Satisfaction''s most vocal detractor Keef himself? So a song such as The Jaynetts' 'Sally Go Round the Roses' was probably dismissed by its own creators as just one of ten thousand girl songs, and needed genii such as Lou Reed and Andy Warhol to pick up the sheer meditational profundity of its twilight 'tweentime structures, and subsume its mysterious genius into their own work. The same thing happened with The Zombies' 1964 epic 'She's Not There', which the band themselves never even came close to revisiting but whose bass parts, drum parts, keyboard stylings and minor-key melodrama were lifted with extraordinary vision and percipient thoroughness by The Doors for a magnificent (and genuinely exploratory) six-album career of sub-Nietzschean, post-Jungian pub banter. As late as 1970, even a comparative neo-veteran like David Bowie could take the unique(!), pseudo-Caribbean stylings of Ray Davies' 'Apeman' and 'Lola' and weld entire concept albums to that singular twelve-string guitar thrum and Welsh-Pakistani ur-whine. If that ain't true genius, then clue me, dudes.

All of which, of course, brings us back to that master of appropriation, Lou Reed. He couldn't sing, so he intoned like Bobby Dylan; when he needed a song title, he nicked a bunch of standards and 'What Goes On' off The Beatles. He purloined the beginning of the Stones' 'Hitchhike' for 'There She Goes Again' and The Vagrants' heavy version of 'Respect' for 'Waiting for the Man', and when Jagger moved into that *Beggars Banquet* vocal territory which Lou couldn't rip, he just got Doug Yule in to do it for him. In that synthesis lies the genius of originality; no matter how many years of intellectual hindsight, tell me who else coulda put that little package together? No-fucking-one! Give Lou Reed the chords and the melody and the hook line, and *still* he made songs that we could never anticipate.

Ain't Hung Up on Originality

So we come to Jamie Klimek and the brief story of Mirrors. There's no point in even discussing originality here, for that was hardly Klimek's cause. He wasn't trying to break down the boundaries of rock'n'roll; rather he was accepting the artistic restrictions set up by The Velvet Underground and working within those limits.[2] Hell, this guy even refused to allow Electric Eels' leader John Morton in the band as bass player because 'he had a mind of his own and I wanted to nip that sort of thing in the bud'.

I'm certainly not damning Klimek with faint praise when I say he walked the path of the Velvets. Would that others could have accepted such 'divine' restrictions and followed blessed elders such as the Lou (and I know, at times, I've been as guilty of stepping off the divine map as the next geek, so include me in all that aforementioned damning). It's just like that T. S. Eliot thing he wrote in his essay 'The Metaphysical Poets', and I know I come back to it again and again, but its genius is essential to understanding rock'n'roll. He said that, unlike ancient cultures, we have a tendency to judge our poets and artists most positively by how *different* they appear from everybody else who has gone before, whereas culture used to appreciate the grand tradition and, therefore, happily accepted the metaphor of an artist clearly following in another's footsteps. So dig the Mirrors *because* they'z like the Velvets, rather than in spite of that fact, and you'll instantly enjoy this record one hundred percent more.

Mirrors opens with 'How Could I?', a 'Who Loves the Sun?' with third Velvets album stylings and backing vocals, Doug Yule bass, Mo Tucker-style drumming, that spindly/melodic electric geetar and an 'I'll Be Your Mirror' gentility. Yet, for all this, the real strength is in Klimek's disarming vocals, which ain't like Lou at all and seem wholly original. At the end, the song speeds up into double time, just like any self-respecting Velvets-loving cats should, only much more believably. Straight away, we must accept the Mirrors' Velvets metaphor, or the band withers before your eyes. Accept it and Jamie Klimek's muse can ride right on top of the whole thing, because this ain't lyrically caught in Lou's thrall, not one iota. Klimek's his own man and he's spoken to by the goddess, the great female, in a manner that the cynical, sometime pseudo-homo Lou could never have approached. Indeed, from that angle Klimek's as much of an anti-Lou as Jonathan Richman's 'I'm Straight' persona was. Klimek's songs are all girl songs, be they about dead Shirley,

2 At least Jamie Klimek never set up the same kind of barriers that Scott Walker created. Hell, I still sometimes wonder how I got through all those opaque Matt Munro vocal stylings to hear the *real* Walker behind it all (musta just liked Matt more than I ever knew!).

star-fucking wannabes Cindy, Cathy, Bobbie and Jackie, or impenetrable female mists, both classical and barbarian.

'All My Life' is the best song on the album. It's a deeply moving mid-afternoon, looking-out-of-the-window, just-my-imagination love song about a muse who is 'always' and 'never' here. It's the Velvets' 'The Ocean', but it ain't. It's the first side of their third LP, but it ain't, because it's far more emotional. Klimek is Dylan as seen through broken Ray Davies shades, while drummer Michael Weldon smashes cymbals to death in a Mo Tucker frenzy and with a confidence only the non-player could summon up.

Looking back, I was a schmuck for not getting the metaphor of 'She Smiled Wild', because its deadly genius is just the sound I was listening to back then. This time it's Robby Krieger's Dylanesque 'Running Blue' voice over any-Velvets (hell, this riff is the *summum bonum*, the fucking every-Velvets!). The sky rains dying seagull guitars and the Kelts run for cover, as Klimek repeats one single phrase over and fucking over again.

Clearly, Mirrors were as much forged on the *Foggy Notion* seven-inch-single bootleg as any other Velvets record. But then again, so was half of the 1977 punk scene. With the accessibility of music on the net, it's difficult for all you young 'uns to understand how mysterious unreleased and bootlegged material was back then. My mate Cott reel-to-reeled the first Roxy Music John Peel session and made us cool cats on the block with our high-quality, thirty-inch-per-second knowledge of such vital stuff. Bowie's version of 'Waiting for the Man' was a Peel session track, only available on an orange Sign of the Pig bootleg, and if you hadn't heard it you had to make believe you had. That seven-inch of 'Foggy Notion' was so legendary I even bought The Count's *I'm a Star* LP for the cover version therein, because anyone who did that song was making a statement of deadly intentions.

'Inside of Here' is that high-camp, Caribbeanesque, 1970 Ray Davies as done by the 1971 *Hunky Dory* Bowie that I was talking about earlier. I reckon this is the ultimate autobiographical song because Klimek remained entirely on the outside of the music industry and would have been a great star had he been given the chance. However, this chance was never to be offered. I feel intense compassion for the guy, especially for the hiccuping smile with which he sings: 'They're eating each other when they want a snack/Yeah, two steps forward and one step back.'

The long-dangly-earring-wearing Paul Marotta changes from piano to organ on the coda, and it's magnificent. It's said that Marotta was given heavy shit for bringing keyboards into the Cleveland scene, but he was one sensitive arranger and player who later moved into the Electric Eels and formed the ultra-abrasive Styrenes as guitarist; so his multiple sensibilities clearly informed much of the Mirrors' sound.

Side One closes with the harmonium and wayward bell-tone blues guitar of 'Fog-Shrouded Mist', a total, total third Velvets LP 'Murder Mystery' meets Nico's 'It Was a Pleasure Then'. Its success is in its creators' utter love and devotion to their heroes. Again, we especially need this music so late on in the Velvets eulogy not only because most so-called Velvets-influenced bands are so one-dimensional (they're basically linear), but also because the originals have been around again and undermined their legend by replaying in arenas what was once 'the moment' but which has now been set in cement. And, for me at least, here at the end of Side One is enough of a new 'Murder Mystery' to be a whole new genre in the making: 'And darkness and darkness and death and confusion/And darkness and light and light and confusion.' Certainly, if schmorks like Aerosmith's Joe Perry and Steven Tyler can get away, for twenty-five years, with such obviousness as a Jagger/Richards carbon copy, it would be churlish not to accept these guys' extremely stylish metaphor.

Side Two opens with the beautiful Hearthen forty-five I so squalidly rejected all those years ago. Effectively, 'Shirley' is the Velvets' 'Rock'n'Roll' with Shel Talmy death-trip lyrics, which are (in any case) half of Lou's *Berlin* trip mixed into an insubstantial Reedian middle eight about 'curiosity killed the cat' which still jar-r-rs my senses. However, the guitar theme is devastatingly pretty, and during the '80s I'd have killed to have written it. Furthermore, the coda is pure Shangri-Las, with dying, caterwauling seagull guitars, grand piano, big washes of drone organ and Klimek repeatedly urging: 'Shirley, I love her/And I miss her so.'

Then we're off into one minute and thirty-two seconds of uproarious, wailing scene squabble that is 'Cindy and Cathy'. The repeated call-and-response chorus of 'Love me . . . Fuck you!' is quiet genius and very funny. It goes on: 'Cindy and Cathy and Bobbie and Jackie/They all wanna get here fast/Tweddly Dee and Tweedly Dum/Dee-dum, dee-dumb, dumb-dumb!'

'I've Been Down' is a 1975 take on the Velvets' *1969* live album crossed with their *Live at Max's Kansas City* LP. You can even imagine Klimek being happy to hear talking and glasses clinking because it puts him in mind of his own heroes' live albums. Paul Marotta does some synth stuff on this track which sounds like a heraldic French horn and really sets you shivering. Again, a superbly obvious, traditional-cum-novelty chord sequence prepares you for Jim Crook's fucking devastating guitar break. He shits such a big load on anything this side of Lou you feel churlish even mentioning the influence. Now, how many times does that happen? And the Crook knows *exactly* which notes to play; this guy is so clearly a songwriter himself first and a guitarist second. I mean, no fucking guitarists are normally sensitive enough to allude to the song melody in a solo; they mostly ride roughshod over it like they ain't ever heard the thing before. But this guy is confident in the way Mick Ronson was.

'Hands in My Pockets' is Mirrors' take on the Velvets' 'Guess I'm Falling in Love', which wasn't even (officially) released when they did their version and wouldn't be for about a decade. As a statement of hipness, as I commented before, you can never beat covering unreleased songs by legends. Strange thing is, it sounds more like The Primitives or Beach Nuts than the VU themselves, and really makes me wanna hear Mirrors' versions of other Velvets stuff.

The album closer is called 'Violent Shadows'; it's so deadly that I want (no, *need*!) an entire album of this stuff. Somebody should take just this song and build a whole band around it. It's Donovan being Nick Drake singing 'Set the Controls for the Heart of the Sun' down a storm drain, as recorded as an out-take from the more outré moments on Nico's *Chelsea Girls*. Got me? Its beauty is utterly devastating, in a weird, Kalacakra manner, and reminds the entire world that nothing is ever a rip-off. It's five minutes long and it shoulda been fifteen! It's the end of a deeply cool album and makes me wanna search online and buy up all the copies I can find.

End of the Road

In the sleeve-notes to the compilation album *Those Were Different Times* Jamie Klimek wrote about a late-summer 1975 Cleveland show billed as 'Extermination Night':

> *The big show. Three bands. Seventy-five cents. Mirrors, Rocket From The Tombs*

and The Electric Eels. Paul Marotta was playing in both Mirrors and the Eels . . . We did our usual excruciatingly loud set, Rockets did their comedy routine and cut holes in each other's clothes, and the Eels (gas-powered lawn mowers, chain saws, meat cleavers, blow torches) exterminated one and all. That's entertainment.

It's tragic to think how unsung every one of those bands would remain until decades after their demise. Of course, tapes were passed around and I've still got all the hand-mades people sent me – I even think of them as the 'real' album covers nowadays. When I asked two of the Monoshock guys what had prompted them to cover a Mirrors tune, it was the exact same thing. The band's Grady Runyan wrote:

I remember the big Mirrors thing being a 'live in '75' cassette. To this day, I don't think that stuff has come out properly or even been booted. 'Everything Near Me' wuz on there, and I think it was Scott/bass who suggested we learn it. For some reason, I ended up the singer and not knowing the words I had to make 'em up. The tape, as a whole, is very good, some would say in league with the Velvets' live 1969 LP.

Rubin Fiberglass concluded that the Mirrors were:

The missing link between the melodic lo-fi of the Velvets and trashy primitivism of The Fugs. To us, they were a classic '70s, Cleveland version of all those unknown, anthologized garage bands of the '60s. We were particularly drawn to Cleveland bands and, while the Electric Eels and Rocket from the Tombs/Pere Ubu captured our most imaginative avant/bombast, the Mirrors lo-fi guitar chunk, screeching solos and floor-tom pummel felt much more at home to our garage-band sensibilities.

In common with one-time obscurities like Japan's Les Rallizes Dénudés, all the Cleveland bands have now become genuinely legendary. Unfortunately, their lack of 'official' releases has meant that fans have generally been in charge of the material, and we know that is not always a good thing. It's meant that the Rocket from the Tombs album was a sink-clogger of unplayable dimensions; a super-concentrated everything's-as-good-as-everything-else Spanish galleon of under-editing. It meant that Electric Eels' 'hits' got subsumed into the (f)art-o-scribble of their free-form sax guano. It also means that the only Mirrors LP currently available is the too-much-already of *Hands in My Pockets* (a reissue overseen by fanatics so fervent they even named their label 'Overground' in homage to the original bootleg!). However, because Mirrors were so damned catchy, this last album mentioned is deffo the best of the litter and worth checking out; hell, it's listenable all the way through, if you really wanna know!

September 18 1975 was the last date Mirrors ever played. Jamie Klimek felt the band was getting nowhere; Cleveland Council did not issue black armbands.

When Paul Weller's Style Council released the abhorrent *Cost of Loving* LP in early 1987, the reviews were so bad he had the nerve to compare his misunderstoodness to that of D. H. Lawrence half a century before. Having suffered similarly many times myself, but – like Weller – always from *within* the record industry, I would suggest he should've listened to Mirrors if he wanted to understand true outsider rock'n'roll. Being told by Polygram's managing director that your new LP sucks, while he's drinking his coffee and standing on his plush carpet, has gotta be a damn sight better than having the doorman eject you without even the stockboy hearing your demos. Such was the fate of the Cleveland bands, and, dammit, can't you hear it in their sounds?

Discography

'Shirley' b/w 'She Smiled Wild' (single, Hearthen Records, 1975)
Mirrors (Underground Records, 1982)
Hands in My Pockets (Overground Records, 2010)

New Gods

Aardvark Thru Zymurgy

(World Theatre, 1977)

SIDE ONE

1 Origin (7.22)
2 Visions of My World (2.26)
3 Strange Forces (3.01)
4 Core (2.34)
5 Phosphorescent Is the Chamber (6.39)

SIDE TWO

1 Within the Zodiac Zone (4.32)
2 Last Day as a Whole Person (2.27)
3 A Dozen Eggs (4.28)
4 Brain and Spinal Column (8.02)

The American Midwest finally caught on to the Summer of Love just as London and New York were spawning punk rock. As in Eastern Europe, Germany and Japan, many American Midwesterners in 1977 were still looking back to those heady days of '67 with a glazed nostalgia, a romantic memory of a time they probably hadn't given a hoot for while it was actually a happening thang. Some forward-thinking, backwards-looking rock'n'rollers attempted to create the spirit of that rebellious time by copying the old music wholesale, bands such as Canada's Simply Saucer (the Barrett Floyd), Cleveland's Mirrors (The Velvet Underground) and Boston's The Modern Lovers (the Velvets again), each one driven on by a sole excellent songwriter at the helm who saved their band's ass from becoming mere pastiche by the power of their individual personalities and sheer songwriting talent. Others such as Electric Eels and The Styrenes aped the abandon of the '67 spirit by coming on with an entirely new sound, a sound hooky both in its riffage and melodies, but so sonically divorced from the then-accepted musical currency that they too would need another twenty years to be understood. Somewhere in amongst all of this were groups like Cleveland's Rocket from the Tombs, who copped from both ends. From their recent past, Rocket borrowed the sounds of The Stooges, Kiss, Montrose and the MC5; from the future they copped lo-fi recording techniques and still-taboo subject matter, then burned their cultural candle down from both ends simultaneously. This 'somewhere-in-between' has long been the subject of Head Heritage Album of the Month reviews, Electric Eels, Mirrors, Simply Saucer and Rocket from the Tombs all having had the light shone upon them at one time or another. But I've not yet investigated the flipside of that coin; that is, the USA's equivalents of bands like Japan's Yonin Bayashi or Prague's Plastic People of The Universe, mid-'70s bands whose aesthetic dwelled in an imaginary universe in which The Velvet Underground, The Doors, The Mothers of Invention, Morton Subotnick and Karlheinz Stockhausen had all got themselves booked for the same festival and all accidentally performed simultaneously. Like that German Velvet Underground compilation with the fake Roger Dean sleeve which I detailed in *Krautrocksampler*, the mixing of the metaphor was not considered inappropriate. Which is where New Gods come in . . .

Shaman Doorkeeper of the Ever-Shifting Goalposts

New Gods sounded like they'd shoe-horned every post-'67 heavy rock'n'roll art statement into their band just through their sheer desire to celebrate it all. From *Absolutely Free*-period Mothers to *Electric Storm in Hell*-period White Noise via The Zodiac's *Cosmic Sounds*, the *United States of America* LP, a dozen *musique concrète* LPs and the whole of the early '70s, everything was grist to New Gods' mill. Analogue synthesizers swirled and farted, totally fogging up the vocals and undermining the perpetually descending/ascending In-A-Gadda-Da-Sunshine-of-Your-21st-Century-Schizoid-Lord-of-This-World-ness of their 'N.I.B.'

New Gods' music was like Hinduism, constantly threatened by wave upon wave of successful new invaders, each leaving their cultural mark, irrigating and edifying but ultimately becoming subsumed into the general polytheistic whole. And so, with its dizzying arsenal of cultural references and perpetually shifting undertow, New Gods' LP *Aardvark Thru Zymurgy* is a truly psychedelic masterpiece. Never mind what instrument is making which sound, on this New Gods album we don't even know where one track ends and another begins. Mind manifesting? I should coco! Not that they'd even started out as New Gods, of course – that would be too convenient. On stage, they were The Eyes, a Pennsylvania quartet with a blond, seventeen-year-old guitarist called Tim Rimer, bass player Keefe Marabito and Marc Cosco on drums. But The Eyes had a visionary at the helm, and a shameless super-confident visionary at that. This guy was a T. S. Eliot of his time, a cultural kleptomaniac who sucked up all the good juice from everything he ever read, heard, inhaled, touched or tasted and distilled it all into saleable potions for limited distribution in his area. He was shamanic and brilliant and beautiful – really fucking gorgeous actually – and (like Mizutani of Les Rallizes Dénudés) he knew one day that the world would catch on to his errant muse.

New Gods' visionary leader was called Todd Clark, and he sang exactly like Ray Collins of the Mothers being Jim Morrison – a drunken, portentous baritone with twenty bazillion lyrics bombarding the listener into submission. I would guess that people often told Todd Clark he sounded like Morrison, and I would suspect that he would not have given a damn. I mean, Clark also sounded like Arthur Brown quite a bit, but – to once again paraphrase T. S. Eliot and his essay 'The Metaphysical Poets' – we nowadays have a tendency to judge artists only by the unique elements they bring to the table, not (as the druids believed) by the traditions they have chosen to follow. Patti Smith was the first major example of a rock'n'roller who celebrated their influences rather than hid or denied them. Unlike good old Plant'n'Page, who stole equally from white folkies to make up for ripping off their black brothers, Patti wore her art on her sleeve, in her poems, on her record covers . . . The traditions she had chosen to follow? Well, the Japanese would have said Patti was taking The Way of Keef, The Way of Rimbaud, The Way of Lou, and ultimately creating The Way of Patti. Similarly, Todd Clark was another confident motherfucker who didn't care, taking The Way of Jimbo, The Way of Bob Moog and The Way of Zappa and melding it all into The Way of Clark. And a pretty fair way it was, or so it would appear to me. So when The Eyes came to make their studio LP after months of getting tight from shows across the Midwest, Todd Clark got into greedy-motherfucker mode and invited his organist mate Chris Lagoe to the sessions to cop some of that Manzarek sound he had always so cherished, then invited pianist

Dennis Kovach for some more Ray-type tinkling; plus Todd himself went overboard with the electronics and had a theremin and a big Moog set up for the sessions. Todd Clark had seen Mickey Dolenz play a big Moog on The Monkees when he was a teenager, and its bubble-bubble-toilet-trouble had created the kind of rage in him that nothing else could.

So here were The Eyes all ready to record, but the Visionary has major other plans and other (my least fave word in current usage, but what the hell, here goes) 'issues'. Sure, Todd loves The Zodiac's *Cosmic Sounds*, but all that astrology is a crock. Didn't Jimbo himself call it 'a bunch of bullshit' on *Absolutely Live*? Well, with regard to Todd's ethnic heritage, he's part paleface'n'part (what we then termed) Red Indian, brothers'n'sisters. So Todd has a big fucking problem with what he calls the 'spurious predictions of Eurocentric astrology [holding people] in pseudo-scientific bondage'. So, unknown to The Eyes, he's gonna record his anti-'Catholic-dominated tyranny' rant/poem 'Within the Zodiac Zone', as well as settling a few other scores with Whitey along the way.

Well, The Eyes get in the studio and don't know what's hit them. Guitarist Tim Rimer's all bent out of shape because here's this guest organist getting all the fucking solos, and when he's not the sound is so manipulated by Our Visionary Overlord that Todd's Moog and theremin squooshes are obliterating all the band's carefully laid plans from the rehearsal room. But it's fucking working so well they cannot complain. Fuck the Summer of Love, this is genius because its psychedelia is true and real and totally disorientating. Man, do you even know what song we're playing? No, keep strumming, brother, Todd knows what's going on.

The seven minutes of 'Origin' which open the LP offer a lo-fi, stop–start über-clatter, like punks playing '21st Century Schizoid Man', as Todd Clark stumbles in with the worst mic technique since Lou 'Neatly Pumped Air' Reed piped up as John Cale's backing singer for 'Lady Godiva's Operation'. I've no idea what Todd's singing but it sure as hell sounds important. Kind of like Cyrus Faryar's 'Nine times the colour red explodes like heated blood' on the opening to *Cosmic Sounds*, but here we have the original lyricist singing his own words, so that's a million times better for all those requiring authenticity. The song soon takes off into that instrumental freek-beat shit-storm in the middle of the Mothers' 'Brown Shoes Don't

Make It', but here electronics have replaced those old-fart woodwinds. Next up, 'Visions of My World' is two and a half minutes of Morrisonisms, but that's acceptable (I guess) as Big Jim was at least an Honorary Redman, dontcha thunk?

'Strange Forces' is an organ salute to the tenth anniversary of the Summer of Love, and comes over just like 'Indian Summer' meets any of *Strange Days*, especially when the bass to 'Unhappy Girl' kicks in, and you gots to wonder how the guitarist ain't just mashing the head of the guest organist. 'Core' is dominated by treated piano and rhythm changes that obliterate the entire backing track *and* the vocals.

Side One concludes with the amazing 'Phosphorescent Is the Chamber', almost seven minutes of gonzo underworld travel, including a drums'n'theremin solo that could be ten minutes longer and still be too short. Hold on, hold on . . . The first side is done already? I'm not sure I remember any of it. Let's flip it back to the beginning again and try to gain a foothold on this crumbling sandbank of sound. But no, seven plays later you still end up just as dazed and confused.

Side Two opens with the sub-Sabbathisms of 'Within the Zodiac Zone', the aforementioned anti-horoscope ditty supported by a chick singer who – because she can't keep up the nursery-rhyme rhythm – renders its remedial-playground rope-jumping just as mysterious as the 'difficult stuff'. Todd gets very Zappa on this, kind of like The Seeds doing 'Who Are the Brain Police?' but scuzzy and lo-fi and FX'd to the max. Besides being possessed of a fucking brilliant title, 'Last Day as a Whole Person' is formed from concrete poetry and a backwards Moog rhythm track, creating dread and confusion where before there was only confusion. You can see the young Todd watching Mickey Dolenz on that fateful *Monkees* episode, not knowing what circus boy was unleashing upon his melted plastic brain.

Theremin opens the doom of 'A Dozen Eggs' (what a fucking great title, *again*!) and we're right in the middle of Side Two of The Zodiac's *Cosmic Sounds* as done by one of those bands on *Pebbles: Volume Three*. Of course, those schmucks could never have strung together such class comments as 'this Catholic-dominated tyranny', but – as ever – the Clark poetry is again undermined/rendered more mysterious by the sheer weight of electronica bombarding the speakers.

But the greatest piece of the LP has to be the last eight minutes of the epic 'Brain and Spinal Column', a poem based on a nightmare Todd's wife once had, in which Todd adopts a kind of Screamin' Jay Hawkins voice over Hendrix guitar riffage as played by *Earthquake*-period Uli John Roth, or maybe the Be-Bop Deluxe of *Axe Victim*. Now c'mon, kiddies, who else writes lyrics so simultaneously crazy and edifying (and, yes, you gotta discount me)? No fucker – even The Doors – coulda melded proto-metal riffage with such erudite barbarianism. Man, I reckon if Glenn Danzig could dispense with some of the bogus Billy Idol/Ian Astbury galumphing and get on a Todd Clark trip, we'd probably see some seriously listenable shit for a change. 'What divides truth from illusion?/ It's your brain and spinal column/ What leaves senses in confusion?/It's your brain and spinal column.'

It's a beautiful way to conclude such a dramatic piece of prolapsing twelve-inch mind-death. All we can hope for, nay, demand is that some one-hundred-and-eighty-gram vinyl company, like those Shadoks fetishists, contact Todd Clark and redo it just as originally released, because the man more than deserves it.

What Else, Then?

I have another Todd Clark LP in the racks, from almost eight years later. However, by the time of 1984's *Into the Vision* LP, Todd had eschewed the Morrison fixation, gained about thirty pounds (he wasn't heavy, just less stick-thin than previously) and mutated into a keyboard whiz. It's totally different music – electronic still, but employing that rototech eight-bit bullshit '80s technology that seems charming to you younger folks but the sound of which most my age would shudder at. However, *Into the Vision* still features some great loud guitar courtesy of ex-Rocket from the Tomb axeman Cheetah Chrome, and Todd cops a few William Burroughs samples for his wonderful electro-poem title track. Moreover, there's another (utterly different) version of 'Brain and Spinal Column', featuring Pere Ubu's Allen Ravenstine on EMS synthesizer, and a superb track entitled 'Death Hovers', which Todd nowadays describes as 'my satirical attempt at writing metaphysical pornography in the purposefully ultraverbose high-bro style of an outrageous poet such as Walt Whitman'. C'mon! It seems we might have a contender here for Head Heritage's honorary Vachel Lindsay Gnostic Poetry Award. And with regard to the dodgy '80s sound of *Into the Vision*, I myself override the problem by playing the record on a mono Dansette-type, cheapo-cheapo affair, through a Simms-Watts four-by-twelve speaker, thus restoring maximum garage to what would otherwise be lost to the world of Nik Kershaw!

Todd has had one of the most erratic and difficult-to-catalogue careers in rock'n'roll, his LPs appearing under many different names – The Eyes, Todd Clark Group, Todd Tamanend Clark, New Gods . . . – and it was only when a new compilation of his work entitled *Nova Psychedelia* was released that I realised I'd known some of his stuff already. Nowadays, Todd's shamanic musings are catalogued better than ever. Many have complained that the double-CD set *Nova Psychedelia* (released by excellent and meticulous motherfuckers Anopheles) should have been edited, but I ain't one of them. Edited? Who is gonna be the editor? Who's got the power to stand up and dismiss such mighty revelations, the Lord hisself? Nah, brothers'n'sisters, when you gotta mighty mouth such as The Clark roaming the planet you need the *totally unexpurgated* works with which to live. And, although it all maybe sounds initially like über-drool to those seeking instant karma, those blessed others on a timeless quest for the sonic Grail will – from the moment the needle drops on our man's works – recognise that they *need, need, need* every bleep, fart, cough, bubble and exhalation from the Moog and mighty gob of Todd Tamanend Clark.

Discography

'Flame Over Africa' b/w 'Two Thousand Light Years from Home' (single, 1975)
'Secret Sinema' b/w 'Nightlife of the New Gods' (single, 1980)
'Flame Over Philadelphia' b/w 'Oceans of She' (single, 1985)
Stars (1975)
New Gods: Aardvark Thru Zymurgy (1977)
We're Not Safe (1979)
Into the Vision (1984)
Nova Psychedelia (2005)

Pentagram

First Daze Here

(Relapse Records, 2001; recorded 1972–76)

1 Forever My Queen (2.24)
2 When the Screams Come (2.59)
3 Walk in the Blue Light (5.35)
4 Starlady (5.15)
5 Lazylady (3.48)
6 Review Your Choices (2.57)
7 Hurricane (2.05)
8 Livin' in a Ram's Head (2.16)
9 Earth Flight (2.51)
10 20 Buck Spin (4.57)
11 Be Forewarned (3.27)
12 Last Days Here (6.08)

Take a look at the longhair in the centre of this LP sleeve and see his Iggy t-shirt . . . in 1972! That hard, youth! Then cop these sleeve-notes by Pentagram's Geof O'Keefe, babies, and tell me yooz not intrigued immediately:

It was 30 years ago, in the fall of 1971. Blue Cheer had lost both their fire and guitarist Leigh Stephens, Cream had disbanded, and Hendrix had been dead a year. But a new wave of sound and fury had begun to emerge in the form of bands like Black Sabbath, Uriah Heep, Sir Lord Baltimore, Dust, the Groundhogs, UFO, Scorpions, Budgie, Bang, Stray and the Stooges. And influenced by these bands and many, many others, Bobby Liebling and I sat in a friend's house . . . when it suddenly dawned on us: why not start a new group, playing all original music influenced by the bands we loved!

Ingrown Sociopaths Hanging from the Tree

This Pentagram record is that same kind of mop-up Album of the Month created for Electric Eels and Mirrors, in that none of these groups ever made a 'proper' album at the time because they lived in the world's biggest cultural desert, the US Midwest. However, whereas the Eels' music was ignored because they were actively doing their damnedest to wind up blue-collardom, and Mirrors were treading too much on the toes of Kinksy Velvetdom when even those two originators were themselves in a backwater, Bobby Liebling's Pentagram was deadly melodic, proto-metal that would have been huge and mainstream had they ever got that first LP away.

A single listen to *First Daze Here* reveals the kind of compulsive refusenik hookiness that the best rawk is always imbued with, from the automatic writing of Steppenwolf's 'Born to Be Wild' to the road trips of Montrose's 'Bad Motor Scooter'. This Pentagram music ain't unknown because it's difficult in any way; it's unknown merely because of the obscurity of the pond from which it chose to ooze. Yup, unfortunately that simple wrong place/wrong time syndrome seems to have been Pentagram's stumbling block; and their home town, Arlington, Virginia, weren't never gonna see the rise of its own mavericks without them all first relocating, Alice Cooper/Janis Joplin-stylee, to some rock'n'roll centre before returning, be-limousined in snotbag splendour, to accompany their own single-finger salute.

And so, for Pentagram, although five of the songs herein were culled from a single recording sesh, even getting into a proper studio was always the biggest deal. Indeed, some of the very best stuff on this record was caught live in their rehearsal room – probably the *only* place they coulda sung what they wanted without being paranoid that some urbane studio engineer wasn't smirking behind smoked glass.

That steaming, hi-hat heavy, recorded-in-our-gang-HQ element only makes the sense of desperation more real. And, as Pentagram's only contemporary single releases came out under different monikers (Macabre and Boffo Socko) in the misguided attempts of local entrepreneurs to hoodwink the population that they was pushing something brand new, so the sense of utter cultural abandonment was made even greater! The great shame is that without that big-label deal, Pentagram never got into a position to do the unwieldy, lengthy deathtracks that surface only when you ain't having to load the gear in and out of the studio, but leaving it all set up for a coupla days and settling into your own corner behind the percussion racks and Leslie cabinet. Still, maybe Pentagram's sense of urgency is there precisely because they never could do that comparatively bourgeois shit! I mean, although they do sound superficially like Sabbath in a too much 'Grease it out' kind of way, Pentagram didn't sound anything at all like the sludge Blue Cheer spunked out. In truth, this lot sounded mostly like a slower Dust, only a fuck of a lot better[1] because they took the more obviously *goyisch* side of Dust, such as the odes to shagging camels and the learning to die songs and the suicide songs, and did them better (hail, babies, Bobby Liebling musta sung Dust's 'Suicide' in the shower two hundred times at the very least). Pentagram also trimmed the excess cling-ons off the Dustian butt (but not all, natch), thus streamlining it, distilling it and making it coherent and believable.

Pentagram's songs are mainly short and brutal and flow from the Nornian fountainhead of Bobby Liebling, whose name I drop regularly in these reviews because he's got the kind of one-off vocal and muse-based lyrical sensibility that only such Captain Scarlet, 'shamanic other' types as Sean Bonniwell seemed to capture on record.[2] When Bobby says he's gonna die tonight, you know he's gonna kick it! He'll resurrect for shit damn sure, but that don't undermine a damn thing. When I use the term 'shamanic', you gots to understand the shaman ain't always successful, but the mere fact that he's cruisin' for a bruisin' puts him right out of the regular space of the average human being.

As I wrote of Faust in *Krautrocksampler* all those years ago, aiming for the stars is so far beyond what people generally do that you can't beat on someone when they don't actually achieve it. Bobby Liebling was Lugh, and his light reflected directly into the songs. As he sang on 'Walk in the Blue Light':

Now you're confused so I'll set you straight,
Many men die 'cause they left it too late
If you don't know what I talk about,
Walk in the blue light, you can find out.

Motherfucker! It's not 'too, too, too to put a finger on', as Tommy Verlaine once sang. Give Bobby Liebling four lines and he says it all. Moreover,

1 Whereas Dust's team of Kenny Kerner, Richie Wise, Kenny Aaronson and the future Markie Ramone were better musicians, producers and arrangers than Pentagram, they was also way too eclectic and suffered (Bang-stylee) from the need to prove they could muso along with the worst of them. Also, despite the images of Viking dwarves and Germanic lettering, they still had a mawkish tendency towards the kind of Leiber and Stoller sentimentality that eventually got Kerner and Wise drummed in to produce Kiss' second LP, *Hotter Than Hell.*

2 I always imagine Pentagram doing a version of The Music Machine's 'Dark White' because it has that perfect mix of Gothic Yardbirds vocal, an elusive Freyjan Priestess as its subject matter, *and* it builds and it fucking *builds*!

there is a stomping refusenik heathenism herein that particularly smokes my pole because I grew up in the West Midlands, where those same attitudes that stopped Pentagram were found in large doses, nay in fucking overdoses. Hard to explain in the twenty-first century, but growing up in the middle of the English West Mid of the early '70s bred a weird sort of anarchy of surrogate cough-mixture trips and Amon Düül II. The biggest thing in our school was when my mate Barry Clempson's older brother joined Humble Pie. That the Pie were brown-nosing the sub-sub-basement of the Everyblues was hardly the point, dahlings. In our minds, we were collectively on a major label and it was fast times at Wincott High from here on in!

Contextualising the Motherfuckers

The first time I heard Pentagram was on the compilation *A Gathering of the Tribes*. Their maudlin death trip, 'Be Forewarned', particularly stood out among the other stuff because it was like an ever-descending sibling of 1970-period Love's *Out Here* version of 'Signed D.C.'. It took a traditional 6/8 minor-chord sequence, stuck an ur-bass rumble underneath and sibilant Zildjian cymbal, tinnitus-inducing percussion over the top, and told a traditional tale about kidnapping your intended love in a manner redolent of 'The Rape of the Sabine Women' (only this weren't no *Seven Brides for Seven Brothers* whitewash, motherfuckers!). Even the presence of Josephus' sixteen-minute 'Dead Man' across most of Side Two couldn't deflect the power of these three and a half minutes of doom and judgement; and, boy, was Bobby Liebling Judge Mental![3]

So, when you listen to this Pentagram record, remember always that,

3 By 1982, the hip East Coast compilers of the great psychedelic garage compilations (*Pebbles* et al.) were, like Lenny Kaye with *Nuggets*, starting to break out of their self-imposed time restrictions and had begun throwing some serious heavy shit into the works. They'd realised that the US Midwest had never even 'had' the '60s, let alone got over the repercussions. Like the Krautrock and Japanese music scenes, all the Sabbath/Bang/Blue Cheerisms had, in Middle America, merely been subsumed into the whole post-Stones catalogue and shit out the other end in true teen-rebel, proto-doom style, somewhat akin to Sean Bonniwell's black-clad Music Machine on a Troggsian death trip. But the real difference was this: it weren't no teen angst any more, 'twas the howl of the West delivered by real grown men crying like several singular voices in the wilderness.

although most of it comes from one 1973 session, the rest was culled from a whole bunch of stuff created between 1972 and 1976. I don't mean this as some kind of apologia for the band, babies, I mean the exact opposite – that this weren't no progressive-rock that 'improved', therefore tidied up, as it went along, and there's no lessening of sonic impact in the later tracks.

First Daze Here

The LP starts with three of the five songs captured at their March '73 recording sesh; they give the album its real coherence. However, the record hits its peak later on, so give it time if this stuff don't smoke thy pole immediately. 'Forever My Queen' opens up just like Bang doing Sabbath in that remedial, Bleib Alien-meets-Sabbath's 'Future Shock'-style – a grunge-aholic trawl through the lowest grade of Iommi riffs. Vincent McAllister solos wildly and inappropriately all through and then it just fades and fucks off in my favourite kind of AM radio fade – three seconds, max. Then off into the next less-than-three-minute bliss-out in the shape of 'When the Screams Come', complete with Bill Wardian Bibles-at-the-sofa drum fills and Sabbalong time-changes. Man, these guys are screaming out for an LP of their own, but there are not even bones for these dogs!

Then slowly out of the mists comes the sub-Joy Division/*E Pluribus Funk* Sabbalong of 'Walk in the Blue Light', in which Vincent McAllister exposes his bassist-turned-guitar-hero provenance with another Bleib Alien riff you always thought Ace Frehley woulda been knocking out before his Kiss days (not true, I'm sure). In fact, that whole Roky Erickson/Bobby Liebling thing that the Swedish band Witchcraft had going really manifests here in the atmosphere of 'Walk in the Blue Light', enjoying a real soaring clarity and openness that Sabbath obviously never approached because of their über-metal groovelessness.

Then 'Starlady' kicks in. Recorded three years later, weez talking about a totally different, blazing, auspicious rock experience that sounds like a band that's huge. Gone is the autistic, post-adolescent, in-yer-boots vibe, to be replaced with a horned-god confidence that screams and struts. Also, here we got another extra guitarist called Marty Iverson, who adds considerable weight to the sound and pushes the whole Pentagram trip into a Dust-as-played-by-Montrose experience, even something like the Australian *Ugly*

Things compilation-period of MC5/ Yardbirds-influenced groups. I know I keep punishing the Dust metaphors, but Liebling's voice is uncannily like Richie Wise's at times.

The fifth track is that classic 'Lazylady' single they recorded a year before as Macabre, and comes on with another 'Walk in the Blue Light', morons-on-the-frontier riff (play 'em back-to-back – they're virtually the same fucking riff: excellent!) over an Ace Frehley 'Shock Me'/'Dark Light'-style throwaway vocal that meets dirty Frank Zappa around the time of *Overnight Sensation* (although this sucker is a year before that Mothers LP) – extremely charming and funny it is, too. This is the toon in which Liebling disses his chick and kicks her out, so she buys up the whole apartment block he lives in and has him kicked out, too. Nice . . .

'Review Your Choices' is the fourth track from that same session that spawned the first three tracks on this disc. Again, we're deep in Sabbath territory, both lyrically and in its per-riffery. Sounds like Liebling never leaves the first four frets for his songwriting and Vincent McAllister is a committed ex-bass player when it comes to copping, then staying true, to the Liebling lick. He also exceeds at soloing like a flailing moron between each vocal delivery. Satan's coming round the bend in this one, and there's a man with a pitchfork, and . . . oh, whatever, I obviously suck this dung into every orifice with more gusto than most, or you wouldn't be getting it served up as Album of the Month.

Two months after that main sesh came the same Boffo Socko alias seven-inch 'Hurricane' that appears on Fly Agaric's 2002 *Guitar Explosion 2* compilation, and is just Hendrix-filtered through Iommi's week-old socks. It's deeply excellent, relentless, by numbers, and irksome that it ain't internationally known. A brief, two-minutes-and-five-second classic; fade and outta here . . .

Then it's time for two of the three best tracks on the whole record, both recorded in their rehearsal room with sometime extra guitarist Randy Palmer. 'Livin' in a Ram's Head' (excellent fucking title, Herr Liebling) has a steaming, incessant freight-train quality you wanna keep playing over and over and over. Man, if they got more of this rehearsal-room stuff in the can, clue me druids, I gots to know! The following track is 'Earth Flight', which coulda been spunked out in the late 1960s and appeared on *Pebbles Volume Five*, or the aforementioned *Ugly Things* compilation, or any classic hard-rock LP of the time.

It's monstrous and full of demons, and worthy of ripping off forever.

'20 Buck Spin' is the last of the five-track session from March 1973, and, man, does it smoke my unyielding pole. Vincent McAllister's SG is more burning here than Iommi's ever was (honest!) *and* this guy never has to resort to soloing *over* his solos, as Iommi did countless times (whaddya mean, I cain't diss Iommi? Only after twenty years did Iommi's solos become classic through sheer overplaying, and I'll challenge any non-motherfucker to disprove my unhasty assertion!). Someone should release these five tracks as a seven-inch, thirty-three rpm, European-style picture-sleeve maxi-single, just so we can judge Pentagram on a contemporary 1973 level and understand the songs in context. This band will surely be revisited again and again in the next few years and will, like lost greats such as The Blue Things and The Swamp Rats, become an accepted part of rock's great canon like the little glitch that held that first LP up weren't fucking owt at all.

'Be Forewarned' is up next. What do I say? I been listening to this on heavy rotation for more than two decades and it is demented and suffused with the kind of incandescant glow that marks it out as the work of the great. Batman-meets-'Lucifer Sam'-as-played-by-heavy-period-Love is not exactly obvious, kiddies, and I think we see here the reason that Fleetwood Mac's 'The Green Manalishi' influenced everyone (except its own writer): it has that Alice Cooper/*Love It to Death* interweaving minor-key Dervish quality that we all try to cop, but rarely even glimpse.

Then we conclude with Pentagram's finest hour by about ten bazzillion miles. 'Last Days Here' is a beautiful, gleaming jewel of a death trip, with Bobby singing like he's staring out of some spectacular ice palace and ain't never coming back to the real world. He's Mithra trapped in the mountain, he's Loki with the poison raining down on him, but there ain't anybody there to wipe it away in this particklier scenario. This song is imbued with a sense of tragedy you rarely hear in heavy-rock. For those who don't quite get it . . . whatever. But, if you ever approached that post-everything vacuum, that empty cathedral in your head, that hollow, unspeaking, unblinking, unhuman emotionless inertia that even Iggy could only hint at in the flatness of 'Sick of You', then you truly *need* this song in your life. If Pentagram had only done this one song and been killed in a plane crash thereafter, we'd still be celebrating it fifty years from now. And, when Bobby takes it down from his dazed, almost whispered tenor to a flat, shark-eyed, semi-spoken baritone and states 'Said it's bin a little bit too long,' you feel the ice melt, then refreeze instantly, and you know in that moment how tragic human life is; how intolerably short human life is; how the moments of adolescence that resurface in adult life must be celebrated and further celebrated, then howled about, shrieked out, screamed out . . . Man, we are dead and in the fucking ground for so long . . . *No, no, no, no, no, no!* Gimme life and gimme the six minutes of this toon on endless rotation.

Aftermath

I feel a little cold right about now, babies. After such deeply moving sounds, you just wanna sit quietly and not even think. Imagine how Bobby Liebling, Vincent McAllister, Greg Wayne and their hugely poetic drummer Geof O'Keefe felt about never getting to spunk this stuff across the coasts of the USA. Dammit, it makes me sad. In various Liebling-led guises, they continued at a local level on and off for years. They even went through some dodgy incarnations as a horror-rock band, before this Relapse reissue got them together and gave them a chance to sift through the past. It was Stephen O'Malley who alerted me to its existence and I furry-freaked the first time I played the sucker.

A newly recorded album, *Review Your Choices*, came out in 1999, featuring re-recordings of their classic stuff plus a bunch of new toons. Then Greg Anderson's Southern Lord label put out *Sub-Basement*, which I've played a few times and is excellent, although how these albums will hold up over the years I can't say, as I ain't had them nearly long enough. *Sub-Basement* includes compelling versions of 'Buzzsaw' and 'Drive Me to the Grave' which anyone would wanna have at home. However, much better than all this, for me, are the two songs they contributed to *Blue Explosion*, that Blue Cheer eulogy CD, namely 'Feathers from Your Tree' and 'Doctor Please'. Both versions are revelations and excavate the chaos from the Cheer originals without losing out, although, for me, you can't really do the former justice without at least approximating Ralph Kellogg's absurdly grandiose dub pianos, however righteously proto-MC5-ian the vocals are. However, their choosing to do a version of 'Doctor Please' seems more than a little poignant with the news from my dear friend Herr O'Malley that all the years of substance abuse has meant Bobby Liebling has had to have both arms amputated! All I can say is such a bizarre sting in the tale has gotta have a mythological provenance waiting round the bend![4]

Discography

As Macabre:
'Lazylady' b/w 'Be Forewarned' (single, Intermedia Records, 1972)

As Boffo Socko:
'Hurricane' (one-sided promo single, Boffo Socko Records, 1973)

As Pentagram:
First Daze Here (Relapse, 2001)
Review Your Choices (Relapse, 1999)
Sub-Basement (Southern Lord, 2001)

4 According to Sunn O)))'s Stephen O'Malley, happily this amputation scare turned out to be just that . . .

Rocket from the Tombs

The World's Only Dumb-Metal, Mind-Death Rock'n'Roll Band

(No label; recorded 1975)

1 Raw Power
2 So Cold
3 I'm Never Gonna Kill Myself Again
4 You Didn't Bleed
5 Thirty Seconds Over Toyko
6 What Love Is
7 Ain't It Fun
8 Life Stinks
9 Dead Boy Down in Flames

'*One of the most seminal American bands of the 1970s.*' (Richie Unterberger, *Unknown Legends of Rock'n'Roll*)

'*One of the noisiest combos ever to emerge from any heartland . . . must've seemed like Martian music at the time . . . snatches vengeful riff-roisterousness from the Stones, Sabbath, Blue Cheer, Blue Öyster Cult, Hawkwind, the Velvets . . . then heaps more distortion on top.*' (Chuck Eddy, *Stairway to Hell*)

They never had a record out when they were together, and they split up in 1976 before punk could adopt them, which it wouldn't have done in any case because they were longhairs and they dug Kiss. But they made an album of sorts which I've played constantly since somebody gave me their 'tape' in 1982, and it should be in everyone's Top Fifty of all time, and surely, one day, it will be talked about as though it's a standard.

I've seen the 'album' in so many differently titled cassette and vinyl guises, from *Life Stinks* to *A Night of Heavy Music* via *The World's Only Dumb-Metal Rock'n'roll Band*, that everyone is confused, so I figured now was the time to set the story straight about this Cleveland band whose 'only common ground was the love of hard groove rock and overdrive dynamics',[1] according to their lead singer, David Thomas.

Half the group, Peter Laughner, Craig Bell and Thomas himself (then known as Crocus Behemoth), were chasing the sound of The Stooges and the MC5, while the others, Gene 'Cheetah Chrome' Connor and Johnny 'Blitz' Mudansky, were totally immersed in the Kiss-type metal of the day. The result was a kind of musical stance which has subsequently been written out of American and British rock'n'roll history, but which crops up at the heart of Krautrock – that of the post-Altamont, longhair, metal refusenik, as celebrated on Side Two of Patti Smith's 1976 album *Radio Ethiopia*, but never so in evidence as here on this 1975 performance.

The Cleveland of late 1974 had been the scene of numerous Stooges shows, and yet a climate had been created where local bands either played Top Forty songs or died. So when two local rock journalists, Peter Laughner and David Thomas, formed this post-MC5, post-teen-angst psychotic reaction, there was, in their first year together, only the facility to play five live shows. And, of course, no one wanted records by them, so the closest they got was a radio broadcast on their local station, WMMS-FM, taken from a two-night loft recording made in February 1975. It is this recording on which Rocket from the Tombs' entire legend stands, and this is what I'm reviewing as Album of the Month. Of course, it rocks deep into the beyond, but more than that it sustains over the years. When I told my wife that I wanted to put this on, she was smiling like the whole Detroit scene just walked in.

First off, I have to tell you that this lo-fi statement is the hissiest album you have ever heard. The bass climbs the walls and obliterates whole vocal lines, while the guitars seethe and penetrate the ears like a High Rise live recording. Only the Electric Eels approximate this kind of sound, and they were also from Cleveland, and at about the same time, too, so what the hell was happening there? Perhaps the confidence of this recording comes from the band's purposeful reaction to everything else which would have been broadcast on WMMS that night, indeed that whole year, and possibly ever.

So Rocket from the Tombs ham up the beginning like it's the start

1 As reproduced in *CLE* magazine.

of 'Kick Out the Jams' and scream 'brothers and sisters' in semi-unison like the MC5 aping the Godfather of Soul, before setting off on an instrumental, *Raw Power* rip of Cresta Run intensity. The song then careers into the slow, wailing, incontinent dissidence of 'So Cold' – an inward-looking losers' anthem by young guys with no expectation of being heard, least of all by their local peer group. The bass oozes and splurges round the room like they've got vats of it spare in the basement just waiting to gloop up any song they might think is too straight.

Then they blast into the rock'n'roll guitar riff of 'I'm Never Gonna Kill Myself Again', with five seconds of acceptable sonic shmeer, before, sure enough, bassist Craig Bell emerges from that mysterious bass-ment with a fresh dollop of Tony Visconti/Trevor Bolder overplay. Remember how Tony Visconti played bass on those early Bowie albums? He was never the ablest of bass players but his co-producer's position meant that rock'n'roll's hoariest bass clichés were transformed into giant's steps, glitterstomping across the sonic landscape, inspiring Trevor Bolder to similar heights/lows on the subsequent Bowie LPs. Well, here in the Rocket from the Tombs' loft, lack of control means the guy with the loudest instrument wins, and he who dares is always Craig Bell. Right on!

Next up comes the dum-dum of 'You Didn't Bleed', another anthem by unknown losers whose heroes are more famous losers. This song sees them get down in the mud, musically and vocally, until everything drops to just the lead-booted bass line, which is met by the whole band muttering and schmuttering the song title like some bastard offspring of Pooh and Piglet on that day they walked round in circles looking for the heffalumps and the woozels. Nothing gets more Stooges than this, but I'm talking about Mo, Shep, Curly and Larry.

Then we get into really strange territory. 'Thirty Seconds Over Tokyo' would emerge, one year later, as the first single by Pere Ubu and cleared the way for the real rot'n'roll to set in. Avant-rock? Fuck that! Here, they take it and break it and shape it as 'Psychotic Reaction' played by Led Zeppelin's afterbirth. It grows fins and swims out of reach like nothing you ever could imagine. Hell, it even ends with a drum solo! Again, they get quieter than The Stooges ever did, although the level of recorded hiss precludes their approaching true Doors-like dynamics. But you know what? They really give it a go, and to such admirable proportions that it kicks Pere Ubu's dick into the dust.

'What Love Is' tears off Glenn Branca sonic sparks for a few seconds before uncontrolled Stooges urges overcome them, and the seemingly unloved and never-to-experience-it Crocus Behemoth starts ranting about how he wants us 'to know what love is'. Then the band make sounds that show that they figure love and Viking warfare are the same thing exactly. This is two years before Johnny Rotten, and the singer's vocal is two hundred times more shamanic. Jack Hawkins' tracheotomy was more musical than this.

Of course, it's hard to sink lower than this, but they do. How? They just get super-asshole Peter Laughner to sing instead. He has an acceptable rock'n'roll voice, but manages to bring us further down by delivering a song of such solipsism that you wanna kill him before he kills himself (which he did, three years later). The song is called 'Ain't It Fun' and Guns N' Roses recorded it years later for their *Spaghetti Incident* covers album, so you can get where it's coming from. Musically, it's a direct rip of The Stooges' 'Open Up and Bleed' – kind of acousto-electric meaningful with such one-line winners as: 'Ain't it fun when you know that you're gonna die young,' and the ultra-compassionate: 'Ain't it fun when you tell her she's just a cunt.'

Mercifully, Crocus Behemoth returns for another Laughner song, the magnificent 'Life Stinks', in which he tells us that: 'Life stinks/I can't think/I hate The Kinks,' over a raw bass and vile-ass organ-thing, then returns for a second verse and suddenly: 'I love the Kinks . . .' The two feelings ain't really as opposite as they sound, and, besides, early rock'n'roll coherence never claimed to be that of anyone beyond their teens. Hey, I love the Stones and I hate the Stones; Laughner sums up his feelings in eight words, and you can't get less addled than that.

They finish this recording in true style with the magnificent 'Dead Boy Down in Flames'. A by-now-standard lone rock'n'roll guitar collides head-on with the un-standard Craig Bell Visconti-bass roar/raw, and we're off again into the Stoogeland of yore. Crocus Behemoth bellows 'Dead Boy' more atonally than Rotten howled 'I wanna be me', and the song collapses into an unaccompanied, overachieving, rhythmless/formless guitar solo, like the middle of Sir Lord Baltimore's 'Pumped Up' – only it never resolves or returns to the beat; it just leaves you hanging there and that's the end. For me, perfection was never the tooled lintels of Stonehenge, it was the rough Mother Nature of Avebury. Listen to this album and you'll see the same argument in sound.

Postscript

Soon after this recording, the two factions of the band split up and formed into Pere Ubu and The Dead Boys, taking certain songs with them, each adding what it saw as the missing dollop of sonic vibe. I have a live tape of Rocket from the Tombs playing the Agora Ballroom in Cleveland, on which they perform what became Pere Ubu's 'Final Solution'. With three decades' hindsight, it's fair to say that neither of the offshoots even approached what this tape does, although the pre-art-wank, early Pere Ubu got close occasionally.

Rocket from the Tombs were out of time and ahead of their time, which means that combining stun-guitar rock'n'roll with cosmic, apostate rage is a still-coming, up-coming thing. I'd advise you all to form your band now!

Sand

Golem

(Delta-Acustic, 1974)

SIDE ONE	SIDE TWO
1 Helicopter (13.42)	1 May Rain (4.29)
2 Old Loggerhead (8.21)	2 On the Corner (4.26)
	3 Sarah 1: Passacaille
	4 Sarah 2: Per Aspera Ad Astra (10.40)

When Gento and Yogi finally fled back to their homes in Bodenwerder, in Lower Saxony, they were looking for normality and safety. As members of the burgeoning Krautrock scene, they had loved their Cologne show supporting Can, and believed that their band, Part of Time (P.O.T.), could only become bigger and better. But they were all from the fantastic land of Baron Münchhausen, a beautiful rural area whose biggest local town was the fairytale Hamelin, from whence had come the legendary Pied Piper. And, although each was intrigued by these industrial cities in which they had been called upon to perform, they had grown up playing in the woods and ancient quarries of the mysterious Weser Valley. Yes, they wanted to play the new rock'n'roll, but they were still mistrustful of the druggies and weirdos who permeated their new lives – lives defined by student demonstration, anti-Cold War attitude and communal living. So, when the remainder of Part of Time decided to move to Berlin, both Gento and Yogi freaked out and quit the band.

Of course, this left Part of Time's now-Berlin-resident Papenburg brothers, Ludwig and Ulrich, in a real fix. Both were excellent musicians, but how should they proceed?

The band's lead singer, Johannes Vester, was a visionary lyricist, but he was no musician. True, he contributed a mean short-wave radio to the soup of their live sound, but it was hardly going to help now that the drummer and organist had both run back to the forest.

However, this was the experimental Krautrock scene of 1972, and anything was possible. Can's manager, Manfred Schmidt, had been enormously impressed by Part of Time's performance in Cologne. He had sat up half the night listening to Johannes Vester's notions of where experimental rock'n'roll should go next. And he had introduced Vester and the two Papenburg brothers to Klaus Schulze, who had in turn encouraged their plans to move to his own city, Berlin, where anything was possible, and the weirder the better.

Thus, Sand was born – a cosmic and drummerless trio with a lead singer who played VCS3 synthesizer and sang mysterious and pedantic English lyrics in a voice like a Frisian Puritan reared on Melanie Kafka and David Bowie. Sample lyric: 'He is an old loggerhead/Actually long ago he is dead.' Reviewer's comment: 'Nuff said.'

On arrival in Berlin, these three longhairs beat a path to Klaus Schulze's front door and asked him to produce their first LP, to be entitled *Golem*. Why did they want to call it that? Well, Golem was a mysterious Jewish figure from the sixteenth century who had been fashioned out of the earth. The members of Sand used 'Golem' as a verb to describe the transmutations which occurred when they played together. In the words of Johannes Vester: 'To experience with the unknown, to give life . . . that was our impulse . . . [those lyrics expressed] exactly what was in our mind when we Golemned.'

And so it happened that Klaus Schulze recorded five strange and extended ambient ballads by a trio of little people from Lower Saxony, who each knew precisely what sound they wished to achieve. Some of the songs hung around from their days as Part of Time, but these, now without drums or organ, were considerably extended in duration in order to consciously create 'reduction, frugality, monotony, even mantric principles and elements', as Johannes Vester would later comment.

As the results sounded like nothing else ever heard, they would all be quite happy. And, quietly and seemingly quite easily, they achieved this goal. For *Golem* is a beautifully mystical and hauntingly empty record, inhabiting those same pre-industrial landscapes in which they had played as children. The songs were occasionally propelled by picked, glassy acoustic guitars and pulsing monolithic bass, as though powered by the heartbeats of frost giants delicately picking their way through their ancient Saxon township in outsize and ill-fitting seven-league boots. However, as often as not, the music was left to hang in mid-air while haunting, weirdly translated lyrics, strangely sung in some undefined post-apocalyptic space-cockney, sauntered and cooed out their bizarre message over washes of belt-driven synthesizers and arhythmic, agricultural ur-folk music.

It must also be understood that this Sand LP was recorded at a time when Klaus Schulze was actually being paid by Membran Records of Berlin to experiment with the famous Kunstkopfstereophonie, or artificial-head, binaural listening system, in which a whole other world was placed in the headphones of those listeners who wanted to go beyond the quadrophonic sound reproduction of the day. There was a plethora of recording and mixing aids being used in the early-to-mid-1970s, many of which followed on naturally from the 1960s hi-fi industry boom, and also through the sonic desires of experimenters such as Karlheinz Stockhausen. This culminated in a situation whereby many different composers, utilising any number of variously sized loudspeakers placed in different configurations around the audience, gradually allowed the technology itself to dominate their work rather than enhance it. Fortunately, although the binaural head technique did compromise the final mix of many of these LPs, the effects achieved when wearing headphones are still remarkable today. It really does your head in. So, when you listen to this Sand LP, get the cans on, babies – it's a stone groove of ambulent proportions. Unfortunately, although Delta-Acustic, Membran's experimental offshoot, simultaneously released several other experimental-rock LPs, it is said that the Sand LP is by far the most achieving and entertaining.[1]

Golem begins with 'Helicopter', in which the phased vocals and twittering VCS3 of Johannes Vester set up a sound worthy enough to

1 Though I have heard none of the other Delta-Acustic LPs, those which have been recommended to me are *We Hope to See You* by Seedog (Delta-Acustic 25-125-1), *Planet of Man* by Code III (Delta-Acustic 25-125-1) and the sampler *Kunstkopf Dimension* (Delta-Acustic 10-130-1). This last one includes all kinds of sound experiments beyond stereo and quadrophonic.

accompany some newly imported space religion. A few minutes into this comes the electronic pulsings of Ludwig Papenburg and the strummed bass of Uli Papenburg, rhythmic but wholly uninterested in the 4/4 beats of rock'n'roll. Their sea-shanty listing ship rocks from side to side, as Johannes Vester takes up the story:

In the sky is flying high a blackbird with a
dusty cry,
On the hills the ravens croak while satyr
plays a dreadful joke,
By the water damp fog whirls,
See the smoking steaming earth,
And the air is dark and strange and cold.

Where does this guy get his pronunciation from? Is this a regular voice in Bodenwerder? Are orators of this type ten-a-penny round his neck of the woods? Or does a Johannes Vester inhabit the peripheries of every neighbourhood? Around eight or so minutes into 'Helicopter', a whole other rhythm takes over and we're suddenly pitched into a world of the recent dead. Now Vester is some north European shaman summoning reluctant spirits out of their graves. Just as Odin pissed off the sleeping goddesses with his acts of midnight seething, so Johannes pops up to do the same to poor old sleeping Allfather himself.

Next comes that crazy 'Old Loggerhead' song, which kicks off with the eeriest harmonica and synthesizer-cross-the-swamp. Down come Uli Papenburg's slow, descending bass chords as Vester begins his next strange tale of shadowy forest characters at the edge of sleepy Dark Age townships: 'He scraped a living in a ramshackle cot/Outside the village near the mystery wood.'

Of course, Old Loggerhead's behaviour is far too anti-social for the locals, themselves guilty of all kinds of clandestine habits. And Vester continues his tale:

Once some fellows stalked up to his shack,
They used caution,
Took the old beaten track,
Painted a white cross on the brittle gate,
So they marked the place of imaginary fate,
And they returned to their peace-loving folk,
Reported excited on the nocturnal joke.

Hearing Vester pronounce the phrase 'once some fellows' is a revelation in itself, and when he tells of Old Loggerhead's disappearance with a 'sinister giggle' the effect is quite superbly chilling.

Side Two opens with the Alpen folk of 'May Rain', a strange cross between Pearls Before Swine and Witthüser & Westrupp, with a melody siphoned directly from Can's 'Vitamin C'. Mallet-balalaika and picked, wintry acoustics hurry along this hook-nosed song like long-coated spirit-Fagins on some unknown stroke-of-midnight mission to the gates of Hel [*sic*].

By the time we come to 'On the Corner', Vester's dialect has become cross-continental. He moves happily and effortlessly from a kind of Brummie-Swiss Syd Barrett to cartoon Norwegian milkmaid (and her cow), via South Africa and the Amish – and sometimes all in the space of one line of lyrics. 'On the Corner' is the catchy one. Y'know how certain songs sound like singles not because they're overtly commercial, but because they are just not nearly so fucking weird as the stuff that's gone before? Well, 'On the Corner' is that guy. It starts with boogie drum machine, moves through several (catchy) rhythmic changes, then, out of the blue, settles on the single most jarring and inappropriate Cajun-soul beat you ever did hear. You hear it the first time and laugh. Then you whizz back in case you misheard. Then you listen one final time for pleasure and the sheer audacity of *that* beginning. Finally, you hear the entire song, and, by the way, it is great.

'Well, I'm standing on the corner with my feet soaking wet,' sings Johannes Vester, over a soul bass line and an acoustic guitar and not much else. Maybe his voice is just a fucking genius joke because the guy sounds like a sheep-shagger. I'm not saying he is, but he sounds like the biggest hick-yokel ever to be allowed in the recording studio; he makes Trio's 'Da Da Da' sound truly worldly wise and city slick! And when we get to the line about Johannes having 'a pain in my bones', he really makes the overly mannered pronunciation of Marc Bolan and Donovan sound bog-standard by comparison.

The album closes with a ten-minute, two-part epic called 'Sarah' – a sort of *Not Available*-period Residents, lost-child-goddess-in-the-attic-of-the-world tale. Part One asks, and answers, the same question over and over again: 'Is it you, Sarah?/ No, it's the storm.' The sounds are atmospheres which fall and rise like the breathing of the twilight wind on the Marlborough Downs. The music is the movement of the sun glimpsed from some ancient eminence in that final hemi-second before it dips below the horizon. And, of course, by the middle of this song it has become quite clear that Sarah and the storm are one. And even though Sarah the Storm Giantess has picked her way ever so carefully through their neighbourhood, she has still 'uncovered all the fields' and 'petrified trees'. And so, under cover of darkness, Vester repeats endlessly over the fade-out that Sarah is '. . . gone with the stream/Sarah is gone/ Sarah is gone/Sarah is gone . . .'

And so the *Golem* LP concludes. Sand had a truly eternal sound; like the Montgolfier Brothers hanging above nineteenth-century Paris in their balloon, it is so close but so out-of-reach that you could imagine them all blowing away at any moment – a life-threatening experiment which seems superficially simple to achieve.

Unfortunately, it is nowadays quite impossible to buy this LP in the original format. So please be aware that the recent Sand reissue suffers from that horrid modern phenomenon: extra tracks . . . Oh yeah! You get no sense of the single-mindedness which Sand used for their original muse. There's not even a nice big thirty-second gap between 'Sarah' and the following piece. Be warned: you get unnecessary demo versions of LP tracks aplenty plus a (very nice) unreleased solo LP by Johannes Vester.[2] This lot all comes under the banner *Ultrasonic Seraphim*, which you have to buy to get to the real deal. That said, several of the tracks are really fucking great. It's just a shame that it all gets mish-mashed (and even horribly cross-faded at times) in the dreary name of 'good value'.

Still, it would be horribly churlish of me not to praise this reissue, because I myself wouldn't even have had a copy otherwise. So enter the world of Sand with both feet jumping and you'll descend into quicksand – keep your hands free and close to the CD eject button – but dig this fucking weird Saxony sound and fill your heart. You know it makes no sense.

2 Don't ask why, but this solo album was recorded under the name Johannes Vester and His Vester Bester Tester Electric Folk Orchestra.

The Illustrated Armand Schaubroeck

A Lot of People Would Like to See Armand Schaubroeck . . . Dead

In early 1977, I used to wedge myself into the tight space in the back room of Probe Records, in Liverpool, sorting for hours through the import racks filled with shrink-wrapped weirdness, all too overpriced to buy but filling my punk head with mystery to the point where anything shrink-wrapped became desirable for its sheer out-of-reachness. Albums by The Residents and Chrome rubbed shoulders with obscurities like Ron Pate and the Debonairs and The Afrika Corps, and all manner of mighty weirdness, till even the import-only copies of Cheap Trick albums looked good enough to steal. But, amongst all those weirdos, one album always stood out as being even weirder. For a start, it was a triple album in a gatefold sleeve, and the front showed a photo of a smiling, curly haired Lou Reed-ian punk in his late twenties, with a poorly executed fake bullet hole right through the centre of his head and fake blood cascading down his face. Turning it over, the handwritten lettering pronounced: 'Armand Schaubroeck Steals.' What the hell was this all about? Even if I'd had the money, I was no way about to pay over seven quid to find out. And so, on every Probe visit, this mysterious album passed through my hands until I was desperate to know what it contained. No one at Probe knew, and neither would they open the shrink-wrap to unlock this mystery. So time passed until another album by Armand Schaubroeck appeared with a sleeve of equally weird proportions – hell, in some ways it was even weirder!

I Came to Visit, but Decided to Stay

The new album was called *I Came to Visit, but Decided to Stay*, and showed Armand, dressed as a vicar, lying on a grave in a fake cemetery, in fake snow. He was resting his head against the cross, staring at a photograph of a nun, which he held in his right hand, while his left hand was firmly clinging to a bottle of some alcohol or other. On the rear of this non-gatefold sleeve a similar shot showed Armand freaking out with grief, and the songs on the credits announced a Schaubroeck-ised treatment of Edgar Allan Poe's 'The Bells' and a version of 'Auld Lang Syne'. Again, the shrink-wrapping acted as a natural barrier to my investigation, and so this second album also became lodged in my unsatisfied brain.

No one else was even interested, and all my punk mates presumed that it must be shit because we were living in fundamental times and Armand even had a heavy-metal guitar with him in his grief, leaning against the stone cross in the snow. But more time passed and there were so many records to buy during that period that my from-a-distance obsession with Armand got put on hold. Until early 1978, that is, at which time his new album appeared mysteriously at the back of Probe, and this time with a title which no one could claim to be unimpressed by . . .

Ratfucker

When I first saw that brand-new copy of Armand Schaubroeck's *Ratfucker*, I knew, then and there, that it had to be mine. I even tore off the shrink-wrap and looked inside, knowing that this action meant that all the Probe staff now considered it unsellable to anyone else but me. *Ratfucker!* What genius was contained inside? Straight away, I saw that the album was dedicated to another semi-hero of mine, the late Peter Laughner, who had started Pere Ubu and then killed himself through sheer physical self-abuse. And there, on the inside sleeve, taped on with love, was a free, shocking-pink plectrum, inscribed with the single word 'Ratfucker'. Wow! Even Armand had surpassed himself this time. I took the album to the Probe staff, who put it away for me until I could afford it. And so, just one week later, I placed it lovingly on to my turntable.

Yes, the record was great; a masterpiece. Hell, Armand said 'fuck' at least twenty times in every song. He said it so gratuitously that I was shocked. And his music was a bizarre combination of Lou Reed, Iggy Pop and a disgusting bar band. What was it all about? I didn't know, but I didn't care. I was finally listening to Armand Schaubroeck and enjoying it!

The album was meant to depict life on one block of Armand's city, and took snapshots of small-time gangsters amassing their measly fortunes at the expense of terrorised locals. The opening title track had Armand as the underworld boss talking to a bunch of businessmen from a furniture convention from out of time. All are here to get laid by whatever means necessary and, throughout, Armand brags psychotically about being able to bring them anything, just so long as you tell him 'what you want, what you want, what you want!' Other songs, such as 'Gigolo Gigolo' and 'I Love Me More Than You', depicted Armand as a rent boy of advancing years, doing anything to keep his over-fucked ass at the top of the pile. 'Buried Alive' was pure Iggy wailing and complaining, while the whole soundscape was American rock with wailing-siren synthesizers and burning, ernie-ernie-ing guitars. Apart from the sicko 'Pre-teen Mama', Side Two was entirely given over to an equally sicko, fourteen-minute-long death epic called 'The Queen Hitter'!

The Shadow Knows

Living in Prospect Vale, off the Prescot Road, I was in a Liverpudlian netherworld of my own uninhabited by other hipsters. Walking the two miles into the city centre every day took me past a record shop called Reddington's Rare Records, which was mainly dedicated to country-and-western music. But when you got inside and really looked it was possible to find Mothers LPs and all kinds of other weirdness for less than one pound fifty (at a time when Mothers LPs were at least one pound eighty in Probe!), and I even found my first Scott Walker LPs there, for eighty pence each. Anyway, this one time spent trawling through Reddington's racks brought me face to face with a second-hand copy of that aforementioned Armand Schaubroeck triple album. Who the fuck shells out over seven quid, then sells it to a country-and-western shop on Prescot Road? I was dumbfounded and even a little scared to imagine the kind of shadowy weirdo who would have done this. Whatever, I handed over the two pounds fifty for the triple album and walked back home directly.

In the cosiness of my Prospect Vale bedsit, the story of Armand's teenage years gradually unfolded.

over the three albums. It was a fucking autobiographical rock opera with spoken words between each song, all re-enacting the story of how Armand went to jail for stealing. Of course, now I got it. Armand had been so scarred by this happening that, almost a decade later, he was still writing about it and calling his own band Armand Schaubroeck Steals. *Weirdness.*

The album began with Armand in the confessional box, owning up to having sex with himself and with a girl, and stealing things, committing thirty-two burglaries, including robbing a church. Then the church theft was re-enacted before Armand launched into a classic, Cajun harmonica-driven Velvets-type song called 'King of the Streets'. Man, I flipped out at the sheer Gothic, nightmarish, horribly more-ish obsession of it. He's screaming out to Jesus for mercy; he's walking down the road to hell, and the most beautiful gospel-meets-the-Velvets'-'Sunday-Morning' singers are waving him goodbye with big smiles on their faces.

The rest of the album carried on in the same obsessive vein, with wondrous songs like 'Streetwalker', 'God Damn You' and a mantra-like dirge called 'I Wish to See Colour', in which the jail-trapped teenage Armand yearns to leave prison just long enough to get away from its grey walls only '. . . to see colour, to see colour/I wish to see colour'.

Other songs made up of endlessly repeated phrases populated the album, giving to it a devotional, religious feel. One song, called 'We, Like Lost Sheep Are Drifting', suggested that Armand was seeing this exorcism through to the end. Even a song about Armand and his girlfriend, Suzie, making love for the last time before he goes to prison took on a mantric, dirge-like quality. I was astounded by the album and wondered where Armand's place in music could possibly lie – especially in those free-for-all days of 1978.

Dear Julian, Please Kill Me

Reddington's Rare Records soon washed up a second-hand copy of *I Came to Visit, but Decided to Stay.* Of course, it must have been from the same shadowy source as my second-hand triple, but every visit to that store saw me eyeing each culty-looking character with suspicion. Was *he* the weirdo who buys then sells Armand albums? Or is it *him* with the one leg and monocle?

I Came to Visit, but Decided to Stay was yet another of Armand's unlikely psycho-dramas/rock operas. This time, he played the part of a priest called Father Michael who had fallen in love with a nun named Sister Jennifer. But she was 'married to Jesus' and 'she was wearing his ring', so it was a sin for them to be lovers. Of course, killing herself would leave Sister Jennifer in purgatory, so Father Michael kills her to put her out of her misery; then he decides to visit her grave and *decides to stay*. It's a simple enough story if you're a genius/lunatic like Armand Schaubroeck, and the record was never off my turntable. Like Lou Reed at his best, Armand's music transcended his muse. Here, he was pitched into an otherworldly maelstrom of over-reverbed country and western, just like taking a mushroom trip at that very second-hand record shop which had delivered him to me.

I was, by now, obsessed with everything Armand. So I wrote to him at the Mirror Records address printed on his album sleeves and waited. Within the month, a huge file of Armand Schaubroeck-ness came through my door: press cuttings, stickers and more plectrums. But best of all were the signed photos and the command: 'Julian, whenever you're in Rochester, N.Y., please kill me. I ain't never died before.'

Armand, I love you, man. It's you and me forever.

Second-hand Ratfucker

Fuelled by personal correspondence and my unknown benefactor at Reddington's Rare Records, I embarked on a policy of Total Armand. When Reddington's delivered to me the inevitable used copy of *Ratfucker*, my brother Joss got a very welcome X-mass gift. When my young mate Yorkie one day accompanied me into Probe with too much money in his pockets, I conned him into spending the full seven quid on that first and unbought triple which had lain there unplayed for so long. I even managed to find a rare forty-five by Armand's first band, The Churchmice. Recorded in 1965, this ball of phlegm showed Armand and his guys to be weirder than even I'd imagined. 'College Psychology on Love' was a raw-cuss and wordy, pre-Velvets stumble, while 'Babe, We're Not Part of Society' was irate and uncoordinated teenage socio-bollocks of the highest order.[1] Then Yorkie outdid me, and bought a Mirror Records'

1 If you ever find a copy of Antar Records' garage compilation *Gone 1: Colour Dreams*, that's my copy of 'Babe, We're Not Part of Society' right there, which Cally used as his master copy.

Armand Schaubroeck single which featured his mate Jerry Porter singing lead vocal! Whoa!

Live at the Hollywood Inn

In the 1970s, any self-respecting rock'n'roller issued at least one double live album, and Armand Schaubroeck was not about to be the exception. And like the Seeds and the 13th Floor Elevators before him, he was not gonna be put off by lack of a big audience or record sales. So when I discovered the paint-splattered *Live at the Hollywood Inn (Rochester, N.Y.)* album I was in no way surprised to discover that the audience was the loudest thing on the record. They respond to the gentle opening chords of 'Elmira Bound' as though they've seen Mother Mary dancing with the Boss: they're howling and wailing and reacting to every little moment and lyrical nuance that Armand can muster. The version of 'Streetwalker' is almost drowned by the fake applause, yet it somehow adds to the obsessive overachievement of that crazy, late-'70s period of Armand Schaubroeck's life. The monochrome front sleeve shows him looking like a punk doctor about to barf on his patient, and the band plays like permanent outpatients on a terminal Saturday night.

By now, I was up to my neck in Armand Schaubroeck stuff, and still the torture never stopped. A dizzying album called *Shakin' Shakin'* was soon to come, the sleeve like some punk take on the Vertigo swirl label, and only three long songs per side, each one an unresolved boogie! Where was his head at? Where was mine at for buying this stuff? I don't know, but I'm so glad that I did. For, before you could ask, 'Wha'appen'd?' Armand Schaubroeck was gone. He'd released all these albums between 1976 and 1978, and suddenly there were no more. When I formed The Teardrop Explodes, I searched around America for his stuff, and no one had a clue. Only Yorkie and my brother had played his stuff, and we were a weird triumvirate with a backlog of Armand history to share.

Leaving Liverpool, I played Armand to my wife, Dorian, and anyone else who would listen. His songs appeared on any compilation tapes I'd make for friends, and I even used a title of his for a *Jehovahkill* song, 'Cut My Friend Down'. But I've never forgotten any of his music and it still rings through me today, as clear and as brutally poignant as ever. I searched for him online and he's now designing guitars; he looks pretty successful at it, too. Armand Schaubroeck – you will always move me!

Discography

A Lot of People Would Like to See Armand Schaubroeck . . .
Dead (Mirror, 1975)
I Came to Visit, but Decided to Stay (Mirror, 1977)
Armand Schaubroeck Steals Live at the Hollywood Inn (Mirror, 1978)
Ratfucker (Mirror, 1978)
Shakin' Shakin' (Mirror, 1978)

Simply Saucer

Cyborgs Revisited

(Fistpuppet/Cargo, 1989; recorded in 1974)

SIDE ONE

1 Electro Rock (4.12)
2 Nazi Apocalypse (3.10)
3 Mole Machine (4.25)
4 Bullet Proof Nothing (2.59)
5 Here Come the Cyborgs (Part 1) (3.45)

SIDE TWO

1 Here Come the Cyborgs (Part 2) (6.45)
2 Dance the Mutation (4.28)
3 Illegal Bodies (10.12)

Like a number of previous Albums of the Month, *Cyborgs Revisited* by Simply Saucer seems to be available in multiple versions. I have two different variations and have been told of a third, which I have not yet seen. I wrote the review below while listening to my favourite version. Simply Saucer released no LPs during their own lifetime, so each future configuration will also include the (mounting legion of) fans' eye views, which is fair, I guess, especially as most record-company A&R people are really just power-wielding fans with delusions of objectivity.

Recently, in an attempt to at least temporarily purge myself of the Japrock which chronically seeps around our house on the Downs and clogs up the ears of the neighbourhood and obliterates the dawn chorus, I bought the excellently repackaged and remastered Velvet Underground double CD *Fully Loaded.* I hadn't listened to the Velvets in years – a conscious decision based on their needlessly un-mythical return as a U2 support act in the mid-'90s. Lou's a louse, Lou's a scab, Lou's a dry husk of his former self, etc. But *Loaded* shoulda given me no such head trips – it was always a Doug Yule-sings-Lou Reed-in-the-manner-of-*Beggars-Banquet*-period-Mick anyway, so how could I be disappointed? Yet I was. I'd been listening to such full-on contemporary rock'n'roll that the extra CD just couldn't command my attention, its half-finished, half-arranged, bass-less or bass-heavy studio dryness wilting under the pressure of twenty-first-century expectations. I turned to the original album, and that was little better. Not only had I never heard *Loaded* on CD before, but my teenage (and only) copy was a cheap, second-hand buy from 1976, on the German Midi label, with a big, fat, black border and a legend proclaiming: 'Original Rock Classics – The Velvet Underground FEATURING Lou Reed'. I knew every pop, fart, bleep and blemish – I could even sing the skips. I didn't want digitally perfect *Loaded* at all, so I filed it away.

But hearing Doug's rendition of Reed's lonesome-cowboy tales of the great outdoors and of the neurotic Burroughsian great indoors did somehow make me yearn for something similar but less familiar. Just as putting Mick Ronson's 'Billy Porter' forty-five on the turntable can sometimes be the only way to slake my Diamond Dog-eyed glam thirst, so I now needed a 'new' or alternative *Loaded.* And, once again, it was to *Cyborgs Revisited* by Simply Saucer that I immediately turned for the right kind of homage-with-staying-power.

Canada's Simply Saucer offered the same kind of originality that was present in other post-glam outfits such as early Cockney Rebel or Neil Merryweather's Kim Fowley-ish Space Rangers. And, just as both Steve Harley and Merryweather used their Bowie infatuation as a mannequin on which to hang their own personal lyrical fetishes and stylish musical neuroses, so did Simply Saucer's Edgar Breau conjure up a whole raft of imaginary Cannuck ne'er-do-wells to travel with him and his group on their extremely idiosyncratic musical travelogue.

But whereas cosmopolitans such as Londoner Harley clothed it in a Biba 1974, faux-Franglais of violin and Spanish guitar, and LA's Merryweather filled all the spaces up with Mellotron 400 and dive-bombing, fake Mick Ronson apocalipstick, so it was the ultra-provincial Edgar Breau's destiny to bring some kind of Modern Lovers take on decadence to downtown Hamilton, Ontario.

Was that possible? Well, by mixing his Lou Reed fixation with lashings of Barrett-era Floyd and early Roxy

Music B-sides,[1] Edgar Breau cooked up an art-rock as coolly-uncool and as bifocalled as Jonathan Richman's first Modern Lovers LP, or even the beguilingly amphetamine and over-arranged provincial garage-prog of The Soft Boys' *A Can of Bees*.

From the limited perspective of this retrospective album, it's fair to say that Breau was an excellent songwriter and a man of great musical taste. The story goes that when Simply Saucer booked a session at Daniel Lanois' Hamilton studio in July '74, Breau brought in Velvets and Stooges albums to show how he wanted them recorded. Breau's voice sounded like Lou Reed being Mick Jagger; Doug Yule being Mick Jagger; David Bowie being Mick Jagger; even Jim Morrison being Mick Jagger. And, within the (self-imposed?) narrow confines of his guitar playing, Breau conjured up some truly great rhythm and lead. His 'Now I'm Lou/Now I'm Sterling' stance surely predated punk by so many years that his friends and contemporaries must have adjudged him a mere rip-off, little knowing the necessary myopia required to pull off such a feat. And he was a neck-wrenching *Monster Movie* at the wah-wah pedal, pulling it off in the same way that no others could, except, perhaps, Can's Michael Karoli.

Breau's other great strength was as a canny band leader. He chose highly unlikely musicians to accompany his muse, and gave them plenty of space. I hate to imagine how limited was his pool of prospective musicians in 1974 Hamilton, yet Breau somehow found three equally forward-thinking, psychedelic soul brothers in Neil DeMerchant, Kevin Christoff and the mythologically named Ping Romany. Local Canadian writers still talk of them performing a weird mixture of Velvet Underground/Syd Barrett/Can/Pink Fairies material in their formative years, which was hardly the way to the top in the London of '74, let alone Hamilton, Ontario.

The splatter-clatter drumming of Neil DeMerchant is at the amphetamine heart of Simply Saucer. He seems to have had a kit made up entirely of snare drums. Simply Saucer rhythms sound as though several thirty-piece teenage marching bands

1 The early Roxy B-sides, such as 'The Numberer' and 'The Pride and the Pain', appear to have inspired Eno's *Here Come the Warm Jets*, possibly even too much in places. Still, patchy as Brian Brain's song career was, that first LP's still worth it just for 'Blank Frank', 'Dead Finks Don't Talk' and the definitive 'Baby's on Fire'. The rest of that stuff, fergetaboutit!

are here to terrorise your neighbourhood. DeMerchant squirms and swivels around the beat like Cheap Trick's Bun E. Carlos copping dollops of Buffin during his astounding 'Walking with a Mountain' period – but with a stick up his ass.

On bass, Kevin Christoff sounds as though he probably thrummed and clawed at a Gibson with the treble position hacksawed off – all looming boom-boom – while the truly odd-man-out was the bizarrely named Ping Romany on 'electronics'. No keyboards for this guy, Romany claiming his inspiration came from 'Stockhausen, Sun Ra and Eno'.

At this pre-punk, pro-muso period of the '70s, even Eno was still coyly referred to as a 'non-musician'. So we can only imagine the self-conscious sniggers that would have emanated from the casual watchers of Simply Saucer's Hamilton shows, as Ping Romany delivered mind-numbing whirrs, blips and glitches from his 'electro-palette of sonic scree', as his champion, Bruce Mowat, called his sound, over a decade later.

The turbulent, stop–start careers of Arthur Lee's Love would seem like so much plain sailing to the members of Simply Saucer, as employees at Canadian branch offices of the major American record companies all ran for cover at the very suggestion that Rick Bissell, the band's manager, was coming in to play them some demos. Indeed, the indifference of Simply Saucer audiences was nothing compared to the hostility and vindictiveness shown by people in the Canadian record industry. By 1975, the show was off the road and in the ditch. New members failed to rescue Simply Saucer from 'too little work and too much substance abuse', according to Bruce Mowat. Indeed, the only contemporary release under the name Simply Saucer would arrive a full three years later, when the rise of punk prompted the release of the ominously titled 'She's a Dog' forty-five. Unfortunately, by now only two of the original members remained, and the song is righteously excluded from this otherwise all-1974 compilation.

Cyborgs Revisited opens with the very Barrett-Floydian clatterstompf of 'Electro Rock', an extremely catching pop song with a riff kinda like the Stones' 'Dandelion' and lyrics about some guy called Gypsy Jones throwing stones at the moon. There's also a Mr Smith, a girl called Suzie and Jesse James exchanging his brain, and a whole bunch of characters doing stuff that Lou Reed and Syd Barrett would have been proud to have them do. Breau's voice is in Jonathan Richman-meets-Doug Yule mode here, until the song ups its pace into an entirely new gear and the whole thing becomes an early-Floyd-ian workout with Roxy-period Eno brewing an electro-storm in a DDT-cup. Neil DeMerchant's drumming has him on 'en-snare only' mode, as Breau's lead guitar scoots between rhythm-Barrett and lead-Barrett, unwinding down a DeMerchantian percussion tunnel. Breau's wah-wah playing is fucking casebook stuff, while the Ping Romany synthesizer is looming and looming and de-glooming. Finally, at the height of the freak-out, the pop-minded Breau deludedly attempts a neat ending, in which the starship tries to make a three-point turn back into the song, fails and crash-lands; but Breau sings the final verse anyway. What the fuck, the last verse? Sure. Didn't I tell you?

'Nazi Apocalypse' starts off with a riff copped directly from 'Lucifer Sam', as Breau relates his tale of Hitler from Eva Braun's point of view. Here, he's Peter Hammill in snotty, Armand Schaubroeck mode. 'I'm cyanide over you/Bye-bye baby, baby, so long,' he coos. 'Nazi Apocalypse/Adolf and his henchmen in their crypts.'

Then off we go into a swooping, lunging, city psychedelia which dissolves into another of DeMerchant's snare-drum-only clatterstompfs. They surely pick riffs of extreme estimation and always whip 'em off in nothing flat, Breau's wah-wah again fuelling the fire as Ping Romany's sheets of synthesizer build electric fences of impenetrable sonics – you can see through them but don't cross over or they'll burn your brain.

'Mole Machine' is an instrumental not unlike Can's 'Matilda Mother', here given the *Here Come the Warm Jets* treatment. Ventures/Davie Allen and the Arrows-themed guitars emit from a Mike Curb soundtrack and combine with further clatterstompf drumming to create a Joe Meekian take on space-rock. This is an early and Utopian, pre-'Planet Earth is blue and there's nothing I can do' view of space. Canadian, I guess . . . Zoony loonies hang and natter with groovy Carnaby Street babes, until ugly space Munsters emerge from their Bakelite coffins and do the science lab, baby.

'Bullet Proof Nothing' is more Doug-meets-Jonathan, but this time on The Partridge Family bus. Then it gets all electric and DeMerchant clatters his snare drums as they Stones it up and Breau entreats his maybe missus to 'Treat me like dirt/I'm a point-blank target for your mindless abuse.' It's like something from that lost Cale period of the Velvets – that lumpy, early version of 'Andy's Chest' sound.

'Here Come the Cyborgs' opens with flowering, solo monophonic synthesizer to present an Edgar Breau song of extreme catching-ness. It's more of that Velvet Underground of 'Foggy Notion', and you know some relation of his is about to marry a midget's son any moment. Don't leave the room, as the second half of the song is a different kettle of gunk entirely – it's sludgy, unresolved blues with scales and a tail.

'Here Come the Cyborgs (Part 2)' is a different song with that cyclical riff thang that turns up in Iggy's song 'New Values' – rudimentary rock with two chromosomes missing. Take me. Edgar's in a *Beggars Banquet* soap opera with a 'Gimme Delta Shelter' twang from nowhere at all. Then the riff stop–starts into a slop trough that even the 1978 Soft Boys woulda kicked into touch. Yuck. I love it. Imagine getting the dirtiest 1966 Dodge Charger (or maybe Plymouth Barracuda, it's the same thing), taking all the badges off and pretending it's a Mark II Sunbeam Alpine. You've got it taxed and insured but you've hand-painted it matte white and left T-Cut smears on the windscreen. That's the fucking sound of this song. Breau starts intoning 'Here come the cyborgs' like he's watching them file out of Cyborg School and we should bully the underachieving fuckers. Right on.

I guess 'Dance the Mutation' is the album's 'best' song. It opens with a Stonesy take on a Beatles riff, as Edgar Jagger sings a sloppy tale of sex in unhygienic places; it's a catching thang that has you itching with the sheer scabies of it all. Hey, this is not Mick Jagger at all; it's bloody Bowie being Jagger on *Diamond Dogs*. It's fucked; I love it. Ping Romany even plays some super-hook on his synth. He's actually playing *music* on that thing. Even the floor shudders at his feet – actually, Breau tells us this in the song. It's like *Let It Bleed* and you wish Edgar Breau hadda made it big. He's the kind of songwriter who woulda got better with success – it woulda bred a confidence and, by now, we'd all be accepting of him as the Cannuck third punk (after Neil Young and Burton Cummings). Dammit!

'Here's some heavy metaloid music,' announces Edgar at the beginning of 'Illegal Bodies'. It's about the future. 'Unless you have a metal body/They're not going to allow you to walk the streets,' he notes, before adding the cutest 'No kidding'. Then a fast'n'high-strummed Stirling rhythm kicks in and they hoedown on one chord as the most delighted Breau declares:

'What a fantastic movie I'm in/ What a fantastic scene I'm in.' It's an 'on-the-one' bolt-thrower with the pumpingest piston bass and a suppressed synthesizer which bubbles and undercuts and takes its time and waits for its moment and maybe any minute now until, until, until . . . whoa!, here comes the fucking electric fence again, guys'n'gals. We duck'n'cover, then run from this electrical chicken-wire and get safe behind the sofa, which is too cosy and deludes us. Ping Romany is building a sonic hothouse with about ten square miles of chicken-wire around the compound. Let me in. Let me out. Whatever, it's all the same thing!

The rhythm drops down to a steaming 'Train Coming Round the Bend' when, suddenly, Keith Richards and whoever his best friend is that day get thrown outta the old caboose, like the Chuck Berry hack he could often be, only to be replaced by an Edgar Breau in Lou Reed shades and a knitted, occult-symbol'd roll-neck sweater which his pagan aunt made for him. Breau turns his guitar into a crop-sprayer and gasses the audience with yet more immense streams of DDT and later claims that he'd merely supplied the suggested dose. With the band as OD'd as the audience, the song is tied up neatly with a coupla riffs from 'Dance the Mutation' and they finish.

This live, in-concert ending to the LP finishes with a declaration from Breau: 'Thanks, we'll be back in just a few minutes.' Thirteen million minutes later, I ain't holding my breath . . . They came, they saw, they left. Oh well. Simply Saucer rocked Hamilton in the '70s, but now they're here to rock you. They done gone international twenty-six years later. Better late than never! Better to be a proto-has-been than a never-was. And, baby, indude they *was*!

Sir Lord Baltimore

Kingdom Come

(Mercury, 1970)

SIDE ONE	SIDE TWO
1 Master Heartache (4.37)	1 Kingdom Come (6.35)
2 Hard Rain Fallin' (2.56)	2 I Got a Woman (3.03)
3 Lady of Fire (2.53)	3 Hell Hound (3.30)
4 Lake Isle of Innisfree (4.03)	4 Helium Head (I Got a Love) (4.02)
5 Pumped Up (4.07)	5 Ain't Got Hung on You (2.24)

As Unsung regulars will know, Sir Lord Baltimore's one-off barbarian 'classic' *Kingdom Come* has long informed the pages of my rock'n'roll writing and my Brain Donor trip. Indeed, I appropriated *Kingdom Come*'s gatefold inner illustration of the one-eyed Odin for both the Brain Donor album and as the motif on Unsung's home page.

In 1969, three longhairs from Brooklyn, New York, were thrown off the stage of Bill Graham's Fillmore East for being what that now legendary promoter described as 'pus'. The trio was named Sir Lord Baltimore and they'd just recorded a flawed but fantastic first album, *Kingdom Come*, which combined the most histrionic, proto-Kiss, proto-David Lee Roth vocal acrobatics ever, with enough Stooged-out proto-metal to last any sane band a lifetime. Did you ever wish that 'Speed King', 'Highway Star' and 'Fireball' were the only songs Deep Purple had ever recorded? Did you ever feel that everything Blue Cheer recorded after Side One of *Outside-inside* was unnecessary, including Side Two of that very LP? Did you ever lament that telling people just how much you love 'I'm on Fire' and 'Atomic Punk' from *Van Halen I* inevitably made them think you secretly loved later sub-Genesis detritus such as 'Jump' as well? Well, search out this album and you've got everything you need in one record.

What does it sound like? Well, I'll tell y'all. The music gets ten out of ten, but the vocals get one hundred out of ten. From the opening notes of 'Master Heartache', it's clear that Paul Stanley, Gene Simmons *and* Patti Smith were at every Long Island gig this band ever played. From the mouth of John Garner, as simple a lyric as 'I know' becomes more spiritually uplifting than Handel's *Messiah* (I'd actually be scared to hear John Garner sing 'I know that my redeemer liveth' – I'd probably be in church within the hour).

On 'Hard Rain Fallin'', the fuzz-ball riffing is marvy, Harvey, but again obliterated by John Garner's impossibly strident and braying delivery. By the time we get to 'Lady of Fire', it's revealed to us that Van Halen was formed specifically because of this song. No doubts. When you first hear Garner scream 'Fire', you feel like every 999 call in the world is coming to your aid and yours alone. It's more than magnificent – it's truly life-affirming. While Richie Blackmore nicked the middle of 'Lady of Fire' for Purple's 'Woman from Tokyo', Ian Gillan even copped the laugh in the last verse for the end of 'Speed King'. Yup, it's just so brimming over with proto-everything.

What are the lyrics to 'Lady of Fire' about? Well, Garner's unable to sleep, takes a walk and meets a prossie who tells him that no man can do it for her, including him. Garner tries and is so fab that she crawls after him forever and will bed no other thereafter. Crap macho bollocks? Not when John Garner tells the tale it isn't. In fact, it's suddenly a whale of a tale, and he's Moby Dick!

So why did Bill Graham kick them off stage all those years ago? Was it the controversial lyrical stance? Was it the Garn's overwrought, macho singing style? No, I don't believe so. Brain-dead bluster was a common enough lyrical style in '69/'70 for no fucker to have given a damn. No, it was probably that they were simply a pile of living shit when it came to playing on stage. For a start, John Garner was a singing drummer. This in itself is almost a crime against rock, unless you're the greatest genius that ever roamed the planet – and even Iggy had to put down his drumsticks before he became the Pop we know and love. If you are a singing drummer, you can wield enormous power and slow songs up in really unlikely places, then hang 'em up for hours while you growl through particularly meaningful bits, like Joey Smith did so successfully with Speed, Glue & Shinki. But John Garner and Joey Smith are still the only two I know who got it right, and Bill Graham's Fillmore antics kinda prove Sir Lud weren't the live force they were on record.

The other possible negative aspect of Sir Lud live woulda been replicating the formidable assault course of multi-tracking which Louis Dambra put his guitar through. We ain't exactly talking guitar–bass–drums on this record. Brother Louis builds it and builds it so intricately that the original guitar is almost un-locatable under the sheer weight of otherness. By the second LP, he'd even got his kid brother in to do some supporting licks. Indeed, it was surely Louis Dambra's collection of riff-upon-riff-upon-riff-upon-riff which gave this album its stupendous drive. Even The Misunderstood or the Page'n'Beck Yardbirds never managed the sustained sonic assault which Dambra attains on this Eddie Kramer-produced throbfest.

I could write twenty thousand words about this one album (and probably will, one day), but, for now, you must know that there was a time, around 1969/1970, when Sir Lord Baltimore managed to fuse The Stooges' primeval 'TV Eye' free-rock with Van Halen's version of 'You Really Got Me' and Blue Cheer's 'Come and Get It' without missing a beat. Besides, who had titles like 'Helium Head' in 1970? Sir Lord Baltimore did. And, while you're trying to figure out the morass of amphetamine soup they called 'Pumped Up', they pull the musical rug from under you and leave Louis Dambra's bucking-bronco guitar rearing alone and uncontrolled. No drum or bass – nothing.

The album isn't perfect, but it's short. Indeed, it's exactly the same length as the first four Van Halen albums were: seventeen minutes per side – excellent. Yes, there's a terrible acoustic song on Side One, and I even used to think that the title track sucked big logs. But, really, it's as good as the rest, just more painful and strung out and more of everything. So, m'luds, ladies and gentlemen, I here present you an album of sublime rock'n'roll – excruciatingly and gratingly sublime, and that's a fact.

Sir Lord Baltimore[1]

(Mercury, 1971)

Beware of Sir Lord Baltimore *by Sir Lord Baltimore*

Drudes, a couple of months ago I hipped you to a very special album called *Kingdom Come* by Sir Lord Baltimore and asked if anyone could find their second and final LP, called simply *Sir Lord Baltimore.* Well, I got one two weeks ago and – ah! – it's a fucking pile of sub-prog underachievement of international proportions. John Garner's superb finger-up-the-ass, enema-whine is here reduced to the back of the mix and the post-Blue Cheer cross-rhythm has been straightened out to meet Deep Purple's ultimate Friday afternoon. I'm talking disappointment; fuck, I'm crying, guys.

The album opens with a yawn-athon called 'Man from Manhattan' that never gets off the ground and sounds like the third Flash album; eleven minutes of cheap deodorant, with no pay-off, about Jesus and how people can play mean games on others. Oh, sentimental artholes. The rest of the album is mid-tempo brain-rot without one iota of stamina. They're just brown-nosing the blues until the last two tracks, which shine like a firefly's ass in the compost heap. 'Woman Tamer' and 'Caesar LXXI' at least see the Garn back in his boss hoss-saddle, and it gives the LP the chance to end with some dignity. But, even then, they're no great shakes, vocally as subdued as Joe Strummer's voice when Pearlman-ised for the second Clash LP. And hell, wouldn't it have been better

1 I later added this disappointed addendum to the Sir Lord Baltimore story.

if that song had been called 'Man Tame, Woman Tamer'?

N.B. In showing lost and unsung delights, I'm gonna have to occasionally alert you to, and warn you off, certain underachieving phlegm by previously cool groups. Otherwise, some of you will get the wrong Love LP by mistake and listen to Side Two of *Da Capo* and wonder what planet I'm on. The end of 's.t.a.r.c.a.r.' on *Autogeddon* includes a sample of the opening of Deep Purple's song 'Fireball', but that does not mean I suddenly love it all – it's just that I grew up with the *Deep Purple in Rock*-period stuff and still believe it's fifty percent great. Unfortunately, the other fifty percent is macho, white-funk, microbollocks. I'm not a heavy-rock advocate – I'm a shamanic detective in a panic defective.

John Peel Presents Tractor

(Dandelion Records, 1972)

SIDE TWO

1 Shubunkin (2.57)
2 Hope in Favour (2.46)
3 Every Time It Happens (5.54)
4 Make the Journey (9.09)

SIDE ONE

1 All Ends Up (6.41)
2 Little Girl in Yellow (8.01)
3 The Watcher (1.56)
4 Ravenscroft's 13-Bar Boogie (3.08)

I chose this 1972 Tractor LP from John Peel's Dandelion Records label as a symbolic personal thank you to Peel for everything he brought to British culture during his forty years as a DJ. Without Peel, punk woulda most probably been a damp, London-centric fashion squib, reggae woulda stayed marginalised or become commercialised into the toilet, and there would most surely have been no *Krautrocksampler*, because no other radio DJ woulda played Can's 'Turtles Have Short Legs', Faust's 'Why Don't You Eat Carrots?', Amon Düül II's 'Archangel's Thunderbird' or (most especially) Neu!'s mesmeric 'Hallogallo'.

This Tractor LP I've chosen was released on Dandelion at the height of my own teenage psychedelic period, and fitted right in there with the aforementioned Krautrock bands and (most pertinently) with the Pink Floyd compilation *Relics*, whose mid-price release the previous spring had introduced Syd Barrett to my own generation.

The Dandelion label released twenty-eight LPs in the period 1969–72, including one sampler album, but the company's pinnacle of artistic success was undoubtedly this Tractor album. Listen to *Tractor* with twenty-first-century ears and see how deeply psychedelic the underground still sounded in 1972. I wish more English bands had been so far out, but this northern duo's catchy songs, recorded in an overtly unbalanced style, still represent the pre-punk 'us' magnificently; and the LP is still one of the most extreme sonic experiences of its period. Dig.

Rochdale '72 as Refracted Through the Ears of a Teenage Tamworth Krauthead

Throughout 1972, I spent most of my weekends on my back, listening to newly edited John Peel sessions in the caravan outside Martin Cottier's parents' house in Brown's Lane, Tamworth. This was on the other side of town from my Glascote Heath home, and Cott was a longhair eighteen months older than me, and a full two years ahead in terms of schooling. But we were united in our obsession with underground rock'n'roll and had a mutual friend in Herb Leake, whom I'd known since I was three and who lived six doors down from Cott. My parents were highly anti the rock, but trusted me whenever I was with Herb Leake, as his parents were old friends of theirs whom I referred to as Auntie Pam and Uncle Brian. Besides, Brian Leake was the town clerk of Tamworth and the ultimate pillar of respectability (the Leakes had the third telephone number in the Tamworth phone book, Tam 2003, right after the police and fire brigade), and Uncle Brian's name was printed after every officious public noticeboard announcement warning the public not to do such-and-such 'by order of H. B. Leake'.

Cott's parents were far looser, however, and gave over the use of their big static caravan for all the heads in the area. We congregated in the green-and-cream Carlight Cosmopolitan, eating Jaffa Cakes and drinking tea, cough mixture and beer. Cott's Revox reel-to-reel stereo tape recorder and mixer dominated most of the foldaway kitchenette table and saved us a fortune on records as he culled John Peel sessions and rare records from the radio for our endless parties. As my mother was a teacher with her own high expectations, weekdays at Cott's were a no-no for me and were reserved exclusively for homework. So I would always have to rush to complete essays and other stuff every night before 10 p.m., whereupon the Peel show could begin and send me off into outer space until midnight.

Then, one night in mid-1972, John Peel played a track that was more mysterious than almost anything I had ever heard. It was the music I thereafter wanted played at my funeral and was most certainly the sound of a soul approaching the canopy of heaven as it left the earth for the last time. And yet it turned out that this sound had been captured and retrieved for us all to hear by two young guys called Jim Milne and Steve Clayton, from Rochdale (up north), who called themselves Tractor. This heavenly music was a piece called 'Shubunkin' and was a portal to the underworld that John Peel played on his show every night seemingly for weeks. I say 'seemingly' because every Tamworth head who lay skint in Cott's caravan was listening to the reel-to-reel of Peel's show. So maybe the heavy rotation was actually of our own doing. Moreover, Peel made great play of the fact that this Tractor sound had been created not in your regular recording studio, but in a Rochdale attic by the band's old school friend, John Brierley, obviously the new Joe Meek with attitude enough to reach the moon!

Anyway, Cott, Herb Leake and I decided that we needed our own copies of this LP and took the Midland Red 116 bus into Birmingham the following weekend. We whizzed down to The Diskery, near Digbeth bus station, where all the local DJs deposited their unwanted free LPs, and I sifted through the stacks of brand-new-but-already-discarded vinyl until I located a prized white label of this new Tractor record for an ultra-cheap one pound twenty-five pence. This was a superb result for rock'n'roll, as white labels were symbols of Total Underground Cool. Without the proper printed Dandelion label there to guide me, I left a blob of marker pen on the side that began with 'Shubunkin', and that became the ultimate beginning to any LP in my collection. The album was flawlessly cosmic except for the dodgy, bluesy filler that ended the record, and even this – entitled 'Ravenscroft's 13-Bar Boogie' – was somehow acceptable because it was clearly a thank you to John Peel's patronage, Ravenscroft being Peel's real surname. And, while I was turning most of my classmates in 3-W at Wilnecote High School on to Tractor, my soul-sister, Nicola Farndon, from neighbouring 3-O, was basking in the reflected glory of seeing her cousin John Fiddler singing Dandelion Records' sole hit single, 'Pictures in the Sky', on *Top of the Pops*, with his hippie duo, Medicine Head. It was the closest Wilnecote High School had come to experiencing rock'n'roll royalty since the previous autumn, when Martin Clempson, of, 4-W, had announced that his brother Dave had just left Coliseum and joined Humble Pie. We wuz really cooking!

Except for one thing: in my rush to Total Tractor Understanding via my Peel show-informed infatuation, I never once noticed that 'Shubunkin' was not the first track at all, but was the opening of Side Two! It was clear as day if you looked at the track titles on the back of the LP jacket, but the euphoria and white label conspired to create a mystery that has meant that, even now, decades on, I always play this record 'Shubunkin' side first. Indeed, it would seriously damage my mental health to up-end the whole thing right now. So please accept my metaphor herein, as this John Peel-inspired Album of the Month would never have the same psychic power if I were to allow its true configuration to take precedence over my long-standing personal mythology with this particklier slab of vinyl.

Another major comment that should be made most forcefully regarding this LP is that the so-called duo status of Tractor should really be called into question, for two reasons. Firstly, I remember the disappointment, several months after our initial Tractor trip, when Cott finally acquired a copy of a Dandelion Records LP by the pre-Tractor The Way We Were, from 1971. In places, despite featuring the same Milne/Clayton line-up, the record was virtually a folk LP, and (lyrically especially) a fairly twee one at that. Occasionally it did hit some post-Cream moments, but nothing at all spectacular, perhaps being closest in style to early-'68, *On the Threshold of a Dream*-period Moody Blues playing The Human Beast (which is real charming in its own way but not what you'd consider in any way mind-altering). Not only was none of the Amon Düül II-like guitar mayhem of the '72 Tractor LP present within this earlier album's grooves, but the fabulous resonance of the more delicate Tractor sound was reduced to a fairly perfunctory 'well-recorded' acceptability. The point to be made from the evidence on this earlier LP is that Tractor had subsequently given over a large part of their trip to studio engineer John Brierley and his so-called 'home-made' attic studio, which clearly played a huge part in achieving Tractor's awesome and primal yawp. What was merely overground and detectable on *The Way We Live* had, by the following year, become stomped so far into the ground that only bare Dionysian screams could be detected somewhere far below that frozen earth. Indeed, heft this Tractor disc on to the turntable right now and you'll soon notice that at least half Tractor's sound was achieved through the on-board tone generators and overdrive pedals whose magic was worked in by Brierley at every opportunity.

'Don't Let the Man in the Grey Suit Deceive You . . .'

Even at this late stage, 'Shubunkin' is still, for me, the ultimate neo-Telstar theme-from-the-heavens, beginning like something straight out of early Ash Ra Tempel 'Amboss'-land, with cosmic drones and infinite hum setting us up for the launch of some imaginary spacecraft. Through the impenetrable soup of sound, a euphoric, stellar slide-guitar theme kicks in, driven along by Steve Clayton's splatter-clatter drums, something like those Dervish fills that Terry Ollis used to scatter wantonly around Hawkwind's *In Search of Space*. Like I said before, play this at my funeral and I'll be beyond the canopy of the Earth in less than sixty seconds.

The track then segues seamlessly into another entirely different piece of music, with Jim Milne's vocals coming across like some late-night country-and-western singer mixed way back (Bob Lind's 'Elusive Butterfly' springs most immediately to mind), before the whole track suddenly surges forwards in volume and Milne's charming northern accent calls from one speaker while his answering dulcet tones choirboy us to death in the other. This part, known as 'Hope in Favour', soon disintegrates into some malevolent hoedown redolent of Alice Cooper's 'Halo of Flies', before rough-cutting into the acoustic drive of 'Every Time It Happens'. Here, the song is an amorphous, impressionistic, almost fey piece, heavily bolstered by extreme Brierley engineering and wafts of magnificently harmony-laden, whirling guitars that wail and wail below the city walls. Again, it's the unorthodox mixing and sheer unreachable mystery that nails us to the bed, before 'Make the Journey' begins a raga-thon (rewritten) version of Episode Six's beautiful 1966 single, 'I Hear Trumpets Blow'. This renegade take, however, blows Ian Gillan's pop period right out of the water with a phenomenal guitar burn-up and more of those insanely over-the-top, clattering Clayton drum fills and delightful harmony vocals, as a freight-train rhythm, straight out of one of those early 1960s Argo Records EPs, fades out of some Isambard Kingdom Brunelian tunnel, and the whole of the previous forty minutes flashes before our eyes in the form of cut-ups and snatches from various songs.

And on to Side Two – which is really Side One – oh, you know what I mean. Coming on (again) like Hawkwind's 'You Shouldn't Do That', with tone generators and bleeping underground noises, 'All Ends Up' crashes in with a massive, Phil Spector-type buzzsaw guitar rhythm undercut by more splatter-clatter drum fills from Steve Clayton, before setting off on a super-paranoid tale of The Man and how to avoid him. Suggestions for not getting ripped off: don't remotely engage The Man; don't even step into the portals of his office; don't believe his words whatever they are and you'll be safe . . . ish. Funnily enough, I know from experience what they mean, and they were right, although staying in Rochdale and doing an LP every few years throughout the coming '70s and '80s on a tiny independent label does seem like a pretty bleak alternative to me. Whatever, 'All Ends Up' has that insanely claustrophobic and hugely over-dubbed sound that (experience tells me) you can only get from working in studios with huge limitations. Excellent indeed, and really one of the best ways to achieve high rock'n'roll magnificence.

Although the epic eight minutes of 'Little Girl in Yellow' kicks off like the heads' answer to Jake Thackaray (complete with a fey acoustic, northern-accented tale of fairies and goblins), it's soon blasting into the grim reaper, scythe-wielding territory of 6/4 electric-guitar rhythms, and we could be in the middle of one of those epic Krautrock LPs by Kalacakra or their ilk. Is this the best piece of music on the entire record? Probably! Massive guitar solos undermine everything but the rhythm of the hi-hats, and the sound gets more heavy-rock than any heavy-rock band on a major label ever could or ever did. Think of the ever-changing sound on Speed, Glue & Shinki LPs or even 1969's somewhat similar St. Steven LP, wherein everything temporarily disappears down a shock corridor before emerging, blinking and bleary-eyed, into the cold light of day. This is a severely psychedelic mixing-desk freak-out in the best Dieter Dierks-stylee, and could only have increased in massiveness by lasting for the whole of the side.

Unfortunately, this otherwise monstrous and mind-manifesting LP finishes disappointingly without style or consideration of any kind, first with the acoustic drivel of 'The Watcher' ('He knows that willingness in others is a blessing'? Even in 1972, oh puh-leaze!), and then by the cod electric-blues of the aforementioned 'Ravenscroft's 13-Bar Boogie'.

The first mentioned could easily have been on *The Way We Live* and is trite shite indeed, whereas the final track at least has the charm of being acceptably generic boogie of The Yardbirds' 'Nazz Is Blue' variety. However, as this Album of the Month only achieves its place in light of the sad passing of Tractor's mentor, John Peel, let's offer up a bit of compassion and state this: when six of the eight tracks are as good as those offered within these grooves, it would take someone more churlish than I to (in these circumstances) give the final two underachieving tracks a merciless kicking. Instead, let's just blank them out and pretend the whole LP is a riot from beginning to end, and hope that M'Lud John 'Ravenscroft' Peel is currently spinning his favourite vinyl for the angels and devils of both heaven and hell as we speak. Because we have kenned John Peel all these past years, and we have listened, learned and been changed forever. Hey, John Peel, wherever you are, we salute ye!

Discography

The Way We Live: *A Candle for Judith* (Dandelion, 1971)
Tractor: *Tractor* (Dandelion, 1972)

The 1980s

Rarely this millennium have I been driven to put pen to paper regarding anything recorded during the '80s, possibly because I was, during that period, hugely busy with a full-time rock'n'roll career, a new wife and the constant threat of being jettisoned from the music business for underachievement and prevarication. Whew, but it's true. So now listen up, all you future rock'n'rollers, if I gots to tell you only one thing of career use in this book it's this: the first five years of a musician's career are critical. And at *any* time you can be out on yer arse, even successful types. Listen up, babbies, pay your dues best for those first five years by being always interesting, interesting and downright fascinating, OK? Not fucking kiss-ass to the suits, never accommodating those suet puddings; always mesmerise them, keep them fascinated. And don't dare take your place in the stellar biz for granted, or they'll heft you oblivion-wards at the first hint of a too strange magic.

Although Anton Corbijn photographed the cover of my first solo LP, *World Shut Your Mouth*, it sold virtually nothing. So Polygram Records were *not* impressed when I wanted the second album's cover shot at a location just 600 metres west of it. And for *Fried*, I was butt nekkid under ye turtle shell. I got around it by being cheap, brothers'n'sisters. So cheap they even let me shoot a third cover (*Saint Julian*) just two miles to the north. Loverly. Also, regarding personal magic, remember that daft cunt Babybird from the '90s? Der. He had a song called 'Too Handsome to Be Homeless', and I knew that was where the sucker was headed: homelessness. You bring that Neg Magick down upon yourself with such declarations, and you will be cosmically afflicted. 'Whom the gods notice, they destroy,' declared Philip K. Dick.

Anyway, the '80s were for me mainly a method of getting over the Death of Punk and the Death of that movement's Revolution (such as it was). Like many, I embarked on a series of highly retro musical obsessions that celebrated a less beaten generation than my own. My only large published work before the '90s was 1983's *NME* essay 'Tales from the Drug Attic', 4,000 words of bile and drooling cerebration [*sic*] of all the no-brow, sub-Troggsian, hitless longhairs that the USA had thrown up. I also endured several micro-Krautrock revivals and a right to-do with American funk, but the only contemporaries during the '80s whom I continued to hold in high regard were those musicians who'd consciously avoided any interface with the commercial whatsoever. But I knew from the trajectory chosen for me by the gods that such a route was entirely impossible for me, because the overall catchy-bastardness of my own songs placed me within reach of World Hitsville and all of the tours, filming and cultural opportunities such success would afford me. Without these opportunities, my '80s Underground Musician *Weltanschauung* may well have remained too low key to facilitate time off for researching such non-general books as *Krautrocksampler* and *The Modern Antiquarian*. So enjoy these random '80s observations and reports and let us praise the gods that even in those dark times there remained apostates who had dared to reject Bruce Springsteen's P. T. Barnum snare-drum sound.

Electric Manchakou

(Spirit of Punk, 1993)

SIDE ONE

1 Murder (1.38)
2 Sudden Bummer (2.28)
3 Sexy Sucky (2.20)
4 Cripple Death Dwarf Must Pay (4.20)
5 Landlord (1.05)

SIDE TWO

1 I Won't Break (2.11)
2 Fucking with Four Eyes (1.40)
3 Animal Man (2.03)
4 She Said (1.38)
5 Hey (3.09)

After a coupla months of dark metal-informed sonic wipe-out, accompanied by several ingestions of various psychedelics and trips down into the underworld, I thought I'd do myself – nay, all of us – a huge favour by picking something psychically lighter than usual for Album of the Month. So strap back and listen to this lost acetate of barely post-teen garage thunder, and let its nth-ooziasm clear your psychic custard. And ja, mein hairies, it is the shortest LP in the world, but I think that's because it says its bit, doesn't labour the point and fucks off right quick. In a world where arduously long records are the norm, ain't it great to return (albeit temporarily) to the breathless brevity of George Orwell's mythical two-minute hate song, played by morons with problems on the same level as the Ramones.

The band takes its name from the Japanese term for fraudulent business practices, including deception, cheating and trickery. So now ya knows!

Cover Your Tackle with a Joey Ramone Wig

Obvious, Electric Manchakou was too fucking obvious for words. Stooges wannabes; a one-trick pony;

a two-single deal; case closed. Maybe so, but I'd vociferously beg to differ. For, if London-based Italians Electric Manchakou were Stooges-obsessed – which they most certainly were – they manifested not in the all-too-typical, ain't-I-rad ennui synonymous with most of the genre of acolyte dead-beat artists (GG Allin via Steven 'Stiv' Bators), but rather with the same exuberance and pristine confidence that the sound of The Velvet Underground informed the early songs of The Modern Lovers, or the neatnik way in which speccy Buddy Holly was obsessed with Bo Diddley. In other words, Electric Manchakou burned with a wide-eyed enthusiasm rarely seen down among your regular line of Dee-twat mung-worshippers.

Led by the tall, gangly and vacant-looking pretty-boy Marc Duran, alongside his trusty, inch-high, guitar-slinging sidekick El Tel Tannier, Electric Manchakou was a brightly youthful and unworldly spark, possessed of teen glamour and a curiously athletic, un-nerdy, high-school sheen of confidence. Did they take drugs? Nah, not even sniffing glue just yet . . . they were still on the weekend trips of Benylin Expectorant and dad's QC sherry. Whereas The Stooges' garbage was ill-making enough to have had to be contained in a rusting Chernobyl skip overflowing with chemical slop, Electric Manchakou's was, by comparison, a clean, moulded-yellow-plastic waste-paper basket filled with unfinished essays fused together with chewing gum and cum-ingrained tissues. Were they like Eater? No, they were too young and pre-pubescent even to be horny yet. Like The Undertones? Nah, that band were too gauche and Jilted John-ish to be as sexy as these horny Manchakou motherfuckers; moreover, the Derry boys were just too achieving and disciplined. Indeed, it's mighty obvious from Manchakou photographs and song content that they was just too damned busy shagging to have wrestled much time to write such things as songs. What about the frivolity of The Damned, then? Yup, weez getting closer . . . How about the secretly delighted, fake ennui of the early Damned doing 'Fan Club'? Sure, that's solipsistic and self-obsessed and proto-Emo enough to fit my Electric Manchakou analogy. Furthermore, the Manchakou may have had a thing for limited editions of six hundred and sixty-six copies, but demonic they never coulda been. On one record sleeve they even appeared in their winter cosies! Now, would Iggy have ever been seen on a record sleeve in his dressing gown? No, never; especially not on his debut.

But the cake-splattered Damned sure would. Plus, being post-punk, the Manchakou were also always gunning for the clean overdrive of Alan Vega's first two solo LPs, too. That simple space-rockabilly which propelled Vega's self-titled debut and its classic successor, *Collision Drive*, is fetched up here within the grooves of the Manchakou. And, as on Vega's classic, Electric Manchakou also employ the pure, hiccuping sound of Suzi Quatro's 'Primitive Love' – a sound that can only be brought on by recording loudly and quickly with few instruments, each one louder than the other.

But you know what? Fuck Stooges wannabes, this Electric Manchakou was something else again. Like Lou Reed and Ron Asheton, El Tel Tannier was one of those great punk rhythm guitarists who was obligated to be seen to play lead. Moreover, the melodies of singer Marc Duran always grabbed the listener from the first instant, his asinine repetition guaranteed to insinuate itself into your brain merely seconds after it had first invaded your lugholes. And Duran never let a lyric get in the way when a scream, holler or irksome Kim Fowley-ian belch could suffice. Barks, barfs, pops, screeches, any outpouring of bile-based squark would do for Duran. And maybe they were Stooges acolytes, but these barely post-adolescent Italians wanted also to be the cheerleader-dating younger brothers of *Back in the USA*-period MC5 (clean production'n'all) and of the debut Dictators LP, *Go Girl Crazy* (i.e. with parents supposedly still doing their washing, and them dry-humping their way to a bruised bell-end because full penetration wasn't yet an option).

These greedy Manchakou motherfuckers also wanted to be every volume of those *Pebbles*, *Back from the Grave* and *Chocolate Soup for Diabetics* compilations (not forgetting *New England Teen*, natch), every Troggs single and every Buzzcocks forty-five. Plus, they were also (just about) grown-up enough to recognise the need to incorporate that pounding 'Declaration of War' funk that Reichführer Ronald Rank Asheton had introduced into his aborted (but oft-genius), immediately post-Stooges project The New Order (the Detroit '75 incarnation that often wore full German outfits, and who were all ex-MC5, ex-Amboy Dukes and ex-Stooges).

If yooz only paying attention to the Electric Manchakou singles, then perhaps you're justified in dismissing this bunch, because the first one – 1989's 'Hey' – was generic in the way that all but the most inventive songs of Metal Urbain can nowadays seem a little samey; while the second forty-five, 1990's 'Animal Man', was (even with its catchy-bastard chorus: 'I'm an animal man/I love my shit') another too-safe bet achieved with a pickup rhythm section, limited studio time and no proper distribution from a tiny record company. But it's a safe bet that the real reason they were ignored is because no one else was in that headspace at the time. Gathered together across the two sides of an LP, these Manchakou dopes start to make sense.

'Rock'n'roll Is Such a Serious Thing'

Side One opens with the one and a half minutes of 'Murder', a classic sub-Stones bozo anthem in the Speed, Glue & Shinki tradition. It's a song which Brain Donor have covered. Over a too, too loud fuzz riff, Marc Duran declares, 'I'm walking down the street/And I'm looking for wild shit.' In the second verse, Duran's 'still walking down the street' as El Tel Tannier takes up the axe and reduces a few itinerant locals to a bloody pulp. Two minutes and it's gone.

Next up, with its raging warrior, wah-wah funk and repeated chorus of 'Antiseptic you', 'Sudden Bummer' is the aforementioned dead ringer for The New Order's 1975 epic 'Declaration of War'. This Manchakou track is barely contained by its even more extreme looped-up drumming than the MC5's Dennis Thompson was able to bring to Asheton's demented vision. Vocally, 'Sexy Sucky' is pure solo Alan Vega hiccuping his way through a seemingly endless glossary of throwaway clichéd asides, but performed over an almost *Spiral Scratch* buzz-saw ramalama, full of underachievingly simplistic but charming lead-guitar breaks, its relentless, fast-strummed rhythm guitar also echoing the Velvets' *1969* live LP.

With 'Cripple Death Dwarf Must Pay', the Manchakou finally hit the kind of long, monotonous, 'Pablo Picasso'-meets-'Mother Sky' drone-groove you always suspect may have been a part of their live set, but might not have made it to disc. Well, here 'tis in all its tunnel vision, replete with lupine howls right out of Joy Division's 'Interzone'; the sort of thing that Mono Man's DMZ could have done so magnificently, but in reality ('Don't Jump Me Mother' and 'When I Get Off' aside) served up all too occasionally. Marc Duran coughs up phlegm, cackles, almost barfs, then yells something about a mysterious 'freak who is running wild', and you get the impression it's the same underworld character as the dangerous sub-dude who often populated David Johansen's Dolls songs (especially 'Jet Boy' and 'Frankenstein').

Side One concludes with the one-minute-long 'Landlord', musically an astute *summum bonum* of the entire 1960s; something like The Stooges' 'Loose' conflated with a more compressed version of Can's 'Full Moon on the Highway' or White Heaven's classic 'Out'. And utilising Grace Slick's 'Greasy Heart' in a Sounds Incorporated-stylee never hurt my old band, The Teardrop Explodes, so I ain't about to rag on the Manchakou for doing precisely the same, because it remains a formula for reaching instant exhilaration.

Side Two kicks off with the ramalama of 'I Won't Break', its sole lyric being 'I won't break/And I don't care.' Yeah, Marc, whatever you say. Songs this straightforward dig such a simple trench of sound that the brief middle-section guitar solo comes over like a major work-out – that is, before Duran's hog-grunts and donkey-brays kick the main riff back in. Interestingly, the opening chords of the immaculately named 'Fucking with Four Eyes' sound like the kind of massive orchestral samples that Duran would employ in his later solo career. But, here we are, belting along down the same old highway, this time with a strange and frantic disco bass line. Then, the barely two-minute duration of the aforementioned 'Animal Man' gets about as pubescent as it could ever be, its lyrics being repetitions of the phrases 'I'm an animal man/I love my shit' and 'I'm an animal man/I love my dick.' More howls and raging guitar wipe-outs follow, and then they're gone. 'She Said' is a revamp of 'Sexy Sucky' and an obvious Duran fave, as he re-recorded it for a later solo LP.

Well under a half hour after it all began, this sole Electric Manchakou album finishes just as it started, with the humming-voiced 'human guitar' solo and rising, three-minute garage riff of their debut single 'Hey'. In context with the rest of the LP, this is an epic, its ascending guitar riff and overloaded chord-organ doing the American garage scene the way only Europeans appear able to do. It's inevitably over too soon and weez reduced to spinning the same disc again and again for our kicks. Damn.

Afterwards?

Subsequently, the tall and gangling Marc Duran relocated to Buenos Aires, where he nowadays makes weirdo, solo Krautrockesque records that sound somewhere midway between L. Voag's *The Way Out*, a more rock'n'roll Der Plan, and those bizarre Dieter Mobius/Conny Plank collaborations. Cut-up voices and even samples of *The Faust Tapes* resound over ambient ballads with beautiful female singing, often heftily undermined by reedy clarinets and/or Duran's adoption of an atonal tenor somewhat akin to Steve Martin's *Absent-Minded Waiter* voice. Elsewhere, eloquent strings, reminiscent of John Cale's *The Academy in Peril*, wander in then out, as electro-reggae pulses dementedly over pseudo-sexy vocals delivered in a Jane Birkin/Serge Gainsbourg style and double-tracked, sped-up, fake 'children' sing playground poems over which Duran intones in a deeply portentous, George Clinton/*Maggot Brain* voice.

Here and there, Manchakou tracks occasionally appear in dissolute form, and poems rise and scatter words around the place as chaos takes over. I've got three of these Duran solo LPs: 1997's *Ladies and Gent*, 2003's *Sturm und Drang* and 2004's *L'Amour Trash*; each contains much of excellence, although virtually nothing is left of the muse that informed his Electric Manchakou days.

Marc Duran's is one of the most singular solo trips I've come across, and majorly supports the case for the Manchakou having been unfairly written off at the time as Stooges clones. Indeed, rather like Washington State's Tight Bro's from Way Back When, Electric Manchakou appear to have been created by a pair of deep thinkers who intentionally set out to make the world think they was a bunch of dummies. Nice.

Discography

Electric Manchakou:
'Hey' b/w 'She Said'/'Murder' (single, Innocent, 1989)
'Animal Man' b/w 'I Won't Break'/'Landlord' (single, Helter Skelter, 1990)
Electric Manchakou (Spirit of Punk, 1993)

Marc Duran:
Ladies and Gent (Innocent, 1997)
Sturm und Drang (Innocent, 2003)
L'Amour Trash (Innocent, 2004)

Factrix

Scheintot

(Adolescent Records, 1981)

SIDE ONE	SIDE TWO
1 Eerie Lights (4.05)	1 Over My Shoulder (And Out of My Life) (3.10)
2 Heavy Breathing (4.58)	2 Ballad of the Grim Rider (4.17)
3 Center of the Doll (4.56)	3 Snuff Box (4.43)
4 Thin Line (2.20)	4 Phantom Pain (5.05)
5 Anemone Housing (2.21)	

Gothedelick K.O.

Travelling through the USA with The Teardrop Explodes during the years 1980–82, and always in a psychedelic condition, I was strongly aware, through my meetings with umpteen kohl-eyed, LSD-informed, edge-of-towners, that the more extreme elements of the West Coast American underground were in the process of appropriating many facets (both musically fundamental and sartorially stylistic) of the equivalent English and New York scenes; but subsuming them all into a uniquely 'Gothadelick' melange of their very own. And so it was that on the terrifically heatful American Pacific coast, incongruous long macs and the Germanic funk of the northern English scene came to be conflated with the more obviously Banshees/Cure-ified darkness and dyed black hair of the post-punk south of England, and the wailing, wall-eyed, immediately post-Blank Generation stares of arch NYC, so-jazz smackies, to manifest in San Francisco as groups such as Patrick Miller's disturbing Minimal Man and Messrs Bergland, Jacobs and Palme's even more disturbing Factrix.

Alongside such artists as Monte Cazazza and Boyd Rice, the aforementioned were responsible for creating unearthly and unexpectedly vampiric blends of A Certain Ratio's 'All Night Party' forty-five, Throbbing Gristle's 'Slugbait', Cabaret Voltaire's canon of Krautdub, the Detroit rock-through-an-*Eraserhead* filter of Chrome, the *No New York*, do-nothing distorto-epic that was Mars circa 'Hairwaves', and the micro-orbiting dirges of Pere Ubu's 'My Dark Ages', 'Chinese Radiation' and 'Laughing', etc. If the *Edward Scissorhands* soundtrack had been supplied by Hollywood musos using Factrix's *Scheintot* LP as their blueprint, it would have created a perfect snapshot of the hairbrushed, post-punk twilight zone that was the '70s/'80s gateway.

Unfortunately, however, Factrix's wonderfully greedy metaphor was undermined by their sheer extremeness. Despite opening their career with the amazing industrial funk assault of their debut single, 'Empire of Passion', Factrix wasn't ever gonna be a singles band. Coming across like English post-punks playing an all-night Final Solution gig at the Acklam Hall, they really shoulda been treading the same stages as Clock DVA, pragVEC, early Manicured Noise (pre-Steve Walsh version) and their ilk in order to get anywhere. From my own experiences from late '78 onwards, those were days when Fast Product-style bands made three or four singles before they started to make a dent in anyone's consciousness. The intense rivalry spurred people on, but Factrix was six thousand miles from where the boys were.

True, Bergland and Palme had begun life as part of Patrick Miller's Minimal Man project, playing four shows in that configuration, but even the rivalry generated after their split was never gonna be enough fuel for their flames. From the gathered evidence, even after supporting such illuminati as Cabaret Voltaire, Arto Lindsay's screechy DNA and Australian ur-primitives SPK (SoliPsiK), the overall Factrix career was apparently such a downer that it temporarily destroyed the mind of each member and saw them return from their only tour homeless and (it is said) destitute. Unfathomable and unlistenable to all but the most ardent adepts (and subscribers to the Sordide Sentimentale label, natch) at a time when almost everyone in the real underground had at least opened their ears to accommodate the coming industrial sounds, the Factrix trio's miniscule output and often almost rhythmless take on all of the above-mentioned artists made the group virtually unreachable; so much so, indeed, that they have become forgotten over the past decades and not even been celebrated with a CD re-release until very recently[1] – and even then not in their original musical sequences.

Both Sides of the Portal

However, time itself is the real judge of true art, and those *No New York* 'art terrorists' are now no more than the archaic fart feasts of yesteryear – temporary jazz sneezes into an already too-damp snot rag. The dismembered music of Factrix, on the other hand, grows more contemporary by the year. And, as their sole LP, *Scheintot*, is as genuinely disturbing and richly disorientating a piece of death-warmed-up as you would ever wish to investigate, I figured now was the time – in these post-Khanatean days – to heft some of its drum-box, death-ray drool your way.

While Factrix was a handsome trio of black-clad Jim-Morrison-on-a-Robert-Smith-trip, deathly post-punks from inner space, playing bizarre, subterranean cemetery non-blues, it was an incredibly precise piece of genius to name their debut LP *Scheintot,* for this is the German equivalent of 'suspended animation' or a 'state of apparent death' – describing the muse-sick of Factrix perfectly. Indeed, Factrix could never have been described as 'drum-machine-driven' in the early-Bunnymen/Sisters of Mercy manner; quite the opposite, in fact. For, while the Scythian guitar of Bond Bergland, the burbling electronic effects of Cole Palme and bouncing octave bass of Joseph Jacobs often created their own propulsion, the drum-box itself often stuttered and spluttered against the beat like some sweating office junior inappropriately and unconsciously plucking at his boss' Newton's Cradle during an important office meeting.

In the midst of all this sonic catering, the interplay between the voices of Bergland, Palme and Jacobs added another horizon of sound, simultaneously human and inhuman, as one band member narrated from the front line while the other

1 Released at the beginning of 2003 by Germany's Storm Records, the double-CD set *Artifact* includes the whole of the *Scheintot* LP on the first disc, commencing with their forty-five debut, 'Empire of Passion', and its B-side, 'Spice of Life'. Terminally disorientating and zoned out of its tiny mind, this package reveals many of the tricks that those few *Scheintot* fans could have only guessed at down the years. The photographic sequence that led Monte Cazazza to his final LP cover shot is particularly arresting.

two sung, droned, intoned and plainsonged (plainsung?) together. Like a scene from *Poltergeist*, Factrix music conjures up the disjointed sounds of a haunted house with perpetually bizarre goings-on, as increasingly bored TV journalists narrate the previous day's activities from the safety of the garden gate. It was these simultaneously personal and impersonal perspectives that drove the Factrix muse on and on.

But that weren't nearly enough for these Poe-faced kiddies; no, dear me no. These druids had to go umpteen seven-league-boot strides further and illustrate the back cover of their LP sleeve with a tomb-rubbing from the back of Ralph Hamsterley's bizarre, sixteenth-century Oxfordshire grave at the chillingly named Doddington ('farm ['ton'] at the judgement centre ['ting'] of the dead ['dod']'). Then they had their sinister mate, Monte Cazazza (himself a twilighter supreme), set up a front-cover photograph that involved a naked female friend seemingly being disrobed by an ancient skeletal hand so perished that wire was necessary to clamp them dry bones together. Obviously informed by Mik Mellen's bizarrely unfinished Cleveland industrial photographs of the mid-to-late '70s, this half-seen-through-a-semi-closed-door vision of their world propels the listener into a dream landscape somewhat akin to that sacred phantom downland conjured up on The Residents' *Not Available.*

'It Was Taking Us to Some Very Dark Places'

For the creation of the ultimate possible form of rock'n'roll music, I've always reckoned on needing a balance of about sixty-five percent tradition to about thirty-five novelty. In this way, your song can still be propelled along by a candy-assed cliché of a hook line that everyone reckons to have heard a zillion times before (the traditional element), because the context in which that cliché finds itself is unbalanced enough to bring something entirely new to the party (the novelty element). The greatest purveyors of rock'n'roll always seem to have adhered to this formula: Suicide, Prince, Outkast being great cases in point, with The Velvet Underground still being urpractitioners of the Ult.

However, such simplistic rules go right out of the window when addressing the so-called experimental music scene. Indeed, I'd probably have to go simultaneously in both of the other directions if asked to make the case for presenting *The Alchemical Instruction Book for the Optymum*

Methodes of Reachyng Most Effectyve Experimental Musics, and say that travelling along the way marked 'one hundred percent cliché' is possibly even more effective than the route that follows the signpost reading 'one hundred percent novelty'. In other words, just as Kimmy the Fowl's *Outrageous* was a spoof psychedelic death and resurrection trip that still functioned as the real thing, so, in the same way, can true psychedelic disorientation be genuinely achieved simply by putting together a rigorous assortment of such obvious ingredients as Sabbath doom chord changes and Hammer horror sound-effects, weak-shit bubbling drum-boxes, portentous Lizard King proclamations, squirrly analogue ARP-ness and Brion Gysin-style early cut-up doomalogues about rotten and drowned muses; all of it done while wearing white face, black clothes and hairstyles à la Tristan Tzara. Which is why Factrix, a trip forged entirely from slugs and snails and puppy-dogs tails, can be so successful artistically *and* useful psychically. Yup, even if it's ultimately just a Pyrrhic victory for rock'n'roll, listening to 'Horse Latitudes' as performed by autistic adolescents in Charles Manson's box-room is always gonna be a worthwhile exercise to your most seasoned inner space traveller.

Taking a look at the Factrix trio's instrument list (and the manner in which it is described) is itself a journey through their own prolapsing minds:

Bond Bergland: guitars, vocals, tape treatments, viola, radioguitar, percussion, drum machine, processing, zither, teakettle.
Cole Palme: vocals, glaxobass, multimoog, tape treatments, drum machine, processing, amputated bass.
Joseph Jacobs: bass guitar, fretless bass, drum machine, vocals, tape treatments, pennywhistle, migh-wiz, saz, doumbek, flute, percussion.

Like the early Chrome experiments, to which guitarists John Lambdin and Gary Spain often added disconnected, droning electric violins, the many defocusing elements offered by this floating Factrix line-up disabled the listeners' ability to judge the music on any level other than the effect of the overall sound. Indeed, so disconnected was the Factrix sonic stew that sometimes the only graspable and protruding reference point (perhaps a doomy guitar hook, or maybe a repeated yet still unearthly vocal) instantly became massive and almost poppy to the listener, purely because it was being made by something from within the realms of their own experiences. It's a bit like those Residents-produced

Snakefinger records that came out on Ralph Records around 1978, insofar as we all imagined his phantom backing band to be ghostly, unreachable alien Muppets, but at least Snakefinger himself was a guitarist/singer, albeit one who inhabited cartoon landscapes.

Admittedly, *Scheintot* is hardly the kind of LP that should be given a song-by-song description, save to say that, in context, 'Ballad of the Grim Rider' sounds like a Top Ten hit merely because it has a graspable form (and don't get me started on the Odinist imagery that pervades their entire oeuvre). But *Scheintot* is a record that deserves to be experienced several times, preferably in the darkness and in a state of near exhaustion (and/or informed by psychoactive chemicals). Its only failure, in the dark light of the early twenty-first century, is in being a half-hour too short – and even that could be remedied by several back-to-back airings without overly wearing out the (so-called) hook lines.

Sitting some way between Germany's ultra-playful Der Plan and Throbbing Gristle's Gen-driven death music, the underlying, heart-beating non-groove that informs all Factrix music is always a truly human one; a beeping crab-skank that takes you forever two steps forward and three steps back. But, if you accept the Factrix metaphor of suspended animation and give yourself to *Scheintot*'s unyielding form, you will soon reach below the incurably arch vocals into a pre-temple-building, nomadic (and still-glacial) netherworld somewhere close to that archaic place where the Frost Giants played and the Trickster kept his prick stuffed into a box that he carried around on his back. Let me take you down, 'cause I'm going too!

Discography

'Empire of Passion' b/w 'Splice of Life' (single, Adolescent, 1980)

'Prescient Dreams' b/w 'Zanoni' (with Monte Cazazza) (single, Subterranean, 1983)

Scheintot (Adolescent, 1981)

California Babylon (with Monte Cazazza) (Subterranean, 1982)

Artifact (Tesco, 2003)

Two tracks ('Night to Forget' and 'Subterfuge') appear on the compilation *Live on Target* (Subterranean, 1980)

Melvins

Lysol

(Boner Records, 1992)

1 Hung Bunny (10.59)
2 Roman Bird Dog (7.60)
3 Sacrifice (6.07)
4 Second Coming (1.15)
5 The Ballad of Dwight Fry (3.10)
6 With Teeth (2.67)

For Melvinites Only? No, Unless All Shall Be Melvinite!

In 1992, with the release of *Lysol*, Melvins nailed the ritual for the next decade. For, as primo anarcheologists of the sub-sub-culture, it was Dale Crover and Buzz Osbourne who located the order in which the next frontiers should be tackled; they who beat the bounds, as it were, lassoed all the disparate ingredients and shoved them into the big rock pie for younger brothers Sleep and school-mates Earth – Zen ur-slackers, hitching a ride in the snug back-pack of Thor. But whereas Earth seems nowadays slow in a slothful way (a pitcher of Tennent's washing down the largactyl), *Lysol* was metaphysically immense and exerted intense tectonic pressure, like some five-day, heavy-metal cricket match, with Lemmy bowling and Philthy Phil as crazy-eyed wicket-keeper. Tossing a hail of concussion grenades through Buzzo's permanent flame-thrower of sound, Dale Crover is four drummers at the best of times. But, on *Lysol*, he was joined in the rhythm battalion by the Generalissimo of bass military coups, Mein Hairy Joe Preston.[1] And so they shall wear ye down . . .

Lysol was the new fundament, the new archetype, sealed by druids and delivered via Olmec hunchback

1 Joe Preston's mythical place in the ritual forecourt of the Melvins was guaranteed simply because they put their Kiss-styled solo LPs out round about the same time as *Lysol*.

(the good-luck variety, natch). But, despite the shock of *Lysol*'s affronting newness, Melvins somewhat sugared their colossus by the inclusion of superb versions of Flipper's 'Sacrifice' and Alice Cooper's 'The Ballad of Dwight Fry'. Despite this, *Lysol* was still essentially one enormous and segmented creation, fashioned from an unfolding and non-linear (and in places skeletal) performance that ebbed and flowed, dipped and swayed, and used, at all times, incredible dynamic ranges. Consider the vast tidal waves of sound that pummel and permeate this record and understand the enormity of a rock act so confident that it dared, in '92, to begin its new album with seven minutes and fifty seconds of virtually unaccompanied Tony Iommi-isms: wave upon wave of them. It's not the difference between Kiss and Super Kiss, motherfuckers. I ain't simply talking Ace's new shoulder pads here. It's the next evolutionary stage, between Super Kiss and Supra Kiss, that weird and cosmic other time around Kiss's brilliant but arch super-flop, *Music from 'The Elder'*.

Like Starchild Paul and the Gene around the time of the aforementioned LP, Melvins, at the time of *Lysol*, understood themselves better than ever; indeed, well enough to make rigorous demands of their audience. Again, I cry, who else with any career expectations whatsoever in 1992 released records that commenced with virtually unaccompanied, free-form guitar riffery that demanded eight minutes of concentrated listening from their bedroom audiences? That's right, motherfuckers, no one at all. When *Lysol* was released, Melvins intuitively knew that they were at the top of their game. Hey, that's why they chose that name. *Lysol*, fer Chrissakes . . . the stuff is a killer, a drain clearer that destroys in a slow, disgustingly painful way. Lysol killed one of my all-time heroes: American poet Vachel Lindsay drank the stuff. And naming the record thus almost killed it for the Melvins when the Lysol Company threatened to sue. In retreat and hastily recalling the LPs, then taping over or magic-markering out the offending name, Melvins were shocked but relieved to discover they soon had a cult on their hands.

Like all the greatest shamanic art, this record operates between worlds . . . many worlds, and the *Zoso/Led Zeppelin IV*-style album title mix-up only increased this mythical effect. Was the record still called *Lysol* or was it now just *The Melvins*? With remarkably poetic justice (for both the artists and the rock'n'roll audience), the righteously formed sonic ritual of *Lysol* has turned out to be most surely Melvins' most pivotal recording of all. For this record was, in 1992, most serpently the new rock'n'roll blueprint, and – although already twenty years old – will continue for many more years of active service. Follow its moods and directions and you will have half an hour of high ritual at your fingertips.

Treat it with reverence, and keep it away from other records, even those made by Melvins themselves. Keep it next to other unique, alchemical prescriptions such as Sleep's *Jerusalem*, Blue Cheer's *Vincebus Eruptum* and Black Sabbath's *Master of Reality*, and use it as often as is required. Oh, and remember, chil'en, if you are going to buy just one Melvins record for your collection, be sure you make this the one.

Before I quit, please allow me a moment for a flight of fancy, if you have the time. I wanna try to place Melvins in their correct context, if you will. And I'll first need a little bit of historical to and fro and overview, too . . .

OK, as ye heathen with a grievance against the organised religion and a belief in the will of rock'n'rollers and other activists to change things, it's my estimation that by the mid-2050s, the Way of Sabbath will have become recognised by society as a strange but acceptable route for a young heathen man to follow. The mass return of organised religion in the early twenty-first century will inevitably have spurred true rebels and stimulated refuseniks to defy the incoming conservatism by acts of flagrancy and non-collective thinking. And some will inevitably fight religion by making their own beliefs into a religion. For example, another most useful route for the Western artist would be the Way of the MC5, a warrior troubadour route ideal for troubled, adventurous young men whose ideals involve an excess of moral fibre and individual bravery.[2] Even hardy outsider heathens would start to consider the possibilities, as the government, recognising the Zeitgeist and themselves raised on loud rebel music, cut tax breaks to those who admit to practising 'rock'n'roll'.

Guaranteed, in this new reality that I'm imagining, would be an almost equally important religious path known as the 'Way of Buzz'n'Dale'. Yup, in forty years time, Melvins will be up there with

2 The MC5 will also be prime architects of the new temple rituals, for it was they who recognised the power of drama with their unique melding of political rally and soul revue.

the true greats, celebrated as part of the All-Time for their outstanding (and sustained) services to Gnostic rock'n'roll. Sustaining any long artistic career in a heightened state is problematic, but the Melvins – regardless of many lean artistic periods – have always eventually risen/sunk into shamanistic newness, reborn again and again. Melvins are a sect diabolick, a gateway, a divine portal between innumerable worlds, an outrageously confident and worthy cosmic interface between punk, post-punk and Sabbathian heavy metal; a gateway between accepted classic dark-rock, Kiss/Alice/'Green Manalishi'-stylee,[3] and the far-flung future (i.e. *now*, motherfuckers). They were 'Standing outside the boundaries of rock'n'roll and aiming their sounds inside,' as Greil Marcus once put it. And *Lysol* is Melvins' greatest and most sacred gift to future heathens, for its tones and vibrations, taken together often and in large doses, offer listeners the key to Eternal Cuntedness.

3 Melvins have also covered Kiss' epic 'Going Blind', from *Hotter Than Hell*, as well as one of my all-time pre-teen favourites, 'The Green Manalishi', Peter Green's last note to the world before he descended into hell.

Van Halen

Atomic Punks

(Oscar Records, 1982)

SIDE ONE	SIDE TWO
1 On Fire	1 Somebody Get Me a Doctor
2 Feel Your Love Tonight	2 Ain't Talkin' 'bout Love
3 Runnin' with the Devil	3 Eruption
4 Atomic Punk	4 D.O.A.
5 Little Dreamer	5 You Really Got Me

Although it's obvious that the optimum deal I coulda dealt ya woulda been a thorough and cohesive analysis of the first four Van Halen LPs, I gotta say a number of things precluded my doing so. For a start, although *Women and Children First* and *Fair Warning* are both virtually faultless records, it's gotta be said that *Van Halen II* was a monumental fudge that took about eight months too long to record, and (although it contains some great songs) I simply never listen to the thing. Secondly, magnificent as the first LP is, in resequencing it for the remastered series, so that the three strongest tracks now open the record, it is not only proof that Warners and Van Halen themselves got it wrong the first time, but hell, it almost makes the thing an entirely new record. While 'Runnin' with the Devil' is just about the greatest (and most bass-heavy) career opener of the 1970s, if it's taken the protagonists over twenty-five years to realise what every Van Halen head always intuitively knew when making C90 comps for mates – that is, following 'Runnin' with the Devil' with 'Atomic Punk' and 'On Fire' – then should they have really bothered at this late stage? Personally, I think they should have said 'sod it' and left well alone. I mean, however shrill and ridiculous the lead vocal is, would you – at this late stage – accept the metaphor of resequencing *Kick Out the Jams* without 'Rambling Rose' opening the LP? Isn't resequencing a neurotic something that should be confined to the beginning of careers?

The third and most obvious reason for not reviewing all four of the main sequence of LPs is the reappearance of this old *Atomic Punks* vinyl bootleg in two other forms, first as *Young and Wild*, then as *Pasadena Partyslammers* on New Jersey's highly prolific Seidr label. So why bother? Hell, you get great versions of songs from the first LP and they even do justice to 'Somebody Get Me a Doctor'! Awl-fucking-righty!

'Humans Are Always at Their Best When They're Ascending Towards Something'

The great thing about this *Atomic Punks* LP was always the way the rhythm guitar dropped out when the solos came in, leaving the mogadon bass of Michael Anthony as sole supporter of the song's chord sequence, thereby rendering Edward Van Halen's shards of shattering-Red Arrows-windscreen guitar aerobatics less Olympian and more Lokian. To be fair, much of the first studio LP did just this and gained hugely from the cast-adrift element of chaos that it brought to the party. But as an antidote to the parts that got rhythm-guitar support (as on the second LP), this *Atomic Punks* bootleg reveals what a freeform racket they could brew up. Man, the amazingly confident harmony vocals sound even greater when you've lost all sense of their context.

I tell you, this boot is the proof that if the Japanese free-rock brigade could only get together with a twenty-first century Mann/Weill or Chinnichap for a coupla days, we'd all be down on our padded, elasticated, high-kicking hands'n'knees with gratitude – or my name ain't Britney Houston. But afore we appraise *Atomic Punks*, a quick mench for just how we should approach it. Because this lot are a right mystery, and as many of you will *not* be down with Van Halen, I want y'all to be in on the collusion. So, first, I should clue ya to avoid collision.

By Defining, Then Accepting Your Metaphor, Your Restrictions Will Release You

Zep did it with 'D'yer Mak'er', The Stooges did it with 'We Will Fall', Kiss did it with 'Beth' and Van Halen did it with 'Ice Cream Man'. That is, they stepped outside their own self-imposed boundaries and brutalised their own metaphor. Of course,

Queen did it so often they transcended every genre and got what they deserved/demanded – and played Sun City. But the point here is that the success of the best Van Halen records is all alchemical; that is, they only failed *when* they stepped outside the metaphor. So long as the songs contained the pre-determined codes – off-kilter riffs, amelodic, chromatic strato-guitar solos, showmanic, look-at-me vocals and faultline-punishing ur-bass – Van Halen *could not* fail. If they had a problem at all, it was just that they had two shamans in one group and both shamen were showmen. For, as K. Rasmussen asserted in his 1929 book *Intellectual Culture of the Iglulik Eskimos*: 'Every great shaman must, when asked and when a number of people are present, exercise his art in miraculous fashion in order to astonish the people and convince them of the sacred and inexplicable powers of the shaman.'

I ask you, is it just me, or was the brevity of the first four Van Halen LPs (generally about sixteen minutes per side) for some deeper shamanic reason? Were they displays rather than entertainments, in the same manner that the Jesus and Mary Chain's early 'shows' were really displays, thereby setting them beyond judgement by being only fifteen minutes in length? Did (Warners in-house producer) Ted Templeman get to produce them because he was their Mr Bollocks, or was it because his name revealed him to be a temple-man? I mean, this sucker weren't no rawk guy; he'd even produced Beefheart's soul LP, *Clear Spot*. And did Ted get credited as 'Tad' Templeman on the label of *Fair Warning* because of some band in-joke that his production technique was (perhaps in some very ancient Keltic manner) turning him into the 'tad', or father, of the group?

I ask these questions because, reading David Lee Roth's autobiography, *Crazy from the Heat*, back in 1999, I was surprised at the sheer depth of mystical understanding that he had brought to a supposedly intuitive rock muse. He wrote about getting down on his hands and knees and scrubbing every arena stage before a show, just so he'd have a direct relationship with the wood on which he danced. Roth wrote about Alex and Edward Van Halen goofing on him and telling him there were people in the organisation to do that shit for him, but Roth still had to do it at every show. And yet here was a man who'd spent his whole career giving the impression to the public that to have been seen to have been emitting anything less than a truly transcendental shallowness at all times would have meant appearing before the Great Wazzir of the Things that Creep Guild and having his 'Licence to Dry Wank' revoked. Here was a man whose determination to haze the line between womaniser and woman-molester allowed almost no one with their own IQ to even approach his band's music without severe inner questioning; whose bound and chained god-self (photographed by Helmut Newton, no less, rather than rock-aristocracy snapper Ross Halfin) appeared on a three-by-four feet poster in all copies of *Women and Children First*, and whose slavish commitment to his deplorably self-serving Dave TV schtick got him ejected from the group he so obviously adored playing with.

Man, I love the guy for all of it. Like my old neighbour, Pete Burns, who could argue with me for fully forty-five minutes about how The Electras' version of 'Action Woman' kicked The Litter's version into hyperspace, then pout with adolescent ennui and whine about his nail polish when Will Sergeant joined in the very same discussion, David Lee Roth is just one of those guys who not only always knew his place in the cosmos, but – more to the point – also knew his *perceived* place in the cosmos and weren't gonna be shifted for no fucker.

In contrast, Edward Van Halen would just let his guitar speak on his behalf. Indeed, when he played lead on Michael Jackson's 'Beat It', the first anyone in the band knew was when it was announced on the radio after first being aired. And, when we speak of Edward's singular guitar genius, we ain't even talking beyond the fretboard itself. Hell, this geek's day-care ideas for instant, packing-tape guitar decoration will run the bills up over close to a fiver if Van Halen ever get to album number sixty.

But maybe, in spite of their differences, David Lee Roth and Edward Van Halen were two Lokian faces of the same fire god, with Edward playing the Logi for Marty McFly, when he needs to 'persuade' his teenage father, in *Back to the Future*, by utilising the entirely freeform 'Eruption'. That's why dear old Dave TV is crazy from the heat on the photocopied cover of *Atomic Punks* – his buns are scorched from the burning Logi behind him.

Proglodytes of Pre-ecstatic Euphoria

This album, recorded at the Pasadena Civic Auditorium, on December 29 1977, opens superbly with simultaneous whoops from Roth, a cheering audience, splatter-chatter drums and a harried MC (already ducking from the dive-bombing guitar and) declaring a state of rock'n'roll. 'On Fire' cranks up its post-Sir Lord Baltimore riff-upon-riff-upon-further-riff-castellated attack, the Garneresque *'figh-yar'*, fire-fight operetta and hither'n'yon chaos riffola all immediately better than the fantastic album version (especially as the Attisian backing vocals of the hugely unsung Michael Anthony are note-for-eunuchised-note perfect). Indeed, without the ideal studio setting, Lord Edward's harmonic, in-between riff is more Manuel Göttsching than expected, and all the better for it, dammit, especially as Roth is 'Hangin' ten now, baby/ As I write your sonnet' . . . OK, so he could be singing 'ride your sonic wave', as some have claimed, but listen up, Shakespeare, ain't it far more likely that Roth would be writing proto-wipe-out poetry to his mystery muse?

The braying-ass guitar riff of 'Feel Your Love Tonight' is soon propelling us into equally cartoon, post-coitally nostrilled lead vocals, with backing vocals so wonderfully unbalanced and overachieving that they rival Scott Thurston's over-rehearsed and over-expectant vocal moves on *Metallic K.O.* (Who was drooling whom, there? I mean, expecting to harmonise vocally with Iggy, in 1974? In those days, harmony for Iggy meant not setting fire to the stage.)

Next up, 'Runnin' with the Devil' is almost as hollering-from-the-deepest-fjord as the album version, but as its spirit in concert (so driven by the sheer abandon of Alex's hi-hat assault) can't hope to emulate the almost *Closer*-like atmosphere of the record, we gotta be satisfied with this merely terrific version. 'Atomic Punk' is just magnificent, despite the beginning being marred by Edward's lead cutting out and the stutter-riff uttering a stuttering too far. However, as the lead breaks throughout this song are just about the greatest union of melody, yawp and cosmic fitfulness he ever achieved, it's righteous to hear that (even in the face of perfection) there remain within Edward several extra squalls of thang still to be fashioned upon each riff. Then Alex knocks out a competent drum solo and they're off into the last track on Side One.

The strange, upside-down cabaret-soul of 'Little Dreamer' always seemed to me like Las Vegas Dread Zeppelin in blackface. The backing vocals are just 'too, too, too to put a finger on', but you gotta question a metal band that can 'shooby-dooby' as well as Van Halen. Especially as, in hindsight, it's all too easy to blame Roth, but here, at the close of Side

One, it ain't him sumptuousising in the background.

Side Two opens by sucking us into the Sir Lord Baltimorean 'Somebody Get Me a Doctor'. Freed from its second-album bondage and fixed with a six-inch syringe full of the good John Garner juice, what a heathen racket this is! I mean, this song is just a festival of utter confusion – I wish I didn't know it and I'm jealous of those who might be being introduced to this song for the first time via this particular version.

'Ain't Talking 'bout Love' is where the garage meets the heavy-rock. The guitar solo is pure We the People and the riff is pure 'Don't Fear the Reaper' as played by Montrose. Again, the studio version had a strange, otherworldly atmosphere that no concert could capture, but this is redressed by the sheerly polished, sabrine finish of the metal exoskeleton they've fitted to this concert version. Meanwhile, 'Eruption' is a thing of even greater concert beauty than on the record. It's longer, too – more braying and mule-like, far less Frehleyan and far more Blackmorean than I'd previously supposed (although about thirty times faster when you actually do the sonic comparisons). And every fucking note is there, too . . . Edward Van Halen! Edward Van Halen!

'D.O.A.' comes in as raw as Nishinihon, or any of your favourites on *Bleach*, or Baltimore's 'Pumped Up', with scattershot guitar flying around the auditorium like there's two guitars playing the riff. After all this reconciliation of the late '70s with the early '70s, it's actually quite a weird scene to hear them encore with The Kinks' 'You Really Got Me'. I was never a particularly big fan of their version on the first LP, purely because it seemed out of context – but here it fits in like UFO's raw early take on Bo Diddley's 'Who Do You Love'.

And so endeth the record; as per usual with Van Halen, far too soon. But the phenomenon has been sighted if not closely inspected, and we at least have the luxury of spinning this sucker all over again from the start.

And Another Fucking Thing . . .

Now, what we need is a whole bunch of poorly recorded concerts from the *Women and Children First* and *Fair Warning* period, preferably with vocals way loud and guitar to the moon. Dammit, we need a Les Rallizes Dénudés-style, ten-CD box with twenty-three versions of 'On Fire' and a Neil Young/*Arc*-ified, multimelded, twenty-five-minute 'Eruption'. After those first four LPs, Van

Halen's last two records with Roth fell so far outside their own metaphor that it was like they'd never ever had it writ in blood on the walls of their clubhouse. *Diver Down* was bar-band filler of the most abject variety (how can I live without more covers of 'Pretty Woman', 'Dancing in the Street' and 'Where Have All the Good Times Gone'?), while the curious *1984* expected us to accept the wholesale metaphor change from Guitar Eddie to Synth Eddie and suck on 'Jump''s Genesis-play-The Who-by-numbers. And although it was unfortunate (but not tragic) that Dave TV fell the wrong side of the shaman/showman line, there were at least plenny of similar cases down the rock'n'roll path to allow fans to prepare themselves for Roth's, erm, TV personality. Moreover, after the initial glitz blitz of incredible acrobatic stunts and wall-hangings, it was pretty clear that Dave TV weren't ever gonna be scraped off the side of Mount Rushmore and brung down in a stars'n'stripes body bag. The guy was just too good at his schtick.

So, engulf your ears at the spinning, silvered doorway that was Van Halen until 1982, and grab any/all C90s of their early shows (preferably recorded with compressor mic, natch) to swim in the rich sonic imbalance that their myth-straddling muse provided. For, as Roth wrote in *Crazy from the Heat*: 'We are always at our best when we're ascending towards something.'

As a former turtle-shell-wearing amphibian, I don't entirely agree with that; but I'm more than happy to accept the guy's metaphor.

Essential Discography

Van Halen (Warners, 1977)
Van Halen II (Warners, 1980)
Women and Children First (Warners, 1980)
Fair Warning (Warners, 1980)

First LP-period bootlegs
Atomic Punks
Pasadena Partyslammers
Young and Wild

The 1990s

As my enlightenment on the night of 22 December 1989 CE coincided rather nicely with the fall of Margaret Thatcher via the April 1990 poll-tax protest, of which I – or rather Sqwubbsy – was such a large part, the '90s kicked off for me with such a flourish and a flash that its political broadsides were colossal enough to echo personally throughout the coming decade, nourishing and nibbling away at popular culture through road protests, animal-rights activism and the like. Hell, I even got to present *Top of the Pops* with Newbury bypass protesters, causing more viewer complaints even than that dude from Cameo's codpiece. No shittttt! The programme producer was demoted to radio, no shitttt! Anyhow, my shamanic self and my political self having been birthed virtually together (or certainly over consecutive months) in those early days of 1990, it has become impossible for me, therefore, ever to disassociate one from the other. And so the early '90s is for me an inspirational place full of strung-out dudes clad in fluorescent yellows, fluorescent oranges, beads, hats-on-backwards, the lot. It's been noted that the '60s didn't really start until 1963, and didn't retreat until 1973. Evidence of the shittiness of the '80s is right here, therefore, in the virtual Revolutionary State that UK youth found itself in at the onset of the '90s. Running out of the '80s they were, kiddies! Running! Running like the wind away from that fucking grey, expressionless, death-camp selfishness.

Copendium's musical representatives of the '90s could, therefore, be seen as a thorny problem. For none has a political motive or motif, unless you class Psychick TV's *Kondole* as a soundtrack for that righteous period when Genesis and Paula P-Orridge were picketing Brighton Dolphinarium. But as I scan these '90s reviews more carefully, then so does the personal politics of each one of these singular artists reveal itself, for each one of my '90s entries was performed by Truth Seekers for whom Kapitalist remuneration was barely a consideration. And safe it is to say that, with the sad exception of VON LMO, each and every artist contained in this section has surfed the twenty-first century successfully thus far. Moreover, several of them have turbo-charged their trips considerably. On downsizing to a duo, the now-guitarless Sleep trio extended their Sabbathian meditations still further and became the righteously titled Om. Monoshock devolved into Liquorball, into Bad Trips, into anything Grady Runyan wanted, and all of it continues to be of hefty use. The previously AC/DC-obsessed Tight Bro's from Way Back When devolved into the spellbinding Nudity, their extraordinary singer recently migrating to the still awesome Melvins. My favourite changeling of the '90s pack, however, remains our lad P-Orridge, whose current guise as Dionysian frontman is as successful as it is unlikely. That will to be what you wish to be, babies. That will to be what you *will* be.

The Badgeman

Ritual Landscape

(Paperhouse Records, 1992)

SIDE ONE	SIDE TWO
1 Grey Area (8.25)	1 Seethe Shanty (4.29)
2 Liturgy (5.33)	2 Auto Da Fé (6.04)
3 Black Song (9.38)	3 Tumuli (3.57)
	4 Swarm (13.53)

I've attempted to make this record Album of the Month on two other occasions, but both times I was eventually dissuaded at the eleventh hour because the lead vocals seemed to let the overall sound down. However, throughout the years I've come back to this record again and again, and, on each return, I've always played the whole thing through and found it to be totally life-affirming. So it seems to me that the singing may only appear to be weak nowadays because most of the music I listen to is replete with vocals of the full-on, howling-at-the-moon variety. Judge for yourselves, of course, but listen to the sound as a whole and the noise this quartet unleashes on *Ritual Landscape* is surely right up there with most of the so-called best post-punk music thus far released.

South Wiltshire's The Badgeman took their name from the mysterious figure (said to be) standing behind the bushes upon the infamous 'grassy knoll' which overlooked the stretch of Dallas highway on which J.F.K. was assassinated. Some conspiracy theorists, believing that they could see the glint of a police badge there in the foliage, concluded that the president's death was not the work of Lee Harvey Oswald but of 'The Badgeman'.

Awake from Your Dreams and See What You've Done

For the Gnostic rock'n'roller, i.e. those of us whose long-term obsessions with electric rock music are primarily concerned with unleashing the wild spirit within us, not by running to epiphany via the safety of some long-established religious system (Christianity, Buddhism, Islam, etc.), nor by following some even dodgier New Age cult (Wicca, Kabbalah, etc.), but, instead, by activating the godlike higher self within us by dancing, sweating, moshing, drugging and head-banging our moronic lower selves into righteous oblivion, I would suggest that The Badgeman's *Ritual Landscape* is of major use to us on two important counts. Firstly, repeated listening to the music contained within these grooves will take you precisely where you need to go (that is, 'above' and 'below', simultaneously); and secondly, it is a splendid symbol of how rock'n'rollers can, when they put their collective psyches together, push each other into achieving at least twenty times more than they had achieved previously.

For not only was this remarkable *Ritual Landscape* album an incredibly cohesive and spectacularly rigorous artistic statement, but – even more remarkably – it was also brought forth from the most unexpected of quarters. The album was delivered in 1992 by the same four young men whose releases of the previous two years (on album, single and EP) had been barely worthy of comment; neither good nor bad, but certainly never previously containing anything more than a spirited hogwash of late-'60s and late-'70s-informed bedsit, indie-girl-song pleasantries entirely in keeping with the rest of this band's (for me) too retro-obsessed generation. Until the release of *Ritual Landscape*, that is.

Suddenly (and as though by magic), all of The Badgeman's twee and syrupy jangle-pop was jettisoned, along with their generic, scattershot, all-purpose indie titles ('Cupid's Exploding Harpoon', 'Sean's Seen the Light', 'Extraordinary Girl', and so on), replaced instead by incredibly poetic and lyrically insightful, heathen, nay, actively pagan folk-dirge dances, each of which was propelled by the weightiest of post-punk/Peter Hook/Pete de Freitas rhythm sections (with the titanic rumble of Hawkwind's *Hall of the Mountain Grill* bass sound . . . sheesh!), and each track bearing such grave [*sic*] titles as 'Tumuli', 'Liturgy', 'Seethe Shanty', 'Auto Da Fé', and the like.

Furthermore, where this group's songs had previously been mainly of the two- or three-minute variety, their new, heavy oeuvre now regularly clocked songs in at between seven and thirteen minutes. Indeed, so huge was The Badgeman's seemingly overnight transformation from eight-legged-groove-machine into sky skrying, wandering priests of the Wansdyke that even their new promo photos could not disguise this new ecstasy and endeavour: guitarist John Packwood and bassist Simon Wigglesworth portrayed backs to the camera, obsessively enveloped in a life-or-death struggle with their instruments (early Jesus and Mary Chain/Pop Group-stylee), as blissed-out singer Neale Hancock slumped across the foreground, his eyes tightly shut and his lion's mane of hair thrown back in obvious communication with the heavens.

However we interpreted the evidence, this new version of the band had no more in common with its earlier incarnation than a streamlined rocket aircraft shares with a biplane. Moreover, like Warsaw's legendary metamorphosis into Joy Division, The Badgeman had achieved this spectacular new enlightenment without making even one change to their personnel. But, whereas the phenomenally accelerated change from post-WWI-style biplane flight to futuristic proto-space-rocket could be deemed to have taken place in barely a decade,[1] even the most optimistic types among us would have to admit that this scary achievement had only occurred due to the accelerated technological priorities brought on by WWII. So what kind of psychic wars did the members of The Badgeman live through between 1990 and 1992 in order to update their collective psyche so eloquently and so comprehensively? Or was their Salisbury home so close to Stonehenge and Old Sarum that the groans of the ancestors inevitably came roaring through their PA during rehearsals?

Perhaps we should remember the early-'90s context in which The Badgeman worked in order to ascertain just how huge and how high

1 As late as 1936, the Heinkel aircraft company was supplying the Luftwaffe with their He51 biplane fighters for use in the Spanish Civil War, despite that aeroplane offering a maximum speed of 205 mph. And yet that same company had, by 1944, implemented production of their Heinkel 163 Komet, capable of almost 600 mph.

was that upward leap to the material on *Ritual Landscape*.[2] But, then again, perhaps I'm precisely the wrong person to do the contextual detective work, as I've been listening to this record regularly since I happened upon it back in the summer of 1993, a period when I was still giddily in thrall to the British landscape and each waking moment appeared more and more plagued/blessed by my ever-mounting list of essential prehistoric temples yet to be visited in these islands for inclusion in my tome *The Modern Antiquarian* (then still five long years away from publication). And, when my eyes lit upon the CD version of *Ritual Landscape* while in an Edinburgh record shop, right after a tour of the Highlands and Islands (the Orkneys, Shetlands and Hebrides) of Scotland, I immediately recognised that it shared a kindred spirit with my own work, breathing a sigh of relief that such an album not only existed, but had even gained a full release on so cool an independent label as Paperhouse Records.

Better still, *Ritual Landscape* soon revealed itself to be a work of brutal but gargantuan beauty, a quintessentially English heathen folk-racket of the most muscular post-punk variety, and of a type such as I'd not heard conjured up since gigs with my long-lost poetic northern brothers (most especially) Joy Division, Echo and the Bunnymen, (Steve Reynolds' tragically unsuccessful) Colours Out of Time, and others of their vainglorious ilk. Like these aforementioned bands, the music of *Ritual Landscape* eschewed such obvious tactics as lead-guitar breaks and Dionysian choruses in favour of highly arranged and ominous displays of collective percussion rushes, or swirling, Dervish-like song annexes over which barnstorming, ur-rumbling bass blitzes remained the sole beacon of tangible and traditional melody.

Badgeman tracks such as 'Black Song' were declarations of poetic intent, songs about the duty of singing the song 'that has to be sung'. Choruses, where there were any, often

2 I know that the haphazard but incredibly highly-paced recording sessions for my own *Peggy Suicide* album, one year earlier, had precipitated huge self-doubt in my old friend Rolo of the Woodentops, who'd himself been in the process of recording an almost all-electronic album (under the band name but without the band), i.e. until he saw the über-primitive manner in which I was recording and became fixated on doing the same (much to the chagrin of our shared manager, Seb Shelton, who was bankrolling the Woodentops' project).

appeared at the end of the song itself, earnest declarations of intent created to be sung collectively and with extreme gusto by the entire assembled company, as in the tail-out of 'Liturgy' and (even more emphatically) on 'Auto Da Fé, whose rousing chorale was as wide-eyed and defiantly guileless as Dexy's Midnight Runners' 1981 *Projected Passion Revue* period:

This is our song we're singing,
This is the truth we're bringing,
This is all ours but we'll do it for you
If it's too heavy, we'll give you a hand,
If it's too hard, we'll help you understand,
The birds for the air and the men for the land
. . . the men for the land.

Ritual Landscape

And, after just a couple of listens to the whole record, *Ritual Landscape* so captured my heart that this new Badgeman sound enveloped me and dragged me down into my own personal underworld, psychically waylaying me in a manner that I had not been forced to address for over a decade, but which left me thirsting once more for that too-brief, late-'70s period when Pete de Freitas and Joy Division's Ian Curtis had still been so very alive, present and correct on the many early concert stages that our bands had shared.

Other than *Ritual Landscape*, nothing of The Badgeman's era alluded to those heady days of northern post-punk music, apart, perhaps, from the occasional Woodentops tune, and certain moments on the album *Jo in Nine G Hell* by the post-Loop ensemble Hair & Skin Trading Co. And so, during those early years with this record, every time I spun it I yearned with a gnawing hunger for my own lost scene, for that brief period, in reality barely more than a decade past, yet so very long ago that I was forced to ask myself if it had ever existed at all. And, although I adored each hearty and collectively declaimed Badgeman chorus, and inwardly hailed their brotherly declarations of unity on the sleeve of *Ritual Landscape* ('percussion: allofus'), still I knew, as their elder, that such a period of time would be all too brief. Moreover, each time the final bars of their lengthy record began their long, long, fade, I would once more feel left alone, inconsolable and bereft; stricken with a feeling of utter cosmic loneliness, trapped by the reluctant recognition that even though that spirit was once more moving among us, nevertheless these hopeful young men, with the weight of the world resting on their too-slight shoulders, would be forced to endure – just as my own generation had been – having that great spirit broken.[3]

Yes, *Ritual Landscape* exerted that kind of extraordinary effect on me each time I played its bizarre, post-John Barleycorn Wessex song-cycle which had dared to strike out for the unknown future by first invoking our distant ancestors. From time to time, down the years, I have often been pushed to meditate on what happened (or didn't happen) to these four young Englishmen, whose final album was so anachronistic, so very pagan, so poetic, so humble and yet simultaneously such a barbarian classic. Did The Badgeman even rate this work highly themselves? Then, after mentioning *Ritual Landscape*, briefly, during my review of Litmus, in December 2004, I learned something of The Badgeman's fate when I was contacted by their bass player and lyricist, Simon Wigglesworth, who told me that the band had imploded right after *Ritual Landscape* had failed to ignite, and noted that they'd even been J. Cope fans.

Well, gentlemen of The Badgeman, wherever you all are now, I'd like to take this perhaps too-late opportunity to salute you all and thank you for your fine achievement. Yes, your final album was criminally under-investigated on its release, but I'm positive that time will prove it to have been a work of enduring genius. Why, the evidence sits right there before me on my turntable. For here is one Wessex-based motherfucker who has never stopped listening to *Ritual Landscape*'s effortlessly epic and life-affirming declarations.

3 As I noted on the sleeve of *Rite 2*, the collective experience of 'broken hope' is often a far more powerful and resonant one than that of 'hope'. As the Russian poet Yevgeny Yevtushenko once commented to Bob Dylan, 'Broken hope unites people rather than hope, because broken hope people have experienced and hope they haven't really experienced.'

Monoshock

Walk to the Fire

(Blackjack Records, 1995)

SIDE ONE

1 Crypto-Zoological Disaster (8.20)
2 I Took You to It, Baby (3.57)
3 Hong Kong (3.23)
4 Astral Plane (5.07)

SIDE TWO

1 Tom Guido Philosophically Stoogely (3.10)
2 Leesa (7.49)
3 Separate Beds (9.09)

SIDE THREE

1 Molten Goldfinger 965 (4.27)
2 Walk to the Fire (5.06)
3 Chicken Lover (3.10)
4 Sea Monkeys (5.34)

SIDE FOUR

1 International Hello (8.09)
2 I Want It All (8.48)

In my quest for the Grail of rock'n'roll (which will, at this rate, most likely turn out to be a roughly hewn, late-Bronze Age, Scando-Zarathustran mead jug currently lying unrecognised somewhere and doubling as piss-pot), I've been doing my best to do-as-you-would-be-done-by and grant each artist their metaphor in order to inhale their best intentions. Therefore, for this Monoshock review, and in the face of massive evidence that their mainman, Grady Runyan, vastly prefers the vinyl medium, I have chosen to observe rock'n'roll protocols and the breaks created by said vinyl medium. As a huge fan of Mr Runyan's other band, Liquorball (who also subscribe to what Mr Runyan himself would term the 'lowbrow, avant-garde aesthetic, à la *Vincebus Eruptum*'), that approach seems to me to be the most honest and true to Mr

Runyan's trip, specifically because his three Liquorball LPs ain't yet even had CD release, and because I myself tend to play the double-vinyl version of *Walk to the Fire* most of all.

Tree-Dwellers of the Future

When the developed world staggers to a close in a hundred or so years' time, it's gonna be the children of Monoshock and their ilk who return to the trees first. Sure, they ain't gonna be any happier about the situation than anyone else, but at least the acts of their recent ancestors will have somewhat prepared them for that dire situation. The evidence I have that they'll be safe and out of reach, several branches above everyone else, can be found within the icky grooves of the music of their great-great-grandfathers, who were led by the ur-ancestor himself (the rock'n'roll writer, guitar hoodlum and all-purpose snot-gobbler), Mr Grady Runyan.

Monoshock's 1995 album *Walk to the Fire* not only talked it with a shaman title to die for, it walked it with such consummate ease that even *Funhouse* sax player Steve Mackay would later come a-knocking on Grady Runyan's door. And although amp spill, a dogged refusal to let the drums be heard and sleeping with your record collection are all admirable, you need vocal and guitar riffs as timelessly mature as those on this Monoshock record in order to simultaneously heighten *and* lower the consciousness of the listener.

That Grady Runyan is a writer, and a poetic writer at that, only reinforces my belief that rock'n'roll has long since passed the days when incoherence and spiritual autism were enough to qualify you as one of the greats (Ian Curtis, for example). Rock'n'roll is now old enough to have snatched the spiritual mantle from both jazz and the avant-garde, *and* to have subsumed both of those art-forms into its gasping, greedy, needy veins.

Monoshock were to rock'n'roll what those Miles Davis 1975 wah-everything, Japan-only-released, double-vinyl monsters (*Get Up with It*, *Agharta*, *Pangaea* and *Dark Magus*) were to jazz. That is, they were superfluous to the fucking intellectuals, but spiritual carbohydrates for the ones who knew. Carbohydrates? Yes! Because they give us the staying power, and the staying power is the transcendental otherness that the merely intellectual can never come close to grasping. Any whooping wannabe can come on all 'I'm-gonna-write-the-epic-poem-which-sums-up-the-neuroses-of-the-world', but that's just the Woodstock moment talking. However, tell that idealist that their poem will take three long years to complete, and see the burning in their eyes fade in an instant. No, no, no, sustaining through fires, floods and the sheer outrageous boredom of everyday dish-doing, crust-earning, bill-paying child-rearing is what I'm talking about. And for that you need fuel, and lots of it. Which is where Monoshock come in: as Grady Runyan puts it, 'The key to being a real punk; I'm talking about not caring about what anyone thinks or even what you think [my underline], because it's all subordinate to what you gotta do.' What you *gotta* do; exact-a-fucking-mundo.

Tear the Fart Apart

They may have only made this one huge, double LP, but Monoshock got to *Walk to the Fire* via four horrendous rackets of seven-inch singles. And, through it all, between 1988 and 2001, Grady Runyan simultaneously ran the 'sad free wail' of Liquorball's errant muse. Liquorball are not for the faint-hearted, so we'll come back to them later; and as this is a Monoshock review, we'll have a quick look first at those noxious, badly pressed singles[1] to see how they got there.

First off, 1994's 'Primitive Zippo' is just wonderfuel. It opens like the Barrett-era Floyd playing 'I Wanna Be Your Dog', then hurtles along like The Neon Boys' 'That's All I Know Right Now' meets the Buzzcocks' *Spiral Scratch* EP, with soloing guitars over a Lemmy-like bass which does what the guitar would normally do. The two tracks on the other side are pure paint-by-numbers rewrites of the A-side. Excellent.

Next came 'Soledad', which is just like something off *Walk to the Fire*; that is, Hawkwind doing the 13th Floor Elevators' version of 'You Really Got Me', with an MC5/James Brown-type 'I wanna see a sea of hands' beginning; a blueprint for perfection. 'Yeah, damn . . . I said *now*!' screams Grady, before it all drops down into the familiar time-change quagmire and wallows like a pig in shit. The B-side, 'Lighting a Match in the Year 4007', is more of the same bile: Electric Eels chords, dual vocals, insane rhythm changes *and* a certain craftsmanship in the songwriting that predates that shown on the most recent Comets on Fire album.

'Corney Weekend' is the weakest of these four singles, but it's still excellent. It sounds like a no-wave band playing The Mystic Tide, and

1 'The fidelity on the original singles is so incredibly poor it makes *Walk to the Fire* sound like bona fide audiophile material' (email from Grady Runyan).

is far more controlled than the other singles. With distinctly different label art and sound, I was even tempted to think it might be by a different Monoshock. The B-side, 'Grandpa', exhibits the same vari-speed rhythms, and the vinyl is a dead ringer for a Liquorball forty-five in my collection. Maybe Grady was on sick leave from his day job as the world's most intuitive non-career mover.

'Model Citizen (Nitroglycerine)' is the Stones' 'Rocks Off' played by the Spiders from Mars, as recorded direct to C90 cassette by Electric Eels' John Morton. The B-sides are lesser, although one sounds like Van Halen's version of 'You Really Got Me' and the other is called 'Hawkwind Show'. Nuff said.

Walk to the Fire is a barbarian classic (what an oxymoron, ya moron!) that brings a smile to your face, a sway to your hips and a lump to your dong from the moment you put it on. This record is as life-affirming as a noisy early-morning fart on a London rush-hour Tube train: rasping, stinky and utterly impossible to ignore; indeed, *Walk to the Fire* is 'enhanced by a very poor and unclean production job', as its main protagonist once wrote of someone else.

My daughters have almost become immune to such vibrant aural passive smoking as Taj Mahal Travellers, Group Ongaku, Stockhausen and Father Moo and the Black Sheep; to them, it's just novelty compost you close the door to escape from. But open the door when Monoshock is playing and I get an earful from them. Like Comets on Fire, Chrome, Electric Eels or Rocket from the Tombs, Monoshock are more incendiary because they take the traditional and fuck with it in a way that Mr Runyan himself has described as an 'engaging display of cave-fuzz'. That is, they take the familiar and rummage about until an unholy alchemy has been achieved.

Walk to the Fire opens with a kind of 'Non-alignment Pact'-like mess of feedback, stop–start drums and worried, shake-appeal howling, before 'Crypto-Zoological Disaster' kicks in a 'Silver Machine' boogie that ain't no boogie at all. Twin vocals start complain-complaining about something inaudible and we're off on the voyage. Mr Runyan is joined by Blackjack Records label boss Scott Derr on hogs-grunt, Lemmy-type bass, and the renta-slob Rubin Fiberglass on drums. Monoshock's Hawkwind-inspired roots[2] show through with the

2 Monoshock and Liquorball also appeared on the *Assassins of Silence/Hundred-Watt Violence* Hawkwind tribute LP, released on Ceres Records. While Monoshock's version of 'Psychedelic

sax-playing-through-an-oscillator of the magnificently named Aluminum Queen. Mr Queen does for Monoshock what Tommy Hall did into his jug for the Elevators, and what Nik Turner needed Dik Mik and Del Dettmar's help for in Hawkwind. However, Monoshock get round this problem by making Aluminum Queen's space-warbling louder than anything else in the mix. It's a device that Noel Harmonson, of Comets on Fire, would pick up on a coupla years later with his Echoplex.

'I Took You to It, Baby' is huge and fast, with a riff to kill for; the Pistols' 'Liar' reduced to no chords and twice as rapid. Dual snot-bag vocals complain-complain over schplutter-mutter drums and you don't have a clue what they're about. Like Electric Eels' 'Accident', they conjure up something you don't quite wish to address.

'Hong Kong' is the Buzzcocks' 'Time's Up' with *High Rise Live* guitar tone and fabulous lyrics, only a slither of which I can fully make out: 'Got another strange idea/Cut off my head so I can't hear.' Twin punk vocals always clear my custard, and this is the best example in years.

They conclude Side One with 'Astral Plane', sinking even lower than Electric Eels did on 'Spin Age Blasters'. However, Monoshock's song is even better than the aforesaid because of its scabies-catchy, slug-slow riff and tortured cowboy vocals. Guest violinist Doug Pearson swerves this sucker right off the road, and Scott Derr picks up his bass bugle and single-handedly demolishes the atonal ugly-pathetic-ness of the entire Laughing Clowns' oeuvre with several of the sweatiest, tromboniest horn solos yet put on tape. 'I saw you baby on the astral plane/You read my dreams just like a magazine.'

Side Two responds to this achingly awful genius by opening with the almost acoustic, Stones space-rock of 'Tom Guido Philosophically Stoogely' – further dual vocals over an amphetamine 'Street Fighting Man' structure and, hey, even some production ideas, including additional guitars and overdubbed tambourine from Liquorball bassist Feast. Whoa!

Warlords (Disappear in Smoke)' is just all right, Liquorball's go at 'You Shouldn't Do That' is sub-dude and almost instrumental. Far more interesting than either of these is the astonishing version of 'Born to Go' by free-rock singing drummer/genius Ed Wilcox and his mighty Temple of Bon Matin in its most embryonic stage. This version takes the proto-punk original and raises it into something worthy of Comets on Fire. Hell, it even shits on a lot of Bon Matin's *Cabin in the Sky* LP.

And with a couple further references to 'You Really Got Me' they can't really fail now, can they?

'Leesa' opens with the whole band singing this girl's name over and over and over, high and falsetto and half asleep, while Aluminum Queen oscillates in an Allen Ravenstine/EMS manner and out of the gloaming rises your ultimate utility instant Hawkwind riff. 'Leeeeee-sahhh! Leeeeee-sahhh!' coo the half-wits, like the Montague gang singing up to Juliet in an effort to blow Romeo's cool and have her drop him. And, boy, do they succeed. Seven minutes into this blitz, she's packed up and settled for an arranged marriage.

The song which closes Side Two is a huge revelation of the Runyan psyche, and it's a tortured, damned masterpiece. Beginning incongruously with the bass playing the riff to Greig's 'In the Hall of the Mountain King', 'Separate Beds' is also the trickster in the pack, the Lokian spirit moving unexpected, unwatched and surely as uncalled for as on The Stooges' 'Anne'. A beautiful and massively dark tragedy and an end-of-the-affair song straight out of the Armand Schaubroeck songbook, this is an epic minor-key masterpiece of true devastation. Here, Grady Runyan reveals himself as a major songwriter who could probably stand up in the 'real' world, if he could even muster up one iota of respect for that place for long enough. A cover version of this would be a huge country-and-western hit – in my dreams, baby.

Side Three opens like 'Iron Man' meets 'TV Eye' meets the theme from *Batman*. It's called 'Molten Goldfinger 965' and it wipes my shitty ass. Hardly any vocals and all of them submerged in the Aluminum Queen's own fug. Again, Mr Runyan has rifled through the Bodleian Library of Rock Riffs, and checked out every one of them – he ain't about to take these suckers back, nor pay the fines.

The deeply brilliant and highly melodic title track is a Stacy Sutherland-type, sub-aqua ballad straight out of *Bull of the Woods*. Imagine the Elevators' 'Rose and the Thorn' with 'Living On' production and you're somewhere close to the mystery of this track. Again, it's got that easy melody that makes you think Grady's been piling 'em up for this very rainy day. And Ethan Miller musta copped a thang or three for his Comets on Fire vocal technique. Imagine a reverbed, dead-man-walking blues riff with sarcophagus vocals and splatter drums – excellent.

Then we come to the furiously inbred 'Chicken Lover'. 'This is a song about people making love with animals,' declares Grady. Cue all instruments copping a few barnyard sounds; then an abrupt stop. 'I shot you in the back when I caught you with my chicken lover,' says Mr Runyan, and off they stomp into a blues-fuelled space tirade. 'I suspect one man's natural tendencies are another man's dementia,' Mr Runyan concludes.

Side Three's closer, 'Sea Monkeys', is like something off Side Two of Pere Ubu's *The Modern Dance* – think 'Chinese Radiation' or even 'Laughing'. This is a rhythmless complain-athon with a wonderful bass riff and drums that only relieve us halfway through.

And so we come to the final side of this behemoth. It is here, on the two eight-minute Technicolor yawns, 'International Hello' and 'I Want It All', that Monoshock most nearly approach their sibling band Liquorball. I say 'nearly' – and it must be very carefully noted that while both of these Side Four epics are an unrestrained headrush, they in no way approach the *Electronic Meditation*-period Tangerine Dream, low-church, Mithraic blood-letting that Liquorball so deeply represents.

'International Hello' fades up slowly out of the murk, a slow blues, 6/8 thunderstorm of drums, then suddenly accelerates into the kind of relentless, caterwauling guitar destruction you need to physically experience. Most of the album was recorded at The Insane Cat studio, in San Francisco, with the exception of this one overflowing canister of fresh garbage, which owes its dubious birth to a place called The Practise Pad. Never book this place; they have one broken compressor mic and no toilets. Hey, I could listen to an entire sixty minutes of this stuff and still want more. Scott Derr's untamed bass rears up and attempts to throw him out of the saddle, but he ain't having none of it. These guys may be influenced by Hawkwind, but this stuff makes Lemmy and Dave Brock look like stuffed owls in an antique boutique. Rubin is close to a heart attack, and who the fuck knows what Aluminum Queen is doing here: it all suffuses together in one incandescent glow. Margaret Niffisent, but you can call me Mag. All those Japrock, mainliner Heino snobs should suck at these guys' priapic altar!

'I Want It All' completes the circle with an intro of Pere Ubu atmosphere – 'Chinese Radiation' again. Farts and bubbles continue until, at one minute fifty-five, we're back in 1975, grooving on both sides of the Atlantic simultaneously with the proto-no wave of the Cleveland sound, by way of the Hawkwind-plays-Neu! of 'Opa-Loka'. It's a call-and-response song with semi-yodelled vocals and yelps: 'I want it all (I want it all)/I want it all (I want it all)/I want it all.'

Again, this could have done with being the whole of an album side, but I'm greedy for Grady'n'co. and sad to see the back of them. What an album, what a sound, what a moment captured. The truth is, Monoshock was gone forever after this one long glimpse of genius, as Grady Runyan returned to his stupor-dooper day job in Liquorball . . .

Yeah, Liquorball; how to review them? What can you say about a trio that calls an album *Live at Hitler's Bunker* but features the word 'bull-shit' so prominently on the sleeve that it's reviewed everywhere as just that? How do you respond to a band who's *Liquorball Fucks the Sky* LP has no song titles and instead features the legend 'Get Well Soon' on its labels? And if even the single release has no titles and only a handwritten sticker announcing the luminous vinyl within, you know there's something afoot. Especially when those records truly explore the kind of atonal, low-trauma music that hung around only briefly even in scenes like that of turn-of-the-'70s Germany (Tangerine Dream's *Electronic Meditation*, specifically). Conrad Schnitzler, in your bass-player incarnation, we need you! Until then, we got Feast on bass for Liquorball, and he's a total genius, with ne'er a nod of respect for 4/4, 3/4, 6/8 or even 1/2 time. If Chuggz' home decorating is redolent of the way he plays the drums, then he's right now hammering in screws and painting lounge walls without moving the sofas or easy chairs.

A bunch of *Q* journalists got mad at me over my *Krautrocksampler* stance, in which I declared that every Tangerine Dream record after *Atem* was blandorama synth-fizzle. Hell, you bourgeois things that creep, gimme T. Dream with the trouser tracks or gimme death! Yup, one listen to that first Liquorball LP will confirm that my assertion was not only fair but was possibly a little too compassionate. For Liquorball is one free-rock travesty you just gotta get a hold of and ingest with abandon.

Except for one single, on which they sounded like Monoshock and he sounds like a refusenik David Lee Roth, Grady Runyan the poet is here reduced/elevated to the kind of shamanic, E.T./Gollum figure which competes admirably with early Yoko.[3] So while *Liquorball Fucks the Sky* is deffo

3 That Grady Runyan finishes Side One of *Liquorball Fucks the Sky* screaming 'Why?' over and over unaccompanied does not (to me, at least) suggest his being even influenced by Yoko's own

my fave, *Live in Hitler's Bunker* takes them into even newer territory because it features the superb, low-church organ playing of Steve Watson. What a keyboard star this guy is; loud and proud and totally without peers.

Liquorball is obvious, funny, pathetic, shitty, wanton, dedicated, unbothered, unsophisticated, unyielding, unnecessary, anyone-could-do-it-and-no-fucker-does-so-they-obviously-can't, beyond-a-joke genius that everyone should buy at least one copy of in their lifetime. In my brief email correspondence with Grady Runyan, I asked him why these LPs weren't out on CD yet. His response was about as perfect a reply as there could be: 'I thought about reissuing *Fucks the Sky* and *Hauls Ass* on a single CD simultaneously, one right channel the other left . . . I wonder how that would *sound*?'

Do it to it, Mr Runyan. We neeeeed!

Discography

Monoshock:

'Primitive Zippo' b/w 'Change that Riff' and 'Nobody Recovery' (single, Womb, 1994)

'Soledad' b/w 'Striking a Match in the Year 4007' (single, Blackjack, 1994)

'Corney Weekend' b/w 'Grandpa' (single, Dolores, 1995)

'Model Citizen' b/w 'Hawkwind Show', 'Everything Near Me' (single, Bag of Hammers, 1995)

Walk to the Fire (Blackjack, 1996)

Liquorball:

'Willie the Worm' b/w 'The Slug Brothers' (Blackjack, 1991)

Liquorball Fucks the Sky (Blackjack, 1992)

Liquorball Hauls Ass (Blackjack, 1994)

Live in Hitler's Bunker (Blackjack, 1997)

'Why?', which concludes in a similar manner. Rather, it suggests to me that screaming 'Why?' repeatedly is instead the ur-holler, a *summum bonum* of every shaman, and that the word 'why' became the ultimate question simply because of its instant and ultimate sound. However, only a proper battle of the shamans could prove this one way or another – although it's a damned good idea, whatever. For the experiment, I'd propose Kan Mikami (Japan), Cotton Casino (Japan), Grady Runyan (US), Alan Dubin (US), Ed Wilcox (US), Christian Vander (France), Mani Neumaier (Germany), Freya Aswynn (Netherlands), John Balance (Britain) and myself, natch.

Aftershock

Following this review, Grady Runyan emailed me with news that I'd gotta few things wrong. When I asked him if I could temporarily add these messages in place of a total re-edit, he was charming and agreed. So here ya go . . .

Whoa Julian, you really know how to heap it on....... I for one consider our horn majorly blown..... which is to say thanks for the coverage...... but now that I've wiped the juice off my leg, I'd like to straighten out a few things........ don't worry, it needn't fuck with any mythology-raising (yours or ours)........ it's just that I don't want someone/something else's credit, especially considering the potential durability of your slather.....

OK.... the main thing is, Monoshock was first and foremost a group, a gang, a party, a tribe, a UNIT...... there was no appointed leader, nor would one have been tolerated. Band processes were collaborative: We were most defiantly NOT a one-(sha) man show and no one was a rent-a-anything, especially Rubin Fiberglass........ he is in fact the author of almost every lyric that you quoted, and the singer thereof t'boot! Find his lead incantations on 'I Took You To It', 'Hong Kong', 'Tom Guido . . .', 'Walk To The Fire', 'Chicken Lover', 'Astral Plane', 'Separate Beds', 'Sea Monkeys' ...... in other words, he's ALL OVER the bleepin' record!.......... Me, I only scram lead on two songs the whole album......... assorted yelps, roars, gurgles and coos notwithstanding, they're just part of the landscape........

Feast did NOT provide extra guitar or production ideas (?) to Tom Guido, or any of our tracks for that matter...... tambourine yes........ and speaking of Feast, the true Loki of this scenario if there ever was one, that is in fact his 'Why' that so fittingly closes Side One of Fucks The Sky....... not mine...... those are also his lungs you're hearing on both L-Ball 7-inchers, not mine....... perhaps Feast is the ur-gollom you seek (though if you still choose me as your cosmic rock'n'roll shaman, I can promise urine-stained carpeting in every basement and a swedish flying saucer on every amp)........

'Corney Weekend' ain't us. You may have noticed I did NOT include it in the 7-inch discography you asked for........ this was not an oversight. The part about it sounding like Liquorball is perhaps the most cosmic of all........

Let it be known that your enthusiasm is most welcome (being compared to a fart ÄND Miles Davis is indeed one for the grandkids), but your blatant fact-lack and lopsided delivery is kinda shafting my fellow tribesmen. Clueing your readers to the credit-where-credit's due-ness of it all might help........

GR

(PS – You need to hear the Sternklang album – 3/4 of Monoshock + 4, no-holds-barred from '94......)

To which I replied:

Hey there Grady,
Sorry I wronged a few rights and disserviced the others – I figured you'd be so deepinaheart of the solo LP, you might not give two hoots for me surfacing da 'shock at this moment. I added up four and four and made one! Your being a poet-ruffian also helped delude me.

No, that's not actually it at all. It was difficult to keep emailing you with what-I-thought-you'd-see-as petty queries, so I perused the album sleeves and that's what I came up with. I only credit Feast with tambourine, if you read it one way (though it can be read the other way now you alert me to it).

If you wanna give me those guys' addresses, I'll do a 'sorry gentlemen' to all of them. And I will – of course – do a re-edit in the best rolling-publishing traditions of the Int'net.

'Corney Weekend' was THEE cosmic curveball. I've had that record since it came out and didn't give it the time of day. Consequently, I dissed the WALK TO THE FIRE album for years and was about to heap in on the pile of slush on its way to Notting Hill Record & Tape Exchange, when the Blackjack label caught my attention, and the WALK TO THE FIRE title kind of put me in the mind of Comets on Fire (who owe a debt to you, bigtime, I would think). Anyway, having a Yank missus and knowing the name Monoshock has a place in teen jock culture, I was initially wary, listened over and over, but figured – eh, it's the same band having temporary delusions. Believe me, it was the mottled vinyl what finally swayed me, guv!

Send me the addresses – I'll do the right thing.

Back at ya!

JULIAN

This was Grady Runyan's final message before NASA pulled the plugs on us:

If you are really serious about a re-edit, you may want to include the Sternklang LP..... it's kinda like an extended Monoshock session, 'International Hello'-style. There is a unique Monoshock track on 'Fuck That Weak Shit, Vol. 3' too.

I had secretly hoped for the day Corney Weekend be attributed to us (I believe Scott owns a copy)......

More trivia: Ed Wilcox played drums for Liquorball once, and the results were issued on CDR: 'Tora Tora Tora' (Radon, 2000; rec. '96)...... 'You Shouldn't...' on the Hawk/trib comes from a primordial 50-minute rendition, CD & LP have completely different excerpts....... and don't forget the first Liquorball single......... you want a copy of my one and only solo show?

Thanks for making right......... and for the coverage in the first place,

GR

Psychick TV

Kondole

(Temple ov Psychic Youth, 1989)

1 Part One (23.00) 2 Part Two (46.00)

Towards the Infinite Beach

Commencing with a series of seemingly random-but-actually-sequential bursts of Lokian analogue synthesizer snarls, cavorting, sparking, flashing and exploding across vast universes of oceanic reverb, and all attended by a watery gaggle of volatile, self-immolating limpet-mine sonic acolytes, whose tinnitus-inducing, overly self-important auditory declarations seethe and chatter like caffeinated suicide bombers re-enacting scenes of Oskar from *The Tin Drum*'s most infantile drumming tantrums, this fabulously ambulant album's musical journey through soupy underworlds and foggy dimensions actually acts out the South Australian myth of Kondole the Whale, and how – through his own monumental selfishness – the blowhole in the top of his head came to be created, pierced by the spear of a frustrated and hungry hunter whom the whale had gypped.

From memory, I can recall only The Residents' equally mythographic and monumental LP *Eskimo* having previously attempted such a spirited act of cultural retrieval, and even their (nothing less than) heroic white-vinyl testament, in all its gloriosity, its mind-manifesting gatefold art and its adoption of authentic Inuit glossaries, still never glimpsed the sheer psychic usefulness and all-purpose healing qualities of Psychick TV's *Kondole*. Phew. For over an hour, *Kondole*'s titanic undertow drags us into the myopic world of the bottom-feeders and keeps us there, declares us all gill-men and lets us grow fins.

Moreover, I believe that without

repeated listening to such epic instrumental sagas as *Kondole*, our aging brains will eventually seize up and petrify. It's as though, through too much TV, or just sheer neglect, our brains experience some equivalent to waxy build-up, coagulating most unfortunately into a kind of scabby psychic shield around our doors of perception, denying us access to all but the most familiar concepts and thoughts. Regular doses of *Kondole*, however, rupture this overly protective brain coating and readmit those fancies that children and teenagers access effortlessly throughout their daily lives.

So welcome to the undersea world of Genesis P-Orridge, circa 1989, a culturally kleptomaniacal, post-New Age rave-up of such velocity that our psychic hero actually *became* – during this pre-'90s gateway – his own Kondole the Whale, a perpetually feeding, gate-mouthed leviathan inhaling whole substrata of lost, arcane information at once, so as to digest, comprehend, then barf them forth coherently (and in edited form) to the next generation; reviewed, rejigged and turbo-charged for the coming age.

During that ultra-fertile 1988–92 period, Genesis P. struck both artistic *and* psychic gold in several areas with his hi-energy, wide-net, cultural fishing techniques. Besides the brilliant deep-space ambulence of *Kondole*, Gen embarked on a Thomas Carlylean policy of high-visibility hero worship, enflamed by his Brian Jones records and pilgrimages, thereafter hooking up with various (invented) DJs in order to create massive Acid House double CDs (such as *Jack the Tab*, *Tekno Acid Beat*, *Towards Thee Infinite Beat*, *Direction ov Travel* . . .), thereby successfully appropriating rave culture in order to demand the wholesale road-widening of its psychic usefulness beyond the then-current (although wholly admirable) football-stadium-as-henge mentality, with the vision of integrating such radical notions into the absolute everyday.

At that cross-decade of the coming '90s, Gen was also most righteously deploying members of the Temple ov Psychic Youth as a picket-line with which to get the Brighton Dolphinarium closed down, *and* all this time was himself on the verge of getting kicked out of the country for one too many radical acts. But then, only the radicals have ever changed culture. For, like the radish in the soil, radicals exist at such a deep cultural level that their influences cannot be excised merely by several judicious snips. For their thoughts, their ideas will – by the time the authorities have even become aware of their presence – have already slipped down even deeper into society's ur-consciousness.

For over forty years, Genesis Breyer P-Orridge has been weaving his spells throughout popular culture, but his art will probably only receive fair judgement posthumously thanks to the wild and (intentionally) distorted image he's built for himself. But what could be more beautiful than the fact that such a sustaining and chronic radical as Gen could have provided us all – in the form of *Kondole* – with a piece of truly *necessary* everyday listening? Surely, brothers and sisters, this artful record's sheer usefulness provides us with ample (and exhilarating) evidence that the radical artist does not deserve to be dismissed under society's catch-all term 'outsider'. Dear me, no. For, as evidenced by the forty-plus-year presence of Genesis P-Orridge at the very wellspring of Western culture's most radical ideas, such rare cultural giants as he deserve nothing less than to be eulogised by the blessed name 'insider'.

Sleep

Dopesmoker

(Tee Pee Records, 2003)

(*Dopesmoker* – originally titled *Jerusalem* – was recorded in 1995)

1 Jerusalem (a.k.a. Dopesmoker) (60.03)
2 Sonic Titan (9.36)

Also in double-vinyl form:

SIDE A
Drop Out of Life (21.10)

SIDE B
Creedsmen Roll Out Across the Dying Dawn (20.11)

SIDE C
Marijuanaut (21.08)

SIDE D
Sonic Titan (8.57)

If yooz highly influenced by another group's sound, there are two methods for forming your band. You can apologise and have a sense of humour about it, or you can be so much more full-on than your predecessors that you surpass them by the release of your second LP. Sleep chose the second route and succeeded magnificently.

Although the double-vinyl artwork is huge, gatefold and magnificent, the CD version of *Dopesmoker* is the best option overall, because you can get utterly narnered once you've put it on and not have to get up for almost an hour and ten minutes.

'Get High, Crank It Up, and Listen'

When my all-smiling, all-visionary, all-grimming partner in sonic grime, Stephen O'Malley (of Khanate, Sunn O))) and Burning Witch), sent me this Sleep album as a gift in 2003, I immediately thought it was the most ground-breaking record in years, because it took an essentially unmeditational musical form (i.e. early Black Sabbath) and sacralised it into the highest form of barbarian sonic code you could ever wish to trip out to. It monged my senses within the first five minutes, then set about my inner structures with the sheer weight of its adamant repetition and monotony.

The CD featured one, sixty-minute-long Sabbath rehash, plus a nine-minute in-concert extra to wake you at the end, in case you'd fallen asleep under the sonic assault of the main track and your home was burning down. 'What pragmatic motherfuckers,' I thunk to myself. You could chew up some of the good hash and neck a few beers and lie in bed and sleep to it, leave your body to it, probably even shag to it, although I was too busy to set up such an experiment. But it was such a forever trip that the whole room, nay the whole of my life, soon became secondary to this one seemingly eternal track. It was neither fast nor slow, operating somewhere between Black Sabbath's own self-titled track from their first LP and the Flower Travellin' Band's own, more ambient, sludge-trudge version of the same song from their 1970 LP, *Anywhere*, then gradually built into a rhythm something akin to *Master of Reality*'s 'Lord of this World' and 'Into the Void'. However, there was, herein, an added bonus in the drumming of Chris Hakius, whose utter relentlessness allowed the sound to transcend Sabbath considerably and obtain a total hold on this listener's mind. After hearing so many recent so-called Sabbath imitators whose muse really appealed to me intellectually but always ultimately failed to make me instantly replay the suckers (Boris, Electric Wizard, Gonga), this Sleep album seemed to be the realest of real shit and then some . . .

As a Krautrocker who'd always professed to have preferred *UFO*-period Guru Guru's extended Sabbalongs to the real thing, I realised that these San Jose lunatics had taken their own proto-metal into much the same LSD March-type territory, then continued out of that music's city limits across the railway tracks and out into netherlands where even Mani Neumaier woulda never thunk to venture. Furthermore, the lyrics (all ten repeated lines or so) offered the kind of accessible, pseudo-religious genius that started genuine religions:

Drop out of life with bong in hand,
Follow the smoke to the riff-filled land,
Drop out of life with bong in hand,

Follow the smoke to the riff-filled land.
Proceeds the Weedian – Nazareth,
Proceeds the Weedian – Nazareth . . .

Do those words represent a new low in redundant amphibian shamanism or what, motherfuckers? Gimme, gimme, gimme – and then gimme some more. When I was a kid, making 1/72 scale model plane kits by Airfix and Revell, I used to paint flies with Humbrol gloss and watch them drag themselves around slower and slower until – finally – they dried up underneath the sheer weight of the glossy overalls I'd painted them into. Now, listening to *Dopesmoker*, I was a fly dying of paint inhalation and loving every exoskeletally en-crisping moment. Lying comatose and aware of nothing but the thousands of glow-in-the-dark stars on my bedroom ceiling, I wondered what could have been behind such a fundamentalist statement as *Dopesmoker*.

Of its three creators, I visualised them (in my hash-mashed mind's eye) inhabiting a world in which the first four Black Sabbath LPs had become sacred testaments on which to base their entire belief system (this wasn't really too hard to envisage – Mormonism and Rastafarianism were based on far less). But then, as I sunk deeper into Sleep's San Jose psyche, I began to think . . . Imagine that you first came to these four Sabs LPs not in their British Vertigo swirl guises, but in their US, Warner Brothers versions, with the first LP losing its gatefold and (therefore) controversial inverted cross, but (more positively) Side Two opening not with the original, slightly incongruous Fontana forty-five 'Evil Woman, Don't You Play Your Games with Me', but with the far more typically doomaholic, stop–start, Iommi-heavy, multi-part B-side, 'Wicked World' – an altogether more auspiciously damned beginning to the second side of such an iconic rock'n'roll debut. Imagine, if you will allow me to continue this metaphor, that, being a teenage American stoner and already of the opinion that, being in possession of the aforementioned quartet of LPs, you have your hands on some sort of holy sonic reliquary umpteen times greater than Islam's piece of sacred meteorite at the centre of Mecca's Haram enclosure, you begin, as time goes by, to read more and more into the titles of those 'extras' that Warner Brothers had insisted Black Sabbath added to their tracklisting to stop the general public from thinking they wuz buying some too-short LPs. Imagine how the addition of those extra, US-only titles on *Black Sabbath* ('Wasp', 'Bassically'), *Paranoid* ('Luke's Wall', 'Jack the Stripper'), *Master of*

Reality ('The Haunting', 'Step Up', 'Deathmask') and *Volume 4* ('The Straightener', 'Everyday Comes and Goes') to the already murky official Sabbath tracklisting contributed further confusion to the thorny question of exactly when songs ended and others began; so much so, in fact, that each already oft-changing riff-athon now appeared to meld seamlessly, tidally, into the next, until your teen-addled stoner cranium saw, heard and inhaled it all as a single, ever-undulating, ever-spiralling, ever-squirming Midgardian Worm of sonic oil-spill, building and building layer upon relentless layer on a seashore, until the whole beachscape, complete with sunbathers, coastguards and concession stands, had been lacquered under a one-metre-thick, obsidian-black layer of petrified chemo-gunk . . .

I visualised Sleep in their pre-Sleep configuration, their teenage stoner minds fixating collectively on these first four Sabbath LPs to such an extent that certain repeated words in the song titles became iconic mantras to be treated (Bridget Riley-stylee) as repeatable motifs almost in the psychedelic manner of six-thousand-year-old Western Atlantic passage grave art. In this mood, titles such as 'Sweetleaf', 'Behind the Wall of Sleep', 'Planet Caravan', 'Under the Sun', 'Warning', 'Snowblind',[1] 'Luke's Wall', 'Supernaut', 'A Bit of Finger', 'Tomorrow's Dream' and 'The Wizard' become a useful, jugglable commodity on which to hang your own variant of Geezer's lyric, of Iommi's heavy, up-the-neck, wound-string Gibson SG riffs, and of Bill's Bible-throwing drum fills.

I heard evidence within these Sleepian grooves that a genuine cult had grown up in San Jose, a cult dedicated to the results of Black Sabbath's controversial decision to rip off[2] a song title ('Sweetleaf') from Clear Blue Sky, their eighteen-year-old Vertigo label-mates, and write it not as a soft homage to grass but as a riff-heavy, 'pot as *the* sacrament', John Sinclair/MC5ian-type Odin-receiving-the-wisdom-of-Urd's Well, *thank you, thank you, you-saved-my-life*

---

1 Sleep recorded a version of 'Snowblind' for the Earache Black Sabbath Tribute album *Masters of Misery*.

2 I don't use the term 'rip-off' as a putdown, by the way. The Clear Blue Sky song had a great title and nine minutes-plus of not much else. However, as it also began their album, you've got to admit it's about time The Butthole Surfers did the right thing and fulfilled both their destiny and this trilogy with their own album-opener entitled 'Sweetleaf'.

shaman's gift to the goddess eulogy. I imagined that on hearing Ozzy's Echoplex'd coughs at the beginning of the song, and the desperation in his voice when he sung to Sweetleaf, 'I love you . . . you know it . . ./ My life was empty . . . my life was down . . ./My life is free now,' the cult-that-would-become-Sleep had heard it as such a rallying cry from within that it finally motivated their otherwise total pot-refusenik butts enough to get up from the couch long enough to lay down some extreme sonic monotony on behalf of the vegetation goddess who had spoken so eloquently to them, their few close stoner mates and Messrs Osbourne, Butler, Iommi and Ward. But after I'd imagined all of the above, I had to stop imagining such things because this thing had actually happened and the results were amazing.

Then came the cruncher: this *Dopesmoker* album was an old recording from 1995 and was the culmination of years of Sleep's collective (and terminal) Sabbophilia. Yup, there was loads more great Sleep stuff, *and* they'd stuffed their label (London Records) with this sucker by scoring unbelievable amounts of the green, inhaling it all, then buying even vaster amounts of the Orange (amplification, that is) and recording one, fifty-two-minute-long track entitled 'Jerusalem' which they then delivered to the label on a DAT tape contained in a porcelain skull bong wearing a US military-police helmet. Legal wrangling took over and miserable London Records suits wearing extremely brown trousers eventually dropped the band, who then had on their hands the greatest bootleg since High Rise's aberrant live double, *Not Wearing a Hard Hat in a Hard Hat Area (That Hard)*. I needed to do some sonic investigation, and I knew it would be one of the great joys of recent history. Indeed, it was . . .

Behind the Wall of Yawn, or Sleep, Volume One

So here's the dope, dopes. Once upon a time, there was a punk-rock band called Asbestos Death who came from San Jose and featured Luke Cisneros (bass, vocals), Chris Hakius (drums) and Tom Choi (guitar). They hooked up with Matt Pike (guitar) and changed their name to Sleep after a coupla singles, when Choi left and was replaced by the religiously minded Justin Marler. Sleep signed to the same tiny Tupelo label that had fortuitously picked up the European rights to Nirvana's *Bleach*, and for production hauled in the excellent Billy Anderson, deffo the Eddie Kramer of proto-doom, nay of all things heavy.

Volume One begins with a tape of Buddhist monks followed by clanking, metal, religious themes, everyone but the drummer singing simultaneously. The songs are mainly generic hard-doom with an added flavour of Middle Eastern twang, and the whole thing pretty much stayed down on that level for three-quarters of an hour, asking questions like 'What is a soul?' in a proto-Khanatean manner. This early period is 'almost there', but it's ultimately also too 'inventive' and too experimental to really nail what Sleep would go on to be really about. With the added guitar of Justin Marler, they actually made far less noise, were not really (quite) so monolithic and even copped a little jazz twang here'n'there (Iommi-stylee, natch), which ain't nearly so bad as it sounds. Indeed, as a first LP they got it together pretty good. Still, when they added 'special thanks' to Geezer, Iommi and Bill Ward on the back sleeve, it was not so much reflected in the music herein, but at the very least their addled minds were clearly already thinking to the future.

You Can Call Me Al, or Sleep's Holy Mountain

Fortunately for all of us, Justin Marler's decision to enter a monastery, soon after the release of the first Sleep album, dramatically changed the sound of the group, and in a manner that could never have been anticipated. Gone was the previous emptiness and gone was the interplay between Pike and Marler's guitars. Enter, instead, a determination to fuse early Black Sabbath monolithomania with genuine astral projection. Bass player Luke Cisneros now became the sole singer of the band, wrote an album's worth of meaningless (and, it has to be admitted, largely *shit*) lyrics, and changed his name to Al Cisneros (which means, in Spanish, 'Towards those who work with swans'[3]). In Al's new guise as the stalker of the swan people, he immediately became not the Ozzy vocal clone we could have anticipated, but the driving, alpha-shaman ur-force behind an entirely

3 Suspicious that this was the possible meaning, I asked my good friend and Spaniard, Annexus Quamm, about the translation. He wrote: 'Yes, literally *cisnero* would be a person who works or deals with swans; like *vaquero* works with *vacas* (cows) and *porquero* with *cerdos* (pork, pigs), both rather old-fashioned terms. [This] makes sense to me in a literal way.'

destiny-led troupe of demented masters of reality.

And so, *Sleep's Holy Mountain* opens with the superb confidence of 'Dragonaut', with its 'Lord of this World' riffola, with changes aplenty and the kind of speeding-horse-arrives-at-saloon slow-up on the second verse which I thought only Speed, Glue & Shinki's Joey Smith would ever dare execute. Weirdest of all is the way the song drops down to conclude in a wah-bass solo redolent of Geezer's 'A Bit of Finger', and you almost expect 'N.I.B.' to power in any second . . .

Suddenly, the Sleep sound is all of its own, bearing the same relationship to Sabbath as The Doors did to The Zombies' 'She's Not There'. In other words, they've totally subsumed the Sabs influences into their trip but belched out something that is entirely theirs. Furthermore, you can't meditate to Sabbath but you can to Sleep. True, they still ape Sabbath structures and even feature an 'Orchid'-style guitar instrumental ('Some Grass'), but, by limiting their Sabbath rehash (basically combining 'Into the Void' and 'Lord of This World') and also aping that particularly rigorous telegraph-wire bass sound that producer Rodger Bain copped for Geezer on *Master of Reality*, they simultaneously achieved the same ridiculously crunchy sonic interplay that Geezer's bass and Iommi's SG achieved therein *and* beat it all to a bloody pulp. Indeed, Sleep's wholesale appropriation of 'Lord of This World' is even more inventive than Tony Iommi's rescue of the main riff from The Pretty Things' 'Baron Saturday'[4] for 'After Forever', because they actually annex the entire section (rhythm, vocal line, the lot) in the same way that High Rise did with The Electric Prunes' 'You've Never Had It Better' for their own 'Outside Gentiles'. When David Thomas wrote Pere Ubu's 'Final Solution' over Blue Cheer's version of 'Summertime Blues', he was saying the same thing – this is a perfect rock'n'roll track and I'm gonna treat it as public-domain folk music on which to scrawl my call sign. In other words, to paraphrase T. S. Eliot again, talent merely borrows whereas genius dares to steal.

4 There are lots of Pretty Things riffs awaiting a good pillaging because, although the band was naturally heavy, they got caught up in adding all kinds of psychedelic detritus and extra sections. You gotta admit that The Stereo Shoestrings did a great job by taking The Pretty Things' forty-five, 'Defecting Grey', and sodding off all the sub-Barrettisms, streamlining the riff and releasing it as 'On the Road South' – one of the greatest speedball paranoia trips ever.

Jerusalem, *or the Lyrical Coming-of-Age of 'Al Cisneros'*

After *Sleep's Holy Mountain* caused a big stir and they'd invented the term 'stoner-rock' (or so I believe), some pretty heavy management took over control of the band and signed them up to London Records, who saw the promise of a big underground band and laid upon them extreme amounts of loot. Now, a note in the booklet of *Sleep's Holy Mountain* ('If you have Orange amplification for sale contact Sleep through Earache Records') should, perhaps, have forewarned everyone, but Sleep now took the cash and laid out thousands for this Holy Grail amplification (all finished in delightful orange-coloured '70s cases, as my contemporaries will so well know). When most groups sign to a major label, they become (in the words of Mark E. Smith) 'like peasants with free milk'. The records are made to suit the company, and some bands even freely admit to working for the man (Mott the Hoople always referred to Island Records as their 'employers', and Lynyrd Skynyrd's second LP even featured a song entitled 'Working for MCA'), so it must have come as a something of a surprise to London Records when their new power-trio signing from San Jose chose to spend all their money on new equipment and pot, and delivered an album that contained just a single fifty-two-minute track entitled 'Jerusalem'. Gone was the generic lyrical vapidness of much of *Sleep's Holy Mountain* (gypsies, druids, dragons, whatever) and incoming was the type of sacred coding that 'Al Cisneros' had previously alluded to only on the song 'From Beyond', on which he intoned, 'Stoner caravan from deep space arrives.'

This was his new direction for 'Jerusalem', and it was fucking magnificent, funny as hell, religious as a motherfucker and as appropriate as you could wish for. Moreover, here on 'Jerusalem' he was happy to confound us all with constant reggae/Rasta lyrical allusions, sometimes coming on more like Ras Michael and the Sons of Negus than a metal band. The *Jerusalem* album is peppered with lyrics like: 'Creedsmen roll out across the dying dawn/Sacred Israel, Holy Mount Zion,' and 'Earthling inserts to chalice the green cutchie/Groundation soul finds thrust upon smoking hose.'

Even the phraseology gets pretty dialectal on lines such as: 'Judgement soon come to mankind/Green herbsmen serve rightful king,' or 'Now smokes believer/the Chronicle of the Sinsemillian.' I really dig it because it's not only refreshing, it's also geographically appropriate to laud your drug of choice in a latitudinally correct manner. Fucking on the case or what, this lot? Now how unhung-up is that? Oh, fuck it, I'm gonna type out the remainder of the lyrics for you to have a gander at:

Creedsmen roll out across the dying dawn,
Sacred Israel, Holy Mt. Zion,
Sun beams down on to the Sandsean reigns,
Caravan migrates through deep sandscape,
Lungsmen unearth the creed of Hasheeshian Lebanon.

Desert legion smoke covenant is complete,
Herb bails retied on to backs of beasts,
Stoner caravan emerge from sandsea,
Earthling inserts to chalice the green cutchie,
Groundation soul finds thrust upon smoking hose,
Assemble creedsmen rises prayer-filled smoke Golgotha.

Judgement soon come to mankind,
Green herbsmen serve rightful king,
Hemp seed caravan carries,
Rides out believer with the spliff aflame,
Marijuanaut escapes earth to cultivate,
Grow room is church temple of the new stoner breed,
Chants loud robed priest down on to the freedom seed,
Burnt offering redeems – completes smoked deliverance,
Caravans' stoned deliverants,
The caravan holds to Eastern creed,
Now smokes believer,
The Chronicle of the Sinsemillian.

Drop out of life with bong in hand,
Follow the smoke to the riff-filled land,
Drop out of life with bong in hand,
Follow the smoke . . . Jerusalem.

While it's no wonder old London Records furry freaked out, you gotta wonder what they'd expected it to be. I mean, did these knob-hounds think they wuz gonna like the results? Furthermore, you also gots to wonder why they didn't just put the sucker out and wait and see. With all this shit going down and *Jerusalem* being removed from release schedules, Sleep slowly and inevitably pulled apart and disappeared. Cassettes and a rogue CD of *Jerusalem* managed to find their way into the underground, and the word oozed out that this was the shit. By then, Sleep were gone and their legend as unsullied truthseekers could only build from there into the sparkling thing that it's become today. And while Messrs Hakius and Pike have continued in other musical forms, the world of doom still awaits the first moves of 'Al Cisneros', whose inactivity now stretches back into the mid-1990s. Rise Above Records released the full, fifty-two-minutes-and-eight-second version of *Jerusalem* in 2002, followed by this earlier, more extreme mix in 2003. Clocking in at three seconds over a full hour, and retitled *Dopesmoker*, methinks this is the best it can get. Also, those of you new to Sleep's work will probably find *Sleep's Holy Mountain* ideal, easy 'daytime' listening, reserving *Dopesmoker* for those long, dark evenings at the back of your mind. Ooh yeah!

Temple of Bon Matin

(No label, 2006)

1 Ex-Man/F.U.N. (5.16) (from *Thunder Feedback Confusion*)
2 Lion Brand (5.04) (from *Thunder Feedback Confusion*)
3 Gunnison (3.06) (from *Infidel*)
4 Born to Go (5.57) (from *Assassins of Silence*)
5 Light of This World (10.53) (from *Thunder Feedback Confusion*)
6 After Heaven (4.19) (from *Enduro*)
7 Miss Rev (6.04) (from *Enduro*)
8 Breed Love (4.04) (from *Infidel*)
9 Crucethon (4.34) (from *Enduro*)
10 Jacobite (8.57) (from *We've Got the Biggest Engine*)

Yes, I know it's another compilation I made up myself, but what the fuck, I'm trying to serve the artist, and if they can't rustle up something that nails their metaphor in a single 'best of'-styled LP, then so be it. Shit, I'm hardly one to talk after all these years of veering all over the road. But Ed Wilcox has now been a favourite for a decade and I gots to at least hip you to his existence before the whole shit-house goes up in flames.

Love Is More Than Words, or Better Late Than Never

Is it too much to ask percussionist/fine art major/poet/lecturer Ed Wilcox to perhaps let one major parp loose so that I could write proper words about it? Or is the leader of Philadelphia's Temple of Bon Matin always gonna be just 'too, too, too to put a finger on'? Am I destined to approach his canon of recorded work every nine months or so, whack together yet another Cope anthology of personal favourites – different every time, natch – then stall at the tail-end of the piece just because it don't do that man Wilcox justice? Or do I just say 'fuck it' and tell you all that this singing drummer, Ed Wilcox, is a living sea shanty, a raggedy-assed Huckleberry Finn-meets-Huckleberry Hound who, as leader of this Woden's Hunt from the backwoods, conducts himself with the same impeccable Ginger Baker-meets-Keith Moon, heathen-glitterstompf rage as the Mongols of the Golden Horde displayed while careering across the Iranian Plain?

Throughout Bon Matin's twelve-year career, Wilcox's whistleblower voice has yelped and hectored, urged and cajoled, like 'Did He Die'-period Sky Sunlight Saxon, or a *Dub Housing*-era Crocus Behemoth wading through a swamp of *musique concrète*, howling impressionist, hoedown lyrics ('Caligari's Mirror'-stylee) as he urges on his ever-changing pack of lo-fi mongrel synthesizer dogs and back-alley guitar kitties (and let's not forget the squealing parps of his occasional ornery horn sections, either), always towing behind his Iron Age battalions of rusted-up Dodge and Plymouth chariots a hang-gliding spectral army of free-jazz phantoms and experimental sonic ancestors, numbering among them the members of *Doremi*-period Hawkwind, 'We Are Time'/*Y*-era Pop Group, *Live in Hitler's Bunker*-period Liquorball,[1] *Alien Soundtracks*-period Chrome, each and every Monoshock-on-forty-five, *Disaster*-period Amon Düül, Exuma The Obeah Man, *Metal Box*-period PiL ('Careering' and 'Poptones' especially), *Strictly Personal*-era Don Van Vliet (the tail feathers of 'Kandy Korn', deffo), *Om*-period John Coltrane and The Residents of *Fingerprince* (à la *Petals Fell on Petaluma*-period Harry Partch multiplied by Zen).

Imagine Creedence's 'Pagan Baby' with three analogue synthesizer players and Mitch Mitchell on drums, all sent through Comets on Fire's Noel Harmonson's Binson Echorec unit, and you're homing in somewhat on the obscurant Wilcox sound. Imagine that same treatment unleashed upon Hanoi Rocks' immaculately decadent, lo-fi 'Self-Destruction Blues' (Andy McCoy's lyrics refracted through the instant Google translator . . .) and you hit the nail on the head once again.

My cosmic assertion that the best rock'n'roll is achieved via an equation of thirty-five percent novelty

1 Ed Wilcox played with Liquorball on their live album, *Tora Tora Live*, released in 2000 on Radon records. This three-piece powerhouse affair featured Marlon 'Feast' Kasberg on bass and sirens, alongside Monoshock legend Grady Runyan, and consisted of one violently explosive thirty-nine-minute track.

and sixty-five percent tradition was never so perfectly realised as in the music of Temple of Bon Matin at their best. Now, of course, being a defiant motherfucker, Ed Wilcox's music often falls way outside that aforementioned magical alchemy, alternately creating overdoses of unlistenable dins or overly devotional backwards/backwoods, inbred folk music (campfire *musique concrète*, anyone?), but as Mister Ed's muse can only be discovered by those willing to probe the deepest recesses of the Internet, we gots to imagine that only those hardiest perennials of souls are – fifteen long years into the trip – still making the effort to listen to his venerable barbarian free spirit.

Ed Wilcox may have termed his band 'space-metal' (perhaps in deference to the early UFO compilation of the same name), but his claims that the group takes as much of its inspiration from Judas Priest as from Sun Ra is disingenuous to say the least. Indeed, Ed's days of the big riff seem long behind him and, surely, the act of making music that sounds like the alchemical melding of the seventeen-minute, unedited version of 'LA Blues', a.k.a. 'Freak', by The Stooges into Mahogany Brain's twenty-one-minute-long 'Burning the Vibes' would, from the reactions of your fellow musicians alone, disavow you of any such notion. Indeed, Ed Wilcox has occasionally recorded whole LPs without so much as a single memorable riff to their name; albums on which 'chanting like negroes in the forest, brightly coloured' seems to be his only *raison d'être*; albums where Exuma the Obeah Man fronts the formlessness of Can's 'Aumgn'; albums where the ESP-Disk ravings of Cro-Magnon's stupor-duo classic 'Caledonian' take over for a whole fucking LP side (*We've Got the Biggest Engine*, *Bullet into Mesmer's Brain*); dirty-ass ambient records that seem to exist purely as a metaphor for the useless and vilely scruffy post-industrial hinterlands that lie, nay wallow between the city conurbations and the rural landscapes beyond. Moreover, these records are real because – in his many and ever-changing day jobs – Ed Wilcox is the poet of the in-between, the forklift-truck driver, the manual labourer, the high-level, itinerant ranter busking a blue-collar living in order to subsidise his music.

So why am I writing about this low rider named Wilcox, if his career has been, is and (possibly) always will be such a hit-and-miss affair? Surely there must be plenny of *caca* more deserving to be bigged up during this particklierly bland portion of the twenty-first century? No. There truly ain't anybody out there more deserving than Ed Wilcox and his hand-painted, semi-industrial drum kit. Shit, I'd have written these words years ago if I'd been able to reach where his music is capable of taking us. However, this is not music of the *now*, brothers and sisters; it is truly music of the *forever*. Ed Wilcox will be making music for at least another decade before he hits his peak and makes something we can all take from; in the meantime, all the real heads can stick their craniums in his bass bins real early, here and now, and look forward to what is to come.

Herr Wilcox being himself an AC/DC fan, Doggen and I have long wished to do a power trio with him named Temple of Bon Scott, but visa problems set that back, and the best I can do is alert you to his ever-curious muse, mostly irritating and unapproachable as it may be. If there's a real problem with the subterranean Ed Wilcox thus far, it's that the Judas Priest clichés he hears are still all in his head and need to be shat out in the company of such turds on a bum ride as me and the Dogman.

This Compilation Sucks: America's Most Loudness

I'd be dead wrong to suggest that these toons I excavated from my sizeable Bon Matin collection in any way truly reflect the band's oeuvre as a whole. Hell, kiddies, it's all down to chance and technology here in Lord Yatesbury's pad. For a start, I ignored totally all the songs from *Cabin in the Sky* (which I love, by the way), purely because I ain't got the technology to transfer the vinyl on to digital for y'all. Indeed, my scratched-to-heil vinyl copy of *Thunder Feedback Confusion* wouldna been represented either if it weren't for the righteous intervention of Surefire Distribution's Ron Schneidermann, whose ecstasy and apostasy regarding The Wilcox clued me to this locust-abortion technician in the first place. That Ron's own transfer from vinyl is itself a crackling, popping miscarriage of sonic justice makes me feel a little better, especially as it suggests that every copy of *Thunder Feedback Confusion* was not pressed conventionally, being instead hand-grooved by southpaw orcs with alcoholic DTs, labouring seventeen hours per day in the sweatshops of Mordor. Furthermore, I was reluctant to heft too much of the unconventional Bon Matin smearage your way for fear of turning you off afore ye'd even commenced the trip. So this so-called 'anthology' is top-heavy with early stuff, almost bereft of mid-period songs and under-representative of the newer, *Infidel*-period squawk.

Sure, Temple of Bon Matin started life as a duo and graduated, for their first LP (*Thunder Feedback Confusion*), into a power trio, but they thereafter made records as a twin-drumming quintet (*Enduro*), before engorging, by the late mid-'90s, into a florid and perspiring nonet (*Bullet into Mesmer's Brain*, *We've Got the Biggest Engine*, *Cabin in the Sky*), replete with three synthesizer players, three guitarists and the guest stupor-star, punch-drunk punk-rock singer Mikey 'Mayor of South Street' Wild.

That Ed Wilcox would not choose to call himself a pragmatic motherfucker is evidenced by his so-called comeback LP, 2004's *Infidel*, on which he still managed to shoehorn six members into the group, making the Temple neither a practical touring outfit nor a viable rehearsing or recording proposition. To my melted plastic way of thinking, this lack of the practical is what makes Wilcox's utter dedication worthy of both your time and mine. He's clearly the US underground's equivalent of George Clinton's Parliament, circa the outlandish and cash-consuming 1978 Mothership tour, and should be lauded for it (if some mentor/patron gave him shed-loads of cash, I'm sure Ed would blow it on a choir and/or arkestra worthy of Sun Ra himself). Long may the temple survive, be it in brick, stone, wood or even soluble-tablet form. That I have made no attempt to describe individually each song contained within this demonstration disc has more to do with the elusive nature of this band than any true laziness on my part.

Temple of Bon Matin, brothers and sisters. Look out for their new record around 2015 and it should all start to be coming a little clearer.

Discography

Thunder Feedback Confusion (Siltbreeze, 1995)
Enduro (Bulb, 1996)
Bullet into Mesmer's Brain (Bulb, 1997)
We've Got the Biggest Engine (New Noise, 1999)
Cabin in the Sky (Bulb, 2001)
Infidel (Spirit of Orr, 2004)
Assassins of Silence/Hundred-Watt Violence (Hawkwind tribute compilation, Ceres, 1995)

Thrones

Sperm Whale

(Kill Rock Stars, 2000)

1 Oso Malo (4.28)
2 Nuts and Berries (3.08)
3 Manmtn (7.00)
4 Acris Venator (2.18)
5 Django (2.45)
6 Ephraim (4.16)
7 The Anguish of Bears (4.11)
8 Obolus (11.45 or 45.47)

Considering Joe Preston's Thrones project has, in the past decade of our Album of the Month review series, regularly cropped up throughout main texts and footnotes, it's more than a little remiss of me to have waited so long before getting it together to devote an entire review to this primal mover and earth-shaker. In truth, however, I've tried several times to write a review of Thrones, only to give up halfway through. That changed after I saw Preston play in Bristol, in 2006; the experience was so liberating that I threw off all my previous fears and determined to set to and deliver as soon as possible. I figured that even if the review was merely average writing, y'all still needed to be clued into this super druid.

One Ubiquitous Motherfucker

Thrones is a phenomenon; a one-man, programmed heavy-metal phenomenon in which a former member of rock icons Melvins and Earth has chosen to lead his audience to endarkenment by the most circuitous and hazardous road imaginable. Not for Thrones the obvious Sabbath, Kiss and Alice Cooperisms of so many of his contemporaries. Instead, armed mainly with a hugely overdriven (and be-horned) BC Rich bass, a variety of vocoders and multitudinous other vocal effects from deep within the ancestral sepulchres of Hanna-Barbera, Disney and AAP, and sporting a truly religious attitude to drum programming that makes the Seventh Day Adventists seem positively Anglican, Joe Preston, on all of his Thrones recordings, bestrides a fertile river valley like some mythical being, shod with giant-sized motorbike boots, on one side of him a mountain surmounted by a temple dedicated to The Residents' *Duck Stab* EP period ('Sinister Exaggerator', 'Bach Is Dead' and 'Elvis and His Boss' slowed to thirty-three rpm), while on the opposing conical hill is situated a similar temple to the movie soundtrack of *A Clockwork Orange* ('Theme' and 'March from . . .').

Although Thrones was forged in the same fires that have, over the decades, yielded such metal mental cases as Sleep, Melvins, Earth, Sunn O))), Khanate and their boisterous ilk, Preston's 'band' regularly strays far outside its 'official' stamping ground in order to gorge itself on tasty treats from entirely foreign sources, barfing up hairballs the size of Edgar Froese's 'Metropolis' from his Kraut-glam epic double LP *Ages*. Unlike many artists who spread their net so wide, however, the fundamental Thrones sound is comprised of such electro-fist-fucking bowel-throb and tinnitus-inducing cymbalism that wherever Preston steers the project, the original influence is immediately transcended purely by the unique rendition of the so-called rhythm section (no one but Preston programmes drum machines with such a curiously caffeinated/amphetamined/maximum-strength Dexatrim ear for detail). This obsessive tendency made his cover of Blue Öyster Cult's Michael Moorcockian epic 'Black Blade' (released on the Southern Lord compilation *Day Late, Dollar Short*) nothing short of masterful, injecting a groove where previously there was none, and making the nightmare lyrics sound like his own personal experiences; moreover, on that same album Thrones dared to cover the single decent Ultravox song ('Young Savage'[1]) ever laid on magnetic tape, proving to me his worth as a musicologist and master of excavation. And another fucking

1 For those too young to know, the John Foxx-fronted early Ultravox had first appeared in 1975 as the glam-rock, post-Biba-styled Tiger Lily, who recorded for Gull Records. Their sole single, a horribly arch, sub-Bryan Ferry version of Fats Waller's 'Ain't Misbehavin'', reappeared on the shelves in mid-'77, and was just visible enough to embarrass the band, and Foxx in particular, who had formerly tried to make it under his own name, Dennis Leigh. In Liverpool, the audience contribution to the chorus of 'Young Savage', when played out at Eric's punk club, was: 'Spring cabbage . . . Spring cabbage!'

thing: Preston's brief time in the Melvins yielded their impossibly overachieving (and impossible to follow) 1992 masterwork, *Lysol*, a single thirty-one-minute proto-doom blueprint of a track replete with another great cover of hard-hearted Alice's 'Ballad of Dwight Fry', from *Love It to Death*.[2]

It was also during their brief Melvins tenure that Buzzo, Dale and Joe put out their own Kiss solo-album-styled records.[3] Joe's it was that copped the biggest feels with its massive, side-long album closer 'Hand's First Flower', a draft version of future Thrones material if ever there was one. Like all great artists, keeping track of the Preston oeuvre is a fucking nachtmare, as he hops from one non-corporate project to another, with ne'er a thunk for the poor impoverished collector, even jumping briefly aboard Matt Pike's Bronze Age headbangers High on Fire, for Odin's sake!

Which is why this Album of the Month is being served up by me – your ornery but pragmatic motherfucker – as promised, as your best way into the Temple of Thrones by way of the sacred twin EPs *Sperm Whale* and *White Rabbit*, herein reduced to one CD album. In their originally released format, the four songs from *Sperm Whale* were all written in celebration of bears ('The Anguish of Bears', 'Nuts and Berries', 'Oso Malo' ['bad bear'] and 'Ephraim'), while *White Rabbit* contained the Buzzo-styled vocals of 'Man Mountain', the cover of Luis Bacalov's amazing spaghetti western theme song from the 1966 Sergio Corbucci movie *Django*, the brief, Space Invaders-sounding instrumental 'Acris Venator' and the forty-five-minute-long 'Obolus' (more than half of which is a field-recording tail-out of cicadas clucking in the olive groves), named after those massive, cumbersome rods that the ancient

2 *Lysol*'s sleeve also proclaimed a version of the Coop's 'Second Coming' from the same *Love It to Death* LP, but it turned out to be one of Buzz's wind-ups.

3 As an Englishman who's been married for well over twenty years to a Yank, I'm still highly aware of how mysterious it is to we Limeys just how much Gene Simmons' vocal style has informed the metal generations. As Kiss didn't mean squat to my comrades, they always thought my wife's Kiss and other glamour-come-lately types were cultural lowlifes. Being married to an American also forced me to re-evaluate such pop-whore bands as Slade and The Sweet, both persona non grata as far as the British rock pantheon is concerned, but lauded as the real deal in Detroit and LA.

Spartans used in place of money to stop people turning into greedheads.

Exeunt Joe Preston, Pursued by a Bear

Like *Alraune*, its predecessor, *Sperm Whale* opens with the kind of statement that sends some gentle souls running out of the room, 'Oso Malo', featuring the kind of sledgehammer, programmed drumming that can only make its point in a digital format as the vinyl would inevitably jump all over the place. From the off, generic alien voices chunter to each other in a slowly descending staff elevator as the Preston horned bass charges down a spiral staircase armed with a claw hammer, attempting to block their exit, the merciless punctuations of programmed cymbals sounding as though – as he runs – he's offing random flies and roaches (and taking out chunks of the wall simultaneously) with that same horrific weapon.

'I'm pleased you appreciate good wine . . . have another glass,' says an arch and cultured English voice as 'Nuts and Berries' kicks off into a kind of Beethoven melody, horribly upended by bass crunch and catchy-bastard, vocodered vocal refrain. For me, this is like *A Clockwork Orange* at its finest: violence and aversion therapy and bass from the sub-basements of Berlin's Bunker.

The seven minutes of 'Man Mountain' (or 'Manmtn', as it's billed) follows; a raging vocal rant about something I can't fathom, propelled solely by the epic Preston bass offage. Harmony vocals and a disturbed, traditional melody lend the song a feeling of compassion that makes the listener both disturbed and concerned . . . just what the fuck is going on here, and should somebody do something about it?

The two-minute-long 'Acris Venator' (or 'steadfast hunter') inhabits a space somewhere between the opening of Amon Düül II's 'Dem Guten, Schönen, Wahren' from *Phallus Dei* and generic moon-landing theme music, bleeping like an alien's car alarm forewarning its owner that chav ne'er-do-wells are plotting its imminent seizure.

After that, 'Avon calling' tubular bells announce the arrival of 'Django', a programmed, 6/8-time spaghetti theme sung in Spanish and propelled by ludicrously overstimulated drum fills, while 'Ephraim' is an almighty bass rendition of 'lone bear lost in the woods' music, Preston playing a mournful harmonised melody over a pulsing and woofing repeated sub-bass note, followed up by the crushing riffage of 'The Anguish of Bears', again, the programmed drumming busting your brain until the whole track opens out into a kind of sub-bass, Mick Ronson orchestra of sweet harmonies. A drum break from the bowels of Mother Earth heralds a screaming aeroplane disaster, before the main riff returns at half the speed and the track tails out in some truly sweet and fully charged vocal/bass/percussion afterburn-up.

The album closer, 'Obolus', commences with pure *A Clockwork Orange* Teutonics; the multi-tracked voices and extraordinarily beautiful harmonies standing midway between Walter Carlos and Seventh Wave's epic medley 'Camera Obscura/Star Palace of the Sombre Warrior'. This huge, three-minute beginning lasts just long enough for the ensuing Thrones riffage to throw us, as the sweet choruses continue, although now accompanied by the agents of sub-bass hell. This vocodered theme continues deep into a kind of doom take on industrial Krautrock, until the cityscape becomes enveloped in mists and the darkness of nature takes over. The lone voice of an Ancient informs us that an era has passed, the gravel-chewing voice of some sub-sub-subterranean 'other' agrees and the entire soundscape is taken over by the clucking of cicadas. It's a truly fabulous finale to this epic voyage, and one that concludes far too soon.

We can only hope that Joe Preston reinvigorates his Thrones trip in the near future, for his music is epically cinematic and effortlessly reaches the highs and lows of rock opera without ever needing to stoop so low as to purvey any actual narrative. To Joe Preston, I cry: 'Mein hairy, I salute thee and thy sub-basso profundo! Voyage onwards, continental drifter, for we shall follow you wherever . . .'

Right fucking on!

Discography

'The Suckling' (single, Kill Rock Stars, 1998)
'Reddleman' (single, Punk In My Vitamins, 1999)
'Senex' (single, Soda Girl, 1999)
'White Rabbit' (EP, Kill Rock Stars, 1999)
'Spermwhale' (EP, Kill Rock Stars, 2000)
Alraune (The Communion Label, 1996)
Sperm Whale/White Rabbit (Kill Rock Stars, 2000)
Day Late, Dollar Short (Southern Lord, 2005)

Tight Bro's from Way Back When

Runnin' Thru My Bones

(Kill Rock Stars, 1999)

SIDE ONE	SIDE TWO
1 Hurricane (2.13)	1 Hayseed Rock (2.16)
2 Workin' Overtime (1.55)	2 Witchy Potion (2.16)
3 That's a Promise (3.03)	3 Shake (2.40)
4 Gimme Luv (2.39)	4 So Sneaky (3.22)
5 Strut (3.48)	5 Coo Coo Ha! (2.46)
6 Drop to My Knees (2.16)	6 Light That Fuse (4.05)
7 Rip It Up (2.28)	

You Can't Kill the Undead

So my missus is cruising Pandora.com looking for the new noise (by way of the old noise, natch), and she comes running into my bedroom blasting this proto-Sonny Vincent, sub-Slade 'Get Down and Get with It' out of the tinny speaker of her laptop, buzzing like a motherbiatch. Even at pin-drop volume, this is a deffo instant find of the year, but I hang fire on any official judgement until I have the machine hooked up to the big speakers, at which time the Slade connection recedes faster than the Morecambe Bay tide (or Dave Hill's comb-over), as the bass kicks off big time, and the twin lewd/simultaneous rhythm-guitar-mangle spewing out is immediately harder than MC/DC or the AC5. Harder and faster, brothers and sisters . . . demented, manic, strung out, brazen, braying and barking at the moon – as though the R&B and soul influences of both of those aforementioned groups had, in the thirty-five years since their heyday, been honed down and burnished, paraphrased and ultra-distilled into a sonic über-liqueur, then siphoned through the next decades of punk, metal, grunge, no wave and hardcore before finally being vomited out at two hundred mph, like some vicious Friday-night curry/lager combo spray-jetting on to the pavement. Merciful relief! Moreover, caterwauling up a banshee hoodoo over this arcane free-geek shit-storm is one ardent polysyllabic motherfucker of a so-called singer who has even more to harp on about than Axl 'and-another-fuckin'-thing' Rose on 'Don't Damn Me'. Sheesh! At his shrieking highest, this sweat-hog gobstar yowls more stratospherically than Brian Johnson and, at his mid-rangiest (this guy don't do low), is a signed'n'certified, caffeine-free, maximum-strength Robby the Tyne (make the Future Now mine!). Meanwhile, mere moments later, M'lady is already on my laptop skrying eBay for evidence of their produce – indeed, before I've even ferreted out the brand name of the delinquents responsible for said protection racket geysering forth. Hey, do these seer/suckers even acknowledge such protocols as a band name? 'Oh ja, mein hairy,' says the lady wife, 'they'ze called Tight Bro's from Way Back When.' A catchy-bastard moniker for sure, thinks I, and – within mere minutes of having even apprehended their existence – the Cope household has summoned up several armfuls of eBay buy-now, including EPs, shared seven-inch forty-fives and two long-players.

Three months down the line, Tight Bro's from Way Back When have become such a fixture here we got burns of the two albums blasting Dorian's side of the house, while the seven- and twelve-inch vinyl lays permanent waste to the living room and temporarily forces my daughters to relinquish gorging themselves on such TVOD as Drake & Josh and Fatso Raven. Plus, these old guys from Olympia, Washington, gotta name longer than Bullet for My Valentine and Bring Me the Horizon, which earns me mucho post-Emo credit points indoors. Better still, in the cold light of day, the MC5 and AC/DC references, important – nay essential – though they be to the Tight Bro's' metaphor, are revealed to have been no more than a chassis over which these guys have dropped a hotted-up George Barris car body and installed a V16 engine. And besides, without The Who underneath it all, what were the Five or the Young brothers, and who's counting anyway? Furthermore, several rotations later, both of the Tight Bro's' albums are shown to be such overdriven monuments to oblivion that it's taken me ages to decide which one most justifies the Album of the Month gong. In the end, I decided it had to be this debut, because it has no cover versions and, most of all, the vinyl edition contains a classic kids-versus-The Man cartoon strip in which the Tight Bro's appear as white-knight paladins of rock'n'roll whose commitment to the music is so evident that even Mr City Hall bows down before them and lets everyone party till dawn. Even better, a passing grey-haired old biddy gets giddy from the rock racket and discovers that Tight Bro's have cured her arthritis! 'Uh-oh!' says the cartoon version of singer Jared to the reader. 'Looks like we've created a rock'n'roll grandma!' Now who, apart from ultra-cool cunts such as me'n'Gene Simmons (see *Citizen Cain'd*'s 'Dying to Meet You' and 'Deuce' from Kiss' debut album), dares to celebrate the grandma in modern music? Tight Bro's, that's who, motherfuckers!

These guys were the epitome of everything rock'n'roll – five utterly confounding, metal-informed, hardcore punks who released records on the same labels as refuseniks such as Thrones, Half Japanese, Melvins and Sleater-Kinney, but raging against the inevitable self-righteous PC of all such successful scenes by coming on like lobotomised slaves of Slade who would play ZZ Top's 'Tush', on stage, whenever anyone broke a string. That such greedy slobs can have their cake and eat it, simultaneously straddling two seemingly entirely opposing worlds, says as much about the greatness of rock'n'roll's Wide Berth Approach as it says about the Tight Bro's themselves, and their record label, Kill Rock Stars. No, that label never advocated doing away with the Rock itself, just the purveyors – and, as any nice trawl around the Viking mead hall would always attest, we let the minstrel sing the song and if it's good enough we won't kill the fucker.

That Shit Is Played Out

Runnin' Thru My Bones is Album of the Month because it's the raging best of two fabulous turn-of-the-millennium recordings (the other being *Lend You a Hand*) in which Tight Bro's from Way Back When sensationally recaptured the kind of high-energy hard-rock that pervaded the concert stage of 1969–71 but rarely – including even Sir Lord Baltimore's incendiary *Kingdom Come* – made it on to vinyl in any truly sustained manner before the punk watershed of '77, after which time the riff became almost the sole domain of metal, while the scalding, post-Keef, *Raw Power* chord sequence became requisitioned by the so-called punk scene.[1] However, two-and-a-bit decades later, the five Tight Bro's from Way Back When (hereafter known as T.B.F.W.B.W.) marshalled their forces around two former members of Olympia hardcore band Behead the Prophet No Lord Shall Live (got the vinyl, need the t-shirt!) to create this mind-boggling, post-everything jizz-fest. Behead the Prophet's bassist, John 'Quitty' Quittner, and guitarist, Dave Harvey, thereafter fucked off all the musical experiment and the worthy and wordy lyrics of their former band (whose LP *I Am That Great and Fiery Force* still sounds like über-superior spew, by the way), replacing it with the hoary, timeless clichés of motormouthed, kinky Afro'd frontman Jared Warren, ex-bass player/singer with Karp. However, claiming this shit is a mere DC or MC5 clone or a *Nuggets/Pebbles* (or, more to the point, a *Hipsville 29BC* or *Back from the Grave*) throwback/wannabe is to entirely miss the point. Rock at its best is meant to be derivative, motherfuckers!

Think about it. Without the Stones there'd have been no Stooges and no Doors; without Hendrix, no Blue Cheer or The Who's *Live at Leeds*; without *Live at Leeds*' 'Young

1 The operative word here is definitely 'sustained'. Until after punk, even AC/DC LPs contained only brief moments of the kind of energy needed to compete with Tight Bro's from Way Back When. Being originally released on the December '75 Australian-only album *TNT*, the demented 'Rocker' sounded entirely anomalous next to its truly sedate neighbours on the internationally-released *Dirty Deeds Done Dirt Cheap*. Indeed, even after punk's broadsides slammed the rock'n'roll world for six, AC/DC's first, punk-informed, October '77 LP *Let There Be Rock* still contained a coupla slowies. Moreover, 1978 saw DC decelerate once more when they returned with the fifty-five mph, sixteen-wheeler, freightliner tonnage of *Powerage* (along with *TNT*, still my personal favourite). And, much as I love *If You Want Blood You've Got It*, live LPs are always full of old songs played twice as fast, so surely we have to exclude it. Of course, any number of early garage-rock bands produced killer moments of sheer adrenaline – from the demented singles of '60s bands such as The Wig ('Crackin' Up') and The Outcasts ('1523 Blair'), to James Williamson's edition of The Stooges around 'I Gotta Right'. But to sustain such energy over an entire LP only happened after punk, and even then, always at the expense of melody and song – something the Tight Bro's could never be accused of. I suppose that only by finding their way to their (some say) retro goal, via hardcore and metal, could Tight Bro's have reached a music of such intense pace – dragging half their fans from previous hardcore bands (Behead the Prophet were terrifyingly fast) would surely have goaded each one of them on to play harder and faster every night.

Man Blues', no 'Black Dog'; without Blue Cheer's *Outsideinside*, no *Kick Out the Jams*; without Led Zeppelin, no Guns N'Roses; without Montrose, no Van Halen; without The New York Dolls, no Sex Pistols; without Black Sabbath, nothing at all . . .

So, despite the pictorial evidence of an initial DC fixation found in T.B.F.W.B.W.'s press clippings (Dave Harvey's wielding a Malcolm Gretsch, while Quitty plays an Angus Gibson SG), ultimately this LP is so exhilarating and intensely bombarding of the senses that it sounds like nothing but itself. And besides, it's fashioned by north-western boyos inbred by years of Sonics and Kingsmen forty-fives. Which is probably why Jared's vocals ultimately sound like somebody accidentally played The Novas' 1965 single 'The Crusher' at seventy-eight rpm – so mangled, so garrotted, so eye-bulgingly shit-yer-pants that W. Axl Rose sounds almost baritone by comparison.

This debut LP was recorded by a subterranean, gristly, five-dicked, ten-armed, tensile nocturnal marsupial that gobbles up its young and fills its pouch with personalised plectrums. After the muddy mush of their debut EP *Take You Higher*,[2] new engineer Stuart Hallerman brought a brilliance to the T.B.F.W.B.W. sound – and didn't these guys rise to the occasion? Commencing with 'Hurricane''s maelstrom of accelerating snare drumming, *Runnin' Thru My Bones* then proceeds across the rock'n'roll horizons of the past forty years, like a parched sun guzzling up all the moisture in its path and leaving only scorched earth where rivers and lakes used to be. 'Hurricane' is the Five's 'Sonically Speaking' through a Guitar Wolf filter, but always with a Ray Charles heart that just burns

2 And yet, despite the enormity of that debut LP achievement, when Tight Bro's opened their recording career with a fairly generic, DC-like EP entitled *Take You Higher*, on the tiny Olympia label Ten-to-One, for shit damn sure no one could have foreseen that this debut LP was gonna offer such an outrageously squirmy electric eel of a sound. Indeed, on 'Take You Higher' the anguished, insane vocals are undermined by the fairly inconsequential backing track, while 'I'm in Luck', while full-on, is ultimately rendered goofy and ersatz thanks to Jared's vocal asides. However, 'Chicken Little Lied' is fucking excellent, something like the Young brothers playing Cactus' heavy version of 'Long Tall Sally'. Perhaps righteously, though, the best of the four and closest to the album material was the EP's closing song, the unused LP title track, 'Runnin' Thru My Bones', which steams like *Rubber Legs*-period Stooges playing a Highway Robbery cover. But still nothing can have prepared fans for that debut LP.

with a truly methylated spirit. The flat-out burn-up of 'Workin' Overtime' is another 'Whole Lotta Rosie', while 'That's a Promise' is suffused with such an incandescent, anguished and stratospheric rock beauty that it brings me almost to the brink of hope for this planet. Motherfuckers . . . I DO believe! This song is the *High Time*-period MC5 playing '19th Nervous Breakdown', rewritten as a battle hymn to the White Goddess by Fred 'Sonic' Smith and sung in Rob Tyner's 'Over and Over' voice. And they don't back off. 'Gimme Luv' is like feeding Led Zep's 'Communication Breakdown' through the end of 'Won't Get Fooled Again' via 'For Those About to Rock', while 'Strut' – despite approaching mid-tempo regions – still burns just as intensely as everything that's come before, as the Bro's (over a soul strut of epic proportions) conflate several classic rock'n'roll lyrics together (mainly Gene Vincent's 'Be Bop A Lula') in the same manner as Purple's 'Speed King'. Thereafter, the song tails out with a wonderful harmonica and call-and-answer chorus in the mandatory, Young brothers' donkey-braying stylee.

'Drop to My Knees' is hotter than heil, an inflammatory berserker's boogie with hard right/left-panned lead-guitar breaks and an *ernie-ernie*-ing 'Radar Love' drop down. It's powered by a hugely thunderous and ornate Stoogedom, with Quitty supplying what he calls 'Neo-Fascist guitar licks', of the oodly-oodly variety, loudly in the right-hand speaker. It's outrageous how a band can plunder such *Rockus Genericus* yet still come up sounding exactly like themselves and nobody else. If yooz a bunch of talented hardworking motherfuckers, you can heap cliché on top of cliché and all you get is originality.

'Rip It Up' concludes Side One by raining down a hail of drums and bass, before Kiss' 'King of the Night Time World' fuses with a Sandy Pearlmanised Clash gone ten times more stratospheric, as Jared's voice rips through Alice Cooper, Gene Simmons, more Axl, bitsa Janis . . . hell, brothers and sisters, through every fucker and no fucker-at-all. This Warren guy is a fucking original, sucking at the fountainhead of every rock move since Ike's 'Rocket 88'.

When 'Hayseed Rock' opens Side Two, we begin an epic cruise through what may one day become a medley of modern classics. This opener is what Silverhead's 1972 boogie probably woulda been around the time of *Sixteen and Savaged*, if those rock tarts coulda got out of the Biba changing rooms for long enough – like an even more monolithic version of Mott the Hoople's monumental, Guy Stevens-produced live ramalama before Bowie fiddled with 'em.

'Witchy Potion' has a twin guitar lead/rhythm worthy of Sonic and Brother Wayne, while the two minutes and forty seconds of 'Shake' is pure frat-rock dorkdom, evidence of Jared Warren's assertion that 'Tight Bro's only do "obscure" covers by bands that are featured in magazines like *Ugly Things*.' Dunno why they left it off the CD, but it helps confuse the issue even further, which is always nice.

With its eternal *ernie-ernie*-ing guitar wail and arch-retro chorus, 'So Sneaky' is what The David Johansen Band's 'I'm a Lover' woulda sounded like if they'd substituted Johnny Thunders or Steve Jones for Syl Sylvain as their touring guest star, and added The Dictators' Handsome Dick Manitoba on dual vox.

'Coo Coo Ha!' is probably the closest to a standard soul classic that the Bro's have come. With its catchy-bastard chorus ('That's right!/ Certifiably loony!'), this song will be regularly covered in fifty years' time *and* be mistaken for a lost Barrett Strong forty-five. Moreover, the 'Call Me Animal' Television-style key change into the fake tail-out is inspired as a motherfucker and killer to the *n*th degree.

Runnin' Thru My Bones finishes with yet more epic soundtrack as the slide-guitar-powered 'Light That Fuse' careens across the highly polished floor, held together only by Justin's wilful jungle drumming, some pure Sir Lord Baltimore overdubbed guitar strangling and the Tight Bro's' collective commitment to layering the track with as much percussion as (that reference again) the Five's 'Sonically Speaking'. Is this a barbarian classic or watt, motherfuckers? Ja, mein hairies – signed, sealed, delivered, they're *ours*!

A Little History of T.B.F.W.B.W.

Unfortunately, despite touring as much as they could and holding down day jobs in the process, the Tight Bro's appear to have hit lean times fairly soon after the release of *Runnin' Thru My Bones*. It's for this reason that drummer Justin Olsen felt compelled to jump ship before the recording of *Lend a Hand*; and also why this second LP was delayed until 2002. However, by the time the album recording had been booked, even new drummer Ian Vanek was long gone and had been replaced by the still short-haired and not yet Ted Nugentised Nat Damm, later to become infamous as drummer with Seattle's Viking-styled death ragers, Akimbo. It was most probably during this miserable interim downtime period that T.B.F.W.B.W.'s career went AWOL; just when they shoulda been picking up new fans by recording LP after LP after LP, working on the same kind of punishing schedule that informed the early careers of Grand Funk and Kiss. If the innate strength of your albums is that they sound as blurrily generic as Tight Bro's' LPs do, you gotta go at it like a scrum of bastards or take the consequences.[3]

Ironically, despite its late release, the second Tight Bro's album is virtually as raging as the first. I stated earlier that I avoided reviewing *Lend You a Hand* because of the cover versions, but that's mainly because Tight Bro's originals are themselves often as catchy as the cover versions, perhaps even more so. But the Bro's were always covering other bands' songs in live shows, having played Slade's 'Gudbuy T'Jane' in their early days, and their recorded version of Joe Tex's 'Show Me' is a timeless monsterpiece that blows my tiny mind. Ironically, *Lend You a Hand* concludes with a slightly inferior version of The Animals' prison lament 'Inside–Looking Out', which was covered with far greater oomph and panache by Grand Funk Railroad and Scott Weinrich's The Obsessed. Apart from that one disappointment, however, *Lend You a Hand* is still almost as vital as the debut.

So, whatever happened to T.B.F.W.B.W.? Well, the short answer to that, brothers and sisters, appears to be 'nuthin' much'. If we're to believe the hagiographers and mythologists of the World Wide Web, my favourite Tight Bro of all – guitarist John 'Quitty' Quittner[4] – is a 'professional window cleanser', while singer Jared 'Handsome Dick' Warren 'got tired of not having an instrument in my hands' and teamed up with Melvins/Thrones/High on

---

3 Accused of making twelve consecutive LPs that all sounded the same, Angus Young told one interviewer that he had not been keeping up and that it was, in fact, fourteen LPs that all sounded the same.

4 Quitty is my mainman because not only is his favourite guitarist James Williamson, but he also 'gets' David Lee Roth, which says fucking everything about a person, in my book. Of Roth, Quittner once wrote: 'He is the blueprint from which all subsequent LA hair bands were designed . . . The runnin' around on stage, the "I love to party" persona, the bodacious blond mane, the pouting . . . all of it! And my man's Jewish to boot.' Nuff said.

Fire legend Joe Preston to form The Whip. Olympia myth also has it that his day job is spent 'Busy, as a hair volumizer', obviously capitalising on his tight 'fro from way back when . . . In the meantime, drummer Nat Damm mutated into a Viking and currently denies having even worked with T.B.F.W.B.W.,[5] while bass player Sean Kelly 'is a professional hill roller, tumbling down some of the steepest hills in the greater Olympia area, just to make sure the safety standards are met for America's youth'. Nothing is known of guitarist Dave Harvey, although rumour has it that he's in France with his Senegalese girlfriend, living out his Linda and Sonny Sharrock fantasies. Interviewed before he disappeared, Harvey's response to the question of a possible Tight Bro's reunion was unequivocal: 'We are so done. For years now! However, if Glenn Frey and Don Henley can put their acrimony aside for a whole tour, certainly the Tight Bro's can be half the men they are some day.'

Do it, gentlemen. Not only are you brilliant and unsung, but y'all got the best un-famous lead vocalist since Woody Leffel split up Granicus back in 1974. Search out that motherfucker, steal his bass, hire him a decent PA and pronto, Tonto! (He should still be allowed to find time to do The Whip, so long as the ever-multi-tasking genius, Joe Preston, is involved.) And if Jared really is a 'hair volumizer' during the daylight hours (which I kinda do wanna believe), then wrench his Nicky Clark hair-straighteners away from him and heft them through the salon window. Even if he's gained a hundred and fifty pounds and had a sex change, it don't matter none – singers of Jared Warren's calibre, the match of Bon Scott, Rob Tyner, Janis Joplin and Brian Johnson, just don't crop up every day. This guy's voice is gold dust and we want it now!

Ironically, Tight Bro's woulda done much better in the music biz had they been halfway decently styled. However, had they been sex gods, they probably woulda slowed down their thing to attract the ladies and fifty percent of the appeal woulda been sucked right out the

5 Nat Damm is also a successful designer of posters and album sleeves, with a huge CV of clients, including Melvins, Liz Phair, Jello Biafra, Gwar, The Hanson Brothers, Evan Dando, Death from Above 1979, The Ponys, High on Fire, Comets on Fire, Eyehategod, Nina Hagen, The Subhumans, The White Stripes, Teenage Fanclub, Ash, Wolf Eyes and Whitehouse. But his time with the Bro's was so bad that he'll nowadays even admit to designing for shit like My Chemical Romance and Devendra Banhart, but still deny any history with T.B.F.W.B.W.!

window. Still, when you got as keen and kick-ass a bunch as T.B.F.W.B.W. watching from the wings, mouth agape at Sleater-Kinney's magnificent rebirth, we can only hope that Tight Bro's get goaded into thinking they could come back even harder than first time around. Indeed, I wanna see an ocean of hope out there, beloveds, because we truly *need* such Olympian brothers! Until then, motherfuckers, at least we still got AC/DC.

Discography

Take You Higher (EP, Ten-in-one, 1998)
Runnin' Thru My Bones (Kill Rock Stars, 1999)
Lend You a Hand (Kill Rock Stars, 2002)

Universal Panzies

Transcendental Floss

(Head Heritage, 1998)

1 Krautrock Lovesong/Hallowed-undgallowed (18.49)
2 Star-bard and Grounded/I Won't Mourn Outside Your Door (15.29)
3 I Crave You (6.26)
4 Cunnyan Crags (11.06)

Happenings Ten Years' Time (Or So) Ago

As evidenced by the mawkishly sentimental outpourings of Peter Hammill's 1975 album *Over*, when the rock'n'roll poet is abandoned by his long-term partner and muse, his poor audience may well be forced to endure a whole LP awash with torrents of sickening self-pity and self-doubt from the solipsistically self-absorbed. That is, unless the rock'n'roll poet in question happens to be a psychically tough (if physically slight) Anglo-Irish Tynesider with a penchant for Krautrock, The Clash and donning heels'n'lippy in order to wind up the local Newkie Brown swiggers in their regulation black-and-white-striped footy shirts. Please step forward, Christophe F of Universal Panzies. In these rare cases, the journey of the artist becomes entirely capsized by his state of affairs, and the recorded results manifest as a neurologic cleansing, nay, a transcendental flossing of the brainboxes of both poet and audience.

And so it was on this sole Universal Panzies Head Heritage release that Christophe F bequeathed us – a magnificent concept album, the first three-quarters of which he spent wounded and brooding upon his sudden abandonment (ugly duckling-stylee) over a highly urban and linear post-Neu!/post-Can, all-purpose motorik beat, before finally emerging triumphant from the dungeon-like city gloom, sun-drenched and bedazzled by the truly rural and heathen daylight of epic, eleven-minute finale 'Cunnyan Crags' – Christophe now reborn as the transcendental seer upon his own land; the Songer, the Speaker of Timeless Truths, garrulous as a motherfucker and thrice as feisty! Me, a swan? . . . Ha, go on!

And you know what, brothers'n'sisters? By celebrating Universal Panzies' *Transcendental Floss*, I feel I've orchestrated something of a righteous act. For the Panzies' album contains within its epic grooves pretty much everything Head Heritage has long aspired to represent and deliver: transcendental, Krautrock-informed, mind-manifesting rhythms, overachieving guitar bombast, saccharine-sweet, Joe Meekian keyboard themes, muse-informed lyrical devotion to the goddess, sheer (post-Queen Elizabeth but pre-Brain Donor) astral glamour of the most Odinistic kind, and always in a manner that projects highly unbalanced sonic overload. Indeed, it's just the kind of sound that current underground bands such as Nudity, Shiva's Tongue and their ilk allude to. On *Transcendental Floss*, however, Christophe's Universal Panzies even managed to turbo that already-hefty metaphor, uniting the by now timeless, driving, linear and motorik Krautrock sound with enough outside elements to render a musical stew not just invigorated but entirely their own – dub elements in the *Transcendental Floss* mix forever firing off fusillades of random King Tubbyan sparks of bass, sub-bass and wholly over-powering guitar power chords, while the mainly mid-range lead vocal occasionally suddenly manifests as the loudest whisper your earhole would ever wish to experience.

The album commences with the gargantuan 'Krautrock Lovesong', in which the lonely, pulsing, post-punk bass of the divinely monikered Rock Stewart X-Mass prepares the way for drummer Boy Fried to enter the fray, Laughing Clowns-style, with his splatter-clattering, Jeffrey Wegener Confederate snare drumming. Spangly guitar from the F and string synth from M'Lady Mandy Neuschnee usher in the poet's intimate pronouncements on the band's intended forthcoming astral projections until – *whumphf* – the whole song defenestrates into the kind of icy and subterranean sonic trough that would even have caused Martin Hannett to cluck. As though Dennis Bovell had applied his *Y*-period Pop Group production techniques to the Bunnymen's *Heaven Up Here*, Universal

Panzies declare their dynamics in such certain terms that the listener's mind immediately makes its decision either to hurl such a singular CD into his fireplace, or accept the coming tsunami with good grace.

Gradually, a motorik air emerges from the core/*coeur* of the song until, at precisely eight minutes and thirteen seconds in, the whole band surges up into a new gear and the La Düsseldorfian themes of 'Hallowedundgallowed' kick in, big time. For nigh on the next ten minutes, the Panzies become barely more than a vehicle for Christophe F's guitar madness, as he assails us with the kind of neck-wringing more reminiscent of Blue Cheer's Leigh Stephens than any of the usual kosmische guitar heroes.

Next up comes 'Star-bard and Grounded', which (according to the artist) began as the Panzies' take on two of my own songs, 's.t.a.r.c.a.r.' and 'Safe Surfer'. However, it's highly apparent that their greedy and melted plastic brains had also scoffed up major elements of The Doors' 'LA Woman' and Funkadelic's 'Maggot Brain', before the resulting queasy stomach saw it all barfed back out again as some disturbingly dystopian Technicolor yawn – a maudlin but heartbreakingly beautiful poetic, sci-fi common-law divorce sung over an enormous music, but one which is so majorly informed by the limited capabilities of the players that part of its true power is contained in the fact that it proffers the kind of sublimely regal and cosmic ineptitude rarely captured on tape. Like East Germans learning rock'n'roll on a crystal radio, picking up only random, distant, US military pop radio stations, the Panzies' performances unite Ramones-level musicianship with Pärson Sound expectations. On 'Star-bard . . .' they bring forth a bubblegum trance music somewhat akin to King Tubby attempting to add blazing Eddie Hazell axe to a thirty-three rpm versh of Boris Gardner's 'Elizabethan Reggae'. Phew! Around seven minutes into this maelstrom, the Panzies – courtesy of keyboardist Mandy Neuschnee – once again change gear drastically, this time into some kinky, Russky hi-steppe that takes in mucho cranky Plastic People of the Universe-style spike-a-delick jamming, until the whole schmeer devolves into the Can-plays-J. Morrison highway blues of 'I Won't Mourn Outside Your Door', an eight-minute-long'n'linear complain-athon punctuated occasionally by some Lora Logic-level rudimentary saxophone from X-Mass and a coupla divine glam descends that, in the ensuing collision, somehow manage to meld together *In Search of Space*-period Hawkwind with *Continental Circus*-era Gong.

Following this apocalypse, the six minutes of 'I Crave You' offer a superb soul-purge that woulda made sense on any late-'70s Berlin dance floor. 'It doesn't hurt at all/It doesn't hurt at all/I'm so pleased to say that it doesn't hurt at all,' chants the F, both vainly and numbly, as the backing voices spell out the song title ('*I-C-R-A-V-E-Y-O-U*') over and over and fucking over again. The vibe here is highly reminiscent of post-Damo Can, but, being possessed of a hugely catchy-bastard, call-and-answer, Tamlaesque chorus, 'I Crave You' comes up smelling only of itself. And as the song's urban driving rhythms recede, so does the sound of the city's nightlife also fade; the clanking horns and the clinking glasses and the uppers and downers and the in-your-face city problems dissipating, diluting and dissolving into nothing . . . to be replaced by the oboe-driven and extraordinarily bucolic sound of the heroic, eleven-minute finale.

Entitled 'Cunnyan Crags', this song finds the poet far out on the moors, propelled by pastoral horn melodies, psychically informed by the ancient landscape and . . . free at last. He walks abroad, hesitating at first amidst the newfound beauty, hardly believing that he's broken away. But each stumbling step across the heather makes him stronger and more ready to take on the outside world again, until – at seven minutes and seven seconds – Christophe F becomes the Seer of the Ages, spewing out the names of the high places that surround him, his words tripping up his tongue at times, but still he rants on like some hilltop rock'n'roll Wordsworth, while the oboe-driven Panzies collectively summon up the ghosts of the ancestors, whose bold strides urge him on and on. It's one of the most exhilarating and beautifully touching album closers I've ever known, and made all the more poignant because it was not to be repeated again at any commercial level. But, herein, Christophe F and his glamorous cohorts created a veritable Pandora's box of words and music, and one that will one day gain its true legend among the people of the north-east.

Whatever Happened to . . .

Many have asked me what became of the Universal Panzies. In truth, I don't rightly know. On and off, I've known Christophe F for nigh on thirty years now, and his health has never been too good, his cohorts never too consistent and his geographical location never too appropriate for the kind of poetic lifestyle he requires. But, while his obstinacy and refusal to move south have hindered Christophe's overall trip, certain other musical peaks – his many privately pressed Panzies EPs, his contributions to my 2000 South Bank festival *Cornucopea*, and 2001's L.A.M.F. album *Ambient Metal* – show that Christophe's artistic spirit will only truly be broken by bodily death. And, as one who truly appreciates just how few black-sheep artists there are among us, I for one would rather he remained safe in the land he knows (and loves so well) rather than dutifully engage with a ruthless outside world that gobbles up the meek, the mild and the messed-up, only to gob them out as useless and undigestible soon after. For while Christophe remains here with us, he remains useful to us all, even if it's only in an advisory capacity.

VON LMO

Red Resistor

(Variant Records, 1996)

1 Mass Destruction (9.43)
2 Flying Saucer 88 (6.53)
3 X + Z = 0 (31.12)
4 Atomic Sound (5.17)

Prepare to be boarded, motherfuckers. VON LMO came out of a decade of suspended animation to make this album, so give it a proper listen, brothers and sisters. This VON LMO druid's had a sixty-year-plus career-of-sorts and employs the kind of artless vocal delivery that's gonna make a few of you duck in fear for the future of your culture. But don't be afraid, because he's the saviour. And, no, he doesn't scream any louder than the next moron; he just drones on and on at the same sustained and insulated maximum volume. Think Cyrus 'Nine times the colour red explodes like heated blood' Faryar, on The Zodiac's *Cosmic Sounds*; Jim 'When I was back there in seminary school' Morrison; Burton 'I wanna do it to a duck in a twelve-ton truck and fade away' Cummings; or maybe even Lou '. . . neatly pump air' Reed's mic technique for his response vocals on the Velvets' 'The Gift'; then refract the whole schmeer through Patti's 'Radio Ethiopia/Abyssinia' title track and multiply by ten thousand.

Moreover, VON LMO rams home his message (on behalf of some higher galactic authority, apparently) about advancing the human psyche, and always with that same monotonous level of brute force on each song, whatever his generic Axis, Bolder, Woodmansey, Ronson backing may be proto-plodding. And, no, VON LMO ain't one for nuance 'cause it reads too much like 'nance', and this is one No Romantic weez talking up. Also, he most surely *is* heavy metal, the way the late '60s defined it (Brian Butterfly/Brute Cheer), although modern nu metallers'd probbly hate him and spurn him because he's a Utopian.

VON LMO claims also to have been born in two places at the same time – to Sicilian parents in Brooklyn, NY, in 1924, and also simultaneously on the planet Strazar. Well, I'm a spaceman myself and I've been to both his birthplaces and they both stink, so give this oinker VON LMO a break because, to turn Howard Devoto's lyric on its face, although he 'came from nowhere', he sure as hell ain't 'going straight back there'!

This review is dedicated to Mitch Fogelberg, a.k.a. Rubin Fiberglass, Grady Runyan and the Seth Man – all of whom already know all this stuff.

Beam Me Up, Scotty, There's No Foil on the Kit-Kats!

This genius Album of the Month may be fifteen years old, but it sounds as though it was recorded yesterday, or, equally, in Ancient Sumer, five thousand years ago. And, for the artist himself, what a fuck of a long time it took in coming! As portentous as *Two Thirds* (Myers and Percy's monumental, six-hundred-page-long 'Neolithic monuments are the works of Martians' paperback) – in other words, full of sound and fury but deffo signifying something, although possibly not what the original creators intended – VON LMO's 1996 monster classic *Red Resistor* is as fucked-up a piece of monolithic religion as ever was barfed out from below the Bo Tree by the Buddha. Riffs the size of moons batter lyrics the size of planets, while Titans and Frost Giants scatter before this man's Jupiter-sized Humvee.

His aristocratic band (a real Chernobylity) here on Earth features David Tamura, on so-called guitar, Robert Lee Oliver II, on seven-league bass, and multi-man drummer Howard 'Crash' Valentine, who collectively manhandle rock'n'roll's stinking, rotten corpse into a darkened cell in Abu Ghraib prison, anally rape and torture it – on behalf of freedom (natch) – while filming it on modern Super-8, as VON LMO alternately intones 'Advance yourself' messages interspersed with 'Be afraid, be very afraid' messages, peppered with his trademark speed-of-light guitar solos (or is that speed-of-sound? Whatever, it's the same difference). The all-new nine minutes of 'Mass Destruction' are followed by seven minutes of the all-old 'Flying Saucer 88', which is a children's-playground-powered, *nya-nya-nyee-nya-nyah* assault, undermined still further by the half-an-hour-plus of 'X + Z = 0' (even throwing in some of 1977's 'We're Not Crazy' by Red Transistor around the nineteen minute mark), all of the aforementioned being so clod-plodding that the five-minute-long LP closer 'Atomic Sound' seems as positively streamlined as Neil Merryweather's Space Rangers hommering the James Gang's 'Funk 49' by comparison.

In VON's world, where any colour is bad, the saxophone of ex-cohort Juno Saturn is long gone, as are any approximations of musical scales or the lyrical subtexts of the earlier works. Moreover, this entire band plays icky no-wave riffs (mixed with anti-climb paint that won't wash off and which causes rashes) that float about in the ether and cause dead zones to rise up around them. And, all the time, VON is screaming lyrics about our need to advance ourselves; indeed, the legend 'Advance Yourself!' shrieks from every corner of every piece of artwork on each and every VON LMO record jacket, as VON advances upon us like Michael Ryan advancing down Hungerford High Street, backed up by a spectral army comprised of Mongolia's Golden Horde. Surprising? Perhaps, but really, how could we ever be *that* surprised by a guy whose debut LP opened with the barmiest libretto since Robert Calvert plainsonged Hawkwind's *Space Ritual* into the record shops back in '72? Dammit, we gots to print in full those first-off LMO words from back in 1981 for the CinemasCoptic [*sic*] vision they conjure within the larger place of our minds:

Six million years ago today,
A message was seen travelling through space,
Transcending time,
Moving faster than the speed of light,
Breaking the sound barrier,
This message was known as the Future Language,
And we are here to deliver this message to you . . . now . . . [pause of the gods] . . .
LONG LIVE HEAVY METAL!

Now I know what some of yooz thinking, punks . . . that this LMO (pronounced 'Elmo') druid's just an uncultured yokel; a Daft Vader who considers breaking the sound barrier (740.5 miles per hour) and travelling faster than the speed of light (186,281 miles per second) are pretty much the same deal because all that stuff goes faster than his kid sister's fixed-wheel tricycle. Me, I thunk the same thing for a few listens, until I heard LMO's later 1990s albums and saw that this fucker had – over the course of two decades – bigged up his original trip ten thousand-fold and brought it on to a whole new level of gunky ostentation, up/down with the rest of we planet squatters. Now, listening to that first LP armed with the new knowledge of his '90s oeuvre makes that intro text seem damn kosher – indeed, it was possibly (to my way of thinking) intended as a cosmic curve-ball to hoodwink the unwary. And, if you take the LMO's complete canon of recorded work – 1972–96 – then it's as violent and barbarian a piece of sonic football hooliganism as ever stomped that single slab of granite that calls itself the Central European Plain (gotta be VON's Transylvanian ur-Heimat, fer shure), and CEO VON LMO is head locust and chief slasher-and-burner with a one-string razor many of you will wish he'd left at home. And yet I find his wakeful barrage of incessant and staccato clod-hopping so tremendously invigorating that I've been listening to the thirty-one minutes of 'X + Y = 0' on heavy rotation for the past coupla weeks. Oh, the days just fly past.

To be honest, until I wrote about Monoshock, VON LMO meant no more to me than Nena's '99 Luftballons' or that 'Rock Me Amadeus' Euro-hit dude with the jerky walk. Indeed, I'd dismissed this VON LMO as yet another late-'70s, sub-Lene Lovich, sub-sub-Devo-alike with an unpronounceable name and a rent-boy cohort called Juno Saturn on bad, bad (terminally undergrad) sax. Too much of the *Future Language* LP had reminded me of Devo doing X-Ray Spex, and the interim years had been informed only by a very average single from '94, which sat in the back of my seven-inch collection, sounding something like a very unsure *Collision Drive*-period Alan Vega doing Kimmy the Foul, displaying a so-called 'industrial' sound so weak that Nine Inch Nails wouldna wiped their senile granny's arse with it. But, as Grady Runyan, Rubin Fiberglass, Scott Derr and Aluminum Queen (collectively the very great Monoshock) had obviously made such an effort to collaborate with this Pyramid of Geezer (and failed miserably at it by their own admission), I figured, at the very least, that VON LMO warranted a thorough aural excavation by my good self. So, when *Red Resistor* plopped through my postbox, I dutifully plugged in my headphones and depressed the stylus of my prototype Sony Sonic Pessary (hey, pals – no needle-sharing!) and . . . whaddya know? This guy weren't Stiff's answer to James 'Fat' Chance and the Contortions after all!

Sure, VON's whole modus operandi was informed by the same poisoned-with-*Round-Up*, withered branch of the anti-rock world tree, but, whereas Chance's semi-formed *No New York*-period 'Flip Your Face' gem wuz ultimately no more than three minutes of snack-o-smacky, populist underachieverdom, dear old VON El the Mo copped several Fleet Air Armfuls of the same Afghani off-road dust, epoxied a Beatle wig on his balding noggin in a Kimmy the Fowl-stylee, and turned the whole Shitty, Shitty She-bang-bang into a third (and fourth and fifth) way to the stars (I knows it – I've test-driven this sucker!). Which ain't half bad considering he's never had a moment's earthbound success in all of his (un)natural . . .

A loser in a losers' scene, LMO even got dropped from that 1978 *No New York* LP that Eno produced,[1] in favour of such deliteniks as DNA and Mars. While these irksome, unhip-squeaks wuz getting a pair of tracks apiece, LMO was getting zip. Which is why I'm a little dubious when I read on one of VON LMO's posters a quote about him from the *New York Post*: 'Radical revolutionary music at extreme high volume intensity representing tomorrow's generation.' No way. I think he just made it up and attributed it to the *Post*. Claiming that The Muppets' character Elmo was based on him is another of this future cave-dweller-fella's mantras, along with the assertion that Devo and Sonic Youth both studied his 'future language' without his permission, after being clued in when copping a glimpse of his 'International Transmitting Symbol For Universal Sounds ®'. According to the sleeve-notes of the remastered *Future Language* album, he's currently suing Bill

1 If I'm talking about the release of the *No New York* LP strictly from the point of view of a member of the Liverpool punk scene, you just gots to excuse me, as that was very much the angle it hit me at. People there fell into two categories: the ones who hated it and ignored it, and the ones who hated it and bought it. I occupied a rarefied third, one-member-only category, because I loved it. I loved the staring eyes of Bradley Field (of Teenage Jesus and The Jerks) most of all, but also held The Contortions' James Chance's black eye in particularly high esteem. D.N.A. front-man Arto Lindsay's albino, African-famine victim deffo won me over, as did Contortions' guitarist Pat Place's Cherry Vanilla-like out-of-focus-ness and Gordon Stevenson's widow's peak. The music was, unfortunately, somewhat less engaging. Teenage Jesus were entirely great and shoulda done four LPs in sixteen months and *then* split (the first album woulda had thirty-four songs on it, as would the second, while the third would've been ten songs on one side and one longee on the other, and the last LP woulda been silence performed by no original members). In what passes for reality, The Contortions opened *No New York* and scored big with the first two songs ('Dish It Out' and 'Flip Your Face') before, most unfortunately, the record became Side Two of Pere Ubu's *The Modern Dance* (the fat witness whining arhythmically as opposed to the full-on, Stooge-ified, post-Rocket from the Tombs thing).

Gates for stealing his inter-galactic peace logo – go, VON, go!

And yet, after a series of stop–starts with a coupla decades in-between, this prize-winning intuitive non-career mover has gradually built up a proper discography (of sorts) with which we can judge first his intentions, and then his achievements. This Album of the Month reveals the level of commitment that this guy has to the message. That he hasn't ever felt the need to cloud the issue with tunes or instrumental variation is proof of dedication to the point of vocation. However, as merely sustaining this level of mung-worship since the late '70s requires a super-human determination, let's first look back at the VON LMO that I so long ago dismissed as a peripheral *No New York* dork, excluded from his own scratch'n'sniff-athon.

'Reverse Trappology', or 'What Do You Want from Life?'

According to the Variant Records-approved biography, 'The VON LMO Story', VON 'was born in the black light dimension in 1924. In 1925, at the age of three, he began his musical studies on electronic violin, sixteenth level piano . . .', before bringing his musical career to 'an abrupt halt' experimenting with the building of rudimentary space ships. 'It was in one of these self-constructed ships that he left Earth to explore the universe. He crash landed on Saturn, where he met and studied orchestration with the late Sun Ra.' From here, the bio reveals, VON LMO travelled to the planet Strazar, before returning to Earth, where he was influenced by the Glenn Miller Big Band to 'wed his message to the big beat . . .' and where 'Sixties encounters with unidentified forces, UFOs and positive force fields convinced him to BECOME the big beat; so he became a reverse trappologist.'[2]

LMO formed the band Funeral of Art in 1970 and flew to London, where he found no success at all (what I've heard is spacey and alien but also corny as hell). He spent a coupla years creating the infant karma of Pumpo, whose musicians were all first-timers in rubber suits, banging on chainsaws and powersaws. Their sole, 1974 LP did shit, at which point he formed Why You . . . Murder Me? and began to lose his hair. Coming simultaneously out of New York's Brooklyn

2 All quotes are from the Variant Records-approved 'The VON LMO Story', c/o Variant Records, POB 3852, Redwood City, CA 94064-3852, USA.

suburbs, yet influenced by the wilds of Planet Strazar (which is entirely composed of meteorites with a caffè latte core) was always a chore for VON to reconcile, as Strazarians are all gay and love graffiti the way the English love their gardens, and not screwing around is a prisonable offence there. So, ever the refusenik, VON LMO married a beautiful Afghan hound on Venus and innocently returned to Earth, where he honeymooned in Mecca, thinking, nostalgically, that he'd show his newly beloved that piece of sacred meteorite in the middle of the Kaaba. Of course, Islam is a princely religion with roots neither in farming nor pastoralism, so dogs, to Muslims, are useless and, therefore, perceived as extremely unclean animals. So when VON, in a fit of rebellion, was busted for graffiti-ing 'Allah is not gay' on the Kaaba walls, the Islamic patriarchs broke the neck of his brand-new Ibanez Iceman guitar, shoved his new canine wife's pooper-scooper up his arse as punishment, and deported her to the restaurants of Korea, with 'Allah is one hungry Motherfucker' tattooed on her shaven butt. Heaping this series of indignities on top of VON's discovery that baldness is considered unattractive on Earth (he sacked his Venusian manager for allowing him to have appeared bald on his first LP, *Future Language*) was almost too much for him – which is why he nowadays combines his Utopianism with wanton scaremongering. Indeed, so Zelig-like has VON become in the past two decades (claiming regularly to be in suspended animation in order to explain his disappearances, and allowing his movements to become untraceable) that the disparate strands of Amerika's 'Axis of Evil' – North Korea, Afghanistan and Iraq – are now thought by the CIA to have been too bizarre to have been conceived of in the White House, being instead a VON LMOian concoction to pay the world back for having been so thoroughly dissed. Indeed, VON himself is now under suspicion of being a genuine cosmic trickster of Lokian proportions, and, perhaps, one who knows well enough the rends in the cosmic fabric to come and go at will, and who possibly created Tin Machine while inhabiting one of David Bowie's more solipsistic dreams in retaliation for the Thin White Duke's unwarranted continuing success on Planet Earth.

VON has also come under fire from the occult community for reducing author Stan Gooch to a burned-out shell living in a Swansea trailer park, and making it impossible for J. K. Rowling to write anything decent in less than seven hundred pages. Personally, I think there's still enough evidence to prove that VON LMO is one of the good guys. His best album to date being this magnificent *Red Resistor* suggests that it was influenced by his (albeit unsuccessful) collaboration with Monoshock[3] from the previous year,

3 Rubin Fiberglass gave me this account of the Monoshock/VON LMO collaboration, which I felt needed to be printed in full for the sake of posterity. Herr Fiberglass wrote:

> '[VON LMO's producer, Peter] Crowley approached us about the possibility of LMO coming out to San Francisco to do some shows using us as his backing band. That VON LMO would emerge from the black light dimension to seek us out as his backing band was pretty impressive, and we gave the plan a collective thumbs-up. I don't remember the exact date that LMO came out (I could find it if you want), but he showed up at Scott's pad in red smoking jacket, jet-black wig and very dark sunglasses. He didn't remove any of these items that evening, and ultimately stayed in character the entire weekend. We rehearsed with him that first night, having already practised the songs a bit under Crowley's direction, and talked about strategy for the shows, etc. As we spent more time with him that first evening, however, it became increasingly apparent to us that LMO took his persona so seriously that he wasn't much more than a big self-parody. That being said, he could still sing with style and intensity, and he knew how to make his guitar go screech and skronk in a metallic sort of way. Even so, it was soon made quite clear to us that our germinal, expulsive, chaotic approach to music was at odds with LMO's desire for backing by technically proficient, anally-retentive studio hack robots. I think there were 2 shows and a live radio performance set up, and LMO seemed to see the weekend as a worldwide showcase for the return of "VON LMO". He also seemed to be feeling a lot of pressure to be presentable in a strictly professional manner, and in turn was on our backs constantly to whip us into combat readiness. As our time together wore on, the situation became very "us against him", as he had proven to be a dictator and we became disenchanted with, if not hostile toward, this VON LMO reality. We played the radio show, and as I recall, there were some problems. I don't remember whether the show was live or taped, but I do know that later that evening, or the next day, LMO insisted that the station destroy any tapes and not air them. I don't remember the performance being poor, but the tension between his need for technical proficiency and connect-the-dots playing, and our belief in raw, emotional, unselfconscious intensity on the one hand, and self-deprecating humility, on the other, really interfered with any potential chemistry, and made the performance stilted and emotionless. In all honesty, I think we were crestfallen. We'd had pretty high hopes for the collaboration. But, following the LMO-deemed radio disaster and our deteriorating relations with him, either a show was cancelled or it was just decided that the whole collaboration would be re-evaluated. At one point things were finally so bad that we threatened to bail on the big Sunday show. LMO was treating us like slaves and it was just so contrary to our musical approach. After a

so – his plastic wig and perpetual shades aside – he's clearly still very much informed by the good people of Earth, and (most especially) the most grungy, mung-worshipping people of Earth at that.

We can but await his next move with excitement. I'm planning to visit Amerika next year, so hopefully I can seek this guy out and we can together investigate a few of that continent's more hidden ancient portals. Until that time, brothers and sisters, 'advance yourselves' with all the VON-informed music you can ingest; and if this write-up jerks VON's turkey enough to bring him after me, well, I'll keep y'all posted . . .

Discography

(With Red Transistor) 'Not Bite'/'We're Not Crazy' (single, Ecstatic Peace, 1990 – recorded in 1977)
'Cosmic Interception'/'Ultraviolet Light' b/w 'Inside Shadowland' (Variant, 1994)
Future Language (Strazar, 1981)
Cosmic Interception (Variant, 1994)
Red Resistor (Variant 1996)
Tranceformer 1978–82 (Munster, 2001)
Max's Kansas City, 9/11/81 (Seidr, 2004)

---

flurry of meetings and calls, we finally all agreed that the ultimate performance would consist of a 45-minute "International Hello" style maelstrom segueing into Red Transistor's "We're Not Crazy". Looking back, I think that all the tension really helped to make for a blistering performance. Grady was at his peak, as he and Aluminum Queen appeared to mock LMO viciously yet subtly behind his back while on stage. Grady affected some bizarre, gender confused guitar playing persona . . . I'd have to revisit the video to recall any of Aluminum Queen's specific performance antics. While we played, there was a video (produced by LMO) showing VON LMO and some kind of CGI aliens floating in space, etc. LMO brought out a drill at some point and applied it to his guitar, which struck me as kinda conventional. Finally, the chaos imploded and became a volatile version of "We're Not Crazy", which was really fun to play as we were so energised and emotionally spent. The fact that it was a sold-out show and that the kids seemed to be real into it was definitely a plus. I think that in the end we were glad to have been a part of the experiment, but were also relieved that the collaboration had finally run its course. As a post-script, I should add that the VON LMO weekend coincided with my upcoming University exams and a number of graduate level papers due that following week. I was left with no choice but to indulge in a form of study aide that enabled me to go without sleep the entire weekend. Yes, those were dark times. Yes, I was in pain.'

The 2000s

Perhaps I tend to judge these past ten years of Underground Music as particularly exceptional because the twin successes of *Krautrocksampler* and the rise of the Internet have conspired to send enormous numbers of underground artists my way with requests for a review. Being suddenly inundated with mucho new CDs and twelve-inch vinyl, I was initially shocked by the veritable tsunami of contemporary music worthy of being Head Heritage Album of the Month. But was this really the case? Was I right to be so astonished, so blown away by the likes of early Comets on Fire, Sunn O))), Orthodox, Khanate, Sunburned Hand of the Man, Gunslingers, Om and The New Lou Reeds? Or was I simply being hoodwinked by its brand-newness? Hindsight and umpteen creative listenings later, I'm happy to report that all of the aforemenched music of the 2000s was real and running on a full sac; indeed, as turbo-charged and remarkable as any of previous rock'n'roll generations. Hell, a good deal of the more lysergic offerings of the early twenty-first century actually cacked big logs from a great height upon the heads of many so-called original British and US '60s 'Psyche Classics'. Crazily and unfairly, the records of many of these Moderns were often far better than those of their originator counterparts simply because the previous technological restrictions and record-company commercial demands were now entirely lifted. And with no expectations of daytime radio play nor even the hefty budget of a national poster campaign to fret about, the music, not the career, once more became the sole *raison d'être* for the focused and determined rock'n'roller. Twenty-minute tracks? Go ahead. Phasing for the entire song? U-betcha! And tragic it was that so much fucking epic music managed to pass enjoyed through my stereo yet still unreviewed and un-noted. Unfortunately, while I can still enjoy any amount of under-achieving sub-sub-sludge trudge and never consider jettisoning the disc until album's end, only certain Sleep-alikes and Khanate devotees can still impel me to spew forth on paper. And, after the outrageous success of *Krautrocksampler*, modern music bearing any remote resemblance to those Neu! rhythms is still guaranteed to send me running into the next life.

Pentagram

Sub-Basement

(Black Widow, 2001)

SIDE ONE	SIDE TWO
1 Bloodlust (2.30)	1 Go in Circles (5.16)
2 Buzzsaw (2.29)	2 Mad Dog (2.17)
3 Drive Me to the Grave (4.30)	3 Tidal Wave (4.40)
4 Sub-Intro (4.00)	4 Out of Luck (3.54)
5 Sub-Basement (6.00)	5 Target (5.10)
6 After the Last (3.43)	

Who does Bobby Liebling think he is? Or, more to the point, *what* he is? Is it only in his later years that Pentagram's leader and primary songwriter made the connection between his real self and the ghastly underworld figure portrayed on the inner gatefold of Pentagram's 2004 album *Show 'Em How*? Or did Bobby Liebling always suspect that he was more, much, much more than the 'dinosaur relic stuck in the twilight zone' that cruel contemporaries (successful mechanics and computer operators, most likely) and chiding, older authority figures have been accusing him of being for the past four decades? Rock'n'rollers of the '70s were all victims, at some point or another, of accusers who pulled the 'grow out of it' card. I identify personally with Bobby Liebling when he sings on the title track of this LP, 'Some think of me as fried/But it's a choice of my own.' Right on, brother motherfucker!

However much I think I'm making sense to the world at large, there'll always be those who dismiss it as ravings from the underworld. But whereas I recorded my first songs (The Teardrop Explodes' *Sleeping Gas* EP) in '78 and had some measure of instant success, Bobby Liebling recorded his first songs in '72 and did not. Separating me and Herr Liebling was a thing called punk, a would-be anarchic phenomenon which freed things up considerably. That Bobby kept plugging away year after year, clawing his way up the slope often only to slip back down again into what he calls the 'sub-basement', suggests to me that he believed in rock'n'roll not because it was the only thing he could do, but because, come the Norse goddess Hel herself or high water, it was Bobby Liebling's destiny on leaving this world to pass through the portals of paradise as Mr Bobby Motherfucking Liebling, rock'n'roll star.

It is by now a given that, thirty years hence, Bobby will – even among the future equivalents of orthodox rock rags such as *Mojo*, *Spin* and *Rolling Stone* – have long ago taken his place in the rock pantheon. For it's surely the destiny of the true artists to navigate their way not through but *around* the temporary trail of slimy shit that celebrity slugs contentedly ooze along on. And – like Scott 'Wino' Weinrich, Mizutani of Les Rallizes Dénudés, Joe 'Thrones' Preston, Todd 'Tamanend' Clark, and precious few others – Bobby Liebling is one of those primary navigators we must salute again and again for exhibiting the dogged determination to not lay down and die but to keep the motherfucking pot simmering so we all can have a little taste. Ooh ja!

You wanna buy a classic rock'n'roll LP, kid? Well then, let me introduce you to one of the greatest heavy-rock LPs not recorded in the '70s: *Sub-Basement*, m'dears. It takes all the elements of underworld investigation that the likes of Ozzy, Alice and Iggy found themselves making by accident in the post-Altamont, anti-Woodstock, post-Manson, 'shit, the '60s didn't destroy the greedheads (and/or religion) after all' malaise, then it digs a little deeper into the cold earth, then a little deeper still, down into the crust, until it hits the granite firmament itself, puncturing a main artery deep within the underworld that jets forth a fountain of menstrual Earth Mother blood, gushing with such a ferocity that you got hell on tap.

Sub-Basement breaks none of rock's boundaries; it just examines those boundaries with the attention to detail and thoroughness of a farmer checking his wire fences, fearful of having his bulls rustled. In the cold light of the early twenty-first century, Pentagram were thus able to redress their situation via the filters of younger bands such as St. Vitus, Sleep and The Obsessed, allowing

Uncle Bobby Liebling a free refresher course in what he already knew like the back of his hands (which needed an Oil of Olay update in any case). Pentagram's members get their *Sub-Basement* ideas precisely from that re-examination, as Bobby Liebling and Joe Hasselvander round up Woden's Wild Hunt from the far corners of their fields, checking the numbers are right (count the horns and divide by two, brother), giving them all a pedicure, removing pebbles from their hooves, practising a kind of hindsight-informed rock'n'roll animal husbandry that pioneers such as Alice and Ozzy never could have foreseen, then distilling it all until there's just a tub-full of pure essence left to smear all over your amphibian self and yooz ready to kiss your surface-dweller ass goodbye. Going Down, anyone? Uh-huh!

Sub-Basement is an album you feel you've heard before even before your first play through. Indeed, when I first heard the record a few years ago, it was so immediately familiar that I virtually dismissed it as being unnecessary. But *Sub-Basement*'s genius eventually overwhelms even the most hardened rock fan, for it bristles with surprises and novelties, yet courts every hard-rock tradition in the most supremely confident manner. It's an end product of hard-rock executed by druid motherfuckers who've worked their craft for years upon years. It's a solidly well-researched 'I'm Living It' declaration, but it's much more. *Sub-Basement* bears the kind of superficial resemblance to Black Sabbath that the new Mini or VW Beetle share with the early post-war originals; that is, while the LP admits its own antecedents, they're actually entirely different beasts built to navigate an entirely different set of problems thrown up by entirely different times. Unlike Bobby Liebling, who's by now wallowing in the nitric ooze and even Golluming up a little ur-flame down there in the pale-green light, Ozzy and Geezer felt bad about finding themselves in the mire; they were almost like second-generation ska band Madness in their determination to 'bend not break the rules'; the Lord's watching and he's disappointed in us. Back in 1970, in 'Paranoid', even a total freak like Ozzy was still so post-Christian guilt-ridden that he blamed himself for any imperfection: 'I can't see the things that make true happiness/I must be blind.'

Thirty years on, Bobby Liebling cuts himself some slack, brothers and sisters, because – like Wino Weinrich – he's done with the martyring and he's glimpsed the Reaper so many times and lost so many friends in the process he's just glad to be alive for however long the be-scythed one chooses to allow him.

More than a few words must be said about the brilliance of *Sub-Basement*'s sonic execution, especially as its musical arrangements and performance thereof were all down to a single person, namely long-term drummer Joe Hasselvander. Joe joined Pentagram in 1977, when the original long-suffering line-up had finally fled the Liebling madness for good. But, by the late '90s, drummer Hasselvander was usefully integrated as guitarist/bassist as well, which means that every dip, every sway, every magnification and inflection is amplified by the same assured hand. And we ain't talking some dude clanking along to a drum machine, motherfuckers. These recordings ooze with organic symmetry of the highest rapport. Furthermore, this Hasselvander guy keeps such an arsenal of rock moves in his school locker that he's in danger of being rapped on the knuckles by the rock teacher for not sharing with the other kiddies. Like Iommi did every godforsaken day, and like Scott 'Wino' Weinrich, Dave Chandler of St. Vitus and Sleep's Al Cisneros and Matt Pyke at their peak, Pentagram's Joe Hasselvander electrifies *Sub-Basement* with a seemingly effortless series of ever-increasing riffage, ducking and swerving around whatever Uncle Bobby chooses to sing. And as Bobby Liebling is an excellent songwriter on his own, the combination is an extremely vicious union of the minds, something akin to Odin and Thor walking abroad on a long-haul mission.

Sub-Basement opens with the short'n'snappy, classic catchy-bastard barrage of 'Bloodlust', two minutes of hit song, faster than Sabbath ever played, more in the tradition of MC5's 'Call Me Animal' via The Obsessed's 'Indestroy' filter. 'I was the finder and the keeper,' sings Bobby, 'I never thought that I would need to be the creeper/But my keeper turned out to be the Reaper.' When such brilliant opening lyrics put the stunners on us, the scene is more than just set; it's coagulating before our eyes. The Liebling 'old man' voice soon kicks in; you know, the one that sounds like Eugene Chadbourne singing The Race Marbles' 'Like a Dribbling Fram'. It's gotta be one of my favourite rock devices ever, and *Sub-Basement* is riddled with that aged, withered yawp. Indeed, the voice is there again on the second song, 'Buzzsaw', which could be (may be?) a genuine old Pentagram song. In a flurry of stick clicks and paradiddles, 'Drive Me to the Grave' blasts out of the crypt as, over an 'Ace of Spades' beat, Uncle Bobby remains in his 'old man' character voice to tell the tale of how 'baby's never coming back', so can the chauffeur of doom please drive right up to the freshly dug hole in the ground? Bobby goes on about having 'five bad points' (on his driving licence, I'd imagine, if he's got such a cavalier attitude to driving around graveyards) as the slamming rhythm and Iommi howl urge the hounds of Hasselvander onwards.

The album then shifts down and down into first gear with the electronically eerie, almost ambient doom-beauty of the 'Sub-Intro' instrumental; kind of like Joy Division playing the themes from Reverend Bizarre's 'Strange Horizon' on the ocean floor. Finally, the title track bursts through the wall and we're into one of Pentagram's best-ever burnt offerings. Total, unashamed Sabbath at their peak, replete with Bill Ward chucking-Bibles-at-the-sofa drum fills.

Side One concludes with 'After the Last', a trudge that coulda stepped straight out of The Obsessed's songbook, in which the ultra-world-weary Liebling's so shit out of luck that he's struggling across the open fields with snakes in his boots and the Christian mob on his heels. Moreover, there's a Cromwellian darkness covering the land and the medieval church bells are tolling out his number: 'Come in Number Thirteen, your time is up.'[1]

Side Two opens with the massive 'Go in Circles'. Man, this is the dopium – the kind of song that's so good, it sounds like a legendary bootleg of some radio edit of about five excerpts of other songs, over which some husky-voice announces totally dispassionately: 'This Sunday at Irving Plaza: heavy rock with Pentagram; tickets available from Greaser Dave's, Record Barn and Hawthorns.' Does it sperm your worm? I should coco!

---

1 I live right next to Yatesbury church, a sixteenth-century building surrounded by a graveyard, with a sixth-century Saxon settlement buried on the opposite side of the road. When I walk the three miles home from Avebury on a Monday evening, I can hear the bells tolling across the wide-open landscape, and the twilight mists along Barrow Way can really creep me out. When I wrote 'My Wall', for Sunn O)))'s *White One* album, I just took mushrooms and wandered around the landscape for about six hours to get inspiration. When I returned, in total darkness, our local witch was standing motionless in the middle of the empty lane. She is seventy-two, with white hair, and yet, for one moment, I was convinced that she was a beautiful, alluring babe; not for the first time, either.

'Mad Dog' follows, an old Pentagram song I only know from their live LP *A Keg Full of Dynamite*, and they stick to that 1978 arrangement for this version. It's a classic two-minute, braying, twin-guitar assault, like Zeppelin playing something off Side Two of Sir Lord Baltimore's *Kingdom Come*. The opening line's a classic, get this: 'Help me out/I need some rearranging.' No shit, Sherlock.

'Tidal Wave' comes on like The Obsessed playing garage-rock, with Bobby howling about how he's been 'stuck in the no-win cave'. Whoa, in Liebling's cock-on-the-block worldview, there are caves for both winners and losers? It sounds like he's trawled up weird memories of some long-lost Ancient Greek fight to the death.

'Out of Luck' is the mutt's nuts, a wonderful, archetypal Pentagram lament which could be from any period of their existence. Here, Bobby Liebling sounds like something on the second Dust LP until, suddenly, Joe Hasselvander's overreaching and shimmering guitar makes gallows apples of the whole track, yanking it into a kind of '7 and 7 Is' ascending chord sequence; it's a truly, transcendentally beautiful moment.

The album's closer is the raging genius of 'Target', five minutes of Highway Robbery-inspired mayhem that spills out into an ever-accelerating 'I'm a Man'/'Psychotic Reaction' flip-out, the way the Robbery did on the second half of 'Ain't Gonna Take No More' or their accelerate-athon 'Lazy Woman'. It's a magnificent end to this marvellous album; indeed, even more so when you recognise that it's all the work of one single musician.

Other Faces of Pentagram

It's difficult to offer an overview of recent Pentagram albums without regretting the re-recording of so many early songs. Of course, Bobby's decades in the wilderness mean he's now got the chance to reach out to a new audience, but the presence of old material does tend to de-fang the new LPs, as though it was felt they needed shoring up in some way. One thing is certain about Bobby Liebling: he's often better now than he ever was. However, for those on a real Pentagram trawl, the first stop should be made at Italy's Black Widow Records website,[2] for therein lies the key to all things Liebling.

2 Black Widow is at www.blackwidow.it.

A Keg Full of Dynamite *and* Review Your Choices

A Keg Full of Dynamite is a pretty good live album which was recorded in 1978 by the second incarnation of Pentagram. It contains great versions of 'When the Screams Come', '20 Buck Spin' and 'Mad Dog', and you also get the studio version of 'Livin' in a Ram's Head' tacked on to the end. Nice. In the habitual Pentagram manner, this ain't no mobile studio recording, but it surely shits logs on the various bootlegs that have been around in the past years.

Also available on Black Widow, *Review Your Choices* is the excellent name of a truly brutal LP made by the Hasselvander/Liebling duo two years before *Sub-Basement.* The opening tracks, 'Burning Rays' and 'Change of Heart', are the closest that Pentagram have ever got to the sound of their beloved Blue Cheer, albeit once more through something of a *Master of Reality*-informed St. Vitus/Obsessed filter. Indeed, it's a shame they felt the need to re-record their classics, 'Livin' in a Ram's Head' and 'Review Your Choices', for the former's presence so early on in the running order considerably undermines what the first two tracks have achieved, while concluding Side One with a considerably inferior 'Snowblind'-ised version of the latter leaves the listener with the feeling of a compilation, as the amazingly heavy 'Yen Sleep'-like scream-dirge of 'Gorgon's Slave', and the equally holocaustic and almost alienatingly chromatic 'Mow You Down', tend to get lost in the shuffle.

Happily, Side Two returns us to mung-worship, and the general sound is of a heavy juggernaut struggling through impassable roads. Tunes – where there are any – creep in and out of the ether, as Thor hammers crescent-moon-sized horseshoes from his smithy at the roadside, and The Liebling comes across like a solitary, wandering, unfunky James Brown, grunting and huffing'n'puffing to himself as he struggles through life's unfertile pastures. Again, the side is disrupted by an unnecessary reworking, this time of their early-'70s classic 'Forever My Queen', herein robbed of its erstwhile finesse as original guitarist Vincent McAllister's finely honed, polished-marble licks are humourlessly concreted over and relined with Hasselvander's sonic breeze-blocks in order to realign the song with the album's overall slug-it-out metaphor. Still, the rest of the record is gloriously slimy, as the brutal 6/8 waltz of 'Downhill Slope' casts the listener down and down into the shrill, 'Into the Void' seal-clubbing of 'Megalania', then down another notch into the truly Roky Erickson-esque madness of 'Gilla', a kind of mutant radio interview with The Liebling you just don't wanna hear, let alone act as the LP's terminus. Overall, though, despite the re-recorded 'filler', *Review Your Choices* contains some of the best Pentagram moments ever.

Show 'Em How

For a number of reasons, I shouldn't comment on Pentagram's 2004 album *Show 'Em How*, featuring an all-new line-up. Personally, 'Last Days Here' was always so moving to me because it was sung by a young man who genuinely thought he was quitting the planet. Sung thirty or forty years later by the same dude, you tend to feel, 'So what?' That said, I've learned enough about The Liebling to know never to casually judge him.

Child of the Darkness

A final mention should be made of the Black Widow Records' album *Child of Darkness* by Pentagram offshoot Bedemon. Although patchy and sonically erratic (having been culled from various rehearsal-room recordings), Bedemon's one release contains some excellent insights into the methodology of the early Pentagram scene, revealing just what out-and-out rock fans they were. Based around the loose aggregation of original guitarist Randy Palmer and drummer Geof O'Keefe, with constant input from Bobby Liebling, the album contains alternative versions of 'Drive Me to the Grave', with entirely different music and melody and a brilliant, *Raw Power*-inspired burn-up entitled 'Time Bomb'. While Bobby Liebling lets loose the latter song just like the Ig, he also sings a poignant, Dust-type ballad, 'Last Call', like some beautiful, early-'70s heavy chanteuse. The record is flawed and messy the way Stooges boots such as *Rubber Legs* and *She Creatures of the Hollywood Hills* are flawed and messy, but they're sure as hell listenable.

In Conclusion

There ain't no conclusion, motherfuckers. Unlike many rock deadbeats who signed their five-album major deal then snuffed out (artistically or just plain died) after the difficult second statement, the jury will be unable to make a judgement on the oeuvre of Uncle Bobby until his cold, clammy body is laid in the earth. Even if he were, in twenty years' time, coughing up blood in the incontinence ward at the geriatric sanatorium, this Sir Lord Janitor of Lunacy could still come up with his best rock move yet. As I'm want to say, probably too often, 'rock'n'roll ain't necessarily a young man's game'. But, with regard to The Liebling, it's possible that he'll continue to inform our lives with rock'n'roll from beyond the grave.

Matt Baldwin

Paths of Ignition

(American Dust, 2007)

SIDE ONE	SIDE TWO
1 Weissensee (10.39)	1 Eulogy and Dark (6.01)
2 Jealous Woman (4.33)	2 Rainbow (14.23)
3 Winter (4.08)	

Coma Toes

From the very first moment I dragged the vinyl out of its too-tight shrink-wrapped, cut-and-paste, sub-sub-*Mind Games* cover, I knew Matt Baldwin's take on his role as new guitar god was gonna be way different to the approach of his acoustic-driven contemporaries. Hell, even the accompanying twenty-four-by-twelve-inch poster that fell out with the record was a statement in itself: Matt standing there – all six feet four of him – long-haired, open-mouthed, hands-on-hips, glowering and gormless as Ozzy's 'What The?' pose on the inner gatefold of *Paranoid.* Sure, the iTunes genre category on my iBook stated 'Folk', but the twelve-inch vinyl, in every way, screamed out 'ROCK!'

For a start, what folk artist would choose to commence his debut LP with a ten-minute cover of Neu!'s 'Weissensee', let alone conclude the first side with a monster, dobro-driven, feedback-overloaded version of Judas Priest's 'Winter', effortlessly summoning up nothing less than the post-Blue Cheer, Mae West swagger of Randy Holden's seminal *Population II*?

Sure, the attendant press release could attempt to schmooze us with claims of Matt's shared role as part of the spearhead of some neo-folk, neo-John Fahey revival, but the aural evidence was totally in opposition to any such braying. Yes, I'm happy to admit that a delightful, John Fahey-styled approach lies at the very eye of each hurricane performance, but what about that *noise*, motherfuckers – the fucking noise that swirled and ached and oozed and cranked from zero to one hundred on certain tracks? Had his record company not even noticed the fucking electric ur-racket that wellied out from underneath the soft white underbelly brought forth by this man-mountain Pyramid of Geezer? Hell, kiddies, on *Paths of Ignition* this so-called folkie Matt Baldwin druid is nothing less than a one-man heavy-metal band, a Stormin' Norman, raging liquid fire across the deserts of the first Gulf War; a flame-thrower-wielding stormtrooper at the gates of Moskva, fighting for his life and surrounded by scores of belligerent Russkies with starving huskies, each waiting to pounce on his meaty butt were he not more slithery than a bag full of KY'd cobras.

A highly amphetamined and paramilitary Nick Drake filtered through Karlheniz Stockhausen's ring-modulator he may be, but cosy, folksy moments with Matt Baldwin? I think not. I've played this album over and over, and it worries me the way they'z trying to pass him off as the new Leo Kottke, or maybe Steve Howe; not because it's an irrelevant allusion, but because – with such a media approach – so many true guitar-worshipping motherfuckers out there in rock'n'roll-land won't even give Matt the time to spin his disc when they clock that 'folkie' tag. Besides, however much you try to conflate then accelerate Steve Howe's 'Mood for a Day' with 'The Clap', it just ain't never gonna sound like Matt Baldwin, because Steve Howe just never sounded that *hungry* . . . Howe needed the combined arsenal of Messrs Bruford's drums, Squire's proto-Jean-Jacques Burnel bass and Wakeman's combination of Mellotron, Moog, Hammond, Steinway et al. before that fey twerp would have dared to attempt a fifteen-minute piece like Matt's LP concluder 'Rainbow', whereas, on said track, Matt takes on the trek entirely alone. Brothers'n'sisters, it's fucking heroic. Moreover, therein Brother Baldwin shows us that he wields the yawp, the power, the *sh-sh-shakes*, the precision and the know-how to take it all the way and then some.[1] I even heard he's taken some flak for presenting more structure than some current

1 On his desperately needed hols a coupla weeks ago, Holy McGrail fell into a super-stupor while under the influence of this record, and woke up laughing his head off at the sheer ludicrous overachievement going on before his very ears.

writers care to appreciate; well, fuck that, because this is all gold.

At his peak, Matt's Leo Kottke-at-his-most-grinningly-demented, tigers on Vaseline, slithery slide work sounds for all the world like he's appropriated some Titan's coffee mug and is scree-surfing down a rusty hillside of old goldmine rail-tracks on it. Elsewhere, Matt veritably hammers the strings, at times nearly clawing those fuckers off the fretboard in his need to coax, cajole and bully the maximum result from his poor, tortured geetar.

Highly perversely, Matt Baldwin himself chooses to call his own music 'New Age', and I like that because I can appreciate this true punk's decision to side-step the genre question by opting for the most annoying one of all. But, to all you truth-seekers out there, this here reviewer would be being far more honest (and useful) to y'all and your own record collections if I simply declared the obvious: these great fists of Matt make Ben Chasny sound like Marge Proops by comparison, and nope, this racketeer ain't a one-man band in the modern Black Metal tradition of Bathory and Furze – and he sure ain't just reviving J. Fahey and L. Kottke, neither. So rush out and score yourselves this album on any format you wish, and just make sure you totally ignore the claims of others that this motherfucker is some kind of folkie, however much the 'genre' button on your iTunes attempts to hoodwink you. U-know!

Boredoms

Vision Creation Newsun

(Birdman, 2000)

The first time I heard this album it was like a deluge overload euphoria had descended from the highest heavens and whipped me, screaming, whirling, teenaged and drooling, into my first acid trip/hard-on/astral projection and into a region of unfathomable and untameable *newness*. I didn't even know what the singer's words meant; I had the record but didn't even know what it was called; I'd heard all seven songs and thought they were one long piece (I still don't know the individual titles). I felt like the mystery of all music had been boiled up over one Hindu kalpa (8,640,000,000 years of human reckoning) and then distilled through this Boredoms album. I fell asleep listening to the album and woke up several times while it was playing, only to fall asleep again, overwhelmed and tearful and with a butterfly belly of surging, gnawing passion.

In the middle of the night, my toy doubleneck (which I used for all the too difficult parts of the L.A.M.F. album) fell over on its face next to my bed. I shot up in bed and looked down at this riffing orange toy playing familiar music, alone and unprompted. Then I jumped outta bed and grabbed the thing and took it (still riffing) to the farthest corner of my bathroom and closed the door. I lay there, motionless; I couldn't sleep; I needed to create a new sound . . . 'Needed . . . to create a . . . new sound'; is that what Boredoms were singing? What was that lyric? 'A new sound . . . sound, sound, sound . . .' At shamanic 4 a.m. I put the record on and listened on headphones, loud as hell. No way could it possibly sustain the sheer mystical feeling of those first coupla listens. No way at all . . . IT FUCKING DID!

The record begins with a single voice imparting the words 'New sun!' Then it's off into the single greatest rush of music since the last millennium. This time I listened again and again, without falling asleep, until the sun came up and the birds were dawning their chorus thang, and I was a reborn earthling.

So, what does it sound like? I dunno – maybe as if *The Faust Tapes*' most euphoric, uplifting moments were digitally tape-sped into some kind of Beyond Time.

You know how you occasionally read a review of some new Fall LP and they say The Fall are back on form and you just gotta hear this particular record, and you get all excited and hopping 'cause if The Fall just got genuinely back on it (even briefly) u-know it would be a pagan free-for-all to live for. And it even has intriguing song titles like 'Dame J. Burchill Art Gulag' and a supposedly great cover version of Don Covay's 'It's Better to Have (and Not Need)'. And, in that brief period between reading about the album and hearing the album, you're a kid again, with a kid's dreams, as a whole world of possibility (not just musical) is thrown up in front of you. Then you hear that new Fall record and it's just more embittered, semi-mystical, coded, fraudulent ramblings about nothing, nothing, NOTHING . . . *But* it does not matter because you've still enjoyed *and* lived fully through those moments of possibility.

Well, this Boredoms album offers all those moments of possibility *and* it achieves them. Those of you who always wanna dig my Album of the Month but then get disappointed because its way too weird, or not weird enough; too rock, or not rock enough; too obscure, or not obscure enough . . . well, this is the album for you! You are all gonna get down on your knees and crawl to my front door after this one. Crawl, crawl, crawl . . .

How do I know? Because I've listened to this album so many times and just kept coming back and coming back, and it never fails me. I played this fucking record so much on the last tour that I had to consciously *not* put it on before every set, or risk appearing like some teenybopper asshole with one CD in the collection.

This is truly enlightened music which encompasses the loftiest rock'n'roll moments of every entirely necessary group of all time without sounding like any of them.

Imagine those heights of ludicrously optimistic utopianism achieved, occasionally, by the Mellotron'd Hawkwind of *Warrior on the Edge of Time*'s first side; the pre-Velvets, menstrual-cycling of The Jaynetts' 'Sally Go Round the Roses';

the eternally rainy-day mono-stare of 'Hiroshima', from Flower Travellin' Band's classic *Made in Japan* LP; the strangely Chuck Berry-based, hard-cissy weeping vision of Justin Hayward's 'The Story in Your Eyes' by The Moody Blues; the eleven-minute guitar destruction of 'Love Is More Than Words, or Better Late Than Never', by the late-period, heavy version of Love, led by Arthur 'I'm-one-of-the-greatest-lyric-writers-of-all-time-but-right-now-I'm-gonna-shut-the-fuck-up' Lee; the cartoon-y but nonetheless real sense of loss on The Residents' 'Ship's a'Going Down' from *Not Available*; the one-off, death-trip despair of Slapp Happy's genius forty-five 'Johnny's Dead'; the unlikely, overloaded Spanish galleon, over-arranged enlightenment of Sabbath's 'Spiral Architect'; the someone-help-me-help-me-help-me-please 'Puppy Love' effect at the gasping-for-air tail-end of The Tubes' 'White Punks on Dope'; and the breathtakingly ever-upwards power-surge that is 'You're in America', the opening track from the first Granicus LP. Imagine all these things, and then imagine them compressed and digitally enhanced and sampled and used purely to empower you – *pow!* – used in order to bring on an emotional pow-wow, equivalent to applying a psychic garlic poultice to your poor, fuzz-bitten inner street plan.

Who are these Boredoms? Well, they've been around for two decades and they're led by a figure called Eye. Eye? Aye. And, clearly, there's only the one Eye. And they've been a punk band, and they've been an all-percussion, chanting shamanic ensemble, and they've had twenty years to prepare us for this. And are we prepared? No, no, no . . .

How do you describe true psychedelia? Do I write: 'There's one beautiful period on track four when the whole group becomes Hawkwind on "Silver Machine", rising upwards in a space-boogie which digitally transforms itself into that percussion and guitar freak-out from the middle of Chicago's "I'm a Man" forty-five (by the way, if you haven't heard that cover version of Spencer Davis' finest moment, get it now, now, now – it is still a transcendental, earth-moving moment from a group that is otherwise utterly unworthy of consideration).' Do I write that? No. There's a whole vibrational otherness coursing through this record which, if I'm stretched to compare, again reminds me of *The Faust Tapes*. But, really, it's just the sound of fine, fine music made by people who live at a higher level than every other fucker.

Sure, those other reference points

I've thrown in are there to ground the review in whatever the real world is. But *Vision Creation Newsun* is a masterpiece. And I mean that in the old sense. It's a masterpiece insofar as it creates a new genre. A new die has been cast. It's a sustainable sonic orgasm where before there was no sustainable sonic orgasm. Other musicians can now rip off this masterpiece (I surely fucking will) and humanity will be higher because of it; nothing less.

Album of the Month . . . Album of the Year!

Comets on Fire

Field Recordings from the Sun

(BaDaBing!, 2002)

1 Beneath the Ice Age (9.20)
2 Return to Heaven (6.29)
3 The Unicorn (3.51)
4 E.S.P. (6.42)
5 The Black Poodle (10.22)

Iggy Pop is not just a daft cunt – he's a cruel, corporate whore with the nuclear industry's level of arrogance. To you, Mr Osterberg, I scream: 'When old twat rock'n'rollers have underachieved their way through the past twenty years, doing the cock-out routine and coming on like fitness freaks, their audience requires that they should do the honourable thing and croak.' But instead, in the face of no new songs and nothing whatsoever to say for the next twenty vacuous orbits of the sun, Herr Oster-fucking-berg-with-time-on-his-hands decides to cast his magical dip-stick over the previous decades of genius in order to fuck up whatever he got right in the first place. Therefore, His Arrogance decides to take a *Brick by Brick* (I'm trembling even typing the words) meets *American Caesar* (u-wish) overview and add what informed its cod meaningfulness (and I'm talking about 'Mixin' the Colours', you fucking legendary no-mark) and welly several shovelfuls of that proto-crud at the beyond-insane genius of *Raw Power*, thereby reducing its eight, needle-jumping-out-of-the-groove, toppier-than-top-end, brown-trouser tracks to the level of a merely achieving, five-star Andy Gill *Q* magazine review.

Well, Mr Pop, it seems to me that you *have* a big bell-end because you *are* a big bell-end, so may the wheels of the industry which for so long rejected you crush you like a bug for so cluelessly destroying what informed our pre-punk ears – you suck . . . and I mean your own tadger. This Comets on Fire review is for you, half pint.

You're Ugly and Your Mother Dresses You Funny

Hawkwind too hippie for you? Simply Saucer too drippy? The singer out of Pere Ubu just too fucking fat (so what if they was Rocket from the Tombs, and Peter Laughner wrote 'Life stinks/I hate the Kinks')? Comets on Fire are the new kids in town, and they'z better, better, better. Of course, two albums doesn't mean this lot are about to sustain a long career in showbusiness (which still ain't what the Rock is about), but all of the above ancient hairies managed their place in our hearts not through longevity and quality of second sides, which all of them failed miserably at; but for such brazen sonic juxtapositioning that all of our poles got smoked down to the root and left us panting for more, be it by those main protagonists or by any passing rip-off merchants who thought they could ape it.

So, Comets on Fire deserve our gratitude, firstly for their distillation of all the best rock riffs since High Rise's take on Blue Cheer, and, secondly, and most of all, for adding to it that very '70s instant Stockhausen, nay, that shrill atonal *otherness* which only Del Dettmar and Dik Mik for Hawkwind, Ping Romany for Simply Saucer and Allen Ravenstine for the Ube ever managed to sneak past their lead singers (even Eno never managed it in Roxy Music, being instead reduced by North Sea Ferry to a backing singer for at least half of *For Your Pleasure*, before being cloned by Eddie Jobson for their rehash third LP).

Here, the 'non-musician' (remember when they were called that?) is a genius named Noel Harmonson, whose sole instrument is an ancient Echoplex, which takes up at least half of the Comets on Fire Sound. On the second record, he will foist upon us oscillators, intercom control panels, so-called 'hippie drums', chanting and even Jew's harps. But just for this first LP, he's making do.

U Watt?

Comets on Fire appeared in 2001 with their debut, self-titled vinyl. Their 'singer', Ethan Miller, is also their (formidable and remarkably un-egotistical) guitarist, while their rhythm section, bass player Ben Flashman and (then) drummer Chris Gonzales, make/made a sludge-fest of rock-by-numbers as brilliantly hamfisted as the Spiders' Trevor

Bolder and Woody Woodmansey, or Kiss' Gene Simmons and Peter 'Beth' Criss (of course, thereby granting themselves instant brotherhood with Makoto Kawabata's Nishinihon). And this *Comets on Fire* album was a four-track production right out of 1979 Chrome-world, housed in hand-painted and self-inserted sleeves from independent hell.

On the cover, Miller, Flashman and Gonzales stand in the distance, staring at Noel Harmonson in the foreground, whose head has been replaced by junky electronics. Hey, and Harmonson probably did the surgery himself, as he's still clutching said head in his right hand!

And here, on this LP, everything was louder than everything else, with hiss-torto-vocals, shock-corridor mid-range which wanted to be high end and low end which wanted to be mid-range, and drums which wanted to be Metal Urbain's drum machine. We are talking a sound so sibilant and lo-fi here that it often gets too much, so you have to put on some early Shockabilly for relaxation. Even their record-company PR guy declared that this debut LP was one in which: 'Metamphetamine and schnapps-drenched hippie tunes take it straight into the sonic shit-storm.' That's a press release that kinda grabs you by the poo-poo, huh? It almost beats Keith Altham's 'Narcissus in Metamorphosis' note for *Scott 3*. Does it make ya wanna listen? Yup, me too. Like the name Les Rallizes Dénudés, it doesn't disappoint. To record it, Comets on Fire stuck a four-track TEAC cassette machine in one room, like Donald Ross Skinner did with *Droolian*, which didn't prevent these suckers coming out with the loudest record this side of the Cheer's 'Song Cycle'.

Next thing we know, they'z flagged down a passing hearse and supped on the dead remains of our late, beloved Lord David Sutch, got themselves well bombed out on that goon's pills, and speedily delivered an even better second album, faultlessly named (and itchy with self-understanding) *Field Recordings from the Sun*; 'Wakka-wakka,' as Fozzie Bear would say. Be expectant, be very expectant.

Gone is the extreme-just-to-be-extreme Ibiza sunburn of the first Comets on Fire album, to be replaced with the choicest mélange of *Funhouse* and *Hall of the Mountain Grill*. Those first-album turds on a bum ride have, on its successor, become spectral star-chasers with Pausanius' ticket to ancient truths. In just a few months, they'z gone from three-feet, six-inch Austrolecipethicus types to divine, six-foot-tall temple builders. Sonically, it's a distance thing, like they've moved the horizon several miles back and parked a fjord in front of the microphone. Emotionally and psychically it's the difference between *Unknown Pleasures* and *Closer*, and it's the daring action of forward-thinking motherfuckers.

So there you go; obvious, immediate and totally absorbing. Buy, steal or burn them, both albums are must-haves; I figured I'd better push *Field Recordings from the Sun* because it's newer, easier to find and *much* better. I thought I'd better at least inform you of the presence of that first one, however, because you still need it and it'll only get reissued on CD if irate heads berate those involved. So here goes on the description, and I'll keep it as minimal as I can without frothing at the mouth too much . . .

Comets on Fire

As I've said, while the first Comets on Fire album is a work of barbarian genius, it's nought but a thing that creeps compared to *Field Recordings from the Sun*. First off, it's clear to me that y'all need to know that this first slice of vinyl (originally released in a limited edition of five hundred copies)[1] was uniquely informed by the same Noogie Monster which afflicted every great noise band after 1975: Electric Eels, Pere Ubu/Rocket from the Tombs, Chrome . . . all the usual suspects. Indeed, you can include all those who took from the '60s but wanted to hear it as they themselves had first heard it; that is, stoned and drunk and half-asleep, through two-inch speakers, on late-night radio. It's that same vibration which informed the hiccuping mess of DMZ's magnificent 'Don't Jump Me Mother'; the good-times-were-never-this-bad of *Slade Alive*; the crazed innocence of The One Way Street's 'We All Love Peanut Butter'; The Alarm Clocks' 'No Reason to Complain'; The Bel-Aires' 'Ya Ha Be Be' (indeed, we're possibly talking all of *Back from the Grave Volume 3* here); the pre-teen, Brummie brain abandonment of The Zodiac Motel's (pre-Birdland) *The Story of Roland Flagg*; and every pre-Bob Ezrin Kiss LP.

'All I Need' opens the album, coming on like Chrome's ultimate career move. It's their nightmare, one-minute-thirty kid brother, and it distils the first side of *Half Machine Lip Moves* into ninety seconds and fucks off the extraneous, arty, sonic dry wank to reveal a pristine, still-drying,

1 Brooklyn's fusetronsound.com once held stock of this long-gone LP, but as that was nearly a decade ago you will almost certainly have to resort to eBay . . .

aural dayglow cartoon turd made by a 3D Bart Simpson.

'Graverobbers' follows: a great hulking riff, like The Sonics' 'The Witch' with a fifty-ton, all-day-breakfast-eating, no-neck truck-driver singer reduced to Bernard Cribbins Hornby gauge but still with the same density (and heavier than the singer on The Novas' 'The Crusher', you turkey-necks). 'One Foot' is an eye-popping *Slade Alive*, with Neville 'Noddy' Holder replaced by a cackling and cackily absurd carbon-copy robot. Gleeful like Zodiac Motel's 'Mr Watchtower', it comes with the built-in bozo guitar solo as standard, madam . . .

'Got a Feel In' is one of those 'Babylon's Burning'-like circular riffs that every rock genius (or people like me) just blatantly rip off and credit to themselves. 'Rimbaud Blues' is the last track on Side One, and opens with drums like Captain Beefheart's brilliant slow anvil blues 'Hard Work Driving Man', which Jack Nitzsche wrote for the movie *Blue Collar* – the twenty-four-track Studer tape machines of Warner Brothers' studios here replaced with one very high-quality C90 cassette.

Side Two opens with a ghoulish horror scream and lonely wah-guitar before spewing forth the pass-the-Bisto-mother ramalama of 'Let's Take It All', which is a perfect *Time's Up*, Buzzcockian bar-chord fuck off, combined with loads of Joe Meek short-wave. Then 'The Way Down' takes the reins and batters 'Surfin' Bird' drums into your brain, along with further complain-complain hiccuping from Ethan Miller.

'Comets on Fire' is their fingers-on-the-master-tape, slow-up, slow-down theme tune, with Paul Stanley hysteria vocals and a classy, classy, ever-shifting chord sequence, further undermined by the rather evident Echoplex-tures of Sir Noel. This racket continues until the outrageously confident and magnificent coda, which is no less than Rocket from the Tombs doing 'Twist and Shout'; nuff said – can't say no more (just like the bit on High Rise's 'Mira' when they arrogantly pick up the tail-out from The Amboy Dukes' 'Journey to the Center of the Mind', and a big old rock'n'roll grin splits your face wide open at the sheer fuck-offness of it all).

Then these bastards tear into the Stooges' 'Death Trip' and call it 'Ghosts of the Cosmos', before whipping out another brand-new set of chords, underpinning it all the time with the 'Death Trip' signature at the end of each pass.

Machine-gun drumming swipes us up into 'Days of Vapors', with its feedback, fuzz-bazouki theme, and this whole thing just sorta . . . peters out . . . (except for the totally un-nessa messabout encore, which I shall not dignify with a proper mention, except to say it undermines the power and truth they so carefully built over the previous half-hour).

All that said, the ten songs on *Comets on Fire* make it an essential buy, and no record library is complete without it. Don't think rock's all been done because it ain't – just get this record, you lovers of today. It's a classic you gots to know!

Field Recordings from the Sun

Just one year on, the dawning of an entirely new and completely rejigged Comets on Fire might have been the saddest news of all. Except it ain't anything less than a Total Upgrading. *Field Recordings from the Sun* is made by a higher form of humanity than its extremely excellent predecessor.[2] In one year, they've lost a drummer but gained a saucy auxiliary from America's deepest underground, and made a short-as-a-Van-Halen-album record of monumental authority. Ben Chasny, from the excellent Six Organs of Admittance,[3] has been brought in to oomph the sound, and he even writes one of the songs, while Comets' new drummer, Utrillo Belcher, surely has the greatest name of any percussionist since Skynyrd replaced Bob Burns with Artemis Pyle.

Strangely, this second record opens like Hapshash and the Coloured Coat shagged the ladies of Amon Düül circa *Disaster*, coming on with the Tibetan bells and all kinds of mantric peace'n'lovedovery. 'Wha'happen'd?' you cry, as 'Beneath the Ice Age' New-Ages you in the rectum . . . Then it's kaboom, and you realise it was all just their 'We Will Fall' smokescreen. The real Comets on Fire have landed, and demented and propellent, bass-driven freak-rock is alive and well again. This is *Rubber Legs*-period Stooges, with Scott Thurston replaced by a Hollywood-sized vacuum cleaner. They even credit an alto-sax player called Tim Daly, but he's in too deep to get in the way, coming on more like a subterranean Nik Turner. The whole track breaks down into chaos and finishes in primal punk chanting.

2 If they were to carry on in this upwards fashion, a third volume would have to be drummerless and released only on flourescent mini-disc.

3 Great-looking records, too.

'Return to Heaven' lurks momentarily in lone feedback until a five-metre bass riff enters the fray and brings us to Texan crazoid heaven – a place where everyone listens to *Bull of the Woods*-period Elevators – and all the band members do their best to undermine the beauty of Ethan Miller's 'Proud Mary' melody (which they can't, as their pre-programmed, forward-thinking motherfucker buttons have been welded shut. Damn!). You might think this is jamming, but no way . . . These guys can write songs *and* have superb arrangements, too. Every lickle bit of mess has its place and there ain't an art-wank cul-de-sac in their whole cityscape.

'The Unicorn' is Flower Travellin' Band's version of 'House of the Rising Sun'; that is, a Zeppelin-styled, picked acoustic proto-'Stairway to Heaven'. Beautifully improvised by Ben Chasny of Six Organs of Admittance, it is suddenly overwhelmed by a Viking attack of feedback and electronic interruption. If you know Doggen's mayhem on T. C. Lethbridge's 'Ring of Brodgar', this is in the same pocket, but here some fucker left their half-chewed bubblegum in there and it's got older, ickier and somehow even runnier. Ooh yeah!

Then we're back into familiar brine dommidge with the berserk descending riffs of 'E.S.P.'. Here, Ethan Miller sings like the guy out of Stereo Shoestrings doing 'On the Road South', or maybe Robert from The Zodiac Motel – he's so disturbingly gleeful. The song ends . . . but won't end . . . Bap, bap, bap . . . bap, bap, bap . . . bap, bap, bap . . . bap, bap, bap . . . bap, bap, bap . . . bap, bap, bap . . .

You think 'The Black Poodle' is a weird name for the heavy freak-out which finishes this great album? So did I, until it bit my ass and sent me blarting my eyes out all the way to the health centre. It's here that Comets on Fire employ all of their mercenaries and auxiliaries, and it's here that Sir Noel utilises all his seventeen dollars' worth of cranky electronics. Soon, he is staring Utrillo Belcher out as the two of them engage in a drums and electronics war; but even locked together like horned gods there ain't no way to stop the massed, six-string cult hordes from flooding over the sonic battlements. And, Thermopylae as you like, Ethan Miller has found a back way into the song that's perfect for guitarists. Soon, producer Tim Green is wailing away on 'extended fuzz wah sky solo' and Angie Thurman is strapped into her 'extended stoned white wah solo', while Ben Chasny has commandeered a solid-body for his 'extended attack distortion one solo'. Now, Ethan is standing on the broken battlements of the song, cackling and flicking the 'V's at Sir Noel, who (seemingly out of nowhere) shoots the singer through the heart with a single but deadly flourish of 'intercom control panel'. . .

'Why are we fighting?' screams Tim Green, in a sudden, righteous memory of ancient rock cameraderie. Immediately, the mayhem subsides: 'Because . . .' gasps the dying but still eloquent Miller, 'human beings are like dolphins . . . (cough) . . . always looking beyond the family unit . . . Always reaching for the ultimate combination . . . for the most superb . . . Gurdjieffian example of the dance . . .'

Then, faltering from internal wounds, Miller raises his still-feedbacking axe above his glowing rock'n'roll head and – howling – tumbles one hundred feet into the morass of dead musicians below. This ain't genocide – this is rock'n'roll!

Crow Tongue

Ghost Eye Seeker

(Hand/Eye, 2008)

1 GHOST EYE GAZE:
- 1 Ghost Eye See (5.13)
- 2 Brightless Gaze, The True Vision (6.52)
- 3 The Silverspun Web (4.46)
- 4 Cloud Eye Sight (10.07)
- 5 Beneath Wings, Above Wind (2.13)

2 SEEKER:
- 1 Seeker Chant (9.31)
- 2 Dream Asleep, Pray Awake (6.53)

3 CANDLE, CORPSE & BELL (5.51)

This review is dedicated to Holy McGrail, who clued me into this stuff in the first place.

He's Mad Enough

Many corporate rock'n'roll artists, even some highly respected ones, are well known for agonising over every stage of their recordings, even in the final run-up to completion, as though they're still desperate to keep their precious work from the gaping jaws of the public, insisting on new mix after new mix, then perhaps one remix more, before finally having their first new album in umpteen years prised from their vice-like grip by their record company, thereafter dutifully touring the world and speaking to every kind of media type until the bones of their project have been picked clean.

While extracting a new album from such artists is like getting blood from a stone, just try stopping them talking about it once they've started; and as for beginning another project, forget about it! These cats are so driven by celeb (un)consciousness that they don't even feel they truly exist unless there's a full-page ad in every magazine and an in-depth career overview for each campaign; so their PR machine's gotta keep getting them more and more gigs at the Grand Ole Vegaswood Lig, itself an unholy and interminable cycle of 'ain't we rad?' mutual back-slapping.

In the meantime, truly visionary rock'n'roll artists – often driven by their own self-imposed deadlines – spend their lives clawing their way up the side of the slippery, razor-sharp scree slope to the top of their own chosen artistic summit; finally standing triumphant at last (but all too briefly) atop the peak, before dashing down again in one breathless running tumble and – after re-establishing base camp – doing it all over.

Visionary artists, when they're right there in the eye of the vision, inevitably find themselves surfing some specific and Niagaran tidal wave that pours out of the heavens and cascades into their third eye, filling them up so deeply and so quickly that they are, thereafter, always on the point of drowning, capsizing, overwhelmed, virtually raped to bloody rawness, like they were, in terms of their metaphysical place in the cosmos, no more than some tiny human-shaped toby jug, an upright human cabriolet with the hood pulled back, while the Norse god Thor – after a Friday evening's mead-drinking contest with his buds Odin and Tyr – pisses the entire honey-tinted contents of his distended belly into their head from ten thousand feet above.

Yup, for the visionary it never rains but it downpours continuously, comes down in sheets, flooding out so quickly that the artist may even be forced to launch projects with different names, offshoots, fake ensembles, any-fucking-thing to extract that aircraft-hangar-sized inventory of stuff from inside their head. They gotta kick that Gnostic shit out, so they can . . . start all over again from the beginning, because new information is constantly stacking up in their melted plastic brains. Indeed, the death of each project and the birth of each subsequent one are so essential to the visionary artist that their visions will coagulate and solidify if they are not facilitated by those around them. Constant renewal is essential.

At James Brown's artistic height, so constant were his revelations that he always had a side project (the J.B.'s in their various guises, Fred Wesley solo LPs, etc.) on the go whenever he was recording a major new album. He did this, firstly, for the sake of his mental health, and, secondly, because the formerly dirt-poor James couldn't bear to waste a single moment in an expensive studio. Even the well-heeled-from-birth Miles Davis acted similarly for decades, propelled by inner demons and churning out ideas so fast that over-taxed musicians and recording engineers fell like flies. When the ever-fertile Neil Young recorded, briefly, for the über-corporate-and-proud-of-it Geffen Records, back in the mid-1980s, the sudden pressure to over-promote everything and slow down his natural recording tempo nearly sent Young insane (similarly, when Geffen denied Kurt Cobain the constant renewal that *his* hazardous inner life demanded, nay, commanded, the blond one was forced to take his own life rather than spend the next two years factory-milking the udders of the *In Utero* cow until they were – to his fast-forward-thinking, fertile crescent mind – drier than your dead great-grandmother's tits).

The evidence is strong that the most ingenious of those visionary artists, at their shamanic peak, will employ any and every moment as a springboard, a new catapult to project them ever further into their trip. At three minutes and ten seconds into the title track of The Doors' *The Soft Parade*, Jimbo refuses to allow engineer Bruce Botnick to edit out his vocal stumble about it being 'the best part of the trip' so as to provide us with evidence that he's so deep in that trip he's become almost pre-verbal. Patti Smith provides us with similar evidence in the form of a little giggle and the comment 'It was really great, man' exactly four minutes and thirty seconds into *Radio Ethiopia*'s 'Poppies'. At seven minutes and twenty-four seconds into 'The Lowest Reaches of Our Highest Preaches', from Zodiac Mountain's 2007, avant-commune classic *Lake Winnebago*, poet/ruffian Clay Ruby, rather than editing out an accidental cough, instead turns it into a Vesuvian lava shower of vocaleptics – Ruby becoming like some dog-headed priest, standing on the very landing strip employed to fly Mother Nature's silver seed to her new home in the sun.

Moreover, however righteous their overall trip may be, many of even the most eco-friendly visionary artists care not one jot about how much of their home planet's raw material is used in the execution of that trip, because – right there at that moment – their truth is the absolute; they're delivering, and if they don't birth this lickle babby right *now*, motherfucker, then they will be forced to do a VON LMO and enter suspended animation. All of which brings us to the subject of this Album of the Month: Timothy Renner, a.k.a. Timothy the Revelator – an artist currently 'enjoying' a similar situation and barfing out album after album, project after project, in a berserk effort to soothe his achingly over-worked brow.

Under the earlier monikers Stone Breath and Black Happy Day, occasionally under his own nom de guerre Timothy (sometimes tiMOTHy or timeMOTHeye) the Revelator, or latterly as leader of the duo Crow Tongue, this artist is currently blasting forth huge statements whose importance may not be recognised until years hence. Yes, ladies'n'gentlemen, Timothy the Revelator has something very specific to say, and – or so it appears to this writer – he will build any vehicle in his power with which to say it . . . *all.* 'I am a chancer,' I declared on *Dark Orgasm*'s 'White Bitch Comes Good'. Timothy's chance is *now* and he lives it in the moment. I've heard much of his music, but have never before felt compelled to broadcast an All Points Bulletin. This Crow Tongue album is, I believe, the place to start.

Over an incessant, honking, post-Henry Flynt Appalachian duo-drone, somewhat akin to Tyrannosaurus Rex during their notorious doom-Donovan phase (i.e. Marc Bolan at his most spectacularly portentous and archly Semitic), singer Timothy the Revelator intones seemingly endless declarations of world destruction and blasts invocations out into the universe. Bass banjo drones, hand drums and a spectacular, Old Testament-style vocal delivery are all transmitted our way via the most intensely claustrophobic, almost entombed production. Much of Timothy's other music is far more attractive in the traditional sense (i.e. more palatable) but this particular Crow Tongue release is – to my mind – the most useful entry point to his work; useful enough for me to feel the need to declare possible comradeship with him, despite his having admitted to being a . . . Christian. Cough, splutter, aghast stares . . . Free your minds, brother and sister motherfuckers, as I had to do . . . for the Revelator's Christianity is closer to our heathenism, our paganism, nay, (for many) our damned Satanism than it is to any popery, Anglicanism or foolish Orthodoxy.

In the late '60s, Tokyo's J. A. Caesar advertised his apocalyptic music as a 'Voodoo rock that invokes blood and the memory of blood,' and so it is with Timothy. This Revelator music may claim to be Christian, but what a pagan Christianity it is. For the Revelator embraces both the blood and the darkness in the void, continually invoking the sun, the moon, the twilight, the darkness . . . Hell, kiddies, it's veritably Armenian in its worship of the Christ – or like some throwback to the sort of arcane early Christianity that still had to rub shoulders with the worshippers of bullock-less Attis and his old lady, Cybele, and with the shrill-voiced, effeminate priests of Frey, dragging their god/idol through the muddy fields of Jutland. Timothy's practising an ur-Christianity from back when it was still just one of many cults competing for bums-on-seats, so it had to accept the pagans upon the heath and their desire to worship this new peace god the old way, which to the Armenians, from AD 301 to the present day, has involved dumping headless birds across carved Bronze Age monoliths, themselves Christianised by having been incised with fantastic khatchkar crosses, the smeared blood crusting those exquisitely detailed carved lines. It's Noah sacrificing the lamb on the Tukh Manukh stone altar on the Mithraic hill of Etchmiadzin at the foot of Mount Ararat. It's a bloody covenant, children, a vandal handshake through the hole of the Odin Stone, up at Stenness, on Orkney's mainland; a handshake and the inevitable cutting of flesh/spilling of blood. It's a direct interfacing with the divine godhead – there was no second-hand, la-di-da, vicar-ious remove back then – Gnostic punches monotonously and repeatedly thrown at the unprotected head.

I know I sometimes have a tendency to hyperbolise too soon, so don't mistakenly think I'm already suggesting that Timothy is really a reborn Gregory the Enlightener screaming from the hell hole that was Khor Virap. As evidenced by the brevity of this review, I ain't saying that, because it's way too early to tell, and I don't wanna heft any unnecessary pressure on Timothy, either. Besides, a visionary artist's truth takes at least thirty years to take form in others' heads. I'll tell y'all this, though: the wave currently being surfed by the Revelator could be as useful to us as any I've yet encountered – even that of mein hairy, Stephen O'Malley – in the eleven-year Album of the Month sojourn I've made thus far into the godless lands of the virtual twenty-first century.

Whether or not this shit sticks, only Old Father Time will tell us. Until then, look to the whore rising, salute Odin and the rest of the heroes, kick the gods' lard-arses into touch and hail Timothy the Revelator for being one highly useful son of the bitch.

Death Comes Along
(Psychedelic Inferno, 2001)

SIDE ONE
1 Psychedelic Inferno/Death Death Death (19.22)
2 Children of the Death (3.02)

SIDE TWO
1 Psychedelic Inferno II (14.40)
2 Psychedelic Inferno III (5.01)

Much of the most useful rock'n'roll ever recorded inhabits that unrighteous place where the free-flowing twin tributaries of LSD and psilocybin disgorge their contents into a sludgy and barely moving cultural canal awash with prescribed drugs, smack addicts' discarded syringes and industrially manufactured amphetamines. Rock'n'rollers, poets, musical prodigies, even a few disenchanted priests find their way to this mythical confluence, for the results of hanging awhile on that there river bank are huge for those few souls sussed enough to lurk at such an unlikely cosmic intersection. For this place is where heavy metal and acid-rock meet the avant-garde, where punk-rock, post-punk and no wave meet Beat poetry and free-jazz, and where protest song and current social comment meets the timelessness of the Psalms.

Not Wearing a Hard Hat in a Hard-Hat Area

Born of that same, late-'80s future shockabilly that spawned High Rise, and still going strong as recently as 2006, Death Comes Along are like some voodoo, campfire, buzzsaw, electric mariachi band accompanying the local witch doctor's agonisingly strung-out ritual purge of a demon from a young girl. Their berserk sledgehammer of sound is a totally unique brand of monolithic, gonzoid, Klaus Schulzean, NASA space-rocking, sub-sub-BÖC, über-bozo De-twat Todd Clark-out-bozos-Kim Fowley, sub-machine-shop rock. And they don't have a limited palette, either, following full-on, twenty-minute free-rock blitzes with vocal-only child-scaring and synthesizer-only doom-noodling (their first LP even included full transcriptions of 1930s Japanese military music); and every incarnation is excellent.

Dam-busting avalanches of analogue synthesizers swamp and swirl as ecstatic screams and agonised screeches (both male and female) caterwaul hysterically; single notes of spindly, claustrophobic, psychedelic axe-worship emulsify the atmosphere, orchestrated by super-erratic, splatter-clatter, Crass-style snare-drum bursts, all of it in service of songs about death and the memory of death; songs about violent death and the refuge found in death. Welcome, then, to the half-world of Tokyo's Death Comes Along . . .

Led by the mysterious Crow, a photo of whose life-size face adorns the LP's entire front sleeve, this loose aggregation of seven musicians/performance artists is a true rock'n'roll micro-cult built around the death-obsessed mind of this one man. Furthermore, while only Crow appears on every album track (his lyrical pronouncements mixed extremely prominently – 'Children of the Death' consisting of his vocal only!), of the six other musicians that vie to be heard on the album, only bassist Bondage appears on more than half the tracks, implying that this project may be more correctly judged as the vision of one man alone, save for a bunch of younger helpers.

The band remained underground throughout the early '90s, before finally emerging, shocked and blinking from the sewers of the underworld, in 1994. That first record was the kind of brutal psychedelic voodoo that only the truly desperate feel the need to perpetrate (I'm talking here about an elite and specific bunch of miscreants: John L's performances throughout the first side of Ash Ra Tempel's *Schwingungen* [and most especially 'Flowers Must Die']; Les Rallizes Dénudés during their *Blind Baby Has Its Mother's Eyes* period; Speed, Glue & Shinki's side-long Moog synthesizer suite 'Sun – Planets – Life – Moon'; the most out-there moments on live bootleg versions of The Doors' 'When the Music's Over'; Ya Ho Wha, all the time, for sure; certain moments of Cro-magnon's legendary LP [especially 'Caledonian']; and – most certainly – that huge double-vinyl LP *Necromanzee Cogent*, by twenty-first-century black-metal iconoclasts Furze). However, on that elusive debut album, Death Comes Along further demanded our attention by dedicating the music contained therein to the following: 'Funeral March for Amebix, The Mob, Dirt, Antisect, Crude SS, May Blitz, Flower Travellin' Band, Diamanda Galas, Ash Ra Tempel, Guru Guru, Amon Düül, Black Sabbath and German Oak.'

Ash Ra Tempel? Guru Guru? German Oak, fer Chrissakes? Now, we ain't talking about some neo-Krautrock ensemble here, kiddies, because this disc was released in spring '94, a full year before even my *Krautrocksampler* was published . . . which makes their German Oak reference even more seriously fucking heavy. And what's all this proto-metal these guys are name-checking? Black Sabbath is clear enough, but May Blitz and Flower Travellin' Band? The lady'n'gentlemen of the Death Comes Along ensemble were/are on the case, and then some.

Luckily for our purposes (i.e. this album's use as a meditative device), the second Death Comes Along LP – released seven long years later – was a lot more cohesive and listenable than their insane debut. Gone are the earlier album's aforementioned scratchy recordings of Japanese military music; gone too are the perplexingly irritating periods of so-called avant-garde 'silence', to be replaced here by the kind of mythical cuntedness that renders the truly insane useful and worthy of repeated listening. Indeed, this record is so worthy of its Album of the Month status that I spent eighteen months trying to shoehorn the sucker into the schedule. However, this record has never left the environs of my turntable long enough to be filed away, so here it is right now.

Tokyo Damage Report

Having been released initially on vinyl, this Album of the Month was clearly conceived of as a time-honoured 'game of two halves'. Indeed, like Ash Ra Tempel's first three LPs, it's an entirely schizophrenic statement in that the first side belongs to a free-rock power trio not unlike VON LMO's first no-wave outfit, Red Transistor, playing The Who's *Live at Leeds* with a Nihonese Todd Clark barfing prophecy out front; while the second side is a scary, wordless, kosmische/industrial black-sheep cousin of the title track of Popol Vuh's *In den Gärten Pharaos*, or even Speed, Glue & Shinki's aforementioned 'Sun – Planets – Life – Moon' suite. Just like Ash Ra Tempel, therefore, this duality renders the record incredibly useful for the serious psychedelic explorer.

Burn out into the stratosphere with Side One's space-rock, or abseil down into the underworld through the crack drilled in the crust by Side Two's instant cave recipe.

Let's look at Side One in proper detail. Its near twenty-minute-long opening medley, 'Psychedelic Inferno/Death Death Death', commences with all the aliens-are-landing portentousness of an early Funkadelic LP, as UFO analogue synths and barked Todd Clark via Damo S, Johnny R, P. Hammill and J. Morrison pronouncements, in a Metal Urbain-stylee, prepare us in no way for the ensuing Troggsian space-rock ('Feels Like a Woman' as played by Eno's 'Needle in the Camel's Eye' ensemble) as unleashed by the stentorian and anally-retentive Chain Gang on their legendary Kapitalist forty-five 'Son of Sam' b/w 'Gary Gilmore on the Island of Dr. Moreau' . . . It's Van der Graaf Generator's 'A Plague of Lighthouse Keepers' as played by Lightning Bolt . . . *blatter, blatter, blatter, blam, blam* . . . Was there ever so Crass-fuelled a space-rock as that played by this bunch of Wolf Eyes-ian faith healers?

Man, as an old motherfucker who recorded his first single back in 1978, I gots to tell y'all that rock'n'roll has certainly downgraded superbly since the days of post-punk. I mean, in those back-in-the-days, such stuff as the fucking Nihilist Spasm Band's epic (and arduous) quarter-of-an-hour-long rot-fest 'Destroy the Nations' was considered by most of my Liverpool-scene mates to be on the very edge, perhaps even over the edge, of what was considered to be music. No such debate any more. For while Side One of this Album of the Month is no less gruelling a meditation, the twenty-first-century ears of the real heads have become attuned and accept, nay, *need* such stimulation overload in order to really get down. And, as though the nineteen minutes of 'Psychedelic Inferno' were not scary enough, Crow chooses to conclude Side One with three minutes of the cheery, unaccompanied vocal of 'Children of the Death'. Who knows what he's hisspering on about, but it's long and it concludes with three repeated sentences spoken/intoned in English: 'Children of the Death . . ./Children of the Death . . ./Children of the Death.'

Side Two's a whole other bathtub of beasties from the depths, as fouteen-minute-long opener 'Psychedelic Inferno II' declares from its opening moments, a raging Crow letting loose on his analogue synthesizer and squawking and chattering along in a torrential blitz of shamanic torment, while new boy

Sugiyama gamely tweaks and twirls the dials of his own monosynth like some radio ham frantically recording the co-ordinates of a ship sending out an SOS. Personally, I'd prefer a heavily extended version of this particular track, as it ends far too soon to be of maximum usage, but its near quarter-hour of electric beehive from hell at least approaches the mind meltdown that Takehisa Kosugi achieves on his masterful 1975 LP *Catch-Wave.*

This album concludes with my favourite track of all – the sheer outrageous absurdity that is 'Psychedelic Inferno III'. It's fabricated around a lovely, subtle, *Faust Tapes*-style minor-chord sequence, on which Bondage switches to guitar, joined by new guitarist Yuki and new drummer Kenji. However, the abrasive Crow here chooses to be the intoning priest, aping a fly buzzing in the high vaults of the cathedral, his tone riding roughshod across the loveliness of the chords. However, as Crow's performance becomes more and more *out there*, the track flies out of control like some rock horror movie in which a berserk Dik Mik tone generator the size of Big Ben escapes from its Hawkwind backline flightcase and descends upon London, deafening all who dare to stay outdoors. This bizarre and absurd song is a fabulous conclusion to this bizarre but hugely catchy (and useful) album.

So, what becomes of a band such as Death Comes Along? I'd like to be able to conclude this piece in an upbeat and hopeful manner and say that Death Comes Along is getting more successful every week, but my searches for the band on the Internet have yielded precious little information and only a couple of photos, including one of Crow performing in Tokyo, in 2006, still wearing the same shirt that he's sporting on the cover of this 2001 release. For all of you rock morons whose heroes are intuitive non-career movers, you gots to admit Crow might be right up your strasse! Get down.

Discography

First Live Album (Mangrove Root, 1994)
Death Comes Along (Psychedelic Inferno, 2001)

Gunslingers

No More Invention

(World in Sound, 2008)

1 Into the Garage (2.20)
2 Light Slinger Festival (12.50)
3 King Yaya's Forty Guns (2.48)
4 San Pedro Hallucination (2.50)
5 The Beheaded Motorbiker's Head (2.02)
6 Black Dwarf Man (4.03)
7 Gigolo Albinos (3.51)
8 Auschwitz Boogie (2.52)
9 The Minister's Black Veil (3.01)

My first confrontation with Gunslingers' leader Gregory Raimo occurred in August 2007, when I reviewed his twelve-inch EP *Xperiment from Within the Tentacular*. Released under the spewdonym GR, the ruminations of Raimo's six-string razor therein were slightly tempered both by the lack of other band members and a studio technique that reeked of *The Faust Tapes*. In other words, it was damned wonderful. Well, now Raimo's back, he's armed with a power trio, and he's pointing that Blakean Cerberus straight at us. Uh, look out!

'You Wanna Suicide in Your Room / You Wanna Suicide in Your Car . . .'

In a systematic act of alchemy clearly designed to upstage, in one fell swoop, every budding Asahito Nanjo, every rising Kawabata Makoto, every post-Reck and neo-Keiji Heino, nay, every occidental Japrock wannabe combined, French super-freak and guitar mangler Gregory Raimo has – with this solitary Gunslingers album release – put to shame each'n'every proto-metal musician across this lickle planet with a spiteful racket so accursedly evil, so mischievously demonic, so gurningly and grinningly piss-taking that barbarians across the globe (myself included, natch) can only drool in disbelief and green-eyed envy. For *No More Invention* is nothing less than the sum total of every move culled from every essential no-wave, post-punk and free-rock statement thus far spewed forth on to vinyl and CD. Indeed, being simultaneously post-Beachnuts, post-Primitives, post-Armand Schaubroeck's Churchmice, post-Voidoids, post-Teenage Jesus, post-Doctor Mix and the Re-Mix, post-White Heaven *and* being in possession of a killer rhythm section who understand his singular metaphor, Gregory Raimo suddenly finds himself in the enviable position of being the ur-underground's Man of the Year!

Yup, kiddies, there'll be no sleep tonight for the high-art inhabitants of the lofts, warehouses and basements of Detroit, Manchester, Manhattan, Tokyo, Copenhagen, Berlin, Nagoya, Long Island City and their ilk. Instead, every true genius of the distorted electric guitar will have now been goaded into action and obligated to break out the black coffee, the Red Bull, the sugary teen drinks, the ephedrine, hell, even those amber chunks of raw amphetamine that mad Uncle Tony left behind when last he descended upon the household to make one of his inimitably sweaty veggie curries; all and everything will be appropriated in Rockaholics Anonymous' collective quest to top Gunslingers' incredible maelstrom as unleashed on *No More Invention.*

That good? Uh huh, *that* good . . . It's everywhere and nowhere, bay-bee, and (ahem) it's French . . . Alpine French, in fact, from Grenoble, no less, and I ain't taking the piste! I know, you know, we *all* know the French might not know how to rock'n'roll ninety-nine-point-nine percent of the time, but when they get it right, boy, does it smoke pole! And, like existentialist hero Albert Camus' bizarre death in the back seat of a massively expensive Facel Vega HK550 supercar, Gunslingers' *No More Invention* is a raging and fumingly Gallic summation of all things righteous, nihilistic and stylishly paradoxical, simultaneously. For a start, its tumbling and stumbling rhythmical idiocy should be the last sound a body requires just before bedtime; nevertheless, it's become one of my preferred methods of meditation. Moreover, as the father of teenage daughters who regularly lambaste themselves with two-hundred-and-fifty mph riff pile-ups, I was nevertheless shocked to hear fourteen-year-old Avalon describing *No More Invention* to her sixteen-year-old sister Albany as 'music of the devil'. Sheesh! What truly occult goings-on must be genuinely occurring within the micro-folds of this record for such descriptions to be happening naturally between teenagers who rarely express anything less than total ennui when confronted by my own preferred choice of listening? And you know me well enough by now to understand that this Odinist heathen motherfucker ascribes *nuthin'* to the Devil, unless it's music born of a voodoo so unearthly, so off-kilter and so reeking with post-Christian damage that its purveyors could only have intended such results.

Well, so it is with *No More Invention*, kiddies. For this Gunslingers' disc rages with references to Lucifer in much the same manner as our beloved Blue Öyster Cult chose to do throughout their career. Herein, Lucifer is not only invoked as the beautiful Keltic godman we enlightened types have come to accept, but also as the still-evil Crosstian opposer of all things good. And, contained in that mysterious netherworld doorway, the music of Gunslingers rages and rails against *everything* (positive and negative), one moment surging forth soul-sparks of life upwards into the heavens, the next shifting direction furiously and drilling into the very crust of the Earth with all the gay abandon of a McAlpine earthmover.

Pragmatic motherfuckers these guys ain't, children. They commence their debut LP with the two-minute hate of 'Into the Garage', then jettison all reason by following it with the record's longest piece, the apocalyptically cunted (and Lucifer-dedicated) genius of 'Light Slinger Festival'. Thereafter, separating each successive song from the next is as futile as time-shifting back to the '70s and attempting to point out Billy Bremner's shorts as they spun around in the Leeds United washing machine. We're talking Total White-Out, ladies'n'gentlemen; the kind of swirling snowblindness only Roald Amundsen's South Pole expedition could have imagined. And what does it sound like? Well, as the aforementioned 'Light Slinger Festival' is the Mother of All Fuckers and the longest song on the disc, let's first address this one track and establish, firstly, why its contents are so damned essential, and, secondly, how we Jonesing wannabes can make one of our own just like it. Here goes.

First, score yourself a copy of the late Love double album *Out Here*, and remove the near-twelve-minute amphetamine-fussy guitar burn-up of Arthurly's 'Love Is More Than Words, or Better Late Than Never' from Side Three. Next, ruthlessly excise that track's soft outer covering (i.e. the bit called 'the song'), then place the rest (i.e. Gary Rowles' viciously and heroically inspired, dragster-on-a-skid-pan axe-worship) in a shallow wok and baste that hi-cal sucker until the spitting fat is showering all and sundry. Next, reduce the insane results to a sickeningly rich broth and decant it into a large syringe. Finally, inject the whole sticky mess up the puckered ass of the current indie scene and *stand well back* . . .

With twenty–twenty hindsight, of course, Gregory Raimo's methods of navigation could not have been more obvious. For Raimo has, in ultra-simplistic terms, merely excavated his way through the path of least resistance, skirting around anything 'too, too, too to put a finger on', and thusly skateboarded down free-rock's main street, appropriating everything labelled 'iconic', 'moronic' or 'Property of Sonic Youth'. But Raimo's true genius lies in his incredible self-confidence, his greed (nay, his *need*) and his determination to render so many of these public things his own; that – in an act of cultural kleptomania somewhat akin to T. S. Eliot's *The Waste Land* – the stellar moments of all guitar jizz are (from this Year Zero onwards) *all his*!

You can almost hear this Grenoble savage screaming: 'Robert Quine? He's mine!' as he crams a dog-eared copy of Richard Hell's *Blank Generation* seven-inch EP into his revolutionary nap sac [*sic*, *sic*, *sic*], carefully wedging it in alongside all the other essential and inevitable spiky detritus: Friction's *'79 Live* album (especially 'Big-S'), Reck's vocal blueprint for rendering J. Rotten's 'Bodies' vocal style entirely one's own; High Rise's *Speed Free Sonic* and *High Rise 2*, for the production (non) values; the Reid brothers' 'Upside Down' forty-five (but played at seventy-eight for the rush and roar); Metal Urbain's tinnitus epic 'Paris Maquis' seven-inch, for the disorientating shock value that a 6/4 riff can bring to buzzsaw punk rock (heart-stopping time-signature changes pervade this Gunslingers' release); Chain Gang's 'Son of Sam' 45; Tom Verlaine and Richard Hell's 1974 Neon Boys' single 'That's All I Know Right Now' – all topped off by The Velvet Underground's 'I Heard Her Call My Name' (to be deployed by Raimo as proof to Gunslingers' hapless drummer that it's OK for his incredible playing to have been rendered almost entirely inaudible for the entire duration of the proceedings).

That Gunslingers have achieved all of their distillations in just nine songs and in less than thirty-seven minutes implies that the magickal and mystical qualities of many early AC/DC and Van Halen LPs may not have been merely accidents or coincidences; perhaps they were truly Gnostic rock'n'roll devices. So do please listen with reverence and care to this Album of the Month and try to find the time to sink deep, deep down into its ether. For, despite the ironical title, *No More Invention* seethes, rages and constantly hollers out great eternal, druidical truths (and with such effortless style) that future record libraries without a copy of this LP will risk being declassified and shut down instantly.

Of course, I am now forced to conclude this review with the one single (time-honoured) word that befits such a glamorous and clamorous art statement. *Yowzah!*

HAARE

The Temple

(Freak Animal, 2004)

1 The Temple (20.01) 2 Satori (19.37)

Despite its initially terrifying sound, such were the instant spike-o-logical effects of this Haare album on my melting plastic brain that I have – for several years – stood on the verge of making it an Album of the Month. As its freshness receded, however, and as newer and almost equally novel ritual cuntedness plopped itself on to my CD player, it became difficult to justify Haare as my choice. However, when two brand-new discs of similar musical direction arrived at my door,[1] I knew that I should be doing Haare's leader, Ilkka Vekka, an enormous disservice if I chose either of them ahead of his startling oeuvre. Humming and haare'ing about the house, I finally remembered that Vekka had, on the record's inner sleeve, righteously declared: 'DESTROY FASCISM.' Of course, this statement of intent immediately forced my hand . . . *The Temple*'s time had finally come.

A Sort of Conduit: A Wormhole Which Provides You with Answers to Questions You'll Never Know

The astonishing ritual music of Finland's Haare sounds as though it was commissioned by Mother Nature herself as the officially approved soundtrack for the creation; y'know the kind of thing – the rending of u-shaped valleys by titanic and

1 The two records are Nordvargr's *In Oceans Abandoned by Life I Drown . . . To Live Again as a Servant of Darkness* (Essence Music 008) and Lngtché's *Music for an Untitled Film by T. Zarkkof* (Etude Records 012).

unstoppable glaciers; the abrupt rising of the oceans by some distant planet having suddenly been knocked out of orbit; the unexpected displacement of ancient peoples by an instant inundation of their traditional homelands; or perhaps the sound of the over-packed and heaving floors of the mythical Ark filled to the brim with terrified animals wailing piteously, as Noah the great biblical patriarch and his legendary sons struggle, seemingly endlessly, to raise the venerable hulk's sagging bottom from the muddy floor of the Mesopotamian plain.

In Haare's world, analogue synthesizers boil and simmer, theremins shriek and funeral bells toll for some long-forgotten calamity, as free-form bass and electric guitars wriggle and ancient cassettes, half-caked with the detritus of untended playback heads, struggle to project their sacred encoded messages.

To call *The Temple* 'orgasmic' would probably call into question this author's sexual needs, but its gargantuan presence is so totally mind-manifesting, so debilitating, so brain-crushingly complete that any description short of such purple prose would render the effects of this review far short of Haare's musical effect; indeed, 'metaphysical orgasm' would be closer to a true description of this music's worth, or my name's not John Donne. For, in the presence of Haare's music, even time stops short and draws back to contemplate, while eternity kicks its heels and wonders just who is this human pretender, this sorcerer's apprentice whose music dares to emulate the very sound of the Big Bang itself? Like some giant roadie tearing off a piece of five-mile-wide gaffer tape in order to plug temporarily the hole in speaker cones the size of the weather-station telescope at Jodrell Bank, Haare's kosmische noise is, to me, as enormous as was the terrifying wilderness of Cumbria to Daniel Defoe's desperate-for-orderliness seventeenth-century mind.

No, it's not a casual listen, and that's a fact. But then, when was ritual ever intended to be casual, except perhaps to the good old Anglican Church, wherein all the mystery (along with every archaic poetic phrase) has been excised and substituted with a chat, a matey parable and a nice hot cup of tea? No, no, no, this Haare music is a truly high ritual of the northern variety. And so, when exhausted at the end of the working day's protracted problems and petty issues, it's to *The Temple* that I regularly turn for the psychic equivalent of colonic irrigation. Haare's is truly a healing music, a restorative up the psychic jacksie that awakens in me the Plumbing Cosmological.

After working increasingly long days, whose hours are punctuated by the endless intake of coffee, sugar, dairy and alcohol, and smoke inhalation, the blood of your average city dweller turns into a right old chemical toilet which needs to be evacuated, and pronto, Tonto. And so this record becomes the Psychic Enema which eliminates from my mental blood reservoir all bodies unnecessary and toxinous [*sic*], as down and down sinks the body juice contaminated merely by living to the full edge of my over-expectations. Do I sink John Lennon-like down the *A Hard Day's Night* plughole with the water? No, the violently restorative music of Haare ejects my foul breath, casts out my psychic farts, and evacuates each clinger and dingleberry, replacing all with the shining innards of a superman.

Safe in the eye of this hurricane that trustworthy Haare has established in my everyday environment, I happily surrender my guttering and drainpipes, my roofing and shiny surfaces, all processed (filtered, sand-blasted, however you wish to envision it) and returned to my care, brand spanking new, via this all-purpose acme of products that goes by the name of Haare. And if the opening twenty-minute title track is an immense craft of metaphysical beauty, then the ensuing nineteen minutes of 'Satori' are even more merciless in their excoriation of each listener's inevitable build-up of psychic plaque. Indeed, like the music of early Sunn O))), Khanate, Nordvargr and their ilk, Haare's sound could (and, in a more enlightened society, should) be issued on prescription in place of all those Mother's Little Helper pills (Devil's Little Workers more like) that your average NHS GP foists upon depressives with alarmingly casual regularity. Do you need a phial or a whole bottle of this stuff? Who knows, but it works, and more again, a double dose, will perhaps work double-fold.

For myself, I know nothing else by Haare but this one record,[2] but it has stood me in good stead for several years. Indeed, its comfort is its usefulness at all times, and there's not much out there quite like it. During its first

2 I know of (but have never heard) Haare's debut single, 'Sacred Mushroom Clouds', which was released (in the highly limited edition of two hundred and seventy copies) on the excellent Finnish label Kult of Nihilow, best known for three excellent doom albums by Fleshpress and another outstanding LP by Tyneside's glorious doomsters Marzuraan.

plays I was far too in awe of its effects to rate its worth, too delighted at its mere existence to make any estimation of its wider significance. For only through time and repeated plays could its importance be assessed. But now, many, many months onwards, firm evidence of *The Temple*'s importance is shown through my need to return again and again to this bizarre behemoth.

And so try listening to *The Temple* while lying twatted beneath the sky after a long work day. For the sake of the experiment, seek not oblivion but only the edge of oblivion, as a drunken-oaf shepherd would lie immobile as his persistent but trustworthy old sheep dog – aware of rustlers in the locality – gnaws at one of his master's socks to ensure that he never sinks into sleep's abyss. So the sheep dog in this case would be Haare, not nibbling flesh, most certainly never taking a bite and never drawing blood, but neither yet giving up the nibbling for a moment, even to take a leak. That is the trustworthy heathen epic music of Haare; a loyal hound, a magical beast in this beautiful, fantastic, brooding, desperate, searching life. Return to it, ready for exploration, after a regular dose of Haare.

Harvey Milk

Special Wishes

(Megablade Records, 2006)

SIDE ONE
1 I've Got a Love (3.44)
2 War (3.12)
3 Crush Them All (5.28)

SIDE TWO
1 Once in a While (3.22)
2 Instrumental (3.22)

SIDE THREE
1 The End
2 Love Swing (6.04)

SIDE FOUR
1 Old Glory (4.20)
2 Mothers Day (8.39)

Although this band takes its name from San Francisco's first openly gay mayor, tragically assassinated back in '78, this album has nothing to do with him, it being a repository of superb, heathen sheet-metal stomp. Apparently, this lot split up in '98, but have now reformed at the behest of bassist Steven Tanner.

Casual listeners should give this record a chance to unfold – these guys know what they are doing.

Crush Them All

I've never heard any of Harvey Milk's previous material and, as evidenced from my note above, had no idea what to expect from this American trio. Their records are extremely difficult to find and appear to have been released on a whole bunch of disparate indie labels. But, from the proof of this record alone, Harvey Milk is a gigantic beast of incredible power; a rock machine comprised of equal parts glam (which occupies the second part of the record) and slow, slow metal (which takes up most of the early stages). At first listen, Harvey Milk appear to occupy a singular place in the rock pantheon, standing directly between the slow trudge of the Melvins, the post-trudge of Thrones and the ecstatically pedestrian glamour of Mick Ronson's 'Angel Number 9', from his second solo LP, *Play, Don't Worry*. Indeed, four songs – 'Once in a While', 'The End', 'Old Glory' and 'Mothers Day' – exhibit the kind of Mick Ralphs-meets-Bill Nelson-meets-Ronno glam descents that only the truly sentimental could be capable of. And yet the members of Harvey Milk have gone out of their way to obscure this fact by cleverly sequencing *Special Wishes* so as to give the listener the initial impression that it's gonna be monomania from start to finish. So I include this here note to the fainthearted: give this record a chance and you'll reap your reward in rock heaven (i.e. hell).

On *Special Wishes*, the seal-clubbing drums and blunderbuss bass collide with the same tectonic plate-crushing as Joe Preston's most intense programming for Thrones; indeed, in places it even approaches the cranium death of Khanate, courtesy of a rhythm section comprising Paul Trudeau, on Dale Crozer-level numbs'n'concussion, and Steven Tanner, on sub-bass fury (remember never to invite these two to a summer sleep-over, as their fly-swatting techniques would inevitably bring down the walls of your house). Harvey Milk is, furthermore, propelled by the post-glam, post-grunge, post-apocalyptic visions of songer/writer/axe-wielder Creston Spires, whose singing sounds something like John Cale, Kurt Cobain or High Tide's Tony Hill; that is, traditional, Middle English/transatlantic, masculine and baritone, but drawn out to garrotted levels, as if every verse was performed with his head already in the noose and a be-hooded executioner in attendance.

The band's southern roots and double-tracked wailing guitars immediately suggest that Lynyrd Skynyrd influences should be somewhere in evidence, but that's far too easy a call, and is no more than a mirage that fades like heat haze on a summer road when investigated fully. In truth, nothing about Harvey Milk is laid-back enough to be Skynyrd-informed. Even at their most pissed off, Ronnie Van Z's boys still had the funk, and considerable amounts of it. For the three gentlemen of Harvey Milk, however, the closest any of them could ever get to cutting a rug would be getting up off the couch to grab a beer. Sure, if Harvey Milk had been around in the early '70s they'd most probably have signed to Phil Walden's Capricorn Records but, even then, you can just guess that these contrary motherfuckers would have rejected The Allman Brothers' party line in favour of bunking off for an evening of fake pagan rites with the late Ron Goedert's White Witch.

From time to time, this *Special Wishes* album also invokes the spectre of heavy-duty progressive-rock, as the three protagonists often take their arrangements into pure Yes territory and keep it there for minutes at a time. However, just as Flower Travellin' Band's enormously barbarian take on King Crimson's '21st Century Schizoid Man' eradicated every last drop of jazz-jizz from the original, so do Harvey Milk banish all of the la-di-da chorale, Jon Anderson/Rick Wakeman elements in favour of a Chris Squire/Bill Bruford mathematical balls-to-the-wall approach. Ja, mein hairies!

Special Wishes is a stunning record that begins in the kind of pure metal territory that reveals no sentiments whatsoever, and remains there for the first three songs. 'I've Got a Love' and 'War' are harsh and gleaming stentorian assaults on the listener of the kind that suggest that this will be the monolithic standard of sonic attack throughout. However, the arrival of the cartoon senselessness of 'Crush Them All' unites those same metal hammer attitudes of the first two songs with a hugely pop sensibility, as though Kurt Cobain was waving a copy of Melvins' *Houdini* in front of their noses. This is the pivotal point of the whole album, the moment when Harvey Milk emerges from behind its Buzzo'n'Dale fixations and demands a whole other lane on the rock'n'roll highway.

Once 'Crush Them All' finally subsides, the outrage continues in an entirely different manner, as swooping and sentimental glam-rock twin-lead guitars announce 'Once in a While'. From here on in, Harvey Milk exhibit a Zen attitude towards their arch display of dynamics, ranging from total and utter nihilistic destruction to pin-drop silence. 'Instrumental' is a stone classic; shit, these guys could do something off ELP's *Brain Salad Surgery* and still make it sound current. And when, on 'The End' (my personal favourite), they combine Thrones' method with a 'Shine on You Crazy Diamond'-style mega-ballad, even this Floyd-hating psychopath has to admit they'z on to something. 'Love Swing' sounds like Speed, Glue & Shinki's 'Stoned Out of My Mind' – I mean, it's *that* slow (although nowhere near as cunted and punky, but then, could anything be?), it's even like The Move at their most unhurried ('Brontosaurus' meets 'When Alice Gets Back to the Farm' – the roots of glam or what?). Admittedly, the spectre of the Melvins always remains close at hand throughout the course of this album, with the exception of the dodgy, anti-war honesty of 'Old Glory', which contains lyrics so gauche, so unutterably arch and cringeworthy that I gots to love it. On 'Old Glory', Creston sounds about as genuine as Gary Numan on that album sleeve where he's shocked by the little pyramid. Moreover, from the manner in which he orchestrates this song, it's clear that Creston Spires himself is obviously aware of its embarrassingly twee side. Still, I'm the last person who can ever complain about such things, and the song's tail-out is a magnificent racket to encounter.

The album concludes with the eight-minute, orchestrated epic 'Mothers Day', whose gorgeous organ-and-strings introduction prepares us for a pleasantly settled, John Cale-style elegy, only to cut us to the quick with the kind of glam-rock intensity that Melvins exhibited circa *Houdini*'s version of Kiss' 'Goin' Blind', but multiplied sevenfold to include all the guitar-strangling so beloved of James Williamson, on his and Iggy's 'Joanna', of Neil Merryweather's Space Rangers and of High Tide's Tony Hill at his most raging. Apparently, this record took an age to write, rehearse and release, and it shows; gentlemen, you've wasted nothing and made every second count. This music is essential and should be on everyone's X-Mass list.

I do have one caveat: I wish the sleeve wasn't so shit. I mean, you're supposed to be making some dosh off this, and everyone'll just burn copies because there's nothing essential on the cover. OK, that's my only complaint, and that's only because I'm an old motherfucker who believes that rock'n'rollers should get their dues, not play the amateur because their fans didn't feel the 'item' itself was essential and that a burn was sufficient. So a picture disc next time, please, and plenny o'glamorous shots and pop biogs (Creston's favourite percussionist, etc. . . .), got me?

To the wider world, these guys are back and – while most of us never even knew they'd been away – their return is guaranteed to make the Western world an unsafer place. Right on!

The Heads

At Last

(Rocket Recordings, 2004)

SIDE ONE (MEDLEY: 25.30)	SIDE TWO (MEDLEY: 22.54)
1 Dissonaut	1 Filler
2 Quad	2 31st
3 Fuego	3 Stodgy
4 Troppo Amrio	4 The Ritual Is an Artform, Is It? (Parts 1 & 2)
5 Vibrating Digit	

Two albums vied for this Album of the Month, both released by those yippiefied distorto-guitar FX behemoths known as The Heads. One record was called *Thirty-Three* – a digitally edited maelstrum remix of Heads music that seemed to squeeze in somewhere between Neil Young's outrageous and arhythmical *Arc* and Dieter Dierks' attempted Cosmic Jokers' take on The Scorpions' monster weird-out *Spiders on Phasing*. But whereas The Heads' twenty-part *Thirty-Three* takes bite-sized chunks of their music and spins its wah-everythingness into a tight web of disorientation that effortlessly accesses your melting plastic brain, the normally over-achieving and thoroughly abnormal Dieter Dierks made *Spiders on Phasing* so overly heavy on the electronics that the poor old Scorpions were left with the kind of munting detritus that could only get the Spanish Archer from both Cosmic Jokers fans *and* their regular hard-rock tribe – seriously underwhelming those moustachioed longhairs expecting more 'Dark Lady'-type fare. And, as Brain Records housed this so-called 'remix' twaddle in a beautiful, fake Peter Geitner-style sleeve in a cynical attempt to align Meine and co. with the Krautrock scene,[1] the real Scorpions fans (of *The Tokyo Tapes*, *Lonesome Crow* and *In Trance*) are left high and dry!

In the end, being a pragmatic motherfucker myself, I too decided that opting for a curveball like *Thirty-Three* as an introduction to The Heads' music would be just too confusing for everyone. Instead, I opted for the comparative safety of *At Last*, a record just as horrid as the aforementioned, but far more in keeping with where The Heads' career is taking them, intuitive non-career movers that they so obviously be!

OK, Gentlemen, Cockhenge . . . *Where Is It?*

For some years now, Wessex's finest mung-worshippers, The Heads, have been promising us a heavy-rock album entitled *Cockhenge*, with a pop-up gatefold cover. Sadly, this artefact has not yet been forthcoming; indeed, I've stopped holding my breath for fear of turning the same shade of cyan blue that has graced almost every Heads album. Had the release of *Cockhenge* come about, however, I have to admit that, regardless of the quality of the music, such a disc would immediately have become an Album of the Month. In a Western culture in which even the most intellectual of us possesses an Inner Moron that needs regular exercise, The Heads would – with the release of *Cockhenge* – have proved themselves as true possessors of the exo-moron, a stubborn Eeyore-like hard-shell of ecstatic stupidity discovered thus far only around David Lee Roth, Joey Smith of Speed, Glue & Shinki, Doggen and myself.

Unsatisfied but resigned to a long

1 The link between heavy-rock and the experimental underground is always a difficult one to reconcile, as I discovered recently from the public's reaction when I went out in a Neu! vest, motorbike boots, sleeveless leather jacket and WWII German officer's peaked cap. About eight years ago, I was talking to the late John Balance, of Coil, about how UFO's first LPs (*UFO*, *UFO2*, *UFO Live* and the *Space Metal* compilation) are, stylistically, like typical Krautrock records, both in their sleeve designs and their use of massively long tracks (some stretching to between eighteen and twenty minutes). Anyway, Sleazy Christopherson overheard our discussion and he suggested that the ultimate reconciling image between heavy-rock and the underground must therefore be the sleeve to UFO's 1975 album *Force It*. Being a dodgy pun alluding to the American for 'tap' ('faucet'), UFO asked Hipgnosis to design the cover, and Sleazy (being one third of Hipgnosis) asked his friends to be the cover-star couple getting it on in the lav. So the faceless duo is actually Genesis P. and Cosey Fanni Tutti from Sleazy's old band Throbbing Gristle. Now, tell me that ain't a know-verwhelming rock revelation!

wait for *Cockhenge*, I, in the meantime, meditated patiently on The Heads' aforementioned over-use of cyan blue (generally united with vicious red in the manner of Amon Düül II's *Phallus Dei*), occasionally slavered and drooled over the hippie babes that nakedly disgraced Heads' album artwork, and admired this band's concise adherence to their own metaphor. Loop meets The Pink Fairies is always a fine place to begin a career, but an even greater place to finish it . . . To finish it . . . To finish it . . . To finish it . . . Yup, that's how repetitious these Heads can be. And, unlike pretty much every other rock'n'roll band, The Heads began slowly and then just got, nay, get better and better, their last two albums having totally eclipsed all of their early work.

At Last . . . *Or, 'Fuck Bloodrock, Let's Have It All Away!'*

This Album of the Month heaps space-rock cliché upon heavy-rock cliché upon psychedelic, proto-metal cliché in a manner so bereft of guilt, so untainted by fashion, so un-ironic that it transcends its inspirations totally and just becomes sonic environment. Indeed, in my present, recently re-psychedelicised state, I have at times been driven to forget I was listening to this record, and have risen from the floor to put it on when it was in fact already playing. Of course, regarding The Heads' use of multiple clichés, it would be disingenuous of me to suggest that this band was unaware of its stance. Hell, they'z from Bristol, not the Orkney Islands. But, as *At Last* has appeared already deep into their so-called career, it's possible that these gentlemen just thought, 'Fuck it, no one's gonna notice anyway' – just like Sleater-Kinney appeared to have done with their Sub-Pop album *The Woods*. Or maybe guitarist P. R. A. Allen has given up looking for what he once called 'That heavy psych sound that we haven't managed to achieve before due to time and financial reasons.'

So, The Heads have given up on engineers and studios and have instead recorded a concise career overview in their rehearsal room, Asahito Nanjo-stylee, although possibly not through one single compressor mic, à la Mr High Rise. Overwhelmed by the vats of raw mid-range (and none of it in sealed containers) that inevitably build up during such projects, plus having been thus relieved of such industry standards as bass-end and audible vocals, The Heads have suddenly descended into the underworld in a truly Odinist manner; that is, they've retrieved nine polished jewels from their past canon of work with which to present us an entirely new long-player. Ja, mein hairies, *At Last* has brung forty-eight minutes of extremely useful tinnitus meditation to our twenty-first-century rock'n'roll party.

It's not just for stoners and gas-guzzlers either, m'dears. As with Side One of Chrome's *Alien Soundtracks* and Loop's *A Gilded Eternity* (especially Side Two's 'The Nail Will Burn' and 'Blood'), I've spent hours lifting weights to *At Last*, doing stomach exercises to it, hell, you can even just lie on the floor with your partner and in–out to it. Fantastic – and cheap, too.

This whole deal they then released on cyan-blue vinyl (natch) in an equally cyan-coloured gatefold sleeve that presumptuously (and wholly correctly) appropriates for its inner artwork the all-time best rock cartoon; that is, the sleeve of Bloodrock's *Bloodrock U.S.A.*, an early-'70s snooze-athon so bereft of meaning and artistry that The Heads truly did the only decent thing and relieved that LP of its single positive asset.[2] Even better is the front cover, which – economical motherfuckers that The Heads are – posterises the photo of the cunt-cupping hippie chick on the cover of their own *Everyone Knows We Got Nowhere*, and logo-ifies her still further.

The beginning of *At Last* is a true *summum bonum* of all things underground; a dark, milky ooze of a cosmic thang that unites Tractor's 'Shubunkin'[3] with Blues Creation's twin-guitar-havoc-laden 'Atomic

2 To be fair, *Bloodrock U.S.A.* does have a few excellent, Mark Farneresque moments of brutal, late-Grand Funk merit. However, this is my opportunity to assert that most of those much-applauded, early-'70s, so-called heavy classics, such as Leafhound, Bang, Dust, Crushed Butler, Third World War, Bloodrock, Poobah, etc., are nowadays regularly eclipsed by twenty-first-century heavy rock'n'roll. Indeed, of the ancestors, only those exo-morons such as Black Sabbath, early Grand Funk Railroad (*On Time*, *Live Album* and the red *Grand Funk* LP, mostly), Joey Smith's Speed, Glue & Shinki, early Flower Travellin' Band (*Anywhere*, *Satori*, *Made in Japan*), early Blue Cheer (*Vincebus Eruptum*, *Outsideinside*, Side Two of *New! Improved!*), Randy Holden's *Population II* and 'Crash Course in Brain Surgery'-period Budgie seem to have been so sonically fundamental to the rock'n'roll canon that they will not one day be bettered.

3 I well remember, back in November '93, the look of disgust on Rooster Cosby's face during the recording of my *Autogeddon* album, as we A/B'd between my own 'Kar-Ma-Kanik' and Tractor's 'Shubunkin' in order to get Rooster's drums quiet enough. Needing to err on the safe side, I made sure the drums were even quieter than Tractor's; indeed, so quiet were they that when Mark Geiger – my A&R man at Def American – heard the master, he suggested that such a space-rock song would probably sound better *with drums*!

Bombs Away' as refracted, inevitably, through Hawkwind's *Space Ritual* lens, which was itself copped from Floyd's 'Astronomy Domine'. Pay no attention to the tracklisting at the head of this review, by the way, for it all sludges from one unidentifiable tantrum into the next in the same manner as the 'Up' medley on Kim Fowley's *Outrageous* and Van der Graaf Generator's supposedly ten-part, twenty-minute freak-out 'A Plague of Lighthouse Keepers', from *Pawn Hearts*. Even though these Heads tracks have appeared in different form across half a decade of studio LPs, here they're all reduced to individual tentacles of the same octopus. For example, the immaculately titled opening track 'Dissonaut' (originally from 2002's *Under Sided*) has so many different parts that any attempts at excavating a beginning or an end can only be a wind-up, especially as the 'official' baton-change slides so seamlessly into 'Quad' (from *Relaxing with the Heads*) that it just feels like a middle eight. The version of 'Fuego' is herein reduced to no more than just a pulsating gear-change in the 'Psychotic Reaction Part 2' tradition. However, those with no foreknowledge of The Heads' oeuvre will hear it all as one performance piece. Moreover, giving a title to each separate and wholly unidentifiable piece creates as disorientating an effect on the listener as we mung-worshippers could wish for, and keeps us pinned to the carpet, croaking 'What the?' out of one corner of our mouths as the drool slides inexorably down the other. Indeed, semi-oblivion just lets it all burn out your stout cortex with never a thought that these might be songs what some scumfucker actually wrote; that is, until the singularly blazing chaos of 'Vibrating Digit' brings Side One to a merciful conclusion.

The thrilling motorpsycho yatter of 'Filler' opens Side Two and contains Simon Price's finest lead vocal thus far recorded – a Kim Fowleyan, shrieking'n'hawking heart attack somewhere close to *Outrageous*' 'Barefoot Country Boy'. Price normally sings with a soft and educated West Country burr that maybe even he ain't aware of, but here he's puking Niagara Falls with Viagra chomping his balls as his vocal delivery becomes subsumed into the rock every-head of De-twat, Delta, Sahf London, Liverpuddle spike-o-babble. Uni-directional guitar feedback then directs us towards the nearest Detroit riff and we ascend a sonic moving staircase towards a major-chord penthouse aurally decorated with Warholised screenprints of Van Halen's version of The Kinks' 'You Really Got Me'. This tense, wah-wah'd masterstroke is 'Stodgy', which even features audible lead vocals, before segueing seamlessly into the first part of 'The Ritual Is an Artform, Is It?' It's somewhere between Brain Donor's 'Pagan Dawn' and Jimi Hendrix's 'Are You Experienced?', and I'd like a whole remix LP of just this track.

Suddenly, peace descends, although the high-volume silence is horribly interrupted by Indian sitar, before some Islamic sultan righteously offs the players' hands for failure to rock, and we descend into the relentless, nine-minute, circular chordal burn-out of 'The Ritual Is an Artform, Is It? Part 2', with which *At Last* concludes. This is as close to old-school space-rock as The Heads ever go, at times approaching the fury of first-album Ash Ra Tempel or even Hawkwind's 'Born to Go'. But always that wah'd-to-fuck midrange slays you beyond the call of duty. It reminds me of the instructions printed on the inner sleeve of Yonin Bayashi's 1973 debut album *Ishoku-Sokuhatsu.* Not only does it state 'This record should be played loud!', there's also a diagrammatic tone control with the bass turned *all* the way down and the treble turned *all* the way up! That note applies equally to this Heads LP.

But, hey, despite my umpteen comparisons with other rock'n'roll groups, The Heads have a trip that is entirely their own – and *At Last* is one hell of a launching pad. Try and find this record on vinyl if you can because the two sides are equally useful and each contributes to the well-being of your mental health, especially for users on a heavy repetition trip.

In Conclusion

Back in 1996, when they first dumped *Relaxing with the Heads* at our back door, I listened but was not charmed – the music was potentially large but the production needed to be a lot more shitty and, dammit, you could hear Wayne Maskell's fucking drums, almost as loud as on a Gaye Bykers on Acid record! Nowadays, he's got it all in check, admitting to no more than having 'a specially made snare that emits radio waves every summer solstice'. Anyway, after that first LP I didn't catch up with what The Heads were doing until 2000's fabulously titled *Everyone Knows We Got Nowhere* showed they were not much closer than before, but at least still on the right track with titles such as 'Kraut Byrds'. Even better was 2002's *Under Sided,* which produced a great song, 'Bedminster', about a part of Bristol that people visit only when looking for cheap off-cuts of carpet with which to do up their sheds. I liked it even more when I read in an interview that these Bristol nutters admitted to crediting all their songs to the whole band because it was the way Black Sabbath did it, and that they'd named their own record label Sweet Nuthin' after the legendary song by Fred 'Sonic' Smith's amazing and largely unsung Sonic's Rendezvous Band. But it still wasn't the knockout punch. However, I gots to say *At Last* is one desperate motherfucker of an LP and more than deserving of its Album of the Month accolade. I only hope these self-styled dissonauts continue along their delightful hell-bound trail. Being from Wessex, they certainly have plenny o'portals in which to locate the underworld. In the meantime, fellow motherfuckers, please applaud The Heads for their sustaining dedication to The Trip. A decade is a long time to continue with the same line-up without losing the plot entirely, so evidence is strong that these gentlemen, having finally found the path, will remain upon it for a good few years to come. And, by opting for the great sonic leap sideways and downwards quite deep into their career, *At Last* has taken this group to another level of pop artistry.

Khanate

(Southern Lord, 2002)

1 Pieces of Quiet (13.22)
2 Skin Coat (9.36)
3 Torching Koroviev (3.38)
4 Under Rotting Sky (18.18)
5 No Joy (11.32)

Altaic Shamen Have Crossed the Bering Straits

I got it. I finally got the fucking sludge-trudge death-march I been looking for these past coupla years, and I'm so grateful to be able to put it on the stereo. It's so great to know it exists. Great to grate on your trickster self – this music is Loki burning Odin's asshole and not even bothering to run. Hit me, motherfucker. I'm more than a ghoul – I'm the vege-fucking-tation, the very soil. If you ever wondered why Dylan Carlson called his band Earth, well, now you know – it's because the shaman of the nomads could only lie in rotting sentience once he became the shaman of the agriculturist. Wandering suddenly had its limits.

Commencing in guitar noise worthy of pure microphone feedback, insultingly loud, slow, slow, refusenik longhairs stand and kick the living shit out of each other for fifty-six minutes. When I shocked this CD on to my hi-fi, this stuff seeped into my room and ruined my black carpet, climbed the walls and graffitied my framed Kiss sleeves, oozed hideous colourless mung over the carved head of my intolerant horned god Bu, then mated with my herd of doublenecks as they stood proud and erect in their shrine. Keep the bedroom door shut, for Non's sake, or they'll ruin the fucking bookshelves in no time at all.

Have you ever felt that Alice's 'Black Ju Ju' was right on the money but 'I Love the Dead' was vaudeville Vincent Price? Me too; but not any more. Alice was just struggling (twenty years too soon) for words when there was not yet a vocabulary. Ever wished that Sabbat had slowed down not just a bit but so far *beyond* that they approached standstill, that every one of Martin Walkyier's words became a painful dental operation just to articulate his erudite Wodenisms? Yeah, fucking me too! Well, u-goddit!

Make no mistake, this band is one bunch of learned, know-just-what-they'z-doing psychonauts. You don't name your group after *the* most successful period of Mongol rule without having tapped (consciously/unconsciously) into the historically provable fact that the shamen of the Altaic mountains were tying their horse to precisely the same kind of tree as the proto-Woden before his tribe of Asir left their homelands and made the trip north-west to Scandinavia. And you surely don't call a song 'Under Rotting Sky' without having tapped into the actual well of Urth itself.

Khanate call themselves a 'proto-dirge' band, and this is the first sludge-trudge supergroup of the twenty-first century. Taking a temporary break from the once Earth-obsessed ambient doom grunge of Sunn O))),[1] Stephen O'Malley has brought his magnificent guitar and sheer healing vision to Khanate. Steeped in album-sleeve design and sonic installations, O'Malley is an ever-rising occult force.[2]

Blind Idiot God's Tim Wyskida provides the kind of antirhythms which Hansel and Gretel woulda created if they'd wandered through the woods leaving a trail of Ziljian cymbals instead of breadcrumbs, and Old's Alan Dubin is massively un-credited with 'vokills' (for me, his range is somewhere between Okinawa assault weapon and Spina de Mul music box, via the wind, the sea and the Black Mass). All this rage is somehow battened down by the telegraph-wire bass of Scorn's James Plotkin, who contributes both form *and* formlessness. Throughout the album, it's like he's stopping the music from returning to

1 Sunn O))) have an LP on the Southern Lord label called *Flight of the Behemoth*. If anything, I prefer it to their wonderful album *ØØ Void*. It sounds like two longhairs in a WWI biplane towing a rainbow.

2 Stephen O'Malley is also responsible for the *Fungal Hex* soundtrack, which accompanied 2001's installations at the Jeleni Gallery in Prague. For those of you with a love of ambulent sensibilities, this is another CD to get yer mitts on.

its proto-Sunn O))) state by erecting makeshift sonic walls – the musical equivalents of beachfront canvas wind-breaks.

Slow Is the New Loud

So what does it sound like? It sounds like orchestrated root-canal work. It sounds like Speed, Glue & Shinki digitally slowed down to cloud speed. It sounds like gloss paint shrinking as it dries over a haplessly incautious housefly. It sounds like Gene Simmons vocally accompanying his own live bass solo while being injected with industrial-strength doses of largactyl.

The bass is a meditation on Dennis Dunaway's intro to 'Guttercats vs. The Jets', from the *School's Out* LP. I'm so romantic. I'm so off the beam. But it's that bass tone, played by the awesome James Plotkin, which holds down and underpins everything. Fuck, everything else goes out of the way to undermine everything else. Stephen O'Malley's guitar always returns, homing-pigeon-like, to its subterranean roost. *Braaaaaaanggggg!* Then off it goes again to hammer the sky with the same sniffy arrogance and rejection of 4/4 rock'n'roll as Flower Travellin' Band managed on their version of Black Sabbath's proto-trudge epic 'Black Sabbath'. Hey, now that's a more than fairly accurate point of reference, come to think of it. I love the drums to death for their Rooster Cosbyan refusal to use the snare as anything but an armrest. Hell, even Tim Wyskida's credit just says 'hammers'. Thor? Tork? Tarawn? Nah, all three, and simultaneously.

'Pieces of Quiet' opens the album with thirteen minutes of the kind of mythological events which the Christians must have unceremoniously and very hastily erased from their translations of the Norse myths. You quickly get the feeling that the Wodenist temple at Old Uppsala would have been strewn with lyrical notes such as these, pinned to the hanging bodies. It has the same grisly humour as the part in the *King Gautrek* saga when successive generations of relatives are each committing suicide by diving over the well-named 'Family Cliff' on 'the way to meet Odin' rather than endure any more pain. Like *Gautrek*, this album is definitely post-Christian, in both its humour and its irony, yet it's miserably human and true all the same. The riff sounds like some digital nutcase tape-stretched one of Black Sabbath's 1971 contemporaries into some under-exposed, sixty-percent half-world ('Future Shock' by Bang,

'Dogman' by Monument,[3] 'Watching You' by Kiss and 'Woman Tamer' by Sir Lord Baltimore[4] are the kind of songs which immediately come to mind).

By the opening strains of 'Skin Coat', they've broken through the doors of perception into some cold-storage chamber for sarcophagi. The vocals shiver and shake like Dubin's been shut in this place so long he's been reduced to a kind of amphibian form, armed only with its own mirror, purring and gibbering in solipsistic jubilation, 'I exist, I exist, I exist . . .' Everything disappears at five minutes and fourteen seconds to reveal O'Malley's brilliant introverted and inverted, arpeggio'd guitar coda, low-key and self-serving as Loki, while (gradually and very slowly) in comes the sibilant vocal refrain: 'I'm wearing a human shield/I put you on/I'm wearing . . . a human shield.'

I'd guess this is my favourite song on the album. Poetically brilliant, it shines like some dark beacon in the surrounding Dark Ages fug and uses the wonderful image of the flesh of the body as the 'human shield'. This is post-Saddam imagery which is so damned pop-art you just feel there should be a whole other music invented calling itself just that.

Then they're off into the brief, wordless interlude they call 'Torching Koroviev': a 'Horse Latitudes' for the New Age of the New Age. The libretto calls it 'an instrumental', but that's just the applaudable hang-ups of Alan Dubin breaking through. From the listeners' perspective, sounds such as '*sssssssssnnnnnssssssnnnn*', '*ttthhsssssss*', '*norhhhhhhhhhhhhhh*' and '*aflehhhhhhhhhhhhhhh!*' count just as much as any of the other sonic gurning which permeates the fabric of this record. And I guarantee that all Japanese rock'n'roll translators with any self-respect whatsoever would conjure

3 Regarding Drone Syndicate's reissue of the Moses album, I gotta tell you it's a fucking smoke-screening waste of time. Keep well away. Even buying a patchy heavy album like the first Monument LP will yield two monsters in 'Dogman' and 'Gimme Life'. But the Moses LP is fucking Arrows without the TV series!

4 It may be unfathomable, but it's still true that two of Baltimore's three greatest sludge-trudges are both on their appalling second LP *Sir Lord Baltimore*. Besides the ultra-trudge 'Kingdom Come' title track of their brilliant and amphetamined first LP, that second album weirdly comes to life only at the end of Side Two, in the form of 'Woman Tamer' and 'Caesar LXXI'. And how!

up at least a half-page of lyrical possibilities from 'Torching Koroviev''s three, Dubinal minutes of primal grunt.

And then we're off into an eighteen-minute descent into Groa's mound that goes by the name 'Under Rotting Sky'. Blazing feedback gives way to ever-lowering, widdershins, de-spiralling Bronze Age guitar, as the Dubin's voice summons up scorched, pig-Latin ritual words. Around five minutes in, the whole thing gives way to the slowest of slow guitar-chord refrains as . . . Dubin . . . breaks into . . . Well, he calls them 'Pseudo-Latin Ramblings', but I'd strongly disagree. We're in Kan Mikami territory here, and Alan Dubin is deep-toning some kinda ur-Sanskrit from beneath the canopy of Indo-European culture. There ain't no such thing as 'pseudo' anything when you get this deep in. On my own shamanic crawl-trawls, I would absolutely lay claim to have touched my amphibian self – and these Dubinal vocalisms are trustworthy, dangerous and brazenly confident. Officially, the libretto reads:

Now I'm under rotten sky . . . Now I'm under rotten sky,
Choke, choke, want you choke,
Change, face to blue,
Sky empty, blanket of you – blanket of nothing,
No . . . stars . . . out,
Choke, choke . . . want you choked,
Blanket of nothing covers your face change – it's blue,
We're choked, me and you,
Sky empty, blanket of me – blanket of nothing,
Our face change, it's blue,
We're choked, me and you . . .

Sure, that's what it looks like in Western script. In reality, each word is a ceremonial code-cypher bellowed out every ten seconds over some ur-stockbreeding 'tween-time, punk-chew-ate-ed by bullish free-rock power chords . . . 'Choke, choke, choke, choke/Want you choked/Choke choke, choke/Want you choked/Choke, choke, choke/Want you choked/Choke, choke, choke/Want you choked.'

Does it get plainer than this? Or do their live shows feature a centrally placed Yggdrasil on which to garrotte the audience? The only way they could be more in yer face would be to call the track 'King Vikar', and half the fucking audience would still be none the wiser.

After that, we can only expect Khanate to maintain their trip into the lowest consciousness. Any more and we'd probably be asleep, or our cultural automatic-dis-engage alarm systems would spring into operation, and we'd find ourselves outside in the street waiting for the emergency services.

And so, on the mantra they call 'No Joy', Khanate become a hunting party of ghouls who have decided to split up in order to smoke out their prey. Now, they are four separated aspects of the same spirit circling the churchyard at 4 a.m., determined to bring down the walls and force the lofty heights of the a'spire down into the dust. The guitar takes one route and we travel with it, as the Dubin brays, coyote-like, in the lychgate. Suddenly, we're right in there with the Dubin, as he pisses under the bleeding yew. To the west the bass and guitars undermine the walls of the kirk, and all this time the drums of Tarawn clatter across two horizons, yet the cymbals remain inside our heads. An almost imperceptible movement, but I'm sure I saw the walls beginning to sink. Round and round and round, anti-sunwise, plough the guitar and bass, like the stockman undoing all the farmer's work – but slow as slow, and controlled, always controlled. Until . . . like the last rays of winter sunset, the stone kirk sinks inevitably into Urth . . . Urth . . . Urth . . . Urth . . . Urtha . . . Urtha . . . Urtha . . . Urtha . . . Urtha . . . Urtha . . . Urtha . . . Urtha . . . Urtha . . .

I Gots to Tell Ya

How to use this music is of paramount importance. Take your headphones and Discman and give yourself to the hillside. Lie amongst the soil in a sleeping bag for the safety of your bodily self. This ain't music to enjoy – but we ain't Christians and we ain't about to martyr ourselves, either. Use this music like a prescription and let it work for you. If you have the facility, wear headphones *and* have the speakers playing on full bass. Also, remember: this ain't music to free the spirit. This is for the forward-thinking motherfucker who accedes to George Clinton's credo, 'Freedom is free of the need to be free.' Like the Normans said to the newly vanquished Saxons, 'You ain't our slaves. You're just un-free.' It's the same with the Golden Horde-period which inspired this group to name themselves Khanate. Indeed, the Khanate t-shirt should probably take the Coca-Cola logo and simply replace that single word 'Enjoy' with 'Endure!'

Jex Thoth

(I Hate Records, 2008)

1 Nothing Left to Die (5.10)
2 Obsidian Night (2.43)
3 Separated at Birth (3.21)
4 Son of Yule (4.09)
5 Equinox Suite (15.07)
   a The Poison Pit
   b Thawing Magus
   c Invocation Part 1
   d The Damned & the Divine
6 When the Raven Calls (3.56)
7 Stone Evil (6.12)

As a Beautiful Princess Crosses a Bridge Under Which Four Great Trolls Are Performing Doom Metal . . .

Both fuelled and be-fouled by lo-fi, post-C90 amp buzzing, heathen doom-plod-from-ye-hayloft, but propelled and sung into being by a bona fide rock goddess anchored in those glorious traditions laid down according to Amon Düül's Renate Knaup, Jefferson Airplane's Grace Slick and The Savage Rose's Annisette Hansen, by way of Heart's Ann Wilson, the music and vocalising of this remarkable Jex Thoth quintet is nothing less than a divine emanation of all things great in postwar Western humanity's return to its heathen roots – the band's music being a supreme sludge-trudge of the *Master of Reality*, 'Into the Void' persuasion, as though created and performed by four enormous Yeti trolls of northern Denmark's icy Skagerrak coast. Moreover, these are four Bobby Liebling-class warrior trolls from atop whose muddy, '59 Caddy tail-finned oxcart parcel-shelf some bewitching and be-daisied Fjordal priestess declaims in perfectly clear tones her most recent visions and extraordinarily high hopes for the future to a spellbound agrarian population, who – on seeing her pass by their field systems looking so resplendent and so well protected – rest briefly upon their hoes, temporarily free from the drudgery of every day; they gaze out across the drystone walling, their near-suffocated minds inhaling, although only momentarily, but nevertheless long enough to have, in that micro-millisecond, imagined complete resuscitation and rescue from their (hopefully only temporary) predicament. Ho hum.

As rural as fuck, as heathen as a cunt and thrice as mysterious, Jex Thoth's is a strange ministry. I imagine this quintet's audience dwelling in scattered, out-of-the-way homesteads, rarely coming together as a community, thus obliging this itinerant quintet to spread their barbarian information out to their congregation by any means necessary; for their music contains few highs or lows of the urban variety, and replaces obvious hooks with insidious melodies that emerge, then take over our melting plastic minds.

Not for Jex Thoth the Metallic K.O. Instead, their very rudimentary but extremely evocative and primal sound is circular, beating-the-bounds, ever-returning to earlier themes, pummelling their audience not with a single punch to the head but through a series of muffled and hazy blows to the lower torso. It's a war of attrition. The music of Jex Thoth seems designed to be heard only in brief snatches, as though the musicians had been expected to hawk it from farm to farm, day after day, month after month, their hoary themes gradually . . . ever so gradually intoxicating their recipients for want of any other tunes to be had in the neighbourhood. But, while it's good work for the trolls when they can get it, it's damned peculiar that such a divine chanteuse should have chosen – of her own free will – to hook up with such a gang of ne'er-do-wells. What's all this about? Well, like the aforemenched rock goddesses of Yore, Jex Thoth singer Jessica – despite the crystal clarity of her voice – appears, both in spirit, lyrical persuasion and goggle-eyed worldview, to share far more in common with the grave-loitering Ozzy, the Promethean Arthur Brown, the First Nation shaman Todd Clark, the gods' antagonist Peter Hammill and six-feet-under Uncle Bobby Liebling than with any contemporary female singers of note, except the timeless and undead Nico, of course.

That Jessica could be possessed of such a fabulous larynx and yet still wish to run with such muckrakers as seven-foot-tall bassist Grim Jim, one-armed drummer Johnny Dee, one-eyed doom keyboardmeister Zodiac and one-fingered axe wielder Silas Paine would be the strong and fiery evidence that she's a *natural* through'n'through, a star-crossed child of Freyja and Loki, were it not for the fact that this singer once yodelled for the strange folk ensemble Wooden Wand. Ah, so there's clearly more than just *need* here; there is also an intellectual undercurrent, a separate agenda.

And, while this simple morsel of info immediately places the music of Jex Thoth into the category of 'Former Undergrounders Going Metal in a Knowing Stylee', so does the evidence of Zodiac Mountain's Clay Ruby at the production helm confirm that all in Jex Thoth's Thorean wedding party bag is not quite as it seems. Which hips us to the evidence that yet more enlightened seekers have broken through that same megalithic facade that Svipdag/Odin discovered back in the eighth century and have consciously chosen to descend 'Into the Void' in order to Rodger Bain their former Paul Rothschild sensibilities.

Stranger still, the most striking element of this entire project is the almost inept, proto-chancer nature of the musicians involved. Kids, these dudes ain't cleverly playing down; this is plainly all they're capable of. And, like the early LPs from bands such as The Stooges, Blue Cheer, Tiger B. Smith and UFO, this gives Jex Thoth a hefty and wonderfully 'over-overdubbed' sound that truly smoked ma pole right down to the cheroot! And always so entirely rural and unroofed; indeed, the closest that Jex Thoth get to sounding remotely urban is on their excellent cover of Bobb Trimble's apocalyptic 'When the Raven Calls', written back in the '80s by everybody's favourite Most Promising Canuckian Who Never Sustained It, but the original versh is far transcended herein by the vast, early Curved Air wah-riffery and Jessica's über-ominous Gracie circa *Crown of Creation* vocal delivery ('Lather' meets 'Greasy Heart', anyone?).

Elsewhere, this remarkable ensemble defines its parameters tightly at all times, mainly strutting down that same Hard Rock Highway as St. Vitus, Pentagram, Flower Travellin' Band, Sabbath and the like, but never averse to corralling some of that old avant-rock as presented by outsiders such as late-period Fugs and/or Prague's Plastic People of the Universe. Indeed, an important note should be made of the manner in which this album's enormous and multi-parted fifth track, 'Equinox Suite', portentously commences with a huge Krautrockian theme in the style of the Plastic People of the Universe meets Todd Clark's New Gods period, before settling into a bizarre Caledonian melody as played by peak-period Van der Graaf Generator (the scything fuzz guitar echoing

VdGG's Jaxon saxophone). Kids, in the manner of its rough garage recording this is almost the underground folk of Alex Harvey's 1969 'Roman Wall Blues', although wedded to that same kind of classic Scottish 'Auld Lang Syne'-style folk melody in the same manner that Armand Schaubroeck employed for his own, hugely Gothick version on the *I Came to Visit but Decided to Stay* album; and get that mawkish mewling lead guitar spewing out of Jex Thoth's speakers! Guitarist Silas Paine is one confident motherfucker, daring to unearth such lost underclasses of hard-rock feeling in the same manner as berserk, axe-wielding, homicidal schmaltzmeisters such as Amon Düül II's John Weinzierl and Flower's Hideki Ishima. Stranger still, 'Son of Yule' emerges from its typically Thothian and shambling Pentagram/Sabbath gait into an unlikely Patti Smithian take on 'Electric Funeral', only to descend once again into the earlier riff, but this time informed by a Jon Lord, circa *Fireball,* doom organ accompaniment as low church and fundamentalist as that of Reverend Bizarre.

Like the original Alice Cooper quintet,[1] Jex Thoth is – at least superficially – a democratic ensemble that relies on each musical element as much as the next in order to achieve its slushy, wayward brilliance. But it's that knowing element, no doubt injected by producer Clay Ruby, which constantly repositions the band and makes its utterings so useful to us.

Where next for Jex Thoth? Well, with their well-oiled arsenal of Amon Düülisms at the ready, I could well imagine this band rendering superb cover versions of The Savage Rose's emotionally shattering 'A Trial in Our Native Town' and Ozzy's 'Revelation Mother Earth' at some point in their career. And, if that comment is nothing more than wishful thinking on my part, you can at least imagine from that comment how highly I have come to regard this wonderful new record. Better still, as the magnificent gatefold artwork was rendered by Reverend Bizarre's own vocal legend Albert Witchfinder, we have further evidence that this quintet is currently sat in the lap of the Motherfucker!

1 I'm talking, of course, about the Alice Cooper quintet in which singer Vince Furnier was barely one-fifth of the drive and talent, beside songwriter-guitarist Michael Bruce and Messrs Dunaway and Smith, surely the least fêted but greatest Krautrock-styled rhythm section in hard-rock.

LIQUORBALL

Evolutionary Squalor

(Rocketship Records, 2009)

SIDE ONE
Evolutionary Squalor Part 1 (18.49)

SIDE TWO
Evolutionary Squalor Part 2 (17.01)

You're Ugly and Your Mother Dresses You Funny

When my spies first told me Liquorball were back together after a full decade of silence, Lordy was I ever suspicious. Why on earth would the band wanna compromise three boner fido, snot-gobbling, classic 1990s LPs (*Liquorball Fucks the Sky*, *Live in Hitler's Bunker* and *Liquorball Hauls Ass*)? I mean, with hobo/hunk/drummer-supreme Mitch Fogelman out of the picture, couldn't Grady Runyan, Feast and co. just give the project a new name and leave us old-timer fans to drool upon our Zimmer frames in a blissful oblivion of stoner incontinence? I mean, those old Liquorball LPs hurt and were even quite psychically dangerous to own. Moreover, if the music contained within their grooves had been housed in artwork true to Liquorball's sound, then they woulda come enfolded in sleeves of asbestos brick, laminated with anti-climb paint. I mean, back in the day, this band was one hoity-toity beast, so following up three epic barf-athons this late in the day could easily have been as lame, tiresomely muso and merely achievingly so-so as both the reformed Rocket from the Tombs and Television.

Oh, the sleepless nights, the gnashing of teeth, the cold compresses to the forehead, brothers'n'sisters. I was a neurotic mess until I flipped this brand-new sucker on to my Garrard SP25 and turned the volume knob way (the fuck) *up*. Hmm . . . the first few minutes had me worried. Where were the strangled-by-barbed-wire guitar riffs that the Runyoid had previously served up as briskly and matter-of-factly as SpongeBob SquarePants on a Krabby Patty OD? Where was Feast's fabulous sub-Shockabilly, sub-sub-Eddie Murphy 'It . . . Was . . . The . . . Dukes' pre-garrotted grunting? Where were those extremely troublesome non-riffs that had petered out into seemingly ever-unfolding soundchecks or those one-man (*any* man) displays of sheer stubborn showing off? Where were the random stop/starts? Before the end of Side One, however, my fears subsided as the latest addition to the sacred Liquorball canon gradually insinuated its weasly ways into my melted plastic brain.

So let's cleanse the palette and start all over again; get this straight from the start. No, the external cuntedness that was the old Liquorball's trademark has vanished entirely, as have the Marzuraan-style lumpenprõle grunt-athons that made these protagonists so, well, subhuman. However, while the music of Liquorball is nowadays definitely made not by stewed orcs at the end of a three-week-long Prague stag, we can (believe me, kiddies) still rely on the good judgement of Grady Runyan always to play the intuitive non-career-mover card and shift the whole schmeer so far sideways that, while he's still putting the boot in, this time around it's with a totally different type of steel toecap. Nice.

Featuring just two untitled, sidelong tracks, the All New Adventures of Liquorball 2009 still manages to showcase the aforementioned Feast, albeit in a highly reduced role, here featured solely on bass, alongside former violinist Doug Pearson, who is nowadays Etch-a-sketching freeform synth doo-doo across the heavens with his Wiard 300 modular. Methinks Doug is to Liquorball what Aluminum Queen was to Monoshock. Cranking up the vibe still further, Liquorball has cleverly inveigled former Hives . . . sorry, Stooges free-sax player Steve Mackay into the band in the 'special guest' role, like some Scrappy Doo-styled rewrite designed to lend added pep to the old formula. And there's the rub, brothers'n'sisters. For it don't half work a treat! In one fell swoop, Liquorball has – with the addition of this mythical squawker – barfed forth precisely the kind of highly sustaining sub-sub-free-jazz scrawl that we all thought woulda died forever after Miles Davis corrupted us with all those mid-'70s post-Krautrock/proto-no-wave double-vinyl behemoths such as *Agharta*, *Get Up with It* and *Dark Magus*.

Yup, the Monster Munch'n'Pepsi Max teenage tantrum version of Liquorball is dead, replaced instead by high-endurance older guys with a low budget, a fixed time limit and a desperate need to shit all the cack out of their overcharged minds while caught collectively in the sweet maelstrom of each other's combined whinnying. Is it fantastic? I should coco!

Recorded quite basically with the musicians all set up between the tight LP racks of Grady Runyan's Californian record store, *Evolutionary Squalor* is comprised of two, ever-unfolding, ever-building, ever-regrouping pieces which greedily and intuitively cram into their performances the best bits of every Krautrock powerdrive, every surf instrumental, every Cleveland 1975, pre-punk roar, every free-jazz (Archie Shepp, Miles Davis, Art Ensemble of Chicago, etc.) lick, and then batter the thing until you can't tell whether it's a plaice or a haddock. So while Iggy from 'the Pru' is still lamenting the loss of his cash cow following the death of Ron Asheton, fellow Stooge Steve Mackay has followed his heart to Ventura, California, playing a major role in reigniting this old Liquorball project by contributing so much stellarly twatted sax that we old-timer Stooges nutters need no longer stare listlessly off into space imagining whole LPs of 'Freak', 'LA Blues' and 'Asthma Attack'. Babies, if they so chose, these Liquorball guys could do it for us! In the meantime, we can all haul ass (as the Runyoid would no doubt term it) down to the local vinyl emporium and cop this mighty *Evolutionary Squalor* LP: forty minutes of Taliban-level *no compromise.*

Better still, Liquorball have even upped the ante somewhat. For, whereas the old Liquorball sounded like nothing on earth, this new ensemble sounds like nothing in the universe. If you buy one vinyl LP this year, revolutionary motherfuckers, make it this one. And if it sells well, maybe we can persuade Messrs Runyan, Feast and co. to record a whole slew of these suckers; imagine these mad cunts once they're back in the saddle! Gentlemen of the ensemble, many thanks for this hellride; like that excellent first batch you hatched back in the day, *Evolutionary Squalor* is most serpently gonna give us all many years of listening pleasure, not to mention hefty psychic usage.

Multi-tasking? U-betcha!

Early Discography

'Come Fly with Us' (single, Blackjack, 1990)
'Willie the Worm' (single, Blackjack, 1991)

Liquorball Fucks the Sky (Blackjack, 1992)
Liquorball Hauls Ass (Blackjack, 1994)
Live in Hitler's Bunker (Blackjack, 1997)
Bulbjack (seven-inch compilation, Blackjack, 1994)
Assassins of Silence/Hundred-Watt Violence LP/CD
(Compilation, Ceres, 1995)

Nathaniel Mayer

Why Don't You Give It to Me?

(Alive Records, 2007)

SIDE ONE

1 Why Don't You Give It to Me? (5.07)
2 White Dress (3.30)
3 I'm a Lonely Man (4.39)
4 Please Don't Drop the Bomb (2.39)
5 Everywhere (3.38)

SIDE TWO

1 What Would You Do? (3.28)
2 Doin' It (8.51)
3 Why Dontcha Show Me? (7.01)

This Is Not a Parody

This Album of the Month is nothing less than a heroic act, being both an extraordinary art statement of cavernous Detroit psychedelic soul *and* a major mission of cultural retrieval. For, with the help of four contemporary musicians at least twenty-five years his junior, veteran Detroit R&B star Nathaniel Mayer has, with this single LP, lifted himself out of the worthy but old-timer, chicken-in-a-basket soul-revue scene and been delivered into the welcoming hands of the drooling and mightily entranced underground. And believe me, kiddies, retrieving the voice of Nathaniel Mayer for our own delectation establishes the musicians in question as true culture heroes; so let's scream out major hails to The Black Keys' Dan Auerbach, SSM's Dave Shettler, The Dirtbombs' Troy Gregory and (most especially) to mainman and prime mover Matthew Smith. For, despite claims to the contrary, even Mayer's 2004 LP *I Just Wanna Be Held* still suffered from boring, nay, dutiful sax, dull 'authentic' guitar tones and songs written in the retro/retread soul vein. Well, not any more! Now, it's welcome to weeping, dual fuzz guitars, proto-punk garage rhythms, nuclear burn-ups of free-rock De-twat, topped off with a changeling R&B guy whose vocal range takes in everything from Screamin' Jay Hawkins to Dionne Warwick, via George Clinton, early I-Tina, Ray Charles and James Brown by way of The Monks.

Why Don't You Give It to Me? is an instant party and an instant classic, an immensely stoned groove and an exhilarating and swampy hybrid of the early call-and-answer, heavy soul of Funkadelic (the first three albums), the cacophonous glam-soul of John and Yoko's *Sometime in New York City*, the fuzzy earnestness of very early ('Heavy Music'-period) Bob Seger, the abandoned lyrical free-association of Kim Fowley's berserk psychedelic soul revue on *Outrageous*, plus the murky voodoo gunk of 'Night Tripper'-period Dr. John.

Yes, from its very first sub-sub-Chocolate Watchband/early Stones-like opening bars, this new Nathaniel Mayer record screams '*Here I am!*' Better still, after his aforementioned stilted 2004 album *I Just Wanna Be Held*,[1] it's enthralling to hear this veteran, sixty-four-year-old Detroit R&B singer finally united with a truly sympathetic backing band, chock-full o'garage-heads who've been raised on such errant fuzz-arama garage compilations as *Pebbles*, *Back from the Grave*, *Hipsville 29BC*, *Off the Wall*, *Turds on a Bum Ride* and their glorious ilk, suddenly lending Nathaniel the kind of guitar-heavy, demented, amphetamine yawp that forces his own performance sky high. The results are no less than immediate and spectacular. Indeed, from the moment Nathaniel Mayer nobbled me with the title track's lyrical opening gambit – 'You gave it to him/ Why don't you give it to me?' – well, I knew this artist was a shoo-in for Album of the Month, just as long as he didn't fuck up the remaining thirty-six minutes *too* much. Ja, mein hairies, this slab of vinyl is truly one motherfucker of an album.

---

1 Released on Fat Possum Records in 2004, *I Just Wanna Be Held* was a brave but failed attempt to capture Nathaniel's live sound on record. Unfortunately, the band was too straight and 'authentic' to have any real resonance with today, and the album is something of a one-trick pony, only Nathaniel's brutal version of John Lennon's 'I Found Out' somewhat anticipating the sound of this current record and making me think he'd do an even better job on Lennon's other soul masterpiece of that period, 'Well, Well, Well'. However, those wishing to check out *I Just Wanna Be Held* will probably enjoy the James Brown-sy 'You Gotta Work' and the strange album closer 'What's Your Name', which contains a futuristic funk that comes across like early Talking Heads playing the Berlin soul of The Rolling Stones' 'Shattered'.

Side One of *Why Don't You Give It to Me?* commences with the title track, whose enormous, bats-in-the-belfry, bell-tone guitar riffing and cranky, leaden drums immediately set the listener on edge, before our hero steps into the spotlight and immediately crouches down on one knee to confess his pain to his coy mistress, the half-written abandon of Nathaniel's lyrics (spawning such couplets as 'You made him a happy man all across the land') reinforcing our suspicion that this record's producers knew they had limited studio time in which to make this record before the whole shithouse exploded in their faces.

Next up is the Electric Manchakou-style teenage exuberance of 'White Dress', another work-in-progress being sketched out before our very ears, like some wide-eyed and ageless shaman/woman cooing and billing in wonder at the opposite sex, over three minutes of 'Shake Appeal'-period Stooges, replete with hand-claps and endless questions. This is followed by 'I'm a Lonely Man', four minutes of the most shameless (and tuneless) *Back from the Grave*-stylee garage voodoo, as Nate vamps and grunts the song's title over and over.

Next up, the chorale-and-heavy-riffology of 'Please Don't Drop the Bomb' is pure early Funkadelic, ambient ice-rink funk, while Side One closer 'Everywhere' is three and a half minutes of boys-being-chicks backing vocals and wide-eyed asides, and sounds like a wonderful hybrid of John Sinclair's super-exuberant late acolytes The Up playing a song by Leslie West's soul-garage outfit The Vagrants.

Side Two opens with the 'Knock on Wood'-styled 'What Would You Do?', another lost classic riff, followed by the weird, nine-minute-long West Coast free-rock of 'Doin' It', whose cheese-grater wah-guitars, bubbling bass, clatter-chatter drums and bell-tone-blues lead axe all conspire to create a wild, almost proto-Comets on Fire rush that sounds like it coulda come off any of the best Detroit rock LPs any time in the past forty years. No wonder this record has been filed under 'Rock' on iTunes. Indeed, only on the seven-minute-long closer 'Why Dontcha Show Me?' does Nate return to his sultry soul roots. Commencing with a Ray Charles-styled piano-only opening coupla verses, this exquisitely crafted and sexy song suddenly metamorphoses into a percussion-heavy bossa nova, somewhere between Tim Buckley's 'Sweet Surrender' and Timmy Thomas's 'Why Can't We Live Together?'. This record is one mind-manifesting rock behemoth, but the confidence of this final statement lifts the entire LP up another coupla notches still.

In Conclusion

With regard to where Nathaniel Mayer takes his next step, well, we probably shouldn't set our hopes too high considering Mayer's first hit, 'Village of Love', was way back in 1962, thereafter ambling and shambling through long periods of bandlessness, giglessness, even homelessness. However, even a perfunctory trawl through Nate's current YouTube performances suggests that this sexagenerian singer is once more enjoying himself enough to attempt to sustain what he's currently achieving. And, on the huge evidence of this wonderful Album of the Month, we can only cross our fingers and selfishly hope that he barfs out a few more in this present stylee, before the (inevitable?) next crash. For the time being, however, we need only take a cursory glance at rock'n'roll history to feel a sense of optimism. For example, we only gotta look at Alex Harvey to see the renewal that an old-timer could achieve just through taking on a much younger backing band. Later, at the inception of punk, mother-of-two Vi Subversa split up her cabaret duo and lead her own outfit, The Poison Girls, all twenty-odd years younger than her, and became the co-leader of the 'new punk', alongside Crass. We have to hope that Nathaniel's current ensemble can find time in their busy careers to stay around and keep him buoyant.

What has made *Why Don't You Give It to Me?* so successful is the abandoned yet still dignified character that Nathaniel brings to the party; so much so that none of the producers has felt tempted to cast him as a mere eccentric outsider, a path trodden by so many lesser talented or less honourably-minded mentors. That's one reason why this particular Album of the Month is so fucking refreshing. Instead of recruiting as lead singer for their new project the gangliest local youth with the biggest garage-rock LP collection in his basement, these enlightened and currently successful rockers have come together to back a forgotten sixty-four-year-old R&B singer, a man of undoubted songwriting talent and possessed of a genuinely extraordinary set of vocal chords, but whose luck has been intermittent, to say the least. That three flourishing contemporary rock'n'rollers should have sought out and championed such a lost hero is, in itself, heroic, and Dan Auerbach, Troy Gregory and – most especially – Matthew Smith should be praised to the skies. That the chosen artist should rise to the occasion in such a manner is even more thrilling, which is why I say to Nathaniel Mayer: 'Bravo, Lord Motherfucker, and deep gratitude for laying this righteous thang upon us.' Amen.

The New Lou Reeds

Ohio Is Out of Business

(This compilation was created by Julian Cope and comprises his favourite songs by the New Lous)

SIDE ONE

1 Stranded in Ashland (3.10)
2 Teenage Metalhead (3.22)
3 Delaware Must Be Destroyed (3.09)
4 Looking for a Boogaloo (5.34)
5 Bury Me with My Bong (6.03)

SIDE TWO

1 Naw, Syke (1.33)
2 You Don't Have to Die (5.26)
3 Hate Fest (3.25)
4 Ohio Is Out of Business (5.28)
5 Sawbuck in Memphis (5.17)

In an effort to distil more succinctly The New Lou Reeds' somewhat rampant and scattershot muse, I've culled these ten songs from the band's 2003 debut LP, *Screwed*, 2006's *Top Billin'*, their 'disappointing sophomore album' (the band's description), and 2007's cassette-only EP *Moonshine'n'Miracles*. I coulda picked fifteen songs or even twenty, I guess, but these ten taken together make a heavily rotatable and tight-ass compilation with which I can feel proud to petition readers/listeners, many of whom probably have highly limited free time and one eye too many on the download, as opposed to the bongload.

English Rudeness Versus American Rudeness, or 'Why Stick Two Fingers Up to the Man When One Will Do?'

When Minnesota singer/guitarist Steve Kuchna came to Cleveland, Ohio, and formed his exceptional 'avant-truckstop' power trio, he musta known that naming them The New Lou Reeds was tantamount to shooting himself in the foot moments before attempting to run a marathon. Indeed, naming your band after one of rock'n'roll's greatest All Timers is such a clear act of self-sabotage that the outside world has just gotta read such a statement as the most vainglorious intuitive non-career move that any artist could make. Perverse to the point of rendering himself culturally invisible (try looking for The New Lou Reeds on Google, motherfuckers), Kuchna next opted for the virtually unreadable stage moniker Stephe DK (pronounced 'Steve Decay') and set about establishing a band that sounds almost as fanatically unlike The Velvet Underground as any you could wish for. For, while The Velvet Underground always sounded stubbornly urban, emphatically free of blue notes and studiedly removed from their songs' subject matter through Lou Reed's perversely observational, post-Dylan monotone, each bluesy, back-porch opus by The New Lou Reeds casts Stephe DK as a man drowning at the Kafkaesque epicentre of his own lyrical maelstrom, forever being dissed by rock promoters, bar-room chicks with bad attitudes, cops with too much time on their hands and government men with their eyes on his stash. And each New Lous' track comes replete with some of the greatest guitar playing I've heard this side of John Fogerty, Mark Farner, Stacy Sutherland and Neil Young, but rarely if ever informed by Lou Reed himself. Brothers'n'sisters, there's an inspirational yawp in the guitar playing of Stephe DK that is so goddamned painful and real that, were his songs merely instrumentals, hell, they'd still be essential. Which is why, in naming his ensemble after that old Velvets duffer, Brother DK is most assuredly buddying up to such legendary glam descendants as Les Rallizes Dénudés' Mizutani and Half Man Half Biscuit's Nigel Blackwell in the self-non-promotion/anti-hero stakes, working his butt off in a deli by day, getting paid squat for long-distance gigs in Knobshine, Indiana, and Drywank, Colorado, by night, and even releasing virtually unobtainable cassette-only albums such as 2007's *Moonshine'n'Miracles* to a jaw-droppingly disinterested local population.

Dammit, fellow motherfuckers, I love The New Lou Reeds, and I care about this Stephe DK guy one helluva lot. I'll admit that even I find his songwriting often haphazard and patchy, and his three long-playing statements so far released are unlikely to set the world on fire however much I hassle your reluctant asses to go out and buy his work. But, brothers'n'sisters, he's always listenable and always valid and, once you get used to his singular flat-earth worldview and that . . . ahem, voice, well, you start to see his incorrigible micro-world-weariness as an essential part of your musical backdrop; a bit like the manner in which Neil Young and Van Morrison fans just have to accept the whole schmeery oeuvre in order for the genius of the best bits to have any context.

For the past half-decade, I've made a sustained and valiant attempt to act as a paladin for the new American underground's so-called neo-folk/anti-folk/what-the-folk movement – the post-Sunburned Hand of the Man generation, as it were. But the fantastic music barfed out by these feral, backward backwoodsmen and hairy-underarmed daughters of the new revolution has been constantly undermined by the super-lame lyrical stance (if you can even call it that) summoned up by these otherwise righteous troubadours. Indeed, in the pre-Obama climate, merely being seen to be anti-Bush appeared to be considered political enough for their overly earnest *Folkjokeopus*. Which is why the braying über-whinny of The New Lou Reeds appears so damned refreshing from here in beleaguered ol' Blighty, where we don't have the three-thousand-five-hundred-mile Atlantic Ocean security blanket protecting our asses from touchy fundamentalist berks who be-burka their babes.

Now, I ain't claiming that The New Lou Reeds are any more heftily political than the aforemenched (mainly wonderful) free-fuck outfits, but at least the New Lous ain't claiming to be revolutionary neither. But (and it's a big hairy 'but', kiddies), I have to ask who is the most real American folk singer of the day? It sure ain't Howlin' Rain or Devendra Go-Kart. No, for my money you only have to listen to one pass through the lyrics of The New Lous' Stephe DK to learn more about the guaranteed No Future of twenty-first-century mid-America than any of the songs of those other too la-di-da so-called lyricists. Fuck the cocaine allusions, revolution's children, these songs by The New Lou Reeds are about scoring food, getting ripped off daily by the Man, and getting laughed at by rock chicks 'cause you're too damned ugly to command their respect. America, I love your underground folk scene, but as an English observer wishing to learn about where the new colony is at, it's when I listen to the words of this rock guy's songs that I learn a whole lot about your culture, real quick; so the evidence is strong that he's gotta be the realest folk singer among you. OK, so now I'll shut the fuck up and get on with the review . . .

Post-It Notes from the Edge, or 'So, What's It Sound Like?'

Ohio Is Out of Business commences with the blistering, over-driven, motorik menace of 'Stranded in Ashland', a post-*Vanishing Point*, three-minute road movie built around one of *the* hottest Stratocaster, single-coil guitar riffs yet barfed out into this twenty-first century; indeed, it's so hot that the cops are soon on our hero's tail, hauling his driver friend off to the nearest town to pay a fine, but not before having unceremoniously dumped Herr DK at some sub-'76 truckstop, when the poor stoned sucker should be heading for a much-needed vacation. 'What the fuck!' he screeches inchoately, his mind close to meltdown, all the while effortlessly excavating classic riff after classic riff, like the Elevators' Stacy Sutherland playing Montrose's 'Bad Motor Scooter'. What a way to begin! 'Stranded in Ashland' is an all-time classic, a veritable '71 Dodge Challenger (orange, natch) with every inch of its black vinyl roof polished to perfection.

Next comes the epic polio-strut of 'Teenage Metalhead' – an over-caffeinated, 6/8-time, finger-pointing glitterstompf; a jarring, caterwauling lyrical demolition of small-town America's everygoth community by this too-unsung guitar genius who demands his right to kneecap anyone and everyone who thinks they're gonna make it just because they 'Can really rock out on air guitar' (although I gots to admit, kiddies, that it was this song that most inspired, nay, *drove* me to my current state of deluded über-rock cliché sartorial inelegance when I first heard it back in '03).

Like all of Stephe DK's songs, 'Teenage Metalhead' features some remarkably acerbic and snotty asides, but this one surpasses even his stellar standards with this out-of-the-blue couplet: 'Driving a Camaro and getting high/Without warning, a wizard walks by!' I mean, c'mon!

Next up, 'Delaware Must be Destroyed' fades in like a cartoon biker-slug riding a souped-up vacuum cleaner; it's just a righteously dum-dum fuzz-tone riff over which DK declares his sheer mystification that natives of the aforementioned state even admit to its being their home ('New Jersey is a motherfucker/But this is just plain wrong'), let alone presume to wear it as some badge of cultural honour (George Thorough-good, is that the best you can claim?). Like our own Nigel Blackwell, from Half Man Half Biscuit, Stephe DK shines a flashlight into the unknown shadows of his too-oft applauded culture, only to recoil in horror at the nest of vipers he's discovered, pausing only to (in the inimitable words of Kiss' Stanley Starchild) '. . . uh, *move on*!'

All of which brings us to the biggest and baddest track on the whole album: that sagging twenty-stoner known as 'Looking for a Boogaloo'.[1] This song (which opened the *Top Billin'* LP) abandons the sleek, spring-chicken, early coupé version of The New Lous, replacing it with a new family saloon/sedan arrangement, somewhat along the lines of FoMoCo's momentous decision to replace the original 1955–57 Ford Thunderbird two-seater boulevardier concept with the big-assed, '58 four-seater. Ousted from The New Lous' rhythm section were the skinny Cross brothers (featured on this compilation's first two tracks), replaced by more hardy veterans of the Cleveland scene, bass player Ed Sotelo and drummer Jeff Ottenbacher. Moreover, a whole host of auxiliary musicians would hereafter be employed to boost the sound, which has – thus far – become somewhat straighter overall but all the better for it. Indeed, 'Looking for a Boogaloo' is a huge rock'n'roll song in the vein of Mott the Hoople's wonderfully cumbersome *Mad Shadows* period, i.e. it's far more accepting of its Jerry Lee roots, and just gets on with it in thee most unhung-up manner. Besides, when a poet of the calibre of Stephe DK is singing (James Brown-style) about filling his stomach before getting high and getting down, we really *do* have to worry about the future of the American Midwest!

Luckily for us, brothers'n'sisters, Side One closes with the soon-to-be standard 'Bury Me with My Bong' – six-minutes of bombed, acid campfire, replete with chick-singer chorale and communal bonced giggling. Like

1 I have occasionally seen The New Lou Reeds compared to Pere Ubu. I suspect that this is mainly because of both bands' use of extraneous tapes and effects and their both having hailed from Cleveland, but also because of the (alleged) similarity of Stephe DK's vocal style to David Thomas' illegal ur-whinny. I disagree with it all. Sure, The New Lous had an epic acoustic ballad entitled 'Peter Laughner' on their first release, but that's hardly evidence of musical similarities. If there's any link, then perhaps it's in Stephe DK's genuinely post-punk lack of respect for the song's key, his guitar playing occasionally exhibiting a genuinely exhilarating (and obviously intentional) atonality consonant with the cantankerous EML synthesizer whine produced by Allen Ravenstine throughout the early Ubu LPs. However, this is a fragile link, if one I felt it essential to address.

my own 'I Gotta Walk' (from *Autogeddon*), 'Bury Me with My Bong' begins with the burning and inhaling of the blessed sacrament, afore ye bard kicks in with his righteous declaration that he won't want 'some phoney priest hanging around' at his funeral, just his close friends and an ounce of the finest green thrown into the casket. Herr DK then proceeds to explain how, on his arrival at the pearly gates, 'Me and St. Peter/We gonna fire up a blunt,' while the aforemenched ladies of the chorus bill and coo the classic line 'Sit in salvation 'n' burn one with the Lord' over and over and fucking over again. Now, that's what I'm talking about!

Side Two opens with the comparatively slight, ninety seconds of 'Naw, Syke', its slightness mainly down to some ironic pro-crack banter which is as funny and (to these ears) as essential as Speed, Glue & Shinki's equally cunted 'Doodle Song'. 'Are those drums in tune?' whines DK to drummer Ottenbacher, who shoots back: 'Are those shoes in tune?' Then we're off again into further addled tales of twenty-first-century Middle America with the blues heft of 'You Don't Have to Die', a behemoth of a track that opens with the scorching lines: 'Behind the wheel of my car?/I watch my ass getting bigger/I think I'm choking on a hamburger/This is my time/And it's good to feel it all passing me by.' Again, the new New Lou Reeds' rhythm section adds an incredible weight both to Herr DK's primal riffery and his atonal Allen Ravenstine-isms, punctuating each downbeat to create a notably heavyweight insistence, as Ed Sotelo's muscular, rising bass carries the entire melody of the track.

Then follows the solo acoustic poetic declarations of 'Hate Fest', a kind of valiant post-Nirvana, post-post-Mafe Nutter hail to 'the men and their guitars', as a 'Las Vegas Basement'-style background of sound-effects tapes of garrulous canteen diners rattling their condiments, crockery and cutlery conspire to create the illusion of some forgotten minstrel anti-hero forced to court the Mrs Mop vote. It is fabulous, indeed.

Next we're off into the stinking monolithic blues of this compilation's title track, an autobiographical explanation of how our hero arrived in Cleveland over fifteen years previously and has, from that day until the present time, unsuccessfully dedicated his life to escaping the city which shackles him like a weakened dwarf standing knee-deep in a skip full of setting toffee.

This compilation concludes with

'Sawbuck in Memphis', the tale of an epic road trip to a gig in distant Memphis, where the three band members were rewarded with the princely sum of ten dollars (the 'sawbuck' in question) by the stingy promoter who'd lured them there. Over a jaunty off-the-peg country-and-western backing track, Stephe DK tells the tale, straight and simple, until the truth wells up and overflows, and, for one brief moment at least, this post-punk prima-donna lets forth a slew of atonal guitar tsunami worthy of his band's ur-namesake. Silence ensues as DK chastises himself for losing it temporarily, and the song returns once more to its jaunty, well-mannered pace – although the hitherto unperturbed listener is, thereafter, never completely at ease.

In Conclusion

I trust that, presently, those of you with the correct paraphernalia easily to hand will sit in salvation and burn one for Herr DK and co. at least once during the record's rotation. Hopefully, you'll return again and again over the next month, perhaps check out the band online or even make a daily pilgrimage to Head Heritage's temple to this too-unsung hero. Hail, Stephe DK, thanks for sustaining your errant but inspired muse this far into the twenty-first century. And one final thing . . . all praise to your men and to your guitar.

Discography

Screwed (Exit Stencil, 2004)
Top Billin' (Exit Stencil, 2006)
Moonshine'n'Miracles (EP, Shandi, 2007)

Om

Variations on a Theme

(Holy Mountain, 2005)

1 On the Mountain at Dawn (21.16)
2 Kapila's Theme (11.56)
3 Annapurna (11.52)

I officially restarted my second psychedelic period on January 1 2005 by chewing up two large portions of Mexican mushies and proceeding into the underworld, at whose portals I did espy a large, spectral Viking ship floating in deep space, manned by several translucent rock'n'roll musicians armed with the sonic equivalent of *Star Wars*-style light sabres. By 5 a.m. I was convinced that rock'n'roll – although inappropriate for much of the straighter population of the world – was still the best way to enlightenment for those itinerant few whose lives depend on travel, change and inconstancy. It was, therefore, with great joy that I discovered the return of these two poet musicians – the über-Weedians, if you will. Gentlemen, it's been a too-long hibernation . . . Welcome home!

Two-Thirds

Breaks the new month with southern sunrise refracting, slowly tracing arc-lights of Mithra across Rinde's frozen belly. Yup, after disappearing into the underworld at the end of the last millennium, the great Dionysus is reawakened and has risen from below Mount Parnassus . . . It's true, motherfuckers. Chris Hakius and Al Cisneros – two-thirds of San Jose's legendary Sleep – have finally returned from the dead after over half a decade. They'z been reborn as the Sacred Twins, Om, and we all gots to start writing in that same elegant, spewdo-religious psychobabble in deference to this fact. And, if that sounds like I ain't totally down with this album and its higher aims, then excuse me reinforcing my assertions by quoting my own review of Sleep's *Dopesmoker*, on which I found the lyrics of Al Cisneros to be truly 'The kind of accessible pseudo-religious genius that started genuine religions.'

Yup, I am yet again worshipping at these guys' pragmatic altar of eternal usefulness. Indeed, I love everything about this record: its sound, its persistent, mid-tempo sludge-trudge (what they themselves call 'a transportive series of differentiated verse with sets of solid groove'), its vocal mantras and its total devotion to taming time. Indeed, even the clichéd but perfectly righteous sleeve, with an It's a Beautiful Day-style lone eagle in the sky and almost New-Age lettering, snags me by the cobblers. Both pertinent *and* righteous simultaneously, this is most surely one supremely meditational album. For whereas Sleep's guitarist Matt Pike attempted to banish the ghost of his old band with his highly rock High on Fire power-trio project, Messrs Cisneros and Hakius have instead taken their previous Sleep trip further and honed it down to a guitar-less yet amazingly complete Rickenbacker bass/vocals and drums sound which – like the best reggae – knits itself into both the ether and the air surrounding it and, taking the fifty-two minutes of Sleep's 'Jerusalem' as its blueprint, presents a sound that is so bold and obvious you wonder why no sucker had copped this idea before.

But, like all the greats, the usefulness of this level of invention is only evident when presented ultra-confidently to the listener by those originators themselves. And so the magnificently named Om project kick-starts itself as full of attitude, as if Sleep had merely shed another guitarist (as they did with Justin Marler between their own debut and *Sleep's Holy Mountain*) and taken a sabbatical in order to trim off further fat stored up during their pan-millennial hibernation.

Long Dark Evenings at the Back of Your Mind

Moreover, the later re-release of 1995's 'Jerusalem' in its massively excavated, extended and re-evaluated 2003 form, retitled *Dopesmoker*, has by now put so much space between the *Sleep's Holy Mountain* period and this debut by Om that there is no longer any need to make even oblique references to their Sabbath origins, save, perhaps, for mentioning that their trudge was undoubtedly initially informed by the low, low, highs of *Master of Reality*'s 'Into the Void' (in which Tony Iommi so subsumed his Gibson SG into Geezer's bass frequencies that Cisneros has easily nailed the sound with one single distorto-Rickenbacker).

By the release of 'Jerusalem', Cisneros had dumped any remaining Ozzy-styled vocalisms in favour of his now celebrated and convoluted high priest of the ganga, 'Proceeds the Weedian' vocal delivery that bears no relation to any other rock'n'roll vocal style. Cisneros' earlier devotion to Holy Land and Middle East imagery ('Sacred Israel, Holy Mt. Zion', 'Hasheeshian Lebanon', 'Prayer-filled Smoke', 'Golgotha', etc.) and Atlantean, Hindi and biblical references was always far removed from the concerns of the typical heavy-metal lyricist. On this Om debut, the lyrics have been pared down to just a couple of passing arcane references (Lazarus, Vedic Sun . . .) that seem to have been employed more for their ability to conjure up instantly 'other' associations, rather than for any specific meanings. Indeed, looking back to 'Jerusalem', the evidence is that Cisneros had the effects of the pot, and its reggae associations, in his mind rather than anything deeper. What other metaller would allude to the 'Groundation soul' in his lyrics, let alone intone about taking hits from 'the green cutchie'?

Whatever, these strange lyrical allusions remain steadfast products of Cisneros' desire for shamanic flight and enthral the listener on this Om voyage. On 'Annapurna', Cisneros intones: 'I climb toward the sun to breathe the indrawn universal,' and 'The flight to freedom gradient raise the called ascendant.' Just as twentieth-century liberal Anglicans adapted the King James Bible in an attempt to make it more approachable to we Moderns, but accidentally rendered it secular and useless in the process, so Cisneros cunningly cloaks his words in such a stylised and seemingly arcane second-language translation-speak that his otherwise fairly obvious poetic allusions are raised towards the Blakean.

On the massive opening track, the initiate watches as the 'summit upholds the canopied skies of a new day'. 'Kapila's Theme' summons up more 'Jerusalem' with lines such as 'Sight to freedom rises descender,' and the tortuously fabulous mouthful 'Prevails flight resplendent/Sails the shrine effulgent windship.' Get down! Indeed, that last winner reminds me that much of the power of these words lies in the confidently concise nature of Al Cisneros' outrageous glossary. Such lines as 'Accretes the ground nerve skein,' and 'Approach the grid substrate the sunglows beam to freedom' are so commonplace in this man's work that you really gots to accept his own publicity hand-out, in which he declares that the power of the lyrics is not in their meaning but in their ability to 'serve as symbolist vehicles to a state outside the field of time and space'. Delivered in this chanted manner, instant psychedelic vision is indeed conjured by such wild imagery as: 'Striates into the sky on outwards spires reaching/Under orbic vermillion sun migration on the wings.'

The Flight to Freedom

It should be noted that this first Om album is very much that: a debut on which to hang big hopes of further massive offerings. In many ways, Cisneros and Hakius have sensibly aimed not too high, working again with doom-meister Billy Anderson and pruning the gargantuan offerings of late-period Sleep into palatably ingestible sacraments for our repeated usage. Indeed, I've had the record on permanent repeat these past two weeks and listened to it integrate with the video-blue walls of my bedroom as its vocal mantras have caught on the sharper objects upon those walls, enveloping them ever so gradually, like a persistent spider pursuing and finally catching an increasingly sleepy, late-November fly. That having been said, the great centrepiece of this Om debut is still a highly charged and high-reaching piece of zoner-rock. This, the aforementioned, twenty-one-minute-long 'On the Mountain at Dawn', with its ten verses and repeated mantras, could surely never have come from the inexperienced minds of first-timers.[1] And, if the gentlemen can achieve such spectacular results with simple bass, drums and vocals, we can only hope that the fruits of subsequent bong voyages are the kind of rampantly overachieving stunners that can equip our innermost mung-worshipping selves right on into the next decade.

So give these gentlemen two rounds of applause – firstly for their new album, and secondly for their determination to accept that their metaphor was righteous enough in the first place to *get back on it*!

---

1 I remember reading how disappointed Tom Verlaine was when he was forced to reduce the original 'Marquee Moon' down from its intended seventeen verses. Well, bub, I reckon the time is right, in these post-Cisnerosian times, to unveil that sucker and have it putter right back into the graveyard. Replace the feyness of the Eno-produced demos with some of the gasoline sludge-trudge that Om are spilling out right here, and Verlaine and co. would be good for another decade, although I Shirley ain't holding my breath.

Orthodox

Gran Poder

(Alone Records, 2005)

1 Geryone's Throne (27.28)
2 Arrodillate ante la madera y la piedra (11.36)
3 Oficio de tinieblas (1.26)
4 El lamento del cabrón (16.56)

Beneath the Sandstone Bedrock and All-Pervasive Bull Worship . . . Something Stirs

Unlike Nordic heathens such as Sunn O))), High on Fire, Khanate, Marzuraan and their Wodenist kin, the bound Mediterranean pastors of Orthodox – in their dark, pagan worship of the Madonna and her infant Christ – are attempting to wrestle control of their God away from the stranglehold of the Pope's church, placing it instead in the hands of blood-letting, sexually engorged, free-thinking motherfuckers.

Gran Poder ('Great Power') is as overwhelming a debut as any I've encountered these past ten years or more. Indeed, this first Orthodox release is a raging and debilitating sonic stag hunt – the beast of any of the doom-metal genre I've thus far encountered, *plus* its bowel movements emanate from the dry arid regions of southern Spain, where the Reconquista and the Spanish Inquisition still inform the local popular metal psyche with as strong a grip as the Viking manner in which Thor, Odin, Cromwell, Martin Luther and John Knox still irrigate the anti-monkish/anti-popery of our own northern lands.

This Orthodox debut is astonishing – an ever-becoming, ever-outpouring sludge-trudge, free-rock blitz, cascading cauldrons full of Choukoku no Niwa's now legendary drum-led epic 'Fukurou' over a hugely mannered, Sleep-style riff-athon, via Sunn O)))'s seminal ('two longhairs in a WWI biplane towing a rainbow') *Flight of the Behemoth*. It's as though some Thor-sized Tommy Vance was courting the goddess Hel herself, making out with a lake of honey mead and a vat of opiated goulash containing four score and ten oxen and twenty sheep's heads.

Orthodox is a power trio whose sonic larder is filled to the brim with such cold-storage '90s basics as Melvins, Sleep, Trouble, Earth, Sunn O))) and Thrones, plus they've added to the mix the inevitable ur-trudge of early Sabbath, *Dance of the Lemmings*-period Amon Düül II and Yankee Sabbalikes Bang ('Future Shock'), with unconscious nods to early Japrock deadbeats Speed, Glue & Shinki ('Red Doll'), Joey Smith's Filipino walking-dead band Juan de la Cruz ('Wanna Take You Home') and Flower Travellin' Band's even-more-strung-out-than-the-original versh of 'Black Sabbath' or (again) Flower's own 'Hiroshima'. In addition, Orthodox have taken Neil Young's *Ragged Glory* feedback endings and welded them in parallel to create Queen Elizabeth/Slomo-sized flame-outs, lashing them to the end of each track. Yup, Orthodox have copped their metaphor and nailed the coffin lid shut on that sucker in one single CD release.

Moreover, on top of these staples, sprinkled like a frosted winter icing, come the exotic ingredients from outer state – let's try Boredoms' digital *Faust Tapes*-like sleight-of-hand located on *Vision Creation Newsun*, but let's avoid yer typical Cookie Monster doom singing and substitute a ghostly, stellar, vaporous heat-haze vocal, more so even than Joe's post-Plant screech on Flower Travellin' Band's *Satori*; yup, a Catholic vocal more redolent of Demis Roussos' eerie, desert-citadel yodel on Aphrodite's Child's massive 1972 double LP *666*. Bassist/singer Marco claims to have been most inspired by Lemmy and Venom's Cronos, but his own achievements on this record are several octaves higher and more mysterious than either.

However the band achieved this barbarian classic, Orthodox obviously worked hard to nail their own ultra-specific metaphor good and proper right from the off. Unsurprisingly, their own press release reveals a group of fundamentalist musicians whose ur-riff was deeply hewn and strait-jacketed with limitations from the off; and it's a concept which they have achieved, and in spades, claiming to provide 'a liturgic music with obsessive repetitions, minimalism, feedback, distortion and endless drones creating a primitive feeling that leads to trance and remains as a perfect soundtrack for every dark point of Christianism: oppression, sin, suffering, guilt and pain'. Well, gentlemen, you've just about done the whole fucking deal on this record. But Christian this disc truly ain't; this shit is more of the half-light Christianity you find in the Iberian outer reaches, the kind where the local priest leads the local virgins to a great stone with a pathetic crucifix shrivelling in the noonday sun upon its summit; the kind of Christianity in which a statue of the local saint is curtly transported on a pony and trap to the nearest holy well and let down on a rope and told to make the rain . . . or else! The Mediterranean regions are full of this kind of errant, so-called Christianity, and Orthodox done captured the whole trip hook, line and sinker.

Inspired by one of those Black Rune stories you get on the net featuring characters with names such as Bryton and Merlin, 'Geryone's Throne' is the killer opener that woulda sent Orthodox straight to the top of the class were it the only song they ever offered up to us. It contains all of the aforementioned inbreedients in a twenty-seven-minute endurance test that first psychedelicises, then refashions the listener's brain using any electric means possible – even, at times, reducing itself to no more than thunderous cymbal crashes. The mighty techtonic upheavals of Khanate are here replaced – especially on the second track ('Arrodillate ante la madera y la piedra') – by a kind of Teeth of Lions Rule the Divine-style splatter-chatter of arhythmical drumming that so engulfs the track that only brutally simple riffage can haul both listener *and* musicians out of the quagmire.

Orthodox are even confident enough to offer us a third track, which comes in at under two minutes in length ('Oficio de tinieblas') and which comprises only stentorian snare drums and simplistic drone piano. Best of all is the humour of the sixteen-minute closer, 'El lamento del cabrón', which – by employing the same geek's bright spirit as Dylan Carlson snagged by slowing down Skynyrd's 'Freebird' for Earth's 1995 classic 'Ripped on Fascist Ideas' – here allows this Spanish doom-trio to cop Link Wray's 'Rumble' and drive it at the same speed as a low-geared street-cleaning wagon. Elements of Stephen O'Malley's e-bow fixation and even moments from his *Fungal Hex* Prague installation surface from time to time below the shattering husks of drum/guitar assault, as Orthodox temporarily tame the sonic Horned One under a fusillade of San Miguel bottles and holy water.

It's one Hel of a record, m'dears. And one that sets its stall out for others to come and try to better. Hey, the evidence is clear, ladies and gentlemen; rock'n'roll will never die and heavy metal has barely started. All we need now is to slay the religious beast once and for all and the rest, as they say, is a breeze. Sideways, motherfuckers, and don't spare the Born Again Cretins!

Aftershock: A Road Trip with Orthodox and Annexus Quamm

Three days after the completion of the above review, I found myself in Seville, Spain, in the company of US über-refusenik Jello Biafra, Spanish poet Annexus Quamm and the three gentlemen of the Orthodox ensemble. My performance at Seville Spoken Word Festival had been a wild one (natch), followed by an evening of drinking, pointing and portentous introductions to each other (Biafra's opening gambit to me: 'Hey, that's a fucking Flower Travellin' Band shirt!') in which the recurring motifs were Melvins, Alice Cooper's 'Halo of Flies' and that ur-doom classic always and forever looming, Flower Travellin' Band's *Satori*.

Orthodox's singer and bassist Marco pointed out to me that their titles are all taken from various phases of the Easter festival that occurs in Seville, as are their black shrouds – each one replete with knotted cord and looking somewhere between a full-face burkha, Sunn O)))'s grim robes and the favoured outfits of the Ku Klux Klan. It's for this reason that the Orthodox guys were somewhat nervous of being photographed in central Seville, and even more so by a photographer in a WWII German peaked cap . . . But my mission was essentially this: to present Orthodox in their uniqueness; that is, a band of doomsters from outside the Nordic realms, a bunch of rebels whose own Catholic landscape had never been trod by protestants against the stupidity of Christianity, and whose population remains enthralled by the Papa and all that he is said to stand for. With patience, we managed to achieve the required shots in front of one particularly brightly yellow-painted Madonna before I took the three musicians up into the Neolithic hills outside the city, where we achieved the triple Mithraic salute to the sun while facing the legendary Seville summit known as the Hill of the Shepherdess.

Throughout the road trip, *Satori*

was blasting across the hot, arid dust-scape of this city, known by locals as 'The Frying Pan of Spain'. All you northern heathens, please be aware of this: the southern Mediterranean reaches need you to come and soil their land with your fucked-up sound. Orthodox is pretty much alone in its mission, but they are righteous, energetic and, most of all, young . . . Nuff said. Let the shit come down!

Ramesses

The Tomb

(Invada Records, 2005)

RAMESSIDE	SKULL SIDE
1 Black Domina (11.10)	1 The Tomb (7.02)
2 Witchampton (8.59)	2 Cult of Cyclops (9.14)
	3 Omniversal Horror (6.14)

Please excuse the particularly personal nature of this review, brothers and sisters, but this record has occupied a strange position in our household since last November. Indeed, I tried writing about this disc before X-Mass and just couldn't get the sentiments into words. So it's a bit long-winded, but heartfelt to the max.

The Nothing Out of Me

These were the beginnings of my history, siblings: last November, quite different a night for a Friday, spent in the company of shaggy hill-men and vamps of the half-life, sonic missionaries from the sub-basement who had finally cracked open the granite pavement that seals the floor of the underworld, bringing forth hordes of trolls from under the bridge between *Nevermind* and the Melvins' solo LPs. These were to be several strange hours in which insight was to be burned, watched from behind my own mask as searing comprehension interfaced with slack-gobbed oblivion and bovine bull-roarer delinquency held hands with sweating, post-coital, nostril-flaring amphetamine ingestion; the right kleine nacht for a little death, as it turned out, and all because Khanate had just turned up. Turned up? Ye Gods, they was loud . . . on eleven and then some.

As I entered the mead hall, masoned in wood, that Bristolians call The Croft, I espied the radiant flames of Stephen O'Malley at the other end of the bar, not the yellow blaze I've listed previously but a deep, subterranean blue. Above his beard, those jewelled, Irish eyes of SOMA gripped mine and we saluted our re-engagement in a junk of 'motherfuckers' and other ardent but outwardly incomprehensible semaphore slanguage. 'Dubin's become the Nightshitter,' muttered SOMA, cryptically, but I grasped his metaphor immediately. Indeed, anyone who has already seen Khanate in concert would have done the same, for Alan Dubin's dedication to the looping bark could grasp where emanates his seat of power. I saw the outwardly affable Dubin soon after, but gravity pulled The Nightshitter inexorably towards the bog, and soon the four Khanates took their place upon the low stage, blew and ritually enslaved our minds with strategic moves and those great tectonic collisions of sound that only the Khanates can fashion.

Seeking refuge, I moved into, occupied, then squatted a deep doorway, accommodating my high-peaked German WWII cap, but could not applaud the merciless rage of the four Khanates. Entranced and informed by hell below, I could only low as cattle low, while the remainder of the audience adopted the English tradition of opting not to notice my bovine boos. Ecstasy rose up and out of me with each tectonic collision brought forth by the four Khanates, and by the conclusion of their concert I was the riddled one, full of questions and more questions.

On the street, hours later, the rear of my Chevrolet four-by-four was packed to the hilt with SOMA's gear and we blasted off into the dim night down the M4 corridor to my Yatesbury home, upon Marlborough Downs. 'I booed all night,' I explained, for this had not been the lowing of failure but of almighty and rigorous success. The clapping and the exuberant cries of 'Awl right!' were inappropriate for such perpetrations of ruin. But the punishing gruel served up by the four Khanates had precipitated them into a deep underworld of gloom, and I feared for their mental health on the roads of English rock'n'roll. I articulated to SOMA that the well-being of James Plotkin, Tim Wyskida and Alan Dubin could be at stake if all they had with which to combat their demons was lukewarm moto-slop and local beer. For SOMA, I didn't hang from such fears – his career in Sunn O))) and his wonderful marriage to the marathon athlete Anne Kugler, and his now-famous design of grand LP sleeves, altogether exhibit a pragmatism of the long-term quester, knee deep in excelsis. But I was still happy to guide SOMA down from his Khanate world with a road trip to Holy McGrail's place in the Yorkshire hills and the fashioning of some ur-drones at Doggen's Nottingham studio. And when, in a thunder storm, I handed over SOMA to Heathrow's Terminal Three less than one week later, I felt – as I once more navigated the M4 corridor, headed west – that these were still early days in the experiment.

Yes, the heathenising process of the West is now well under way, but its major protagonists still write the rules, and shall do so for the next decades.

Exhausted from driving hundreds of miles in a torrential downpour in prescription shades (my new soft contacts shrivel up in my eyes like the bollocks of a New Year's Day swimmer in the Serpentine), I disrobed and was about to sink lifeless into the bath when I realised that the fury of the rain would take its toll of the contents in the non-watertight rear compartment of the Chevrolet four-by-four. Hastily donning my all-weather gear, I staggered across the cobbles as Thor's mighty platform boots stomped across my path. Throwing open the tailgate in the vicious wind, I grabbed my sodden overnight bag and noted several distinguished articles that swirled around in the twisting waters of the unlit rear compartment. I collected up all of this hitherto unknown loot and rushed indoors. Inside the warmth of the kitchen, I realised at once that Khanate's Bristol promoter – Invada Records' CEO, Fatpaul – had, at the load-out, one week before, very kindly plied me (unsolicited) with all kinds of vinyl goods – LPs and seven- and twelve-inch singles – all of which had been shaking about in the soup of my four-by-four for over a hundred and twenty hours.

I gathered them all up and gingerly separated each element, leaving them to dry slowly in our Jockeyhouse annex. But when, next morning, I beheld the pieces, part of each item had returned to the primordial ooze whence it originated and I reluctantly consigned all to the trash. Everything, that is, except one lone warrior – a twelve-inch picture disc whose survival had depended not on the strength of its easily warped cardboard sleeve, but whose entire vibe was contained behind clear plastic sheeting, the image of its three band-member protagonists staring out at me from a wooded location. Moreover, the designer had specifically centred the photo so as to place the central hole right between the eyes of the central figure. Pleasant details, methunk, and I gave it a spin . . .

Pastor of Muppets

Slowly at first, but right from the off, I warmed to the sound that these backwoods boys made. With no idea from whence they originated, and still recumbent with exhaustion, I lay on the bed and stared up at Kentucky Jim Bennett's fine-art depiction of the doubleneck guitar as horned Pan. The opening bars of this sole surviving picture disc put me in mind of Joy Division playing the chords of Yes' Kraut-styled instrumental 'Wurm' or even Amon Düül II's more overt, Peter Leopold-propelled metal graspings on *Dance of the Lemmings*, and my pampered spirit tap-danced with the lightness of its touch. That reggae rimshot drumming was something else again . . . But then, sixty-nine seconds into the track, as a mighty upsurge of sonic wind caught me off guard, the great cloven-hoofed iron horse kicked off from its starting gate and, with all the mythical power of Sleipnir – Odin's eight-legged steed – the track climbed a full twelve decibels in volume, as vocals of the über-Cookie Monster variety declared undying undeath to the inbred members of its shortbread audience. What the? I was soon drowning under the avalanche of sound as the previously twinkle-toed drumming multiplied into umpteen mighty Burundi warriors on acid.

Where was this tsunami of a band from? Who were they? Did I know them already? I'm sure they're called Ramesses on the sleeve; wasn't there a band called Ramesses in the '70s, on Vertigo? What the fuck is going on? Meanwhile, in their simple, elliptical lyrical declaration, the enormous and monolithic ur-Gollum vocals appeared to be describing – over and over and fucking over again – nothing less than merciful Allah himself selecting a young believer for service to the sacred crescent as a human bomb with which to wipe away the infidels: 'Step into the white light/Move into the white light/Step into suicide.'

It was the most Godlike vocal I'd heard in years, literally *like God*, and as scary as the God must be. Furthermore, the harshness of the Martin Hannett-style production and the imbalance of sound all contributed to this grand feeling of being in the presence of truly uncompromising evil. The genius of the lyric repetition was simply this: in replicating those same words over and over, the libretto was (no more and no less) an instruction, nay, a demand from a cosmically higher force made to a reluctant minion. The lyric gave no room for questioning, and the mantric manner in which the order was barked left us in no doubt that the song would have continued for however long was necessary to get this simple order across to the 'victim'.

Now that the solipsistic, overly demanding, metal ur-growl of Cookie Monster, once the sole realm of Sabbat's Martin Walkyier and his ilk, has been successfully appropriated by most every metaller worth his rock salt, from the rurally acoustic country-and-western death metal of Austria's wonderful Cadaverous Condition[1] to such sonically disparate young bands as Trivium, Marzuraan and The Chariot. But nothing, *nothing*, had prepared me for the sound of this song, which I would later discover was entitled 'Black Domina'. I sank, obliterated, into the mattress, skewered on the tightly turned springs and physically oppressed by the weight of this band unknown. Incognizant of the realm from whence they'd sprung, I languished for a further twenty minutes on the bed, incoherent, drool-smeared and gonzoid, as the diamond needle dragged itself around the vinyl gutter, seemingly caught forever in a locked groove of its makers' own device. It was – in half the time – as exhausting, obliterating and complete as Venom's side-long 'At War with Satan', just as dynamic and sure-footed, but in a whole new league of heavy.

In order to achieve the epic nature of 'Black Domina' (and the ensuing 'Witchampton'), Ramesses seemed to have put Sabbath's 'Cornucopia' through a dark, Scandinavian Joy Division filter, in much the same way that Finland's Reverend Bizarre had put *Volume 4*'s 'Snowblind' through the same dark, Nordic/Mancunian sieve in order to achieve their massively hypnotic doom ballad 'Strange Horizon'.

1 All of Cadaverous Condition's releases have much in them to be recommended. However, their seamless move from thunderous electric music to rural acoustic is perhaps a bit much for casual tastes, and I would suggest investigators begin with their LP *The Lesser Travelled Seas* (Perverted Taste, 2001). That said, their 1993 debut, *In Melancholy* (Lethal Records), is also superb, as is their 2006 LP *To the Night Sky*. But for sheer acoustic, mythical drama, cop a copy of the split ten-inch, all-acoustic mini-LP that they shared with the American band Changes, released in 2004 on the Eis & Licht label.

Finally, I struggled upright for just long enough to take the only option open . . . and spun that sucker for a second time.

'We Are All Doomed'

As the twenty minutes of music concluded once more, I at last shifted my delicate frame off the bed and beheld that shitty, wipe-yer-arse-on-it cover which Invada Records has the nerve to call 'a poster'! With simultaneously Orwellian and Crowleyian poetic thoroughness, my copy was number 101/666 and the name of this LP was *The Tomb*. The single track to which I had become so attached was actually two songs that segued together, the aforementioned 'Black Domina' and 'Witchampton', the latter title being the name of a Dorset village I know, located not far from the Neolithic henge at Knowlton, the one with the Norman church built at its centre and with yew trees on its banks. The music, the vocal delivery, the lyrics and the production had all conspired to create in this 'Black Domina'/'Witchampton' piece a timeless and menacingly barbarian classic; an underworld season ticket with guarantees.[2]

Successive multiple rotations of this LP side convinced me that Ramesses had captured one of the great heavy-rock classics of all time, literally a new height in low-brow culture; an 'Into the Void' for the early twenty-first century – but, in its epic nature, even greater and even more useful to the pragmatic motherfucker. No, this was not quite Sleep's 'Jerusalem', but it certainly

2 Also, in small lettering set aside from the main information text, were written the simple words 'We Are All Doomed'. Yes, yes, yes; these guys knew precisely what they were doing. For this was doom in all its barbarian splendour; doom at its most finely drawn; doom not as death but doom as judgement – *true* doom. For the Doom of the Scando-Germanic tribes of the Dark Ages – the Normans, Vikings, Jutes, Saxons and Danes – manifested most clearly in the Domesday Book of 1086, which the victorious William the Conqueror used to make a list of everything Saxon that he now considered to be his own. To the Scando-Germanic tribes, 'Doom' always meant 'judgement' and is the reason that Russia's Viking-informed culture still calls its parliament the 'Duma'; why the Icelandic law seats are called 'doom rings'; and why the high law seat of the Orkney Isles was situated at the geographical centre of a lake called Loch Doomy (and also why I concluded my 1993 LP, *Autogeddon*, with the lyrics: 'All love is doomed/All love is doomed'). Of course, love is not always destined to die . . . but it *is* (I believe) always destined to be judged.

transcended Om's 'On the Mountain at Dawn' for sheer navigational usefulness. And my need to play the song twenty times a day was the evidence, motherfuckers. I could go to the other side of our house and find my missus punishing the same song at all hours and on that same heavy rotation.

Then I did me some research and dug the fullness of my discovery, ladies'n'gentlemen; and what a confusion these Ramesses boys present – almost as psychedelic and confusing as their music. For a start, this lot was almost Electric Wizard, except without singer Jus Oborn. That is, they were the Wizard but they weren't. Birthed in February 2003, after the mysterious demise of their legendary former band, bass player Tim Bagshaw and drummer Mark Greening had sought out another like mind from their Dorset Heimat, namely the foul-mouthed singer Adam Richardson, whose manimal presence on the 'Ramesside' had so captivated me and created such initial confusion as to where they wuz coming from. I'd never been a massive Electric Wizard fan, despite my late mate, the highly esteemed King of the Underground, Trevor 'Harmonia Mundi' Manwaring, blasting me with them any moment he got the time. It wasn't an antipathy I had; it was just that they never really grabbed me by the poo-poo; they made all the right noises (the Geezer/*Master of Reality*-period bass especially, alongside the Bill Wardian drumming) and the long songs were nice, but maybe the vocals weren't quite *it*, for me.

Anyway, Ramesses' story was a super-convoluted thing, to be sure; the drummer was the same Mark Greening as before, but the Wizard's Geezeresque bass player, the aforementioned Tim Bagshaw, had now become Ramesses' guitarist, with obvious and immediately stratospheric effect. But most pivotal of all was the introduction of this Adam Richardson, ur-priest of all Cookie Monsters and Pastor of Muppets, on whose vocals Ramesses' sound so depended. More so, indeed, because this motherfucker could play the bass, too, and therefore kept them in power-trio mode – the loveliest of all the rock-band forms, I think, nay, assert.

Side Two or Thereabouts

So why am I reviewing a picture-disc LP and not the similarly named CD release? Well, the vinyl sounds better, is more analogue and, therefore, is more sonically graspable (natch). But here it gets even more complicated because . . . (pause for breath) having settled into the Ramesside for about two weeks, it was disconcerting to have to approach the Skull side of this LP. Absent, on the second side, was the boxy, sibilant, thrill-seeking garage sound of Side One, here replaced by a pristine, gated thunder, recorded with typical bombast and thoroughness by doom legend Billy Anderson (for whose work on every other record I've heard I'd willingly ritually sacrifice Chelsea players, but not here). Everything that had spilled over on the Ramesside and left my bedroom walls coated with an icky, past-its-sell-by-date, stomach-churning mystery had, here on the Skull side, been banished by a Roman Andersonian thoroughness, so that the vats of raw yawp that had so defied my ears was here replaced by clearly clinical destruction. It was as though the slow, messy devastation of the Somme had been superseded by precise and all-pervasive atomic warfare (you know how shockingly hi-fi Sabs' *Volume 4* had at first seemed when you were still in bed with the cassette-copy-from-hell that was *Master of Reality*), and I struggled to get a grip with the other material. For me, this other side was still pale in comparison to 'Black Domina'/'Witchampton' precisely because it's not as *much* as it should be. Ja, mein hairies, the riffs are still fucking evil and still like pointlessly epic rushes into massed bayonets, but I want them to be twice as long – Om-length, at least, Orthodox-style, preferably, and then maybe even some more. However, I was then disconcerted to discover that my favourite tracks had already appeared on CD on the December '03 release *We Will Lead You to Glorious Times*. Collected herein, the two tracks were even more outstanding, head and shoulders above the much shorter 'Ramesses II' and 'Master Your Demons', although those two at least possessed the same sound and sense of over-recording.

Weirder still is the fact that those of you who buy *The Tomb* CD will miss out entirely on the flagship tracks, because they were on the earlier release. So you have to buy the twelve-inch picture disc because it's a far better sound, far better package and a far better mix of tracks. Got me? Hey, ultimately you just gotta get your collective asses down to the padded seats of the Bournemouth Opera House to enjoy these wolverines in a barely semi-upright position. At *Rome Wasn't Burned in a Day*, I managed to present Sunn O))) in a sumptuous theatre, where layabouts could lay and endure in comfort (and I still gotta do it for Khanate), but this Ramesses trip is obviously barely into second gear, and I reckon we're gonna see some huge, huge stuff that will, one day, even relegate the pitch-black Bible-burning of 'Black Domina'/'Witchampton' to a footnote in their history.

Rite on!

Discography

We Will Lead You to Glorious Times (This Dark Reign, 2003)
The Tomb (Invada, 2005)

Residual Echoes

(Big Drum, 2004)

SIDE ONE

1 Beginning and Slant (12.30)

2 The Diamond Drops (11.28)

SIDE TWO

1 Fish Don't Swim (1.23)

2 This Is Not a Start (1.07)

3 A Start One & Two (3.29)

4 A Stardt Three & Three and a Half (8.09)

5 A Better Substitute for Butter and Ending (6.09)

From my dugout, it seems that almost the only put-your-head-above-the-surface people nowadays seem to be modern Americans, their manifest destiny being to their credit and detriment also. Here at Poundland, however, we don't want any euros, and neither – so it seems – do Europeans, because it's costing them all a fortune. Even my Italian publishers say so, so it ain't xenophobic, babe. But when will we get America's next poet-Dylan to rival textually such massive instrumental deliveries as the below described? I mean, Guns' errant and *Raw Power*-ish 'One in a Million' is still my fave of theirs, even if it makes Alexis de Tocqueville turn in his grave (and I suppose Axl's erudite and earth-shaking 'Don't Damn Me' was an apologia of sorts). So, all ye wise-ass crackers with a neo-black butt shakin', you gits gots to be out there and lay some 'Ant Rap' down, and you ain't gonna be Devendra Banheart fer shit damn shure! C'mon, boobies, I'm coming over the Atlantic to search you out, so clue me soon-time.

This review is dedicated to the late Trevor Manwaring, underground prime mover and champion of the English scene, and also to Brian

Turner, self-styled shock-jock of WFMU, who turned these suckers loose on me in the first place.

This Is a Start

Does the music of Residual Echoes sound like the ultimate inner soundtrack issuing forth from the collective unconscious of readers of this review? Yes, the maximum, the *summum bonum*, the All Golden, perhaps, for some, the highest. With the release of this major debut from San Francisco's Residual Echoes, welcome to the New Year, motherfuckers! Moreover, there's no sexism or racism within these grooves, no songs of scarred old slavers whipping the women, no rampant Priapus crowing over his sprawling and reluctant fellatresses; just good ole rock'n'roll for the trepanned men and women of this twenty-first century. Verily, when the barmy, fuzz-faced, post-everything of Residual Echoes first razed my teepee to the ground a coupla weeks ago, I was too busy hiding behind the sofa to notice that they wuz dragging behind their chariots the festering corpses of their rock'n'roll heroes in a splendid effort to keep we commentators on the scent. And all came marching through my stereogram imprinted into that cracking old-timer format . . . vinyl! Unquenchable thrills!

The music of psychedelia (and, for some, the absolute beginnings of heavy metal) truly only lurks in the sounds of the in-between. And what is more 'in-between' than the days December 26 through 30, when even old Auntie Maiden Maud has no real inkling what the clock says and when even the CEO of McDonald's washes up, drunken on the piss, his house number forgotten in the taxi; he's a right fucking state . . .

This is one more than for the Seth Man; indeed, even our own Comets on Fire fan will redeem his Our Price Records voucher in preference to plucking from www.midheaven.com, and suchlike, the vinyl-only *Residual Echoes*. Who are those guys, some of them girls, who make the rattle of death seem easy meat compared to this, their debut rock'n'roll record, without need of remix, printed sleeve nor even labelling for the sides? Hey, brothers and sisters, you got it and it's crossing your lawn now, humbled and stumbling, Post-It notes from hell writ only on the sly side of a passing fox, fixing to die.

Here, in the grooves of *Residual Echoes*, lie the scrambled fragments of minds informed by the passing Cleveland taxi radio blaring *Hall of the Mountain Grill* as performed by the Electric Eels, with the ur-whinnying

David E on 'first time musette'. Or was it the intro to Chrome's *Half Machine Lip Moves* blaring through the Dansette of Ed Wilcox, as accompanied by the three-prong synthesizer attack of Temple of Bon Matin's *Bullet into Mesmer's Brain*-period nonet? Residual Echoes is the psychedelic, the utmost, the highest confusal beyond worlds – more even than juxtaposing a Sudafed/Actifed-informed bellyache with 'Why Don't You Eat Carrots?' during John Peel's first Faust phase, all those years ago; by the same post-Monoshockian wall o'noise that VON Elbowed Messrs Miller, Flashman, Harmonson, Chasny and Belcher in the face during that 'tweentime between Comets on Fire's own vinyl-only debut and the sublime *Field Recordings from the Sun*.

The leader of the sect-like Residual Echoes, purveyors of this illegal product, goes by the name of Adam Payne. That's right, Adam, the First Man of this the first year, who is called 'Payne' in the ass of humankind. He has monster bollocks that shake, and his only respite from such discomfort is to plague us all with a kind of *mucus concrète*, something like Utopia Carcrash playing Hapshash and the Coloured Coat playing Stockhausen's *Hymnen*, or maybe something like the Japanese Group Ongaku's album as played by their more rhythmically motivated Amalgamation brethren; but being also an inbred love-child of Amon Düül I's most ramshackle *Disaster*-period and Amon Düül II at their most proto-metal (nay, two inbred offspring, if you count the Karuna Khyal and Brast Burn sacred twins [who themselves bring in 'I Walk on Gilded Splinters'-period Dr. John as refracted through the lens of Mr Obi's Exuma]). Yup, the rhythm section of this Residual Echoes band gallumps along looser than Hansel and Gretel laying trails of crumbs along the forest's ferny floor.

Imagine sandals of the 'open toad' variety, the foot broken with many individual toffee-hammer blows across each separate bone, rather than by one giant, flattening weight. This is the sound of Residual Echoes. Their bass is not impressive and stops soon after commencing. Next, however, debilitating synthesizers geek'n'splutter like this Adam guy has no choice but to up-end his own muse, and militant, free rock'n'roll descends upon us from the boiling metal cauldrons that Adam has prepared earlier in anticipation of our soon-come future nomadic sauntering enquiringly at the base of his city walls. Jericho, for Adam Payne, will only be destroyed when we tame his barking mad fixation and wrestle this devil to the ground. Buried up to his neck in sand, he will then admit to fear and apologise for his sins. Down, sinner, down, down . . . We are the invaders and you are only the carrier of ill information. Baleful stares . . . Desist at once as we crack your long cranium and bleed from the issuing wound enough to stall your demonic holler. Boy, you will obey us! Treating the Lord like some big, drunk director is not the way forward, but somebody gots to do it. Otherwise, you err on the side of a culture happy to bleat at each other: 'My invisible god is more important than your Invisible God.'

You want me to translate that idea? Okey-dokey, Lord of the Gallows who hangs out until judgement day – no, not just bodily death, but death everlasting; it's back to the Bronze Age, in other words; death in *this* world. Get this into your system, quick, and learn from the tsunami that Mother Earth unleashed upon south-east Asia – Residual Echoes will only get big when we buy many copies and chart it higher than Girls Aloud. Overturn the system when you paint out all the road signs in white and let religious maniacs stop the show because it calls their god 'cunt'. Free your mind with the music of Adam Payne, and history stops dead. This music will cure you of time, gentle people. Only then, at the enforced stasis of history, can life truly begin.

I've Got the Rock'n'Rolls Again

But enough information; in order to help Adam Payne play simultaneously the part of many backing members of the group Residual Echoes this recording also features others such as Tom Cabela, whose shirtless drumming adds to the rebel yell of 'Start One'. On 'Stardt Three and a Half' comes the drumming of Marcello, whose overdubs are formed of so-called 'flutophone', and what's that? Like Comets on Fire, the unique music of Residual Echoes has created a sect malignant, allied sourcery and nourisher of dread. *This* is the way forward, like Ozzy throwing peace signs and screaming 'We love you!' between songs and even between lyrics. For the in-between times are the doorways, where the results begin and soon multiply into a dozen chasmic orgasms for the ears and, very soon afterwards, also for the mind. Yes, for the mind. Good will prevail only when rock'n'rollers have shown that hell ain't a bad place to be!

Translation: the Pope is a witless battery half-man in a battery car, creating more saints these past years than any other Pope ever, in a splendidly incorrect and half-baked manner, dreaming that such action is the way to thwart the incoming heathenism. The result is total devaluation of the idea of canonisation. It's an excellent fuck for organised Mediterranean religion (although of little mark to those saint-hating Proddiz); excellent push for the rock'n'roller. Join up the ranks of fast-flowing music-heads and leave your fear of the physical far behind. With this unbelievable folkloric, cosmic jam-rag, Residual Echoes joins Monoshock and Comets on Fire in the pantheon of the geographically suitable divinities fit to suck at the juicy tit of Mutha Urd and grace the slopes of Mount Ararat, all back members carved Mount Rushmore-stylee and staring out like guardian angels across Armenia's cities in the dust.

2005 certainly started as auspiciously as you'd ever dreamt could happen. The Faust was back and his doors were open. As Ettore Rosboch said, as it struck him that first moment that the jam-rag should fully occupy Side Two's vinyl allotment: 'It's that simple. And it's that urgent.'

I'm Zoroaster and they can all – Christianity, Islam, Judaism – fuck right off!

Riharc Smiles

The Last Green Days of Summer

(Steinklang, 2004)

SIDE ONE

1 Ouverture – The End of Winter (2.58)
2 The Last Green Days of Summer (3.53)
3 Join Us (4.39)
4 Armageddon Is a Sunny Day (5.24)

SIDE TWO

1 Magic Circle (3.59)
2 Crossroads (3.43)
3 Epilogue (4.32)

In the Beginning of the End

If the so-called 'dark folk' scene was ever to be summed up in a single recorded statement, then it was surely done best by this limited-release, vinyl-only album[1] from Austrian songwriter Riharc, back in August 2004. Coming on like the loner bard of Brittany's well-populated Kevrenn Alré, Riharc's opening gambit was as shrill and mid-rangey as their massed bombard band, and just as infectious and enthusiastic. Indeed, if ever I picked an Album of the Month purely because of the sheer amount of times I'd spun the disc, then this would be the geezer! Perhaps it's the brevity of the album – barely a half hour in length – or perhaps it's Riharc's smiling vocal delivery; whatever, the sounds contained within *The Last Green Days of Summer* have always sent my ever questing and lusty inner being directly to an imaginary heathen land, as gorgeously clichéd as County Meath's

1 The record was also made available in a limited wooden-box edition.

legendary Hill of Tara, and as truly free of Christian piety as Christopher Lee's Summerisle, in *The Wicker Man*. For the songs barely contained herein are catchy as a bastard, the women's voices plaintive and urging, the drum-led (and hurdy-gurdy'n'accordion-fuelled) instrumentation being both an all-purpose catch-all of Kelto-Viking enchantedness *and* a delightfully inventive potpourri of anti-popery, while Riharc always has more than plenty to say for himself, and always in as charmingly poetic a manner as you could wish for.

Does it do what it says on the tin? U-betcha! And, if the Apocalypse is anything like Riharc describes on this album, we heathens are gonna be Ragnarocking into our collective last ditches in a communal state of mind near on as happy as ye Christians, but blind drunk and bullock naked! Apparently, while this ensemble was always intended to be Riharc's positive statement to the world, he also had another negative/nihilist outfit ready in the wings named Riharc Snarls (or something like that). But, as I've scoured the Internet in vain for evidence of any such thing, perhaps the poet contented himself with the extreme success of this sole project. I can't say I'd be that surprised, as *The Last Green Days of Summer* reveals a trip as thorough, charming and as determined as any on the dark folk scene.

For years, I had no more Riharc in my record library than a single, credit-free promo CD version of this album, sent to me back in the day by Steinklang's label boss Markus. That is, until I scored a delightful vinyl copy from Cold Spring's olde yeBay shoppe, which came complete with colour libretto and list of musicians. Until then, not knowing who had played what and how had always been something of a drag, but it had at least given me a few years in which to let my imagination run riot.

Of all the levels on which this record achieved so highly, for me *The Last Green Days of Summer* worked best because it seemed to be a journal of this time; i.e. it conjured up not hoary and forgotten ancient standing stones trapped behind overgrown yews, festooned with gnarly thorns, tied with wire fences and barely visited, but, instead, made me think of the freshly mown Eisteddfod fields of north-west Wales, their newly erected bardic stone circles awash with local village children; or the handsome (although slightly liberty-taking) council-erected neo-dolmens of the north Netherlands; or even the over-fastidiously thatched houses of that same area; in other words, this Riharc Smiles record peddled a completely confident, post-Christian, *now* paganism rather than crouching, slightly hangdog, in the shadow of some rather dubious, guilty restoration of a wannabe but ultimately unreal past, in denial of Wodenist hangings and sacrificial blood-letting (as so much modern neo-paganism chooses to do).

Even better, Riharc's voice throughout this record even exhibits a lovely Faust-do-ballads quality, as though the poet had learned his English via a slightly anglicised American relative (or an aunt's ex-GI boyfriend), lending his clipped pronunciation and slightly lost-in-translation words an even more mysterious air. Unfortunately, that quality was sadly absent from the sole other track I knew by Riharc Smiles: a spirited but slightly perfunctory electro-performance of 'Wir Rufen Deine Wölfe', which appeared on the Ahnstern Records double LP of the same name. Besides, I'd far preferred Sturmpercht's own ultra-portentous, acoustic'n'marching-drums version that opened their own release, *Geister im Waldgebirg*.

Anyhow, as I'm here only to praise the smiling one, let's take a brief look at *The Last Green Days of Summer* and see what pleasures it contains . . .

Imam Schmimman, I Want Me Mam!

Riharc's album commences on some gusty Heimdal hilltop, as massed snare drums and braying bombards belch forth life across the hayfields and sheepfolds scattered far below, the sacred breath issuing out and onwards to the distant horizon, infused as though by some gigantic, nay, titanic spirit of Mother Urd in possession of a valley-sized comb and paper. Then we're whirled out of our senses into the Medieval, one-chord death dance of the title track – four minutes of cartwheeling acousto-drone and caterwauling, Anglo-Viking jig, replete with enthusiastic yelps and cries of 'hey', as the anguished but smiling poet Riharc declaims his intentions: 'The dance goes on forever now/ Until the morning comes.'

With its punishing cries, its persistent percussion and its spangly Spanish guitar, this gem could happily continue for another quarter hour, but we're immediately cast once again into the cosmick tingle-tangle as the forever waltz of 'Join Us' descends, and the female vocals and bagpipes crowd around Riharc and lament for the existence of the great ancestors beneath the earth, then proceed to lament for those who are alive but lonely and removed from society, the disparate groups throughout this Mother Earth who – despite their disenchantment – still rail against those who pillage from the Now and leave nothing for what will soon be Becoming.

Side One concludes too soon with the massed bandoneon march of 'Armageddon Is a Sunny Day', in which we are informed that Mother Earth's final hours as a human sanctuary will be spent under bright shining blue, the inevitable and chaotic cacophony of gunfire and explosions overwhelmed by the intensity of this predicted sunshine: 'No need for us to cry/Armageddon is a sunny day.' Again, the single minor-chord drone throws our heads into a veritable meditative whorl, although the descending notes on the second half of the song tear at our heartstrings and drag us down and down into a prehistoric underworld vault of overwhelming melancholy. But, like overly caffeinated English city dwellers at a west of Ireland wake, our obstinate and kicking defiance persists, so thoroughly has Riharc's music raised our psychic hackles.

Side Two kicks off with 'Magic Circle', the only traditional song on the record, and a piano-driven, minor-key ballad at that. At first, belligerent backward troll vocals undermine the niceness of Riharc's delivery, but this soon gives way to a genuinely beautiful song that points out just what Judgement may entail:

And what of dreams, my friend?
We think our days will never end,
But in the evening there is still,
A final meeting on that hill,
Where we have to show,
Where we have to say,
Where we confess and then go away.

War rears its head next, as combative drums and then the lyrics of 'Crossroads' broadcast the tale of a quarrel at some obscure and lonely forest junction. As the repeated choruses develop over further marching drums, male voices and enormous gongs, the fight gets further out of hand and develops into a fully fledged battle – Riharc and his cronies eventually relieved to have got out of there alive.

And so – far too soon – we come to 'Epilogue', the final track of this superb debut LP; and what a song it is. The returning wind arrives, as the hilltop poet is this time accompanied by piping flute and a noisy (Rosedale?) chord-organ that brings to mind that epic Kevin Coyne death ballad 'Are We Dreaming?'.[2] Again, the lamenting Riharc describes the

2 'Are We Dreaming?' appeared on Kevin Coyne's 1978 Virgin Records LP *Dynamite Daze*.

last day on Mother Earth as viewed from high atop his lofty perch, as the sounds of the landscape are slowly sucked out and over the distant whore risin' . . . If ever a record left the listener demanding more, then this be a true candidate.

I just have to admit that *The Last Green Days of Summer*, like the Ramones' debut LP, is as complete in its concept and execution as any of my true favourites, and that it's only my own greed, nay, *need* for Riharc's sound that leaves me gasping for more, more, more.

Sacrificial Totem

Hurqalya

(Katabatik, 2004)

1 Ritual I (13.41)
2 Ritual II (14.53)
3 Ritual III (24.04)
4 Ritual IV (21.20)

Without fudging, without sleight of hand, without consciousness this brief review came in at exactly 666 words.

Genre: Blackest Ambient Metal

Place this disc upon thy stereo system and watch the so-called real world first recede then evaporate in mere moments, as the undead Ancients of the Underworld reawaken, then emerge triumphant to restore their bizarre death dance to our landscapes. For Sacrificial Totem rage cataclysmically across our speaker systems in enormous, weather-sized sonic tempests that exhibit more life force than even the most ardent proto-metal or no-wave free-rock, and their calamitous sound is a key to clearing away all the slack, all the cack and all the psychic plaque that the extraneous and unnecessary moves of the modern world build up around our senses, divorcing us from the sheer ecstasy of the exterior by numbing us with sweet, sticky melodies and rhymes of unrealistic hope.

Sacrificial Totem's sound is not the sound of human individuals at honest endeavour, but the sound of the gods creating the world, nay, the universe on eight-bit sampling machines, typing in the codes of the future on battered word processors retrieved from local charity shops. There's no need to believe this stuff was created on human instruments, brothers'n'sisters, for the single most continuous auditory experience brought forth by Sacrificial Totem is a mysterious sound that alludes to the Great Blacksmith himself igniting and reigniting his newly invented welding torch over and over and over. It is alchemy, brothers'n'sisters. Did the concept of insemination of the female by the male gain credibility only after the (probably accidental) application of heat to meat and to metals had taught humankind the idea of fusion? That's the kind of thought that manifests in my mind when Sacrificial Totem's singular sounds burn brightest at the base of my melting plastic brain; for this is the most useful of all rock'n'roll, and should be taken only in the officially prescribed doses.

To reach the vastness of the four tracks 'Ritual I', 'Ritual II', Ritual III' and 'Ritual IV', imagine first a fraught and still grief-stricken Odin hoovering Balder's grave, then accidentally dropping the brush attachment so that it swings down out of reach into the human world, where it proceeds randomly to suck up trees, streams and small homesteads, anything in its path, until the tetchy god finally retrieves it, hauls it in, then blasts the contents back down below. The sounds made by this black-metal outfit from the American North-West offer further strong evidence that it is the metal scene which has become home to the true keepers of the avant-garde flame. For this mysterious Sacrificial Totem outfit, these renegade black-metal devils of the North American forests, unleash in their music the same eternals as did Messrs Roedelius and Moebius on 1971's enormous *Cluster 1* or Haare's tumultuous *The Temple*, back in 2004. Indeed, while meditating to the four rituals contained on this *Hurqalya* album, I've been twice delivered into the slavering jaws of the mythical Fenris wolf, and glimpsed what could only be described as 'my conclusion' due to this savage sound. To all the anthropologists who study shamanism only at the peripheries of culture – Siberian, Inuit, Lapp – I declare this: there is now enough evidence of shamanism within rock'n'roll culture for you to dismount your lofty perches and look closer to home. Would you consider a study of Christianity valid if the information had only been gathered from the edges of Christian culture? No! Only at the centre of culture does the ardent flame of the practitioner beat at its brightest; elsewhere it is in danger of becoming an ingrown and niggardly thing. Even a cursory glance at the antics of the wee, wee Free Church of Scotland, practised in the name of Christianity up in the Outer Hebrides, will show this to be true. And so, instead of looking to the edges of culture, search out the most powerful declarations of rock'n'roll music from the scenes of the West and steep yourselves in their mysteries. Therefore, the most useful current tool of the twenty-first-century shaman belongs to the unlikely genre: blackest ambient metal.

Solar Fire Trio

(Invada, 2006)

SIDE ONE	SIDE TWO
1 Breakthrough (26.13)	1 External Threat (25.43)

For those of you on an electric trip, this Album of the Month may come as a shock simply because its proto-metal is played on acoustic instruments. For those of you on an acoustic trip, its blurting sound may be anathema simply due to this band's sheer unsignpostedness. But approach this record as a head-clearer and watch the demons rise up out of your skull and clear off, post haste, as the Solar Fire Trio first mush your branium, then Dyno-rod it with a transcendental floss.

Music Is the Healing Force of the Universe

Hail to the visionaries, motherfuckers. Hail to those who wanna start the reconstruction. But, and it's one hell of a big butt, in these times of dogmatism and corporate smotherfuckers, let's also remember to hail the explorers, the musical nihilists, those who dare to stand at the edge of the abyss and . . . surf downwards. 'Fuck replacing shit,' they scream. 'First let's just destroy.' And in this twenty-first-century world of believers – and Kamikaze believers at that – let's put our hands together for the sons of chaos, confusion, assault and sonic battery.

Welcome to the world of the Solar Fire Trio, brothers'n'sisters, an imaginary world in which the free-jazz of the mid-'60s made heroes and gods of Archie Shepp, Albert Ayler, John Coltrane and Pharoah Sanders; a Walter Mitty world in which 1967's witty 'The Psychedelic Saxophone of Charlie

Nothing'[1] had every young 'un on the block picking up an alto or tenor sax instead of a solid-bodied electric guitar. The Solar Fire Trio are punks, punks and more punks, and their debut LP is the mutt's nuts, the pig's business and the cat's arse. These gentlemen ain't no gentle men; they're Blue Cheer to John Coltrane's Hendrix; they're The Stooges to Archie Shepp's MC5; and they're The Fugs to Albert Ayler's Mothers of Invention – got me?

Let's get one thing straight from the off: Solar Fire Trio is not jazz. Forget about the two saxes and drums line-up; these mung-worshippers ain't even 'jazz' the way smacky James Chance conceived of it. No, Solar Fire Trio is rock'n'roll – brutal, North African, tribal rock'n'roll in its most singular form (they should have a naked lead singer/dancer at the front who utters not one word). Solar Fire Trio is R&B at its most devolved and free-form, running the voodoo down, down and ever further down. Solar Fire Trio is devolved and dissolved Detroit soul, as hard, gleaming and polished as the shiny bell-ends of their righteous horns. Solar Fire Trio is a power trio not in the 'So jazz' Cream mould but in the 'So what?' Musica Transonic mould. This is 'religion, brutality and a dance beat', as my erstwhile mentor and former manager of Liverpool's Eric's Club, Roger Eagle, used to call it.

Yeah, Liverpool: Solar Fire Trio is comprised of three Liverpudlians with a biker-rock attitude to free-jazz, or is that a free-jazz attitude to biker-rock? Come to think of it, this music probably owes more to the behemoth soul of Grand Funk Railroad than it does even to John Coltrane's superhuman cacophony. Is the Solar Fire Trio playing a medley of classic soul and R&B on this LP? It certainly sounds that way. As though each player were wearing headphones connected to the same communal iPod, Solar Fire Trio plays together apparently united by some deeply ingrained inner soundtrack that only they can hear. Imagine early Blue Cheer jamming along, with Eddie Floyd's 'Big Bird' as their inner road map, so they could all hear where each other was at while

1 Released in 1967, on John Fahey's Tacoma Records, Charlie Nothing was the spewdonym of author Charles Martin Simon. Although the artist himself didn't take his album seriously, its release on Fahey's label meant that the heads adopted it as a heavyweight contender in the 'new jazz' stakes.

the audience remained none the wiser. Indeed, with regard to free-jazz, only John Coltrane, around '67, is in any way as brutally wanton as these jackbooted thugs. Besides, this Solar Fire Trio stuff seems to be as much informed by the tumultuous Mars/Friction side of no wave and post-punk as it is by jazz. Indeed, like the legendary Klondike & York album *The Holy Book*,[2] the only jazz elements here are the instruments.[3]

But who are these madmen who kick the bejaysus out of jazz? Well, they ain't completely unprovenanced, brothers'n'sisters. For starters, it's Ray Dickaty, a.k.a. Ray Moonshake, a.k.a. Ray Spiritualized, who nails that tenor sax, soul riffing like there's an entire section there, occupying the mid-range and baritones, as fellow brass player Dave Jackson free-squeeks the alto sax into Patty Waters'/Yoko Ono's attic; these two Jack Horners barely kept in check by drummer Steve Belger, who lays down the kind of bass-less soul rhythms that only the most confident drummers dare execute. Belger is to Solar Fire Trio what Guy Evans was to the nihilistic soul of *Godbluff*-period Van der Graaf Generator, or what Tony Williams was to his own bass-less power trio, Lifetime.

If Solar Fire Trio were true jazz, not punk, there'd be some redundant, ever-descending, ber-doom-doom-doom-doom upright bass plunking away in the background, but these gentlemen know a big-ass double bass would add nothing to the yawp, *plus* it would stop them from roaring up and down the country in their old, beat-up, silver Mercedes estate car, earning the dollar. So, instead, Ray Dickaty often takes on the role of the entire horn section single-handed, blowing with such a supreme rock confidence that Dave Jackson's alto sax is allowed to soar

2 The Klondike & York LP *The Holy Book* allows Chad Stockdale's single tenor saxophone far more space than Solar Fire Trio, often providing a horizon of analogue synthesizer as the sole 'context' for the drums'n'sax's free-forming. Released on Weird Forest Records, this exhilarating vinyl album must surely be due for a CD reissue.

3 Everything in this primal soup screams out the name Nihilist Spasm Band, a Canadian group whose 1968 LP *No Record* I copped for one pound eighty pence back in 1978 and proceeded to lambaste everyone on the L'pool scene with whenever they, stupidly, dropped in for tea. Like Solar Fire Trio, Nihilist Spasm Band was an out-there ensemble with a penchant for jamming along to their own collective inner soundtrack, and whose fifteen-minute barrage 'Destroy the Nations' was included on the Canadian nihilist film *No Movie.*

off into Van Halen-ish stratospherics, like Gerd Dudek on the title track of The Wolfgang Dauner Septet's *Free Action*.[4]

Yup, like over-opinionated Jewish fundamentalists at a circumcision rite, Messrs. Dickaty, Jackson and Belger have pruned it all back to the basics, not only removing the piano and all of the landmarks that such a chordal instrument brings, but also removing all other musical rafts that could possibly give listeners something/anything to hang on to as the stormy seas rage around them. As I previously mentioned, it all sounds like these guys have been listening to '67 John Coltrane septet stuff through a broken Dansette with only the treble control and one speaker working. These stoned motherfuckers done fucked off McCoy Tyner's piano, Joe Brazil's flute, both bass players, and reduced the rest to a heady and distilled broth of just Pharoah Sanders' tenor sax, Elvin Jones' drums and Coltrane's own tenor.

Under a stairwell on a connecting floor, somewhere between the attic where The Stooges recorded the seventeen-minute version of 'LA Blues' and the smoky basement jazz club in which Albert Ayler performed his Plastic People of the Universe-like 'Holy Ghost'. . . that's where Solar Fire Trio currently dwell. Too rock to attract be-beret'd Little Miss Heartbreaker/Homemaker types and too jazz to court the living rock goddess. For our purposes, brothers'n'sisters, that's just where we need them to stay – well hung at dawn, betwixt and between, forever standing at the tuning fork in the road, three open toads, horny for the horn.

Where Next?

In conclusion, brothers'n'sisters, I have one plea. If yooz about to make a purchase of one free-sax blurtathon, then please make sure it ain't by 'Trane or Archie or Albert but by the Solar Fire Trio themselves, because these guys is living this racket and schlepping its slithery, Lokian

4 Like the Coltrane references, Wolfgang Dauner's move outside jazz into free-rock began in 1967, when his drummer was still Mani Neumeier, soon to form Guru Guru. Indeed, while the 1967 MPS Records LP *Free Action* is still entirely located in jazz, the Dauner Septet echo John Coltrane's ensemble but with entirely different instruments: Gerd Dudek's tenor sax is often indistinguishable from Jean-Luc Ponty's vertigo-inducing violin, and the lower registers swerve like tigers on Vaseline as Jürgen Karg's bass fuses with the cello of future bass star Eberhard Weber.

torso up and down the motorways of the UK as we speak. And, furthermore, what better reason is there to buy a record than to know that it's a piece of contemporary art parping its vibrations directly into the current of the post-everything twenty-first century, its cascading avalanche of pure white snow pulsating through the overly caffeinated veins of popular culture.

Call me a kibitzer but, for the future, I'd love to see Solar Fire Trio bringing in a little order to random moments, maybe a little Teo Macero-style orchestration and portentous instant ritual in the style of John Coltrane's *Om* introduction, something to wrestle meaning from the chaos, if only to let the whole thing be subsumed back into that chaos. Or maybe they could try something really fucking contentious, like Mary Maria Parks' vocal contribution to Albert Ayler's *Music Is the Healing of the Universe.* Perhaps that's just my own sense of the ridiculous, and I shouldn't foist any trip on these full-on motherfuckers, especially as I've heard two other tracks by this bunch – the sixteen minutes of 'Vanishing Point' and the twenty minutes of 'Incitement to Life' – which showcase the trio in a more lyrical mood and which would make an ideal second album. Perhaps the best thing about Solar Fire Trio is that they exist at all. Rock'n'fuckin'roll, as they say.

Sunburned Hand of the Man

Jaybird

(Manhand, 2001)

1 Featherweight (7.18)
2 The Jaybird (16.53)
3 Soss, the Quilled Investigator (11.30)
4 Eggshell Blues (18.31)
5 Leaving the Nest (8.46)
6 Too High to Fly No More (14.06)

The Burren

Do not travel on the N6 to Galway, unless you use your own fiscal year. In general, the roads of western Ireland are so bad that no Irish drivers ever bother to pick up any real speed, for fear of giving themselves the kind of 'modern' expectations which would be instantly shattered by the gaggles of insistent biddies for whom it is an offence to ever have their motor vehicle struggle beyond an unsteady thirty-eight mph. Keeping to a schedule on the N6 to Galway can only bring calamity. Indeed, so long ago did Galway drivers give up making demands of other road users that nowadays signs appear at junctions entreating drivers to 'Please stop at the red light.'

Of course, this is all excellent practice for supposedly cool English, Welsh and Scottish holidaymakers who (located on the Emerald Isle for a limited period) soon find themselves goaded into displays of horrible Germania, nay proto-jackbooted Nazism. And many's the time I've attempted to drive a particularly impassive Galway driver off the road, using everything from shunting and headlight-flashing to post-New Age mantras such as 'Pull the fuck over, you cunt!' But it never works, and the brain cells lost on the journey have, inevitably, always been mine.

But travel just south of beautiful Galway town, down the N18 towards

Gort, and you'll find an entirely different reality taking over. For rising up to the west, just over the border into County Clare, is *the* most magical and confounding landscape – a faerie-dusted and deserted upland consisting of nothing more than mile upon desolate mile of blue-grey karstic limestone. Once this land was host to woodlands and dense vegetation, and the fine megalithic monuments which still lie scattered around bear witness to its place as a former home of early humanity. Overfarming and deforestation eventually caused the vegetation to retreat, and nowadays, at sundown, it is only the odd ignorant tourist who can be seen standing outside the legendary Poulnabrone dolmen. For the locals well know that it would not be right to upset the ancient spirits – and no one but those on the quest wish to be seen here after dark. Not at . . . the Burren.

My Swampy Massachusetts Home

The Burren is a time machine, and the Burren is a time*less* machine. And nowadays 'The Burren' is also the name of an Irish pub in New England, given to throwing its doors open to all and every vagabond musician who wishes to ply his trade there. And, true to the spirit of ye olde original Burren, three thousand miles to the east, this neo-Burren is also home to bizarrely dressed makers of ritual and fertility dances.

Tonight, there are at least twelve people on stage doing this thing that sounds like early Funkadelic's 'Music for My Mother' meets Dr. John the Night Tripper's 'I Walk on Gilded Splinters', while Brian Donnelly, a 'do-nothing doodad' (as the locals like to call him), skanks around the tiny stage getting in the way. Sometimes he's wont to blow a mean saxophone, or even (at his most compassionless) parp his Aboriginal didge. But, just for tonight, Donnelly Do-Nothing is a tiny Cajun bingo caller in reggae trousers and stovepipe hat, one gozzie eye staring directly up to the heavens.

There's a horribly more-ish analogue synthesizer astrally vamping somewhere in the mix, putting me in mind of Roxy Music's mighty '73 groove 'The Bogus Man'. Elsewhere in the smoky clutter of The Burren's cramped stage the audience can just make out the shadowy, almost-mummified figure of one 'Critter', as he shakes his pea-filled gourds and whacks his frame drums. He's always been known as the 'Echo voice spirit', since the others found him alone in a dry river gorge, beating on a hollow rotting log and intoning wah-mouth mantras. Next to Critter, the dress-wearing and tattoo'd figure of Chad Cooper toasts reverb'd proto-biblical messages into his mic and shakes his sticks and bones, occasionally lashing out at his skin drums. Behind Cooper and the Crit lurks Cousin Rich Thomas on baby rattles and shakers. Sometimes they'll let him pound at his geetar because he's everybody's cousin and it would be pointless to try and stop him in any case (but they keep him turned down lower than Brian Jones on the *Beggars Banquet* sessions – just don't ever tell him!).

So you've got all these percussion guys *sh-sh-sh*-shaking and a-grooving like The Residents on the back sleeve of *Fingerprince*, and that still ain't enough for 'em. They need the drums, and they need 'em now! So the remarkably un-weirdly named Phil Franklin plays one of the drum kits that are set up and keeps it sensible (don't believe it – for his day job he's also an award-winning delivery boy at Ramadan Fast Food), while the other kit is occupied by the Reverend John Moloney, a fine record producer and seer/sucker of western Irish descent. This Moloney dude is the one who got them The Burren gig in the first place, and it is he who produces their records, although he's still wondering why none of this sounds in any way like the mélange of Melvins and Sonic Youth which he was led to believe he would be tapping into when Sunburned Hand of the Man started, back in '94. In fact, to begin with they'd been called Shit-Spangled Banner (x-o-fucking-lent name!) and there were just the three of them – how the fuck had they ever swollen to the size of Sun Ra's Arkestra?

And now, as the bass crawled up the sweaty walls of The Burren and the music dipped into a bizarre take on Captain Beefheart's sublime 'Mirror Man', Moloney scanned the rest of the barely lit stage and considered it all. Half of these dudes are playing African percussion and drums and shakers and whistles and Turkish vau-vaus, and all these suckers are unconsciously chuntering a mean love-grunt, like Oscar Peterson when he's in full flow, and all this is drifting across the PA like an inbred, unschooled version of The Wild Tchoupitoulas. Meanwhile, the ascendant groove is now screaming around the PA like fly agaric in a liquidiser – as though Joe Gibbs has left Retirement Crescent to join Rosko Gee and Reebop for some late-Can 'on-the-wan' of stellar proportions. Forget the percussion credits, who's taking the blame for the stink of creosote and the digital distortion?

Ah yes, being in The Burren, it's

the geological fault of some other guys I ain't even bothered mentioning yet. How could I be so crass? There's Bo Hill picking on Stratocaster wah-guitars through glassy Fender amps, or brittle-sounding Telecasters though glassy Fender amps; and there's Silk Pontius fuzzing everything up with his 'down low phase guitar'; and how about the immaculately named Mark Orleans, who spends most of his time busking at the entrance to the club, only occasionally deigning to whip it out for some furious and astral sky-writer solo.

Of course, this ain't a band so much as it's a scene of people coming and going. I could name a whole other bunch of protagonists down at The Burren, but the stupefied reader would only become weary of too much information. So I'll close this descriptive passage with the simple comment that Sunburned's anchor is provided by this mighty bass wielder called Bobby Thomas, who has co-produced all of the Sunburned oeuvre with the Rev. Moloney.

Two-track Recordings, Direct to CD-R

It should be noted that one of the best series of communal free-rock grooves ever recorded was made in one long, psychedelic weekend in 1969 by those Deutsche peace'n'love fuckers Amon Düül I. Indeed, those fabulous unisexers were still releasing highly achieving double LPs from said lost weekend as late as 1972! So it should come as no shock to learn that the best grooves yet unleashed by Sunburned Hand of the Man were all recorded direct to two-track tape recorder around the period 2000–1. As I quickly learned from dealing with such errant genii as Rooster Cosby and Michael Mooneye, the real work always consisted in putting these guys in the right state of mind to get their thang down, while simultaneously keeping one eye on the recording engineer to make sure he was getting on to tape every riff, lick, fart, squeak and toot. Sunburned Hand of the Man have one advantage over all of us, and that is their ever-present audience at The Burren, predominantly made up of locals, other musicians and even errant Sunburners waiting to be served at the bar. This whole trip allows such inconsistent luminaries as Tony Goddess (wonderfully credited as 'Synth Ra') and West Coaster Doug Ross (on wah-organ) to turn up whenever they feel like it, bringing a whole other sonic dimension into the process.

Of course, there has to be a downside to all this immediacy, and it manifests here in the lack of regard to detail in the finish of Sunburned 'product'. Peculiarly, I don't mean that their albums are not nicely 'finished' – they are actually quite exquisite for handmades, exhibiting 'proper' printing and good-quality labels. No, Sunburned's problem is that almost every one of these major-league grooves finishes as abruptly as The Beatles' 'She's So Heavy'. Just as you're drifting quietly in some super-consciousness, another clunk of instant silence springs you back into life and yet another hefty sixteen-wheeler funkathon fires itself up and idles briefly before leaving the warehouse.

But, of course, this is all by the by in the great quest for the contemporary shamanic thang, and Sunburned Hand is surely that. And, just maybe, these punks intend to keep us on our psychic toes.

Why Jaybird *Is Album of the Month*

From the off, we should be in no doubt that *Jaybird* is one motherfucker of a psychedelic trip. Its grooves run rings around Saturn and its bass penetrates Uranus; its songs have no let-up and listeners never know which ones they're listening to – indeed, it's the confusion and timelessness of this record which makes it such an achievement. Also, the mix of *Jaybird* is thoughtlessly daft enough to challenge '70–'71-period Funkadelic, or the best mid-'70s dub.

Unlike the road-warrior abandon of Comets on Fire (whose power is their seemingly unstoppable celebration of rootless travel), Sunburned Hand of the Man is a sedentary thing made by people in one place.[1] Like The Wailers' bassist, Aston 'Family Man' Barrett, these guys come over confident enough to celebrate their sense of settlement. Indeed, in the case of Comets on Fire versus Sunburned Hand of the Man, it's definitely a hunter/nomad versus settler/farmer thing. To sum it up, Sunburned would build bridges that their children's children would use forever, so long as the children of Comets on Fire had not long ago laid waste to those bridges and all the land around them.[2]

1 Nevertheless, the Reverend John Moloney told me that both bands were then recording material for a shared album.

2 OK, so this is just a metaphor you have to accept in order for me to make my point. I ain't claiming Ethan Miller and co. *actually* live in some shitty, Hawkwind-type, 1960s AEC Reliance coach with all the seats taken out (like the one belonging to Dave Brock, which I went on with Dave Balfe in 1980 to sell them some acid. Believe me, it was horrible).

Anyway, *Jaybird* opens with a seven-minute bugger of a bass line with the same tone as Yarborough and Peoples' 'Don't Stop the Music'. 'Featherweight' is the name of the song, and it features a fine, fine circling guitar motif most reminiscent of Funkadelic's 'I'll Bet You'. An underachieving but hugely catchy, sub-Philly flute keeps it just this side of African Head Charge, as they replace Grady Thomas, Fuzzy Haskins, Ray 'Stingray' Davis and Calvin Simon with crowds of chanting percussionists, each one on an entirely different trip (and all of mixed ability). Like all Sunburned's stuff, 'Featherweight' stops abruptly and shakes your concentration before the biggie kicks in.

'I can't sleep at night/I can't even remember their name,' laments the voice at the beginning of the magnificent, seventeen-minute-long title track. Sounds like this po' little New England boy went to sleep with a statue of Rose Kennedy beside his bed and woke up in downtown Washington with a huge poster of Sir Nose Devoid of Funk staring down on his candy ass. Hail, this don't sound like a mixed-race band, more like mixed species, with bull-in-a-china-shop percussionists – a veritable chimps' tea party of crockery smashers. Yes, brothers and sisters, this is *the* track. This is the sound that maketh The Man. The mix overwhelms everything in the room, banishing all Funkadelic comparisons, and has you smashing your Chambers Brothers 'Time Has Come Today' record in an act of sheer 'Oh-butt-U-R-sohhhh-obsolete' abandon. Dig this fucking groove and ride it long and hard! Where's the twelve-inch vinyl, Reverend Moloney? We needs it . . . *RIGHT NOW*!

Next up, 'Soss, the Quilled Investigator' is a latter-day 'Danse Kalinda Ba Doom': eleven minutes of gris-gris that's more in the righteous zone than any Tom Waits' Beefheart-fixation could ever hope for. Over-recorded and fuzzed out, we're talking more like Karuna Khyal and Brast Burn here, as the unbalanced Ry Cooder slide geetar rises out of the swamp and nabs the babby right out of the mother's arms. Then a lone organ builds and builds this funereal dirge as the haunted and distracted figure of Groa begins to hover over her burial mound. Then, out of the blue . . . clunk! Sack that fucking editor, boys.

The first few minutes of 'Eggshell Blues' feature only stereo shakers and people ordering bar food. Settle down, now, settle down. But we got eighteen minutes to fire this sucker up, so lose your city-dweller expectations and understand that smoky bar-room chitter-chat can be a meditation too! And meditate they do . . . bringing the mix to a slow, slow simmer, then ever-so-gradually stirring in the very delicious sweet'n'sour Cajun sauce. Apparently, at the end of this track they dished up the distillation of the rhythms and served it out to the audience.

'Leaving the Nest' takes its unlikely rhythm from Kim Fowley's Napoleon 14th hit 'They're Coming to Take Me Away' and adds distant drone mouth, which wheels around The Burren like an unmanned, 1/73 scale model spy plane in the dome of some medieval cathedral. Slowly, the congas and funky knuckle skins begin to belt out a welting crack-a-crack as Chad Cooper consults his charts and intones deeply into the inhale-atron, Critter sighing like an analogue synthesizer from his rudimentary dugout round the back. These two shamans act in vocal tandem to reinforce the trip, but beware of the Critter, for (as the good Dr. John Creaux, the Night Tripper, famously reported) he 'will act as a second guardian angel unless you overwork him'. Close to nine minutes of this shake appeal carries us into the massively bass-heavy and epic quarter-of-an-hour-long closing track, 'Too High to Fly No More'. A big old cylindrical bass line up-ends the track and we're soon approaching Meters territory. What's that portentous post-spiel that Cooper's bellowing out? He could be calling the drunks in the front row a 'coupla Nazis', but just as likely he's asking the waiter for a 'coupla nachos'. Sounds important enough; just play on, brothers.

And so Cooper of the congas, and Critter of the shakers, and Cousin Rich of the rattles, and Franklin of the traps, and the Reverend of the rhythm all pound and beat their meat for one last champagne handshake, as Messrs Orleans, Bo Hill and Pontius of the wires scrub their 'lectrick washboards cleaner than clean. Ah, but unknown to them all Cousin Bobby of the bass has had one funky butt cheek on the fader all along, and it's tipped the scales in his low, low favour. Our unbalanced Album of the Month grinds to a halt without so much as an inch of flab, and the audience sink down in their seats, exhausted and spent.

But Don't Forget About Wild Animal

If *Jaybird* is the Man's one-hundred-percent real deal, and you dig the holy shit out of it, brothers and sisters, then I should clue you into its ninety-percent sibling in the form of *Wild Animal* (or *The Wild Animal*, as it's called on some copies). It may be flawed and pock-marked by seething enthusiasm and the worship of one too many deities at once, but *Wild Animal* is nevertheless a total orgy of a thang. If they'd put this and *Jaybird* out as a sumptuous two-CD set, we'd have the first genuinely erotic cum-athon of the twenty-first century.

'Bound' is the massive, nine-minute piece that opens the album. It begins like an Islamic Velvet Underground – all chromatic strings over a huge, cosmic groove of bells, wah-guitars and fjord-deep sonorous synthesizer. Imagine Pärson Sound playing Les Mogollar and yooz getting some way close to the mighty groove that it creates.

The incredible ten minutes of 'Gay from the Waist Up' which follows is more of that 'Bogus Man'-type, percussion-based Krautrock; all spindly Michael Karoli guitar and hugely reverb'd, Promethean cries of who knows what . . . Then we're off into yet more madness in the shape of 'Intending to Spend Three Months of the Winter on a Yacqui Reservation', as Chad Cooper overshoots and gets lost in Llandrindod Wells ('Hey, who's that guy with all the GG Allin tattoos on his neck, boyo?') – it overwhelms your speakers and you wanna simultaneously smack both the guitarists for their audacity and take 'em home for a good meal.

Further 'on-the-wan' mayhem kicks in during the eight minutes of 'Austin Wiggins Junior Hayride', which even includes a little audience response at the end. Then we descend into the seven minutes of low-spark-of-high-heel-boys which is 'Groove from a Hovel'. Imagine trying to smuggle Cheech and Chong over the Mexican border from insane Tijuana to ultra-straight San Diego. Only Cheech has been chewing on the amber cooking speed and won't shut the fuck up for a moment because he's wearing headphones and singing along to the *Grease* soundtrack. So the musicians have to groove louder and louder and louder, but all the while Cheech is more and more into his thang. He's gittin' *dowwwn*, momma: 'I love you/We love you,' he screams. The track finishes with the perfunctory applause of the police as they open the rear doors. 'Thank you,' says Cheech as they put on the cuffs.

Unfortunately, this otherwise amazing disc just kind of peters out. The last two tracks are duds, cute but rotten, like Can's 'Ethnological Forgery Series' (what's the point?). 'A Better Organised Sexlife' is a five-minute-long film theme from an imaginary movie about a Louisiana preacher trying to collect enough money from his inbred congregation to stop their church sinking into the swamp. You guessed it – the church sinks. Make this song twenty minutes longer, gentlemen – yooz just getting started. The last song is lesser, being untitled, too camp and too short. So ixnay on the anglais ongs say, but still a fuck off into deep space from our swampiest New England brethren. Get this sucker, too.

Inner Nutshell

The rest of the Sunburned Hand's oeuvre is a disparate bunch of releases, as we should expect from characters whose project bands are described as ranging from 'acid metal gospel' to 'skateboard/troublemaker'. Indeed, I'm only glad they don't try and put every aspect of every offshoot band out under the Sunburned name. As it is, an album like *The Agoraphobic Christcycle* is released under their name when, in fact, this heavy, heavy artefact is virtually a Chad Cooper solo album, being a venture into deep freak-out synthesizer over samples of street-corner fighting and arguing, and (what sounds like) rat torture. The Coop made most of it himself on a 'hot' Korg Polysix, so where it fits within the overall Sunburned Hand of the Man canon is anyone's guess, although the rest of the band seem quite content to present it under their name. The Rev. John Moloney described the album to me as 'Some heavy electronic Americana pulled from the archives.' Nuff said.

Looking back into their catalogue, 1997's *Mind of a Brother* is a lot more cosmic and subdued, still hugely rhythmical but way more ethereal. Elsewhere, it really reminds me of L. Voag's legendary 1979 album *The Way Out*, with tidal waves of sound coming and going, while their ne'er-do-well Donnelly Doodad clucks his sax like the metal chicken that attacked The Clangers' soup. I'm not at all keen on 1998's *Piff's Clicks* (each of its songs recorded directly to DAT and chosen by their soundman, Cliff Kaelin), which sets up camp somewhere between the acoustic free expression of Taj Mahal Travellers and the acoustic soupy mantras of Harvester, but with the definition of neither.

To my mind, the 2003 twelve-inch *Headdress* also fails, but this is simply down to the limitations of the vinyl format. You know how Timmy Thomas' 'Why Can't We Live Together' feels like it's twenty-five minutes minutes too short on the seven-inch vinyl? Well, it's the same deal with this. Like a sampler that never allows them to get into their stone groove, each track comes over like an 'excerpt', then moves on before you can get a grip on anything. The vocals become irritating because their insistence only pays off when yooz ten minutes into a Sunburned track. It ain't the band's fault, musically, but, to my way of thinking, they shoulda made it a double LP or even triple. And I'll bet the original grooves were hugely more extended, so maybe there's a double-CD version waiting to get chucked out.

Much better to my ears is 2002's junk-band jamboree *The Book of Pressure*, which is fucking marvellous, although far more fucked-up than any of the other albums I've mentioned. The five-minute title track opens the album, with Chad Cooper's psychobabble coming on like The Godz performing 'Eleven' or The Fugs around *Tenderness Junction*, and it quickly descends into Nihilist Spasm Band territory. Cooper totally cuts it as a visionary preacher, and on this album he's joined only by Messrs Bo Hill, Moloney and the cousins Thomas. The vast majority of the album is taken up by the relentless, multi-part school play known as 'The Ten Glens', whose lead instruments are shaker, hand drums, Subbuteo players shaken in a cup and communal whistling. *The Book of Pressure* closes with a short, melancholy acoustic-guitar piece, in what seems like a cynical attempt to wipe your memory clean of the previous half-hour's molestations.

Closure, We Need Closure

So there you are, me babbies: Sunburned Hand of the Man. They may release any old trouser tracks from time to time but they'z also truly capable of moving the firmaments when the Muses get to them – and get to them they have done over and over again. Believe me, it weren't no fluke! My advice is to get *Jaybird* first and *Wild Animal* next, and then read all and everything you can about this mob in case I got my head stuck temporarily up my ass while writing this thing.

Discography

Mind of a Brother (Manhand 001, 1997)
Piff's Clicks (Manhand 002, 1998)
Jaybird (Manhand 003, 2001)
Wild Animal (Manhand 004, 2001)
The Book of Pressure (Manhand 006, 2002)
The Agoraphobic Christcycle (Manhand 007, 2002)
Headdress (Record Records 6, 2002)

Vibracathedral Orchestra

Dabbling with Gravity and Who You Are

(Released 2002 on VHF Records)

1 Hypnotism in Your Hips (4.00)
2 Let Steam Rule and Luck Lose (8.01)
3 He Play All Day Long (5.47)
4 Bombay Stores Disco (3.17)
5 Fingernail R'n'B (2.54)
6 The Body Is the Arrow, the Arms Form the Bow (14.08)
7 'Mutual Amnesia Sugar' (5.52)
8 Hall 7 Broke My Heart: True as God (2.26)
9 This Is Where No One Worked Out (4.07)
10 Mystical Coughing (7.25)
11 Going Out Intending to Dig (3.40)

The first time I heard this record, its compulsive rhythms and debased, ragged raga immediately sold it to me as a righteous Album of the Month. Seven listens later, I was still convinced. Its title, *Dabbling with Gravity and Who You Are*, describes the Vibracathedral Orchestra trip perfectly, for this whole groove changes depending on whether you are listening in the bath, in bed or even in the concert hall. However, the more I have listened, the more I have realised that this is music that does not need much by way of description; indeed, it could be off-putting to do so. Instead, listeners just need to be alerted to the fact that it exists.

No Freak-Out

'The records should sound like bootlegs, as if recorded by somebody who passed a group rehearsing or jamming and then cut the recorded material wildly together.' (Uwe Nettelbeck, talking about his ur-vision of Faust, in 1972)

Although this lot have been called everything from a punk band (smart-arsed bollocks) to a hippie freak-out collective (careless bollocks), the most striking element in the work of Vibracathedral Orchestra is their extraordinary focus; it's as though they have just one riff and they're gonna play it till they all die. The musicians swap instruments all the time, and still the groove continues, however much the shades and tones of the music change.

This is music as a shamanic aid, made as much for the players themselves as for the listeners. But as I'm writing from the listening perspective, I have to inform y'all that this is music to get you there. Every track sounds as though it has always just 'been there', it's just you ain't quite tuned into its peculiar frequency until now.

Vibracathedral Orchestra also employ a system of rough-cut editing which is fucking magnificent – as ragged as Sunburned Hand of the Man, but intentional. The effect is something like that of *The Faust Tapes*, in that each piece is deeply inspiring and groove-some but rarely outstays its welcome. Imagine a rough-cut compilation of This Heat's 'Music Like Escaping Gas' spliced into Far East Family Band's epic *Parallel World* of Klaus Schulzean grooves, into *Rite 2*'s eternal 'Ringed Hills of Ver', into Faust's seemingly automaton-generated 'Krautrock', into Speed, Glue & Shinki's free-floating, Moog-generated 'Sun' suite, into Organisation's *Tone Float* clatter-skank, into the drum things of *Disaster*-period Amon Düül, into the shake-appeal dub of *Half Alive*-era Suicide, and yooz getting close to the bubbling, meditational caffeine that is Vibracathedral Orchestra.

It's this insistence that makes Vibracathedral Orchestra so *not* a freak-out band. Freak-outs involve all kinds of wasted blurts of cantankerous refusenik moves, and often with as many unharmoniously unsynchronised moments as there are members of the group. Not so with Vibracathedral Orchestra. For this is measured music with no highs or lows (or if there are any they are carefully edited out). If they were Christians, they'd be on a John Wesleyan trip and stand in opposition to gospel music. If they were Muslims, they'd all be circling the Kaaba and calling for the Dervishes to be kicked out once and for all. There are no solos and no individuality rears out of their locked grooves.

They Drone (One)

Vibracathedral Orchestra are from Leeds, which is a city of enlightened souls and stupendously stupid footballers. I got married there once, in the late 1970s, and still have a lot of extremely forward-thinking friends in the city. I don't know the members of Vibracathedral Orchestra, but the evidence says they are extremely confident and together in their trip. This even reveals itself in the packaging of the albums, some of which are beautifully housed in standard jewel cases, while others have been achieved by cleverly appropriating unique options provided by companies such as Ikea, the group stamping its style upon them.

Musically, the refusal to provide any 'lead' instruments allows the generic Eastern percussion and drums of Neil Campbell and Mick Flower to drive the sound, while Bridget Hayden's violin and Adam Davenport's synthesizer and shawm-like clarinet add weaving drones. Julian Bradley plays guitars in styles that range from tumultuous strumming through to Michael Karoliesque, single-note funk, occasionally adding further generic Middle Eastern-ness with his extremely un-Augustus Pablo-like melodica. This musical range is also often supported by Campbell's flute-like Casio.

By the way, I use the term 'generic' very positively, for half of the success of this music is its magpie attitude that nothing is beyond appropriation. Indeed, when they invoke the sonic gods of some particular region of the world, there is never any such attempt to replicate. When a reedy wail from the local mosque is added to a raga guitar, you can be sure that it's the drums of Amon Düül I, or a generated, Cluster-type synthesizer drone, which will provide the support. This ain't no musicological study.

Dabbling with Gravity and Who You Are

There may be thirteen song titles on this album, but it all works as a whole. John Peel once read out the names of *The Faust Tapes*' songs, but no one knew them at the time. So, for this Vibracathedral Orchestra album, I was even loath to specify individual song times and titles at the beginning, but being the fucker who always says you gotta accept the artists' metaphors, I can't be saying one thing and doing the other. Anyway, brief explanations of the sound of each piece should be enough, so I'll try and be economical with my praise.

'Hypnotism in Your Hips' opens with all-swaying, Indian belly-dancing and snake-charming reed-isms. The cross-cut edit drops you straight into it and you feel like a cyber tourist in a two-dimensional bazaar. Next up, the eight minutes of 'Let Steam Rule and Luck Lose' is one of their hugely exhilarating, Terry Riley-meets-Pärson Sound, single-note howls. The Orchestra revisits this sound good and often, and the manner in which this song slows down suggests it may well be an early take of the jam which spawned their amazing 'Baptism Bar Blues', which we'll come to in a moment.

'He Play All Day Long' is pure, first-album This Heat, or Cluster, as generated keyboard shakes your shangalang and drops a confetti of suspended chords over the listeners, while a mile-wide tambourine flaps and fusses. This holding pattern continues with a slow cross-fade into the 'Ethnological Forgery Series'-like, pseudo-sitaraga of the aptly titled 'Bombay Stores Disco'. Next up is a Zoroastrian funeral dirge named 'Fingernail R'n'B', a plucked violin and curtains of sound-effects transporting some mythical patriarch across the Styx in his burning longship.

Then it's a ferocious wakey-wakey which cross-splices you out of the trance into the 6/8 time of 'The Body Is the Arrow, the Arms Form the Bow' – over fourteen further, magnificent minutes of shredded, Pärson Sound strings and post-Velvets holler, as that gigantic hollow-bodied tambourine again threatens to flood the concert hall. Waves of Bridget Hayden's strings engulf this track like Chie Mukai and Tony Conrad joined in halfway through on erhu and violin, respectively. Personally, I'd be happy with a full half-hour of this sucker, which (incidentally) does a very un-Orchestra thing and actually ends!

'Mutual Amnesia Sugar' is extremely well named, being a deeply resonant non-groove of deep stasis, shot through with an overpowering seam of baritone synthesizer drone. Only a distant scabies violin melody breaks the moods as it valiantly attempts to scratch an itch that's just out of reach.

Then we're segued into the mysterious, duelling raga banjos of 'Hall 7 Broke My Heart: True as God', which is just two and a half minutes of relapsing post-echo.

'This Is Where No One Worked Out' is more of the same bile. An apparently random, stentorian, Balkan-type acoustic guitar provides the rhythm as aircraft-drone synthesizer attempts to drown out a tone generator and a solitary flautist. All this then cross-fades into the marvellously titled 'Mystical Coughing', whose beautiful seven minutes of low church organ/harmonium drone is the kind of suffocatingly oppressive, John Cale-period Velvet

Underground sound which Lou Reed so successfully Stalinised out of the band as soon as he got the power. I wonder why?

Just as you think it's never gonna end, an old-fashioned cash register invades the proceedings and the chimps' tea party concludes with the bouncy, wannabe forty-five 'Going Out Intending to Dig'. This is massive Krautrock of the early Amon Düül/*Psychedelic Underground* variety, or even Circle without that ludicrous, Freddie Mercury-type singing. You should just buy this album and be done with it, brothers and sisters. Once it insinuates itself into your brain, I'm sure your automaton will send you off to check out another of their oeuvre before you even know it yourself.

They Drone (Two)

For a moment, I thought the heavier and slightly more obvious *Music for Red Breath* might make a better Album of the Month, until *Lino Hi* perplexed me and confused me. And so it was that the newness and evenness of *Dabbling with Gravity and Who You Are* won through. The former albums are both the kind of sonic monsters that sit right next to the dark stuff in your collection and leave strange stains on the CDs either side of them. Both of these albums sound like two huge, hunched giants with pudgy hands, each playing drones on barn-sized synthesizers, as tiny humanoids rush about interrupting the sound with percussive toys, pitch-pipe squarks and sprinkles of distant drum clatter. *Music for Red Breath* is slightly less fully realised than *Lino Hi*. Indeed, the latter album might be their best of all, but I just don't know it well enough to make that judgement yet. I do listen to it a lot, however, and it seems like the most sonically rich.

Lino Hi is real intensity in ten cities, and should be the potential second purchase of any would-be Orchestra groupies. It came out on the American Giardia label and delivered the most un-Orchestral sound so far, dizzying the senses with long super-vibrations of post-Spaceman Three wah-everything – a shudder-thon of fundametalism. The opener is the eight-minute, slow violin scrawl of 'Can I Put My Thumb in Your Pudding Please?'. This is a place I could stay for a long, long time.

It's followed by the rapid-paced, six-minute-long, This Heatian drone of 'Roll On, Roll Off', and the nine-minute fury of 'Chasing a Rabbit', which introduces flugelhorn and hollow tom toms to marvellous effect, before dropping into more typically

Orchestral stuff such as 'Padded Like a Starlight Saint'.

'Airy Way' returns to the exotic, Cale-esque drone of the opening song, while 'TB Radio from a Shady District' is yet more extended drone. Then 'Sink Me' rolls off beyond the quarter-of-an-hour mark with more deep-space trauma. This is the kind of piece which twats you with a wall of noise and which should accompany every mental breakdown. 'Pink Twinkle' cheekily adds a Velvet Underground 'Heroin' chord sequence to stun the listeners at the album's close. A long fade to oblivion shows even the Orchestra have the occasional moment of compassion.

The live album *Long Live the Weeds* illustrates just how well this music works in concert, especially without the benefits of their cross-cut editing technique. Its hugely long drones are sonic catering of the highest order – it's as though several chefs are standing around their simmering vats, stoned and staring.

MMICD is the weakest of the bunch. Here, the group eschewed song titles entirely, opting instead for a more of-the-moment form of cataloguing, in the manner of such ensembles as Marginal Consort, East Bionic Symphonia and Taj Mahal Travellers; you know the kind of thing I mean. The ethereally tough chorale that opens the disc is called '02/09.1'. Then we're off into typically flute'n'spoons-shaking Vibracathedral territory with such titles as '02/02.2', '03/10', '18/10', etc. Cute, but hollow after the fuck-dog-pig of the other stuff.

Single Releases, Solo Projects and Various Vinyl Appearances

Vibracathedral Orchestra on seven-inch single is a mixed blessing because the medium is generally outside the parameters of their experiment. Drone music in shortened form just makes listeners too conscious of the approaching ending. This is because the mind cannot break free, knowing that the conclusion is coming soon, and so anticipates it constantly. I always cite the end of The Beatles' 'I Want You (She's So Heavy)' as the perfect example of a great track ruined by the gimmicky abruptness of its ending (it should have a five-minute fade). And so it is with the mid-tempo, highland drone of Vibracathedral's 'The One You Call the Ghost Train' forty-five. It's all very beautiful, but it still leaves an unsatisfied feeling in the listener. However, 'Oblong 2', on the reverse side of that single, is dynamite: much shorter and more complete, like Comets on Fire's massive, shamanic clear-out, 'Beneath the Ice Age'.

Even more satisfying is the twelve-inch, vinyl-only album which the group shared with the US band Jackie-O Motherfucker (incidentally, featuring pop-artwork worthy of The Residents, Stereolab or Brain Donor). There are just two tracks on the Vibracathedral Orchestra side, but both are superb. The twelve-and-a-half-minute-long 'Wearing Clothes of Ash' is like a piano-led *Paradieswärts Düül*-period drone-athon, with John Cale and Terry Riley guesting on viola and keys. Following this, the sublime 'Baptism Bar Blues' is proof positive that they can rock the riot house with a pure adrenaline rush when the decision is made. Indeed, this seven-minute track is magnificent and should be available to the masses free, or in pill form.

Last year, Neil Campbell's excellent solo LP *Sol Powr* was released to further mess up the guesstimates of who does what in this band. This superb vinyl offering sounds as though Martin Rev had teamed up with Moebius and Roedelius, during their *Cluster II* period. Organs, Casios, cellos (probably) and occasional guitars drive the recording. Were this an official Vibracathedral Orchestra release, it would be one of my favourites.

In Conclusion

So ends my review. If you like music, you're sure to get on like a house on fire with this lot. Also, I'm pretty sure there's lots more from the Orchestra I ain't never heard, and they'll be sure to have had more stuff out by the time you read this. However, if I've provided y'all with a way into these drones, then I've done my job. *Dabbling with Gravity . . .* is the one to start with, but I'm convinced that nearly all their albums could play some part in your future enlightenment. Get down!

Discography

'The One You Call the Ghost Train' b/w 'Oblong Two' (single, tonschacht, 2001)
'Stole Some Sentimental Jewellery' b/w 'David and Jude' (single, split with Low, Misplaced, 2001)
Music for Red Breath (CD-R, 1999)
Lino Hi (Giardia, 1999)
Long Live the Weeds (CD-R, 2001)
MMICD (Ikea packaging CD-R, 2001)

Dabbling with Gravity and Who You Are (VHF, 2002)
Wearing Clothes of Ash/ Baptism Bar Blues (vinyl album, split with Jackie-O Motherfucker, Textile, 2002)

Neil Campbell:
Sol Powr (Lal Lal Lal, 2002)

Vincent Black Shadow

(Heart Break Beat, 2006)

SIDE ONE	SIDE TWO
1 Child of Orion (2.49)	1 Ain't No Law (6.29)
2 Real Wood (5.20)	2 Raoul (2.56)
3 Blow It Up in the Sunshine (3.59)	3 Legend of Sex (4.11)
4 Colours and Feelings (1.10)	4 Drunk in Space (3.09)

This bunch of Baltimore malcontents take their name from an overly endowed, 1936 English motorcycle that crossed Bonneville Salt Flats at one hundred and fifty mph, in 1948, ridden by a mechanic wearing only a bathing suit and sneakers. The motorbike was powered by two five hundred cc engines working together in the form of a hugely belligerent one thousand cc V-twin, located under the rider's seat, which was thus so restricted that one reviewer famously described the engine as looking as though it had been 'forced in with a whip and a chair'. During his short life, my dear, late friend Pete de Freitas, erstwhile drummer in Echo and the Bunnymen, wanted nothing more from life than to be the proud owner of one of these beasts. So this review is for Peter Louis Vincent de Freitas (1961–89). That a band has come along worthy of its legendary automotive namesake is a major result for rock'n'roll.

(I Wanna Be) Gnawing on Bones Like Mark, Don and Mel

OK, motherfuckers, it's official: rock'n'roll is dead, long live rock'n'roll . . . This twenty-first century has finally superseded 1965, 1969 and 1970 . . . and Cleveland 1975, too! It's all been conflated into one single, end-of-the-world *Animal House* party, wherein the frat-rock of The Swamp Rats, The Sparkles, The Sonics and

The Hangmen of Fairfield County nowadays co-habits with the lyrically enlightened post-Doors, post-MC5 early/mid-'70s proto space-metal of Granicus, Groundhogs, Bleib Alien, BÖC and most of Todd Clark's various incarnations. What am I saying? I'm saying, brothers'n'sisters, that the king is dead, long live the king, and all the great truisms and platitudes of the West are henceforth shown to be real . . . Punk's not dead; the north will rise again; don't eat the brown acid; only the industrial heartlands make for classic rock'n'roll; King Arthur's only sleeping; divorces makes winners only out of the lawyers; and that ain't no way to treat a lady . . . I mean, I've had it notarised and authenticated and duplicated in triplicate an' everything! Finally . . . finally . . . finally . . . in Baltimore's Vincent Black Shadow we gotta son-of-Orion lead-singer figurehead, sexy enough to make the (ob)scene kid swoon and the Emo drool, and all sonically delivered by Siamese, twin-lead guitarists formed of Leigh Stephens' bell-custard over a Bill Ward-meets-Scott Krauss-style soul beat that's harsh enough to satisfy even the most overly zealous melted plastic brains of every sexagenerian low-brow with an axe to grind (the kind with a vinyl collection chock-full o'forty-fives by The Wild Colonials, The Primitives, The Wig, The Stereo Shoestrings, The Caretakers of Deception and The Outcasts, plus umpteen anally filed and plastic-covered LPs by Speed, Glue & Shinki, Monoshock, Shockabilly, Terminal Lovers, Tiger B. Smith, Blue Cheer circa *Vincebus Eruptum* and *Outsideinside*, *High Rise Live*, the Mainliner of *Mainliner Sonic*, *Live Album*-period Grand Funk, *Kingdom Come*-era Sir Lord Baltimore, Juan De La Cruz, New Gods' *Aardvark Thru Zymurgy*, Rallizes' *Heavier Than a Death in the Family*, plus any amount of Skydog-styled French boots of The New Order and Sonic's Rendezvous Band).

So sell your motherfucking Bang and (gathering dust) Dust LPs, and pronto, Tonto! That's mostly fifty percent Zep-alike stuff, anyway. And flush your DMZ down the drain, and your Leaf Hound down the pan. No, better still, dump those suckers in a skip so that their market value forces Shadoks to reissue them! Why? Because of Adam Black Savage, brothers'n'sisters; he's the singer with the Vincent Black Shadow and – like Alice and Iggy afore him – he's a sex-bomb to boot, styled and gorgeous and even has his own GHD hair straighteners (the best and hottest on the market, not Nicky Clarke's, as some would claim).

Unlike every other singer in the underground who is *not hot*, Adam Black Savage also has a great attitude towards hygiene, shells out mucho dollar for his hair dye (gotta be Schwartzkopf, natch!) and wears a white shirt that's still as clean when he takes it off at night as when he first put the thing on. And, when yooz laying a horny broad every rock'n'roll night, it's those details (not having surplus PP3s for your wah-wah pedal) that makes your legend grow. You think I'm shucking and jiving ya, don't you, kiddies? Well, I ain't goofing one iota on Brother Black Savage because because because we (you, me, the freaks that count) need each and every figurehead we can muster to prove to the outside world that mung-worship rock'n'roll in the non-corporate sector ain't the mug's game the rock-biz greedheads (A&R twats, CEO cocksuckers, music publishing's old way *agent prevaricateurs* and beaters around the bush) believe it to be.

When you have a quintet as unmercilessly on the right path through the forest as Vincent Black Shadow, all you need to go that extra half-mile to the rocky summit is an Apollonian figurehead, a Dionysian prince of the underworld, a Gerard Way of the Third Way (to put it in Buddhist terms everyone can reach). Who else we got, brothers'n'sisters? Well, I know we've got one über-mod hottie in the form of Plastic Crimewave, who'd most surely cut it on a sartorial level, but even he's too aged, too sage and just too down with Reid Fleming and Flaming Carrot for the tots of today. And, if weez any chance of stopping the already too self-satisfied new American underground from side-stepping the Rock completely and accidentally Franken-morphing into that moustache guy out of Growing (gimme a break!), then Adam Black Savage is the way forward because he has a larynx that sounds like he eats mountains for breakfast, yet, from his look, it's clear that he regularly shags women under twenty-five.

Now, you know me, and I ain't about to lay a 'rock's a young man's game' argument at your doorstep, but it ain't purely the realm of ye oldesters, neither. Motherfuckers, we are representatives of a Heightened Lower Realm. We ain't in the basement with Joey and Dee Dee any more, weez in the sub-basement with Herr Liebling (you seen Uncle Bobby lately? Too scary . . .), and a cadaverous condition is being had by all. And so we need new skin for the old ceremony, new blood for the old veins, and Adam's the only guy wan enough to lure the pouting, sallow youth to our outdoor temples in the groves. Moreover, with regard to the sound made by Vincent Black Shadow, their unrighteous Israeli Wall of Sound issuing forth behind this Great Stone Eater is an ultra-confident, stop–start micro-Detroit machine-shop of the highest order, nay, the newest order! Mix one part of Blue Cheer's 'Out of Focus' with two parts early Pa Ubu ('Non-Alignment Pact', via 'Cloud 149'), then filter all through Beefheart's 'Moonlight on Vermont'. Drain and serve on a bed of Terry Knight production values, and you got this debut LP by Vincent Black Shadow . . .

Music to Bring Down Boeotian Battlements

Vincent Black Shadow is a monumental debut, and damn me if it ain't righteous the way they bring in the whole ship and cargo at just over thirty minutes. Place yourselves in central Greece, brothers'n'sisters, for that is where our tale 'The Legend of Side One' begins, with 'Child of Orion'. High on the broken battlements of Orchomenos sits the heroic, bearded figure of Bobcat Rufus Platt, each drum having been hefted, dragged, threatened and cajoled up to the citadel from the Boeotian Plain below. Bobcat commences a massive soul stomp in the Don Brewer/Scott Krauss manner, and wakes from its slumber the whole of Boeotia, home of Orion. And it's up here high upon the citadels of Orchomenos, ancient capital of Boeotia, that we first glimpse Brother Black Savage searching frantically at the foot of the dusty drystone walling for the eyes of his blinded father, Orion. Insurgents armed with solid-body six-strings join Bobcat high on the citadel and proceed to lambaste the scenery with the kind of braying, Glitter Band-plays-kazoo marching-band guitar snarl that was at its height of popularity in the early post-Christian late 1960s, but which continued to inform the rock genre until the middle of the twenty-second century, via the accidental rediscovery, in 2078, of the *Devotion* LP, an unlikely 1970 hybridised, proto-metal doom epic from the pre-Mahavishnu'd mind of John McLaughlin during his forgotten, Black Sabbath-informed period on Douglas Records.

That's Outer Dave Litz standing in the doorway, his long, dreadlocked hair streaked with dry egg and cereal, for he is the Guitar Muncher and often makes his most beautiful sounds when he's eating the strings. Parallel with Outer is his short-haired, be-shaded counterpart, Dan van Owen. When he's strangling hoary clichés out of his axe, some call him just Dan Owen, but it's the 'van' of vanguard that is the key to this man. And when Dan kicks his middle name into gear, The Van accelerates to new heights.

Over this fully loaded, twin-fuzz, Mekong Delta soul stomp, Adam Black Savage 'fesses up to being the grandson of Poseidon and the son of that great Boeotian hunter who took so much shit from Apollo and Dionysus. It's a barbarian classic, if you'll 'scuse the oxymoron. The ducking and diving, triple riffing of 'Real Wood' kicks in next, a raging Tiger B. Smith, dumb punk-athon, with stop–start rhythms somewhat akin to 'I Want, Need, Love You' by the legendary Australian band The Black Diamonds, but played harder, as though by the *Absolutely Free*-period Mothers.

That bass – what the fuck? A single, torn eight-inch speaker cone recorded with someone's home tape recorder's microphone. Is the Savage yelling 'It's hard work' or 'Sod work!'? Both ways is fine by me, as bottleneck guitars and blistered, bluesy, fuzz-bass underpins the 'American Woman'-styled harmony twin-lead. The Savage screams, 'Tell me I'm a sucker/Tell me I'm a sucker . . .' over and over and fucking over, to its conclusion.

Then, with barely a moment's rest, Savage is singing, 'Heat rays is what we've got going on,' and the small beginning of 'Blow It Up in the Sunshine' suddenly, well, blows up, then opens out into a flattened and shimmering motorik kraut (small 'k') road trip in an open-topped, pre-WWII Mercedes (black with massive fenders), in the style of Can's 'Mother Sky' or The Stooges' 'Loose' – the Savage wishing he was a lightning bug because he's out of control, he's out of control, he's out of control . . . Then, as the urging siren guitars feedback on and into each other in pure, coagulating sonic alchemy, the sky turns red and the Savage's lupine howl announces the sunset, while the feedback guitars, panned now hard right and left, decorate the horizon with the good jismick juice.

Side One concludes with 'Colours and Feelings', a kind of one-minute instrumental 'Boris the Spider' bass-player take on the *Get Carter* theme, which swans in, does a once around the block, then sods off quick. I want more . . .

'Ain't No Law' kicks off Side Two, like Joy Division playing a demented Hawkwind song (*Doremi* period), with effects of the 13th Floor Elevators persuasion, as the catchy-bastard 'Ain't no law/Ain't no law' chorus blasts a seemingly endless repeat;

that is, until they slow it all down to half-speed (this is becoming an excellent habit) and *then* some (Joey Smith-stylee), as the scything, schrieking, feedbacking guitars howl and stratospherise the nacht into a towering, Ack-Ack anti-aircraft-gun search for enemy planes flying too high to be detected up at fifty thousand feet.

Next, we're embarking on the pure *Love It to Death* of 'Raoul', a kind of Alice meets Side Two of the second Grand Funk LP. Darker than the rest is 'Legend of Sex', with its lead bass and Terminal Lovers/ Downside Special rock melody over uncanny and strange chords, eventually dropping down into another classic repeated chorus: 'Does anyone know about the body?'

Some places this band go allow the bass insurgency to climb right up there, freaking out alongside the guitars, leaving excellent room for a fuggy haze of chord-less free-rock to hang about the air-conditioning system and facilitating the entrance of the final song, 'Drunk in Space' which kicks in like early Alice does with the free-rock of 'Return of the Spiders'.

'I know no god,' bawls the Savage over a riff somewhat akin to The Stooges playing a pounding and far more remedial version of 'School's Out'. The Savage would only need to sing 'Let me in' at this point for the Alice–Iggy cycle to be completed, but the twin fifteen minutes of this Vincent Black Shadow are already over, brothers'n'sisters. However, I'll tell you this, gentlemen of the Shadow, you've achieved an excellent and genuine motherfucker of a debut. It's as hard as nails, catchy, obsessive, smart and dumber than almost everything out there. This stuff will be on the compulsory listening list in a few years' time, of that I'm sure. You catchy motherfuckers deserve to go far.

The Samplers

Driven by the unexpected success of 1995's *Krautrocksampler*, and by the procession of CD and cassette-clutching World Freaks who beat a path to my door thereafter, my mind – now encumbered by these mounting piles of sonic gifts from Japan, Italy, Scandinavia and other obscure rock'n'roll sources – gradually began to formulate other samplers which could hopefully, some time in the distant future, appear as mega-features in my Head Heritage Album of the Month. Don't hold your breath, Cope. It's gonna be a slow, slow process. And so, between 2000–2004 CE, I collected and I stored, waiting patiently for the Cultural Coffers to fill up. Slowly, ever so slowly. Even my future book *Japrocksampler* began in this painstakingly slow manner, and for the first few years I was shown little evidence that even a hefty delve into the Japanese music of the '60s and '70s could produce anything more than a substantial magazine-sized article. But throughout those first four years of Album of the Month, a Danish publisher by the name of Ole Knudsen took it upon himself to furnish, nay, indoctrinate me with his own personal overview of the Danish underground. On account of Ole's own musical status within that '60s/'70s scene, many of his recommendations were just too hippie or too prog for my own tastes. But as his persistence synchronised with my Danish research for my tome *The Megalithic European*, I soon found scattered record shops in Copenhagen, Odense and Aarhus that gave me the opportunity to check things out for myself, and the Dansk repository was on its way. Better still, with my discovery of Copenhagen's hippie commune at the former USAF base now retitled Free Christiania, I was provided with a righteous Truth Seeker element, which instantly injected a heroic aspect to the unfolding tale of these distant Scandos. And thus this first breakthrough in the Sampler series came in June 2004 CE, with the publication of *Danskrocksampler*.

Thereafter, each Sampler grew similarly slowly across that decade of the noughties, perhaps a chance meeting with another music maniac temporarily boosting one particular musical reservoir, then another and another, until that time has come when the six beasts that stand before you have stared green-eyed at the successes of *Krautrocksampler* and *Japrocksampler* and are now themselves demanding equal rights of publication. But this Sampler Circus that I have cobbled together, this bizarre *ménage à rie*, though all of my own vision, was not all of my own research. For example, on learning of my intended *Postpunksampler*, Jon Savage petitioned me with enough lost 45s to fill up two-thirds of *Postpunksampler 2*. The precise metaphor for my *Hardrocksampler* owed its origins to endless communications with author The Seth Man, whose own music mission throughout this past decade has – on his Head Heritage-hosted *The Book of Seth* – often mined territory parallel to my own. And my *Japrocksampler* burst forth when a series of hourly phone calls to the late Trevor Manwaring coincided with an impromptu visit to David Keenan up in Argyllshire. Indeed, only the *Krautrocksampler* is all of my own research, and even that was because there was just nothing to go on in those pre-Internet days. But I still believe that the paucity of the information in that book was more than made up for by the kosmische music itself and the heroic tales of each of those startling musicians. However, its lack of republication is entirely due to my current and enduring belief in the book's redundancy. For the *Krautrocksampler* was a cosmic cultural signpost, no more and no less. And like all of the Samplers brung forth in *Copendium*, its success lay in my daring to deploy micro-histories of the musicians *and* to give specific advice on what and where to shell out your shitters. Pragmatic motherfucker, ain't I? So go forth now and snare some more lost essentials from the skyscraper-high top shelves of Lord Yatesbury's Archive, and praise me for giving such shape and spiritual form to your Kapitalism! Yowzah!

Detroitrocksampler

1 The Rationals: Guitar Army (3.18) (1969)
2 MC5: Looking at You (3.05) (1968)
3 Alice Cooper: Long Way to Go (3.05) (1971)
4 The Up: Together (4.23) (1968)
5 The Amboy Dukes: Journey to the Centre of the Mind (3.14) (1968)
6 Don and the Wanderers: On the Road (2.18) (1968)
7 Bob Seger System: Heavy Music (2.39) (1967)
8 The Mynah Birds: I've Got You in My Soul (2.29) (1966)
9 Third Power: Persecution (3.25) (1970)
10 Detroit: Rock'n'roll (5.53) (1971)
11 Grand Funk Railroad: Inside Looking Out (9.32) (1969)
12 The Pleasure Seekers: What a Way to Die (2.14) (1966)
13 Unrelated Segments: Story of My Life (2.38) (1967)
14 Terry Knight and the Pack: How Much More? (2.30) (1967)
15 The Woolies: Who Do You Love? (2.00) (1967)
16 The Underdogs: Love's Gone Bad (2.27) (1966)
17 SRC: Black Sheep (3.47) (1968)
18 Flaming Ember: Gotta Get Away (4.20) (1969)
19 Frijid Pink: House of the Rising Sun (4.39) (1970)
20 The Stooges: Down on the Street (2.47) (1970)
21 Savage Grace: All Along the Watchtower (5.41) (1971)
22 The Frost: Rock'n'roll Music (3.00) (1969)
23 MC5: Borderline (3.11) (1969)
24 Funkadelic: Cosmic Slop (3.21) (1973)
25 Wayne Kramer: Get Some (3.38) (1977)
26 The New Order: Declaration of War (2.48) (1976)
27 Ascension: Get Ready (8.54) (1973)
28 Destroy All Monsters: You're Gonna Die (2.52) (1977)

29 Sonic's Rendezvous Band: City Slang (5.15) (1977)
30 Southbound Freeway: Psychedelic Used Car Lot Blues (2.30) (1967)
31 Bob Seger System: 2+2=? (2.45) (1967)
32 Unrelated Segments: Where You Gonna Go? (1967)
33 Terry Knight and the Pack: Numbers (2.08) (1966)
34 Tidal Waves: Farmer John (2.09) (1966)
35 The Früt: Keep on Truckin' (2.56) (1971)
36 ? and the Mysterians: Girl (2.18) (1967)
37 The Iguanas: Mona (2.39) (1966)
38 The Stooges: Asthma Attack (6.36) (1969)

I should warn you in advance that there ain't no chronology to this tracklisting, just an avalanche of burning, devil's music. I figured I was obliged to commence with The Rationals' 'Guitar Army' on account of its John Sinclair connection and to conclude with The Stooges' 'Asthma Attack' – Iggy's homage to Kim Fowley's expectorating – because only the dutiful would be left standing at compilation's end.

Avebury, Mecca, Jerusalem, Rome, Detroit

Detroit, Michigan, was the epicentre of twentieth-century Western culture, a sacred navel in whose lakeside bosom dwelt the two greatest prophets of their time: the electric-light-bringing Thomas Edison – whose company General Electric remains, to this day, one of the largest in the world – and Henry Ford, whose percipient prophecy – 'I will make a motorcar for the multitude [to] enjoy hours of pleasure in God's great open spaces' – would later be realised in Ford's legendary Model T. 'I'm going to democratize the automobile,' declared Ford early on, although his original intention of bringing forth only eco-friendly, hemp-fuelled automobiles (to be built on his father's vast hemp farm) would soon be dashed by the unrighteous drive of business rivals and cynical partners. But, however tragically the rise of the automobile industry has turned out for we Moderns, let us always remember how Henry Ford's visionary ideas freed working men and women of the early twentieth century – at least temporarily – from the mind-numbing drudgery of their daily grind upon the land.

Created on a mechanical assembly line, the revolutionary Model T reinforced those hoary Puritan values of self-reliance that America's first white arrivals had brought with them to Plymouth Rock, encouraging other car-makers across America to establish their auto-manufacturing plants in Detroit, Michigan. And if it is true, as C. G. Jung attests, that a culture's greatest interests are most evident from the roles of those buildings that dominate its horizons, then the sky-hugging auto factories of Detroit might well be classed as the cathedrals of this brand-new secular age.

During World War II, however, most of the Detroit auto industry was temporarily given over to the building of tanks and warplanes, and it was not until 1948 that the big three car corporations – Ford, Chrysler and General Motors – unveiled their first postwar automobiles. But what automobiles they were! Desperate to shrug off the drab olive and khaki nightmares of wartime, the car-industry moguls rewarded the American public by unleashing upon them highly exotic new products more in keeping with the chariots of Ancient Rome. Big, independent car companies brought forth futuristic chromium steeds with warplane-inspired names such as the Hudson Jet and Nash Airflyte, while new Studebakers even arrived replete with a non-functional propeller boss slap bang in the centre of their bullet-styled facades. Over at General Motors, chief designer Harley Earl went several airmiles further by adding missile-shaped hood ornaments to the first postwar Oldsmobiles, affixing bombsight-style hood adornments and lighting-up portholes to Buick's upmarket Roadmaster series, and – inspired by the USAF's P-38 Lightning fighter – appending miniature tailfins to his top-of-the-range Cadillacs. 'Go all the way, and then back off,' was Harley Earl's enlightened motto.

Electrifying Edisonian Rock'n'roll

Its landscapes and cities untouched by the carpet-bombing which had shattered Europe and Japan, triumphant, postwar America remained splendidly intact: the sole capitalist culture genuinely worthy of eulogising in poetry and song. So, while Oldsmobile founder Ransom E. Olds was an old-fashioned racist who insisted that whites alone be allowed to build cars in his Lansing factory, it was to Oldsmobile's brand-new, supercharged 'Rocket 88' that Afro-American singer Jackie Brenston turned for his subject matter. Recorded in March 1951, 'Rocket 88' is generally regarded as the first true rock'n'roll song. However, despite it being unfairly credited by Chess Records to the entirely invented 'Jackie Brenston and his Delta Cats', the song's rhythms were, in truth, laid down by Ike Turner's Kings of Rhythm, with whom Brenston was merely the sax player. Nonetheless, this record *was* rock'n'roll, and highly barbarian it was, too, propelled through a broken, distorted amplifier by Ike's insistent, urgent, ice-blue, solid-body Fender electric guitar.

Like the car industry, rock'n'roll existed only because of huge advances in twentieth-century technology. And, whereas jazz could have survived the non-invention of Adolphe Sax's nineteenth-century saxophone, the beautiful Fender Stratocaster belonging to proto-rocker Ike Turner would, without the prophet Thomas Edison, have been no more than an ultra-modern lump of wood. Although white society would initially dismiss such outbursts as 'Rocket 88' as 'the devil's music', the song's patriotic subject matter – being a product made in Detroit by a thriving US auto industry – forged an unbreakable link between the new electric music and fast cars. It was true that jazz had also long eulogised car culture, but the future was electric, and from here on in jazz would be caught on the back foot, constantly fending off the 'old-timer' tag on account of its ostensibly acoustic nature. Henceforth – to bastardise the words of Duke Ellington's 1943 jazz hit – 'It don't mean a piss if it ain't got that hiss.' Now, c'mon!

Diss Integration in the Motor City!

Although the feisty youth music celebrated within the grooves of this here *Detroitrocksampler* was mostly made by urbanite Michigan musicians of a Caucasian or Latino background, musicologists have long emphasised the particularly strong Afro-American influence of soul music, gospel and R&B upon the Detroit rock scene, thanks to the pervasive presence in the Motor City of Berry Gordy's Motown empire. So it comes as a shock to discover that local government agencies in Detroit, far from operating integrated and enlightened race policies ahead of other northern cities, had long chosen to keep black and white communities steadfastly apart, citing the events of the city's first race riot in 1863 as their excuse. Thereafter, Detroit's burgeoning African-American population regularly complained about their lack of job opportunities, of police brutality and of housing discrimination.

During World War II, however, Detroit's racist employment policies were forcibly lifted – albeit temporarily – by Franklin Roosevelt's Fair Employment Practices Committee, luring a further fifty thousand African-Americans, mainly from the Deep South, to seek employment at one of Michigan's multitude of aircraft and tank factories. However, a second race riot, in 1943, revealed deep-seated and institutionally racist practices, not least the fact that eighty-five percent of those rioters arrested had been black. And it was the continuance of these nefarious racist practices throughout the '50s into the early '60s to which the black activist Malcolm X referred when he commented in his 1965 autobiography: 'The truth is that "integration" is an image, it's a foxy Northern liberal's smoke-screen that confuses the true wants of the American black man.' Continuing his tirade elsewhere, X concluded: 'I know nothing of the South. I am a creation of the Northern white man and of his hypocritical attitude towards the Negro.'

The Civil Rights era was by now upon Detroit, and African-American leaders seized their opportunities like never before. Whitney Young, for one, transformed the traditionally conservative National Urban League into a radical organisation, using his position as executive director to goad corporations into hiring increasing numbers of black Americans. In Detroit, Young even befriended Ford Motor Company's new boss, Henry Ford II, promising the industrialist in 1966 that, should he help promote integration in Detroit's heavy industry, Young's PR machine would ensure that Ford would be perceived as 'the White Moses'.

Nonetheless, the following year Detroit's third set of major race riots broke out during heavy-handed policing one hot July '67 night. And it was from the poetic heart of this powder keg, this city of perpetual race problems and heavy industry, that all of the music on *Detroitrocksampler* was brought forth, Detroit's apartheid practices and its ambivalence, nay, antipathy towards racial integration, surely contributing hugely to the extraordinary heaviness of even the poppiest songs contained herein. Wayne Kramer, of the MC5, has described the significant status and enormous respect enjoyed by Motown's musicians among his own peers – 'Play like [James] Jamerson [Motown's renowned in-house bassist],' he always urged the Five's Michael Davis. But even to a hip, white insider such as Kramer these Motown guys were remote figures from another world.

So, with all that in mind, let's enjoy the music of *Detroitrocksampler*, and hopefully the city's own unique worldview will – as you read the thirty-eight song reviews – unfold before your melted plastic brains. Dig in, motherfuckers!

The Rationals: Guitar Army
(Genesis, 1969)

Despite lending its name to White Panther poet/guru John Sinclair's classic 1971 book of prison and street writings, The Rationals' opening salvo – exhilarating, futuristic and psychedelic as it was – had only the outward appearance of being the soundtrack to Detroit revolution; as singer Scott Morgan admitted: 'I ain't talking about burning it down, I'm just talking about getting down.' Still, for all you kiddies who know next to nothing of The Rationals, I gots to tell you that by the release of their 'Guitar Army' forty-five, this quartet had progressed in leaps and bounds from their mid-'60s beginnings, delivering white-soul covers of songs such as Aretha's 'Respect'. Moreover, leader Morgan would go on to co-front Fred 'Sonic' Smith's late-'70s group, Sonic's Rendezvous Band – evidence, indeed, of his heavy rep among those motherfuckers in the know. Unfortunately, The Rationals' eponymous 1969 LP could in no way sustain the burning desires of this single, which occupies a rare and blissful space somewhere between power-trio period Mark, Mel and Don and the more tight-ass studio-soul moments of the MC5's patchy *Back in the USA* – that is, if it hadn't been 'produced' into the abortion clinic by Bruce Springclean's corpulent, middle-brow manager-to-be.

MC5: Looking at You
(A-Square, 1968)

Surely one of the noisiest slabs o'seven-inch vinyl ever commercially released, the gratuitous sonic overkill of the Five's 'Looking at You' defeats even The Stereo Shoestrings' vicious 'On the Road South' and The Outcasts' berserk '1523 Blair' for sheer apocalyptic mind-death. Hell, kiddies, while the rest of the Five boys struggle even to keep their 'song' together, Brother Wayne haemorrhages so much feedbacking forked lightning and motorpsycho madness over the track that The Misunderstood's demonic Glenn Ross Campbell musta been suicidal on hearing the results. And trying to compare this with the anaemic 1970 LP versh only makes ya wanna break corporate heads in disgust.

Alice Cooper: Long Way to Go
(Warner Bros, 1971)

Free at last from their merely tiresome,

too overtly Frank Zappa-influenced Straight Records period, Arizona's heavy quintet Alice Cooper took up residence in their spiritual home of Detroit, hired Toronto's Bob Ezrin as producer and set about subsuming the MC5's entire oeuvre into their next LP, *Love It to Death.* Herein, hunky main songwriter Michael Bruce barfed out this Fivean teen anthem, while ghoul-eyed Dennis Dunaway stole the entire show with his pulsing bass lines, and Toronto Bob did his best to capsize the fucker with a twee, piano-boogie middle eight; Canadians, sheesh! Later that year, Detroit's Channel 28 had the pleasure of presenting Dunaway and co. performing an elongated versh of *Love It to Death*'s lyrically perplexing 'Is It My Body', during which singer Herr Vincent Furnier (a.k.a. Alice Cooper) stripped down to the kind of odd, disgusting grundies that even senile old biddies would baulk at. I know. When I played said performance at the climax of *Discover Odin*, my 2001 British Museum festival, several members of the audience walked out and a few complained. Nevertheless, before he nicked his band's name for his solo persona and tried to sell us that rancid, top-hatted, *Welcome to My Nightmare* schtick, old Vince Furnier was a right *Vincebus Eruptum.*

The Up: Together
(Total Energy, 1968)

Hugely influenced by the MC5 and managed by David Sinclair, brother of John, The Up began life back in high school in the mid-'60s as The Citations, until band leaders Gary and Bob Rasmussen hooked up with the Grande Ballroom's stage announcer, Franklin Bach, who became their singer and spokesman. Obviously nervous about having named their band after Detroit's mythical Ford publicity disaster, the Edsel Citation, the band briefly became known as Brand X before settling on The Up as a positive response to hanging out on the politicised campus at Wayne State University. Thereafter, they were invited to support the MC5 at the Grande, and followed John Sinclair's Trans-Love Energies commune when it transplanted to Ann Arbor, where they promoted an exclusively revolutionary image by appearing among allotments of massive cannabis plants while toting rifles and Fenders. C'mon! Nowadays best known for their tribal, red-vinyl single 'Just Like an Aborigine', it is the incendiary rush and propellant roar of 'Together' that provides we Moderns with the greatest evidence of The Up's then-heartstopping stage act.

The Amboy Dukes: Journey to the Centre of the Mind
(Mainstream, 1968)

Ever time he hears this fucking amazing (although admittedly excruciatingly stupid) seven-inch seer/sucker, it must fucking kill drug-free lion-mauler Ted Nugent that twenty-second-century foxes around the globe will remember him not as the Ben Turpin-eyed, chest-beating proto-Angus of 'Dag Nabbit, Who's Manhandled My New Fangled Poo-Mangle' or whatever the fuck it's called, but as the pert'n'wailing, be-suited, spike-a-delic paladin of Sandoz. Bah! It's true, Teddy boy! So, however many racoons ye barbie tonight, you ornery retard from the frontiers of daft, to the world of tomorrow you're forever wedded to singer John Knight's earnest declarations of faith in the microdot. Gotcha, you micro-twat!

Don and the Wanderers: On the Road
(Kustom, 1968)

Hailing from the small town of Belding, about thirty miles north of Grand Rapids, Don and the Wanderers was an exclusively family affair whose world-weary contribution to this here compilation disguises the fact that the musicians involved were all still teenagers and were managed by their leader's father, Russ Thompson. All becomes clear, however, when we discover that 'On the Road' was imposed upon the Wanderers by producer and local star Dick Wagner, who'd originally written and released the song one year previously while leading The Bossmen. This time around, however, Wagner took his protégés into the tiny Audio Studios, in the basement of Cleveland's WKYC Radio, where he fuzzed up the Bossmen's garage stylings to suit the current heavy trends, producing for the Wanderers a classically deranged, lost garage single that still stands head'n'shoulders above almost all of their contemporaries.

Bob Seger System: Heavy Music
(Capitol, 1967)

Yeah, yeah, punks, I know yooz all wondering why Boring Bob, a.k.a. Snoring Seger, lifted Tommy James and the Shondells' 'Mony Mony' for the basis of this superb A-side. But, as 'Mony Mony' didn't appear until almost a full year later – mid-1968 – Tommy James was obviously smoke-screening furiously when he commented: 'Songs like "Mony Mony" aren't really written, they're sort of hanging in space.' Yeah, right; 'aren't really written by me' is what James was trying to avoid saying. Anyway, by utilising a superb piano/bass-guitar riff as the vehicle on which to build his workout, and employing an occasional stop–start lifted directly from Music Machine's 'Talk Talk', Bob Seger created this vast 'song about the song', which was intended to transport listeners 'deeper' into the music than ever before. 'Don't you ever feel like going insane when the drums begin to pound?' wails Seger, as the tension mounts and the vocal collective support the singer's every emotion, James Brown-style. And, all the time, the 'heavy music' – somewhere midway between the all-purpose Cannibal and the Headhunters/Strangeloves party clatter and the pomp of Phil Spector – drags us further and further into that grey area between dancing and fucking. 'Deeper, deeper,' hectors our hero to his girl, to his band and to his radio audience, until – like Cheech and Chong's Basketball Jones – he's calling out across the whole fucking world, rendering all future copies merely 'Phoney, Phoney'. Yowzah!

The Mynah Birds: I've Got You in My Soul
(Motown demo, 1966)

Who knows what greatness might have been achieved at Motown had this unstable and integrated proto-supergroup not exploded in a fit of draft-board and work-permit problems? Still, despite being relegated to no more than one of rock'n'roll's mythical near-misses, the temporary union of vocalist Rick 'Super Freak' James with Neil 'Shakey' Young and future Buffalo Springfield bassist/guru Bruce Palmer inevitably stuffs the head of any Utopian music obsessive with wall-to-wall 'what ifs', especially when the funky contents of 'I've Got You in My Soul' are trotted out as evidence. Shit, this is good: the vocal delivery, Young's harmonica, that compelling groove and, especially, Van Morrison's magnificent song. Recorded in February '66, at Motown's Detroit studio on West Grand Boulevard, 'I've Got You in My Soul' was intended for inclusion on The Mynah Birds' debut LP – the first fruits of a seven-year-contract, allegedly – that is, until the untimely arrest of singer James by US Navy police on a charge of desertion. Bassist Bruce Palmer does at least provide us with one unforgettable image of this lost supergroup at the height of their onstage powers: 'Neil would stop playing lead, do a harp solo, throw the harmonica way up into the air and Ricky would catch it and continue the solo.'

THIRD POWER: PERSECUTION
(Vanguard, 1970)

Talk about a storm in a teacup, guys; I mean, lighten up. While Detroit's Black Panthers were getting set up by the CIA, and the MC5 had tanks at their door, Third Power's singer/bassist Jem Targal screamed 'persecution' just because his friends didn't like the way he played guitar. Hail, kiddies, they even called him names! OK, forget the Nancy subject matter and just dig the fucking Heavy, will ya? I mean, musically this is an 'I Can See for Miles'-style display that's up there with the baddest. Mercifully, there's little in this song of the turgid Mountain and Cream influence known to permeate much of Third Power's other material. Instead, this epic power-statement handles like a purple 1970 Dodge Challenger – at its happiest around ninety mph; indeed, it probably appealed to the very same Vietnam vets that Chrysler was courting. Unfortunately, while Third Power's debut LP *Believe* was occasionally varied and excellent – 'Lost in a Daydream' and 'Passed By' sound like Arthur Lee – the disc made its first appearance while Vanguard Records were experiencing a distribution nightmare which stalled the band's career, proving that Targal's mealy-mouthed friends were right when they said that he was 'never gonna be a star!'

DETROIT: ROCK'N'ROLL
(Paramount, 1971)

Struggling to replicate his massive '60s success fronting The Detroit Wheels, soul singer extraordinaire Mitch Ryder bowed to the heaviness of the early '70s by co-opting the services of local bikers and long-time musician friends to create his 'rough street band' Detroit, whose enormous sound came from its multiple percussionists, female backing singers and the wailing lead guitar of future Lou Reed sideman Steve Hunter. Signing to Paramount Records, the band recorded half of their self-titled debut LP at RCA's Chicago studio, before Toronto Bob Ezrin stepped in to complete the project up in Canada. And it was Ezrin who savvily suggested this vast, six-minute version of Lou Reed's classic radio song, later to be appropriated by The Runaways for their 1977 LP *Live in Japan.* And what a colossus this arrangement turned out to be, as cowbell honked, Hammond organ shuddered and shook and gospel chicks billed'n'cooed, while Mitch brung the house down with his parched, pleading vocals. Released as a single, 'Rock'n'roll' failed to turn around Ryder's failing fortunes and never made the Top Forty. It did, however, find favour with the song's writer, Reed commenting at the time: 'That's the way it was supposed to sound.'

Grand Funk Railroad: Inside Looking Out
(Capitol, 1969)

Disparaged by the contemporary music press for their refusal to give interviews, their naïve trust in mentor/producer Terry Knight and singer/guitarist Mark Farner's obstinately heroic Apache Jock image, it's only by applying twenty-twenty hindsight and employing a twenty-first-century open mind of Anglican proportions that we're forced to conclude that, fuck me, they was good! Yup, all those mid-'60s years spent backing up then-singer Terry Knight meant an almost total absence of the then-prevalent guitar dry wank – Cream's noodling, the albatross blues of Ten Years After's Alvin Lee, Jimmy Page's violin bow mucking about, oh, you name it – Grand Funk substituting, instead, seemingly endless R&B grooves deployed with all the caveman subtlety of the Japanese army during the Rape of Nanking. That their (arguably) finest moment was achieved on this Animals cover versh is not a comment on Grand Funk's inability to write great songs, either; hell, this classy tune has long been the flagship of such other greats as The Obsessed and Tight Bro's from Way Back When. But what draws rock nutters back again and again and again to this nine-minute behemoth is the sheer exhilaration created by Mark, Mel and Don's incredible power-drives. It's as though they were performing extracts from twenty classic soul-stompers, reducing each to the bite-size highpoints required for the nowadays obsolete art form known as 'the medley'. Yup, kiddies, listen to Grand Funk Railroad as though each song was a performance of several medleys and your worldview opens up before you. Indeed, what you'd previously dismissed as heavy-metal overkill actually becomes soul music as played by the USAF!

The Pleasure Seekers: What a Way to Die
(Hideout, 1966)

Raised in the home of jazz musician Art Quatro, in the Detroit suburbs of Grosse Pointe, Suzi Quatro and her sisters Arlene and Patti were all products of the Hideout Club scene, where fourteen-year-old Suzi worked behind the bar selling Coca-Cola. But when Suzi and Patti (seventeen) complained to club owner Dave Leone about the poor quality of acts passing through the Hideout, he goaded them into forming The Pleasure Seekers by securing instrument deals for Arlene and Patti with local music shops, while Quatro Senior bequeathed his precious 1957 Fender Precision bass to Suzi, now the band's lead vocalist. Initially dismissed as no more than a jailbait novelty, The Pleasure Seekers' performances at the Hideout gained fans through the sheer excitement of their performances and Suzi's unyielding vocals, eventually earning them the doubtful honour of playing on a USO tour to troops in Vietnam. Unfortunately, when both of their Hideout Records singles flopped, The Pleasure Seekers were seemingly consigned to oblivion . . . that is, until 'What a Way to Die' – their classic homage to teenage drinking – surfaced in 1980 as the title track of one of the greatest post-*Nuggets/Pebbles* garage-rock compilations. 'Your loving fluctuates, baby/But everybody knows the temperature always stays the same on an ice-cold bottle of Stroh's!' Now c'mon, what right-minder could fail to melt with such inspirational, nay, aspirational lyrics as these?

Unrelated Segments: Story of My Life
(Hanna Barbera, 1967)

Possessed of a singular voodoo that pervaded each of their three forty-fives – 'Story of My Life', 'Where You Gonna Go?' and 'Cry, Cry, Cry' – Unrelated Segments were a highly original group whose songs all revolved around the jarring Dervish tones of guitarist Rory Mack and the self-absorbed lyrics of singer Ron Stults, whose subject matter and mewling, hectoring vocal style would probably have suited a full-length LP better than the seven-inch format. Dammit, this was no garage band, brothers'n'sisters; they played with both the subtlety and daring of a big hit band. And just feel the bubbling, bumping, pumping bass that Barry Van Engelen imposes on the song's final verse; it's quality, m'dears, real quality. Released on Detroit's tiny SVR label, 'The Story of My Life' was received with rapture across Michigan, gaining heavy enough local airplay for the song to be picked up for national release by Hanna-Barbera Records. That the song was no national hit is a crying shame.

Terry Knight and the Pack: How Much More?
(Lucky Eleven, 1967)

What a monumental recording this is. Sheesh! For sheer cussed teenage lip, 'How Much More?' sits right up there with 'Get Off of My Cloud'. And, like The Swamp Rats' legendary

'Rats' Revenge', the snot-gobbling call-and-answer vocals contained herein lend masses of immediate character to the Pack themselves. I don't half wish Tez'n'co. coulda barfed out a few more of these two-n'arf-minute epics. Unfortunately, he and the Pack was too busy chasing the hits . . . which perpetually eluded them. So, between 1965 and '67, the group failed nine times to crack the national Top One Hundred, although in the process delivered to their Lucky Eleven record label a crazily mixed-up string of . . . well, everything, from distraught, romantic piano ballads to calypsos, Mexican songs, terrible, *terribly* English imitations and hi-kwol garage complain-athons. Talk about a mixed metaphor, motherfuckers! For fuck's sake, their scattershot releases even included random versions of such chestnuts as Bob and Earl's 'The Harlem Shuffle', The Yardbirds' 'Mr, You're a Better Man Than I', the Stones' 'Lady Jane' and even Ben E. King's blub-a-long Italian makeover 'I Who Have Nothing'. But still, the public would not buy into Tez's TV histrionics and self-appointed role as the world's first 'air lyricist'. When, at last, our stubborn Knight got the public's thumbs-down message through his thick skull, he returned briefly to his former DJ day job, only to discover that his erstwhile, equally failing cohorts had formed a band called Grand Funk Railroad and asked if he would be their manager. Thereafter, mad at the bastards for making it big without him, Knight proceeded to rip off Mark Farner, Don Brewer and Mel Schacher to the tune of a very great deal. Oh, if only Terry Knight had stuck to garage classics like 'Numbers', 'Love, Love, Love, Love, Love' and 'How Much More?'. The poor guy was murdered in 2004.

The Woolies: Who Do You Love?
(Dunhill, 1967)

Winners of Vox Amplifiers' 1966 'Best Band in the Land' competition, the Dearborn-based Woolies were shocked to discover that their first prize of a record contract and a trip to Hollywood 'turned out to be a big fraud', as group leader Bob Baldori would later comment. Fearful of The Woolies' threats of negative publicity, however, the Vox promoters at least agreed to pay for plane tickets to Los Angeles, where the five musicians hawked their five-song demo tape around several labels before successfully wooing Lou Adler's ABC-Dunhill label. Entering LA's Western Sound Studios the following day, they nailed this stunning Bo Diddley cover and headed for home, where the record would peak at Number Three on WKNR's prestigious 'Music Guide'. Heavy radio play in the Chicago area soon pushed the forty-five into the national Top One Hundred, where it unfortunately stalled at Number Ninety-five. Nevertheless, this glimpse of stardom increased The Woolies' Detroit kudos so much that Chuck Berry requested them as backing band for all future Detroit shows, and Russ Gibb invited them to support the MC5 at the Grande Ballroom's second weekend.

The Underdogs: Love's Gone Bad
(VIP, 1966)

As veterans of Dave Leone's legendary teen dance hangout the Hideout Club, the six-piece Underdogs made their recording debut in 1965, when Leone chose their song 'Man in the Glass' to represent his venue's first venture as a record company. The song's immediate radio success brought Hideaway a lucrative deal with Frank Sinatra's Reprise label, who unfortunately called off their promo campaign on discovering that the song's lyricist, Buzz Van Houten, had stolen the words from a poem representing Alcoholics Anonymous! Reduced now to a quartet, The Underdogs' fortunes continued to rise, however, with the release of two excellent, Bob Seger-produced forty-fives. These discs still failed to sell in quantity, but both received such constant airing on Detroit radio that the band came to the attention of Motown, where producer Clarence Paul suggested they try a remake of 'Love's Gone Bad', a recent near miss for Motown's white chanteuse, Chris Clark. Accompanied by two Motown legends – bass player James Jamerson and organist Earl Van Dyke – The Underdogs stripped Clark's organ-dominated version of its clutter, sensationally revisioning it in the clipped, melodramatic style of The Yardbirds' 'Mr, You're a Better Man Than I', as played by the Funk Brothers. The superb results were such that everyone outside Detroit presumed the band was black. Unfortunately, when The Underdogs were booked on the 1966 'Motortown Revue' alongside such luminaries as Stevie Wonder, Gladys Knight and Martha Reeves, their whiteness merely confounded black audiences, and their single was relegated to a release on Motown's VIP Records subsidiary – this classy slab of garage R&B never even breaking into the pop chart's Top One Hundred.

SRC: Black Sheep
(Capitol, 1968)

Despite its creators having long ago

been relegated to the great list of mighta beens, SRC's wondrous 'Black Sheep' – with its mournfully wailing, fuzz-guitar motifs and arpeggiating, mid-paced organ chords – remains one of the most poetic lost classics of the late '60s. Ah, that glorious chorus . . . Altogether now: 'Black sheep, outcast, misfit, Ishmael/Every stranger each his own tale.'

Beginning his career as lead vocalist for the now-legendary Chosen Few at the prestigious opening of Detroit's Grande Ballroom, alongside guitarists Ron Asheton and James Williamson, SRC's Scott Richardson was rightfully considered a hot ticket among the city's hardest rockers. So it was to Richardson's door that the hilariously named Quackenbush brothers – organist Glenn and guitarist Gary – beat a path when they made their decision to split up their school band, The Fugitives, and get serious. Determined to secure full-time work, the new band was taken under the wing of legendary Michigan entrepreneur Jeep Holland, who – clearly mindful of the impact made by British pop stars Cliff and Keith Richard (a.k.a. Keith Richards) – shortened singer Scott's surname and renamed the band The Scott Richard Case. Throughout the 1968–70 period, Jeep Holland tirelessly pushed SRC as a Michigan-wide band but, even after signing an album deal with Capitol Records, no national success was forthcoming. The reason, from what I've heard of SRC, was down to too much of their music being so-so a-go-go and too many of their songs being simply unmemorable. And at a time when the word 'Detroit' equated to tear-ass, high-energy rock or Motown soul classics, it was perhaps the overly reasonable sound and thoughtful songwriting of SRC which let the band down. No matter, let's remember them for this truly superb Detroit anthem to the underdog . . . nay, to the black sheep, motherfuckers!

Flaming Ember: Gotta Get Away
(Ric Tic, 1969)

Starting out, in 1964, as The Flaming Embers, this white-soul quartet spent half a decade aping black acts in an attempt to persuade Berry Gordy to sign them to Motown, but the closest they could get was when the label bought out Ed Wingate's Golden World and Ric Tic record labels, Flaming Ember getting themselves included in the deal. The band finally achieved national success when 1969's awful 'Mind, Body and Soul' peaked at Number Twenty-six on the

Billboard chart – the equally vapid 'Westbound Number Nine' later hitting the Number Fifteen spot. Here, they're represented by the beautiful gospel majesty of 'Gotta Get Away', a fairly George Clintonesque mega-production worthy of early Funkadelic. Thereafter, Flaming Ember renamed themselves after their most well-known hit ('Mind, Body and Soul') and set about trawling the troughs of the chicken-in-a-basket scene.

Frijid Pink: House of the Rising Sun
(Parrot, 1970)

Embarrassed that his band's demo tape had failed to impress his girlfriend's father, Paul Cannon, then musical director of Detroit's WKNR radio station, Frijid Pink's drummer Richard Stevers was about to make his exit from the station when a guitar blitz at the cassette's end suddenly blasted out of nowhere: a colossally overdriven version of The Animals' hoary anthem, 'House of the Rising Sun'. Perking up at last, Cannon insisted that it was a guaranteed monster hit. 'But it's already the B-side of our current single,' blurted Stevers. Cannon suggested Parrot Records flip the A-side, and within months the song was a worldwide hit – four months in the UK Top Seventy-Five and eleven weeks at Number One in Germany.

The Stooges: Down on the Street
(Elektra, 1970)

In a somewhat pathetic attempt to get some radio play with a seven-inch single, Elektra persuaded former Kingsmen and then-current Stooges producer Don Galluci to add some classy keyboard to *Funhouse*'s opening track. The Don having served up the ur-business seven years previously on 'Louie Louie', no right-minder could then have expected Galluci to daub not frat-garage über-whumpf but hoary, sub-sub-Doorsian Manzadrek all over his own hard work. That Galluci had no idea of the quality of the work he was undertaking with *Funhouse* is strikingly evident from this shameless contribution to Lizard King homage. But, best of all, it combines with that moment in 'TV Eye' when the Ig screams 'Brother, brother' to showcase his Jimbo fixations most succinctly.

Savage Grace: All Along the Watchtower
(Reprise, 1971)

Just when you're sure you don't need another heavy versh of this Dylan monolith, along come Savage Grace to demand, nay, command that you give 'em a listen. And what a vast piece this is, kiddies; nearly six minutes of high-energy, De-twat overkill gets slung at Mr Zimmer-frame's three lickle chords, and still its fabric remains buoyant and uncapsizable. Bother. Still, Savage Grace was a mighty live ensemble, even said to have blown Black Sabbath off the stage when supporting them at Michigan State Fairground, in summer '71. Their records, however, were too eclectic for their own good, and a move to Los Angeles fucked their sound up even more. Back in the late '60s, bearded guitarist Ron Koss, piano player John Seanor and drummer Larry Zack had started out as a jazzy trio named Scarlet Letter, until gravel-chomping howler Al Jacquez joined them as singer and bassist, bringing a truly Ian Gillan-like vocal transcendence to their often too-busy musicianship. Still, any band who coulda bullied this motherfucker on to magnetic tape has gotta be worth its own legend. Yowzah!

The Frost: Rock'n'roll Music
(Vanguard, 1969)

Back in ye glory days, afore his name became inexorably linked to top-hat-period Alice Cooper and Lou Reed, Detroit's Dick Wagner was a Detroit star in his own right, initially, in the mid-'60s, with The Bossmen. However, a change of style to the heavier sounds prevalent later in the decade gained Wagner a two-album deal with Vanguard Records, this superb live track being the title cut of The Frost's sophomore LP for that label. Like the Velvets' 'We're Gonna Have a Real Good Time Together', this arch anthem – recorded in Detroit's legendary Grande Ballroom – is a real classic 'song about the song' which anticipates much of Grand Funk Railroad's soul overkill, and even contains the outrageous lyrical claim: 'Rock'n'roll music is saying what's left to be said.'

MC5: Borderline
(Elektra, 1969)

Supporting Blue Cheer at the Grande Ballroom on June 23 1968 appears to have generated such a seismic change in the musical approach of the pre-album MC5 that Wayne and co. briefly abandoned their R&B/soul roots in favour of ornately arranged cumbersome overkill, in the style of Dickie, Leigh and Paul. That the Five were still immersed in *Outsideinside* is most evidenced both by their *Kick Out the Jams* version of The Troggs' 'I Want You' and this magnificently brutal arrangement of their own 'Borderline', replete with ungainly, stop–start Gatling-gun drumming, proto-Mel Schacher über-bass and note-perfect harmony vocals. Although my first personal interface with the Five was my 1977 purchase of their bootleg Skydog Records seven-inch, which contained an *even more* radical versh, I chose this timeless recording to best represent our fave rock revolutionaries because it was captured on the first day of the White Panther Party's 'Zenta New Year' bash *and* came badged with the Elektra Records seal of quality. Fuck Hudson's, motherfuckers!

Funkadelic: Cosmic Slop
(Westbound, 1973)

A post-Malcolm X teenage Detroit power trio back up a psychedelicised New Jersey doo-wop outfit; how's that gonna pan out? Hideous, no doubt, unless a world genius such as George Clinton is the instigator behind it all. And, despite having endured over a decade without chart success, songwriter and Parliaments leader Clinton held such enduring faith in his thirty-something cohorts Calvin Simon, Ray Davis, Grady Thomas and Fuzzy Haskins that he financed the band himself throughout the late '60s by gaining employment as a songwriter and staff producer at Tamla Motown, travelling home to New Jersey every weekend for shows with The Parliaments. However, when Detroit's Revilot Records offered The Parliaments their own single deal, only Clinton could afford to appear on the record, the rest of the band being too broke to leave New Jersey. Desperate for money, Clinton signed the renamed Funkadelic to Armen Boladian's Westbound label and unleashed upon the world his post-Hendrix, post-Sly, post-Mothers of Invention vision, and, lo, it was righteous, religious and its first three albums – *Funkadelic* (1970), *Free Your Mind and Your Ass Will Follow* (1970) and *Maggot Brain* (1971) – all absurdly perfect. Unfortunately, the band thereafter abandoned its policy of presenting massively long, near-meditational grooves, dumping them in favour of more succinct songs. The fallow period which followed – 1972–3 – yielded the politically charged but musically tame *America Eats Its Young* double LP, then the equally un-visionary *Cosmic Slop*, from whence came this epic, Zappa-influenced title track, also released as a seven-inch by Westbound Records. Real George Clinton fanatics will not, I'm sure, find it strange that I should elect to represent Funkadelic with this song from one of their lesser LPs, for even their patchiest platters still brim over with vision and life-affirming invention. Besides, kiddies, this song's a funk leviathan with Frank Zappa's sense of humour, a world serpent with a forked tongue in its cheek and a deadly sting in its seven-league tail.

Wayne Kramer: Get Some
(Stiff/Chiswick, 1977)

Brother Wayne's 1970s: now that's not something to consider lightly, kiddies. He'd led the mighty Five from their greaser beginnings – through garage-rock, R&B and obsessions with James Brown, free-jazz, Sun Ra, free-love and Trans-Love Energies – to the fifteen-thousand-feet abyss awaiting them all, come the revolution's untimely end. Utopian beyond his years, beyond his culture, beyond his better-educated peers, Kramer gazed through the sell-outs of John Vladimir Lennin and Abbie Hoffman, then jonesed in a state prison after trying to deal coke to the FBI. Which is why this incredible song – a collaborative 1977 'Free Wayne Kramer' campaign between Stiff and Chiswick – reeks with such genuine Gnostic pain and pity for what coulda, mighta, shoulda fucking been. Recorded with drummer Melvin Davis and mega-bassist Tim Schaeff in a Detroit studio sometime in 1975, the wide grooves of 'Get Some' exude an aura so blue it surrounds the vinyl artefact like a fog, and owners are forced to archive it between two Barney the Dinosaur records in order to diffuse some of the disc's tragically chilly Chernobility.

The New Order: Declaration of War
(Revenge, 1976)

Whaddya mean it sounds like someone recorded it off a stereo system, with a hand-held compressor mic? Of course they fucking did! And that someone was probably the late Ronald Frank Asheton himself, desperate for dosh in mid-'74, and everywhere pursued by loot-bearing, French Stooges fanatics. Next thing he knows, there's an import-only twelve-inch LP available through Paris' semi-legal Revenge Records, replete with a deluxe, half-colour sleeve featuring Ron himself, sometime Stooges bassist Jimmy Recca and former MC5 drummer Dennis Thompson, all armed with bayonets in a highly provocative belligerent pose. Unfortunately, by the time this vinyl curiosity hit the streets, around mid-'76, singer Jeff Spry was back in gaol for drug offences, although former Stooge Scott Thurston had now joined up on electric piano. As for the music itself, well, it's fucking brilliant, high-energy rock, fully Ashetonesque and blazing; while the vocal is (ahem) truly something else, as Spry bellows instructions in a sub-Adolf Hitler voice over an air-raid siren, the rest of the band collectively screaming, 'Sieg Heil!' At the middle eight, jazzy, sub-disco drums and bass punctuate the Asheton power chords, and the sheer un-PC-ness of it all immediately transports listeners' minds back to Alex Harvey's similarly bizarre Hitler routine, and some unknown 1974 *Top of the Pops* producer's 'brave' decision to allow The Sweet's Steve Priest to deliver his ultra-camp vocal asides in full SS uniform. Anyway, as good as the music on this LP was, they were clearly never gonna make it big with an unrighteous band name like that!

Ascension: Get Ready
(Seidr, 2003: recorded 1973)

Mindblown by the failure of the mighty MC5, yet forced by hunger to start out all over again, Five rhythm guitarist Fred 'Sonic' Smith and drummer Dennis 'Machine Gun' Thompson hooked up briefly with bassist John Hefti to form the mighty Ascension. With former MC5 bassist Michael Davis now singing lead, and expected by bar owners to play a large percentage of contemporary Top Forty hits, Ascension took full advantage of white funk band Rare Earth's recent massive chart-hit reworking of The Temptations' legendary 'Get Ready' to justify this, their own killer six-minutes-plus version. Grinding Rare Earth's vacuous offering into the dust, Sonic and co. trump Smokey Robinson's entire Motown production with just guitars and overly loud bass. It's a wondrous, blissful overkill, kiddies. A few years ago, a full album of Ascension's live set was briefly available from the always excellent Seidr label: search that sucker out! However, please do prepare yourselves in advance, all you Five fanatics, as it's always difficult to hear an audience confront one's heroes' performances with a totally blank response.

Destroy All Monsters: You're Gonna Die
(Cherry Red, 1977)

Starting out in 1973, at the University of Michigan, Destroy All Monsters was a free-form, multi-media art trip led by film-maker Carey Loren, with non-musicians Jim Shaw, Mike Kelly and female singer/painter Niagara completing the ensemble. Vacuum cleaners, coffee cans, kids' toys and broken electronic equipment were all features of their early live shows, although an avant-garde version of Sabbath's 'Iron Man' got them thrown off the stage of an Ann Arbor comic-book convention.

As every one of them was a long-time Stooges aficionado, Destroy All Monsters invited Ron Frank Asheton to contribute some guitar to their guerrilla ramblings. It was a big mistake. Within the year, Asheton had shacked up with Niagara and sacked all of the other original members, replacing them with musician mates, including former MC5 bassist Michael Davis. Gone were the bizarre and formless sonic explorations, replaced by Asheton's superb axe-wielding, over which the sultry Niagara declaimed her bizarre lyrics in a decidedly woolly, borderline Michigan/Canadian burr. 'You're Gonna Die' is included herein not as the best example of DAM's work but as the most appropriate for this compilation; my personal fave remains their '90s, inchoate'n'exploratory seven-inch version of 'Killing Me Softy with His Song'!

Sonic's Rendezvous Band: City Slang
(Limited Edition, 1977)

It's damned hard to accept that this exhausting and brilliant power-drive was the sole contemporary vinyl release from this quartet of De-twat legends; it ain't much evidence to go on, kiddies. Hell, even the B-side was just a mono versh of the A-side! And yet this solitary 1977 release by former members of the MC5, The Rationals, The Stooges and The Up contained all of the pent-up fury of the Five's 1971 album *High Time*, as filtered through the Year Zero punk blender . . . and then some! And, when the only other recourse to hearing the Sonic's Rendezvous back catalogue is via a multitude of iffy bootleg LPs, it's great to know that this single showcased the band in a manner approved by its founders. So buy those bootlegs, sure, but do your utmost to seek out this official statement. For, despite being let down by lack of cash and real playing opportunities, Sonic's Rendezvous Band was a Gnostic odyssey of epic proportions and a natural high-energy successor to *High Time* in all of its heavy gloriosity. Jesus fuck, this breaks my heart every time.

Southbound Freeway: Psychedelic Used Car Lot Blues
(Tera Shirma, 1967)

Coming across on this record more San Francisco than Detroit, Southbound Freeway's cranky, folky sound was down to lead guitarist Marc Chover, whose obsession with local folk singer Ted Lucas and his band the Spikedrivers pushed the Freeway into their vocal-heavy style and gained them many successful shows at Detroit's folk club, The Chessmate. The band's big break, however, came with the invitation to open for the MC5 on one of the Grande Ballroom's opening nights. Indeed, Southbound Freeway even appeared at the legendary (to some, infamous) Trans-Love Energies 'love-in' on Belle Isle, lining up alongside the Five and The Up. Thereafter, they entered Ralph Terrana's tiny Tera Shirma studios, where they recorded 'Psychedelic Used Car Lot Blues' in one short night's session. The single was a huge hit in Detroit after being picked up by CKLW Radio, enabling the band to play Robin Seymour's hip teen TV show, *Swingin' Time*. Syndicated reruns even saw the single picked up by seven regional record labels across the US, but still the song failed to break into the national Top One Hundred.

Bob Seger System: 2+2=?
(Capitol, 1967)

It's almost impossible, nowadays, to imagine that this superb slice of anti-Vietnam War garage ramalama was the product of boring Bob; that is, until you suss that '2+2=?' was – along with Seger's Dylan protest parody 'Persecution Smith' and X-Mass single 'Sock It to Me Santa' from the previous year – ultimately just another of his highly professional efforts to break into the national charts. Don't let his cynicism spoil your fun, however, brothers'n'sisters; Dylan's capricious, ever-changing muse long ago showed what dividends could be reaped by those with total contempt for authenticity. In the meantime, suck up all the good juices emanating from this seven-inch offering from Seger's then-new outfit, The System, and remember how much the dude brung to the Detroit party before his worthy, right-wing, blue-collar values resurfaced as an ocean of mid-tempo, reactionary gush about a lush American Golden Age that never actually existed.

Unrelated Segments: Where You Gonna Go?
(Liberty, 1967)

Despite failing nationally with their debut forty-five, 'Story of My Life', that song's limited regional success opened the doors to Russ Gibb's legendary Grande Ballroom, where Unrelated Segments played support to such major stars as The Who, the MC5, The Jeff Beck Group, Spirit and The Spencer Davis Group. Returning to the studio for the recording of a second single entitled 'Where You Gonna Go?', guitarist Rory Mack this time unleashed a compelling, Middle European riff that propelled the song with all the fire of a Cossack dance, over which bass player Barry Van Engelen laid an equally catchy, percussive part, as though aping Brian Jones' marimba on then-current Stones records. And again, singer Ron Stults drooled out his epic teenage tale of abandonment and the coming perils of adulthood. And again, the Segments' new single was a local smash, this time being picked up nationally by Liberty Records. Unfortunately, the record stalled once more. And with the failure of this second forty-five, an excellent third single, 'Cry, Cry, Cry', received only token publicity. This superb band folded for good when the drafted Van Engelen was sent to serve in Vietnam in early '69. Pah!

Terry Knight and the Pack: Numbers
(Lucky Eleven, 1966)

At least those poor suckers who bought a copy of Terry Knight's excruciating 'I Who Have Nothing' forty-five woulda been rewarded heftily by the discovery of the mighty 'Numbers', its extraordinarily dynamic B-side. Hell, that bass/fuzz riff has just got to have been quarried from one of rock's all-time-great granite seams, thereafter being fashioned by dwarfs into a solid bolt of forked lightning, flung down from on high directly from the fuzz gods. Over this wriggling'n'pulsing leviathan of a riff, bad Tez gets mad at some little rich girl, piling up list upon list of her daily misdemeanours: too many motorcycles (seven), too many telephones (sixteen), too many planes (twelve) . . . Interesting articles, in context with the killer riffery, but it ain't exactly 'Where Do You Go to, My Lovely?', know worramean?

Tidal Waves: Farmer John
(Hanna Barbera, 1966)

Despite being remembered nowadays only for this excellent remake of The Premiers' hoary 1964 smash, Tidal Waves used the song's familiarity to secure a TV spot on Michigan's teen show *Swingin' Time*. This led to two high-profile Detroit support slots, first opening for The Dave Clark Five and, soon after, appearing third on the bill before The Animals and Herman's Hermits at the prestigious Olympia Stadium. The result was that they transferred from Detroit's tiny SVR label to Hanna Barbera, home of Yogi Bear and The Flintstones. 'Farmer John' was to be their career peak, however; thereafter the band learned an inevitable fourth chord, mutating into the 'heavy' outfit Featherstone, after which nothing more was heard from them.

The Früt: Keep on Truckin'
(Westbound, 1971)

Starting out at the Grande Ballroom, in 1967, as the 'campy hippie band' Früt of the Loom, this weird ensemble began initially as a ropey vehicle for the ruminations of their singer, Panama Red, who darted about the stage like Commander Cody and ran the band's club, 'The Früt Cellar', at Mount Clemens. Taking the music far less seriously than their overall presentation, The Früt were accompanied on stage by a daft-looking, out-of-shape dancer in Red Man get-up, while their eclectic song selections saw them often compared to retro acts such as Flash Cadillac and the aforemenched Commander Cody. Way past their sell-by date, The Früt finally signed to Armen Boladian's Westbound Records (home to Funkadelic and The Jimmy Castor Bunch), under whose auspices they released the *Keep on Truckin'* LP, in 1971. As evidenced by this thin-spread slice of slipshod, sub-Doorsian boogie, The Früt obviously still retained their semi-pro attitude to such tiresome details as how to begin and end songs.

? and the Mysterians: Girl
(Cameo Parkway, 1967)

Tarred with the dreaded 'one-hit wonder' tag they might be, but being in possession of a song of the calibre of '96 Tears' ? and the Mysterians hardly needed anything more. I spent time in summer '77 at Birkenhead's Zephyr Records, buying up several of the Mysterians' obscure Cameo Parkway forty-fives while hanging out in with my erstwhile neighbour, Pete Burns (yup, he fucking adored *Pebbles*-style garage music). All of the Mysterians' singles were worth the price (twenty-five pence), and their remarkable sameyness is still, to this day, only outperformed by that run of early forty-fives by Sky Saxon's lunatic quartet The Seeds. The Mysterians were all originally sons of Mexican migrants from Texas, rising to fame in the northern Detroit area of Saginaw, playing a pumping fusion of Tex-Mex and James Brown to migrant farm workers. So professional and dextrous were the band that over a million copies of '96 Tears' were sold, despite its recording being made – thanks to their record company's impoverishment – in a studio with no headphones, no separate control booth and with no bass drum included in the session's hired drum kit. Against all odds or what? Anyway, please check out the Mysterians' stubbornly futuristic 'Girl' and lament, along with me, that the public's rapturous reception of their phenomenal US Number One smash ensured that Americans would receive their Mysterians dosage in one large helping, rather than over the course of several intriguing garage forty-fives.

The Iguanas: Mona
(Pre, 1966)

Included herein more for musicological reasons than because this sucker's particularly good, this frat ensemble, from whence came Insurio Osterberg's stage moniker, might have stayed more legendary had they not committed it to tape. Still, we can – as we sing along to 'Mona' – consider Scott Morgan's earnest pronouncement that his Rationals had considered offering Iggy the drum seat around '68, then mull upon what the first Stooges LP coulda been, had not John Cale been brown-nosing Elektra's Jac Holzman for a proper house-producer job and forced upon those underachievers a spirited, post-Troggsian teen LP, utterly in opposition to that talked up to biographers these past thirty years by Herr O his-self.

The Stooges: Asthma Attack
(Elektra, 1969)

Left off their John Cale-produced self-titled debut LP, and still unreleased to this day, The Stooges' 'Asthma Attack' was Iggy's spirited, junior attempt to conjure up precisely that same expectorating madness that Grey Wizard, Kimmy the Fowl, had achieved effortlessly on his gloriously unhinged 1968 LP *Outrageous*, released just ten months previously. Unfortunately, although L'Osterberg displays enough of an intimate knowledge of Fowley's truly insane *Outrageous* epics 'Chinese Water Torture' and 'Nightrider' to meld successfully the two into this giant gob-athon, 'Asthma Attack' is not their equal simply because Iggy's let down throughout by the reluctance of his fellow Stooges to abandon themselves to the primal-scream state necessary for such an exercise. Which is a damn shame for the overall art state/ment (as John Sinclair woulda spelled it), but ultimately it's still thrilling to observe Iggy both seeking *and* finding inspiration in the throat-clearing of such a truly world sleaze as His Kimmyness.

Hardrocksampler

1 Aynsley Dunbar Retaliation: Warning (3.18) (1967)
2 Jake Holmes: Dazed and Confused (3.51) (1967)
3 The Up: Together (4.23) (1968)
4 The Flowers: How Many More Times? (7.00) (1969)
5 The Litter: Blue Ice (3.10) (1969)
6 The Helpful Soul: Peace for Fools (10.33) (1969)
7 The Move: Don't Make My Baby Blue (6.04) (1970)
8 David Bowie: She Shook Me Cold (4.17) (1970)
9 Love: Love Is More than Words . . . (11.22) (1970)
10 Bloodrock: D.O.A. (8.29) (1970)
11 Sir Lord Baltimore: Caesar LXXI (5.22) (1971)
12 Hairy Chapter: Only an Officer's Daughter (7.57) (1971)
13 Speed, Glue & Shinki: Sniffin' and Snortin' (2.38) (1971)
14 Budgie: Crash Course in Brain Surgery (2.39) (1971)
15 UFO: Timothy (3.32) (1971)
16 The Mops: Town Where I Was Born (9.01) (1971)
17 Bang: Future Shock (4.40) (1971)
18 Tiger B. Smith: These Days (5.58) (1972)
19 The Troggs: Feels Like a Woman (3.32) (1972)
20 Thin Lizzy: The Rocker (2.41) (1973)
21 Granicus: You're in America (4.08) (1973)
22 Kiss: Parasite (3.04) (1974)
23 Mott: The Great White Wail (5.07) (1975)

As a heathen motherfucker who wants to bid 'bad riddance' to organised religion, it does my heart good to know that some loon somewhere, even as I write this, is currently wailing up an electric storm-from-hell on a loud and distorted solid-bodied guitar, mercilessly wringing the neck of some poor axe in the righteous service of dissing the sky gods.

As these pages are likely to be mainly read by sonic navigators of the first order, on *Hardrocksampler* I've included no Sabs, no Zep, no MC5, no Grand Funk, no Blue Cheer, no Pentagram, no Blue Öyster Cult, nor anything else that might have already been discussed in detail. Instead, I've tried to include a few classy obscurities that many will have heard *about* but perhaps not actually *heard*, plus some heavy stuff that mighta been overlooked because the artists in question were better known for other styles of music.

It's the Devil's Music . . .

. . . and it scares the shit out of Christians and Muslims because the electric beat pummels your heart-driven (and already pulsating) body, exciting your adrenalin into play, with the immediate effect that awareness of your animal side has been awakened. Indeed, one of the bands on this compilation, Bloodrock, had to stop playing their most famous song, 'D.O.A.' (included herein), because the new Christian singer was too yucked out by the chords and the death imagery. Fuck him, guys; you shoulda sacked the sad cunt. Why'd he apply for the job in the first place? Iggy Pop, in explanation of his obsession with rock'n'roll performance, once stated: 'Speakers push the air, and push me too.' Fuck me, you should share a stage with Sunn O))), Jimmy.

Anyway, the better the technology got, the louder the amps became, and the more we all came closer to barking at the moon. Of course, even without the rise of rock'n'roll, those already deeply paranoid religious leaders of the previous two centuries had been barely keeping a lid on us. So, when electric music took over as the main populist entertainment, in the mid-'50s, the new amplification was already on the way to allowing rock'n'roll temples to surpass the size of cathedrals, and the music could challenge Christianity at last. Nice. Louder and louder and louder it became, until The Beatles' legendary 1964 Shea Stadium show was finally eclipsed, in the summer of 1971, by the brute force of the über-populist power trio of Mark, Mel and Don, a.k.a. Grand Funk Railroad.

During that period, the term 'rock'n'roll' was sidelined, used only when referring to the hoary '50s originators. Modern people played 'rock music', and the harder the better. Indeed, time was – around 1970 and '71 – when hard-rock/heavy-rock was so pervasive that every popular musician not playing reggae, bubblegum or opera was inevitably informed by the overamplified sound. Every week, perverse, cartoon hairies invaded the BBC's *Top of the Pops* studios – the show, throughout 1970 and 1971, featuring such anachronisms as Frijid Pink's fuzz-fest versh of 'House of the Rising Sun' (Number Six in the BBC's Top Forty in May 1970), Peter Green's swansong/descent into hell with Fleetwood Mac's 'The Green Manalishi' (Number Ten in July 1970), Black Sabbath's seminal 'Paranoid' (Number Four in October 1970), Deep Purple's sludgy 'Black Night' (Number Two in October 1970), the recently deceased Jimi Hendrix's 'Voodoo Chile' (Number One in November 1970), Deep Purple, again, with 'Strange Kind of Woman' (Number Eight in March 1971), Family's Roger Chapman bellowing out the beginnings of 'In My Own Time' (Number Eight in June 1971), and Atomic Rooster doing 'The Devil's Answer' (Number Four in August 1971).

To the dismay of the general public, these were performers whose idea of recreation involved ingesting massive amounts of illegal drugs (Hendrix, Sabbath), balling horny broads (that's early-'70s slang for shagging groupies, all you youngsters), investigating the underworld as a possible future home (Peter Green), or even committing suicide (Vincent Crane of Atomic Rooster). And I'm only mentioning the truly hairy heavies who struck the esteemed BBC Top Ten, motherfuckers! Which is why, in 1970, even the ever-career-opportunistic Dave Bowie still felt it necessary, nay, essential to address the genre with his 'She Shook Me Cold' (included herein) – and supremely crafted and nailed to the floor it is, too.

But, when everything is heavy, you gots to question just how much of it is real, and how much was just informed by the spirit of the time. Take Deep Purple, for example. I mean, while Ritchie Blackmore had started back in the early '60s with Screaming Lord Sutch and the Savages, and had always played the Occult Godfather of guitar lunacy to some extent, new boys Ian Gillan and Roger Glover had previously been neato, short-haired harmony singers in the saccharine-sweet Episode Six. So long hair and screaming was deffo a sensible career move back then. Talking of saccharine, even disgraced entrepreneur Jonathan King struck big in 1971 with his anthemic/anaemic fuzz-guitar version of The Archies' 'Sugar Sugar', which I saw him perform on *Top of the Pops* under a pink Afro wig. The name of this hard-rock-styled project? Sakkarin – yowzah! All of which brings us to the matter of where hard-rock went afterwards.

Where Did Hard-Rock Go, Daddy?

Well, kids, like a Friday-night tarka dal spillage, it had got fucking everywhere by the mid-'70s. Like drunks on a weekend over-spending spree down the local Indian, everybody's eyes were too big for their bellies and they had ordered far too much. The authorities were in a quandary. So, in an effort to get shot of the stuff, vats of raw hard-rock were sold off to Mickie Most, who used it to prop up his otherwise strictly bubblegum RAK-label releases (Suzie Quatro, Mud, Arrows . . .), and they offloaded another coupla hundred containers to glam-pop auteurs Chinnichap, who used it to turbo-charge The Sweet (whose previous RCA forty-fives, 'Poppa Joe', 'Co Co' and 'Funny Funny', were sub-Archies at best), and they cynically sent much of it abroad (without printed instructions), where it was used to fuel the careers of such walking abortions as Germany's Birth Control, Denmark's Walkers and Japan's Pyg. The remainder they sent to Seattle, where it festered behind security fences throughout the '80s, before bursting out and contaminating youngsters playing near it, thereby accidentally starting the grunge scene.

The rest, as they say, is history. By the mid-'90s, the Sabbath revival was in full swing courtesy of stoners such as Sleep and St. Vitus – musicians who clearly needed to make such a din, even if it meant cutting metalwork classes. And, just as doom band Sunn O))) named their publishing company Sabbath ReHash, those playing hard-rock nowadays are confident enough to accept that there's much to be gained simply by rearranging the pieces of the original puzzle. Indeed, it's becoming increasingly clear to many in the music business that, although hard-rock reached its first peak of popularity in the period 1970–5, the genre is emotionally and physically fulfilling in so many ways that, down the years, newer and newer waves have brought forth novel musical revelations and genuine new stars. Hell, the Finnish band Circle even run their own 'Stoner Rock' project, Pharaoh Overlord, so they can discharge, at regular intervals, a few of the heavy riffs that otherwise coagulate unused in their melted plastic brains. If you'll go along with my assertion that wanking is essential for clearing the custard, then you're probably the type who'll allow me to extend the metaphor and agree that the conducting of a good riff-athon (replete with clichés) can be just as necessary to a musician for spunking out the excess psychic build-up.

In July 1999, after drowning in the eight years of field research necessary to complete my tome *The Modern Antiquarian*, I was so driven to interface with the musically stupefying that I established my own so-called stupor-group – the power trio Brain Donor – with two members of English drone band Spiritualized. It was to be a power trio in the traditional sense, and had been inspired specifically by the first two Blue Cheer LPs, anything by Japan's High Rise, the first, third and fourth Van Halen LPs, Sir Lord Baltimore's 1970 debut *Kingdom Come* and Black Sabbath's 1975 album *Sabotage*. These sounds were our blueprint and we tried not to veer outside this self-imposed field system. Of course, anything featuring my hefty involvement soon brought along a heavy dose of the MC5-influenced Detroit sound, but this was always held in counter-balance by the Van Halen obsessions of guitarist Doggen. And, if that sounds interchangeable, well, that's because it is. Fashions may come and fashions may go, but 'Jerusalem' by Sleep goes on forever. And if Islam in the Middle East and Christianity from America's Midwest ever get too intrusive, we still have the gods of rock to fight them with. They ain't gotta chance! While they're far too entrenched in dogma and traditions from back in the day, our truth will become greater the bigger the PA gets . . .

So let us now turn to *Hardrocksampler*. I'll lay some descriptives on y'all. In order to make this compilation even heavier, I decided that we should commence with a twin-pronged attack, for the roots of both Led Zeppelin *and* Black Sabbath actually lie in that so-called 'Summer of Love', 1967. We all know that Zep's Jimmy Page stole 'Dazed and Confused' off former Tim Hardin and Tim Rose associate Jake Holmes, but it's included herein to show just how much that greedy bastard nicked, i.e. everything from basic song to arrangement, not to mention that mind-holocaust of a breakdown. But, first off, as Black Sabbath's debut LP is (to most people, including me) the ur-text from which all of hard-rock's future bludgeon riffola emanated, then it's certainly righteous to activate this compilation with one of the tracks that most informed Geezer and co. in those early days. So what better way to commence than with Aynsley Dunbar's original seven-inch version of 'Warning'?

Aynsley Dunbar Retaliation: Warning
(Blue Horizon, 1967)

Even earlier than Blue Cheer's flaying debut LP *Vincebus Eruptum*, this original version of 'Warning' is a dark, angst-ridden, Doors-informed, empty pedestrian blues that you could imagine having been released on GNP Crescendo or Cameo Parkway. It's like Python Lee Jackson's 'In a Broken Dream' on largactyl and bad blotter; a lament from Hades to a girl who's most likely already forgotten the poor sap's name. Better still, we finally get the link between the song title and the chorus, as singer Victor Brox howls: 'I was warned about you, baby/But my feelings gotta little bit too strong.' Ah, so that's it. So did Ozzy just mishear these words? Or (and this seems more likely) did he get them wrong initially, get corrected by the band, manager and producer, then perversely follow his own interpretation, whatever? I suspect the latter, because Ozzy weren't the Prince of Darkness for nuthin'. Don't let the Brummie monotones and stumbling gait fool y'all into thinking he weren't no genius . . . Boy, was he ever! That Ozzy cat just knew he was upping the nihilism factor another fifty percent when he changed the original words to this supreme outsider statement: 'I was born without you, baby/But my feelings gotta little bit too strong.' The '90s started right here.

Jake Holmes: Dazed and Confused
(Tower, 1967)

With its seemingly ever-descending-the-spiral-staircase riff and sleep-walking vocal, Jake Holmes' original recording of this song took the listener down into the underworld . . . right down to the source of the Moment. And what a moment! Man, you can hear all three musicians padding around on hell's cold granite floor, each inchoate but brilliant musical stumble registering ten flights above them on the magnetic tape machine of the scientific engineer; each intuitive move caught by technology and imprinted as future codes for all of us rebels against Creation. Working around the anchored, descending bass of Rick Randle, but without a drummer, Holmes and guitarist Ted Irwin extracted all of their percussion effects from the soundboards of their hollow-body guitars, their incredible dynamic range achieved through long nights of onstage experimentation – often playing as many as three sets each evening. Unfortunately for Jake Holmes, on August 25 1967 his trio played support to The Yardbirds, at New York's Village Theatre.

Thereafter, The Yardbirds incorporated Holmes' song into their set and Jimmy Page would release it, and credit it to himself, on Led Zeppelin's 1969 debut album. Every detail, even the guitar-tapping and ricochets of Holmes' version, had been developed and expanded to achieve maximum effect by the none-more-thorough Mr Page. Regrettably for Holmes, when he contacted Page about the authorship of the song, he received no reply. Holmes never took legal action.

The Up: Together
(Total Energy, 1968)

At times up there with late-'60s high-energy white-soul bands such as Leslie West's The Vagrants, The Rationals and the MC5, it's unfortunate that The Up will always exist in the shadow of their great mentor, John Sinclair, destined to remain the Jimmy Osmonds of their scene; a Trans-Love Energies fixture as the even-littler brother band of the MC5 and The Stooges. Still, this 1968 anthem is a match for the energy of live Grand Funk Railroad, while being far more inventive. Over a formidably danceable, 6/4-time hurricane of rhythm, the collective Up members unleash a veritable storm of glorious soul harmonies, each time either changing key upwards or breaking down into a heart-stopping three-quarter time that catastrophies your entirely Motown'd butt. Every great 'Land of a Thousand Mony Monys' soul work-out pales in comparison to this one song.

The Flowers: How Many More Times?
(CBS, 1969)

Not only is this pre-Flower Travellin' Band performance a curiosity and rarity because it features a woman – singer Lemi Aso – in the almost exclusively masculine setting of hard-rock, but it's also a Led Zeppelin cover as performed by Big Brother and the Holding Company wannabes,[1] thereby uniting the previously only intuitive link between the young Robert Plant and his hard-drinking Mama Muse, Ms Janis Joplin. Better still, the six-piece Flowers were all veteran Japanese musicians arduously auditioned by one of rock'n'roll's true freaks, The Flowers' co-singer and mentor, Yuya

1 For their sole LP, 1969's *Challenge*, The Flowers recorded versions of two Big Brother originals, 'Combination of the Two' and 'Piece of My Heart', alongside a take on Big Brother's own (rather simplified) arrangement of Moondog's memorable drone lament 'All Is Loneliness'.

Uchida, placing this performance more on the sustained high-energy level of an Ike Turner showband than mere rock'n'roll, thereby so kicking Big Brother's dick into the dust that comparisons are laughable as they shove Zeppelin's song into 'River Deep, Mountain High' territory. 'How Many More Times?' commences like The Misunderstood at their height, as lap steel guitarist Katsuhiko Kobayashi replicates the stellar tones of boy genius Glenn Ross Campbell, then takes you even higher. I shit you not, this song is orgasmic from start to end. Indeed, the musicians created such a level of controlled hysteria for the song's backing track that the two singers appear to have become, by song's end, temporarily unhinged and truly abandoned. The call-and-answer finale heats up to such emotional levels of near heart attack that the band split about a week afterwards.

The Litter: Blue Ice
(Probe, 1969)

For me, The Litter's 'Blue Ice' and the MC5's 'Looking at You' are the two greatest ever bridges between garage-rock and hard-rock; high-energy songs that defined the latter genre for such future bands as Sammy Hagar's Montrose, but which still had their roots deep in the '60s. It's hard to explain just how 'back in the day' that decade seemed to me in the very early '70s, but, in those days, I didn't want any of it. I wanted only the now! No Rolling Stones, no Beatles; even Led Zeppelin's non-gatefold debut looked old by 1972 (none of that 'laminated in Clarifoil by Garrod and Lofthouse' shite). Until the end of summer '72, that is, when my mate Max Eacock and I were in Devon running his Uncle Chris's café, in Labrador Bay. One day, we stumbled upon a Torquay record shop selling old 'new stock' albums for twenty-five pence each, and we both scored a bunch of 1969 stuff released on the Probe label, selecting purely on price. We both nabbed copies of Probe 1004 (*Emerge* by The Litter), while I also grabbed Probe 1006 (Saint Steven's eponymous album) and Probe 1010 (Zephyr's self-titled album). While the latter LP was unlistenable blues shit with a wailing, Janis-on-helium chick singer (and featured future Deep Purple guitarist Tommy Bolin), Side Two of the Saint Steven LP was evocative, dark-as-fuck genius. However, nothing prepared me for the rush and roar of The Litter, and that record still exhilarates me almost forty years later. Sounds crap to admit, but mostly it's not the songs but the musicianship that stands out. Like the MC5, The Litter displayed more sonic control than almost any of their peers, while Jim Kane's bass lines are something I still rip off regularly. As for 'Blue Ice', even now it's so powerful I laugh when I hear it, especially the tearing and slightly atonal lead guitar and the rising rhythm-guitar chords that still fuck my head, big stylee.

The Helpful Soul: Peace for Fools
(Victor, 1969)

Man, this nihilistic charabanc ride into the heart of darkness makes me wish The Doors' 'Five to One' had been twelve minutes in duration. As empty and monotonous and linear as the *Funhouse*-period Stooges or *Delay*-era Can, the ten-minutes-plus of 'Peace for Fools' is pure trudge-funk; a Krautrockesque, one-chord meditation somewhat akin to The Chambers Brothers playing the latter six minutes of The Rolling Stones' ur-kraut classic 'Goin' Home'. Imagine Kim Fowley producing sixteen-year-olds with an early Funkadelic fixation, only this is a full year before 'Free Your Mind and Your Ass Will Follow'; and it exhibits that same embedded-in-the-earth groove located throughout George Clinton's debut Funkadelic album the previous year. Highly original, despite nicking the bass line from Iron Butterfly's 'In-A-Gadda-Da-Vida' towards the end, 'Peace for Fools' is genuinely tormented, the young singer clearly genuinely disturbed by the dystopian future he's witnessing (or being peddled by the underground). Still, it makes for compelling listening and is, in time, surely destined to become a nihilistic classic.

The Move: Don't Make My Baby Blue
(Regal, 1970)

Figuring that you already knew The Move's primo, low-geared chart-topper 'Brontosaurus', I thought y'all might appreciate hearing what Roy Wood could do to a lovely Cynthia Weill/Barry Mann, Brill Building pop song like 'Don't Make My Baby Blue', originally a 1965 hit for The Shadows! Well, we all know what a cunt for a riff Roy Wood was, but it don't get more convoluted and expressionist than this lickle babby, as our hero weds the obsessive retard blues of The Beatles' 'I Want You (She's So Heavy)' to Blue Cheer's insanely over-played 'Feathers from Your Tree', then directs drummer Bev Bevan to play as though – with each drum fill – he's dotting the 'i's and crossing the 't's of every single word Wood is singing. Dial nine–nine–nine, there's a song in there! Hell knows what the songwriters thought of the end result, although by the time Roy'd finished, Mann and Weill might not even have noticed that it was theirs. It's like Posh and Beckham bought a semi-detached council house and added ballrooms, an entrance staircase, jacuzzis and some turrets – yup, that tasteful. But, boy, ain't it exhilarating!

David Bowie: She Shook Me Cold
(Mercury, 1970)

On my all-time favourite live album, Tom Lehrer's 1958 masterpiece *An Evening Wasted with Tom Lehrer*, Lehrer investigates the folk song as a genre and comes to the valid conclusion that professional songwriters woulda done a much better job. Well, kiddies, cop a load of this behemoth and see what a real songwriter does to a modern electric folk song like 'Iron Man'! For, whatever you think about the Thin White Streak of Piss, like Roy Wood before him Bowie sure knew how to don the mantle of entire musical genres and come up smelling just like the rest of the competition. Tony Visconti's bass carries the track from start to conclusion; Mick Ronson's guitar cuts right across the structure like a thoughtless eBayer wrapping a matchbox-sized parcel with two-inch wide double-sided tape, and the drum fills sound more like throwing Bibles at a sofa than even those of mein hairy, Bill Ward! The arrangement is so tight and seamless that, despite arriving late, travelling market-stall owner Bowie gets all of his wares set out, sold, cleaned up and packed away in just over four minutes; hell, Sabbath woulda still been tolling the bells!

Love: Love Is More Than Words, or Better Late Than Never
(Blue Thumb, 1970)

Out in the cold and off Elektra Records, the 1970 Arthur Lee was cursing having ever straightened his frizz and on a mish to locate his inner Voodoo Chile. Legend has it that when plans for the proposed supergroup featuring himself, Steve Winwood and Jimi Hendrix collapsed on account of the latter's death, Arthur's new Love LP, *Out Here*, turned into a double when he invited stun guitarist Gary Rowles to guest on one track, then turned the whole schmeer over to Rowles and just let the druid rip it up across most of Side Three. Only the truly confident artist allows another to traipse around their hallowed grooves, but Arthur was always in the top three percent and knew it. And you know what? However intense this mind-fogger becomes, Arthur's blessed A–G chords are always chiming away underneath, so you can never truly forget yooz in the presence of Mr Forever Changes.

Bloodrock: D.O.A.
(Capitol, 1970)

It is hard to believe now, but this epic funeral dirge about an edge-of-death plane-crash victim reached Number Thirty-six on the US singles charts! Wedding dreary Sabbath atonalities to Atomic Rooster organ daubs, this has gotta be the most hamfisted epic this side of Grand Funk Railroad's second (and best) studio LP, *Grand Funk*. Which makes sense when you learn that it was recorded by their producer, Terry Knight, and engineer Ken Hamann. It's as eerie and apocalyptic as Salem's twelve-minute 'Witch Burning', or the title track of *Black Sabbath*. Indeed, when singer Jim Rutledge left the band, the haunted mood of the song weirded out new singer Warren Ham so badly he refused to sing it on account of being a Christian. No comment . . . you cunt.

Sir Lord Baltimore: Caesar LXXI
(Mercury, 1971)

Easily the best track from Sir Lord Baltimore's otherwise disastrous self-titled second LP, 'Caesar LXXI' is a true Cecil B. DeMille soundtrack of hard-rock, an archly declaimed tale of early history that only as shameless a performer as the great genius John Garner coulda dreamed of getting away with. Would that the remainder of the album tracks were half as good as this thrill-spill; unfortunately, the album's a void to avoid. 'Woman Tamer' is a great name for a lame duck (and would be good by anyone else, but we're allowed higher expectations when it's The Lord, fercryingoutloud!), but the rest are a pitiful, perfunctory shadow of the songs that (dis)graced *Kingdom Come*'s second side, and 'Man from Manhattan', in particular, is a mighty nothing-going-on abortion. New producer John Linde was the culprit, I'll wager: he not only co-wrote the songs but denuded them of the obsessively overdubbed guitar clusters that the brilliant Louis Dambra had lovingly daubed in his inimitably Catholical manner (nowadays he's a priest, no shit) on the earlier album. Worst of all, Linde straitjacketed the mighty John Garner and made him dump the first LP's subnormal, teenage-sex-addict-with-Tourette's vocal style, reducing the whole performance to the merely orgasmic. If the Garn's vocals on *Kingdom Come* were Joe Strummer circa the first Clash album, then the vocals on this follow-up are the *Give 'Em Enough Rope* Joe, i.e. just a man brung way down by Sandy Pearlman. It's as if they gave Garner downers and a minder. So it's lucky for all of us that at least one song sprung up whose exaggerated subject matter and ostentatious riffing, nay, its entire psyche demanded a temporary resurrection of Priapus.

Hairy Chapter: Only an Officer's Daughter
(Bacillus, 1971)

The immaculately named Hairy Chapter was a quartet of German heavy-rockers who really captured the yearning, burning of the male psyche with this near eight-minute-long display of early-Alice Cooper-style, post-'Green Manalishi' dark riffola. 'Gimme your body/Gimme your mind,' beseeches singer Harry Unte to his girl, imploring desperately that he wants to 'hold your luscious breasts in my hands' as the darkness of the twin guitars takes him down and down into hell. 'I wanna ball you all night long,' the poor sap mewls as on and on drive those dark axes. If you need to know more about these purveyors of anguish, get hold of the record from which this track was lifted, *Can't Get Through*, which I discussed earlier in these pages.

Speed, Glue & Shinki: Sniffin' and Snortin'
(Atlantic, 1971)

The power trio with the best name ever played a music that ranged from electronic synthesizer holocaust to sub-sub-Kiss rock, but three years early. That they erred on the side of the latter is to our advantage, because Filipino singer/drummer Joey Smith is a vocalising genius. Rather than repeat myself, I'm gonna reproduce what I wrote about the song in *Japrocksampler*:

Coming on like Iggy singing over Roky Erickson's pre-13th Floor Elevators band The Spades, Joey's 'Sniffin' and Snortin'' is garage-rock's finest hour both musically and lyrically. Joey hips us to his quest over a tumultuous Texan riff, explaining how he's drinking wine and loading up his syringe on his way 'to a Sunday jam': 'Well, I'll shoot it/I'll shoot it nice and clean/By the time I pull it out of my veins I'm gonna feel so strange.' No shit, Sherlock! Next thing, some street scruff accosts Brother Joey with an even badder proposition. The scruff reaches into his pocket, takes out a wrap and shakes it in the singer's face: 'Let's snort it out of my hand/It'll make you feel like you've never been alive before.' Shrill as a motherfucker, guitarist Shinki Chen kicks in an angular piercing solo and the band takes off like a Viet vet in a '69 Dodge Challenger. Joey's upside down, hanging from the sky, determined to make this his everyday lifestyle: 'Well, I know for sure that I'd never come back home again / And we started sniffin' and snortin' until we turned into skin and bones / Yeah, we been snortin' and sniffin' our brains away.'

Best cocaine lyrics ever . . . shoulda won Joey a half a Grammy!

Budgie: Crash Course in Brain Surgery
(MCA, 1971)

Although probably better known by now as a 1987 Metallica cover version, Budgie's seven-inch original was the kind of two-minutes-and-thirty-seconds that my generation coulda charted with a little more help from the record company. Unfortunately, MCA Records was just a middle-of-the-road Tony Christie institution back then, so the song went nowhere. Still, Budgie's Noel Redding-like singer/bass player Burke Shelley had an amazingly operatic voice for such a half-pint, journalists of the time often drawing comparisons with fellow Cardiff singer Burly Chassis. As you can hear on this song, taken from their self-titled debut LP, Shelley's poetic allusions were damn fine, too, as were other song titles such as 'Nude Disintegrating Parachute Woman', 'The Rape of the Lock' (not the Alexander Pope masterpiece – this one's about authority types threatening Burke with a haircut!) and the coulda/shoulda-been-a-hit 'Homicidal Suicidal'.

UFO: Timothy
(Beacon, 1971)

Clad in stunning Krautrock sleeves by Günter Blum (because they were signed to Germany's Nova label), the first three UFO albums are a goldmine of wondrous teenage bare-bones riffery. The bass propels every track like The Stooges' Dave Alexander or Joy Div's Peter Hook, while the rest sorta just fits around it. Yup, pre-Michael Schenker UFO mined a skinny space-rock seam that was truly 'Into the Void'. Taken from their punky debut LP, the flailing drums and pumping, two-note bass of 'Timothy' is probably the best way in for the doubters. Phil the Mogg intones the tale of the mysterious Timothy, ably illustrated by Mick Bolton's economical-to-the-point-of-austerity guitar, and you just gots to love 'em. Then again, the sludgy, slowed-down-to-a-crawl wah-fest of 'Treacle People' approaches The Stooges' dark ballad 'Anne', so it might also smoke your pole. I know these guys were bluesy, but it was always such a motorik, linear and unresolved blues. C'mon!

The Mops: Town Where I Was Born
(Liberty, 1971)

In which four Japanese former pop stars take their Animals fixation to its peak, excavating Eric and co.'s 1968 live LP *Every One of Us* and uncovering, then reworking it into nine minutes of singular brilliance. I mean, this is pure Detroit rock at its finest: exhilarating, hard as nails, marvellously arranged and replete with umpteen guitar breaks. Shee-it, this woulda slipped seamlessly on to any of the early Grand Funk LPs. Come to think of it, it's too good . . . not leaden enough, if anything. Of course, the problem with these ex-Group Sounds bands was their baggage. This classic is taken from their 1971 album *Ijaniyka*, which unfortunately features only two other full-on metallers in the same style; the rest of the album is stocked up with mushy ballads, dodgy covers and even a comedy number!

Bang: Future Shock
(Capitol, 1971)

Next up, segueing seamlessly and disgracefully, comes the post-'Iron Man' sound of Bang's epic and stupefying 1971 ditty 'Future Shock'. The band was a trio whose producer, Michael Sunday, insisted that bass player Frank Ferrara took over as lead singer from guitarist Frank Gilken because he looked more the part. What a great move! Ferrara's wailing and moaning are all summed up here on 'Future Shock', a song driven at a crawl so tractor-driver slow that you can hear the rest of the songs on this compilation screaming: 'Fucking pull over and let us pass, you bastard, we've got homes to go to as well!'

Tiger B. Smith: These Days
(1972)

Unfortunately, these poor suckers have also got to get past Tiger B. Smith. These German hard-rockers were led by Holger Schmidt, a platform-booted hairy with an only-child, 'me, me, me' complex that anticipated Gene Simmons' solipsistic self-love by at least two years. Moreover, the near six minutes of 'These Days' is yet another 'Iron Man' wannabe, with riffery so endlessly sludgy and slack that it makes the stentorian, wall-eyed bark of The Glitter Band's 'Angel Face' sound folky in comparison.

The Troggs: Feels Like a Woman
(Pye, 1972)

By 1972, The Troggs were so dumped on that even a single especially written and produced for them by Marc Bolan would'na score a Top Seventy-five place. They still had it occasionally, though, as with this song, hidden away on the B-side of an obscure non-hit ('Everything's Funny'). This late November '72 release united Yes' 'Heart of the Sunrise' riff with King Crimson's '21st Century Schizoid Man' and played it so hard that it was like 1969 all over again. 'I never thought you was groovy/I looked at mew like a child,' leers singer Reginald Presley. Had he meant to sing 'looked at *you*' but mistakenly sung 'me' and had to mutate the word? It is possible, but I somehow doubt it; him being Reg, I think he actually wrote down the lyric as 'mew'.

Thin Lizzy: The Rocker
(Decca, 1973)

When I bought this seven-inch, at the end of '73, I preferred it to the extended LP version because the guitar solo was edited down to a coupla bars of phasing FX, thus rendering it all the more dizzying by being so brief. It was the last thing the Lizzy recorded with original guitarist Eric Bell, and the only thing I ever bought by them; but 'The Rocker' features such a total, full-on vocal performance by Phil Lynott that I still shake my head in disbelief every time it comes on. I'll tell you what, though: those old blue '60s Decca labels didn't half look archaic in 1973.

Granicus: You're in America
(RCA, 1973)

Led by hard-rock poet Woody Leffel, it's weird to think that this Cleveland quintet wuz only a year ahead of such proto-punk co-habitants as the Electric Eels and Rocket from the Tombs. Leffel's screeching for the Red Man on this exhilarating and ever-accelerating rocket ride, and promises to 'drop my load' over the whole You Ess of Ay. I'd guess that any male artist musing on the world's injustices will always get the old spunk going, but a pretty full sac this boy musta had. Taken from their sole, self-titled LP, 'You're in America' opened what was a pretty damn good record, full of Woody's visions and righteous anger and desire to leave the small-town attitudes of Cleveland behind. Unfortunately, too many of the songs had something missing, something inconsistent or something weak in the arrangements. Sadly, they split up soon after and Woody is said to have remained in Cleveland . . .

Kiss: Parasite
(Casablanca, 1974)

OK, let's ease off the cruise control for a while and get her up into top gear with 'Parasite', from Kiss' almost-classic second LP, *Hotter than Hell.* While early Kiss was far often far too informed by the self-satisfied, mid-pace Biba boogie of the New Yawn Dolls, at least the Starchild, the Demon and the Wussy could occasionally rely on Ace 'Yes, I have been known to drive at eighty-five mph up the Long Island Expressway in the wrong direction, what of it?' Frehley to joyride some ominous and ruinous discord right up their Tin Pan Alley, as evidenced by the staccato robo-metal of 'Parasite', which is everything and more. Back in those early days, Ace knew his place and only the Gene had the spleen to deliver such a mutant oeuvre. Stand by for that Ack-Ack-gun guitar solo, and do try to catch them playing this song in black and white back in '75 (it's bound to be somewhere on YouTube). What with the synchronised boogie at the end, it's essential.

Mott: The Great White Wail
(CBS, 1975)

When Mott the Hoople carelessly lost both singer Ian Hunter *and* new guitarist Mick Ronson at the end of 1974, it's safe to say no one thought they'd stay together, let alone make a decent album. However, as bassist Overend Watts had been riff-collecting since day one and was also in possession of a formidable library of obscure LPs, he took it upon himself to write a whole album of heavy, post-glam songs, and almost succeeded. Indeed, *Drive On* was an almost totally listenable experience thanks to new singer Nigel Benjamin's incredible vocal range and ex-Hackensack guitarist Ray Major's dedication to the trip. The five minutes-plus of 'The Great White Wail' make for one superb and overdriven motherfucker somewhat along the lines of what Silverhead woulda conjured up if they'd had a proper songwriter. Moreover, it boasts a middle eight worthy of The Yardbirds, and the juggernaut production is so heavy that it's *heevy.* Git down!

In Conclusion

I know I've had to exclude hundreds of obvious hard-rock standards from this compilation. I don't like 'Armageddon', 'Clear Blue Sky', 'War Pigs' and half of the other so-called classics of the hard-rock canon that so many old-timer freaks embrace. Why? Because, as I said in the introduction, much of the music sounds suspiciously like the 'heavy' element was added afterwards and was purely a by-product of then-current musical fashions. Behind the lovely and mysterious 'heavy' artwork and overdriven opening coupla full-on numbers on LPs by revered bands such as Monument and Killing Floor, most of these so-called lost classics contain any number of clunkers (a flute-driven ballad, an overly bluesy, brass-driven growler, a guitar or piano piece included to mollify the university drop-out guitarist's university-lecturer parents, etc.). All of these dubious contents ensured (and with some justification) that *Melody Maker*, *Disc* and *NME* didn't pick up on it back in the day.

And another fucking thing: here we are, today, free of all those turgid Cream influences *and* we've all been filtered through punk and grunge and grown intolerant of half-assed thirty-minute LPs, like those by Bang and Dust, which outwardly aped Sabbath but still included overly large portions of acousto-dreck that appealed to no one's kid sister. Listen to the Vincent Black Shadow debut LP from a few years back and tell me it doesn't kick all those old guys' dicks into the dirt. And only a turd on a bum ride, a dyed-in-the-wool collectaholic, could argue that Sleep's *Jerusalem* hadn't eclipsed most of 1971's musical output by raising hard-rock to the level of High Ritual.

Luckily for all of us, hard-rock is such a poetically essential part of Western music that it's just gonna keep going away and coming back again, a crucial component of culture's ebb and flow. By 2053, we'll probably have witnessed at least another three hard-rock revivals. Why? Because of the decibels, motherfuckers; those thousands of kilowatts that Saint Thomas Edison bequeathed to us Westerners. For fifty years they've shaped, rearranged and enslaved our molecules, just like old Mohammed's Koran has enslaved the Middle East. Those power chords are life and death to us – we *need* them so we can stay sane, motherfuckers!

Glamrocksampler

1 Tyrannosaurus Rex: King of the Rumbling Spires (2.10) (1969)
2 The Move: When Alice Comes Back to the Farm (3.44) (1970)
3 John Kongos: He's Gonna Step on You Again (4.24) (1971)
4 Tiger B. Smith: Tiger Rock (5.17) (1972)
5 Pussy: Feline Woman (2.28) (1972)
6 Lucifer: Fuck You (4.53) (1972)
7 White Witch: Class of 2000 (6.15) (1973)
8 Jobriath: World Without End (3.45) (1973)
9 Silverhead: 16 and Savaged (4.26) (1973)
10 Amon Düül II: Jalousie (3.29) (1973)
11 Argent: God Gave Rock'n'roll to You (6.41) (1973)
12 Pantherman: Pantherman (3.10) (1974)
13 Mustard: Good Time Comin' (2.33) (1974)
14 Iron Virgin: Rebels Rule (3.12) (1974)
15 Dump: Annabella (3.20) (1975)
16 Neil Merryweather: The Groove (5.32) (1975)
17 Be-Bop Deluxe: Swansong (5.53) (1975)
18 Seventh Wave: Star Palace of the Sombre Warrior (3.12) (1975)
19 The Dictators: Master Race Rock (4.17) (1975)
20 Rik Kenton: The Libertine (3.21) (1976)
21 Kiss: Great Expectations (4.24) (1976)
22 The Runaways: Dead End Justice (6.10) (1976)
23 Chrome: My Time to Live (4.21) (1976)
24 Doctors of Madness: Mainlines (15.46) (1976)

By late 1969, those murders perpetrated by Hell's Angels at The Rolling Stones' infamous Altamont Festival, and by the Manson Family up in the Hollywood Hills, were taxing the Utopianism of even the most idealistic hippies. While music pushed ever onward into new territories of avant-garde psychedelic-rock, the practising of free love and anti-capitalist and anti-Vietnam student protests (and riots) had become de rigueur across much of the world throughout the period 1965–8. By 1969, however, the idealistic freight train had hit the buffers. That was the year in which even rock's hardiest experimentalists ceased to proceed exclusively forwards, and, amid all the murders, the cash-ins, the hype and the rip-offs, a question began to loom large: where in hell was the so-called Alternative Society headed?

Adventurous rock'n'rollers in need of a Utopian goal sought solace in that summer's first NASA moon landing. For poets and singers of the new myth, our polluted and post-atomic world was apparently dying before our very eyes, and space exploration was to be humanity's saviour. As the heroes of choice for teenage boys, the gentlemen of NASA temporarily eclipsed even our beloved rock stars; they were no less mysterious, wore even wackier outfits, controlled bigger budgets, and were pushing humanity forwards in a highly visible manner; and, boy, were they using technology![1]

And so, knee-deep in the carnage of '69, the freaks started looking backwards for inspiration, seeking brief sanctuary in revivalist performances of the wild, original 1950s rock'n'roll which had set them on the road in the first place. New megastars Led Zeppelin – inspired no doubt by The Jeff Beck Group's wild, stomping, strung-out version of Elvis' 'All Shook Up' – regularly included their own live versions of The King's songs, while Black Sabbath threw in a jaunty version of Carl Perkins' 'Blue Suede Shoes' among their live

---

1 Just as minstrels of the past had adapted old songs to accommodate the current exploits of their cultural heroes, so modern songwriters, too, made detailed accounts of the exploits of these new heroes. Typically, it was the folk artists who responded most immediately to the moon landings, The Byrds bringing forth 'Armstrong, Aldrin and Collins', while Donovan contributed 'The Voyage to the Moon', The Grateful Dead released 'Mountains of the Moon' and John Stewart offered his controversial homage 'Armstrong'.

set's knuckle-dragging blues epics. In 1969, prog-rock behemoths Vanilla Fudge abandoned entirely their 1967/'68 classical pretensions (typical titles: 'Variation on a Theme from Mozart's Divertimento No. 13 in F Major' and 'Beethoven: Für Elise and Theme from Moonlight Sonata') and spectacular cultural conceits (my fave title has to be 'Voices in Time: Neville Chamberlain, Winston Churchill, Franklin Delano Roosevelt, Harry S. Truman, John F. Kennedy, and Other Voices') in favour of calling their 1969 album (get this!) *Rock & Roll* . . . Talk about abandoning ship! Indeed, within months the Vanilla Fudge rhythm section had formed Cactus, whose gasoline-guzzlin' repertoire included stomping versions of Little Richard's 'Long Tall Sally' and 'You Can't Judge a Book by Looking at the Cover'.

While John Ono Lennon still flew the freak flag with his 1969, Yoko-inspired avant-garde projects, even The Beatles themselves returned to the safety of their raw, rock'n'roll roots for their post-*White Album* recordings, John and Paul even daring to record one of their own rock'n'roll-era originals, 'One After 909', for their final LP.

Where The Beatles went, so the Beatle-watchers followed. The Move's Roy Wood threw off his 1968 obsessions with Love, Buffalo Springfield and the West Coast scene, greased back his long, flowing hair, and proceeded to barf forth his own radically futuristic versions of '50s rock'n'roll in a style that was sultry, alien and brand new. The Move's 'When Alice Comes Back to the Farm' sounded as though it had been fed through a Phil Spector or Joe Meek filter, while their 1970 single 'Brontosaurus' featured '50s elements that were performed so pointedly, and slowed down to such a crawl, that they even rivalled the sludge-trudge of fellow Brummies Black Sabbath.[2]

Surely the clearest evidence of the counter-culture's outright need to cosy up with the recent past was the appearance at the Woodstock Festival of Teddy-boy group Sha Na Na. For this motley bunch of revivalists, with neither a Top Fifty hit nor a successful LP to their name, took to the stage of the most epochal event

2 On the ostensibly twelve-bar-boogie-based Move forty-five 'When Alice Comes Back to the Farm', Roy Wood integrated radical chords and new structures so effortlessly that the song – superficially at least – appeared like an authentic rock'n'roll tune. Look inside, however, and we can see the songs of Ian Hunter and Ziggy-period Bowie staring back at us.

of '60s hippiedom to play their set of nine '50s covers not early in the day, but high on the bill of the final night, sandwiched between new superstars Crosby, Stills, Nash and Young[3] and Jimi Hendrix, whose performance concluded the entire three-day event. The dawn of the 1970s was but one hundred and four days away, but the band playing second from the top of the most legendary '60s festival of them all was going down a storm playing 'At the Hop', 'Jailhouse Rock' and 'Teen Angel' . . .

Remake/Remodel

So the swinging '60s were over and the time was ripe for glam-rock. But, whoa, it was not a pretty sight. Across the pond, a failed London songwriter called David Bowie[4] demanded that rock music be 'tarted up, made into a prostitute, a parody of itself', not realising that such an attitude would ultimately provide a safe haven for all the flotsam and jetsam of the music biz, the walking dead and has-beens of the recent (and not-so-recent) past, artistes [*sic*] who – painfully aware of Sha Na Na's success in front of 'the young people' at Woodstock – now seized their opportunity and rushed to the pan stick and eyeliner in order to try and resuscitate their dormant, nay, dead careers.

What emerged at first was frightful. A former '60s no-mark singer

3 Neil Young played only on certain songs because the film cameras distracted him.

4 While the Bowie of 1969 was still a Denmark Street song hack, peddling compositions and doing a folk act, over in Arizona there was an experimental quintet that went by the name of Alice Cooper (formerly The Spiders), whose lead singer was already 'wearing ladies' sling-back shoes and false eye-lashes and dresses', according to Wayne County. That is, until Bowie – typically – appropriated Cooper's style, then set about obscuring the source of his *The Man Who Sold the World* image by slagging off Cooper as often and distractingly as he could. Come to think of it, it's also highly unlikely that such a shameless art-vampire as Bowie could possibly have been unaware of Alice Cooper's 1969 song 'Return of the Spiders', from their LP *Pretties for You*. So you gotta wonder why, with all his decades of success, David Bowie is still in denial. Even as late as 1993 he was obviously so nervous about the connection that he commented to Suede's Brent Anderson: 'I don't even think [Alice Cooper] tried theatricality, until they saw the English bands.' What a crock! Watch a film of Alice Cooper at the 1970 Toronto Pop Festival; their act was so theatrical that it was in danger of overwhelming the musical content. And yet Bowie's act, as late as August 1971, was described thus by Wayne County, one of his greatest apologists: '. . . the show was really disappointing . . . it was a folky act with acoustic guitars and Mick Ronson looking like a dippy hippie'.

called Paul Raven returned as a shock-faced, portly, tinfoil-bedecked MC named Gary Glitter (achieving his first Top Ten hit at the age of thirty-two), while the no less youthful Shane Fenton reinvented himself as a Matalan Gene Vincent named Alvin Stardust (first Top Ten hit aged thirty-one). Bowie's famous 'parody of itself' quote backfired badly as oldsters across the music scene glammed up, hoping to knock a few years off. When Ian Patterson became Mott the Hoople's Ian Hunter, this former bass player for early-'60s beat group The Apex scored his first Top Ten hit (aged thirty-three) with 'All the Young Dudes', a David Bowie song, no less! When Hunter sang, in 1973's 'Hymn for the Dudes', 'You ain't the Nazz/ You're just a buzz/Some kinda temporary,' he was long in the tooth enough to know what a brief spell at the top would mean. Indeed, Hunter's love of '50s rock'n'roll would ultimately upend his group, turning them into the frightful pastiche that would later beget such walking abortions as Racey and The Rubettes.

But I digress. Thanks to the generation-hopping qualities of glam-rock ('Get up and get your grandma out of here!' bellowed Kiss), even Glasgow legend Alex Harvey, fronting his Sensational Alex Harvey Band (all of whom were ten years his junior), finally made it into the UK Top Ten (after spending several years in the cast of the musical *Hair*), a mere seventeen-and-a-bit years after commencing his professional career by winning a 1958 Tommy Steele lookalike contest. Further south, in Newcastle-upon-Tyne, future Roxy Music leader Bryan Ferry (first Top Ten hit aged twenty-seven) had been signed, briefly, to Polydor Records with his group The Banshees. However, Ferry had spent most of the '60s as an art teacher and was older even than such psychedelic legends as Keith Moon and Syd Barrett. Indeed, even glam-rock's founding fathers, Marc Bolan and David Bowie, had both been professional recording musicians since 1965.

Had there ever been such a mongrel, such a musical mutt? This mechanical, highly stylised and oh-so-knowing version of the 'real thing' . . . could rock'n'roll even survive such a cynical, sell-out phenomenon as glam-rock? Everyone jumped on the bandwagon. Leo Sayer launched his career as a bizarre, scat-singing glam-rock harlequin and was taken entirely seriously. Even already established acts went glam. Dressed as a quartet of Bonnie and Clyde-styled gangsters, Chicory Tip couldn't get arrested, but restyled as glam-rock space aliens, singing Giorgio Moroder's daft Euro anthem 'Son of My Father', they went to Number One. As a bubblegum group, The Sweet had a highly successful career before they discovered glam-rock, regularly assaulting the Top Thirty with sub-sub-Archies, sub-'Chirpy Chirpy Cheep Cheep' abortions such as 'Poppa Joe', 'Funny Funny' and 'Alexander Graham Bell' (a devastating singalong homage to the inventor of the telephone, no less).[5] But as soon as songwriters Nicky Chinn and Mike Chapman wrote a vocal character part for preening macho bassist Steve Priest, the simpering Mae Westian drivel that spewed forth from his mutant mush turned the band into overnacht superstars. Within months, Priest was vying with Mud's Rob Davis for pole position as rock's Most Effeminate Heterosexual, while Mott's Ariel Bender and Slade's Dave Hill sulked and pouted in eclipsed disgust![6]

Thereafter, spewdo-intellectual revisionist authors of the '80s and '90s, intent on rendering '70s glam-rock as a gay phenomenon, denied 'the brickies-in-lippy' reality which was the scene's overridingly heterosexual context, possibly for the simple reason that beautiful people hate the uglies and wanna write them out of the story. Besides, unlike its Wodenist, Midland siblings, hard-rock and heavy metal – genres entirely ignored by the so-called intellectuals – the presence at the epicentre of glam-rock of two such pixies as Bowie and Bolan meant that almost *everybody* (compared to that fey duo, at least) was a 'brickie-in-lippy', including such important glam-rockers as the Adrian Street-esque Mick Ronson; the shark-like Mick 'Woody' Woodmansey; the Edwardian dockside crane Trevor Bolder; Mott's Overend Watts; Alice Cooper's six-foot-five drummer Neal Smith, and hairy-chested songwriter Michael Bruce. So, when you look at these accused, each one is an esteemed and fucking central hub

5 Back in the day, The Sweet always used to protest to the 'real' rock press that their hard-rock roots had been derailed (and obscured) by the careerist methods of producer/writers Nicky Chinn and Mike Chapman, conveniently forgetting that their pre-glam hits for RCA had not been hard-rock at all.

6 The painted lead guitarist is a bizarre glam-rock phenomenon that began with Sensational Alex Harvey Band's Zal Cleminson, then migrated to Kiss' Ace Frehley via Bob Starkie of Australian glam-rockers Skyhooks.

of the glam-rock scene. So fuck that 'brickies-in-lippy' shit.[7]

And so, when film director Todd Haynes revised glam-rock's roots into some Utopian gay impulse with his 1998 movie *Velvet Goldmine*, he was swimming against the tide of evidence in favour of a romantic theory that suited his own sexuality.[8] Of course, we now know from the biographies that many of the main glam protagonists dabbled in homosexuality, but they were clearly just being swept along by the spirit of the time. This spirit was driven not by the artists themselves, but by their gay retainers and designers (such as former Andy Warholites Tony Zanetta, Leee [*sic*] Black Childers and Wayne County), and then goaded into even more radical action by muses such as Marc Bolan's partner June Child and David Bowie's wife Angela. Yes, *wives*! For, even during this exceptionally free period in Western culture, the main protagonists of glam-rock, Messrs Bolan, Bowie, Reed and Pop, were all married. That the surge of glam made gay liberation a real possibility is undeniable, but it certainly wasn't the genre's primary impulse.

Moreover, glam-rock was not a new impulse at all. It was just about getting rock music back on the highway and out of the muddy gulleys and gutters that honest singer-songwriters (ouch!) and authentic bluesmen (wince!) such as Joni Mitchell, James Taylor and Rory Gallagher had steered it into. 'This ain't a parody,' sang Silverhead. Indeed, the spirit of glam was closer to that of Oscar Wilde's aphorism: 'One should either be a work of art, or wear a work of art.'

So, far from heralding anything truly new, glam-rock was actually a return to the traditional; a glittering paladin of rock'n'roll's core Saturday-night entertainment values, preaching sex, sleight-of-hand and oblivion. It was about returning rock'n'roll to its natural, Little Richardian showbiz path, a path it never would have left in the first place if those shitty, so-called serious artists (Cream? I shit 'em) had not waylaid the population with their

7 It's an attitude that's far too close to the kind of muso snobbery of the late-'60s Island Records inner sanctum which caused Guy Stevens' Hereford-derived Mott the Hoople studio project to be mythologised as yokel morons by Traffic in the title track of their 1971 LP *The Low Spark of High Heel Boys*.

8 In Todd Haynes' foreword to Barney Hoskyns' 1998 book *Glam!*, Haynes admits: 'Growing up in the States, I basically missed glam rock.'

faded denim, proto-Coldplay honesty and minging blues authenticity.

Evidence for my claims littered the early 1960s. Audiences of that period demanded such glamour and show from their rock'n'rollers that groups were often able to disguise their feeble playing simply by dressing up. Top of the list was the artless, proto-Alice Cooper 'horror rock' of Screaming Lord Sutch, whose band travelled throughout 1961 and '62 in an ambulance surmounted by a huge pink crocodile, and whose stage act included arriving via a coffin and wearing large bull horns, monster feet and two-foot-long hair. Horror movies also inspired the frock coats and top hats of Jackie Lomax's beat group The Undertakers, who arrived at shows in a hearse throughout 1963. No, this was not yet glam-rock as such, but such extreme showmanship soon goaded others to new highs and lows. Also in 1963, future counter-culture mainstay Twink signed to Decca Records, along with his controversial R&B outfit The Fairies, which featured future Mott the Hoople organist Mick 'Blue' Weaver, while Yorkshire's The Quare Fellows sported bleached hair and outrageous clothes. Thereafter, Beatlemania's overwhelming influence temporarily tamed all-comers (foisting neatnik suits on to all but the wildest), until idiot savagery returned with The Pretty Things' outrageously long hair, manifesting further in The Rolling Stones' outright transvestism for the cover of their 1966 single 'Have You Seen Your Mother, Baby (Standing in the Shadows)'. If anything, glam-rock was about pretending to be homosexual in order to further threaten an already intimidated straight world. It was a concept completely in keeping with the Total Wind-Up style of The Rolling Stones' Brian Jones and the band's mid-'60s teenage manager Andrew Loog Oldham, and something brilliantly envisioned in William Burroughs' turn-of-the-decade novel *The Wild Boys*, whose dystopian future vision depicted Western cities populated by hordes of lawless gay boys Teenage Rampaging in packs.

'Why you all got long hair?' a nervous Essex lad's voice asks The Yardbirds on their terminal forty-five 'Happenings Ten Years Time Ago'. 'I bet you do all right with the crumpet, dontcha?' he continues, semi-sarcastically, semi-obsequiously. Fear of being ritually bummed by hip teenagers . . . the man down the pub's ultimate nightmare.

Anyway, let's get on with describing what goes on in this here *Glamrocksampler*, the contents of which appear in chronological order.

Tyrannosaurus Rex: King of the Rumbling Spires
(Regal, 1969)

Tyrannosaurus Rex's incredible 1969 single was the fourth and final release to feature original percussionist Steve Peregrin Took, and a song on which Marc Bolan anticipated Adam and the Ants' entire Burundi schtick over a decade early. Replete with heavy bass from producer Tony Visconti, and exhibiting a whole new arsenal of orchestral concussion quite unlike that showcased on earlier releases, 'King of the Rumbling Spires' exudes a rush and a roar, nay, a sheer obstinate otherness quite unlike anything anyone (Bolan included) had achieved before. Abounding with bizarre 'tween-time key changes, keyboard gimmickry and brutal stop–start rhythms, this single release unleashed a legion of possibilities into the post-hippie world, and then some.

The Move: When Alice Comes Back to the Farm
(Fly, 1970)

Even hairier but not nearly as pretty as Marc Bolan, The Move's Roy Wood had kept his Brummie bad lads in the charts for three years through a mixture of ingenuity and sheer eclecticism. But, by 1970, the latter was beginning to spread his muse too thin. However, when The Beatles returned to rock'n'roll, in 1969, Fab Four-watcher Wood returned to his ur-fave like a duck's arse to water. Only Wood's die-hard (and damned annoying) eclecticism stood between us and a whole LP of the exquisite, heavy arrangements found on 'When Alice Comes Back to the Farm', 'Brontosaurus' and 'Don't Make My Baby Blue'. 'When Alice Comes Back to the Farm' is a Sid James of a song, its riffs gnarled and toughened with usage; yet its tempo changes and constant gear-shifts are truly what make the song, for me. Somehow, its rhythms also anticipate David Bowie's Ziggy Stardust period (especially the song 'Star'), and the track powers through with an unbelievably oily engine-room ruggedness.

John Kongos: He's Gonna Step on You Again
(Fly, 1971)

Now, as mentioned earlier, we only have to make a cursory scan of the evidence to see that glam-rock's Marc Bolan roots lay deep in the late-'60s Utopian 'street' style of agit-folk singers such as Donovan, P. F. Sloan and New York's own proto-punk outlaw David Peel, whose own metaphor had of late been appropriated by John 'Legendary Stardust' Lennon for deployment during his Me and the Missus and Ten-Score Celebrity Percussionists period, with the Plastic Ono Band's protest love-in singalongs such as 'Give Peace a Chance', 'Instant Karma' and 'Power to the People'. It was upon this commune/commie wave that John Kongos surfed in, scoring two big hits in 1971 with 'Tokoloshe Man' and this ode to the Man, 'He's Gonna Step on You Again'. Kongos' own success inspired contemporary rebel commie activist duos Third World War (Fly label-mates from Notting Hill) and Tokyo's Zuno Keisatsu, a.k.a. Brain Police. Happy Mondays' 1990 baggy versh was similarly monumental *and* was bound to a similarly barmy scene.

Tiger B. Smith: Tiger Rock
(Vertigo, 1972)

Germany's Tiger B. Smith anticipated Gene'n'Paul's Kiss ultra-metaphor way back in '72, as evidenced by this track from their debut LP, *Tiger Rock*. Herein, over riffing so basic every '70s toddler with a kazoo wouldna tried it in case his childminder figured him a retard, singer/guitarist Holger Schmidt declares that the woman who adores him must look elsewhere because he's the Tiger and has to be free. Schmidt then proceeds to ram the point home with the incessant barrage of spew listed below:

Ain't gonna do it,
Just will not do it, just will not do, I just can't do it,
Can't make me do it,
I will not do it,
Just will not do it,
Just will not do it,
Can't make me do it . . . [repeated at least thirty-two times]

Ah, what depths of the human condition lurk and linger at the interface of heavy metal and glam-rock. 'Tiger Rock' is as devolved and low-grade as Bang's tortuous slave-metal riffing on their sub-sub-Ace Frehley mind-death fry-up 'Future Shock'.

Pussy: Feline Woman
(Deram, 1972)

Hot on their tail is the inimitably named power trio Pussy, whose sole, 1972 Deram forty-five was produced by Deep Purple's Ian Gillan. Vocally, this bunch sound Hispanic, although I know they ain't, as the rhythm section belonged to the London band Jerusalem. It's weird how Purple's ex-Episode Six members (Gillan and Roger Glover) both became adept at producing. Anyway, I digress. From Pussy, we move to Lucifer's porno-rock, as it was billed at the time.

Lucifer: Fuck You
(Private pressing, 1972)

Worthy of a place in this *Glamrocksampler* if only for its astonishing Cocksucker Blues-like seediness, 'Fuck You' by lone wolf Lucifer is a slice of avant-blues of the kind that commune bands such as Shagrat probably made every night of their lives. Releasing this shit on seven-inch is another thing again, however, and the record was advertised only in the back pages of certain music and sex mags. I very much dig its awe-ful eternities of silence and its rhymes, but the spoken final verse is truly one of rock'n'roll's most brutally harrowing moments. Nice.

White Witch: Class of 2000
(Capricorn, 1973)

Next, let me tell you how this glam-rock ensemble from Georgia navigated the inevitable problems entailed in hailing from the southern United States. Led by occultist Ron Goedert, the Witch cleverly kept their fagginess to the Alice Cooper/ Silverhead/Rolling Stones type and signed to Capricorn Records, thereby gaining a little of The Allman Brothers' respectability. Coupling this with a huge dedication to describing their pot intake and a tendency to lapse into late-'60s cosiness, White Witch nevertheless contained, in Goedert, a sometimes shamanic singer whose outrageous vocal delivery occasionally outdid even that of Sir Lord Baltimore's John Garner. The track contained herein is from their second (highly patchy) LP *A Spiritual Gathering*, and showcases Goedert's voice at its most elatingly elastic.

Jobriath: World Without End
(Elektra, 1973)

Now if ever there was clear proof that glam-rock should never be revised as having been a historically gay phenomenon, then it's revealed right here in the career of Jobriath, the hapless (although supremely talented) Texan songwriter whom Elektra Records signed as the USA's first openly gay performer. Sure, his debut album was patchy and swamped by hype (did he really sign for half a million dollars?), but Jobriath's rich muse was not deserving of such a truly horrific outcome, one in which the poor lad was so psychically battered that he crawled back into his exquisite shell and refused thereafter to sing any of his songs ever again, living out the remainder of his tragic life singing torch songs under the name Cole

Berlin, before dying of AIDS in 1983. Yes, Jobriath's music was confused, but some of that Texan yawp at times displayed a pure Roky Erickson-ness that was as crystal clear as their shared ur-ancestor, Buddy Holly. Moreover, this track, 'World Without End', anticipated the Krautfunk of David Bowie's 1975 *Station to Station* album fully twenty-four months in advance of the Tin White Machine himself.

Silverhead: 16 and Savaged
(Purple, 1973)

Being a real-life marquis really stopped Silverhead singer Michael Des Barres from properly making it; he just didn't *need* to slum it, he was already rich. Which is a shame, because when he was hard-working he was superb, as evidenced by the extremely dubious but highly hilarious front cover of Silverhead's second album. Anyway, here's the title track of that aforementioned LP, and what a mega-stomp it is! Imagine *Rocks*-period Joe Perry playing a Jimmy Page Zep riff, plus some of the really fine overdriven Hammond that Tony Kaye played occasionally on early Yes records. Nice? Superb!

Amon Düül II: Jalousie
(United Artists, 1973)

By 1973, the glam-rock virus had so taken hold of the music business that even arch progressive underground tsars Amon Düül II made a so-called glam album entitled *Vive La Trance.* Of course, being German allowed their uncomprehending musicians to dress as characters from the *Wizard of Oz*, so long as singer Renate Knaup shopped at Biba and there was enough tin foil, snakeskin and platform boots in evidence. On *Vive La Trance*, Amon Düül II sustained a particularly high level of songwriting for a bunch who'd emerged from the commune scene, none more so than this proto-Kate Bush ballad. I'd rather have had this in the UK charts back in the day than fucking 'S-s-s-single Bed' by Noosha Fox. As ever, Peter Leopold's urgently lyrical free-drumming propels the band in an outrageous manner, as beautiful Renate caterwauls in her best and most Brechtian manner.

Argent: God Gave Rock'n'roll to You
(Epic, 1973)

Continuing to mine for gems at the prog/glam interface, we next find a wonderfully arch (and almost unnecessarily rousing) chorus emanating from Argent's beatific forty-five 'God Gave Rock'n'Roll to You'. Written by the band's guitarist Russ Ballard, this song (all seven minutes-plus of it on the *In Deep* album version) highlights glam-rock's old-age phenomenon perfectly. Ballard had commenced his career as a professional musician back in 1961, strumming for Adam Faith, and still performed with too much of that overly smiley, uncool grimacing self-consciously whenever he realised he should be giving it loads of Jim Morrison cheekbone. But, despite Russ' tendency to come over like a Roy Orbison/ Hank Marvin who'd been immersed in a family-size bottle of Jeff Beck, his long years in the mid-'60s beat-group wilderness invoked in him an almost mawkish sense of self-pity, similar to that of Ian Hunter, which manifested in ridiculously poignant and anthemic rock ballads, all arranged with band co-leader and former Zombie Rod Argent. It's surely Ballard's long career experience that gives the guitar solo herein such a plaintive quality, treading a line between Mott's Mick Ralphs and Tony Peluso's exhilarating fuzz tail-out on the Carpenters' 'Goodbye to Love'. That Argent's biggest (and best-known) hit, 'Hold Your Head Up', had been written by Rod's former Zombies colleague Chris White must have been a constant pain to Ballard, who made up for it thereafter by spewing out hit after vapid, bombastic hit for such acts as Rainbow ('Since You've Been Gone'), Hot Chocolate ('So, You Win Again') and Kiss' Ace Frehley-via-Hello ('New York Groove'). Indeed, the unmasked Kiss themselves rewrote this here Argent hit for their own versh in the 1990s, replacing Ballard's mysterious lyric, 'Love Cliff Richard but please don't tease,' with something far more Yank-friendly. Oh, and check out YouTube for some well-dodgy miming on *The Old Grey Whistle Test* . . .

Pantherman: Pantherman
(Polydor, 1974)

As we move now into 1974, I should mention that the *Melody Maker* review of the first Queen LP was captioned 'The Fag-end of Glam'. That was late summer '73, and yet we're barely halfway through this glam trawl. OK, next up, we have the Netherlands' own singular version of glam-rock in the form of 'Pantherman', a spirited although direct rip-off of Roxy Music's 'Virginia Plain' performed by one-man glam-rock band Pantherman. Like Tiger B. Smith before him, Frank 'Pantherman' Klunhaar was clearly so full of feline attitude that he just couldn't wait to (a) 'Show you my paws,' and (b) 'Show you my claws.' Hell, kiddies, once you fall victim to that hook line ('I'm gonna bite you!') you can see why the Dutch media ignored it. Stranger still, then, that Klunhaar struggled on through a coupla further flop forty-fives before he decided (in his own words) '. . . to put down the Pantherman mask because the concept had not proven very successful'.

Mustard: Good Time Comin'
(EMI, 1974)

Now what was it about the glam-rock metaphor that enabled totally mechanical, robot-like stomp-athons such as this to sit so snugly alongside the music and poetry of singularly beautiful misfits such as Messrs Bolan, Bowie, Harley and Nelson? Mustard belongs to the Blackfoot Sue school of Moronick Toss, and clatters along like a Creedence cassette demo with Kiss' Paul 'Starchild' Stanley on lead larynx. Sometimes the wafer-thin line between hard-rock and glam-rock snags, and bands such as Mott the Hoople, Murahatchibu and Mustard slip through. It's uncanny.

Iron Virgin: Rebels Rule
(Deram, 1974)

Spare a thought for the progeny of Edinburgh's Iron Virgin, whose secondary educations would have been constantly marred by having to defend Dad's dodgy '70s decision to wear a chastity belt inscribed with the legend 'KEEP OUT!'. Yup, a glam-rock band without hits is like a porn star without tits, and Iron Virgin's debut forty-five – a cover of Sir Macca's 'Jet' – was totally fucking buried when Wings' original charted barely a month later. This hasty follow-up received plenty of radio play but still died a death, leaving da Virgin rudderless and adrift with nowt but a pile o'platforms waiting to be reheeled. 'Rebels Rule' is a damned good song, though; it reminds me of the Human League's daft-but-epic 'Empire State Human', or even something by early, Valerian-period Gazza Numan.

Dump: Annabella
(Fontana, 1975)

Next up, we got old Pantherman's sibling on the deck. Yup, Dump is more of the Nederlanders' take on glam, and their all-purpose 1975 single 'Annabella' covers just about every glam-rock cliché. Commencing just like The Partridge Family's 'I Think I Love You', the band's singers thereafter – over a crunching cycle of different glitter tempos – run through a gamut of emotions, ranging from Sean Bonniwell's paranoid baritone on Music Machine's 'Talk Talk' to archetypal, strained,

'Cum On, Feel the Noize'-period Noddy Holder, via a refrain ('He's got no self-control') that entirely anticipates Devo's gloriously teenage chorus (same tone'n'everything) on 'Uncontrollable Urge'.[9] 'Annabella' never charted in the UK, but I well remember it got played to death on the radio.

Neil Merryweather: The Groove
(Mercury, 1975)

Ah, Neil Merryweather . . . so close and yet so far. Like many scholarly musos, the moustachioed Merryweather spent much of the early '70s in loose blues/folk aggregations, organising super-jams with Dave Mason types and generally authenticatin' his soul. Boy, it weren't half drippy and dreary, I can tell you. Then he heard Todd Rundgren's *A Wizard, a True Star* and admitted to himself that the *Ziggy Stardust* album had also really touched a nerve. So, in the grand glam-rock tradition, Merryweather wrote a series of future-dystopia 'vision songs' and declared himself for space, thereafter appearing clad only in Todd Clark-like space captain's overalls, his newly bleached'n'be-fringed barnet only accentuating his defiant retaining of the Old Regime muzzy. Like Ian Hunter, whose Road to Damascus moment had been celebrated with similar splendour, songs about the song proliferated in the new Merryweather canon, while behind him blazed a singular hard-rock act not unlike Mott themselves. Known as the Space Rangers, Merryweather's band was hot, and the guitarist was a sky-high colossus in the style of Bill Nelson. I picked up my first Merryweather in 1998, at a second-hand shop in Devizes, and soon discovered his purple patch had been unfortunately brief. But feast your lugholes on 'The Groove' and agree with me: when he got it right, he didn't half nail it down.

Be-Bop Deluxe: Swansong
(Harvest, 1975)

Next, I feel a little background fact and recent history is necessary to know about this Bill Nelson fellow, in order to best enjoy his song. Prior to releasing the sublime and earthquaking 'Swansong', Nelson had sacked

9 Interesting that the collective singing style on the chorus to Devo's delightful 'Uncontrollable Urge' was adopted, hook, line and sinker, one year later by The Undertones. Somehow, its gleeful innocence suited the delivery and appearance of Michael Bradley and co.

his galumphing Yorkshire glam-rock band, high-tailed it to the Smoke and hired two hotshots on bass and drums. Now he is delivering his second record, with the brand-new line-up. He's so coiled and ready to burst that the record company depict him on the record sleeve as a bound harlequin god attempting to escape the clutches of his restrainers. The record itself he dedicated 'To the Muse in the Moon' – right fucking on! 'Swansong' is surely the most exultant of all glam-rock songs, its breathtaking compositional beauty surpassed by the ludicrous heights to which its composer/performer ascends in order to tell 'Her' how he feels. Sometimes I switch this track off halfway through. No shit, I can't take that level of yearning any more.

Seventh Wave: Star Palace of the Sombre Warrior
(Gull, 1975)

While it would be too gauche of me to describe the early-'70s 'serious' music scene as having been a cultural war between hordes of horny heavy-rockers on the trail of eternal pussy, versus dickless grammar-school boys who carried their hard-ons in their . . . no? There is, nevertheless, still a certain poetic truth to such an assertion. Furthermore, the stalemate was only broken by Eno, a once glorious and exquisitely painted alien whose needs were such that he was full-on enough to demand that we accept his receding, Mekon-like hairline as evidence of both greater intellectual capacity *and* cock'n'ball sac power. So when, in 1973, Roxy's so-called 'non-musician' hooked up with the über-beard nerd-boffin Robert Fripp, the mythically named Eno bestrode such a previously unstraddleable chasm between the boot boys of the metalwork class and the Einsteins of the science lab that it united them briefly on the school playground, to engage (albeit temporarily) in holy conversation. In the meantime, it's hard to imagine, from this musical evidence, that Seventh Wave began life as the clunking, low-grade stoners Chillum, whose sole LP had appeared in a handmade, self-printed limited edition. In their new Seventh Wave guise, this unholy trio occupied a bizarre hinterland in the mid-'70s scene, photographed by Mick Rock and coming on like the most decadent of all the glam-rockers. On this their second LP, one song commences with a direct lyrical quote from Scott Walker's 'The Amorous Humphrey Plugg' ('Plastic Palace Alice'), before descending into *A Clockwork Orange* territory with the help of Van der Graaf Generator's Hugh Banton.

Stranger still, the vocals that open this song sound exactly like Peter Hammill on Van der Graaf's *Godbluff.* And as that album, Hammill's own *Nadir's Big Chance* and this Seventh Wave LP were all contemporaneous . . . well, it makes you think, don't it?

The Dictators: Master Race Rock
(Epic, 1975)

As one door opens, so another closes. I'm talking – of course – about the manner in which the Ramones opened their debut 1976 LP with the same 'Let's go!' chant as The Dictators used to close their own debut album from one year earlier. Nobody noticed because The Dictators' *Go Girl Crazy!* debut was mostly just a ragbag of mixed metaphors, in-jokes and co-producer Sandy Pearlman's stock methodology. Even today, the sound appears at times far too BÖC-by-numbers, while elsewhere it's just a bogus '60s piss-take. Where it scores, however, is on the two tracks 'Master Race Rock' and 'The Next Big Thing', which ape *Destroyer*-period Kiss magnificently and make you wanna Blu-Tack posters all over your ceiling.

Rik Kenton: The Libertine
(EMI, 1976)

With the punk-rock future as predicted by The Dictators already within our grasp, then, let's spare a thought for poor old Rik Kenton, former bass player with Roxy Music. Although a member of that celebrated ensemble for barely six months during 1972, Kenton was still – four years later – trying desperately to summon up a little of the Brian/Bryan magic with his own single, 'The Libertine', for whose EMI sessions the ultra-thorough Kenton hired in several glam-rock institutions as his backing band, including guitarists Chris Spedding and Cockney Rebel's Jim Cregan, along with Bowie/Bolan drummer Tony Newman and 'Walk on the Wild Side' arranger Herbie Flowers on brass and bass. As evidenced here, the charming song itself, while somewhat underwhelming, remains undeniable proof that the glam impulse was still considered to be commercially vibrant as late as 1976.

Kiss: Great Expectations
(Casablanca, 1976)

Glam-rock's preening and solipsistic self-regard surely reached its apotheosis in Kiss' 1976 song 'Great Expectations', in which Gene Simmons anticipated the band's forthcoming Super-Kiss period and described his awe-ful vision of daughters of fine US citizens lusting piteously after his scaly body, so tantalisingly out of reach. If you think Ian Hunter feyed out a little too much on his enormous solo ballad 'Boy', then cop an earful as the demon takes it all umpteen seven-league-boot strides further over the horizon of self-regard. Gosh. Replete with 'Toronto' Bobby Ezrin's astonishingly göyische,[10] nay, Canadian orchestrations and a choir, no less, 'Great Expectations' is epic, cloying, perfect . . .

The Runaways: Dead End Justice
(Mercury, 1976)

When John Peel played this song in summer 1976, I felt like giving up. These chicks were all younger than me, and I still lived at home . . . Motherfucker! Hate Kim Fowley for the dirty cunt that he is, but praise his directing skills to the skies for this hefty slab o'jailbait jailbreak. Taking equal amounts of Shangri-Las' tradition and sheer teenage-girl attitude, Joan Jett and Cherie Curie act out a desperate tale of urchin camaraderie against the Man. Its six-minute duration is magnificent, tense, gauche, inept, daring and brave all at the same time. When this LP was released, my then thirteen-year-old wife, Dorian, played piano in an all-girl band called The Shooting Stars. On hearing this record, she split her band. Nuff said.

Chrome: My Time to Live
(Siren Songs, 1976)

Vocalist/lyricist/songwriter/drummer Damon Edge was the Klaus Dinger of the late-'70s San Francisco scene, and his ultra-sharp view of the alienated future world created in Chrome's music a superb doorway between true gasoline-garage rock'n'roll and the futuristic art house. His voice was punky, edgy, snidey, always harping on and on. However, I've included in this collection one of the tracks from Chrome's 1976 debut LP *The Visitation*, on which Edge employed lead singer Mike Low. Despite it being an utter anachronism within the Chrome canon, 'My Time to Live' is a hauntingly beautiful piece of guitar-heavy late glam, occupying that same upper atmosphere as Uli Jon Roth's inspired *Earthquake* project.

10 'Göyische' is Yiddish (German Jewish) for anything 'non-Jewish' or Gentile.

Doctors of Madness: Mainlines
(United Artists, 1976)

OK, it's mid-'76 and punk-rock is barely months away and The Dictators have already handed on their baton to the Ramones, so, uh, 'Let's go!' Hold on, what's this bunch of ugs doing with a near sixteen-minute-long glam-rock epic? When it's time to move on culturally, there's always a coupla Luddites trying to keep us all back in the day (The Jam, in '77, were just the fucking same). So, while the rest of the 1976 world was gearing up for the forthcoming two-minute hate, Doctors of Madness' Kid Strange, Urban Blitz and co. were down in United Artists' studio, laying stinking, side-long dystopian turds upon our doorsteps. That said, 'Mainlines' is one hell of a movement. Writ into umpteen sections and taking at least three listens before the song even starts to make sense, when it really kicks in, boy, don't it just! It's a shame no sucker gave this song more than a cursory earful back in the day. But then, who had the time when you could say it all in one minute and fifty-four?

Some Conclusions

Hopefully, I've shown here – without taking too many liberties – that glam-rock was an icky flypaper of a term for a genre so widely drawn that it has, in its time, sucked all living things into its gaping, badly painted maw – well, everything in da music biz, anyway. During the period 1970–5, everything was tainted by glam-rock, even such disparate practitioners as the folkie Strawbs, the ultra-serious Peter Hammill and the defiantly imageless AC/DC. And, despite having chided his contemporaries by singing 'You don't have to camp around' in 1973, Todd Rundgren still dared to appear on NBC's *Soul Train* TV show in full drag the following year. Indeed, even Tangerine Dream's granite-like leader, Edgar Froese, ponced out for the cover of his hefty 1974 double LP *Ages*, which at least had the decency to contain a twelve-minute epic entitled 'Metropolis' that aped the Moog music of Walter Carlos' soundtrack for *A Clockwork Orange*.

Indeed, no so-called 'serious artists' seemed truly above slumming it, however temporarily, in the glam basement. I, for one, was mightily let down by the very average, American FM-rock emanating from the grooves of Edgar Winter's glamorously clad, but with zilch glam-rock content, 1972 LP, *They Only Come Out at Night.*

My own route into glam was not through Bowie (already well known to John Peel show listeners thanks to his great BBC sessions and Peel's championing of *Hunky Dory*), but through learning Russian at O level and then seeing Malcolm McDowell behave (and speak) like such an erudite barbarian in the movie version of *A Clockwork Orange.* That movie's uniform of white boiler suits and bovver boots was soon adopted by Led Zep's John Bonham and failed glam-rock band The Jook; indeed, by any provincials who felt the pull of glam but feared a beating by the local casuals.

As the '70s progressed, glam-rock came to mean something different to everyone, from boot boys to space-rockers via moustachioed disco dopes and Eurotrash like Abba and The Brotherhood of Man. Ultimately, glam-rock offered an opportunity for just about anyone to explore – however deeply or superficially – the weird and otherly side of one's personality. Eventually, even glam-rock stage names became super-extravagant and preening, sometimes being composed of a single word, at others being the same name repeated or of the ostentatious, three-part, middle-name-deploying variety.[11]

Glam-rock forced regular songwriters to pimp their works with daft, brutal effects, sky-rocket guitar solos, glitter-stompf drums and meaningless choruses, turning pap into, well, *expressionist* pap! Glam singles became great events, full

---

11 The three-name phenomenon entered glam-rock via Tyrannosaurus Rex percussionist Steve Peregrin Took, who inspired Be-Bop Deluxe bassist Nicholas Chatterton-Dew, Curved Air's Florian Pilkington-Miksa, Queen's Roger Meddows-Taylor, Cockney Rebel's Milton Reame-James and Silverhead's Rod Rook Davis. Except for their singer Fee Waybill, glam-rock latecomers The Tubes were all known by three names, being billed as Rick Marc Anderson, Michael David Cotten, Prairie L'Emprere Prince, William Edmund Spooner, Roger Allan Steen and Vincent Leo Welnick. However, the single name was by far the *most* mysterious of all the glam-rock devices. And, although Mott the Hoople's drummer got there first, the glam-rock single name was undoubtedly inspired by Roxy Music's Eno, whose glamour and spirit inhabited the same otherworldliness as one-name Andy Warhol characters like Ondine and Nico. Jobriath soon followed, as did Curved Air's new guitarist Kirby, The Doctors of Madness' bass player Stoner and Space Rangers' keyboardist Edgemont.

of sirens, explosions and shocked expressions, and themed with mysterious plots and chock-full o'chants that sounded meaningless, but who really knew? Could Suzie Quatro really get so het up over defining what exactly '48 Crash' was if it didn't mean anything at all? And let's just compare The Sweet's pre-glam, rock forty-fives ('Coco', 'Poppa Joe', 'Funny Funny', 'Alexander Graham Bell' . . .) to their glam hits ('Block Buster', 'Teenage Rampage', 'Hellraiser', 'Ballroom Blitz' . . .). While the light emotions of the first four were guaranteed to appeal to Grandma and Auntie Mabel, those latter four were ultra-ludicrous, platform-booted forced marches through exclusively teen domain, designed specifically to annoy Dad as he relaxed in front of Thursday nacht's *Top of the Pops*. As I mentioned, Sweet's Steve Priest even delivered his camp one-liner dressed in a Nazi uniform!

Ultimately, glam-rock may have had no more message than a simple 'Wake up!' But it was unashamedly attempting to be top entertainment at a time when most so-called serious rock was so far up its own ass that even putting on stage clothes was considered gauche by the delicate flowers of the singer-songwriter scene. And, considering David Bowie's enlightened demand that rock'n'roll be reborn by becoming a parody of itself, the reality, as it descended upon the '70s pop charts, was, at times, quite spectacular and inventive. What's more, the fact that we still have trouble defining this superficially simplistic phenomenon is a true testament to its clod-hopping will-o-'the-wispiness.

Danskrocksampler

1 The Savage Rose: Ride My Mountain (5.42)
2 Young Flowers: And Who but I Should Be (5.40)
3 Burnin' Red Ivanhoe: Ivanhoe I Brodbyerne (3.56)
4 Alrune Rod: Du Taler Og Si'r (7.45)
5 Povl Dissing: Tingel-Tangelmanden (10.25)
6 Young Flowers: The Moment Life Appeared (2.16)
7 The Savage Rose: A Trial in Our Native Town (7.10)
8 Burnin' Red Ivanhoe: Marsfesten (5.35)
9 Ache: The Invasion (6.01)
10 Alrune Rod: Hej Du (15.05)
11 Steppeulvene: Itsi-Bitsi (4.54)

My interest in Danish rock'n'roll began by accident, in early '99, when I paid twenty pence for a perfect copy of The Savage Rose's wonder-fuelled instrumental LP *Dødens Triumf* at Melksham's big Dorothy Hospice charity shop, about twelve miles from my home. This album was so unlike The Savage Rose singles I'd heard that I wondered how they'd got to such a place. However, a little research soon revealed that the album had been been massive in Denmark but unknown in the rest of the world. As I travelled through Denmark a few times during the next few years' research into *The Megalithic European*, I made friends with a hip publisher called Ole Knudsen, whom I hassled immoderately to help me navigate the uncharted waters of Danish psychedelia and progressive music. To the Danes, I send salutations and congratulations for the immaculate state of their beautiful islands, and to Ole Knudsen I dedicate this introductory article with many thanks.

When U Ragnarock with Me

While the Swedish late-'60s underground scene has been well excavated in recent years, so that such heavyweights as Bo Anders Persson's legendary Pärson Sound (and their alter egos, Harvester and Träd, Gräs och Stenar) have now been joined by such previously lost souls as Archimedes Badkar and Algarnas Tradgard, the equivalent Danish scene, happening hardly more than a stone's throw across the watery Øresund, has remained severely unsung. That this is a big hole in rock'n'roll will become apparent when you hear the music on *Danskrocksampler* for the first time, for the groups showcased herein had a raunch and invention on a par with the best contemporary British and American bands. Indeed, like the finest Japanese and Krautrock bands, the only notably obscure elements in all these Danish head sounds were their lyrics and their geographical location.

But while Ache, Alrune Rod, Young Flowers and the Tim Hardin/Jacques Brel-styled Povl Dissing carved out successful careers in the Danish music scene, only the Copenhagen-based Burnin' Red Ivanhoe found their records released in Britain, and even then it was within the confines of John Peel's relatively obscure Dandelion label. The Savage Rose, however, went several steps further, gaining a major American contract with RCA and playing alongside Miles Davis and James Brown at the 1969 Newport Jazz Festival. But their subsequent refusal to play out the so-called American Dream (moreover, biting the hand that fed them by playing for the Black Panthers and the PLO) and the band's dignified return to homeland glory acts as a perfect Danish metaphor. For this huge archipelago of low-lying islands, so often considered by the Danes to be relatively meagre territory, is a rich and fertile land that has long been inhabited by a culture strong in moral fibre, tenacity and determination, and a singular desire to do their own thing. So the cultural revolution of the 1960s, although inspired by the beat of American and British rock'n'roll, was soon appropriated by the Danes and used for their own ends.

Denmark's failed attempt to remain neutral during WWII saw its islands invaded by the Nazis, who valued the country's Baltic ports and its high-yielding agricultural lands, which were appropriated to help feed the burgeoning Third Reich. And so post-war Danes were in no mood for further invasions, even if only of the cultural variety. After the war, their governments would set about building the most successful welfare state in Europe, and Danes prided themselves on their open-mindedness and egalitarian attitudes. Like jazz before it, the coming of rock'n'roll culture was embraced in Denmark, not only for its sounds but because it emanated from Afro-American culture and symbolised new-found freedom. It was the eighteenth-century German mystic Johann Gottlieb Fichte who so percipiently commented: 'To be born free is nothing – to become free is heavenly.'

Empathising with the Afro-American freedom riders on buses across the southern states of America, the Danes danced and hollered with the joys of this new freedom, Nazi tyranny still so fresh in their collective memory. From the earliest days of rock'n'roll, Denmark's islands resounded with the new electric sounds. From Zealand in the east to the great land mass of Jutland in the west, via Fyn, Lolland, Falster and Langeland, bizarrely named Danorockers plied their guitar-and-sax-fuelled trade every weekend.

You thought the Swedes had the monopoly on weird names after you read about the Mecki Mark Men? Well, think again, suckers! Throughout the late '50s and into the mid-'60s, town halls and local ballrooms from Skagerrak to Copenhagen advertised Danish rock'n'roll bands and beat groups with such unlikely names as Ola and the Janglers, Ole and the Others, Pils and His Pilsners, Little Freddie and His Rockboys, The Stamping Bricks, Ranthe-Birch's Smashband, The Rookeys, Melvis Rockband, The Dandy Swingers, The Clidows, The Five Danes, The Teenmakers, The Hitmakers, The (Cliff Richard-inspired) Cliffters (!), The Telstars, Sir Henry and His Butlers (who featured their own stripper!), and the seven futuristic proto-Numanoids of X-Group! Eventually, these gave way to worthy, humourless blues bands such as Hurdy Gurdy, Delta Blues Band, The Beefeaters, The Blues Addicts and Gasolin', many of whom remained on the scene during and after the soon to be forthcoming psychedelic era.

Steppeulvene and the Student Riots

By 1967, the effects of the Vietnam War were beginning to severely affect European opinion of the USA, and many American bands returned home under a cloud of depression from having weathered so many insults and questions about the actions of their government. Preaching freedom for Americans while destroying civilian populations thousands of miles away especially alienated the inward-looking Danes, whose youth was now beginning to follow the trend for 'finding itself' in travels to the East. Their figurehead came in the form of the young hippie poet/singer Eik Skaloe, whose wordy songs and strangely female-sounding baritone made his band, Steppeulvene ('Steppenwolf'), sound like Marlene Dietrich fronting Mouse and the Traps. Eik Skaloe was the first of his generation to sing in his native language and – his decision ultimately rendering his muse opaque to the rest of the world – Steppeulvene's 1967 LP, the immaculately titled *Hip*, became the symbol of all things cool and defiantly Danish. Tragically, Skaloe's success in Denmark could not hold back his Odinist wanderings forever and, in 1968, aged just twenty-five, he disappeared while travelling through the Indian city of Ferozepore. Whether or not Skaloe was murdered or died of a self-inflicted drug overdose, the singer became Denmark's own Brian Jonesian sacrifice and his early death symbolically confirmed to young Danes that theirs was a righteous scene.

Although the *Hip* album is musically very dated compared to subsequent bands, Steppeulvene's influence was already vast, something reinforced only by Skaloe's mysterious disappearance at the height of his career. Skaloe is a still-pervasive rock myth in twenty-first-century Denmark, and will always be considered by the original Danish heads to have been 'Brother Number One'.

Skaloe inspired such highly political groups as the Jomfru Ane Band and Rode Mor to sing their own politicised songs entirely in Danish. The latter band featured the refusenik vocalist/poet Troels Trier and released such records as the anti-Vietnam War EP *Johnny Gennem Ild og Vand* ('Johnny through Fire and Water'), about a dead American GI returning from the war unaware that he is a ghost. Unfortunately, although the record's lyrics are highly emotive and successful, the music nowadays seems too old-fashioned and unworthy of a place on this compilation.

Young Flowers, Traffic and the Festival of the Flower Children

In the meantime, the 1966 impact of power trios Cream and the Jimi Hendrix Experience kicked into the Danish consciousness with a new band whose members had all previously played in well-known beat groups. Cast in the role of the first

Danish supergroup, Young Flowers were an often blues-based but otherwise highly original bunch, led by a singing bass player called Peter Ingemann, whose blond Afro had become well known in the Danish beat group UFO. With drummer Ken Gudmand and Jens Dahl on lead guitar, Young Flowers appeared all over Denmark throughout 1967, supporting Traffic and other big British and American bands, before headlining at the Festival of the Flower Children, at Copenhagen's Falkoner Centre, on September 10 1967. Capturing the coveted support slot for Traffic was a major coup for Young Flowers, as the 'getting their new band together in the countryside' modus operandi employed by Steve Winwood, Jim Capaldi, Chris Wood and Dave Mason had become an archetype and role model for every aspiring hippie musician. Photographs of Traffic shot even before they had released records had so captured the imagination of the underground scene that their shows reverberated with the atmosphere of a proto-Monterey Festival. And, with 'Little Stevie' Winwood's hugely credible Spencer Davis Group provenance and soulful Ray Charlesian holler, Traffic's music held an extraordinary resonance for European rock bands, many of whom regarded former soul-boy Chris Wood's hippie reappropriation of the saxophone as an excuse to call in the services of all their hitherto marginalised jazz mates.

By 1968, Young Flowers had hit the album charts with *Blomsterpistolen* ('Flower Gun') and the singles Top Thirty with their forty-five 'Oppe I Traet' ('Up in the Tree'), whose excellent lyrics opened with the line 'Up in the tree/I'm damned well sitting/And I'm far away,' and continued with such classy psychedelic allusions as: 'The darkness is dark.' However, this fairly generic piece of lyrical bunkum in no way reflected Peter Ingemann's lack of taste, and he was genuinely inspired in his decision to use several Walt Whitman poems as the lyrical base for many of the subsequent Young Flowers songs. Their magical delivery of Whitman's 'The Moment Life Appeared' is Donovan-ised and incredibly charming. The other track I've chosen here is their adaption of Walt Whitman's 'And Who but I Should Be', plucked from their second LP, *No. 2*.

The blues side of Young Flowers is typical of this period and does nothing to smoke my pole. But then again, whenever I've listened to this era of rock'n'roll, from Greece's Socrates

Drank the Conium to the relentlessly harrowing and empty Cuby and the Blizzards from the Netherlands, they all really burn it up until they inevitably start 'imposing' their versions of the blues upon us. Maybe only real, black bluesmen had the un-Romanised body rhythms to pull off such raunch. However, when Young Flowers unleashed their loose freak-out style, it was totally full-on and extremely appealing, especially such tracks as the 'Ruckzack'-period Kraftwerk-meets-Klaus Dinger/ Neu!-style phased drumming of 'April '68', the Barrett Floyd-styled 'Overture' and their eleven-minute flute- and sax-assisted 'Kragerne Vender' – a self-styled, monolithic 'freeform jam session' [*sic*] which closed *No. 2*.

In the early '70s, Peter Ingemann did a Chas Chandler and went on to become a successful rock'n'roll manager, as well as becoming part of the hugely successful Skousen and Ingemann duo, whose albums were massive. Unfortunately, the sole LP of which I have a copy is 1971's *Herfa Hvor Vi Star* ('From Where We Stand'), which is really quite bland and flute-heavy, barely computing with the malevolent contortions hurled about by Young Flowers just two years earlier.

Burnin' Red Ivanhoe

How did the Danish free-jazzers – of which there were many – respond to this new onslaught of the experimental rock lifestyle? Rising out of the Copenhagen free-jazz community in May '67, Burnin' Red Ivanhoe was born of the desires of sax player Karsten Vogel and his poet friend Erik Wille to create a concoction of 'avant-garde jazz, beat music, The Who and Albert Ayler'. After many early personnel changes, the be-Afro'd Vogel inveigled the services of longhair drummer Bo Thrige Andersen, Skagerrak little-person and wind player Kim Menzer, archetypal bass-playing quiet man Jess Stæhr, and a blond hippie Viking called Ole Fick as lead singer and guitarist. Although their first record was a relatively slow train coming, in February 1969, Burnin' Red Ivanhoe's debut immediately made its mark by being the first ever double LP on the Danish scene.

Housed in a bright orange gatefold sleeve, with loud, artless US Army *M.A.S.H.*-style lettering, *M144* was as vivid a statement as any in the late '60s, and contained a kind of inspired underground music that would have been at home on the German scene. Dominated by Karsten Vogel's declamatory, David

Jackson-styled alto saxophone and guitarist Ole Fick's Peter Hamillish, changeling vocals (one moment cooing and kittenish, the next strident and belligerent), the Burnin' Red Ivanhoe sound set them right alongside early Can, The Fugs, The Velvet Underground and Zappa's early Mothers of Invention. Burnin' Red Ivanhoe lacked any archetypal lead guitarist, Ole Fick's style being a cyclical mix of Michael Karoli and Sterling Morrison, while their occasional utilisation of trombone, flute and two saxes implied the presence of a far larger ensemble, specifically calling to mind the sounds made by the early 'Brown Shoes Don't Make It'-period Mothers or the *Monster Movie*-era Can. Indeed, the record contains several Krautrock burn-ups, notably the ten minutes of 'Ksiloy'. Moreover, Karsten Vogel's use of Vox Continental organ and the Wille lyric method of continuously straddling the English and Danish languages created a delightfully alienating vibe, hinting at slightly later Eastern European bands such as MCH and The Plastic People of the Universe.

The whole Ivanhoe trip was very self-referential, in a typically jazz way, and seems to have been aiming to reinforce whatever was going on in the idealistic Danish scene of the time. 'Ivanhoe in the Woods' is a massive, sax-driven instrumental take on '(I Can't Get No) Satisfaction', while the opening track of *M144*, which I've included here, is called 'Ivanhoe I Brodbyerne', after a suburb of Copenhagen. As well as this song, I've also selected the extraordinarily beautiful and creepy song 'Marsfesten', whose Julie Cruise-singing-'In Heaven Everything Is Fine' atmosphere is truly Martian.

John Peel took up the Ivanhoe cause with the far jazzier self-titled second LP, which he released on his own Dandelion label in July 1970. Unfortunately, I have not heard that LP since the early '70s, and even then only listened as a Dandelion Records fan. However, the following summer came the band's great collaboration with Povl Dissing on the album *Seks Elefantskovcikadeviser*, which yielded the fabulous version of 'Tingel Tangelmandsen' which is included within the cyber-grooves of this *Dansksrocksampler.*

The Savage Rose

Playing for free for the Palestine Liberation Organisation and the Black Panthers, addressing one of their albums to Malcolm X, refusing to play in Vietnam for the US troops and returning to their homeland after a great, North America-priming *Rolling Stone* review by Lester Bangs would all nowadays be considered career suicide by the unidealistic, sell-your-songs-to-the-advert-guys generic throng that call themselves rock'n'roll artists. However, The Savage Rose was comprised of musicians and artists so talented, but so wilful, that when their leader, Thomas Koppel, still in his music-student guise at the Royal Conservatory, was commissioned to write a laudatory piece in celebration of the school's two-hundredth anniversary and performed it, along with other pieces, before Denmark's Queen Ingrid, he did so with such fury that on the last note of Beethoven's 'Appassionata' his right foot stamped the grand piano's foot pedal clean off its mooring. Koppel's instant reaction to that moment was classic: 'So long, Ludwig, I love you, but I need to move on now and join the living.'

And so The Savage Rose was born. Thomas persuaded his younger poet/film-maker brother Anders to buy a red Farfisa organ and hooked up with four other musicians, including the amazing singer Annisette Hansen, whose extraordinarily over-the-top, proto-Björk/post-Edith Piaf sexual delivery would later be described by Lester Bangs as 'Grace Slick at 78 rpm' and 'Minnie Mouse on a belladonna jag'.[1] Nowadays generally known as 'The Yellow Album', the band's first, self-titled LP was a beautiful but mainly too innocent/too simplistic take on what The Savage Rose would come to represent. Too often, Annisette had to adopt Anders Koppel's male lyrical persona for songs such as 'A Girl I Knew', which was released as a single. However, the second album, *In the Plain*, revealed the true colours of the band's psychedelic, three-keyboard-player, Spectorish onslaught. Imagine Japan's euphoric, Big Brotheresque septet The Flowers if they'd been able to write their own songs, or, perhaps, Guy Stevens' wildest 'River Deep, Mountain High' aspirations written by idealistic anti-Vietnam, post-Frisco refuseniks, topped with the most helium-voiced, mid-orgasming female singer this side of early Kate Bush, and yooz approaching the heights that The Savage Rose occasionally attained.

For this compilation I've chosen their almost-six-minute epic 'Ride My Mountain' to illustrate these

1 Lester Bangs, *Rolling Stone* (October 18 1969).

giddy heights, for theirs was not only transcendent rock'n'roll; The Savage Rose also bucked traditions by taking Phil Spector's three-minute rush and recontextualising it within the sound of The Doors' first albums (effectively 'Light My Fire' to 'Unknown Soldier' via 'Five to One') to sustain a flat-out, operatic rock burn-up that I ain't never heard elsewhere, then or since. The other track that I knew had to represent The Savage Rose herein was their otherworldly, seven-minute, Dylanesque death ritual 'A Trial in Our Native Town'. Here, they again approach a kind of Scando-Germanic doom-trudge with a Doors-meets-early-Siouxsie 'what precisely the fuck is going on?'-ness that is both disturbing in its *Ryan's Daughter* rawness and delightful in its *Wicker Man*-meets-*The Seventh Seal* cinemascopic vastness. Imagine Iggy Pop and James Williamson's proto-Suicide take on Dylan's 'Ballad of Hollis Brown', slow it down some and play it as a backdrop to a film of the German Army retreating from Moscow and you're getting somewhere close. I include here the entire libretto, not for what it reveals, but for what it conjures in the mind of the listener:

A leather strip around your hand,
The great landowner whom you kissed,
The cries out from the battlefield,
Tell me, where did you come from?

Coming right through to the end,
You don't want to resent,
The poor souls that brought you here,
The landscape behind your fingerprints.

You have walked between snakes in the plain,
People everywhere greeted you in vain,
Steal my heart, baby, just roll on,
Just roll on from your native town.

They've been haunting you and drinking,
They've been so careful thinking,
That you shouldn't be alone here,
That you belong to them.

There's the drummer, breathing the air,
There's the man, who brought the chair,
Where you should be seated,
Within the doors of your home.

You sit down in this painted chair,
You're tired, they don't care,
Oh, come out from your hidden place,
They want to kiss you, want to be with you.

The fields are heavy with dust,
Remember the smell from your city lost?
The chain around your naked foot?
Tell me, what do you do now?

You better wait until past midnight,
Tie your mind to me waiting outside the prison,
With the leather strip from your hand,
Wait, I'll come to hold you tight.

With their new American presence, including that show with James Brown and Miles Davis at the 1969

Newport Jazz Festival, The Savage Rose took on two heavyweight US managers who had no understanding of their idealism. The next two years saw them treading water with three generally average LPs: *Travellin'*, *Your Daily Gift* and *Refugee*, the last two being produced, to little effect, by The Rolling Stones' knob-twiddler Jimmy Miller. In this atmosphere of stasis, Thomas Koppel was asked to write a ballet score for the Danish Royal Ballet's forthcoming production of *Dødens Triumf* ('Triumph of Death'). That Koppel had never intended entirely to sideline his classical career is evidenced by the success of his opera *The Story of a Mother*, which he had written aged nineteen, and which was still being performed by the Royal Opera company. With little record-company enthusiasm for the project and half of the band alienated from this all-instrumental project, Koppel single-mindedly approached the score to *Dødens Triumf* as though it were his most important ever work. And so, when Polydor's first pressing of the LP was limited to just five hundred copies, Koppel's initial anger soon gave way to delight as the record went on to be The Savage Rose's most commercially successful album, selling over a quarter of a million copies.

As my first introduction to The Savage Rose, this album still holds a place in my heart, although there's clearly no place for any of the LP's lengthy pieces within the confines of this brief compilation. However, with hindsight and a little research, it's clear that Thomas Koppel had always seen The Savage Rose as a potential vehicle for the kind of music contained within the grooves of *Dødens Triumf*, as evidenced by the eight-minute-long mood piece 'Tapiola' on 1969's *Your Daily Gift*.

The success of *Dødens Triumf* took its toll on the original line-up of The Savage Rose, which gradually diminished from here on in, as Thomas Koppel and Annisette Hansen took over the public face of the band; indeed, as they have continued to do right up to the present day. I haven't attempted to keep up with their muse, and they clearly retain an idealism that keeps them as adored in modern Denmark as they were thirty-five years ago. Listening to the two tracks included on this *Danskrocksampler*, I'm convinced that you will feel driven to further excavate their enormous (and enormously thorough) canon of work.

Povl Dissing

Yeah, Povl Dissing . . . what a hip dude and what a classy name. With his cranky, histrionic, gravel-voiced style, straggly beard, lyrics only ever in Danish and wild flailing arms, Povl Dissing was quickly adopted by Denmark's youth culture as much for the apoplectic reactions he engendered in older people as for the actual sound of his records. And the more the immaculately named Dissing became the subject of prime-time TV impersonators, the more his freakily outrageous, Joe Cockeresque song delivery became synonymous with the most refusenik aspects of Denmark's alienated rock underground. This led to huge sales of his 1969 album *Dissing*, and, in 1970, further success with *Jeg Er en Tosset Spillemand* ('I Am a Crazy Fiddler').

Unfortunately for us, however, Povl Dissing employed the well-known (in Denmark) mid-'60s blues band The Beefeaters as his backing on these important early LPs, creating an almost opaque trip for the twenty-first-century cultural navigator. For, like Steppeulvene's equally wordy muse, Dissing's songs suffer, nowadays, from the sheer light-handedness of The Beefeaters' arrangements and the almost blandly subtle blues garnishes that they add to the atmosphere of the records.

Fortunately, Dissing hooked up with the very genuine sonic terrorists of Burnin' Red Ivanhoe for his 1971 recordings, the steaming results of which fetched up on the magnificent (and, in Denmark, truly legendary) album *Seks Elefantskovcikadeviser*. Here, the music ached with feeling and gave off the kind of gloriously sticky-budded, post-folk psychedelic stink that Jerry Yester's arrangements had brought to Tim Buckley's *Goodbye and Hello* and which Witthüser & Westrupp had summoned on their classic Ohr LP *Trips und Träume*.

I have included herein *Seks Elefantskovcikadeviser*'s very best and most obvious representative, the strung-out ten minutes-plus of 'Tingel-Tangelmanden', a song whose very name conjures up the ancient and orgiastic sexual rites that were so slow to be stamped out in early Christian Scando-Germania.[2] The suppressed wah-voodoo of the Lokian guitar riff comes across like the three-pronged attack of Fleetwood Mac's Jeremy Spencer/Peter Green/Danny Kirwan line-up rejigging the *St. Stephen*

2 Evidence for the Tingel Tangel having once been a ritual phenomenon all across the northern lands can be seen in the trial of the Forfar witches in the seventeenth century. Confessions from the four hanged women stated that they had drunk beer with the devil, whom some of them had kissed, while 'singing altogether a song called Tinkletum Tankletum'.

LP. Moreover, the later stages of this epic piece drop down into a dark, northern forest of sonic emptiness, as Dissing's dissonant groanings retreat and a malevolent blackness takes over. The lyrics of this song, which had first appeared in a far less developed state on Burnin' Red Ivanhoe's own album *M144*, appear to be strings of charming non sequiturs, or even streams of consciousness. However, as I know nothing of the occultural roots of the songwriters, other than their having originated from a free-jazz background, I may be severely underestimating the codes within these lyrics. Although Burnin' Red Ivanhoe's own take on 'Tingel-Tangelmanden' sounds far less psychedelic than this marvellous Dissing version, their dual/double-tracked vocals are still highly charming and a lot like Syd Barrett's declaimed, artless singing on 'Octopus'.

Ache

If you wanna hear some truly weird dwellers on the threshold of the psychedelic/progressive scene, then Ache is gonna be another band right up your strasse. Swimming in the oily wake left by 1967's heavy organ bands, such as Iron Butterfly, Vanilla Fudge, John Hiseman's Colosseum and Keith Emerson's The Nice, Ache was led by the similarly classically trained keyboardist Peter Mellin, who had just graduated from the Danish Academy of Music. Getting it together in the countryside, Traffic-stylee, in January '68, with the teenage Olafson brothers – Finn and Torsten on lead and bass guitars – and their bare-chested drummer Glenn Fisher, early photos of Ache standing atop a Bronze Age hoj, or barrow, were employed to push the band's supposedly uniquely Danish attitude. Furthering this Danish cause, Ache hooked up with ballet dancer Peter Schaufuss, from the Royal Danish Ballet Company, in order to produce the first 'rock ballet'. Opening performances of their two twenty-minute-long, LP-side-long pieces were received with rapturous applause, both at Copenhagen's Royal Theatre and at the Bolshoi Ballet, in Moscow. Indeed, the introduction of the so-called 'rock ballet' is still seen by many Danish heads as evidence of Ache's uniqueness.

The reality, however, was somewhat different and Ache's massive debut LP *De Homine Urbano* ('About Urban Man') almost fitted right in alongside such bombastic second-generation, overwrought Spanish galleons as early Yes and Van der Graaf Generator. Indeed, their opening, side-long epic title track was surely inspired by Yes' frenetic and strung-out take on The Beatles' 'Every Little Thing', and was all the better for it. Strangely, the other side of the first LP was itself called 'Little Things' and unashamedly nicked even more rock moments from all over the place (including Led Zeppelin's 'How Many More Times?'). However, it is unfair to stop there with the descriptions, for much of the music is truly evocative and entirely Norse in its emotional drive and doomy atmosphere, coming on like a much better version of Van der Graaf's *The Least We Can Do Is Wave to Each Other*, with added psychedelic guitar somewhere between Davy O'List and Peter Banks' wired, post-swinging-London, speed-freak sound. Moreover, there is a psychedelic violence and power to Ache that is far more reminiscent of such pre-prog nuggets as The Shy Limbs' incredibly phased 'Shattered' and The Syn's '14-Hour Technicolour Dream' forty-five. Clearly, the members of Ache had much bigger plans in mind than merely ripping the heart out of late-'60s heavy-rock.

I much prefer the more song-based second LP *Green Man*, for its strangely elegant take on *Pawn Hearts*, 'Man-Erg'-period Peter Hammill, which much better sums up the loss of '60s idealism and the subsequent ghetto-ising of the underground rock scene. 'Shadow of a Gypsy', which opens Side Two, best illustrates this 'Man-Erg' obsession and was a massive hit in France. Unfortunately, the *Green Man* LP closes with yet another disappointing heavy cover version, this time of The Beatles' 'We Can Work It Out'. Strangest of all, though, is that the Hammill-esque lead vocal throughout this record sounds not Danish but like a typically well-spoken English northerner! Sometimes, when travelling in that geographically obscure area of south Jutland, Schleswig-Holstein or the most northerly parts of the Netherlands, I have felt like I'm tripping on acid when – on overhearing local conversations that sound exactly like people from the English north Midlands – I've still been unable to understand a single word spoken!

Ache occasionally give me this same psychedelic and appealingly disorientating feeling of alienation in familiar sounds. The biggest problem here is picking a piece of music that best encapsulates the Ache sound, as you really need a full LP side to get where they'z coming from. After much humming and hawing, I settled on 'The Invasion' because its mood best captures the fury and the Scandinavian doom, as well as copping the superb vocal melody from

The Zombies' 'Beechwood Park', from their 1968 Mellotron 400 classic *Odessey and Oracle*.

Alrune Rod

I think Alrune Rod is ultimately my favourite bunch of all these inspirational, whey-faced Danish loons, mainly because their first two albums are real cosmic kicks up the psychic jacksie, their songs effortlessly straddling wildly opposing emotions. In places, Alrune Rod ('Mandrake Root') come over like organ-heavy early Traffic, with Peter Hammill singing Ozzy Osbourne singing Arthur Brown, but whatever they're doing it's never merely a matter of aping their predecessors. Typical of the time, the Rod's first single, 'Pigen Pa Stranden', was a bit of a curveball and quite unlike their real direction. Written by Danish singer-songwriter Bent Birkholm, its huge, stop–start organ cross-pollinated Cat Stevens' 'The First Cut Is the Deepest' with Procol Harum's 'A Whiter Shade of Pale', without laying to rest the spectre of either. Much better was their gleeful, self-penned B-side 'Tael Aldrig I Morgen Med', which conjures up the same Daft Vader atmosphere of Hammill's later 'Imperial Zeppelin'. Fucking beautiful, man!

But it's within the grooves of those first two Alrune Rod LPs, the self-titled debut of '69 and the magnificently spacey *Hej Du* ('Hey You') from the following year, that the band really stretched the cosmic envelope. Both records still exist entirely in their own space and, moreover, don't really touch very much on the styles which their contemporary Danish brethren were dishing up.

Starting out as a staring-at-the-floor quartet of super longhairs, the Alrune Rod quartet featured Giese (guitar and vocals), Kurt 'Pastor' Ziegler (organ, piano) and Claus From (drums), and was led by singer/bass player Leif Roden, who wrote and sang most of their thundering, organ-heavy, doomy Ragnarock like some Skogsnuffar from Skagerrak in an anorak sniffing smack from a rug on a rock. These Danish cosmic rockers created expansive, two-tracks-per-side LPs, with an edge-of-space sound somewhere between early Pink Floyd, an emptier Arthur Brown's Kingdom Come and *Pawn Hearts*-period Van der Graaf Generator, the latter especially so on the quarter-of-an-hour-long descent-into-hell known as 'Rejsen Hjem', which closes Alrune Rod's first LP. Its three-minute-long, ever-ascending, accelerating introduction and Hamillesque vocals are the most instant sounds that these subtle doom academics ever achieved on this first LP. Everything is either propelled or anchored by Leif Roden's bass, which even kicks into a raga-styled cross between 'Paint It Black' and The Doors' 'Not to Touch the Earth' at one point.

Eighteen months later, however, their sound had been augmented by a second drummer, with the immaculate name of Karsten Host, pushing their heavy range further but into far more obviously riff-orientated territory than before, as Leif Roden's massive 'Perlesøen' enveloped the whole of the second side *Hej Du*. Still Hammill-influenced, vocally, the album opened with the seven-minute 'Du Taler Og Si'r', before unleashing the fury of the Van der Graaf-styled title track in its full, quarter-of-an-hour-long splendour.

On this *Danskrocksampler* I have included all of Side One of *Hej Du*, so, pretty please, give this enormous track your fullest attention, for it is extremely essential rock'n'roll and a massive sonic addition to the psyche of your un-average, forward-thinking motherfucker. 'Tis only a pity that the whole of Side Two couldn't be squeezed in as well, for, verily, it swallows my golly.

By their third LP, 1972's *Alrune Rock*, the band had been augmented further, and the modified line-up meant the spacey sound had started to take on far more defined song structures. Geise's atmospheric guitar playing had been replaced by Ole Poulsen, and the mighty organ of Pastor Zeigler had been dumped in some Langeland fjord, to be replaced only by guest percussionists and flautists. But even this record retains a delightfully Traffic-esque, yippie squawk that would be massive had it been recorded by an English or American rock'n'roll band.

Alrune Rod is possibly the most unsung of all the bands on the Danish scene, but they surely have a future place awaiting them in the hearts of Vertigo swirl-heads, Ohr Records obsessives and pink-label Island completists throughout the bedroom scenes of Britain, America, Japan and Europe.

In Conclusion

Naturally, this *Danskrocksampler* article barely scratches the surface of essential Danish music, but we gots to start somewhere and at least this is a beginning. I should probably mention the extremely marginal outsider band Hair, who released one patchy but highly inspired LP, *Piece*, on the Dutch Frost label, in 1970. Although they claim to have been influenced by The Doors, Vanilla Fudge and

Tim Buckley, Hair's bizarre music is actually more entertaining because of the effortless way in which it straddles everything from heavy 'downer' pop to melodic, West Coast psychedelia (Jefferson Airplane mainly, but Mad River's 'Amphetamine Gazelle' also springs to mind), and often bolstered by a full gospel choir. Side Two of *Piece* contains an epic Hammond organ/fuzz-guitar version of Tim Buckley's 'Pleasant Street' by people who can't sing (always a good idea when attempting to ape a singer as fine as Timmy, I feel) and a fractured, eleven-minute take on Big Brother's 'Piece of My Heart' that similarly tries to transcend Janis Joplin's original but never gets higher than 'enthusiastic' . . .

Three subsequent forty-fives saw Hair developing an unhealthy respect for the boogie, despite undermining it at all times with stellar sound-effects and a Utopian lyrical stance ('Come Tell the People' is like Robert Calvert and David Clayton-Thomas duetting [!], while 'Get Together Hand by Hand' is The Guess Who's 'New Mother Nature' as sung by Golden Earring's Barry Hay). Nevertheless, there's some genuine strand of thang resounding in their muse at all times, and the LP cover is surely one of the greatest shit sleeves I ever set eyes on.

Much better, although hardly typically Danish in attitude, was Culpeper's Orchard, an acid-rock quintet of highly developed song arrangers, whose dwarves and Ku Klux Klansmen in the Garden of Eden record sleeve probably sets the all-time standard for rock-band misrepresentation. Their sole, eponymously titled album was a highly involved, heavily vocalled and rocked-out take on 'No Time'-period The Guess Who/late Buffalo Springfield as played by Yes circa *The Yes Album*, with lashings of Procol Harum's 'A Whiter Shade of Pale' and Thunderclap Newman's 'Accidents' thrown in, and (ooh-er) Dieter Dierks at the soundboard. If that sounds horrendous, then it's my fault because it's compulsive and euphoric and wholly authentic.

This lot was led by an ex-pat Yank by the name of Cy Nicklin, whose self-referential trip is occasionally too twee and cloying, but is mainly authentic in a manner similar to that of Burton Cummings and hefts up their trip considerably. Methinks readers of these Cope articles are gonna love or hate this band unreservedly, with no in-betweens. Me, I love this record because I already love and therefore accept its references, but then I loved Be-Bop Deluxe's *Axe Victim because*, not in spite of, its Ziggyphilia.

By 1971, when Danish heavy-rock was giving way to such progressive bands as Alrune Rod, Ache, the Yes-played-by-jazzers sound of Midnight Sun, Day of Phoenix, Secret Oyster and The Old Man and the Sea, the student protests which had continued since the late '60s were beginning to take effect, eventually leading to the proclamation of a 'Free State of Christiania' on a military base on the outskirts of Copenhagen. Operating along the same lines as the Berlin Eins commune of three years previously, this 'social experiment' attracted over one thousand people who agreed to take up residence in abandoned barracks under communal rules. The liberal government accepted the experiment and even allowed Christiania to fly its own flag as a partly self-governed area of Copenhagen. Freetown Christiania, as the commune also became known, was accessible through only two gates, and petrol-driven vehicles were banned entirely. The commune's main drag took the name Pusher Street as drug dealers took up residence at permanent stalls that sold grass and hash openly and cheaply. Although Christiania has stared at possible extinction for the past decade, its tenuous survival these past thirty-one years shows us, like the continuing twentieth-century success of The Savage Rose, that the Utopian spirit of the Danish '60s music scene was a cut above most of the other hip enclaves spawned by rock'n'roll, the freedom riders and Albert Hoffman's accidental bicycle ride. I only hope that this article creates a deluge of new Danish information, for the music I've heard so far does more than a job on my frontal lobes – verily, it trepanneth the bone from mah skullington!

Selected Album Discography

Ache:
De Homine Urbano (Philips, 1970)
Green Man (Philips, 1971)

Alrune Rod:
Alrune Rod (Sonet, 1969)
Hej Du (Sonet, 1971)
Alrune Rock (Sonet, 1972)

Burnin' Red Ivanhoe:
M144 (Sonet, 1969)
Burnin' Red Ivanhoe (Dandelion, 1970)

Povl Dissing:
Dissing (Sonet, 1969)
Jeg Er en Tosset Spillemand (Sonet, 1970)
Seks Elefantskovcikadeviser (Sonet, 1971)

The Savage Rose:
The Savage Rose (Polydor, 1968)
In the Plain (Polydor, 1968)
Travellin' (Polydor, 1969)
Refugee (Polydor, 1971)
Your Daily Gift (RCA, 1971)
Dødens Triumf (Polydor, 1972)

Steppeulvene:
Hip (Metronome, 1967)

Young Flowers:
Blomsterpistolen (Sonet, 1968)
No. 2 (Sonet, 1969)

Notable Danish Singles

Ache: 'Shadow of a Gypsy' b/w 'Over the Fields' (Philips, 1971)
Alrune Rod: 'Tael Aldrig I Morgen Med' (Sonet, 1969)
Burnin' Red Ivanhoe: 'De Danske Hjertvarmere' EP (Sonet, 1969)
The Savage Rose: 'Girl I Knew' (Polydor, 1968)
The Savage Rose: 'Evening's Child' (Polydor, 1968)
The Savage Rose: 'Long Before I Was Born' (Polydor, 1968)
The Savage Rose: 'Sunday Morning' (RCA, 1970)
The Savage Rose: 'Revival Day' (RCA, 1971)
Young Flowers: 'Oppe I Traeet' (Sonet, 1968)

Postpunksampler

1 Metal Urbain: Paris Maquis (3.07) (1977)
2 Zounds: Can't Cheat Karma (2.42) (1980)
3 Subway Sect: Ambition (3.10) (1978)
4 Richard Hell and the Voidoids: Liars Beware (2.52) (1977)
5 The Germs: Forming (3.08) (1977)
6 39 Clocks: Aspetando Godo (3.53) (1982)
7 Missing Presumed Dead: Family Tree (2.11) (1979)
8 Manicured Noise: Faith (3.30) (1980)
9 Jane Aire and the Belvederes: Yankee Wheels (3.05) (1979)
10 Dance Party: Photograph (3.05) (1980)
11 Dum Dum Dum: Dum Dum Dum (2.57) (1980)
12 Crass: Mother Earth (4.12) (1980)
13 Friction: Crazy Dream (4.23) (1980)
14 Hair & Skin Trading Co.: Monkies (3.24) (1992)
15 Electric Eels: Accident (3.22) (1975)
16 Chain Gang: Son of Sam (3.09) (1977)
17 Swell Maps: Read About Seymour (1.27) (1977)
18 The Sods: Transport (2.55) (1979)
19 Reptile Ranch: Saying Goodbye (3.05) (1981)
20 Dalek I Love You: Trapped (3.59) (1980)
21 Colours Out of Time: As if Another World (3.34) (1981)
22 The Wild Swans: Now You're Perfect (3.15) (1980)
23 Armand Schaubroeck: Buried Alive (1.43) (1978)
24 Psycho Surgeons: Horizontal Action (1.47) (1978)
25 DMZ: Bad Attitude (2.57) (1978)
26 ESG: UFO (2.33) (1978)
27 Gaz Chambers: Who's Life Is It Anyway? (11.12) (1981)

Of the multitude of obscure examples of post-punk forty-fives and cassette demos that I archived from Bill Drummond's filing cabinets when he moved Zoo Records to London, those tracks selected for this *Postpunksampler* have been chosen either because they enjoy an important place in my tender old heart, or because there's a decent story behind 'em.

This review is dedicated to Bernard Sumner, whose eyebrow-raising, chewing, singing and spirited whooping during New Order's daring live performance of 'Blue Monday' on *Top of the Pops*, back in 1983, confirmed within my then-cabbaged and LSD-drenched (not to mention virtually career-less) soul that renewal through constant psychic death and resurrection was my only option.

From Punk to Post-Punk: Structures Burned and Structures Returned

First there was punk; it was absurd, ugly and furiously anti-royalist – a highly edgy concept amid the insane media preparations for Queen Elizabeth's impending Silver Jubilee year, 1977.[1] Johnny Rotten's pseudonym, wall-eyed stare and anti-sex stance entirely defined punk's Year Zero. It was new. It was not The Who. Sex Pistols' guitarist Steve Jones even admitted that the band was more interested in chaos than music; who cares? Rotten's Sex Pistols audition had merely involved miming in front of impresario Malcolm McLaren's jukebox. Gurning insanely for the tabloids, it was not the Pistols' music but their chaos; their anti-authority shamelessness; their daring to be perceived more like a circus act than a proper band; their sheer WTF quotient; Rotten's archly anti-social practice of heaving phlegm on to the stage; bawling out anti-royalist lyrics in this year of Jubilee; and rhyming 'Anti-Christ' with 'anarchist' on the Pistols' debut single that ultimately convinced a high percentage of the

---

1 Coming from the small Midland town of Tamworth, I first experienced punk as everyone else in the UK experienced it during that hot summer of '76, i.e. through the distorted lens of the media. From the beginning, I was won over not by the Sex Pistols' music but by their attitude and Johnny Rotten's 'I hate Pink Floyd' t-shirt. Brought up a socialist, but still a royalist, that coupla years' media build-up to the 1977 Jubilee sickened me so much I woulda followed almost anybody with a visionary method of opposing its forelock-tugging, its tinsel and its sheer lies, let alone four guys barely older than me screaming it loud, accompanied by the 'V's! Bring it on!

UK's smart youth that dropping their prog-rock double LPs down the nearest lift shaft and adopting an ironic, self-deprecating moniker was the route to the future: Pig Youth, Johnny Moped, Dee Generate, Steve Ignorant, please stand up.

In terms of walking around getting threatened for what you stood for, punk died when the Jubilee year finished. Thereafter, up sprung post-punk. If Tony Wilson had hosted his own Granada TV chat show back in the Jubilee year, he could – with one future cohort as special guest – have distilled the entire incoherent everyman essence of that original Jubilee punk with this simple announcement: 'Ladies and gentlemen, please welcome Barney Rubble of Warsaw.'

Barney only appeared on one Warsaw record under that pseudonym; his real surname was Dickin. But punk was so blink-and-you-miss-it that when Warsaw's projected LP for RK Records was held up, the band lost their brief window of opportunity for career consolidation, while everybody else had hurried on. Then came post-punk; it was serious and dark. When Johnny Rotten reverted to being plain John Lydon and chose a new band of non-musicians, he had entirely defined the new approach. What a gauntlet to throw down! Poor Steve Spunker, a.k.a. Steve Havoc, had to become Steve Severin. Poor Jimmy Pursey had to become James T. Pursey. Ooh-er, missus! And if Tony Wilson had hosted his own TV chat show back then, he'd have best defined post-punk thus: 'Ladies and gentlemen, please welcome Bernard Albrecht of Joy Division.' Yup, Manchester's Mr Dickin turns out to be a right useful barometer by which to measure the devious twists and turns of the musical period 1977–81.

Back then, the current status of Barney's surname said more about the state of culture than one of the Queen Mother's dresses. So, while the national media's successful suppression of such non-PC, early-1977 punk accessories as Siouxsie Sioux's Nazi armband, Sidney Vish's swastika t-shirts and the outré accoutrements of their Bromley/Weimar ilk had goaded the more PC amongst us to support Rock Against Racism, up in Manchester Messrs Curtis, Hook, Morris and Dickin/Albrecht shamelessly renamed their band after the Nazis' slave prostitutes and did very well for themselves. And if Tony Wilson had hosted his own TV chat show soon after the awful, May 1980 suicide of Ian Curtis, he could have really wound up the Rough Trade lefties thus: 'Ladies and gentlemen, please welcome Bernard Sumner of New Order.'

Cough, splutter, WTF? They can't get away with that! The 'New Order' is another Nazi allusion. Look, don't hassle them; they've lost their singer, they've been through a lot. Besides, no fucker gave Ron Asheton and Dennis Thompson grief when they formed their own band called The New Order, back in 1975. Leave them to their leaderless grief and their Fall-styled female-chancer keyboard player . . .

But no, we cannot leave New Order just yet. For their extremely brave decision to soldier on, singerless, and under a new name, was one of *the* great punk events in rock history.[2] Nothing less than heroic, their decision entirely summed up the nihilistic, groundbreaking DIY attitude that had originally defined punk. Rip it up and start again. Punk proved, to every fucker that lived through it, that anyone could be anything, anytime they so chose. This was new. This was not The Who. And, as Barney Rubble-Dickin-Albrecht-Sumner would have probably been among the first to point out, only the arrival of such an absurdly Utopian phenomenon as punk could have transformed as indifferent a lead guitarist as he to the heights of whopping international vocalist/songwriter. And so, as drab homophobic/homosocial Johnny-come-lately wannabe 'punks' bogusly attempted to Stalinize the original classless, anti-royalist impulse of '77 into that macho, authoritarian, hung-up younger brother forever after called punk-rock, many of the original '77 punks jumped ship. I know; I was one of them. As was my highly exotic friend and neighbour Pete Burns, who's job at Probe Records one year later would put him in the invidious position of having – throughout 1978 – to sell Sham 69, Skids and Members singles to those very same 'Hurry Up Harry' meatheads who daily threatened him for being 'a poseur' (gosh!) whenever they were confronted by his otherworldly mincing along Bold Street's drab thoroughfare.

Sick (literally!) of the same expectorating oiks, The Damned's leader, Brian James, decided his group's debut album, *Damned, Damned, Damned*, had been enough and formed a new band for '78 – a

2 In stark contrast to Messrs Hook, Morris and Dickin's brave decision to start all over, the remaining three members of Ultravox opted for a slightly safer route when their leader/songwriter John Foxx left after releasing three LPs for Island Records. They replaced him with ex-Thin Lizzy, ex-Slik all-purpose rocker Midge Ure, and never looked back.

psychedelic group, no less: the luckless Tanz Der Youth. Meanwhile, The Buzzcocks' Howard Devoto wouldn't even go out any more; he just stayed indoors plotting . . . smoking . . . envisioning . . . Thus, throughout 1978, exotic post-punk groups began to appear totally in defiance of that newly composed, revisionist punk-rock rule book ('Thou shalt not wear this . . . Thou shalt not listen to that . . .' To which post-punk replied: 'I fucking will, mate, and with flares on if I wish').

I ain't gonna name, blame and shame anybody specific for what happened . . . oh, all right then, yes, I will. It was Uncle Joe Stalin, sorry, Uncle Joe Strummer who caused the schism. Yup, once the posh, too-old Clash singer had made his crass (memories of 'Power in a Union'?) appeal to 'Punk rockers!' on whichever Clash single it was, up sprang a whole new generation of uniformed Strummer *Jugend*, all desperate to wear only the gear that Joe wore, to sing only of the subjects that Joe sang about.[3] A public-school-educated diplomat's son, and at least old enough to remember Woody Guthrie, Strummer reached out to the working classes in the manner all British poshies still think best, i.e. act macho, slurp your tea and deny your past. And so, after 1977's Jubilee chaos, the vivid punk vision of the Pistols/Clash/Buzzcocks was absorbed into so-called punk-rock, a tweaked, men-only, Shi-ite version

3 From the evidence contained within *The Future's Unwritten*, Julien Temple's excellent Joe Strummer documentary profile, it seems to me that Joe's abandonment of his role as Generalissimo of punk in favour of pop stardom in the USA was a decision that still baffled even him, poor sod. However, in the cold light of today, it must be remembered that Strummer was still only in his mid- to late twenties when all these decisions had to be made. However decrepit he seemed to me at the time, that's still very young to shoulder such a heavy weight of cultural responsibility. That he'd had the sleight of hand and sheer personal Pol Pot-ness to blank all his commune mates from the 101 house in order to better fit in with the much younger punk scene suggests to me that Strummer would ultimately have demanded of himself a prime starring role in whatever next-big-thing transpired musically, and most serpently didn't wanna have to take a worthy secretarial role – even as General Secretary – in the greatest musical revolution since 1967, and who could blame him? Why play the important but temporary Trotsky to J. Rotten's Lenin when you could be off on your own with your heroic other being Stalin, rewriting the route as you go along, even assassinating your erstwhile 'kamarad' Mickhail Jonesky? Poor Joe S. Perhaps Tymon Dogg came back at the end as a kind of Beria figure. The jury's still out on this one . . .

of its original vision, almost always thereafter to be comprised of obligatory two-minute-hate songs, pub terrace anthems, four leather jackets and four pairs of scuffed 501s. And whatever punk had done randomly during 1977, punk-rock wished ritualistically to re-enact forever thereafter *and* while demanding parity with the form's originators.

In stark contrast to all of this rule-making, the post-punk scene turned out to be a right old Trotskyite experience; a permanent revolution so wild and anti-authoritian we'd have had the NKVD secret police at our doors had we been a political party. Displaying remarkable, inclusionist attitudes, the post-punk scene actually facilitated, nay, sought out the involvement of women, blacks, gays, synthesizers, saxes, congas, art installations, the French . . . heck, even some old-timers! 'Whaddya mean old-timers?' Well, for a start, such English orphan noise-ensembles as Cabaret Voltaire (formed 1973) and Throbbing Gristle (formed 1975) at last found a guaranteed and open-minded audience. Post-punk was a scene in which TG's Genesis P-Orridge could be seen in spirited collaboration with fanzine inventor extraordinaire Mark 'P' Perry, editor of *Sniffin' Glue*. Now, for shit damn sure, Mark Perry was never punk-rock; that guy was always just *punk*, as evidenced by his band Alternative TV's daring, spoken-word live epic 'Alternatives to NATO', and by his pre-Fall v-neck jumper and the sly cover of Kim Fowley's *Outrageous* LP peeking out on the cover of an early ATV single. Indeed, Mark Perry's heady combination of obsessive music fanatic and burgeoning artiste proved to be the perfect blueprint with which to enter this next stage of the revolution.

Like jet-set carrion crows, each trafficking an exotic musical morsel from another part of the world, thrilling post-punk groups appeared throughout 1978, bearing almost no musical relation to the simplistic punk ramalama that had generally been their band members' first inspiration. 'No Elvis, Beatles or The Rolling Stones in 1977,' sang The Clash, but the king-for-a-day pagan attitude of post-punk suggested that 'No Clash, no Damned or the Sex Pistols in 1978' appeared just as possible to those most Utopian among us.

In Manchester, erstwhile Buzzcocks' singer Howard Devoto finally resurfaced, preening at the prow of Magazine's polished neon mothership, a laconic, chain-smoking raconteur fuelled by Dave Formula's banks of bracing polyphonic synthesizers, surely the unpunkest of all noises. Also in Manchester, but unable to compete with such superb musicianship, the non-musicians of Blah Blah Blah – nevertheless desperate to contribute to this inventive post-punk scene – avoided negative judgements from the press by super-gluing their seven-inch record within its sleeve! In London, more first-generation punks abandoned their roots: first the posh, Tunbridge Wells-born, Westminster public school-educated Shane MacGowan dropped entirely his Jubilee year Union flag-wearing for a far more archaic, revolutionary image . . . the drunken Irish poet! Eh, there's always room for one more o'them. Viva authenticity! Come on! Even the archetypal rent-a-punks of Wire, with their stupid, loudmouth bassist, entirely ditched the eighty mph ramalama of their 1977 debut LP *Pink Flag*, instead delivering, for 1978, an album of extremely noisesome and mid-to-slow-tempo material entitled *Chairs Missing*, a record so devoid of the '1-2-X-U' knuckle-head crowd-pleasers of the previous LP that the band's 1978 shows often enraged the new punk-rocker hordes greedy for more of the *Pink Flag*-stylee; fucking heck, this was not the Ramones' *Leave Home*. But then, underneath it all, Wire were precisely the art-school types that the revisionists so detested – hell, even back in '77, their ex-art-teacher guitarist Bruce Gilbert had already reached the grand age of thirty-one![4] Even the Stranglers' Hugh Cornwell was younger than that!

Over in Manchester, in April 1978, I saw the still-teenage Pop Group – each of them baggily be-suited in an *Eraserhead* style – flying the post-punk flag with extreme grace and eloquence, inflicting upon us an incredibly taut set throughout which they united the heavy funk of George Clinton's Funkadelic with the dub of King Tubby, some demented Righteous Brothers-on-quaaludes crooning and the proto-rap of New York's The Last Poets, all of which presented such an unyieldingly pissed-off but politically well-informed worldview that it showed up The Clash's newly released second album, *Give 'Em Enough Rope*, for precisely what it was: old-fashioned. So fucking old-fashioned it coulda been a biplane . . . or a Blue Öyster Cult record. Sheesh! *Secret Treaties* certainly comes to mind. Sure, that

4 In truth, none of Wire's members even approached the *NME*'s then-idealised punk age of nineteen, drummer Robert Gotobed having been born back in 1951, while even bassist (Graham) Lewis was as old as Joe Strummer.

sounds classic enough now, but we'd all cut our hair and followed foul-mouthed Johnny to get as far away from that shit as was possible. Old-fashioned fucking rock'n'roll they were serving us, and were shameless enough to try and pass it off as new; and – far worse – they succeeded in hoodwinking most of the suckers! The 'look' of rebellion, that's all that the majority wanted. I still remember standing in Probe Records the day The Clash's sad slab came out and thinking, 'You fucking sell-outs, with your fucking staccato BÖC drums and late-Mott choruses'; after the thrill of fucking off every adult in Jubilee-land the previous year, who the fuck wanted this bloated and too-long-in-the-recording American FM brain-rot? That the LP's reception in the USA gained the band Album of the Year awards from such arch-bastions of Kapitalism as *Rolling Stone* and *Time* magazines is all the evidence you need to see just how far Uncle Joe's band would stoop to conquer. And after that crock of old shite was released, ex-rockers everywhere seized their opportunity to come in from the cold. Indeed, Strummer and co.'s decision to Pearlmanise The Clash inevitably endorsed the return of all those hoary old '70s big-rock riffs again, this time punked up not in any musical manner but by the protagonists simply donning motorbike leathers. People didn't even bother cutting their hair any more. Was it punk, or was it Thin Lizzy?

Thereafter, music weekly *Sounds* even tried to pass off AC/DC as punk-rockers! Suddenly, it was as though the good-time '70s had never been ousted, and even those fucking sexist geriatrics The Rolling Stones were making a comeback. As evidenced by the thirty thousand sales of Stiff Little Fingers' debut single 'Suspect Device', the Americanisation process was almost complete, for that song (undeniably brilliant as it was) had been built entirely around the main riff from Sammy Hagar's 'Space Station Number 5', readily available on Montrose's debut LP, itself still barely three years old. As Joe Strummer had once sung: 'I'm so bored with the USA/But what can I do?' Er, how about totally capitulate, tailor your songs and entire sound to those corporate Yank bastards and then complain you were misunderstood after you've reaped all the commercial benefits? 'Oh, OK,' says Uncle Joe, who then disappears from our lives for about four years, playing cattle sheds across America. How un-punk was that?

So, rather than re-educating the

UK masses as he'd blathered on about for so long, Strummer's pro-US obsession facilitated all those fifth columnists who churlishly wished only to prolong the Jubilee year's punk festivities, and – worse still – prolong it in a tart, bowdlerised form, all gesture and self-parody. So when Suicide – darlings of the UK post-punk scene from day one – supported The Clash on their 1978 British tour, parochial meatheads to a man rained bottles down on them for providing no evidence whatsoever of being punk-rockers (no geetars, no drums, no motorbike leathers, WTF?). What a tragic episode; a musical Holocaust. At the time, I was depressed as all hell and felt outrageously betrayed. After all those fucking promises, all we got from The Clash were rock'n'roll bromides and Yank imagery. Remembering those Clash/Suicide shows, even today, surely nothing better illustrates the division between what punk's experiment coulda been and what it was now forced to become: merely fast, angry rock played by J. Stalin's proles. Mao woulda laughed, of course (and guessed in advance), but Trotsky woulda turned in his grave. Oh well, it were nice while it lasted.

Let's now listen to some of those avant-guardians of post-punk, those defiant suckers who needed more than just Dr. Feelgood, 'Get Out of Denver' and The Small Faces speeded up to count themselves as revolutionaries.

The songs of the Postpunksampler

But first, after all that fucking spiel, what's the status of this compilation I've chosen to heave in your direction? Well, it's controversial for a start, because I've even included a coupla real early punk things in there and claimed them for post-punk: The Germs and Chain Gang, for example, both put out records in '77 that exhibit such singular performance and compositional trademarks that they coulda been released pretty much anywhere in the 1977–81 time frame. The rest are songs I've played to death over the years, and the list gradually reveals the manner in which various musical options unfolded within what constituted the post-punk scene. Controversially, perhaps, I've also gone quite late in order to show evidence of the continuing persistence of the post-punk spirit even into the rave years. Any way you feel about the list is fine by me; so long as it doesn't just bore you into an early suicide.

METAL URBAIN: PARIS MAQUIS
(Rough Trade, 1977)

Postpunksampler commences with the first ever seven-inch single release by Rough Trade Records: Metal Urbain's 'Paris Maquis' ('Paris Resistance'), a song whose berserk 6/4 rhythms and ever-repeating circular riffery support anarcho-syndicalist lyrics and persistent yelps of 'Fasciste!' throughout. Served up in an anarchist black-and-red bag depicting an inverted Eiffel Tower, this was the second of Metal Urbain's classic sequence of forty-fives, and certainly the only one on which they entirely transcended their Velvets/Stooges obsessions to create a purely Gallic white-light ramalama unjudgeable by any but its own kith and kin. Translating from the French half a decade later, I half-inched the line '*Je juge l'état contre moi*' ('I judge the state against myself') for my own song 'When I Walk Through the Land of Fear'. Oh yeah, and should/could any song conclude more spiritedly than 'Paris Maquis''s final, unaccompanied, strangulated voice crying in the desert: 'Fasciste!'?

ZOUNDS: CAN'T CHEAT KARMA
(Crass Records, 1980)

Hailing from Oxford, Zounds used this seven-inch single as a vehicle with which to nail every post-punk element perfectly, using rickety, sub-funk guitar and a wry mockney accent to disguise a rather finely written pop song (including a superb middle eight). WTF? Well, Crass majored in some pretty smart disguises themselves, so we shouldn't be surprised. Also, like their Crass mentors, Zounds were daring enough to exploit the weedy Terry Chimes drums, last heard on that debut Clash LP, totally in defiance of ninety-nine percent of punk-rockers obliged to find inspiration in *Money for Old Rope*, thereby lending this recording a cleanness that renders its outwardly affable mystery not less but *even more* ungraspable.

SUBWAY SECT: AMBITION
(Rough Trade, 1978)

While Vic Godard never even nearly delivered us the music he heard in his head and talked of so magnificently in the press, his too-intermittent releases were clearly sparser than he wished. We forgave him his sporadic canon because there was always a high enough overall artistic aim involved. 'Ambition' hailed from the second incarnation of Subway Sect, but since nothing exists of the first ensemble that could represent what they presented their Liverpool audience the night they supported The Clash on the 1977 *White Riot* tour, instead I'll lay on ya one of Vic's greatest 'pop' songs of all.

Richard Hell and the Voidoids: Liars Beware
(Sire, 1977)

Poor Richard Hell was never a man in control of his own metaphor. First, Malcolm McLaren stole off with it across the pond and applied it, with more effect, to the far younger Johnny Rotten; then Richard found himself in possession of a possible cultural anthem in the form of his song 'Blank Generation', but was never able to record it successfully. 'I don't mean Blank Generation as in Stupid Generation,' Richard then explained to a fascinated press. 'I mean it as fill in "the blank" that fits you best.' Then he forgot all that, and, anyway, had already alluded to the stupid version by naming his band . . . the Voidoids. Sheesh!

The Germs: Forming
(What Records, 1977)

Struggling at all times to keep their eyes on the mish, but nevertheless delivering the dish, LA's The Germs conjured up a sub-rudimentary, unmusical, experimental people carrier over which 'singer' Darby Crash anticipated post-punk's wise numbskull sound by at least eighteen months. And while *nothing* else during punk was nearly this deadly monotonous, nor so rigorously underachieving, give it a coupla scene-shifts and two years later everybody'd finally caught up.

39 Clocks: Aspetando Godo
(Psychotic Promotion, 1982)

I learned of the German duo 39 Clocks in 1979, when their manager interviewed me in Cologne and pressed their LP and single into my hands. Included herein, 'Aspetando Godo' is that single, and it still captures that distant time when a drum machine did one thing only and you just had to play along. Like the Bunnymen pre-Pete de Freitas, 39 Clocks clearly just jammed and jammed until songs emerged, conjuring up ugly but benign tumours of electric-guitar scrawl that trundle along, occasionally allowing eddies and flows of pretty Velvets 1969-isms to creep in, before reverting inevitably to The Ugliness. Add to this a transatlantic singer/dead ringer for *The Faust Tapes* and you gotcha self an underground hit.

Missing Presumed Dead: Family Tree
(Sequel Records, 1979)

Next up, 'Family Tree' is one

motherfucker of a tour de force and nails, in two minutes, the entire inventory of requirements needed to fulfil the pure post-punk covenant (loud, angular bass; a portentous, non-US vocalist singing about family issues; and slashing, weak white-funk/no-wave guitar). It's strange, then, that this gem was hidden away on the end of Missing Presumed Dead's totally forgettable 1979 four-track EP *Say It with Flowers*. This song's northern sound was so entirely irreconcilable with the skanky high-rise white reggae of the other offerings on the EP that my mate Bernie Connors – while working in Liverpool's Probe Records – declared it to be a parody of The Teardrop Explodes. I disagree. But it's one hell of an eloquent and succinct statement; a real lost classic, methinks.

Manicured Noise: Faith (Pre, 1980)

Jumping ship to Manchester from the London scene, where he couldn't get a look in, songwriter/guitarist Steve Walsh – briefly a member of Sid Vicious and Viv Albertine's Flowers of Romance – hijacked long-time free-form punk band Manicured Noise, then pruned them, rehearsed them and recorded them into a tight, soulful, sax-led Manny take on early Talking Heads. Signing to prog-rock label Charisma's faux-indie imprint, Pre, for a while, Walsh and co. threatened to deliver a killer first album chock-full o'tunes. At the final hurdle, however, they imploded and left us just two rather classic seven-inch singles. This one sounded amazing when played loudly in clubs; I remember assuming it would be Top Ten, then feeling miffed when it did absolutely fuck all.

Jane Aire and the Belvederes: Yankee Wheels (Stiff, 1979)

Thirty-two years ago, the British music press fell in love with a bunch of bands from Akron, Ohio, and the fifteen-year-old Jane Aire was the one whose innate punkiness got to all of them. Stiff signed her for this sleazy, wheezing, avant-garage debut single, and its strangely staggering, piano-led no-wave/Mike Garsonness and strangulated lead guitar have haunted me ever since. The mad, unsung genius behind this single was one Liam Sternberg, whose piano and songwriting should really have been investigated further from the evidence of this recording.

Dance Party: Photograph (Cassette release, 1980)

Future Shack/Pale Fountains boss

Mike Head's music sounded like Joy Division/The Teardrop Explodes until I accidentally left my copy of *Love Revisited* around at Yorkie's, where we practised. Thereafter, Michael was reborn on the West Coast and found his true calling was not to be stuck, Jaz Coleman-like, singing from behind a monophonic synth but (far more admirably) to start learning the whole of Arthur Lee's (then) remarkably unsung *Forever Changes* and exquisite lost/last Elektra forty-five 'Your Mind and We Belong Together'. Joined here by Yorkie on bass, and two others, 'Photograph' was recorded around early 1980, in the same place we'd done 'Sleeping Gas' eighteen months earlier.

Dum Dum Dum: Dum Dum Dum
(Struck Dumb, 1980)

When the drummer-less A Certain Ratio supported my band at the Factory, back in May 1979, singer Simon Topping cloaked their entire sound with some strange hand-held noise-making device, which ne'er left his mitts throughout their entire show. Within the year, however, said device was history and the entire band thereafter hung their shabbily scrawled riffage over the mighty funk rhythms of new black drummer Donald Johnson, the results of which were a magical skronk hybrid that more than did the trick. Sounds to me like Oxford's Dum Dum Dum opted herein for precisely the same route, surfacing with this obvious-but-compelling post-PiL rhythmical racket, all surmounted with glissando guitars and 'fun, fun, fun'-type lyrics delivered in an Iggy/Devoto stylee.

Crass: Mother Earth
(Crass Records, 1980)

The proof of original punk's innate truth was proven, in mid-'78, by the release of Crass' *Feeding of the Five Thousand* EP, on which they mesmerised me with their superb distillation of original punk attitude. As a snob who'd started growing his hair long at the end of '77, I saw Crass, with all their moves – their hypnotic posing, their scary banners, their reserves of substitute vocalists/poets – promoting that EP at Eric's and discovered with something akin to a thunderbolt from the blue that it was possible for really smart and organised adult anarchists to combine Bakuninist thoroughness with all that unharnessed Jubilee year teen pissed-offness, and craft it so tightly, so carefully, so heroically that you could capture generations two tiers below you. Being a daft, tripping cunt, I forgot soon after, but I return again and again to Crass, just so I can revive my flagging Revolutionary Spirit.

FRICTION: CRAZY DREAM
(Pass, 1980)

Blasting forth with their bizarre hybrid of 'Bodies'-period J. Rotten vocals and errant axe riffs straight outta the Mars-meets-Voidoids, *No New York* school, Tokyo's Friction nailed the entire Western post-punk conceit so succinctly to their whipping post not because the band was composed of intuitive first-timers, but because leader Reck had just returned from a brief spell as bass player in a late, late incarnation of NYC's notorious Teenage Jesus and the Jerks. Of undefined age and with a hippie past as long as Withnail's coat-tails, Reck returned to Tokyo having entirely copped Richard Hell's look and attitude (although mercifully not his bass-guitar style) and had a full twelve months in which to build his rep before his fellow countrymen realised that he was just recycling.

HAIR & SKIN TRADING CO.: MONKIES
(Situation Two, 1992)

Proof positive of the post-punk blueprint's staying power was this technically way too late offering from former Loop duo, drummer John Wills and singer/guitarist Neil Mackay. Hair & Skin Trading Co. rarely sounded like they do on this remarkably post-punk assault; they generally dubbed it up and confused the punters with electronic drone bombardments of pure experiment, especially on 1992's *Jo in Nine G Hell* album, whence comes this truly formidable track.

ELECTRIC EELS: ACCIDENT
(Stereo recording, 1975)

Until Rough Trade released the first Electric Eels vinyl, in 1979, nobody had heard these mythical beasts outside their home city, Cleveland, Ohio. So you can imagine how much minds were blown when their cavernous sub-sub-*Spiral Scratch* sound was shown to have been captured on tape four long years earlier, back in barren 1975! Not only is the Electric Eels' canon chock-full of future classics awaiting cover versions, but their songwriting emanated from several highly competitive sources, giving the Eels the compositional edge that will see their standing rise and rise in the coming decades. In 1981, Eels singer David E interviewed me during a Teardrops show in Cleveland; it was in the middle of 'that' tour unfortunately, so I was more than the worse for wear. I do, however, still have the copy of *CLE* magazine he gave me, with a nice flexi of Pere Ubu doing The Seeds' 'Pushin' Too Hard'. Sorry for the nostalgia fest, kiddies; snivel, drool, sometimes it all just seems so long ago!

Chain Gang: Son of Sam
(Kapitalist, 1977)

Chain Gang's 'Son of Sam' was such a stone killer, such a creepy and dyslexic lurch of a tale that a Liverpool cult developed around it. Sheesh, even the silver Kapitalist record label was a bit off. Myself, Budgie and our skinny mate Hughie Jones formed a band called The Young Winstons just for the purposes of performing this song. That lurching, straining riff, that stentorian snare drum . . . was there even a full kit?

Swell Maps: Read About Seymour
(Rather, 1977)

Meanwhile, over in Middle England, Leamington Spa's finest, Swell Maps, descend in 'Read About Seymour', a sonic, home-made, plywood 1:1 scale De Havilland Mosquito, powered by rubber bands and lots of enthusiasm. This is *the* ur-racket; an incendiary riot of dual/even triple in-joke lead vocals intoned by school friends, each of whom musta contributed a lyric. Who the fuck knows what these gentlemen dudes were on? Search me. Their records sounded like Asmus Tietchens producing the Buzzcocks, but their stupid record sleeves pitched them somewhere between The Undertones and a dafter The Fall. This sound, though, is some-fucking-thing-fucking-else . . . and the 'drums and tea tray' credit just about sums these suckers up.

The Sods: Transport
(Polydor, 1979)

Denmark's finest punk band, The Sods generally did 'punk' very well, a smorgasbord of white reggae, Siouxsian guitar noise and Wire ramalama, but all performed with enough conviction to achieve a believable hybrid; even The Sods' name was a clever enough catch-all. Herein, they skank and stutter like De Presse covering The Ruts: a Malcolm Owen-as-Strummer bark doubles as lead vocal, while proto-Joy Division extraneous noise hoses the backing track and urbanises proceedings. Later, as Sort Sol, the same quartet successfully converted to genuine, serious, grey button-down post-punk, but this song nails the *Postpunksampler* metaphor nicely enough.

Reptile Ranch: Saying Goodbye
(Z Block, 1981)

The old cliché about a drummer being someone who hangs around with musicians could well have originated in the Reptile Ranch rehearsal room, their sticks-man obviously having gained his position in the band by telling them it's not what you play, it's what you leave out that makes you a good player. Ah, but not having the heart to kick him out, the other three spiritedly make up for his deficiencies with this highly arranged and intricately composed post-punk song, during which both bass player and organist reach their own individual musical epiphanies and the blagger-guitarist struggles not too hard to mask his own ineptitude, knowing that random cymbal crashes are always funnier. In just over three minutes, Reptile Ranch sum up the entire northern indie scene of two years previously. Nice.

Dalek I Love You: Trapped
(Phonogram, 1980)

In 1978, a few sofas and a lamp standard on Dalek I Love You's defiantly post-everything stage set was enough to cause a schism in the ranks between myself and my compadres. 'You can't do that': you can, they did it. Still, Dalek bassist Dave Balfe came to the mainland, while leader Alan Gill grew pot in his sideboard. Soon after, I was over the water inhaling the sideboard and being introduced to LSD by its owner . . . hmm, perhaps my memory's still got mucho rose-tinted spectacles. Herein, Alan's using Vox Jaguar organ and mucho Dave Wakeling-style tremolo on the old larynx, trying to stop his lady from leaving. He's caught in a sea of typical post-punk soundscapes between Reptile Ranch and Colours Out of Time, but he ain't going down casually.

Colours Out of Time: As if Another World
(John Peel session, 1981)

Remember Colours Out of Time? Nah, nobody else does neither. Yet these poor sods from Crewe, in Cheshire, were several times close to getting somewhere, had they not, every time, scuppered their own chances by changing their own metaphor and (accidentally) becoming a different band. I booked them to support The Teardrop Explodes at Liverpool's Club Zoo on the strength of their first single, a gigantic Detroit chasm of a riff-song with no noticeable IQ of its own. Then they turned up for the show and sounded like us – organ'n'all!

'As if Another World' sees Colours Out of Time in a 'When I Dream' state of mind, soon after which they morphed yet again, this time into a transatlantic sound-alike of those terrible 'Paisley underground' spewdo-psych outfits.

The Wild Swans: Now You're Perfect
(Cassette demo, 1980)

Ah, Paul Simpson's Wild Swans; if only the band had sounded like they did in my erstwhile Teardrop co-founder's head – hell, we'd all still be defending Guernica from Franco! Unfortunately, the music of The Wild Swans rarely performed its intended task, i.e. to rouse the proletariat from their somnambulist slumber, mainly because no amount of fussy arpeggiating from shocked-looking guitarist Jerry Kelly could hide the similarities of each song's structure. Still, 'Now You're Perfect' shows that The Wild Swans, when taken in short doses, displayed a wistful majesty and an urgent, almost caffeinated heart. And all you young '80s heads out there: get that bass player! I'll wager you rarely encounter that level of overachieving in the modern popular scene!

Armand Schaubroeck: Buried Alive
(Mirror, 1978)

Armand Schaubroeck is included here because his 1978 LP *Ratfucker* was dedicated to Pere Ubu's genius guitarist, the late Peter Laughner, and because Armand herein had clearly copped a band sound that actively aped the Bowie/Sales brothers ensemble that Iggy was touring around *Lust for Life.* Better still, on 'Buried Alive' Armand says, in less than two minutes of expletives and gospel-preacher invective, what Ben Elton takes two hours to say on Queen's behalf in their rock-musical abortion. And what's that, mister? Fuck all, kiddies, absolutely *fuck all.*

Psycho Surgeons: Horizontal Action
(Wallaby Beat, 1978)

While most everyone else charged forwards into further storms of avant-whatever, a few obstreperous souls insisted their future vision was, well, *retro*. Some were accepted for their sheer persistence and personality; The Jam, for example, were top entertainment every time I saw them, but they were like Todd Rundgren and Lynyrd Skynyrd, whom I also saw during Jubilee year; I didn't count them on my list. Compared to the newness of everything else, those aforemenched seemed like dinosaurs, especially the moddy jumps that both The Jam *and* Todd traded in! No fucking shit! 'Don't Make Another Bass Guitar, Mr Rickenbacker,' sang Danny and the Dressmakers, in 1980, which I always took to be a dig at The Jam's Bruce Foxton. Anyway, over in Australia, Psycho Surgeons contributed to post-punk's Great Leap Forward by hitching a ride back to 1963 *and* 1973 simultaneously, thereby accessing the combined (and frenzied) attack of both *Raw Power* and frat-rock – that bilious, one-take, between-beat clatterstompf so beloved of The Monks and Japan's more adventuresome Group Sounds bands.

DMZ: Bad Attitude
(Sire, 1978)

Up in Boston, Massachusetts, DMZ also chose the retro route, singer Mono Man doing Iggy and the Stooges' routine at a time when everybody (Stiv Bators, Lux Interior, even Andy Ellison) was still stupid enough to dare. Live, they did it blazingly well, apparently, but on record it was too patchy a concept to peddle in a world currently obsessed with Right Now, and most of the Flo & Eddie-produced LP was recycled/degraded Troggs with far too clean a production. However, two thousand years after the event, when even Curly, Mo and the other originals have turned power-pop or died, this sub-Stooges ramalama still exhibits a remarkable '78 spirit, easily worthy of inclusion in these hallowed ranks.

ESG: UFO
(99 Records, 1978)

ESG is a classy example of what the open-mindedness of the post-punk scene could turn up. Ed Bahlman, in New York, set up this great twelve-inch singles label called 99; I got stuff just because it was on that label. ESG was a five-piece centred around three teenage sisters from the South Bronx. Their grooves were always so minimal that each conga slap was a lifetime a-coming, and their triple-vocal, playground singing was exquisite ('You're No Good' still sends me!). My then future wife, Dorian, saw them umpteen times and says they were great live, too, totally natural. Then, one year later, Factory Records put out this seven-inch single, produced by Martin Hannett, on which they even cross that Can 'I Need More'/Joy Division 'Atmosphere' Rubicon where soul music *is* Krautrock.

Gaz Chambers: Who's Life Is It Anyway?
(Cassette demo, 1981)

This eleven-minute frenzy of harrowing adolescence opened seventeen-year-old Gaz Chambers' *Music from the Death Factory* cassette EP, unfortunately trashing all the other in-joke/oddly titled songs on the record ('Hitler Drove a BRN'!). For sheer persistent discordance and earnest harping, six-foot-four Gaz and his equally persistent but uncredited second keyboardist (the ultra-anonymous T. Ross) are truly hard to beat. And, in answer to all of your inevitable Gaz questions thrown up by the brevity of this review, the answer is 'No'.

Prologue to 'In Conclusion'

With twenty–twenty hindsight, it could be argued that punk and post-punk happened almost simultaneously, especially if we count Subway Sect's steadfastly monochrome support set on The Clash's otherwise ultra-colourful *White Riot* tour, in May '77, as evidence, Vic Godard and co. most serpently anticipating the entire future Liverpool scene with their unconcerned, proto-Will Sargeant shoe-gazing and Eeyorean glumness. Was the sound of 1979 right there, in '77? You're damned right it was! But, looking back on post-punk now, from this great way off, I believe most of us followed Lydon's lead and, thereafter, abandoned anything that smacked of the Sex Pistols . . . or The Clash for that matter. Instead, post-punk looked back into infinity and forwards into the future simultaneously, co-opting James Brown, the Velvets (inevitably), Miles Davis, The Last Poets, The Doors, almost *any-fucking-thing* other than the Sex Pistols, darling!

Post-punk was a haven for orphan poets like Patrik Fitzgerald, Joolz and Manchester's John the Postman, whose raging, unaccompanied, twenty-minute performance of the mouth-piece 'Senegal' was often preceded by a Mark E. Smith introduction of molto hyperbole (Smith: 'Rich foreign stars die in front of their video . . . The Postman IS the music scene!').[5] Unlike the new punk-rockers, anything trad was fucked off in favour of the rad; indeed,

5 By Christmas 1977, Ian McCulloch and I had virtually given up on the Liverpool punk scene and had transferred our allegiances to the far more experimental and active music scene in Manchester, whose thriving 'centre of the city where all roads meet' sucked in every touring band as inevitably as Liverpool – accessed only via the obscure M57 – was bypassed by Patti Smith,

the post-punk scene was novelty-obsessed, feminist and revolutionary. Heck, lads, half the groups featured ladies! Kleenex, The Au Pairs, Delta Five . . . and hard-drinking, feminist ladies, too, so mind your mouth.

Post-punk's purveyors wanted life change, too, demanded it, applied punk reason/unreason to everything thereafter – and scorned tradition as previous intellectual generations had scorned the Ku Klux Klan. Down in our dungeonous former Liverpool punk club Eric's, post-punk revolution started the moment The Spitfire Boys split up: the last day of 1977. From here on in, the post-punk cry was The Desperate Bicycles' own 'It was easy, it was cheap, go and do it!' EMI? DIY!

Like the Puritans and the American Transcendentalists, those frugal-of-necessity ancestors who'd first preached self-reliance, the post-punk generation practised standing on their own two feet. The thrift stores of punk gave way to the thrift of post-punk; even cheap new market-stall threads cut the post-punk mustard if you were a Fall fan. So, while Sham 69 and McLaren's Ronnie Biggs-led Pistols anthems spawned faux terrace shite such as The Cockney Rejects, those with their own IQ scouted about for other desperate souls free-thinking enough to consider the Augustus Pablo-endorsed melodica a valid rock instrument, then set about creating their own radical hybrid music for a fraction of the cash wasted on *Give 'Em Enough Rope*. Heck, at the tail-end of '78, Scritti Politti even printed the costs of their record's manufacture on its cover!

Blondie, Television, Pere Ubu . . . you name it, we missed it, unless we schlepped our asses over to Manny. By the summer of '77, certain aspects of the Liverpool punk scene were becoming highly tiresome for that city's most insatiable music freak, as I became forced to travel to Manchester, Leeds, Sheffield, Birmingham and London to see international bands that really shoulda made the effort to come to me. Hitching across the UK and courting a girl in Leeds, however, it soon became evident to me why Patti, Television, Blondie et al. had opted to give us a miss: whereas all those aforementioned cities were at the confluences of two or more great highways (M1, M5, M6, M62), poor Liverpool was accessed only via the aforementioned M57, whose blink-and-you-miss-it junction/exit was a barely acknowledged tributary off the monolithic highway to Glasgow and the far north. Add to that Liverpool's docks, its port, its Irish influence and large Catholic population, and outsiders soon understand why Liverpudlians tend to be more singular than your average UK city dweller. As an outsider myself, however, you can probably also understand why its, ahem, close-knit artistic community got so claustrophobic that I had to split.

In Conclusion

So here endeth this *Postpunksampler*. To those of you young 'uns who consider I've been too Taliban about punk dates, etc., I beseech you to try to understand that – back in ye punk day – such fundamentalism was essential to fuelling the entire bitchy scene. To have recorded and released a punk forty-five during 1977 validated a musician's revolutionary credentials no end, even if it was a right crock o'cack. Outwardly, Ian McCulloch, Pete Wylie and I ridiculed Liverpool's Spitfire Boys for their painfully weak 'British Refugee' single; but, shit, were we secretly jealous of Paul Rutherford, Budgie and the other two! Then again, I admit to totally lording it over Mac after recording our debut single in 1978, while he had to wait until '79. Mac, in turn, absolutely hammered Wylie in public for daring to print the date '1979' on his first forty-five, 'Better Scream', when the fucker never came out until March 1980! Seeing that, thirty years after the event, and I still feel the glee at having one-upped those bastards. Punk made me that way.

Postpunksampler 2

1 Joy Division: Autosuggestion (6.07) (1979)
2 Blue Orchids: The Flood (4.18) (1980)
3 The Scars: Horrorshow (3.00) (1979)
4 Josef K: Sense of Guilt (3.06) (1981)
5 The Fire Engines: Get Up and Use Me (3.12) (1980)
6 Artist's Studio: Jungle Gardenia (4.04) (1982)
7 Subway Sect: Ambition (2.53) (1977)
8 Tubeway Army: Jo the Waiter (2.40) (1978)
9 Richard Hell and the Voidoids: Another World (5.30) (1977)
10 Mars: Helen Fordsdale (2.27) (1978)
11 Red Transistor: Not Bite (3.48) (1978)
12 SoliPsiK: See Saw (2.22) (1981)
13 Rema-Rema: Rema-Rema (4.21) (1980)
14 A Certain Ratio: All Night Party (3.12) (1979)
15 Theatre of Hate: Rebel Without a Brain (3.49) (1980)
16 Spizzenergi: Soldier Soldier (3.46) (1979)
17 Scritti Politti: 28/8/78 (2.39) (2005)
18 The Sleepers: Linda (4.15) (1978)
19 Human Switchboard: Fly-In (3.12) (1978)
20 DMZ: Don't Jump Me, Mother (3.21) (1978)
21 ESG: You're No Good (3.07) (1981)
22 Kleenex: Ain't You (3.01) (1978)
23 Section 25: Girls Don't Count (4.26) (1980)
24 Ed Banger: Kinnel Tommy (4.06) (1978)
25 John Cooper Clarke: Psycle Psluts (5.42) (1978)
26 Crispy Ambulance: The Presence (12.55) (1981)

Legendary jazz bassist Charles Mingus once told a tale of how, back in the early '50s, some downtrodden, lanky white dude chanced upon the club Mingus was playing, blagged his way on stage, then commandeered his double bass, from which said untutored stranger proceeded to extract sounds and effects the like of which Mingus claimed never to have heard again. No one knows to this day who the dude was.

My story is less mysterious but sadder. In 1979, a smart, cool-looking guy called Richard Sanderson came backstage after a Middlesborough show and gave me a bedroom recording by his quartet, Drop. In his manner, style and quiet confidence, Richard was the Peter Hammill of post-punk, anguished, lean and nobly Norman. I loved every song on the tape and played it to Bill Drummond and Dave Balfe, who rejected it outright for being too much like 'the Teardrops and The Fall'. I was aghast at their not recognising the sheer confidence and succinctness of Drop's songs, but this was mid-1979, when many bands featured 'that' sound. Anyway, I visited Richard and he gave me another bedroom tape on which there were yet more new songs, all of them great. I was by that time experiencing problems of my own, due to success, mainly, but also because I was absolutely caned on acid most of the time and finding it hard even to keep my own shit together. So by the time I'd found time to hook up with Richard again . . . he'd become Edwin Collins! Unlucky!

Unfortunately, the spirit of the artists of those punk and post-punk times was way ahead of the technology and its technicians, so Drop's classic set was never even captured in a studio. Oh, the fucking absolute tragedy! Worse still, there must, inevitably, be umpteen similar sob stories to be told up and down the UK's culturally impoverished landscape. With all of this in mind, let's just enjoy the racket brung forth on *Postpunksampler 2* and give thanks that it was even captured on tape in the first place.

The Songs, or 'And There Will Your Heart Be, Also'

Joy Division: Autosuggestion (Fast, 1979)

By this late stage in the rock'n'roll game, it's surely difficult for younger generations to understand why a legend such as Joy Division should have been forced to share space on a twelve-inch vinyl sampler with two unknown acts. But, yes, you heard right; this exhilarating and truly classic *vox clamantis in deserto* Curtisian call to action known as 'Autosuggestion' first appeared on *Earcom 2*, an obscure twelve-inch EP released by Edinburgh's Fast Records, alongside The Thursdays (who they?) performing Otis Redding's 'Dock of the Bay' and the foul-tasting progressive-rock of Redcar's Basczax. Whoa! 'But why were the Div even on this record?' I hear y'all cry. Well, as Ian and co. had trod the boards the previous year in the guise of the fairly awful and slightly dodgy punk band Warsaw, it took more than a simple name change to convince cynical north-west-scene heads that the Div was a goer. So repaying their dues by bequeathing breathtaking sonic artworks to undeserving parochial post-punk samplers was clearly part of their cosmick covenant on the way to the, ahem, top; (not so) simple as that.

Blue Orchids: The Flood
(Rough Trade, 1980)

As my initial love of The Fall was caused not by Mark's splendid feistmeister bark but by Martin Bramah's fiery, upside-down guitar scrawl and the uni-sexy Una Baines' dithery electric piano, this debut Blue Orchids single, recorded by the post-Fall Baines/Bramah duo, was an event to be taken with great seriousness round our neck o'the woods. And what an opening gambit! Colossally over-recorded French nuns chant arhythmically from the moment the needle hits the vinyl; suddenly the pious bints are cut short by one of the all-time greatest (and most ramshackle) post-punk riffs. Imagine the clattery melancholy of Ringo's 1970 Apple single 'It Don't Come Easy' played not by studio professionals but by enthusiastic hobbyists, whose more-by-luck-than-judgement arrangement has been hastily band-aided together by endless minor/major-chord clashes and decorated with irresponsible lead-guitar flourishes. Amidst all the clatter, the brave middle eight briefly showcases one of Una's delightfully New Age poems – unfortunately mixed too quietly to be audible – before being Spanish Archer'd out of the way by molto incoming Bramah guitar pyrotechnics. Later the same year, the Blue Orchids' debut LP, *The Greatest Hit*, was further evidence of the duo's blazing post-hippie vibe, but their records thereafter became more and more infrequent until, like the house in one of their songs, they sadly just faded out.

The Scars: Horrorshow
(Fast Product, 1979)

From the opening moments of Paul Research's churning, yearning lead guitar into the thunderous, neo-hard-rock bass and drums, The Scars' debut forty-five was a stone classic. Add to that a bizarre (although rather late in the day) lyrical narrative taken from the aversion-therapy scenes of *A Clockwork Orange*, and you soon see why – back in 1979 – almost anything released on Bob Last's Fast label was essential to check out. Bob had already delivered us those early Gang of Four and Human League EPs, but this Scars record was even better. Why so? Well, as a product of the early-'70s O level Russian course, I was delighted when these four Scots teenagers named their debut single after my all-time fave Russky word, 'horrorshow' being a slightly stretching it, Westernised way of spelling the Russian word for 'fine'. Unfortunately, The Scars could never sustain this greatness, despite a spirited (although altogether more commercial sounding) debut LP entitled *Author! Author!*. Singer Rob King would later join the list of Nico's buddies in smack addiction. Ho hum.

Josef K: Sense of Guilt
(Postcard, 1981)

Commencing with a bracingly atonal, Martin Bramahesque lead-guitar signature that parodies The Teardrop Explodes' single 'Treason', Josef K's driving, pulsating 'Sense of Guilt' was a fine post-glam racket, its *Scary Monsters*-like ecstatic, dual-lead vocals telling an undefined tale over ever-returning semi-choruses of rapturous almost-chords. From Blue Orchids to The Chills, A Shallow Madness to Laughing Clowns, great post-punk music was often achieved purely because each musician involved was too selfish, too caught up in the moment or too untutored to contribute tonally to what the others were doing. When the sonic harshness was finally discovered, while listening to the playback over studio monitors, many obstinate and opinionated musicians simply defended their own corners by acting mardy and refusing to budge: 'Are you playing a minor chord there?' 'God knows!' Yup, during the post-punk era, reconciling the irreconcilable was a breeze.

The Fire Engines: Get Up and Use Me
(Codex, 1980)

Edinburgh's The Fire Engines delivered a (suitably) fiery brand of hastily scrawled garage funk that thundered along like an unladen white Mercedes Sprinter driven by a Pepsi Max freak. This particular song's Velveteen stumble even occasionally invoked memories of Messrs Hell and Verlaine's 1974 Neon Boys tumble on 'That's All I Know Right Now'. On stage, the band was even hotter and even scratchier and even younger than you could imagine. However, this studio versh of 'Get Up and Use Me' should do the trick, especially as it's possessed of quite enough fiery Mithraic ramalama for most bands' entire careers.

Artist's Studio: Jungle Gardenia
(Recorded 1982)

Conceived as a duo, along the same lines as The Associates, Glasgow's Artist's Studio followed their countrymen in the Thin White Cop-out's footprints, letting rip with this fabulous period piece which sounds like The Flying Lizards playing 'China Girl' im Berlin. Propelled along by a remedial Chinese water-torture drum-box and an acutely cumbersome and overly ornate bass guitar, the duo tells us a traditional tale straight out of, well, *Heroes*, I guess. While Uncle Ziggy's post-*Let's Dance* abortions may have ruined him for all future generations, boy, did his influence run deep in my own. The reason, as evidenced by the rich plundering encountered herein, is that my generation could never escape the skinny get, because so much of his exotic schtick was – in modified form (natch) – at least good enough to commandeer for yerself. Sheesh, what a giveaway!

Subway Sect: Ambition
(Studio version, 1977)

Included for the benefit of hindsight, this 1977 studio edition, recorded by the original Subway Sect line-up, replicates fairly accurately the sound that so enthralled me on the *White Riot* tour, but which was destined for oblivion after Vic Godard and co. fell out with manager Bernard Rhodes. While the arrangement here is almost exactly the same as that contained within the grooves of the later forty-five (as described in the earlier *Postpunksampler* entry), there's a stuttering, John Maher/Buzzcockian nervousness on this versh which makes me yearn for a proper 'official bootleg', along the lines of Buzzcocks' *Time's Up* album. Still, this'll do me righteously for the present.

Tubeway Army: Jo the Waiter
(Beggars Banquet, 1978)

Commencing in exactly the same

acoustically driven manner as my own 'Unisex Cathedral', Gazza's homoerotic tale of being groped in the gents displays a melancholic Subway Sectarianism that might not be accidental; hell, even the name of Gazza's band is just a far more terraced-up versh of Subway Sect. Located in the boneyard of Tubeway Army's first LP for Beggars Banquet, there's a charming and disarming Desperate Bicycles-plays-*Beard of Stars* DIY quality to 'Jo the Waiter' that stood in fair opposition to the rest of Gazza's clattery, Chrome-informed Thin White Muse. Anyhow, regarding this particular song, the absence of an 'e' at the end of Jo turned out to be a cunning clue: Jo was Gazza's waitress girlfriend of the time. Ah, sweet.

Richard Hell and the Voidoids: Another World
(Sire, 1977)

Despite fielding a musical troupe whose combined ages added up to more than that of the entire Liverpool punk scene combined, Dickie bug-eyes occasionally pursued his metaphor just far enough for the more appreciative among us to get a clue as to what the fuck he was on about. While Hell's lyrics contained herein are clear enough evidence for me to surmise that I'd have hated the existential fucker up close, nevertheless the music and the manner in which it was performed renders this track nothing less than a masterpiece. I mean that in both the modern *and* the old-time descriptive sense. For, despite naming this sonic epic after a dreary NYC daytime soap opera, Richie and his combined Oids (didn't all major fans call 'em that?) herein predicted the avant-clatter of the following year's no-wave scene in Manhattan, not to mention the obsessively heathen haggis-funk of Josef K and The Fire Engines, then still three long Caledonian winters away.

Mars: Helen Fordsdale
(Antibes, 1978)

Delivered to the world aboard Brian Eno's none-more-hip 1978 avant-garde compilation *No New York*, Mars were indeed privileged to arrive on the coat-tails of such an esteemed sonic adventurer. Unlike fellow passengers DNA, with their *Tin Drum*-like kindergarten tantrums, or saxdrûûler James Chance's lousy/unlusty ensemble The Contortions, however, Mars fully deserved their place on Eno's record (and then some) by delivering up to us 'Helen Fordsdale', a veritable blueprint for a ten-year rock career, and all in a two'n'arf-minute song. *No New*

York's other showcased act was Lydia Lunch's extraordinary Teenage Jesus and the Jerks, an example of whose canon of work I should perhaps have included on this compilation.

Red Transistor: Not Bite
(Unreleased)

Poor VON LMO; poor Rudolph Grey . . . Like many no-wave artists excluded from Eno's excellent but too exclusive *No New York* compilation, VON LMO and Grey's wonderful Red Transistor were passed over in favour of some right unadroit twats. Unfortunately, while time has been far kinder to Red Transistor than to most, this still fabulous hunk o'Chrome-play-*Neu! 2* at British Aerospace has been far upstaged by VON LMO's own obsessive, pan-dimensional Black Light trip into the astral salad. I'm talking (of course) about his 1996 track 'X+Y=0'. Still, in context with the rest of the post-punk programme, Herrs Grey und VON LMO acquit themselves marvellously here.

SoliPsiK: See Saw
(M Squared, 1981)

I picked this seven-inch single up in Sydney, during The Teardrop Explodes' 1982 Australian tour, and freaked out at the exhilarating post-Cleveland yawp of the thing. Driven by what sounds like two ARP 2600 synths in parallel, 'See Saw' exhibits a peculiarly proto-Muslimgauzean quality, yet never gets too 'minarets' for parody. The weird thing is, this band was far better known as SPK, whom I've never, to my knowledge, even heard. This one-off single remains a fave, however.

Rema-Rema: Rema-Rema
(4AD, 1980)

Taken from their sole 4AD EP, this obsessively psychedelic slab of 1980 post-punk soul slopped a pungent stew of refusenik chanted vocals and plenny of Suicide's second-album keyboard FX over the hoariest of all soul riffs, i.e. that venerable sucker that Grand Funk had half-inched for their 1970 epic 'Heartbreaker' and which The Doors just couldn't resist re-nicking the following year for 1971's 'The Changeling'. Oh, and all the cranky lead guitars came from future Ant Marco Pirroni.

A Certain Ratio: All Night Party
(Factory, 1979)

I was telling y'all, in the first *Postpunksampler*, about being supported, in mid-'79, by the dwarfishly tiny, baggily be-suited and mysterious drummer-less versh of A Certain Ratio. Well, here's the only released example of that ensemble, and boy does it stink good. The band members were all physically tiny except for the bass player, but when they commandeered six-foot-tall black drummer Donald Johnson to act as a central rhythmical shaft, then covered Banbarra's classic anti-marriage hit 'Shack Up', these little bastards nailed their metaphor down, but good.

Theatre of Hate: Rebel Without a Brain
(Burning Rome, 1980)

Considering this single was produced by Clash guitarist Mick Jones, and the band itself led by guitarist/songwriter Kirk Brandon, quite how Theatre of Hate achieved this extraordinarily heathen sound is beyond my ken. For a start, there are no guitars. Instead, sticky dub drumming propels a harsh, stentorian sax'n'bass riff more reminiscent of *Pawn Hearts*-period Van der Graaf Generator than anything then current. Tuneless, dirgy, haunting and utterly captivating, 'Rebel Without a Brain' is a genre in itself. Still, Kirk and co. were clearly a loosely packed ensemble, as evidenced by their being happy to release an excellent 1981 live LP, *He Who Dares Wins*, despite the band's synthesizer having been nicked from their van just hours before the show!

Spizzenergi: Soldier Soldier
(Rough Trade, 1979)

Top of the Utopian Intuitive Non-Career Mover's list for 1979 was the inimitable Spizz, erstwhile leader of punk duo Spizz Oil, then of post-punk franchise Spizzenergi, Athletico Spizz 80 and The Spizzles. Unfortunately, Spizz made a revolutionary (and admirably impractical) decision to embody the punk myth by changing his band's name every year – ideologically wonderful but clearly useless. For just as each 'new' band was getting known, it was all change. For a while, however, Spizz blasted forth excellent single after excellent single, and 'Soldier Soldier' remains locked in my head as the most spectacular hybrid of disco and field holler. Spizz would probably have been a decent songwriter had he been born at any other time in history, but driven on by punk open-mindedness, he became the Blaster Bates of the scene, operating behind such a truly cartoon image that he remains faceless to this day.

Scritti Politti: 28/8/78
(Rough Trade, 2005)

Back in 1979, when the Teardrops

and Bunnymen played lots of London-area shows for Final Solution, Kevin Millins' underground promotion company, the bills often featured Scritti Politti, along with A Certain Ratio, Joy Division, Orchestral Manoeuvres, etc. However, that earliest incarnation of Scritti was like a post-This Heat/Art Bears-style ensemble, delivering scratchy, agricultural funk instrumentals with earnest, upper-crusty thoroughness. Released on the twenty-first-century Rough Trade retrospective *Early*, this track sums up England in 1978 about as well as any I've yet heard. It's the very embodiment of the post-punk inclusiveness.

The Sleepers: Linda
(Win, 1978)

Obviously sharing the same obsessions with stripped-down soul as early Joy Division, Talking Heads, Manicured Noise and The Teardrop Explodes, San Francisco's The Sleepers took the concept of ultra-austere instrumentation to its very limits on 'Linda', the lead vocals, drums and R. Dean Taylor-like guitar figure being swamped throughout by a monumental emptiness. It's as though a fetishist on the level of Joe Meek or Kim Fowley had been deployed purely to undermine the overall balance, ensuring the listener's sense of extreme tension breaks only when the bracingly atonal lead-guitar theme presents its skinny neck to the metaphorical chopping board. It's nothing less than blood sacrifice.

Human Switchboard: Fly-In
(Under-the-Rug, 1978)

Cleveland's Human Switchboard were a bizarre throwback: a bassless trio whose uptempo soul-organ stabs, garage lead-guitar licks, sweet harmony vocals and clattering drums nevertheless possessed a Motown melancholy. Akin to disco-dancing alone to The Four Tops, Human Switchboard played outsider garage-soul and were Number One in a category of their own. Stranger still, the female Armenian organist dressed in the same 'ee-by-gum' flat cap and unisex jacket as the boys in the band, both of whom sported a freakish, Eastern European migrant fruit-picker image. Not lookers, then, but Human Switchboard nevertheless sounded like they had at least one great LP in them, although they unfortunately disappeared from sight after this solitary seven-inch EP.

DMZ: Don't Jump Me, Mother
(Sire, 1978)

Showcased here at their heaviest,

DMZ coulda been mistaken for a De-twat power trio of the 1970 variety, had they dropped all the Troggs songs in favour of such lost shriekers as 'When I Get Off'. Furthermore, if only Sire Records hadn't co-opted mock-schlock-meisters Flo & Eddie as producers maybe DMZ's sole, patchy studio-LP offering woulda sounded a little more contemporary and competitive. Nevertheless, 'Don't Jump Me, Mother' is a particularly cyclical song in the best Detroit tradition, and most serpently exhibits one of the finest proto-metal drone riffs of All Rock Time, singer Mono Man's urging vocal and Paul Murphy's thunderous drop-in/drop-out drums duck'n'diving and truly elevating this sucker to the stratospheric. Now is that yowzah or what?

ESG: You're No Good
(Factory, 1981)

The minimalist funk of ESG was always served up in such titchy *nouvelle cuisine* portions that I sometimes – back in the day – felt compelled to form a copy band just so there'd be more similar shit out there. 'You're No Good' showcases the sisters at their playground finest, like a fleet of sassy fourteen-year-old smoker-girls rallying behind one of theirs as she gives her greasy, eighteen-year-old boyfriend a right dressing down. Two notes is all ESG needed for this entire single, but, boy, did they get them in the right order!

Kleenex: Ain't You
(Sunrise, 1978)

Can you believe that four Swiss punk ladies going 'Ee, ee' were forced to change their name by the mighty Kleenex Corporation in case the general public mixed the two up? It's crazy, pathetic, obscene, but true. Kleenex were forcibly metamorphosed into Liliput, by which time I was too engaged in my own career to check them out. Herein they were perfect, however, as the band displays crazily catchy-bastard songs, molto amounts of teen-girl playground vocal gush, plus a woozily brilliant musical facility to change tempo rapidly yet highly organically.

Section 25: Girls Don't Count
(Factory, 1980)

Inspired Idea Number One: write some lyrics which diss all the most essential things in life. Inspired Idea Number Two: as a vehicle for your lyrics, construct a highly remedial early Siouxsie and the Banshees-type, sub-'Metal Postcard' riff. Inspired Idea Number Three: employ Ian

Curtis and his manager, Rob Gretton, to produce it, then demand that their mixdown is so brutal that The Glitter Band's 'Angel Face' sounds schmaltzy in comparison. Inspired Idea Number Four: bark out the lyrics with all the wall-eyed gusto of an institutionalised teenage lobotomy.

Ed Banger: Kinnel Tommy
(Rabid, 1978)

Leaving The Nosebleeds in late '77 for a possibly lucrative solo career, punk singer Ed Banger opted for the scenic route to stardom by commencing his chart-busting attempt with a football song. Yup, written from the point of view of a tense footy coach urging and cajoling from the touchline, 'Kinnel Tommy' is a hymn to the heart attack and high blood pressure caused by the narrator's underachieving number nine. Orchestrated with taste and executed with vigour, this Martin Hannett production remains one of my all-time favourite forty-fives. Furthermoreishly, the extremely compelling B-side is a bizarre *musique concrète* boogie about East Grinstead, in Sussex, entitled 'Baby Was a Baby'. I mean, *c'mon.*

John Cooper Clarke: Psycle Psluts
(Rabid, 1978)

Contained within ye Salford bard's magnificent 1978 *Suspended Sentence* debut EP, this side-long poetic tour de force remains one of the Seven Wonders of the punk era, and still makes me yearn for some confident bardic motherfucker to attempt a similar feat. Produced and co-organised/orchestrated by Martin Hannett, Clarke performed his English A-road biker epic over an inspired smorgasbord of drum-box, synthesizers and guitar noise, all so masterfully hand-forged that I cannot reach a useful musical comparison. Imagine Leicestershire rapper MC Pitman toasting over a shambolically punky version of 'I Feel Love', and you're some way to reaching Clarke's singular pleasure centres . . . but not all the way. Interesting note: The Fall's Mark Smith made an entire career out of rewriting Clarke's triumphant declaration at three minutes and eleven seconds into this track: 'For the Gonad-a-go-go age of compulsory cunnilingus-ah!'[1]

1 Knowing absolutely sod all about psychedelics back in the day, I've retained a coupla Mark Smith's letters from 1978, specifically because they were useful at the time for Mark's detailed illustrations of psylocibin mushies. Back then, Mark lived with The Fall's manager, Kay Carroll, who was a lot older and would always add lovely and extravagantly poetic PS's.

Crispy Ambulance: The Presence
(Factory Benelux, 1981)

According to legend, Jesus loves The Stooges, but only journalist Dave McCulloch loved Crispy Ambulance. Yup, the wet-week who told his *Sounds* readers that Ian Curtis topped himself *for them* was, at the time, the only fucker proto-Emo enough to give the Ambulance positive column inches; which is tragic, really, because 'The Presence' still sounds entirely contemporary, skilled in its execution and useful if only for being so goddamn long! Moreover, at a time when bands like The Ruts were being hailed for merely copping The Clash's entire reggae'n'rock schtick, why was the twangy bass guitar of Crispy Ambulance so off limits as to be deemed a drone too far? I mean, we bass players all did it just to get louder on shit amps; it wasn't even Hooky who came first, even though he was emphatically the Supreme Master of the form as handed down to our entire generation via Holger Czukay, knoworrahmean?

In Conclusion

And, with that final mouthful, I shall quit this hefty Part Two, safe in the knowledge that I've (once again) most serpently wound some fucker up who really did deserve to be included herein. Still, there's plenty to listen to, for 'twas a massively fertile time; which is why, ultimately, I'm still a part-post-punk motherfucker with a post-punk wife who I fell for back in '81, when she was just nineteen years old. I reckon Dorian probably bought/scored even more of the above sonic selection than I did at the time. Besides, never having been forced to endure a Teardrop Explodes reunion has, with hindsight, ensured that my cherished memories of these post-punk songs have remained uncontaminated with age.

The Epilogue

In May 2010 CE, after exactly ten years of uninterrupted entries, I decided to bring Album of the Month to a stop, a-feared that my continuing indefinitely might risk compromising the quality of future choices. Besides, my enduring interest in so many of the world's current underground music scenes and the ease with which I was able to justify reviewing at least six new albums per month on my website seemed reason enough to jettison the retro side of my writing attack. What the future holds for my rock'n'roll writing I cannot tell, for no truth-seeker shaman can even suspect when next the spirit of rock'n'roll will take them, let alone when it will next envelope them entirely and cast them down helpless upon its sacrificial altar. For my thirty-three years of rock'n'roll I give daily my extreme thanks to the poet god Odin, who brought me the ode, to the Lokian spirit that enchants me, but most of all to the Diva whose beauty, fertility and timeless and effortless ensnaring of men's hearts has made her the subject of almost all great rock'n'roll songs.

Appendix: Unsung Albums of the Month

Groundhogs
Split
June 2000

Rocket from the Tombs
The World's Only Dumb-Metal, Mind-Death Rock'n'Roll Band
July 2000

Hairy Chapter
Can't Get Through
August 2000

The Electric Eels
God Says 'Fuck You!'
November 2000

Montrose
Montrose
January 2001

German Oak
German Oak
February 2001

Simply Saucer
Cyborgs Revisited
May 2001

Miles Davis
On the One
June 2001

Battiato
Fetus
July 2001

Alice Cooper
Don't Blow Your Mind
August 2001

Magma
Köhntarkösz
September 2001

Boredoms
Vision Creation Newsun
November 2001

Sand
Golem
December 2001

A.R. & Machines
Echo
February 2002

Khanate
Khanate
March 2002

James Brown
The Payback
May 2002

Le Stelle di Mario Schifano
Dedicato a . . .
July 2002

Sir Lord Baltimore
Kingdom Come
August 2002

Comets on Fire
Field Recordings from the Sun
November 2002

Sunburned Hand of the Man
Jaybird
December 2002

Kim Fowley
Outrageous
January 2003

Monoshock
Walk to the Fire
February 2003

Vibracathedral Orchestra
Dabbling with Gravity and Who You Are
March 2003

Black Sabbath
Behind the Wall of Spock
April 2003

Mirrors
July 2003

Van Halen
Atomic Punks
August 2003

Lord Buckley
In Concert
October 2003

Randy Holden
Population II
February 2004

Pentagram
First Daze Here
March 2004

Sleep
Dopesmoker
April 2004

Be-Bop Deluxe
Axe Victim
August 2004

VON LMO
Red Resistor
September 2004

Grand Funk Railroad
Live Album
October 2004

John Peel Presents Tractor
November 2004

Residual Echoes
Residual Echoes
January 2005

Om
Variations on a Theme
February 2005

Factrix
Scheintot
March 2005

Alrune Rod
Hej Du
April 2005

The Heads
At Last
May 2005

Highway Robbery
For Love or Money
June 2005

Blue Öyster Cult
In Your Dreams or In My Hole
October 2005

Henry Flynt and the Insurrections
I Don't Wanna
November 2005

Chrome
Chromeology
December 2005

Temple of Bon Matin
January 2006

Ramesses
The Tomb
February 2006

Orthodox
Gran Poder
March 2006

Tight Bro's from Way Back When
Runnin' Thru My Bones
April 2006

Electric Manchakou
Electric Manchakou
May 2006

Vincent Black Shadow
Vincent Black Shadow
June 2006

New Gods
Aardvark Thru Zymurgy
July 2006

Pentagram
Sub-Basement
August 2006

Solar Fire Trio
Solar Fire Trio
October 2006

Harvey Milk
Special Wishes
November 2006

Various Artists
High Vikings
December 2006

Thrones
Sperm Whale
February 2007

Nico
The Marble Index
March 2007

Sacrificial Totem
Hurqalya
April 2007

Death Comes Along
Death Comes Along
July 2007

Haare
The Temple
August 2007

Melvins
Lysol
September 2007

The New Lou Reeds
Ohio Is Out of Business
November 2007

The Badgeman
Ritual Landscape
December 2007

Friction
'79 Live
January 2008

Crow Tongue
Ghost Eye Seeker
April 2008

Nathaniel Mayer
Why Don't You Give It to Me?
May 2008

Riharc Smiles
The Last Green Days of Summer
June 2008

Matt Baldwin
Paths of Ignition
July 2008

Gunslingers
No More Invention
August 2008

Universal Panzies
Transcendental Floss
September 2008

Jex Thoth
Jex Thoth
December 2008

Billy Miller
Three Visionary Songs
May 2009

Liquorball
Evolutionary Squalor
June 2009

Culpeper's Orchard
Culpeper's Orchard
July 2009

Tom Lehrer
Songs of Tom Lehrer
September 2009

Blue Cheer
The Godlike Genius of Blue Cheer
November 2009

Psychick TV
Kondole
January 2010

Pärson Sound
The Godlike Genius of Pärson Sound
February 2010

Soft Machine
Early Soft Machine
May 2010

(NB *The Illustrated Armand Schaubroeck*: First published July 2000, then again, with images, in January 2003.)

Danskrocksampler
July 2004

Hardrocksampler
August 2008

Glamrocksampler
February 2009

Postpunksampler
November 2009

Postpunksampler 2
December 2009

Detroitrocksampler
November 2010

The Index

(NB Albums and tracks are indexed by artist.
Compilations are indexed under 'Various artists')